W9-CCD-813

Enterprise

ENTERPRISE

The Dynamic Economy of a Free People

Stuart Bruchey

Harvard University Press
Cambridge, Massachusetts
London, England

Copyright © 1990 by the President and Fellows of Harvard College
All rights reserved
Printed in the United States of America
10 9 8 7 6 5 4 3 2

A small portion of this work, undocumented,
appeared in *The Wealth of the Nation: An Economic
History of the United States* (Harper & Row, 1988),
232 pp.

This book is printed on acid-free paper, and its binding materials
have been chosen for strength and durability.

Library of Congress Cataloging-in-Publication Data
Bruchey, Stuart Weems.
  Enterprise : the dynamic economy of a free people / Stuart
Bruchey.
    p. cm.
  Includes index.
  ISBN 0–674–25745–6 (alk. paper).—ISBN 0–674–25746–4 (pbk. : alk. paper)

  1. United States—Economic conditions. 2. Capitalism—United
States—History. 3. Free enterprise—United States—History.
4. Industrial laws and legislation—United States—History.
I. Title.
HC103.B78845 1990   89–11102
330.973—dc20   CIP

To Eleanor

Preface

For a teacher and writer, one of the blessings of long life is the opportunity to summarize conclusions reached after many years of reading and research. The field in which I have concentrated my studies is that of economic history, an area that in the last thirty years has undoubtedly attracted more men and women trained as economists than as historians. To my numerous friends among economists and to their discipline I offer no apology here. Economic analysis necessarily abstracts from the complexities of the real world, holding them at arm's length, so to speak—impounded in *ceteris paribus*—in order to observe the measurable behavior of one or more variables acting under rigorously defined rules. Models or hypotheses so structured have yielded commentaries far more persuasive than roundhouse rhetoric on a number of questions that have intrigued historians over the years—from the costs and benefits of colonial membership in the British Empire to the profitability and viability of slavery, the impact of the Civil War on industrialization, and the economic effects of fiscal policies in the 1930s. But the problems such analysis has successfully addressed have been relatively narrow, short-range ones. Moreover, questions about the nature of the relationships between economic and other variables, pinned to the ground in the models but struggling to rise and speak, have survived the exercises.

No person trained as a historian can believe for a moment that economic behavior does not intersect forces that are broadly social and cultural in nature. The pace of economic development is affected not only by price, wage, and employment responses to the relative scarcity or abundance of capital, labor, and resources but also by popular attitudes and values, the supply of available knowledge, the nature of political and legal systems, and the degree of resilience in the social structure. These factors play on the incentives of people— of workers, farmers, business executives, and men and women in the public sector, as well as of ordinary people—and do much to shape the environment in which an enormous number of decisions affecting economic life are made. The contexts change over time in ways that either encourage or prove inhospitable to feats of enterprise. The proper business of the economic historian is not only to judge which persons, events, and developments ought for the record to be rescued from the heaving seas of the past (because of their pertinence to issues then, now, or in the foreseeable future); it is also to describe and analyze the forces making for change in the contexts in which they have appeared. The task is all the more important if the historian believes, as I do, that the single most significant factor promoting the material betterment of humankind is the enterprise of a free people.

Because my approach to economic history is a broad one, I have over the years incurred obligations to scholars in many disciplines. The notes, I trust, will reveal the diversity of this indebtedness, but there are men and women, at Columbia University (where I taught for nearly twenty-two years) and elsewhere, to whom I owe special thanks because of the suggestions and critiques they offered on occasions ranging from formal seminars and dissertation defenses to casual conversations over lunch.

At Columbia, contributing colleagues in history include John A. Garraty particularly, Eric Foner, Henry F. Graff, the late Richard Hofstadter, Kenneth T. Jackson, Robert A. McCaughey, Eric L. McKitrick, Walter P. Metzger, the late Richard B. Morris, Rosalind Rosenberg, David J. Rothman, James P. Shenton, and Alden T. Vaughan; in economics, Philip Cagan, Donald Dewey, and Norman Mintz; in sociology, Jonathan Cole, Sigmund Diamond, Herbert Gans, Robert Merton, Viviana Zelizer, and Harriet Zuckerman; in political science, Herbert A. Deane and the late William Fox; in business, James Kuhn, Guilio Pontecorvo, and the late Paul McNulty; in law, Barbara Black, Harlan Blake, Louis Henkin, and the late Walter Werner. Scholars at other universities include C. Vann Woodward, Robert Babcock, T. H. Breen, Robert E. Brown, Vincent P. Carosso, Alfred D. Chandler, Jr., Thomas C. Cochran, Joel Colton, Paul A. David, Carl N. Degler, Stanley L. Engerman, David Finn, Louis Galambos, Robert E. Gallman, Tian Kang Go, Jack P. Greene, Morton Horwitz, the late Alice Hanson Jones, David M. Kennedy, the late Frederic C. Lane, William E. Leuchtenburg, Diane Lindstrom, Jerome Nadelhaft, Douglass C. North, William N. Parker, Harry N. Scheiber, James H. Soltow, Gordon Stewart, Richard Sylla, Paul A. Varg, Harold G. Vatter, Harold Williamson, and Gordon Wood. The contribution of John Higham has been so many-sided and has endured for so long that it warrants a special category for him alone.

At the Institute for Advanced Study in Princeton, where I was a member in 1972–73, I became especially indebted to J. H. Elliott and received encouraging criticism from Felix Gilbert and Carl Kaysen. As a 1975–76 Fellow at the Center for Advanced Study in Behavioral Sciences at Stanford, I benefited from the advice of Richard N. Cooper as well as Joseph Pechman and Bernard Wolfman.

For fellowships essential to the leisure required for research and writing, I express my deep appreciation to the John Simon Guggenheim Foundation, the Social Science Research Council, and the National Endowment for the Humanities.

Among my doctoral students, some of whose work is cited in the following pages, I have been enriched by interchanges with Peter A. Coclanis, Randolph Bergstrom, Thomas Dublin, Robert Gross, Susan Lee, Gloria L. Main, Albro Martin, Cathy Matson, and Daniel Pope.

The challenges and problems encountered in turning an initial draft into a publishable manuscript will be familiar to colleagues in the academic world. I hope that one such problem is a rare one: over the more than twenty years during which this book was written and rewritten, I lost the notes to an earlier version of the first chapter. Thanks to the patience and ingenuity of another graduate student at Columbia, Dona Riddick, they were reconstituted.

I am grateful to Carol Rickards of Maine for superb typing and to a number of editors and their associates for indispensable aid at crucial times. I acknowledge the intellectual companionship of my long-term friend at Harper & Row, Hugh Van Dusen. Aida Donald, another friend over the years and Editor in Chief at Harvard University Press, gave me warm encouragement after her first careful scrutiny of the manuscript. Two anonymous readers responded to Dr. Donald's request for further evaluation with suggestions that markedly improved the text. I extend my gratitude also to Jacqueline Dormitzer, Elizabeth Suttell, and Vivian Wheeler for editorial assistance. I am particularly indebted to Ms. Dormitzer for her meticulous editing of the entire manuscript; her feel for the language caught many a stumbling phrase before it fell onto the printed page. The professionalism with which my friend Ann Louise Coffin McLaughlin helped turn an edited manuscript into a book added to my deep appreciation of the things for which Harvard University Press stands. Finally, I acknowledge the help of the reference librarians at Columbia University, especially Eileen McIlvaine, and at the University of Maine.

To all these friends, teachers, and helpers, and to others I may have inadvertently neglected to mention, I express heartfelt thanks. Those whose names appear here are by no means to be associated with the remaining shortcomings of the book.

The last shall be first. The dedication is as eloquent as I can make it.

S.B.

Contents

Tables

Enterprise

1

The Road to Jamestown

On April 26, 1607, three small ships carrying 105 colonists passed between Cape Charles and Cape Henry into Chesapeake Bay in search of a propitious site for a settlement in the land called Virginia. Every schoolchild knows the subsequent story of Jamestown, the first permanent English colony in America. Wracked by shortages of supplies, the hostility of Indians, and quarrels among the leaders, the tiny settlement all but expired in the early years. Yet the settlers continued to search for gold and a passage to the Pacific, and continued to neglect the growing of food. When Sir Thomas Gates arrived after the settlement's third winter, he found only sixty men of six hundred still alive, and the survivors barely able to walk. Subsequently a new supply of provisions and men revived the colony. But when Sir Thomas Dale reached Jamestown in May 1611, he found the settlers at "their daily and usuall workes, bowling in the streetes."[1]

Bowling in the streetes! What accounts for this extraordinary behavior, this playful frittering away of energies in such straitened circumstances? The leaders of the colony themselves believed the answer to be the presence among them of too many ne'er-do-wells and gentlemen who "never did know what a day's work was." On the other hand, many historians since have emphasized the communal nature of the original settlement. Everyone was an employee of the Virginia Company and, while supplies lasted, was fed by the company whether he worked or not. Then, in a change of policy, the company decided to distribute land to individuals. Encouraged now to work for themselves, the settlers changed their attitudes, and the discovery of the export possibilities of tobacco reinforced the change. From 1617 on, inertia gave way to frantic activity, and "the market-place and streets and all other spare places were set with the crop and the colonie dispersed all about planting tobacco." Whether in the New World or the Old, idleness said more about opportunity and incentive than it did about the human condition. One must acknowledge, however, that labor has often counted for little among the values of the well-born.[2]

In the pioneer days of empire, gentlemen and well-born soldiers of fortune were to be found in the American settlements of all the European powers. Their objectives are not difficult to discern. The quest for precious metals and the greed for booty, land, and lordship had been principal driving forces behind the colonial ventures of sixteenth-century Spain. The first arrivals in the New World had been drawn from the gentry and lower classes rather than from the upper aristocracy, and they were mainly men with previous military experience. Perhaps "men of quality" gambled more than other social classes, but whether or not they did, their presence is conspicuous in areas of high risk and quick profit, of excitement, glamor, and constant peril. To the historian of the English in the West Indies, the Caribbean was "a stage for mettlesome gamblers," the "Wild West" of the sixteenth and seventeenth centuries. Gentlemen came to English North America too in the early days, but by the 1630s their number had declined to insignificance. Some were slain by Indians, others drowned, and still others, perhaps the largest group of all, returned to England, their enthusiasm cooled by the prosaic reality of wilderness life.[3]

So far as representatives of the upper levels of English society are concerned, it was not aristocrats or gentlemen but rather those who were "just close enough to establishment in gentility to feel the pangs of deprivation most acutely" who came and chose to remain. They came as part of a new, second generation emigration that commenced in the 1640s. Younger sons without prospects in England and other young male members of substantial mercantile and landed families well connected in London business and governmental circles, they hoped to found positions of social and political leadership upon broad estates in America. And they succeeded in doing so. These men included the Blands, Burwells, Byrds, Carters, Digges, Ludwells, and Masons—indeed, most of Virginia's great eighteenth century names. Limited in their chances for wealth and position in the Old World, they soon achieved both in the New.[4]

What of the others, of those who settled not in seventeenth century Virginia but in Massachusetts Bay and elsewhere? What motives induced their migration? We cannot, of course, be sure. Some did not come to the New World of their own free will. For them "transportation" to America represented a penal sentence for violation of English law. Others were simply kidnapped and hustled on board ship at some English port of embarkation. But the great majority left England because they wished to leave, some of them, no doubt, in an effort to escape inhospitable economic conditions. Many, particularly in the earlier years of the seventeenth century, must also have responded to patriotic appeals to plant "a Nation, where none before hath stood." The importance of numerous sermons and promotional tracts in creating a broad sense of national purpose, although unleashed in considerable measure by promoters, investors, and participants in colonial ventures, cannot be underestimated. Other emigrants, as generations of scholars have agreed, sought as the Pilgrims did a haven in the New World in which to practice their religion in freedom. According to one authority, participants in a later wave of settlement in the closing decades of the seventeenth century "were so largely religious dissenters as to tempt one to say that all of them were."[5]

No assembly of motives can fully embrace the varieties of human experience, can adequately reflect the presence of additional sources of decision such as curiosity, thirst for adventure, or the desire to be free of marital, legal, or other entanglements. More important, it cannot be assumed that any single motive fully explains the decision to act. Most men and women are moved by a number of considerations, and introspection provides little basis for any claim, where concerns of large import are involved, that their relative degrees of significance can be fully understood and precisely known. For John Winthrop, leader of the Great Puritan Migration to Massachusetts in 1630 and conscious founder of a new City of God, the consideration was a material one: "My means here [in England] are so shortened (now my 3 eldest sons are come of age) as I shall not be able to continue in this place and employment where I now am . . . and with what comfort can I live with 7 or 8 servants in that place and condition where for many years I have spent 3 or 400 *li.* per ann. and maintain as great a charge?" By the end of the 1640s Winthrop's far-flung landholdings in and around Boston were more extensive than those of most other men. In his case—and in how many others?—both religious and material motives were conspicuously present, and who is to say how much the one counted as against the other?[6]

Emphasis, then, is a matter of judgment. In my own opinion, the search for social and material betterment will bear a considerable weight, whether in application to the unskilled and illiterate or to their opposites. Unhappily, in all likelihood it will never be possible to part the waters of the vast emigrant stream of the seventeenth and eighteenth centuries to determine with precision the proportion that was skilled and literate. Nevertheless, surviving lists of persons under indentured servitude yield significant information, especially because half of all colonial immigration is very conservatively estimated to have occurred in consonance with this contractual arrangement, under which migrants agreed to work for an individual master for a period of years, usually four, in return for passage to America. Two lists are available, one of which is from Bristol for the years 1654–1686. This list contains the registrations of more than 10,600 servants who shipped under indenture from that port. The second, from Middlesex County, is smaller, containing 812 names for the period January 1683 to September 1684. Study of the Bristol list reveals that it is made up of four groups in roughly equal parts: farmers, laborers, those skilled in both manufacturing and service trades, and youths without trades. The Middlesex County list includes a somewhat greater share of skilled craftsmen and tradesmen, a considerably larger component of the unskilled, and a smaller proportion of farmers and young men. In sum, male servants represented a cross section of a very broad segment of English society. The skill

component among indentured emigrés in the seventeenth century was probably less than that of the next century, but this is what we should expect of
the changing needs of a developing economy.[7]

Although England's "middling classes"—yeoman farmers and husbandmen
and skilled workers such as masons, bricklayers, carpenters, weavers, tilemak-
ers, and practitioners of other trades—did not in all probability dominate the
outflow of seventeenth-century servants, its members had particularly strong
incentives to improve their lot in the New World.

These were the productive groups in England's laboring population. Unlike
the unskilled and the poor, they felt their niche in the social and economic
scale to be threatened. The English yeomanry was not a contented peasantry
tilling the soil with no thought of the morrow. Rather, it was "a group of
ambitious, aggressive, small capitalists," whose "wit, industry and initiative"
marked them as men "distinctly on the make." As we shall see, this was a
period of rapid turnover in claims and titles to landed property. Men were
unusually zealous to improve their position, and the yeomanry of the seventeenth century was advancing further and more rapidly than its forebears. But
it was also a period of "shifting fortunes among the great as well as the small."[8]
Fluidity was perhaps greater than it had ever been before, yet a man could go
down as well as up. When fortune tilted down too far, when yeomen who did
not hold their land in a good tenure lost it, when hard times came to the cloth
trades that had spread over the countryside in the sixteenth century, the
thoughts of many ambitious men turned to America. "I wish I could hear
what condition you live in," an Essex tradesman wrote his Virginia kinsman,
"for I fear if these times hold long amongst us we must all faine come to
Virginia." It is not the totally but the partially dispossessed, it has been well
observed, who "build up the most propulsive aspirations." Responding in a
degree that is impossible to assess to forces that pushed as well as pulled,
significant numbers of Englishmen of initiative and ambition looked to the
New World to restore and improve that measure of well-being that the Old
had impaired.[9]

By 1700 a population estimated at 250,000, largely English in origin, inhabited the seaboard colonies of North America. Some had been born there,
and we are unable to say how many they were in relation to the total number
of emigrés. Nor can we be certain of the number of English who migrated to
Barbados, Jamaica, and the Leeward Islands in the seventeenth century. A
historian of the English in the Caribbean surmises that at least thirty thousand
did so in the first half of the seventeenth century. But the English were not
the only migrants to the New World in the seventeenth century. Small groups
of Swiss, Swedes, Finns, and French were to be found in pockets along the
coast of North America, there were Dutch along the Hudson and in the
Caribbean, and French in Acadia (Nova Scotia) and the Caribbean too. Sixteenth-century Spain had sent an estimated 200,000 colonists to the New

World, mainly to Mexico, Peru, and the West Indies, and the Portuguese had colonized Brazil. Did the desire for social and material betterment play an important part in the motivations of these groups as well?[10]

Surviving evidence is pitifully small, but the chances are excellent that it did. In his *History of New France,* written in 1609, the Frenchman Marc Lescarbot suggests three things that "induce men to seek distant lands and leave their native homes. The first is the desire for something better. The second is when a province is so inundated with people that it overflows . . . The third is divisions, quarrels and lawsuits." Forty-one recently published letters written by sixteenth-century Spanish settlers in the Mexican city of Puebla to their relatives in Spain bespeak the driving force of the settlers' urge for "something better":

> A constant refrain runs through their correspondence: this is a good land. Come! "Here you will earn more with your job in one month, than there in a year . . ," writes Alonso Ramiro to his brother-in-law. Diego de San Lorents, a tailor who had arrived in Puebla in 1564, begs his wife five years later to join him with their ten-year-old son. "Here we can live according to our pleasure, and you will be very contented, and with you beside me I shall soon be rich." Juan de Robles writes to his brother in Valladolid in 1532: "Don't hesitate. God will help us. This land is as good as ours, for God has given us more here than there, and we shall be better off."

Unquestionably, some men sought a way out of poverty, while others "may perhaps have been moved by the desire to escape from the constricting social conventions of a country where ancestry and purity of blood counted for so much." Still others, as the Puebla letters show so clearly, were "men of enterprise and initiative, willing to risk a new life in a strange environment in order to better themselves."[11] The same is true of seventeenth-century Englishmen and the members of other national groups as well.

It continued to be so. According to the British Register of Emigration for the years 1773–1776, when asked "for what purposes they leave this country," 2,532 people (together with their 1,926 dependents) who were not indentured servants and whose purposes in emigrating were recorded—considerably more than half of the latter—replied that they were "seeking to better themselves, or planning to 'plant' themselves on American soil, or hoping to establish a 'settlement' for their families there, or expecting to join relatives with whom they had been in communication, or assuming that they would be able to engage abroad in crafts and trades for which they had been trained." Their historian calls them "a people of hope, not despair." They were "enterprising, not defeated."[12]

The existence of hopeful and resourceful persons speaks volumes about the culture of opportunity which had evolved in England by the century of colonization. Such cultures, widely embracing ordinary men and women, are rare

in history and slow to form. Wholly dependent on the possibility of betterment in the material conditions of life, they make for a social and political
milieu that is favorable to respect for the individual, a respect essential to what
the modern world has come to know as democracy. The evolution of seventeenth-century England's social economy therefore belongs to the history of
America. It belongs also to the history of western Europe, for in the absence
of that past, seventeenth-century England would have been a different country
from the one we know. It is a history which unfolds in pain in the dim light
of the times after the fall of Rome in A.D. 476.

In most of those early centuries, opportunities to translate effort into reward
were confined to the very few, mainly to men of the cloth and the sword. Both
professions were essential, if not indispensable. After the death of Charlemagne in 814 and the subsequent collapse of his Frankish empire, the economic and social life of western Europe was repeatedly subjected to disruptive
forces. Feudal anarchy followed the breakdown of royal power, and constant
fighting left wide stretches of wasteland in its wake. Villages were burned and
abandoned. The French countryside, in the words of Marc Bloc, had "an
undeniably depopulated aspect, riddled with pockets of emptiness. In many
places cultivation had ceased altogether."[13] And not in France alone. Many
other regions of the empire, out of whose breakup would emerge the king-
doms of Germany, Italy, Frankish Gaul, Upper Burgundy, Lower Burgundy,
and Navarre, presented similar scenes of desolation. Invasions by Vikings,
Moslems, and Hungarians compounded the misery and disorder.

In these abysmal circumstances the economy of Europe approached a state
of total collapse. Although we lack population figures, it is nearly inconceivable that overall numbers could have risen; probably they declined, as in numerous local places they certainly did. Monasteries were in ruins, ports such
as Duurstede and Quentovic were destroyed, never to recover. Urban life was
all but dead. Whether even trickles of local trade and circulating coins continued seems uncertain. Hunger, misery, and stark fear must have been the common lot of the common man in this black night of the Dark Ages.[14]

Yet instruments of desolation sometimes become agents of deliverance as
well. In the first place, the impact of invasion gradually spent its force. By the
end of the ninth century the Norsemen had begun to settle down as farmers
and traders in some of the lands they had once terrorized, mainly in Britain
and Normandy. The Magyars were defeated in battles with Saxon emperors,
by Henry I at Riaide in 933 and even more decisively by Otto I at Lechfeld
in 955. Settling in Hungary they accepted conversion to Christianity around
the year 1000.

In the second place, whereas anarchy and civil disruption were the first fruits
of the dismemberment of Charlemagne's empire, the maturation of feudal
institutions in the period between the tenth and thirteenth centuries did much
to bring order out of chaos. Essential elements of these institutions, particu-

larly vassalage and the holding of fiefs from king or lords, were becoming common about the middle of the eighth century, reflecting the fact that the mounting of noble warriors on horseback was essentially a way of organizing society for instant warfare. Not yet, however, did the holders of military power also possess the powers of the state. It was not until the decline of public authority after the death of Charlemagne that the latter fell into their hands.[15]

A system of interpersonal contracts replaced the collapse of sovereignty, the power of the state to govern. Private government, based on private contract, is the essence of feudalism. Those who entered into these contractual arrangements—and only freemen did so—mutually agreed to assume certain obligations. The more powerful agreed to provide protection and justice, the less powerful to furnish stipulated dues and services, especially military service. In time, ceremonial ritual formalized the relationship: the lord granted land—increasingly called a fief during and after the tenth century— to his vassal, and the latter swore fealty and homage. Nearly all lords were vassals of more powerful lords, and nearly all vassals were lords of less powerful vassals. Feudal kings themselves ruled over their vassals rather than over subjects. Nevertheless, in the judgment of F. L. Ganshof, the reciprocal obligations of feudalism helped prevent the complete disintegration of the state in both France and Germany. They also helped preserve a semblance of social organization, in the absence of which economic life would have amounted to little more than scratching to stay alive.[16]

Feudal institutions differed from region to region. They emerged first in the heartland of the Carolingian empire—Burgundy, central France, the German Rhineland—and in these areas their characteristics were essentially the same. Those developing in central Germany, northern Italy, Spain and England assumed special forms. Everywhere, however, they were superimposed upon the larger body of feudal society itself. Lords and vassals, both lay and clerical, while constituting the upper of society's two classes, represented only a small fraction of the population. Peasants tilling the soil, weaving cloth, and engaging in other forms of household manufacturing formed the broad base of the social pyramid. Most, but not all, were unfree serfs bound to the soil, like their children after them. It was their labor that enabled the aristocracy to fight, carouse, and pray. Yet there is another side to the coin. Without the protection and rude justice afforded by feudal warriors, the peasants would have found their labors difficult to perform at all. Serfs ventured to plow and sow because they knew that an asylum existed for their families and their grain and cattle in the circle of palisades at the base of a fortified castle.

Most serfs lived in village communities known as manors, "manorialism" both preceding and outliving feudalism. A manor was a large estate made up of several small villages and perhaps a hundred peasant households that was held by one or more members of the feudal nobility. A typical manor was divided into two or three arable fields, with each peasant household holding long, narrow strips of land in each of them. Intermingled among the strips or held in a compact farm was the lord's land—the domain (demesne). The forest and pasturelands of the village were held in common for the use of all.

Of the obligations owed by serfs to their lords, labor was the most important. Serfs spent a long morning or afternoon three to five days a week ("week work") plowing, sowing, harrowing, weeding, carting manure, or performing other labor such as building fences and repairing the manor house and buildings. During busy seasons, especially at harvest time, the amount of overtime or "boon" work increased. In addition, serfs owed stipulated payments in produce on occasions such as the marriage of a daughter, remarriage of a widow, or training of a son of the lord for the clergy (village priests, however, were often serfs themselves). Finally, fees had to be paid in kind for use of the flour mill, brewery, oven, dye vat, sawmill, fulling mill, and other public utilities owned by the lord of the manor. These fees and other obligations were fixed by the custom of the manor. Although custom might be overridden by the will of the lord, what mattered to the lord was the yield of his estates. Discontented peasants were unlikely to be productive.[17]

Increase in the security of life and property stands at the fountainhead of a remarkable period of economic expansion that took place between approximately the end of the tenth and the middle of the fourteenth centuries. Men and women needed some assurance that the fruits of their labor would not be visited by the sudden frost of war or, when ripened, snatched from them by the caprice of the strong. It is the view of Douglass C. North and Robert Paul Thomas that population growth provides the link between security and expansion. "Where security prevailed," they suggest, "population began once more to increase." A growing population, in turn, "basically accounts for the growth and development of Western Europe during the High Middle Ages."[18]

Still another link is required, however. Security is indeed conducive to population growth, but unless the pressure exerted by the latter on resources generates successful efforts to raise the productivity of agricultural labor, increases in numbers of people will have as their consequence lowered levels of living and perhaps even death from starvation and disease. These dire consequences did not ensue, precisely because a series of remarkable agricultural innovations, for the most part dating from the sixth to the ninth centuries, underwent a process of diffusion among the farming people of northern Europe during this era.

Probably the most basic of the innovations was the gradual substitution of a three-field system of crop rotation for a two-field plan. Under the latter, one of the two arable fields was planted with winter grain while the other was left fallow. The next year the two fields exchanged functions. Under the three-field system, one field was planted in the autumn with winter wheat or rye. The next spring the second field was planted with oats, barley, peas, chickpeas, lentils, or broad beans. The third field was left fallow. "The next year the first field was planted to summer crops, the second field was left fallow, the third field was put into winter grains." The three-field plan thus increased by one-third the amount of land under the plow.[19]

It was in northern Europe that the new plan first appeared in the late eighth century, the two-field system being common in the Mediterranean. By the twelfth century at latest it had been found profitable under both systems to plow the fallow twice to keep down weeds and improve fertility. This increased still more the advantage of the triennial rotation. Peasants handling 600 acres under the two-field system had to plow a total of 900 acres (300 in arable once and 300 in fallow twice) for a yield of 300 acres in crops. Under the three-field system, 600 acres required the plowing of only 800 acres (each arable field of 200 acres once and 200 acres in fallow twice) for a yield of 400 acres in crops.

Since the same peasants plowed 100 acres less under the three-field system, they might be put to work reclaiming additional acres from forests or swamps. Indeed, 75 new acres of arable could thus be added, for when divided into three fields of 25 acres each, total acres plowed amounted to 100 (each 25-acre section once and the 25 acres in fallow twice). The same peasants were thus able to cultivate not 600 but 675 acres (450 in crops), and their production advantage over the two-field rotation rose by 50 percent (that is, 450 instead of 300 acres in crops). In sum, the new plan of rotation raised the peasant's productivity by 50 percent and increased by one-eighth the area he could cultivate.[20]

The spread of the triennial system, inhibited at first by the difficulty of changing existing allotments of strips from two fields to three and by the disordered conditions of the ninth and tenth centuries, thus gave a major impulse to land reclamation, the conversion to arable of land in forests and swamps and beneath the sea (by the creation of polders). As we shall see, however, increases in population encouraged by the productivity advantages of the three-field system and other innovations about to be discussed had the effect, even before the spread of the practice of plowing the fallow twice, of bringing about diminishing returns in local areas already under the plow. Double plowing of the fallow thus added to population pressure on extant resources to encourage the clearing of new land. In addition, a new type of felling ax, developed in the tenth century, may also help account for the great new extension of arable land that commenced at about that time.[21]

Other significant innovations include the heavy plow, the nailed horseshoe, the horse collar, and improved wagons. The first of these made an important contribution to the diffusion of efficient farming in the heavy clay soils of northern Europe. Unlike the primitive scratch-plow, essentially an enlarged digging stick that was reasonably well suited to climatic and soil conditions around the Mediterranean, the wheeled heavy plow turned over the soil and eliminated the need for cross-plowing. Its use saved peasant labor, improved field drainage, and made it possible to open up the fertile soils found in dense, rich alluvial bottomlands. Originating in the sixth century, the heavy plow was taken by the Norsemen in the late ninth century to England and then to Normandy.

Oxen pulled plows, but horses could do so more swiftly. In the moist soils of northern Europe, however, the hooves of horses became soft and easily damaged. Nailed horseshoes provided the necessary protection against wear, and firm evidence of their existence dates from the end of the ninth century. By the late eleventh century they appear to have become common. The usefulness of even a shod horse for plowing or hauling, however, depends on its being harnessed in such a way as to utilize its pulling power. Whereas the yoke harness was well suited to oxen, it was applied to horses in such a way as to press on their jugular vein and windpipe. The solution to this problem was the development in the early ninth century of a rigid padded collar resting on the horse's shoulders.

Plow horses may have been a common sight on Europe's northern plains by the end of the eleventh century; certainly they were increasingly found in England a century later. Their widespread use in agriculture appears to have been intimately connected with the diffusion of the three-field system, for under that system oats—the best possible food for horses—was one of the major spring crops. And since the switching of a village from two-field to three-field rotation was easiest when an entirely new field could be brought under cultivation or when devastated areas were being repopulated after a period of chaos, the increased degree of security that came after the period of the invasions was conducive to improved modes of tillage. As Lynn White, Jr., observes, the widespread replacement of oxen by horses "marked an era in the application of power to agriculture." Their use as draft animals following the advent of improved wagons in the twelfth and thirteenth centuries also lowered the costs of land transport.[22]

Innovation in agriculture not only made it possible to sustain an increasing population but laid the basis for commercial expansion as well. It did so in part by creating goods in quantities that were in excess of the consumption needs of local areas. Barter exchanges on local markets were then succeeded, wherever transport costs did not inhibit their development, by regional and interregional trade. The latter may have been facilitated by the encouragement given to the settlement of new regions by population pressure and diminishing returns in older areas. The pouring of people into empty space and the conversion of forest, swamp and either devastated or inundated areas into arable assumed great volume as well as momentum in the twelfth and thirteenth centuries. By the end of the latter century the empty spaces in France had been settled. In the Low Countries settlement was completed even earlier. Immigration into the empty lands of eastern Europe continued till the mid-fourteenth century, with some lords employing promoters to locate suitable land, divide it into farms and search for settlers. In newer regions such as these, North and Thomas suggest, population was less dense than in older ones. Differences in land/labor ratios, coupled with regional differences in resource endowments, led to varying types of production, which facilitated profitable interregional exchanges of products. The regions of Europe thus benefited from the geographic division of labor.[23]

Whatever the precise balance of contributing circumstances, the volume of production and trade expanded greatly in the High Middle Ages. And with the growth of trade, urban life revived. Merchant caravans had to have places to rest and depots in which to store their wares. Sites of older Roman towns and areas possessing a fortified castle were natural stopping places, especially if located at the junction of roads or confluence of rivers. Above all, as Michael M. Postan points out, the full-time merchants, as well as the artisans who soon followed them into the towns to cater to their needs and to those of rising urban populations, required exemption from the ties and liabilities which restricted the liberty of movement and freedom of contract of the lower orders of feudal society. Town charters were essentially guarantees of these exemptions, so that towns possessing them became places where mercantile transactions could be "judged by a law better suited to dealings between merchant and merchant than were the feudal custumals and common law." Essentially they were "non-feudal islands in feudal seas."[24]

Towns multiplied in number and grew in size in the two centuries after the tenth, and as they grew the feudal seas receded. For everywhere it was commoners rather than noblemen who filled the ranks of the urban business class.[25] With the growth of trade and monetary rather than barter exchanges, labor services began to be commuted to money payments. Increasingly the two-class system of the Middle Ages gave way as a third, middle class strode onto the historical stage. It was destined to become the greatest class in human history, one that would transform the world by producing ever more affordable goods and services that would gnaw away at the ancient deprivation of humankind.

Thus far we have emphasized developments in northern Europe. Some scholars would surely agree that this is where emphasis belongs, for in their view, to cite the words of Lynn White, Jr., it is an "observable fact" that the "focus of Europe shifted in Carolingian times from South to North, from the classic lands of the Mediterranean to the great plains drained by the Loire, the Seine, the Rhine, the Elbe, the Upper Danube, and the Thames." Who can doubt, he asks, that "save for brief periods, the core of European culture has been north of the Alps and the Loire from the ninth century to our own day?"[26] Echoing this point of view, although dating the change from the period between the eleventh and fourteenth centuries, North and Thomas say flatly that the "focus of the development of the Western World shifted once and for all" from the Mediterranean to northern Europe.[27]

It may be countered that words like *focus* depend on the view of the beholder and that there is room for disagreement about what elements deserve a place within the "core" of a culture—whatever that may mean. More positively, a strong case may be made that, significant as are the agricultural innovations and demographic changes that took place in northern Europe, as well as the commercial, industrial, and urban developments they made possible, the ability to finance and to organize and manage pursuits that are economic in character derives substantially from contributions emanating from the Mediterranean, especially from Italy. As Raymond de Roover has written, "In the Middle Ages the leading business men of Europe were the Italians, and their organisation was far superior to that of any of their rivals." More explicitly, "forms of business organisation were less developed in Northern than in Southern Europe."[28] Those Italian business innovations—we shall shortly examine them—contributed to the success of the English colonization effort in the seventeenth century and to the efficient conduct of economic and business enterprise in America long after that.

Southern as well as northern Europe experienced unprecedented population growth during the High Middle Ages, and evidence of change in methods of farming is sufficiently impressive to lead one student to speak of a "minor agricultural revolution" in Italy, Provence, and Catalonia.[29] Furthermore, the continuity of urban life was probably more pronounced in Italy than elsewhere in western Europe. Even in the worst days of invasion some of the Italian cities had managed to survive and to continue their industrial or commercial activity. Then from the end of the eleventh to the beginning of the thirteenth century, one student has written, there occurred "a great advance in urban civilization from one end of Italy to the other. Such was its intensity that even antiquity offers no parallel."[30] By the twelfth century, according to another scholar, Venice, Genoa, and other mercantile cities had "surpassed in wealth the greatest business centres of the classic world." In the late thirteenth and early fourteenth centuries businessmen of the western Mediterranean—Italians far more than any others—had won "unchallenged supremacy in world trade." The sphere of their direct or indirect influence "stretched as far as England, South Russia, the oases of the Sahara Desert, India and China." "It was," says Robert Lopez, "the greatest economic engine that the world had ever known."[31]

Lopez believes that Italy was to the "Commercial Revolution" that took place during these centuries what England was to become to the Industrial Revolution of the eighteenth century, and that just as industrialism appeared first in one country and then spread later to the rest of the world, so the Commercial Revolution "first affected a few Italian cities and then made its way slowly through the rest of Europe."[32] Just how slowly may be gauged by the statement of a student of northern trade that in 1500 there was a lag of perhaps two centuries between the commercial and financial methods of the leading merchants of northern Europe (the Hanseatic merchants) and those of the Italians.[33] "Even a Jacob Fugger left his Augsburg to learn business practice in Venice."[34] According to Raymond de Roover, the Italians were "the first to master" a number of new business techniques, and "as a result, foreign trade in Western Europe became virtually an Italian monopoly."[35]

Organizational and technical changes in methods of doing business are generally responses made by businessmen to underlying change in market conditions, actual or anticipated. The initial response to the expansion of markets in the High Middle Ages had been the formation of temporary partnerships. These were of two types, and both were in common use in several Italian cities in the twelfth century. One, the *commenda*, represented a union between capital and labor, between a stay-at-home investor who supplied the goods and a trader who took them to market and received one-fourth of any profits for his work. The former might "commend" capital to a number of traders; each of the latter might take goods supplied him by many investors. Investors received three-fourths of any profits and traders one-fourth. In the second type, the *societas maris,* the trader supplied part of the capital, usually a third. When he did, he was entitled to the usual one-fourth for his labor and one-third of the remaining three-fourths—that is, one fourth, of course—for his capital, his combined reward amounting to one-half the profits. The essential character of both types of temporary partnership was that they were formed for a single venture; they were "one-shot deals" that came to an end with the return of the trader from his journey to market.

One market he often sought was to be found at the fairs of Champagne. Situated roughly two-thirds of the distance between the Mediterranean and the North Sea and on or near a half-dozen navigable rivers, Champagne was an area through which passed the overland north-south route. Because of its favorable location, and also because the counts of Champagne kept the territory free of wars and preserved order on its roads and rivers, the fairs became the main meeting place between merchants of northern and southern Europe. Here traveling merchants from Flanders and Germany, on the one hand, and from Provence and Italy, on the other, met to exchange Flemish cloth or Scandinavian skins and furs for spices, silk, and other luxury articles from the Levant. Almost every kind of European or Asiatic goods could be bought. Frequently sales were made on credit instead of cash, the purchaser committing himself in writing to repay his "fair letter"—essentially an I.O.U.—at a later fair. Sums were also borrowed subject to similar repayment. The fairs thus played an important part in the development of credit.[36]

The golden age of the Champagne fairs lasted from about 1150 to nearly 1300. Their sudden decline has been imputed to a number of converging circumstances: to disturbances which followed the passage of the region into the hands of the kings of France; to heavy taxation imposed by those kings; to social troubles in Flanders and war between that country and France; and to the development of sea transportation between the Mediterranean and the North Sea. The last enabled buyers and sellers to gather where the ships came in, especially in Bruges, which now became the meeting place of southern and northern sea lanes. Unquestionably, all of these developments, assisted by the rise of woolen textile manufacturing in Bruges and other Flemish cities, contributed to the outcome. Yet there is one additional factor to consider, namely, the effect on business organization and techniques of the continuing expansion of output and demand.[37]

"No student of the thirteenth century," Michael M. Postan has written, "will fail to notice not only an over-all increase in agricultural and industrial production, but also a greater emphasis on production for sale and the spread of more or less capitalistic agriculture on large estates, and the consequent growth of towns, markets, and mercantile classes."[38] Population and urban growth, and new inventions improving the design of machines and making available more animal, water and wind power to increase the production of cloth, leather, flour, iron, lumber, and other commodities, were joining hands with agricultural innovations to raise productivity and expand the volume of goods to be traded on a host of urban markets. For these reasons the traveling merchant became transformed into a sedentary or resident merchant, and the temporary partnership that characterized the twelfth century gave way increasingly to partnerships designed to last for a number of years (the "terminal partnership") or permanently. According to de Roover, this change took place "especially in the overland trade between Italy and the fairs of Champagne."[39]

Sometimes partners or employees were sent abroad to reside in a particular place; at other times businessmen already resident abroad and hence able to serve as agents on a commission basis bought and sold goods, attended to the collection of debts, and served as sources of information on prices and market conditions. Even long before Venetian galleys began in the late thirteenth century to act as common carriers transporting goods to the Low Countries by sea, Italian businessmen had settled in nearly every important city in France, Flanders, and England. Whether this means that reliance on foreign partners outweighed the importance of relationships with businessmen already resident abroad is uncertain.[40]

These changes in organization and modes of transacting business did not sweep aside earlier forms. For example, in overseas trade the *commenda* contract survived for centuries. Nor, even after the advent of the sedentary or resident merchant, did merchants cease to travel. Indeed, Robert S. Lopez depicts the medieval "big business man" of southern Europe, of whom perhaps as many as nine-tenths were northern or central Italians, as "always ready, until old age prevented, to leave his comfortable home to wander *per diversas mundi partes,* wherever business opportunities might call him."[41] Yet the depicted changes were sufficiently general to give rise to techniques so central to the conduct of business that they survived for at least half a millennium in America as well as in Europe.

Traveling merchants had formed convoys by sea and armed caravans by land to diminish the risk of attack by pirates and bandits. When they ceased to travel, they could no longer be present in person to protect their goods. This situation gave rise to the institution of maritime insurance, which made it possible to shift at least some of the risk to underwriters. Other possibilities remained, however. As late as the sixteenth century it was the common practice of Venetian merchants to divide their cargoes, loading parts on different galleys in the same fleet, to lessen the danger of loss from shipwreck. Permanent partnerships also divided the risks of investments by forming temporary partnerships or agreements for joint ownership and agency. The latter practice was to be a common one in the foreign trade of late-colonial American merchants, indeed, of those of the early nineteenth century as well.[42]

The advent of the bill of exchange was a second consequence of the change to the residential conduct of business. Merchants traveling to the fairs of Champagne could take a promissory note from a buyer of goods and then present it for payment at a subsequent fair. When they could no longer do so, they necessarily had to shift from handling promises to pay to negotiating orders to pay. They drew these orders on their debtors and sent them to their partners or agents abroad for presentation and payment. Later they would sell them at a discount to a merchant in their own country who needed to make a remittance abroad. Bills of exchange would thus permit the settlement of international debts (and interregional ones too) without the necessity of locating gold or silver, often difficult to obtain, and running the risks of shipping it. Bills also served as devices by which loans could be made without obvious infringement of the medieval church's ban on usury. Usury meant "any accrual, great or small, above the principal of the loan."[43] In a decretal of 1312 Pope Clement V ruled that lenders could be convicted of usury on the strength of their own account books. Thereafter, various devices permitted greater secretiveness. As Raymond de Roover has shown, interest was concealed in the exchange rate, the difference between the current market value of the local currency in which a loan was made and the foreign currency in which it was later to be repaid. Bills of exchange thus contributed to the mobility of capital as well as to the early development of capital markets.[44]

Finally, but by no means least important, the shift from movement to residence, the widening of investments permitted by that shift, and above all the emergence of more durable units of enterprise gave rise to double-entry bookkeeping. The "immediate result" of the last factor, de Roover believes, "was to make the medieval bookkeeper conscious of the fact that the firm is a unit in itself and that capital and accumulated profits represent the claim of the owners. It thus became necessary to keep track of changes in the owners' equity, either through new investments or withdrawals, and to devise a system permitting the determination of profit or loss, which was distributed among the partners in accordance with the provisions of the articles of [partnership] association."[45]

Double entry did not arrive on the scene full-blown overnight. Rather, the prerequisites of the system seem to have made a gradual and piecemeal appearance in the practice of various Italian firms, "almost simultaneously" in several cities, between 1250 and 1350. The first undoubted example dates from accounts kept in Genoa in 1340, but there are clear signs of earlier development.[46]

The essential nature of double entry can be illumined by contrasting it with the simpler records kept by traveling merchants. The latter consisted merely of notations concerning credit transactions. All that was required to settle the affairs of the temporary partnership was to deduct expenses from the proceeds of sale and divide up the remainder in accordance with the terms of the contract. All this could be done on a scrap of paper.[47]

Ongoing firms transacting business through resident partners or commission agents abroad made multiple purchases and sales from time to time and therefore needed to record sums owed or due the same man (firm) more than just once. Under double entry an account would be opened for each such man (firm) in a book of accounts known as the ledger, each account consisting of either a page divided into two parts by a vertical line or two adjoining pages. The purpose of the line was to separate sums due the firm whose ledger it was from sums owed the man (firm) in whose name the account had been opened.

The sums due were called "debits," a word meaning literally *debt*. (In other words, this account owes me, the proprietor, such and such an amount.) Debits were entered on the left-hand side of the page. Entries on the right-hand side ("credits") recorded the payments either of these sums or of other sums owed by the firm keeping the ledger to the man (firm) in whose name the account had been opened. These entries signified that the account had received credit for the sums entered.

Accounts in the name of individuals or firms were "personal" accounts. A merchant dealing in goods of various kinds also needed "impersonal" accounts for each commodity, one for each shipment of goods abroad ("venture" accounts), for each form of property owned, for profit and loss, and for each of the partners (capital accounts). Obviously the number and kinds of accounts required depended on the scale and complexity of the business. If the book-keeping was accurate, the accounts would reveal not only changes in the form and value of all assets but also liabilities (in addition to credits to personal accounts, there might also be a need for certain kinds of expense accounts), profit or loss, and changes in the amount of capital which each partner could claim to be due him by the partnership.

An integrated system of accounts recording changes in the equity of the owners and permitting the determination of profit and loss is one of two fundamental prerequisites for the existence of double-entry. The other is just what the term *double-entry* suggests: each transaction must be recorded in the ledger not once but twice. Why twice? Because all business transactions themselves involve duality: something is given (that is to say, is sold, goes out) and something is received (comes in). Cloth, for example, is sold—hence the cloth account must be given credit for the sale—and something is received—hence the cash account (or an account in the name of the purchaser if the sale is on credit, or perhaps a "notes receivable" account if a promissory note is taken from the purchaser) must be debited to record the sum received. To repeat, if cloth is sold for fifty ducats in cash, then the cloth account is credited fifty ducats and the cash account is debited the same sum.

Obviously if the bookkeeping is methodically and accurately done the accounts will automatically "balance"—that is, the sum of the debits will equal the sum of the credits. But what was it that enabled the bookkeeper to balance the individual account, specifically the individual commodity account (for cloth, say) or other investment account? As we know, sales proceeds are nearly always either less or more than the cost of the goods sold. The answer is that he used the profit and loss account to bring the two sides of the commodity account—one for purchases (debits), the other for sales (credits)—into balance. Let us assume that sales proceeds exceeded costs, that is, a profit was earned. The bookkeeper had only to total the two sides and subtract the lesser (debit) from the larger (credit) total. He then entered the difference between the two on the debit side of the commodity account—bringing the account into arithmetic balance—and recorded the same sum as a credit to the profit and loss account. This operation fulfilled the fundamental requirement of *double* entry, namely, that for each debit there must be an exactly equivalent or offsetting credit, and vice versa.

Credit entries to profit and loss identified the sources of gain and debit entries the sources of loss. A similar balancing of the profit and loss account itself, and the entering of the debit or credit difference to the accounts of the partners, revealed the extent to which invested capital had increased or declined in the course of business.

De Roover found that the fifteenth-century firms of Borromei in Milan and Medici in Florence "made it a rule to close and balance their books every year," that other Florentine firms did so "every year or so, at least, at more or less regular intervals," and that "the same rule was undoubtedly followed by others." Venetian merchants, on the other hand, often postponed this reckoning for several years. Among Venetian ledgers, however, venture or voyage accounts for overseas shipments are especially conspicuous. When closed to profit and loss, they yielded the most important kind of information which merchants needed to have. For them, an overall balancing of the accounts for the purpose of ascertaining the state of assets and liabilities was less meaningful than an occasional balancing to test the accuracy of the bookkeeping.

The discovery and diffusion of these advanced techniques—the ancient world knew nothing of double-entry bookkeeping[48]—helped make Italians "the leading businessmen of Europe" in the Middle Ages, and in De Roover's judgment made their organization of business "far superior to that of any of their rivals." It was only in the sixteenth century, he adds, that the other nations began to catch up, with the Spaniards and Portuguese in the lead "and the others trailing far behind."[49]

De Roover was not alone in emphasizing the historical importance of the discovery of double entry. Scholars as influential in their day as Max Weber and Werner Sombart believed the advent of capitalism to be closely related to that discovery.

Every economic system, Sombart held, had its characteristic form of organization, technique, and spirit. By "spirit," on which he placed heavy emphasis, he meant the sum of the purposes, motives, and principles which determine human behavior in economic life. The spirit of precapitalism was traditional, it was constricted by custom, and people pursued economic life only to gain a livelihood. In contrast, the capitalist spirit was competitive, acquisitive, and in particular rational. Capitalist rationality was to be seen in its predilection for long-range planning, in a strict adaptation of means to ends, and in exact calculation. Sombart contrasted this with the wastefulness of resources and with the ill-considered use of the means of production characteristic of the centuries of precapitalism. What made rationality possible, he believed, was the discovery and use of double entry bookkeeping. Sombart went so far as to say that capitalism and double-entry were "connected as intimately as form and contents."[50]

Max Weber certainly agreed in part. "A rational capitalistic establishment," he wrote, "is one with capital accounting, that is, an establishment which determines its income-yielding power by calculation according to the methods of modern bookkeeping and the striking of a balance." But Weber also believed other sources of rationality to be essential to capitalism, for example, the rational permanent enterprise, rational technology, and rational law.[51]

We need not here seek to determine the degree to which such an exalted view of the historic importance of double entry is justified. The technique served as an administrative device for reducing affairs of business to order and system, and it appeared on the historical scene when administration itself developed as a necessary ingredient in the conduct of business—that is, after temporary partnerships gave way to permanent units of enterprise. At least, then, it was an efficient tool of routine management. At most, it was an aid to abstract thinking about the relative profitability of alternative investments and therefore helpful in reaching market decisions. Yet too much should not be made of the latter. Not past records of profit or loss but current and prospective market conditions and prices mattered most in predominantly agromercantile economies with relatively little investment in fixed capital, and that amount highly liquid because divided into transferable shares.

Not much appears to be known about the process of diffusion of double entry and other tools of trade, including the advent of deposit banking, from their centers of origin in Italy to other parts of Europe, especially England. It seems obvious, however, that the usefulness of these techniques must have increased with growth in the volume and geographic range of commerce. Familiar trade of relatively short range required little or no change in methods of conducting it unless its volume markedly increased. Long-distance trade, on the other hand, involved longer periods of time to consummate, greater risk of loss, and degrees of complexity that must have heightened the attractiveness of accounting methods capable of reducing it to an orderly system. Double entry originated, after all, in interregional trade.

Little incentive existed for the diffusion of these techniques in the final century of the Middle Ages (1348–1453). This was a period of contraction during which urban centers of trade and industry, the leaders in the economic expansion of the High Middle Ages, underwent a general decline. The previous expansion had been fed by a long wave of population growth that was accompanied by an impressive array of innovations. Now the wave ebbed and spent its force, and population declined both in size and in rate of growth. The consequences of the decline on the standard of living are uncertain. Since most people were engaged in agriculture, one would expect a fall in their numbers to have increased the amount of available land per person—and better land at that, because the reduction of population pressure should have led to the abandonment of inferior soils. If so, higher standards of living for the masses should have resulted. The balance of the evidence, however, tilts against this theoretical expectation.[52]

Above all, the insecurity of the times militated against it. This was an age of war, plague, and famine—of wars more destructive and continuous than any since the last barbarian invasions in the ninth and early tenth centuries, of plagues so devastating as to rank with the great tragedies of humankind. Reaching the Crimea from Asia in 1346, the Black Death spread over Europe during the next four years and then burst out again and again between 1360 and 1400. While the plague struck with particular severity at concentrations of people in cities, seaports, and monasteries, the countryside did not escape and the toll was heavy wherever agrarian population was thickly sown.[53]

Frequent battles added much to agricultural disruption—not by the killing of large numbers of people but by the pillaging and looting and driving to flight of village inhabitants. Periodical depopulation of entire regions and, as in England throughout the late Middle Ages, the abandonment of "a very considerable proportion of land erstwhile occupied" point to conditions opposite to those conducive to material well-being, rising fertility, and family formation. In sum, although a fall in numbers of people ought in theory to lead to better conditions and a renewal of the rate of population growth, the former probably did not occur and the latter certainly did not.[54]

Europe was relatively free of plague—but not of wars!—in the sixteenth century, and in all probability this proved decisively favorable to the resumption of population growth. It is possible, however, that factors of which we have no present knowledge also may have influenced rates of fertility and mortality. Whatever the explanation, a pronounced secular upswing was under way in all countries after 1500. Between 1450 and 1600 the population of Europe increased from some 50 million to 60 million soon after 1450 to some 80 million around 1600. Spain's portion increased from well under 5 million to over 8 million in 1590. The number in the Netherlands rose to over 3 million by the early seventeenth century. In England various tax data and ecclesiastical surveys made between 1547 and 1650 suggest a rise from about 2.5 million in 1500 to about 4 million in 1603.[55]

Despite their aura of quantitative precision, these numbers, certainly in the case of England, are "anything but reliable."[56] Nevertheless, the undoubted fact of population increase prompted writers in many countries to express the fear that a surplus population existed and to suggest ways of coping with the excess. Walter Raleigh recommended war. "When any country is overlaid by the multitude which live upon it," he writes in his *Discourse of War,* "there is a natural necessity compelling it to disburden itself, and lay the load upon others, by right or wrong . . . Wherefore the war that is grounded on general, remediless necessity may be termed the general and remediless, or necessary war."[57] Other writers, as we shall see, recommended colonization. To be sure, many of the authors of sermons, letters, broadsides, and pamphlets were members of the great companies whose interest it was to champion colonization schemes. Despite the possibility that these authors "may have been inclined to draw exaggerated conclusions," however, Karl F. Helleiner believes that their conclusions were based on "observations that were in all likelihood intrinsically valid."[58] "Contemporaries," adds C. G. A. Clay, "were conscious that the country's population was too large and economic opportunities too limited, as is demonstrated by their interest in the establishment of settlements overseas as a means to draw off some of the excess."[59]

It is indeed possible that sixteenth- and seventeenth-century Europe was relatively overpopulated. The word *relatively* must be stressed. It is obvious that Europe today accommodates far more people than lived during those earlier centuries. But most of contemporary western Europe has been "modernized"; it is economically developed—or rapidly developing—and is able to draw upon an accumulated fund of technological knowledge to raise, and raise again and again, industrial and agricultural output per head of population.

What enabled first western Europe and then much of the contemporary world to embark and long remain on this course was the diffusion of improved technological knowledge and practice from its primary source, eighteenth-century England. This is not to say that technological innovation was unknown in earlier times and places. When we recall the substitution of a three-field system of crop rotation for a two-field plan, and the development in northern Europe of the heavy plow, the nailed horseshoe, the horse collar, and improved wagons between the sixth and ninth centuries—to say nothing of innovations in industry—it is apparent that technological change had been occurring since at least the early Middle Ages. And as we shall see in the case of sixteenth- and seventeenth-century England, technical improvement also occurred in early modern Europe.

Yet the pace of change in English agriculture appears to have been relatively slow before approximately the mid-seventeenth century, and slower still in industry—until the beginnings of the classic Industrial Revolution in the last decades of the next century. The advance, that is to say, was not cumulative and self-sustaining; it was not yet possible to invent the process of invention itself. Economic expansion—increases in the volume of output and of trade that accompany increases in numbers of people—is a hallmark of both the High Middle Ages (1050–1300) and of Europe in the sixteenth and seventeenth centuries. But not economic growth, not *sustained* increases in output per capita.[60] It is true that one scholar argued in a notable exposition some years ago that the progress of technology and rate of concentration of industrial capital between 1540 and 1640 in England were "scarcely less striking" than the rate of change associated with the Industrial Revolution of the late eighteenth century. Citing evidence of an "enormous expansion . . . in the output of coal, salt, glass and ships, and of a great increase in the production of many other industrial commodities, such as alum, soap, gunpowder, metal goods, and accessories," he suggested that the growth in the importance of mining and manufacturing in the national economy was scarcely less rapid between the mid-sixteenth century and the Civil War than between the mid-eighteenth century and the Reform Act of 1832. Yet even if we grant that a newly awakened interest in mechanical improvements "spread among all classes in England from the nobility to the humblest artisan," the question of the degree of that permeation remains.[61]

Other difficult questions also remain. Technological innovation should have reduced costs of industrial production, but the extent to which it did so in real terms is debatable. Cost-reducing innovations do not appear to have affected the main manufacturing activity, cloth production. Costs of production in industry probably did rise less than agricultural costs, but agricultural and industrial prices began to diverge before 1540, that is, before the technological advances described could have exercised any effect on costs. Industrial prices continued to lag behind agricultural prices till the middle years of the seventeenth century, but what probably accounts for this is not differences in the costs of production in the two sectors but differences in patterns of demand and expenditure. The demand for manufactured goods was smaller than the demand for land and agricultural commodities. The relatively low industrial demand, in turn, may be explained by the declining real wages of labor, the existence of much subsistence farming, and a high propensity to save on the part of large and middling farmers engaged in commercial agriculture.[62]

One additional ground for reservation deserves emphasis. Available data on the wages of industrial workers, while scanty, suggest that they followed a trend broadly similar to that of the wages of agricultural laborers and building craftsmen. The alleged gap between prices and labor costs once seen as the main source of industrial capital formation ("profit inflation") therefore does not appear to have existed. For these reasons, then, the extent of the application of new industrial techniques has probably been exaggerated. The absence of technical knowledge severely limited the substitution of capital for labor in seventeenth-century England; techniques continued to be backward and productivity per worker low. In all probability, manufacturing industry could not have employed more than one-fifth of the working population, even in 1650, and its expansion thereafter was "quite inadequate to absorb the surplus labor made available by population growth and agrarian change." And if agrarian change was itself one source of the surplus labor force, it is apparent that agriculture, which dominated the economy of the period, could not absorb it either.[63]

The explanation for its failure to do so is complex. To begin with, while much diversity in farming systems was to be found in the numerous regions (Fen, Cheese Country, Butter Country, Midland Plain), two types were basic. Nature itself is responsible for this, for climatically and topographically England is divided into two parts. The region north and west is a land of mountains and moors, of poor, thin soils, and of cool, wet climate. This was grass-growing country, and its inhabitants specialized in the production of sheep, cattle, pigs, and other animals. The region south and east, in contrast, is an area of undulating lowlands and smaller, gentler hills, of richer, deeper soil, and of drier climate. Here farmers had a choice: they might grow cereals (barley, wheat, oats, and rye) as well as grass, and in the sixteenth century this was the country of mixed farming. Highland farmers kept some sheep for their wool but sold most of the rest of their young stock to lowland graziers for fattening. Lowland farmers grew cereals or fattened meat for the butcher while relying on the highlands for many of their store animals. Cattle were driven from the northern counties or Wales southward, and whatever cereals were not needed for the supply of a prodigiously expanding London or the markets of other growing towns were sent via coastal vessel from the south and east to the north and west.

Given population and urban growth, those in a position to do so had every incentive to acquire as much land as possible. The demand for land became intense at every social level, with buying and selling especially active in the south and east, the area earliest to come under the influence of commercialized agriculture. Yet the same lively, observant interest in agricultural markets was apparent all over the country, except for the peerage and the poor. Land changed hands rapidly and shifted from one class to another. Leasing became more popular than ever before and was the means whereby many yeomen gained the use of lands they did not own. Under the influence of land hunger not only sale and rental values but also agricultural prices rose substantially.[64]

Rents varied among farming regions, among different types of estates and terminal relationships, and from time to time. It is therefore difficult to say for sure when a general rise commenced. In some pastoral districts rents may have begun to increase in the late fifteenth century, but a sharp upward movement in arable rents did not occur till the 1520s. For many landowners, revisions of rental rates had to await the completion of the terms of old tenancies; for them, the 1570s and 1580s reveal rent rolls on estate after estate doubling, tripling, and even quadrupling in a matter of decades. In general, there is evidence of a marked increase on the estates of many private landowners in the late sixteenth and early seventeenth centuries. On ecclesiastical estates, rents were generally at a less remunerative level than on private ones, and on Crown lands notably less so. The latter were "regarded less as long-term income-yielding investments than as a means of raising capital and rewarding allegiance."[65]

Both the sale and the rental value of land depended on the potential profitability of its use. The latter, in turn, depended substantially on whether it was the price of wool or the price of cereals that was rising faster. If relative wool prices were favorable, furthermore, those in the lowland area of feasible mixed farming would be encouraged to shift from arable to pastoral farming. During the first half of the sixteenth century the export demand for cloth soared, and in response the relative price of wool moved sharply upward, especially in the late 1530s and the 1540s. In consequence, the profits of pasture farming tempted the larger farmers to overstock pastures previously used in common by all village families or to enclose the arable commons by hedging or fencing the land, thus extinguishing common grazing rights over it ("enclosure"). As common-field arable was turned over to grass, the fall in demand for labor brought unemployment. "In one way or another," in sum, "the small farmer and hired man were edged off the land."[66]

After 1551 the cloth trade declined, and during the second half of the century grain prices were generally sharply higher than those of wool. In these circumstances it became potentially more profitable to enclose land for purposes of arable farming. We do not know the extent to which this was generally done. In Leicestershire, the enclosure of almost half the 31,000 acres enclosed between 1485 and 1607 occurred after 1580. Although enclosure for arable probably did not decrease labor requirements, many copyholders whose tenures were insecure or whose leases had expired, as well as cottagers and other husbandmen, were "edged off the land" in order to make possible larger, more composite farms. In some cases small hamlets might be completely abandoned and larger villages seriously depopulated. The Inquisitions of Depopulation made after the Midland Revolt of 1607 reveal a total of 70,000 acres enclosed in six Midland counties between 1578 and 1607.[67]

Whether land was to be used for grazing or for tillage, it was enclosed in order to reduce production costs. Enclosure was often preceded by the consolidation of strips of land by exchange or purchase. It was often followed by the achievement of increased efficiency. For the encloser was free to do what he pleased with the land throughout the year, instead of having to allow other members of the community to graze their animals on the stubble or aftermath following the harvest. The same objective might be achieved by "engrossing," or amalgamating two or more farms into one. Ironically, although enclosure and engrossing represent responses to the growth of population and the resultant intensification of the demand for land, both caused agricultural unemployment and rural depopulation.[68]

At the same time, both devices contributed to more efficient production, lower costs, and an increase in the food supply. Enclosures of common-field land, the use of lime and marl, the floating of water meadows—a technique suggested by the natural action of rivers in overflowing low meadows—and the practice of "convertible husbandry"—turning arable into pasture for a few years to enable soil nutrients to be restored and then converting back to arable—tended to increase the yield from both arable and pasture. Indeed, one authority characterizes these and other innovations as revolutionary in their effects. The "agricultural revolution," he suggests, "took place in England in the sixteenth and seventeenth centuries and not in the eighteenth and nineteenth." As in the case of claims for an early "industrial revolution," however, there remains the troublesome problem of the degree to which these practices permeated agriculture and produced measurable results justifying the emphasis given them. Other scholars incline to a different timetable. One believes that organizational change and technical advances took place more slowly, with "as decisive an upturn as can ever be detected in the rate of agricultural change" occurring in the mid-seventeenth century. Another acknowledges that the innovations certainly were becoming more widely adopted but holds that, apart from enclosure, it "would be wrong" to infer that the improved methods of agriculture "had more than a limited application in the early Stuart period." He believes that the increase in the country's agricultural output in the two centuries before 1650 "probably owed less to improvements in productivity than to extensions in the cultivated area." But although the sixteenth century did see the embankment of the Greenwich, Plumstead, and Wapping marshes, no very spectacular extension of the area of land under cultivation occurred. The large-scale draining of the Fens awaited the Stuart period.[69]

Thus it is clear that English agriculture did respond to the pressure of population on the land and its resources by introducing improved technical methods, by extending the agricultural area, and by specializing in products giving the highest physical returns. An example of the last is the rise of gardening, that is, the production of fruit, vegetables, and hops in many places within easy reach of the growing London market. It is no less clear that the response was insufficient to prevent increasing unemployment and poverty among the agricultural laboring class. The best evidence for this is provided by the course of food prices and wages. Although in good years some export of cereals occurred, there is every reason to believe that grain and other food prices reflected market conditions in England itself. Their long term trend reveals that the forces making for increased supply moved far more slowly than those making for increased demand. The average price of all arable crops, including wheat, barley, oats, rye, hay, straw, peas, and beans, approximately tripled between 1500–1509 and 1550–1559. By the first decade of the seventeenth century the price of these crops was about six times the level of a century before. The price of cattle and sheep was nearly five times higher at the end of the same interval.[70]

Wages lagged far behind. Data on daily wage rates of agricultural laborers and building craftsmen in southern England reveal that increases in money wages, though substantial, failed to keep pace with the general level of prices. Beginning in the early years of the sixteenth century the purchasing power of the daily wage rate declined, although not continuously. A sharp fall occurred in the middle years of the century, followed by partial recovery. During the decade 1610-1619 the purchasing power of the agricultural laborer's daily wage rate reached its lowest point: 44 percent of its level in the second half of the fifteenth century. In the same decade the building craftsman's wage rate was 39 percent of the comparable level.[71]

Scholars used to believe that the long inflation of prices could be explained principally by changes in the value of money. However, the contribution of monetary factors, though difficult to determine precisely, has very probably been overstressed. The contribution took two forms: devaluation of English coins by reducing the amount of precious metal in them and an influx of silver originating either in central Europe or in Spanish America. Close examination of price behavior during and after periods of currency debasement reveals the relationship to have been a doubtful one. During the period 1542–1551, for example, the metallic content of English coins was reduced by 75 percent for silver and 25 percent for gold. Yet prices did not rise uninterruptedly, and it was not till the end of the 1540s that the general price level moved sharply upward. And since prices on the Continent followed a broadly similar course, the suggestion is that real economic factors rather than monetary ones were at work. Spanish-American silver does not appear to have reached England in large quantities till the second quarter of the seventeenth century, when the inflationary movement was coming to an end.[72]

In sum, it was population growth rather than monetary factors that provided the most essential support for the high prices of the period. Neither the agricultural nor the industrial sector was able to accommodate that growth, and unemployment, poverty, and hunger affected thousands. Elizabethan England presents a tableau in which considerable numbers of people moved constantly from village to village, village to town, and county to county, presumably looking for work. That the spectacle of a restless population, vagrant, poor, mendicant, and sometimes disposed to criminality, became a source of grave concern to the English public and their rulers is evidenced by passage in 1572 of an "Acte for the Punishment of Vacabondes, and for Relief of the Poore and Impotent." Typical of the writings of the period is the complaint that "our multitudes like too much blood in the body do infect our country with plague and poverty . . . our land hath brought forth, but it hath not milk sufficient in the breast thereof to nourish all those children which it hath brought forth." More and more, Englishmen of late Elizabethan and Stuart times began to think of colonization as a means of demographic relief.[73]

Yet colonization is one thing, the possession of colonies another, as late-eighteenth-century Americans were to learn so well. Columbus had discovered America in 1492, over a century before the Virginia Company dispatched people to what became the settlement of Jamestown. How is it that the English took so long to decide on the course of empire? The answer has to do with perceptions of narrowing differences in national power, that is to say, with the evident weakening of Spain vis-à-vis England, with widening commercial horizons, and with an increasingly direct participation by Englishmen in lengthening trade routes. It has to do with the growth of interest in colonization on the part of government and on the part of private persons willing to invest in the transport and supply costs that settlement would necessarily entail. And finally, it has also to do with something more elusive: that conscious pride in national identity and accomplishment that one associates with the age of Shakespeare, Gilbert, Raleigh, Hawkins, and Drake, with the Elizabethan Renaissance.

At the time of Columbus' famous discovery, as indeed throughout the sixteenth century, woolen cloth was by far the most important commodity exported from England. Exports went in two principal directions: to Antwerp and to northern Germany, Scandinavia, and the Baltic. Italian, Ragusan, and French buyers came to London for some of the cloth, but very large shipments, chiefly taking the form of undyed and unfinished "shortcloths," were handled by Englishmen themselves organized in a corporate body known as the Company of Merchant Adventurers. The headquarters of this "regulated company"—so-called because it was an association of individual merchants, each of whom traded on his own capital—was located at Antwerp. On the other hand, merchants of the German Hanse handled almost all exports of the heavy, hard-wearing English fabrics that went to the north. In return for their carrying services, these merchants enjoyed exceptional privileges in London, including preferential treatment with regard to export duties. This was not to last: Hanseatic privileges were first reduced, then abolished. By the early seventeenth century English merchants controlled 95 percent of the cloth trade. A lessening degree of dependence on foreigners, as we shall see, is one of the most important facets of the growing economic nationalism that marks the decades after the mid-sixteenth century.[74]

Most English cloth went from London to Antwerp, the center not only of the international textile trade but also the commercial and financial capital of much of northern Europe. Indeed, economically London was its satellite: as Antwerp grew, so too did English cloth exports. The rapid rise of the Flemish city in the first half of the century was thus paralleled by a remarkable expansion in the volume of exports of English shortcloths, which grew in these years by 150 percent. In the early 1550s, however, came a dramatic reversal. Price and exchange rate differentials between England and the Continent, which had been favorable to English exports, especially in the 1540s, shifted early in the next decade, and the opening years of Elizabeth's reign (1558–1603) found the cloth trade at a level some 30 percent below the peak of the boom. The great expansion was over. With the revolt of the Low Countries against Philip II of Spain, Antwerp's boom also came to an end. Religious disorders in 1566 led many leading bankers to emigrate, and in 1572 the city was engulfed in war.[75]

Until recently, the view was widely accepted that the disorders in Antwerp, by compelling English merchants to search out other markets for cloth in the Baltic and Mediterranean, led directly to a widening of English commercial horizons, which culminated in Atlantic adventures and in colonization. This view retains some of its validity: it is probably true that members of the Merchant Adventurers also invested in the trade to newer areas in the hope that cloth could be sold there. And some was. More important, however, is that, following the disorders, the Merchant Adventurers located their headquarters elsewhere in northern Europe—at Hamburg from 1611 until the nineteenth century—and stabilized at a fairly high level this familiar, safe, and short-route trade. The new cloth markets to the East proved small in comparison. Annual exports to all of them combined did not average more than 10,000 cloths during the last thirty years of the sixteenth century. Over the same period, the Merchant Adventurers' annual exports to northern Europe averaged 65,000 cloths.

It is not exports so much as imports that deserve the lion's share of the credit for the commercial expansion of the Elizabethan age. And it was not the conservative members of the Company of Merchant Adventurers but in the main new men who were its agents. In these senses, the Elizabethan expansion "should be seen to mark an important break and a new stage in the development of English trade." Little if any increase in the volume of trade seems to have occurred. Rather, there took place significant changes in its composition and direction.[76]

Even before the disruption of Antwerp, the Muscovy Company had been formed (1553–1555). The objective of this first English joint stock company—an association of capital rather than of men—was to tap the riches of the Orient by a route free of Portuguese interference. The troubles at Antwerp further encouraged English merchants to lessen their dependence on European middlemen. Spices and other Eastern imports had been purchased previously either in the Flemish city or in Lisbon. Now Englishmen began to go directly to the sources of supply themselves.

The Muscovy Company was followed by the Levant Company (1581) and the East India Company (1600). Once the eastward expansion reached the Levant, it became firmly focused on imports. The main objective of the Levant Company was to bring back spices, silks, and currants to serve the rising demand for luxuries on the part of those with access to the high agricultural incomes of the age. In the late 1590s the average annual value of cloth exports to the Levant amounted perhaps to £50,000 or £60,000. In comparison, a decade before this some English merchants were already importing £70,000 worth of Levantine commodities in a single shipment. Throughout the period the annual value of imports more than doubled that of exports. Imports continued to increase in the 1620s and 1630s, reaching an official valuation (probably understated) of £352,263 in 1630. Cloth exports, in contrast, stagnated, remaining steady at late-sixteenth-century levels. Despite the great opportunities offered by the Eastern commerce, the Merchant Adventurers were earning steady profits from their own privileged commercial line and "had little reason to run the risks or suffer the inconveniences required to build a new trade." The success enjoyed by exporters of cloth to northern Europe and by importers of luxury goods from the East helps explain the slowness with which mercantile interest turned to the profit potentialities of colonial trade.[77]

The conservatism of Elizabeth and her court is to be explained at least in part by the possibility that high profits, won at minimal risk of full-scale war, might sometimes prove the yield of investments in expeditions formed for the purpose of preying on Spanish commerce. From 1570 till the outbreak of open war between Spain and England in 1585, the Caribbean was a scene of intermittent privateering in which Francis Drake was the central figure. Sometimes raids brought small prizes, but Drake's three-year circumnavigation of the globe (1577–1580) culminated in outstanding success. The voyage had cost only £5,000 to equip, and his return cargo of Spanish treasure was worth £1,500,000. The queen's portion was £250,000, and other investors realized a profit at the rate of 4,600 percent! Small wonder that the prime objective of the first colonization effort of the famous lost colony established in Raleigh's interests on Roanoke Island in 1585 was to serve as a base for raids on Spanish shipping. Throughout the 1590s mercantile investments moved strongly into privateering, and the enthusiasm for colonial settlement awakened by the Roanoke plantation declined.[78]

Notwithstanding the susceptibility of Spanish fleets to surprise attack, the power of imperial Spain through most of the sixteenth century goes even further to explain the gradualness with which the English approached thoughts of empire in the West. In possession of the greater half of the New World by virtue of discovery and division with Portugal (Treaty of Tordisillas, 1494), held in awe on account of the ability of its imported treasure in silver, gold, and other valuables to finance the most luxurious court and most powerful army in Europe, Spain and its empire in the Indies invited envy, smuggling, and raiding rather than the more lasting confrontation implicit in a planting of peoples in the areas it claimed. Had not the Spaniards destroyed a small colony of French Huguenots situated on the coast of Florida? And destroyed as well in the battle of San Juan de Ulùa most of Hawkins' fleet following surreptitious trading with Spanish settlements in the West Indies? The whole episode "made clear that the Spanish government would tolerate no interlopers of any kind in American waters." Or on American land. The situation of the Roanoke settlement behind a formidable moat composed of dangerous shoals and inlets might have enabled that colony to escape the fate of the French in Florida. We shall never know; the only thing of which we can be sure is that the Spanish looked for the settlement in vain in 1590, unaware that it had already disappeared.[79]

It was not till the Treaty of London (1604), ending the war between Spain and England, that the first sign appeared of a tipping of the balance between the two powers in North America. Spain would not publicly acknowledge any abatement of its claims to sovereignty, yet its efforts to defend the Caribbean while conducting war in Europe had severely taxed its strength. In the negotiations for the treaty, James I acknowledged Spain's monopolistic claims to all the territory it effectively occupied, but he refused to admit its rights in unoccupied parts of America. One scholar believes that James "must have intended" this distinction to cover the settling activities of the English in Virginia from 1606 onward.[80]

The stage was now set, or nearly so; for requisite or useful experience of various kinds had come by then to the English, even experience in enduring colonization. Emigration to Ireland, especially after 1582, provided the latter, and although the movement into that island had led to disillusionment, bitterness, and war, it had also helped prepare the way for America. Leading West Country figures in the Irish planting such as Humphrey Gilbert, George Peckham, and Raleigh were also to play key roles in the Roanoke ventures. Experience in long and hazardous ocean voyages had been obtained throughout the sixteenth century by fishermen visiting Iceland and the Grand Banks off Newfoundland. More than experience, great quantities of cod had also been obtained for the needy larders of England and the Continent. And even more than that, with the seizure of Newfoundland in 1583 by Humphrey Gilbert, the first English possession in the New World had been obtained.

What was needed now to launch colonists westward were the encouragement and protective support of government, the capital required to outfit ships and sustain the settlement in its first years, and a propaganda campaign that would whip up interest on the part of potential emigrés and investors. Earlier experience proved helpful here too, for as we have seen, ever since the mid-sixteenth century England had been providing public support for private enterprise overseas by issuing charters of incorporation to joint stock companies. In a larger perspective, the two centuries thereafter would define the classic Age of Mercantilism, and corporate charters that conferred monopoly rights of trade in designated areas and delegated sovereign powers of government as well would form important facets of mercantilist practice. Indeed, six of the nine settlements made by Englishmen along the Atlantic coast of North America in the seventeenth century were promoted and initially financed by joint stock companies.

Settlement and trade, the discovery of precious metals and other treasure, plunder of the Spanish Indies, and in some cases the discovery of a passage to other lands or seas were among the objectives sought by joint stock companies. Trade that produced a balance in favor of the home country was of special importance in the eyes of mercantilist writers and government advisers, for as the author of the *Discourse of the Commonweal of This Realm of England* put it in 1549, "We must always take heed that we buy no more of strangers than we do sell them; for so we should impoverish ourselves and enrich them." Especially to be deplored, he continued, were imports of "trifles from beyond the seas" which could either be done without or made at home. But his thought moved beyond luxury goods, beyond "painted clothes" and "perfumed gloves," to include "all kinds of cloth, kerseys, worsted . . . , paper, and all kinds of leather ware . . . and . . . vessls," in short, to include the products of a host of occupations which he favored "setting up." Goods made at home not only put one's own people to work instead of "strangers" but also brought "treasure into the country." An increase in the nation's stock of coin and precious metals was no quaint or fatuous objective in an age when credit mechanisms were not well developed and commercial banks were nonexistent. They enabled mercenary soldiers to be hired and subsidies paid to allies. They provided *nervi bellorum*—sinews of war.[81]

Englishmen came increasingly to believe that the possession of colonies in America would add strength to these sinews, would enhance the nation's wealth and security. In time, colonies would serve as markets for the manufactured products of the home country. In addition, by reducing the degree of dependence on foreigners for valuable materials, colonies would not only permit a net saving in precious metals but would also serve as sources less liable to interdiction in time of war. They would add to the nation's strategic security.

Timber and naval stores were an important case in point. England had long been importing from the Baltic substantial quantities of timber, wax, tar, and hemp, all vital to the shipbuilding industry. Indeed, from the end of the fifteenth century on, English shipping was "unthinkable without east European timber, hemp, pitch, and grease." The country's natural supplies of wood, depleted by shipbuilding, iron smelting, and construction, began to run short about the middle of the sixteenth century. By 1600 the price of timber was nearly three times what it had been in mid century, and by 1650 the multiple had risen to nearly five. The Baltic trade, however, was highly vulnerable to interruption, and great hopes were entertained that the New World would supply the needed quantities.[82]

Of all the commodities needed in England which the subscribers to the Virginia Company hoped would be produced in America, naval stores seemed to be most important. High transport costs appear to have defeated these hopes, but it is interests and motives rather than outcomes that are pertinent to the founding of empires.[83]

Those interests and motives find their classic statement in the life's work of the younger Richard Hakluyt, and he, more than any other single person, is responsible for concentrating the attention of England on America. The enormous influence exerted by Hakluyt and the process by which he gradually came to exert it are well described in the following evaluation:

> His early tract, the *Discourse of Western Planting*, was a bold plea for making North American colonisation a matter for the enterprise and resources of the state as well as of private persons. The plea had little immediate effect, because Hakluyt's opinion was not shared by the queen or her immediate advisers; but for nearly forty years Hakluyt continued to write, to record, to publish, and to advise. He knew most of the leading adventurers personally. The *Principall Navigations* is a monument of historical enquiry, of careful preservation and scholarly editing of original accounts. No other seafaring nation possesses anything like it. To Hakluyt's contemporaries, it was not only a record of past achievements but an incitement to fresh endeavours. His work was complementary to that of scientific navigators such as John Davis and of the geographers and mathematicians, among whom John Dee—who also had direct access to the queen—was pre-eminent. He was followed by a host of other pamphleteers, many of them able and persuasive. The later Elizabethan poets and playwrights in turn took up the song. Gradually influential men in England, statesmen, courtiers, financiers, came round to Hakluyt's way of thinking.[84]

Hakluyt shared the view of many of his contemporaries that England was surfeited with people: "Truthe it is that throughe our longe peace and seldome sickness wee are growen more populous than ever heretofore; so that now there are of every arte and science so many, that they can hardly lyve one by another, nay rather they are readie to eate upp one another." That he also believed the interests of England's cloth exporters would be served by colonization is clear from his dedication of the second edition of the *Principall Navigations* (1599) to Robert Cecil: "Our chief desire is to find out ample vent of our woollen cloth, the natural commodity of this our Realm." Finally,

America would provide a new, cheaper, and more dependable source for needed raw materials:

> The Countries . . . of America whereunto we have just title . . . being answerable in climate to Barbary, Egypt, Syria, Persia, Turkey and Greece, all the islands of the Levant Sea, Italy, Spain, Portugal, France, Flanders, High Almayne, Denmark, Eastland, Poland and Muscovy, may presently or within a short space afford unto us, for little or nothing, and with much more safety, either all or a great part of the commodities which the aforesaid countries do yield us at a very dear hand and with manifold dangers.[85]

The importunities of Hakluyt and other publicists, abetted by the long, sharp rivalry with Spain and the growing nationalism of the age, created a momentum of enthusiasm, a sense of mission in which the projected colonization of America was elevated to the level of national enterprise. It is true that the principal investors in the original offering of stock by the Virginia Company were large-scale merchants. But it is also true that fully one-third of the investors were members of the landed classes. Indeed, the proportion is probably higher, for of 1,252 investors whose social origins it is possible to identify, 560, or about 45 percent, were nobles or gentlemen. In the judgment of the historian who has most recently probed the matter, in the spectrum of motives that inspired the expansion of England, "the gentry were closer to the vision of national enterprise, whereas the merchants were closer to the concern for profits."[86]

This judgment applies with particular force to the greater merchants of London. "At no time," another scholar concludes, "were these men enthusiastic about colonization." It is difficult not to surmise that they found themselves overwhelmed by the wave of national euphoria attending the launching of Virginia. But not entirely: they also had hopes of winning quick profits through the fur trade and the discovery of precious metals. When these failed to materialize, they withdrew their financial support. Within two years of the issuance of a new charter in 1609, new contributions to the joint stock of the Virginia Company dried up. In a period in which London merchants were the principal investors in subscriptions for the East India Company amounting to more than £2 million, the stock of the Virginia Company could not attract £40,000. With the dissolution of the latter company in 1624, the greater London merchants severed all connections with the colonial trades. Why indeed should members of the Levant Company, say, have shifted their capital to colonial tobacco? In 1640 merely 51 men enjoyed a legal monopoly of the right to import currants from the Levant. In the same year no fewer than 330 small men were actively engaged in the colonial tobacco trade.[87]

Small businessmen organized in partnerships, men of initiative who were willing to run risks, took over where the large corporations left off. Shopkeepers, sea captains, and domestic traders of all types entered the colonial trades, sometimes by emigrating to America themselves. They made fitting counter-parts to the thousands of men and women of humble social origins who were investing their lives in the promise of the New World. What came of the investment we shall see in the chapters ahead.

2

The Promised Land

The settlement of America altered the relationship between man and nature not only in western Europe but also in North America and the islands of the Caribbean—the Atlantic community of the seventeenth century. It did so by increasing the natural resources available to the people of that community. The volume of production and trade expanded vigorously as each of the regions pursued its comparative advantage and exchanged its output with others. Of course the populations of the regions were also affected. More abundant foods and raw materials, coupled with the salutary environment of an essentially rural people, encouraged birthrates and lowered mortality rates in North America. Even so, labor shortages persisted, and both here and in the Caribbean white men took the fateful step of importing blacks from Africa. Meanwhile western Europe, for complex reasons that are only partially understood, entered a period of population decline. Numerous social, economic, and demographic factors thus affected the size of populations, their rates of growth, and their geographic distribution. Yet it remains probable that even with minimal technological innovation the rich resources of the New World improved the ratio of man to land throughout the Atlantic community, with consequences in terms of hemispheric well-being and economic buoyancy that are incalculable. Certainly the emigrés themselves enjoyed a greater abundance of land in relation to their numbers than did the peoples they had left behind. And this was nowhere more true than in the English settlements of North America.

In the preindustrial world of the seventeenth century the ownership of land not only sustained the material basis of life but largely determined one's social status as well. In all probability it was land more than any other consideration, except for the vital need for religious freedom, that induced men and women to migrate to America. The leaders of the Virginia Company learned the truth of this after being compelled by the company's lack of success as a trading monopoly to act also as a settlement agency. Recognizing that freehold farmers could not be forced for long "to trade with company stores at company-controlled prices," they nevertheless had been reluctant to distribute land to settlers and postponed doing so till the years 1616–1619. For quite different reasons the founding fathers of the New England towns generally believed that land ought be worked by the community rather than by private individuals, but they too were soon obliged to modify their views. It would be difficult to overemphasize the importance of private ownership and management of land, especially as a means of attracting scarce labor to America. When conjoined with widening markets, they would also sharpen the incentive for productive effort and help elevate the levels of living.[1]

In the beginning of settlement all rights to the land were vested in the Crown, England's claim, like those of other powers, resting on discovery and occupancy. Indeed, the Crown went so far as to hold that the rights of the Indians themselves derived from those of the English, an allegation resting uneasily on the assumption that Christian claims were superior to those of pagans. Thus the charter granted Walter Raleigh in 1584 allowed the colonizers to occupy land "not actually possessed of any Christian Prince, nor inhabited by Christian People," and the essence of the provision was also included in the first charter of Virginia in 1606.[2] It must be acknowledged that Indian titles were often extinguished by conquest, strong drink, trifles, and ambiguous words, that force and fraud often accompanied exercises depriving the natives of their ancient rights. But not always. Roger Williams' compassionate concern for fairness toward Indians is justly celebrated, as is that of William Penn,[3] and a number of provinces decreed essentially what the legislature of New York enacted into law in 1684: "Noe Purchase of Lands from the Indians shall bee esteemed a good Title without Leave first had and obtaineid from the Governour signified by a Warrant under his hand and Seale and entered on Record in the Secritaries office att New Yorke and Satisfaction for the said Purchase acknowliged by the Indians from whome the Purchase was made which is to bee Recorded likewise." Legislation did not put an end to fraud, but made it more difficult for unscrupulous persons to practice it.[4]

In colonial America rights to land often followed circuitous routes into the hands of settlers. The Crown itself transferred title from time to time to proprietors such as Lord Baltimore, William Penn, and the duke of York or to trading monopolies and settlement agencies such as the Virginia Company and other joint stock companies. These recipients then turned over the land to settlers and fixed the terms of their tenure. Except in New England, where the towns intermediated between joint stock company and individual colonist, the principal method of transfer in the seventeenth century was the so-called headright system. However, much land was also bought and sold, earlier and to a greater extent in some colonies than in others, and with restrictions on sales in some places, especially in Georgia and New England. In sum, a free market in land developed only gradually and not everywhere at the same time, with prices varying by quality, location, and time period in ways that are difficult to summarize except for local situations. Surprisingly, land was also leased, tenancy making its appearance at the very beginning of the colonial era.

Headrights date from an effort on the part of the Virginia Company in 1618 to encourage emigration without making cash outlays from its depleted treasury. Under the system any person paying his own way or that of others to America received a grant of 50 acres for each person transported. Thus a man paying for himself, wife, and four children received 300 acres of land, whereas a wealthy individual financing the emigration of 100 indentured servants was entitled to 5,000 acres.[5]

Headrights benefited some people more than others. In some colonies indentured servants themselves received a grant of land at the expiration of their period of servitude. They did so in Maryland, for example, but not as a rule in Virginia. The system, however, easily lent itself to abuse. Some recipients of headrights based their claims on multiple arrivals of the same person. Thus Sarah Law received three hundred acres of Virginia land after "importing" six times a man who was probably a sailor. On a larger scale, ship captains submitted claims that included the names of both fare-paying passengers and sailors, although entitled to compensation for neither group. In other cases fictitious names were used, and, perhaps worst of all, clerks in the office of the secretary of the colony simply sold claims to anyone willing to pay from one to five shillings. According to reports to the Board of Trade in the 1690s, the latter was common practice.[6]

Given the abundance of land in America and the desirability of using it to attract scarce labor, it is hardly surprising that a mechanism for making it available should have been laxly administered. Perhaps the more important question is whether or not persons of moderate circumstances were enabled to obtain land under the headright system. For obvious reasons the question is extremely difficult to answer, not least because of the scarcity of available evidence on the actual distribution of land in the colonies in which headrights were important. Yet something is known about most of the colonies, and in the case of Virginia, a great deal.

We know that in Georgia the trustees at least sought to avoid headright grants exceeding 500 acres, although the rule against them was often evaded. After Georgia became a royal province in 1752, headrights varied from 50 to 5,000 acres, but during a year (1755–56) typical of the early period, more than half the grants were for 300 acres or less, with one of six ranging between 640 and 2,000 acres. In sum, Georgia was not a colony of large landowners. In seventeenth century South Carolina, as in Pennsylvania and Delaware, sale was the chief method by which titles to land were transferred. South Carolina also used the headright system, however, and although in that province some large plantations developed, most allotments were for less than 300 acres. In

Pennsylvania grants were generally for 100 to 500 acres. In Maryland head-rights served as the principal basis on which land was granted till abolished by the proprietor in favor of sales in 1683. Lord Baltimore preferred making grants in large tracts, and in the period prior to 1676 about sixty manors were erected containing an average of about 3,000 acres.[7] Yet grants resulting in manors of that size were quite atypical. The average size of all holdings was about 200 acres between 1650 and 1660, and in the years that followed, the average never much exceeded that figure. In Maryland extremely large estates were uncommon except for those reserved by the proprietor.[8]

Not so in New York. In that province before 1664 the Dutch envisaged the founding of lordly estates (patroonships) of immense size, although also making smaller grants available to less wealthy persons and encouraging the development of municipalities. In practice it was the English rather than the Dutch who erected vast manors, with one governor (Fletcher) granting land in parcels of 100,000 acres per person—and four or five times that much to some of his favorites. One of Fletcher's grants was seventy miles in length and eight miles in width! Others measured fifty and thirty miles. Small wonder that his successor, Governor Bellomont, should have complained that Fletcher "hath made it almost impossible to settle the Country with Inhabitants, there being no land but what must be purchased from his few Grantees, (who never can settle it themselves." Small wonder too that the complaint should have been made (in 1732) that young people were leaving New York every year and purchasing land in neighboring colonies. Under far less grievous conditions of land engrossment, settlers were also attracted from Virginia to South Carolina.[9]

Virginia provides the richest lode of surviving data on the operation of the headright system. In the four years ending in 1623, the Virginia Company made forty-four grants of land to patentees, each of whom had agreed to transport to the colony at least one hundred persons at his own expense. Plantations acquired at this time in consequence of headright grants were comparatively small as a rule, a census of 1626 revealing that the great majority of the estates were between 100 and 150 acres. A few covered as much as 1,000 acres. In the early years after the dissolution of the company, the greatest area included in any one patent was 1,000 acres, and between the years 1626 and 1632 grants usually ranged between 100 and 300 acres. From 1634 to 1650 an occasional grant of 5,000 acres was made, but the average amounted to 446 acres. Headright grants in the last half of the century were decidedly larger, a number of them ranging between 10,000 and 20,000 acres. Their average size reached 674 acres, an increase of 228 acres over the average for the period before 1650.[10]

Much of the increase came during the third quarter of the period; the trend of the final quarter was toward smaller landholdings, some of the larger estates being broken up in order to provide land for children or for servants completing their indenture. Some of the land was sold, however, owing to lack of slaves, indentured servants, tenant farmers, or wage earners to work it. By the end of the century small farms and small landholders had emerged as the largest numerical group in seventeenth-century Virginia. Nevertheless, a small percentage of the population continued to hold a considerable amount of land. In 1703–04 the average size of landholdings in Northampton County was 389 acres; in Accomack County, 520 acres. In the former county, 3 percent of the tithables held 39 percent of the land, and in the latter, 4 percent held 43 percent. Mainly through the headright system or by private purchase, William Byrd I had acquired 26,231 acres of land by the time of his death. William Fitzhugh obtained 96,000 acres during his lifetime and at his death in 1701 left approximately 54,000 acres to five sons.[11]

The amassing of large estates, especially by those able to use positions of influence in the government to obtain grants, appears to have discouraged migration to the colony in the later years of the seventeenth century. According to a report made in 1696 to the Board of Trade by Edward Randolph, surveyor-general of the customs in America, "[indentured] servants are not so willing to go there as formerly." Such was the extent of land engrossment in Virginia that "for many years there has been no waste land to be taken up by those who bring with them servants, or by servants who have served their time." Small farmholders may well have been the largest group among landowners in Virginia at the end of the seventeenth century, but it is clear that their numerical preponderance was increasingly offset by planters with far larger resources.[12]

The colonies of New England afford contrasts at many points with the land systems of Virginia and other headright provinces. They differed from the beginning in their mode and pace of settlement. During the 1630s some ten thousand men, women, and children participated in the Great Puritan Migration to New England. Sometimes an entire congregation came; at other times neighborhoods or families were united in bonds of sympathy and common purpose by religious or political conflict. Life in freedom, indeed survival itself, required the precedence of the group over the individual: "The care of the publique," in the words of John Winthrop, must "oversway all private respects." "For it is a true rule," Winthrop added, "that particular Estates cannott subsist in the ruine of the publique."[13] In the New England colonies values like these led to the adoption of a land system unique to that region. Yet secular experiences also played an important part in forging policies conducive to the interests of groups founding plantations at Plymouth, at Salem, and at other settlements about Massachusetts Bay, along the Connecticut River, on the shores of Narragansett Bay, and elsewhere.

In 1621 the Crown had bestowed on the Council for New England, a joint stock company incorporated that year at Plymouth, Devon, title to a vast tract of land between the fortieth and forty-eighth degrees of north latitude, extending through the continent, and authorized the company to grant out the land to settlers. It was from the council that the Pilgrims, who had landed as squatters on Plymouth Rock, obtained legal rights of settlement. Before another settlement was made, the council sold its territorial rights to the incorporators of the Massachusetts Bay Company, a transfer approved by the Crown in 1629. The Massachusetts Bay Company then proceeded to empower the company's governor and council in New England to allot the land. Thereafter, allotments by the provincial legislature to towns, and by the latter to the inhabitants of the towns, was the most common method by which land was acquired in seventeenth-century New England.[14]

"For the first time in their lives" the inhabitants of an English town— provided the town was located in America!—could assume "that each adult male would be granted some land, free and clear."[15] Practically every husbandman in New England was a freeholder. But this does not mean the land was equally shared. Hardly anyone believed it should be. Whether in England or in America, a fundamental tenet of seventeenth-century social philosophy was "the universal acceptance of the concept of social gradation and a complete belief in its rightness."[16] Few if any would have disagreed with John Winthrop's statement, made in a celebrated sermon while enroute to America in the ship *Arbella,* that "God Almightie in his most holy and wise providence, hath soe disposed of the Condition of mankinde, as in all times some must be rich, some poore, some highe and eminent in power and dignitie; others meane and in subjection."[17] The settlers accepted a hierarchy of wealth and status as both desirable and inevitable.

People of "rank and quality" therefore received larger grants, as did those who had invested more money or ability than others in the enterprise of founding the town, and those with large families.[18] Yet limits were also observed. From the beginning there existed among the families of Andover, Massachusetts, a hierarchy of rank and wealth, yet the selectmen of the town limited the largest houselots to twenty acres and the smallest to four acres.[19] In the Puritan village of Sudbury, Massachusetts, "no one was allowed to be too rich or too poor." In that town three men received 50 acres apiece; nine, 30 acres; and the six men at the low end of the scale, 16 acres.[20] In sum, no one was permitted to monopolize the land to the exclusion of lesser individuals. An assumption held by the town fathers of early Connecticut was undoubtedly widely shared: men with a stake in society could be depended on to uphold laws protecting property and order.[21]

Perfect equality in the distribution of landed wealth was certainly not attained, but the adoption of upper and lower limits on houselot sizes, together with divisions of arable and other lands in amounts determined by those sizes, resulted in a closer approach to equality than was ever again to be the case in so large a number of American communities. Furthermore, the number of acres of land received by the average member of the first generation of settlers exceeded what most men could have expected to obtain in England, where a farm of 50 to 100 acres was a substantial one. A man who lived in Dedham, Massachusetts, for any twenty-five-year span between 1636 and 1686 received from the town between 50 and 500 acres—on the average, 150 acres. A man owning a farm this size was a potential yeoman, a status enjoyed by only a minority of the English rural population. Comparative study of other towns in eastern Massachusetts leads to the conclusion that an estimate of 150 acres for the typical early inhabitant is a reasonable one. Land allotments in Andover were comparable in magnitude.[22]

The form in which the allotments were first made reflected the settlement patterns familiar to the leaders of the towns. All except two of the original selectmen of Watertown, Massachusetts, had emigrated from East Anglia, England where farms were enclosed and subject to individual management. And fully 60 percent of those granted meadowland in June 1637 had come from the East Anglian counties of Essex, Suffolk, and Norfolk. In consequence, although town law gave them the alternative to enclose their grants or feed their cattle in common, they appear soon to have chosen the former.[23] On the other hand, town leaders from English open-field country such as Hampshire, Lincolnshire, and Wiltshire sought to reproduce the nucleated village life they had known in those counties. In this pattern of rural life all the inhabitants resided side by side along the streets of the village rather than on separate and distant farms outside the village center. Besides houselots, the town allotted settlers pieces of arable land in large open fields, sometimes in long strips and sometimes in parcels of varying size and shape. Every man had a similar strip and joined with his fellow landholders in making common decisions on what crop to sow in the field and on its care and harvesting. In addition, inhabitants received strips of meadow and woodland scattered around the village. Year after year the town enacted orders governing pasturage of the common herd and designating which fields were to be planted and which left fallow, the dates by which fences had to be made following the planting and harrowing, and the appointment of fence viewers and other town officers to supervise these operations.[24]

After the initial allotments the town's lands were held in reserve, forming a savings bank of land, as it were, to be drawn on later as needed or desired. At first, divisions came surprisingly slowly, even hesitantly. During the first twenty years the inhabitants of Dedham divided among themselves less than 3,000 acres. Presumably, scarcity of land in England nurtured habits of parsimony rather than indulgence, at least initially. The first generation of settlers acted with similar conservatism at Andover, where, between 1646 and 1662, only 5,160 acres of upland (that is, plowland) were divided.[25] At Sudbury, 89 percent of the land available for distribution remained in the town's bank account after the first division in 1639–1640.[26]

This early conservatism was not destined to last. Whereas Dedham allotted only three thousand acres in the first twenty years, in the next twelve years the town divided five times that amount. Andover allotted only an acre of upland for each acre of houselot in its first two town divisions but quadrupled this amount in a third, and then in 1662 ordered that twenty acres be given for every acre of houselot. Other towns pursued a similar course. Some evidence suggests that the best, most fertile lands were distributed first, with marginal lands following. Certainly later allotments provided many townsmen with parcels of land at a considerable distance from the village. Because distant lands could be farmed on a daily basis only with great difficulty, farmers moved their residences to more convenient locations. They also began to consolidate their holdings into compact farms by buying, selling, and exchanging lots for others more conveniently located. The effect was to diminish the cohesion of the community, to weaken and then destroy communal agriculture in the form of open field systems, and to augment the importance of the individual family settled on its own lands at a distance from its neighbors.[27]

Dispersal from original village centers thus hastened the process by which New England's unique pattern of land settlement was transformed into one characterized by small proprietorships and separate family farms. A nearly total change to individual management had come to Watertown by 1655, and in the 1660s the open-field system was rapidly giving way in Andover and Haverhill. Although the townsmen of Sudbury tolerated open fields for fifteen years, everyone wanted to run his own freehold farm as an independent manager as soon as possible. In Dedham, the common-field system began to disintegrate almost from the day of its inception.[28]

These developments were inherent in a situation in which there was plenty of land for all. Although it is undoubtedly true that the inhabitants of some New England towns only slowly pushed the lamp of their ambition against the darkness of the wilderness, it is not true of all. As Governor William Bradford of Plymouth Plantation noted at the very beginning of settlement in New England, "no man now thought he could live except he had cattle and a great deal of ground to keep them; all striving to increase their stocks."[29] Following a quickly abandoned communal system of agriculture similar to that at early Jamestown, each inhabitant of Plymouth wanted more pasture for his own growing herd and forest lands for timber. The desire for land mounted as fathers wished for their children material opportunities equal to their own. In England the rule of primogeniture had confined this prospect to the eldest son, but in the New World there was land enough for all the sons and generous portions for daughters too. Intact parcels of land were almost never left to any one son. Indeed, when men died intestate, New England law provided for a double share of the whole estate for the eldest son and equal shares for all other children. Thus English law was abandoned for the law of partible inheritance, once more in keeping with early American abundance.[30]

The economic meaning of abundance to colonial American families depended on the quality of the land and the uses to which it was put, on the resources of nature and their own responses to the demand for its products. The largesse of nature had not fallen evenly along the coastal plain where most people made their homes in the seventeenth century. The width of the plain varied from merely 50 to 80 miles in New England, to 100 or more in New Jersey, Delaware, and Pennsylvania, before stretching out to about 250 miles in the Carolinas. Not only did the people of New England have less land available for cultivation than the inhabitants of the middle and southern provinces, but also much of what they had was relatively poor, winters were long and harsh, and the growing season short. The soil was largely glacial in origin, much of it boulder clay and hard to cultivate. Some 25,000 years ago the last continental ice sheet had wrenched off boulders and stones from the mountains across which it moved and strewn them over the lower lands. Besides rocks there was coarse sand; indeed, a wide strip of sand in the southeastern part was almost useless for agriculture. Also in the south and east, however, lay what the anonymous author of *American Husbandry* characterized in 1775 as "very considerable tracts of fine and rich land," a description that well fits the fertile alluvial soil of the Connecticut Valley. In sum, the land that was good was good indeed, but the region had relatively less of it. For most of those who lived there, subsistence was a product of hard labor.[31]

Clearly, New England's comparative advantage lay elsewhere than in agriculture, and once again nature played an important part in its determination. Possessed of a sunken coast full of bays, numerous harbors, rivers with wide estuaries, and forests rich in pine, New Englanders could look to shipbuilding and trade to offset stunted opportunities on the farm. In addition, because the more important food fish were more plentiful in cold water than in warm, the shores of the region and its outlying fishing banks were to prove hospitable to that industry. Not least among potential natural advantages was an abundance of water power. The prehistoric glacier had sent the rivers into strange courses and provided hundreds of waterfalls. These falls would prove unusually dependable, in part because the rainfall of the region was well distributed throughout the year. The glacier had also left upland swamps and thousands of lakes and had made many of the soils porous and thus able to absorb much rain, store it, and release it gradually through springs. A plentiful supply, coupled with evenness of flow, meant that, in contrast to regions below the glacial belt, dams were less likely to be washed out or raceways broken. Natural advantages of these kinds would play a part in the early industrialization of the region at a later time.[32]

The climate and soil of the middle colonies, together with their wider plain, made agriculture a more inviting prospect than in New England. It is true that the sandy earth of New Jersey's coastal plain had discouraged settlement, but the clay soils of the Piedmont, which ran through the northwestern part of the province and on into Pennsylvania, were generally fertile. Coastal New

York was sandy too, but in the interior were to be found "noble tracs [*sic*] of rich black mold, red loam, and friable clays, with mixtures of these soils in great varieties." In the central valleys of both New York and Pennsylvania layers of limestone had decomposed to form unusually rich agricultural land. On the whole, the area between the Potomac and Hudson rivers was the best in the American colonies for the production of food, especially the cereal crops.[33]

To the author of *American Husbandry* the southern colonies shared striking similarities in the characteristics of their soil. From Maryland and Virginia through Georgia the maritime parts of the coastal lowland were sandy and either pine barrens, marsh, or swampland. The soil improved as one advanced toward the mountains, and in many parts of the backcountry the land was "a rich black mould, of a good depth, and highly fertile." The fertility of the lowlands on the river banks of Maryland and Virginia exceeded "every thing in Pennsylvania or to the northward"; the higher lands were sandy "but not therefore barren or of little value," for their moisture was "sufficient even for tobacco." The soil in the interior of North Carolina was "very fine," several of its tracts being "equal to the best of Virginia." Beyond the pine country of South Carolina, an area that was "very poor" and would bear "scarcely any thing but its spontaneous growth," and to the west of its salt- and freshwater marshes spread "extensive meadows of rich, deep land," whose soil possessed an "extraordinary fertility." Yet the deep, black loam behind the sandy coast of Georgia was "of a fertility that even exceeds the back parts of South Carolina." In sum, the southern interior contained soils of unusual richness, and this, in combination with a long growing season, made the region one of great promise for agricultural activity.[34]

In all three regions, however, some prospective tillers of the soil had to face first the trees that covered the land. From Maine to Georgia a dense forest primeval stretched back from the water's edge. "It is a very fine Country," wrote the settler Thomas Markham to his wife in 1681, "if it were not so overgrown with Woods."[35] Yet it would be a mistake to visualize the early colonists bravely pitting their small labor against a Goliath of trees. Many had no need to, for fortunately there existed numerous openings along the Atlantic coastal plain, especially along the river banks; many natural meadows covered with grass, cane, or wild pea vines in the piedmont districts of all the colonies; and clearings that the Indians had been making for centuries in order to grow maize (Indian corn) and vegetables. At Plymouth the first fields brought under cultivation were invariably laid out on natural meadows, Indian burnings, or abandoned cornfields; those who came to Massachusetts in the 1630s sought out salt marshes, meadowland along rivers, natural clearings on the Charles, Mystic, Concord, and Connecticut rivers, and old Indian lands; in Pennsylvania their counterparts in and after the 1680s sought open areas, and in Maryland the Indians allowed the first settlers to use some of their corn land right away and the rest of it after the harvest. Thus many colonists were presented by nature and by the Indians with part of their initial means of production, although the fertility of the Indian lands had been diminished by use. Very soon, however, and for some immediately, increases in the number of arrivals obliged many to carve farmland out of forest.[36]

The Indians taught them to do this by burning the underbrush and then cutting a girdle around the trunks of the largest trees. Stripping away the girdle of bark intercepted the flow of the sap, and the coup de grace could then be administered by kindling fires around the exposed roots. Unable to put forth foliage, the trees soon weakened and died and in a few years were blown down by the wind. Naturally falling trees put life and limb at risk, however, and most New Englanders felled them by ax, burning them where they lay so their ashes might add to the fertilizer provided by the burned underbrush. Early southerners sometimes planted corn and tobacco between the standing dead trees, but seventeenth century New Englanders would not tolerate even the stumps! Indeed, they often left fertile soil unplanted till stumps had been removed and the land was ready for the plow. Stump removal was "undoubtedly the hardest work of the New World."[37] The farmer had to dig around under the roots and then, using from two to four teams of oxen— his own and his neighbors—drag out the stump by brute force.

The Indians not only supplied some of the early colonists with cleared land and a technique for clearing more, but they also introduced them to many crops and provided instruction in methods of cultivating and preparing them for the table. Among the important ones were maize, pumpkins, squash, and beans, all planted in the same field in the North, and crops of the South such as sweet potatoes, gourds, and melons, as well as tobacco and the New World species of cotton, *Gossypium barbadense*. Not confined to a single region, maize was grown almost everywhere. Having dominated aboriginal agriculture, it also became the principal grain for man and beast in all the colonies.[38]Maize was the first crop raised by the English in New England, and by 1629 it was reported from Jamestown that the settlers "finde the *Indian* corn so much better than ours, they beginne to leave sowing" of English grain. The contribution of the Indians was thus a significant one, and from the New England towns to the scattered farms of Pennsylvania and the South colonists relied, sometimes greatly, on their knowledge and suggestions.[39] As an agricultural historian has pointed out, "it was not until the English settlers adopted the American Indians' agricultural plants, cultivation and harvesting methods, and processes of food preparation that they were assured of adequate food supplies."Nevertheless, the agricultural traditions which the settlers brought with them across the ocean were also important. "Indeed . . . it was the *union* of American Indian and European farming that produced the beginnings of American agriculture and provided the essential bases for its ultimate development."[40]

From the very first the colonists had tried to raise English grains—wheat, rye, barley, oats, and peas. The problem, in part, was either insufficient quantities of seed corn—as at Jamestown—or its probable spoilage at sea enroute to America—as in the case of Plymouth. Early lack of plows and oxen was also to blame, for the most effective way to grow the small grains was to sow seed broadcast on ground that had been plowed and harrowed, and then to harrow in the seed. Harrows could be improvised, but probably a number of years passed before a plow was in operation at Jamestown. The Pilgrims had no plows for a dozen years after the landing on the Rock, and as late as 1636 there were but thirty in the whole of the Massachusetts Bay Colony. Nevertheless, husbandmen at Plymouth succeeded in harvesting English grains in 1624 and 1625, and the relative importance of Indian corn, which had been vital to survival in the early years, began to decline. From midcentury on, the typical settler planted roughly half his cultivated land in corn and the other half in traditional English crops, especially wheat and rye. In New England as a whole, Indian corn remained a staple throughout the seventeenth century, but its importance as the principal bread grain was far greater in the South, where wheat and other small grains were little grown.[41]

Tobacco too, of course, was also much more important in the South, and the leading role played by corn and tobacco goes far to explain the prevalence of hoeing and the relative scarcity of plows in the region throughout the colonial period. Indian corn grows best in bunches or hills, made by heaping up earth around the growing plant, and this is work a hoe does best. The hoe was equally essential in the cultivation of tobacco. Each plant was set by hand, and the earliest surviving full account of methods of cultivation, dating from 1671, makes it clear that after the plants reached a certain size, they were replanted in hills, "which afterward they keep with diligent Weedings"—more work for the hoe.[42] The plow did not become a major factor in the tobacco fields till late in the colonial period, and even then the use of the hoe continued to predominate.[43] In seventeenth century Maryland, however, the use of the plow spread among the richer planters of the western shore, perhaps as a result of their preference for wheat bread. Its increasing use to the north and across Chesapeake Bay suggests a rising interest in the market for cereals. Still, even in the 1760s estate inventories in the Chesapeake tobacco country show that fewer than one planter in twenty owned a plow.[44]

In contrast, plowing husbandry typified the agriculture of Pennsylvania, where wheat was the leading crop, and throughout the seventeenth century in New England plowing was considered absolutely necessary. It is true that impediments in newly cleared southern soil in the form of stumps and roots, which they "never grub up," would have made the journey of a plow through the earth a difficult one. But there was no need for plowing. The stumps and roots were allowed to remain because they did not impede the hoes that were used in the cultivation of tobacco and Indian corn. It was not till late in the eighteenth century that New Englanders discovered that Indian corn could be successfully raised among the burnt logs without the use of the plow. Before then, land had to remain in pasture till the removal of roots and stumps made plowing possible.[45]

Plows continued to be in short supply in New England, but it was far easier to alleviate scarcities in that region than it would have been in the South. The original cultivation of strips in common fields meant that plowing could be undertaken, as it had been throughout the Middle Ages, as a community responsibility. Even after the advent of separate compact farms, farms were close enough to one another to permit the owner of a plow to till the fields of his neighbors, and some men specialized in doing so. Had southerners needed that service, it would have been more difficult to perform because of the scattered locations of their farms and plantations. Judging from inventories, the number of harrows in seventeenth century New England was also astonishingly small. But harrows as well as plows could be used cooperatively. Furthermore, seed could be covered and the soil pulverized by a homemade implement of brush and saplings of insufficient value to be listed in inventories.[46]

The great bulk of the tools in use in colonial agriculture were hand tools: hatchets, felling axes, broadaxes, pick-axes, mattocks, handsaws, and whipsaws for clearing forest land; mattocks once again, broad and narrow hoes, shovels, and spades for cultivating the fields; sickles, scythes, and reaping hooks for harvesting; and fans and flails for threshing, besides pitchforks for haying, wheelbarrows for moving dung, and carpentering tools. Implements of any kind were scarce on most Pennsylvania farms till after 1750, but this probably means that most farms were small ones with minimal stocks of equipment.[47] That is certainly true of seventeenth-century planters at the bottom of the economic scale on the western shore of Maryland. In the smallest estates of the early eighteenth century—and these are more than half the total—the ax and hoe are the only implements listed. More affluent planters, though, also had rakes, shovels, and pruning knives.[48]

There undoubtedly exists a close relationship between degrees of affluence and quality of farming. The author of *American Husbandry* observed in 1775, "In America, as well as in all other parts of the world . . . the richer the cultivator, the better will the land be cultivated."[49] Modern studies of agriculture in colonial Pennsylvania confirm the strength of this relationship while also taking into consideration the amount of acreage under production and the quality of the soil.[50]

It remains to emphasize the backwardness of colonial agricultural implements. Heavy, clumsy, and poorly suited to their purpose, they "would have been familiar," a historian suggests, "in ancient Babylonia."[51] A roughhewn stick served as a beam on even the best plows, the beam itself holding another stick fitted at the end with a rude plate of bog iron. An awkward, ungainly tool, it surely must have been difficult to manage. Harrows had wooden teeth, although these were soon discarded for iron ones, cart wheels often lacked tires, and hoes were large and heavy. Such cumbersome implements must have been taxing to the strength of men and animals. And they were largely home-hewn, although shares, coulters, and iron teeth were generally imported from England. Finally, little if any improvement occurred until the very close of the eighteenth century. Not till then did plows appear that would cut even to a depth of six inches, and even then only a few men possessed them. It would be another twenty-five years before they would meet with wide use.[52]

Tools like these limited narrowly the prospect of raising the productivity of those who used them. To be sure, long experience in the use of even primitive tools must have improved one's skill; nevertheless, resulting increases in output per man would have come only slowly and with limited effect. It is doubtful that most farmers aimed for higher productivity. The majority were small producers whose tools were few and whose labor resources were limited in the main to the members of their own families. Yet even small farmers, while primarily engaged in producing food and other goods for household consumption, constantly sought a marketable product and welcomed outside help when they could get it.

The problem was getting it. Because of the abundance of cheap land, labor was scarce and wages high. Land was not equally cheap everywhere nor labor always dear, but in general the colonial laborer commanded real wages that were from 30 to 100 percent higher than those of a contemporary English workman.[53] By enabling workers to buy their own farms, high wages tended to keep labor in short supply. As the author of *American Husbandry* noted, "Nothing but a high price will induce men to labour [for others] at all, and at the same time it presently puts a conclusion to it by so soon enabling them to take a piece of waste land."[54] It is for these reasons that small farmers everywhere essentially depended on their own families for their labor needs. Those who could afford to hire free labor did so, but its inadequate supply, uncertain tenure, and high price soon induced them to look first to bound labor, that is, to indentured servitude, and then to slavery.

The farmers of seventeenth-century New England depended on their own families to a greater degree than did those in other regions. Possibly some of them had the help of a servant or two, but it is unlikely very many did. The pursuit of agriculture in that inhospitable region required relatively less extra labor. Indeed, the country was better suited to raising cattle than to growing corn. Stock raising, of horses as well as cows, sheep, swine, and goats, was even more important than field husbandry. Lumbering was also a thriving industry; indeed it had become one in New Hampshire and Maine as early as the 1630s, and in southern New England many farmers worked at it as part of their land-clearing operations. But these activities were adjunctive to an agriculture lacking a staple whose production in volume would have required a large labor force.

A fair proportion of the participants in the Great Puritan Migration of the

1630s must have consisted of servants under indenture, but the number entering the region thereafter was negligible. New Englanders owned African
slaves too, probably as early as 1638, but there were only a few hundred in
1680, and even in the eighteenth century slaves made up no more than 3
percent of the population. Probably few of these were employed in
agriculture.[55]

In New England, it was the father and his older sons who took care of the
fields. They began the plowing in March, their crude implement and slow-
moving oxen enabling them to finish no more than an acre a day. The harrowing came next and went faster. Planting time extended from mid-March to
mid-May, with some weeding of corn and grainfield in both May and June.
In July and August, the haying months, about an acre of grass a day would be
cut with a long-handled scythe. Harvesting of wheat, rye and peas began in
August and early September, with the use of a hook-shaped, short-handled
sickle. This backbreaking work limited the amount that farmers could reap. A
strong man could cut about an acre a day but could harvest only five acres a
season. Barley and oats were cut with a scythe. The cornfields were turned to
in September or later, with the ears, beans, gourds, and pumpkins picked first
and stored, then the stalks cut down to serve as winter fodder for the animals.
Winter was threshing time, and time also for repairing equipment, spreading
manure on the fields, felling trees, and cutting firewood that would be allowed
to season for use the following winter.[56]

As these diverse activities suggest, the farmer was a jack-of-all-trades. Besides his regular duties in the field, meadow, and barn, he was a woodsman
and an artisan as well. In addition, "there were calves, colts, and lambs to be
ushered into the world, and cattle, great and small, to be ushered out." His
wife was also far from idle. "She ran the kitchen, grew flowers and vegetables
in the garden, killed the chickens, milked the cows (even on the Sabbath),
made butter and cheese, spun and wove homespun—in a word, busied herself
with every phase of household activity." Daughters assisted in some of these
tasks, in the spinning and weaving, for example, and, together with the small
boys of the family, helped in the feeding, milking, and watering of the animals.[57] Except occasionally at harvest time, the wives of New England farmers,
unlike those of the German farmers of Pennsylvania and New York, did not
work in the fields. "Women in New England," as Timothy Dwight primly
announced, "are employed only in and about the house, and in the proper
business of the sex."[58]

Small farmers also dominated the agriculture of the middle colonies, but
probably to a lesser degree than in New England. Most production was for
household consumption, with farmers producing a wide range of crops and
livestock. They thus practiced diversified, mixed farming, as in New England.
But they also had a staple—wheat (and flour)—and the urban and external
demand for these products encouraged the development of some specializa-

tion in the agriculture of southeastern Pennsylvania and New Jersey. Larger-scale farming in these provinces created a greater need for outside help than in New England, and by 1685 nearly half the adult males arriving in Pennsylvania were indentured servants. Many of the immigrants went to Philadelphia, however, rather than into rural areas and farming. Indentured servitude would play a more important part in the agriculture of the middle colonies in the eighteenth century than in the seventeenth.[59]

The staple agriculture of the upper South had the greatest need for labor, and in the seventeenth century most indentured servants migrating to North America went to the Chesapeake tobacco colonies. Men were employed primarily in field work, while female servants cooked, cleaned, wove, and mended, although there is some evidence that they also took a hand in tobacco cultivation. For the first three-quarters of the seventeenth century the plantation system in Virginia was based mainly on indentured servitude. First achieving legal recognition in that province in 1619, indentured servitude won a similar position in Maryland in 1637, in the Carolinas in 1665, and in Georgia in 1732. Discovery of the export possibilities of tobacco created an insatiable demand for labor, and already by 1621 the wages of day workers in Virginia had risen to a level three or four times higher than the maximum wages of day labor set by county justices in England. These premium wages gave tobacco planters an incentive to substitute lower-rate bound labor for free labor. It is true that the cost of importing a man from England was about six pounds, and that provisions and clothes for the voyage and to start him out in the New World amounted to an additional four to six pounds. But the services of bound workers could be counted on for a number of years, in contrast to those of free workers, who might use their earnings to buy land for themselves. Accordingly, tobacco planters could not get enough of them. As the planter John Pory succinctly expressed it, "Our principall wealth . . . consisteth in servants."[60]

In 1624–25 servants in Virginia numbered 474 of a population of 1,200, or 40 percent of the total, and in the earlier years of Maryland the ratio of servants to freemen was about six to one. The largest movement of servants to the colonies in the seventeenth century occurred just before and after the Restoration, although the total emigrating probably never exceeded 3,500 in any one year. Throughout the 1670s, between 12,000 and 15,000 servants labored in the plantations, about 6,000 in Jamaica, with the rest divided roughly equally among the other southern colonies. About one white person in ten was under indenture. Prior to a substantial increase in the number of slaves imported in the closing years of the seventeenth century, indentured servitude—augmented by such involuntary servants as insolvent debtors, paupers, criminals, and the kidnapped, principally children—provided the labor base on which the growing prosperity of the southern colonies rested.[61]

In South Carolina as well as in the tobacco colonies slavery gradually replaced indentured servitude in the late seventeenth and eighteenth centuries, first in field work and then in skilled occupations. The timing of both transitions is best explained in terms of the increasing relative costs first of unskilled and later of skilled indentured white labor. Servants were becoming scarcer and more dear as improving economic conditions lessened their willingness to bind themselves to overseas service. At the same time, the supply of African slaves available for purchase was steadily rising. In the 1680s their price fell to a long-term low because of economic depression in the West Indies and other sugar-producing regions. In addition, falling transport costs encouraged their importation, while the high and rising wages commanded by free labor also helped tilt the balance in favor of slavery.[62]

The importance of the acquisition of skills by the slaves deserves emphasis. Slave imports traversed a rising curve till the 1740s, when the number of newly imported and hence inexperienced and unacclimated slaves formed a declining proportion of the slave population as a whole. This surely tended to increase the productivity of that population. Long before then, and just as surely, the lifelong servitude of slaves gave their work efforts a productivity advantage over those of servants. The latter usually served an indenture of five years and then took with them into freedom the skills they had acquired. Slaves not only gathered experience over a far longer period but continued to apply it for the benefit of their owners. Although we have no measure of it, slave efficiency must have increased as a result of what we would now consider to be a process of compulsory human capital formation.

Just how compulsory that process was has rarely if ever been depicted more graphically than in the terse notations of an eighteenth-century ship captain in his "Trade Book." In the employ of the mercantile house of Nicholas Brown & Company of Providence, Rhode Island, Captain Esek Hopkins of the ship *Sally* traded his outgoing cargo of rum for a cargo of slaves on the Guinea coast of Africa. Even before leaving the coast, death began taking a grim toll of the cargo. The first occurred on April 1, 1765, when Captain Hopkins recorded that "a boye Slave died." On June 8 a "woman Slave hanged her Self between Decks." By August 20 he had already lost 20 slaves of his original cargo of 196. Death continued to stalk the dread Middle Passage between Africa and the West Indies as the captain recorded the loss of 4 more persons before August 28. Then on that date comes the following entry: "Slaves Rose on us was obliged to fire on them and Destroyed 8 and Several more wounded badly 1 Thye & ones Ribs broke." As the *Sally* sailed toward the Caribbean, deaths were an almost daily occurrence. Finally, in a letter from Antigua Captain Hopkins told the story of the last tragic days of the voyage. After the uprising, the surviving blacks were "so disperited" that "some drowned themselves, some starved and others sickened and died." Eighty-eight were dead and the remaining slaves were in a "very sickly and disordered manner."[63]

Quite obviously, not only economic advantage but a far more complex history of prejudicial attitudes and events would also be necessary for a complete account of the origins of a system based on racial differences. That account would also require a history of the intimate connection between powerful interests and the roles of government and law in creating property rights in human beings. Suffice it here to note that after 1660 slavery began crystallizing on the statute books of Maryland, Virginia, and other colonies. And since a cheaper and more stable labor force contributed to the growing prosperity of the South, the legal system must be "credited" in part with this result.[64]Finally, although nothing can assuage the unspeakable inhumanity of subjecting black men and women and their children to bondage during the entirety of their lives, it must be remembered that many servants also suffered. An "impressive number of masters led drunken, dissolute lives and were brutal and sadistic in behavior toward their workmen." The labor extracted from servants was exploitative and often cruelly oppressive because of the planter's desire to squeeze all he could from the limited period of the indenture. With the advent of slavery, the position of servants improved, "partly for the reason that they were not Negroes," surely one of the more expensive alleviations in the history of human pain.[65]

Slavery must also be credited in part for the surprisingly advanced political views of both wealthy planters and small farmers in eighteenth century Virginia. The existence of black slaves in their midst helped unify the free white community, helped generate and support concepts of white equality and republicanism. But, once again, the price was high.[66]

Yet we must not exaggerate the numbers of slaves in the Chesapeake tobacco colonies. In Maryland in the 1720s, three-fourths of the planters owned no slaves at all, and only 13 percent of the slaveholders owned more than five. In Virginia, except for a half-dozen counties where a larger percentage of the households had managed to acquire a slave or two, the pattern of distribution was very close to that of Maryland. Even as late as the 1760s, two-thirds of the slaveholders along the tobacco coast of Virginia and Maryland owned only one to four slaves.[67]

Their concentration was in the lower South, particularly in the South Carolina low country after the rise, first, of rice plantations in the early eighteenth century, and later, of estates devoted to indigo. Blacks constituted only 15 percent of the estimated population of South Carolina in 1670, but within a decade this percentage doubled, and by 1720 nearly two of every three persons in a population of roughly eighteen thousand was black, almost all of them slaves. Most lived and labored in the lowlands nearest the coast, where by 1770 they outnumbered whites more than three to one. In the backcountry, whites held a five to one advantage over blacks.[68]

Again, it was the general scarcity of labor and the abundance of land in a context of rising world demand for tobacco, rice, and other staples, that gave birth to indentured servitude and slavery. To be sure, supplies of capital were not abundant either, but in an age largely innocent of technological change, this was a scarcity whose relative importance was less than it later became. The other two factors—scarcity of labor and abundance of land—governed agricultural life not only in the South but everywhere else in colonial America as well. They induced the farmer to practice an agriculture that was extensive rather than intensive: instead of using capital and labor to increase the output of fields already under cultivation, he put these factors of production to work clearing more land. By necessity he did so slowly and gradually, for, as the mid-eighteenth-century agricultural writer Jared Eliot said, "it is an arduous Work, to clear Land, overgrown with Wood, and drain Land, immerged in Water, and bring it into a State of Fertility." The cheapness of land enabled the farmer to purchase much more of it than he needed right away, and whether in New England or in the South only a fraction of it was under cultivation at one time. And since it was principally in the greater fertility of new land that increases in output per acre originated, this source of productivity growth, like those germane to output per worker, exercised its influence only gradually and to a limited degree.[69]

Once a field had been cleared, the farmer planted it, harvested the crop, and then planted it again, year in and year out, until its yield ran so low that he had no alternative but to clear more land. Probably making use first of that part of the forest from which he had been taking timber for firewood and building materials, he enlarged the area of plowland and then repeated the process "till,"—in the words of the author of *American Husbandry,* he had "run through" his "whole ground," after which he went back again to the piece he had cleared first, which by that time was "half forest and half weeds and grass"; this he cleared again and sowed as before, as long as it would yield a crop. Thus bit by bit the cleared part of a farmer's land increased in relation to the whole.[70]

What the farmer did in America was just the opposite of what he had done in England. There, and in Europe generally, agriculture was intensive rather than extensive, applying relatively cheap labor to relatively expensive land. The European farmer used agricultural methods that reflected the relative scarcity of land, methods designed to extract the highest possible yield from each acre while nursing each into the longest possible life. Accordingly, he allowed his arable land to lie fallow at periodic intervals so that it might regain its strength, and while fallow he plowed it three or four times. When his grainfields were in cultivation, he cross plowed them, that is, gave them a second plowing at right angles from the first. He rotated his crops too, and after that harvest gleaners went through the grainfield to pick up every stray kernel. He drained, trenched, and hedged his fields, developed the beginnings of a science of agriculture and a growing literature appertaining to it, and heaped scorn on the "wasteful" ways of American farmers.[71] The most important set of strictures is found in the pages of *American Husbandry,* (1775), but other critics have not been wanting, then or since.[72]

The "first settlers, with the usual foresight of the Americans," charged the author of *American Husbandry*, "destroyed the timber, as if it was impossible they should ever want any."[73] According to Jared Eliot, an eighteenth-century Connecticut minister, physician, and farmer whose six *Essays upon Field Husbandry in New England* are among our valued sources of knowledge of colonial farming techniques, "when our fore-fathers settled here, they entered a land which probably never had been Ploughed since the Creation; the Land being new they depended upon the natural Fertility of the Ground,—which served their purpose very well, and when they had worn out one piece they cleared another, without any concern to amend their Land, except a little helped by the Fold and Cart-dung." Eliot mildly observed that "our Country yet needs and is capable of greater Improvement in the management of our Lands,"[74] but the author of *American Husbandry* was anything but mild:

> Seduced by the fertility of the soil on first settling, the farmers [of New York] think only of exhausting it as soon as possible, without attending to their own interest in a future day: this is a degree of blindness which in sensible people one may fairly call astonishing.

"All our American colonists are very bad farmers," he concluded; "the American planters and farmers are in general the greatest slovens in christendom."[75] To the German traveler Peter Kalm it was clear that "their eyes are fixed upon the present gain, and they are blind to futurity."[76]

Agricultural historians are agreed that colonial farming techniques suffer in comparison not only with modern practice but also with those of contemporary Europe. Two collaborating scholars sum up, a bit ungenerously, the case against the colonial farmers of New England: "On their poorly cultivated fields little fertilizer of any sort was used, their implements were rough and clumsy, livestock was neglected, and the same grains and vegetables were raised year after year with little attempt at a rotation of crops, until the land was exhausted."[77] By modern standards, another observes, the practices of Pennsylvania farmers were "virtually antediluvian."[78] The planting economy, says a historian of southern agriculture, was "based on deliberate exhaustion of the soil . . . Planters bought land as they might buy a wagon—with the expectation of wearing it out."[79] The consequences were clear. By the end of the eighteenth century almost all inhabited regions in New England had been stripped of their original forest cover, while throughout the older districts of the tobacco colonies "great stretches of barren and gullied fields" quietly testified to the way in which the land had been treated.[80]

Any general indictment, however, is easily overdrawn. The charge that the early settlers wantonly destroyed the timber is unfounded. Many colonists of the seventeenth century had bitter memories of timber shortages in England and displayed solicitude for the forests of America. As a rule, the town authorities of New England, far from encouraging the wholesale felling of trees, "took the most careful precautions against it,"[81] and in Pennsylvania William

Penn's Charter of Privileges (1701) stipulated that "one acre should be left in trees in every five cleared." However, it must be acknowledged that there is no evidence that Penn's regulation was observed "in a single instance,"[82] and that once the memory of England's timber crisis had faded, so too did the enactment of conservation laws and their observance. It should also be remembered that "in a forested land in an Age of Wood, there were few ways to succeed without exploiting timber."[83]

Other distinctions also deserve note. Exploitative and extensive techniques of cultivation were more characteristic of the South than of New England. The rapid increase of population in the small land area of the latter region led early to the employment of intensive and soil-conserving methods.[84] After learning that Indian corn exhausted the fertility of the soil, farmers of New England fertilized it by adopting the Indian practice of burying fish in the corn hills. At Plymouth, though, farmers tended to revert to the use of traditional manures during and after the 1640s.[85] Elsewhere intensive agricultural techniques were also found in areas close to market centers, probably because farmers would have incurred higher transport costs by moving to new and more productive land. In general, however, efforts to conserve the soil did not characterize the behavior of colonial farmers. In Pennsylvania, and probably also in other provinces, fallow often meant land out of cultivation for long periods that had been permitted to revert to bush, and crop rotation patterns were often ill defined, careless, and poorly developed, in a word, far more casual than in England.[86]

Moreover, yields per acre were often small. While they all varied of necessity with differing qualities of soil, seed, and husbandry, they all declined with time and cropping. Farmers who broke ground that had been forested for thousands of years, that had all the humus it could store and a rich loam as topsoil, got big yields from the first crops. Thereafter, yields fell. According to the author of *American Husbandry,* a sowing of 2 or 3 bushels of seed an acre yielded from 25 to 32 bushels of wheat per acre "on good lands" in Pennsylvania. But "on fields of inferior quality, or such as are almost exhausted by yielding corn, they get from 15 to 25 bushels, and sometimes not so much as 15, but this never happens without its being owing to previous bad management."[87] A modern investigator confirms the correlation between the freshness of land and its yield. "Despite the great importance of wheat, yields per acre were low. From newer land twenty, thirty, or even forty bushels per acre were reported; but abundant comments suggest that five to twelve bushels was all that could be expected from old land.[88]

Other sources tell much the same story about these and other crops in other regions. Maize seems to have returned an average yield of 20 to 25 bushels an acre if the soil was fairly good, as in New York and Connecticut, with crops of 40 to 50 bushels sometimes achieved when conditions were favorable. Long Island land heavily manured with fish yielded 40 to 50 bushels of wheat, the best crops reported anywhere. A fair average wheat crop in the middle colonies, however, probably ranged between 10 and 15 bushels, as a rule nearer the lower figure. On the other hand, new land in the Hudson and Mohawk valleys might yield from 20 to 30 bushels. Average yields of wheat from New England were apparently higher than in Pennsylvania and New Jersey, but calculated yields at Plymouth are more sobering: grain yields of 6, 8, and 10 bushels per acre and corn yields of 18. Not only were such yields low in terms of seventeenth century England, they actually seem to have dropped to the level of England's output per acre in the thirteenth and fourteenth centuries![89] The testimony of a well-known farmer of Mount Vernon, Virginia, shows how little this situation had changed by the end of the colonial period. It would be difficult to find a clearer statement of the underlying reasons than in a letter from George Washington to the English agricultural reformer Arthur Young:

> An English farmer must entertain a contemptible opinion of our husbandry, or a horrid idea of our lands, when he shall be informed that not more than eight or ten bushels of wheat is the yield of an acre; but this low produce may be ascribed, and principally too, to a cause which I do not find touched by either of the gentlemen whose letters are sent to you, namely, that the aim of the farmers in this country, if they can be called farmers, is, not to make the most they can from the land, which is, or has been cheap, but the most of the labour, which is dear; the consequence of which has been, much ground has been *scratched* over and none cultivated or improved as it ought to have been: whereas a farmer in England, where land is dear, and labour cheap, finds it his interest to improve and cultivate highly, that he may reap large crops from a small quantity of ground.[90]

The farmers of colonial America must be adjudged innocent of the charge of being wasteful. "Waste" is in the beholder's eye: it necessarily takes its meaning in relation to the value of resources at a given time. Later scarcities are not proper grounds for indicting practices characteristic of a regime of abundance, in which resources freely spent were cheap in comparison with the costs of capital and labor. To have spared the land and the trees while freely spending more costly factors of production would have been irrational. People do not ordinarily act that way, and colonial farmers did not either. They freely spent the land, because there was so much of it that people generally valued it less than they did labor. Later, when supplies of land (and capital too) had increased and population pressure had raised the value of land, it made economic sense to restore the fertility of exhausted acres. And this is what happened. In the closing decades of the antebellum period, marl, gypsum, and other rock fertilizers came into wide use, with the result that thousands of acres once in an exhausted condition were restored to productiveness. Rational men who allocated the resources available to them in a rational manner, colonial farmers did not squander the nation's heritage.[91]

Whether or not they sought to maximize their earnings is less difficult to determine. Almost certainly, most did not. They were subsistence farmers. Most of the food they grew and most of the goods they made were intended for their own use rather than for sale. Yet it was nearly impossible for any farm family to be entirely self-sufficient, if only because items such as muskets and powder could not be made at home. To obtain them, farmers either bartered some of their produce or sold it for cash, the value of the goods involved being expressed in money prices. Where they sold their produce depended on their location and on the difficulty or ease of access to buyers. Farmers close enough to the coastal cities sold in the markets there. Those in the backcountry dealt with the storekeepers in their area, and those farther west did their bargaining with wandering peddlers. Wherever farmers sold, the prices they received were strongly influenced by the prices at which goods were bought and sold in the major markets of the coastal cities. Certainly that was true by the middle of the eighteenth century, but it was probably also true far earlier.[92]

The arm of the market was long, but this is not the issue. The important question is, what proportion of the resources available to them did farmers allocate to commercial production? Surely those located within reach of the growing markets of the coastal cities—the majority of seventeenth-century farmers—were tempted to make this proportion as large as possible. But there were limits to the possible, limits drawn by the tools and labor at their disposal. And since most were small farmers, these limits restrained their ability to respond to the lure of the market. Is it not likely that those limiting circumstances influenced not only their behavior but also their values, so that the greater the degree of production for subsistence, the less the effort to maximize income? Surely this would go far to explain the "limited desires and expectations" of the farmers of Andover. And it would help us understand why those of southeastern Pennsylvania were "a satisfied group of farmers" rather than "maximizing materialists," a people who "found their returns from general mixed farming satisfactory and so felt little incentive to adopt more specialized and intensive kinds of agriculture such as dairying." These farmers "participated in an economic system marked by a strong subsistence component," one in which "most agricultural produce was for home consumption." In Dedham, too, agriculture was "devoted largely to mere subsistence."[93]

The great majority of small northern farmers probably followed a safety-first strategy. In the main they avoided risk taking, specialization, and innovative behavior.[94] There is little or no reason to believe that these generalizations do not apply also to the small tobacco farmers of Maryland and Virginia. Even in the eighteenth century the maximizers would be in the minority, the possessors of broad acres and numerous nonfamily workers, especially slaves in the southern colonies, together with large-scale merchants in foreign trade. But this minority would grow in size as demand deepened for the country's agricultural staples and the economy industrialized.

In the seventeenth century, in sum, agriculture was dominated numerically by small farmers producing goods mainly for their own consumption. How well off were they? Probate inventories of estates throw much light on this question because they reveal the material possessions accumulated during a person's lifetime and on hand at the time of death (unfortunately, inventories for the southern colonies do not include land). Since the monetary value of each of the items was also assessed, it is possible to rank decedents in accordance with their wealth and to distinguish the relatively poor from the relatively rich and from those in between. Let us look at the poorest farmers of seventeenth-century Maryland, those whose estates had an assessed value ranking them in the lowest 30 percent of the wealthholders in that colony. (We can be pretty sure they were farmers because the colony was almost entirely rural.) At midcentury the poorest farmers in Maryland accumulated estates consisting of miscellaneous livestock—about 10 cattle, 8 swine, 2 horses, and, for one-fourth of the group, also an average of 8 sheep—clothing, bedding, kitchen utensils, and a few work tools. The houses in which they lived were small one- or one-and-a-half-story box frame structures which probably consisted of a single room. Although we do not know how much land on average they held, we do know that these poorer farmers were only a little better off at the end of the seventeenth century, by which time the appraised value of their physical personal wealth had risen from an average of £11 sterling at midcentury to £13 sterling.[95]

The standard of living of these Marylanders has been well described as one of "rude sufficiency."[96] Glimpses into lives in other places largely confirm the impression that the characterization is a fitting one for most seventeenth century farmers. Most of the settlers in Pennsylvania were of "middling" means: by 1693 little differentiation of wealth had occurred.[97] In Andover in the closing years of the century, 74.3 percent of the probated estates, including land, were inventoried at less than £600, and 60 percent at less than £400.[98] In Dedham, agriculture was "devoted largely to mere subsistence," and a seventeenth-century farmer might possess, besides his land, "a house of two to eight rooms with a few beds, chests and chairs, a little pewter or silver, perhaps two changes of clothing and a good suit and cloak, a Bible, sometimes with commentaries thereon; . . . a barn or lean-to containing agricultural tools, a cart, bins, bowls, pots, and pans, a few bushels of each of the staple crops, and finally a horse or two, several cattle and five or six each of sheep and swine. His whole state would come to between 200 and 400 pounds Massachusetts currency."[99]

These then were the artifacts of sufficiency, and the great bulk of America's farmers in the seventeenth century had a little more or a little less of them. Still, even rude sufficiency was better than the hunger that was the common lot of so many in the Europe they had left behind, and as landowners they had dignity and independence besides. They worked brutally hard, especially at hacking their farms out of the seemingly interminable forest, but no matter how difficult their labor, it would have brought them lesser returns had it not been for the fertility of America's abundant acres.

In one substantial sense the colonists had not left Europe behind at all. In the beginning, their very survival in the New World had depended on their lifeline to Europe, on food supplies brought with them and subsequently imported. Even after they had forced the wilderness to yield them an ample subsistence, they raised produce for sale, as we have seen, in order to obtain the weapons, iron pots and pans, farming and building equipment, stockings, coats and blankets, and other supplies that could not be made at home or made so cheaply or so well. And while some of this produce found consumer markets in the coastal towns, much was shipped abroad, where its disposal provided credits to pay for imports. Transactions such as these linked the settlers to the exchanges that were knitting the Atlantic community of the seventeenth-century into a series of interdependent markets. These exchanges had to be organized and initiated, of course, for goods and services do not flow of their own accord. Fortunately colonial America was not lacking in the commercial skills required: as in every society, some individuals were more able and aggressive than others, more alert to opportunities for betterment opened by trade. Whether farmer or merchant—or both in combination— such persons reaped material rewards in consequence. So that whereas most men and women of the seventeenth century enjoyed a sufficiency of the goods of life, some won more than that.[100]

The principal markets for colonial produce in the Atlantic community were the British Isles and southern Europe, the wine islands (the Canaries, Madeira, and the Azores), the West Indies, Newfoundland, and the colonies of North America themselves. These markets developed gradually in the course of the seventeenth century as increases in population and income or changes in taste in one part of the community set up demands for goods and services which other parts might fill. The comparative costs of production in the various regions determined which of them would respond to these demands. Thus, although several colonial governments sought to encourage the establishment of wine and silk industries in North America, the efforts failed, principally because of the high cost of skilled labor and the comparative advantage of employing available resources in other ways. Although, as we shall see in the next chapter, legislation was not without power to influence the production and distribution of goods, the fundamental determinants were those of the market.

The needs of the immigrants themselves opened the first important market for the surplus produce of New England. Throughout the Great Migration of the 1630s colonists arrived in the New World with many of their worldly possessions in the form of coin or products of English manufacture such as textiles, leather goods, and ironware. These they were glad to exchange with earlier settlers for cattle, corn, and other goods essential to the start of life in the New World.[101] Then in 1640–1642 the immigrant tide began to ebb. The beginnings of civil and religious reform by the Long Parliament brightened the prospects for religious freedom at home, while the advent of civil war attracted to the army men who considered it a religious duty to defend the cause of the Independents. In consequence, as John Winthrop sadly noted in his *Journal* in 1640, "there cam over a great store of provisions, both out of England and Ireland, and but few passengers."[102] Prices declined with the fall in demand, and before the end of the year nearly all of the specie in New England had been spent for English manufactures. Responding to the "great stop in trade and commerce for want of money," the General Court enacted legislation requiring creditors to accept the products of the region at fixed prices. "By then, however, many debtors had lost their houses, lands, and other possessions."[103]

In this situation various governmental bodies determined to try to encourage the production at home of products which New Englanders lacked the means for importing from abroad. Connecticut required families to plant hemp and flax, and Massachusetts encouraged sheep raising and the manufacture of garments, gunpowder, and glass, besides enacting laws to discourage the wasting of hides. The manufacturing of salt was begun in Plymouth Colony, and, with the aid of English investors, miners, foundrymen, and laborers, ironworks were completed at Braintree, Massachusetts, in 1645 and at Saugus soon thereafter. By 1648 the Saugus plant was producing a ton of iron a day. However, this initial success was rapidly eclipsed by a lack of skilled ironworkers, high costs, and other problems, and the company collapsed in the early 1650s. Other attempts to use the bog iron deposits of New England were made at Taunton, Concord, Rowley, and Pawtucket, but although small quantities of iron were produced at each place, all lapsed into inactivity. Helpful as were these early efforts to manufacture goods at home, it was clear that surplus products of one kind or another would have to be exported if commodities desired from abroad were to be obtained.[104]

Grain surpluses were sometimes available, but they could not be depended on because of the sour and rocky soil and the short growing season. Beaver and other furs had been exported from the Puritan settlements around Massachusetts Bay since the early 1630s, but the trade was quickly exploited and exhausted. Its volume in the East declined sharply after 1660, and by 1675 it was entirely gone. In western Massachusetts the trade reached its peak during the 1650s; in Rhode Island and other parts of New England it declined in that decade and was practically defunct by 1660. Clearly, exports of furs would generate foreign-exchange earnings, but not for long. Freights earned by vessels built in the region and exports of fish would do so over a far longer period. But shipbuilding and the fishing industry were only in their infancy when the Great Migration ended in 1640.[105]

Fortunately, New Englanders were well acquainted with forest resources other than animals. During the 1630s lumbering was already an important industry in Maine and New Hampshire, most boards being sawed by hand. By 1675 at least fifty water-powered sawmills were in operation in these two provinces and in northern Massachusetts, each of them being able to produce between 500 and 1,000 feet of white pine boards a day. Once again, therefore, rich natural resources enabled New World settlers to better their living standards, in this instance by responding to a growing demand for timber in foreign markets. The demand for fish and other provisions was also a rising one, and their supply did not linger long behind the beginnings of the timber trade.[106]

It was the merchants of Boston in particular who after 1640 began to develop first the timber markets of the wine ports and southern Europe and then those of the West Indies, Newfoundland, and England. With more than 1,200 inhabitants in that year, Boston was by far the largest town of provincial America. New York then had an estimated population of 400, Newport, Rhode Island, had 96; and Philadelphia and Charleston were yet to be born. By the end of the century population differentials had narrowed—Boston had 6,700 people, Philadelphia about 5,000, New York 5,000, Newport 2,600, and Charleston 2,000--but the Massachusetts town remained preeminent in shipping and trade. Indeed, it ranked as one of the major maritime centers of the Atlantic world, only London and Bristol, the latter the second-largest port in England, being superior in shipping.[107]

At the end of the century the Massachusetts fleet consisted of 171 vessels totaling 8,453 tons, each ton equaling 40 cubic feet of cargo-carrying space. This fleet probably represented half the cargo-carrying capacity of colonial-owned shipping. Most of it, 124 of the 171 vessels and 6,443 of the 8,453 tons, belonged to Boston. Only New York, which probably owned half as many vessels as Massachusetts, was a serious contender among the towns of colonial America. Philadelphia had undergone a remarkable expansion in population between the time of its founding in 1682–83 and 1700, but its foreign trade was only just beginning to develop. Although English ships dominated the trade of the tobacco colonies, a substantial portion of it was handled by the merchants and vessels of Boston. In sum, besides serving as a distributing center for European goods, Boston also supplied a good deal of the shipping required for the exportation of the surplus produce of Massachusetts and other provinces. As Governor Bellomont of Massachusetts and New York remarked in 1698, "The Bostoners may be said to be the carriers to most of the other plantations."[108]

Boston's timber and provisioning trade with southern Europe and the wine islands after 1640 not only revived the economic life of the Puritan settlements but also served as the major factor in the growth of the New England shipbuilding industry. Because of the wine trade, ships were built for the first time in Boston and Charlestown, and after the mid-1640s the fishing industry also became extremely profitable. In continental ports such as Bilbao, Oporto,

Cádiz, Málaga, and Alicante exports of wine casks were rapidly diminishing. By the early seventeenth century Spaniards had covered the Canaries with vines, and large quantities of staves and heading were needed for the huge pipes in which wine was stored and shipped. Madeira and the Azores had also been cleared of woodlands and were fully planted in vines. New Englanders had been exporting white oak for wet casks—"casks impermeable to wine but porous enough for air to filter through to influence the oxygenation of the wine"—since the 1630s. These cargoes were supplemented in the 1640s by pipe staves, fish, wheat, corn, peas, and other provisions. Returns from exports sometimes took the form of fruit, salt, or iron, with many merchants preferring to draw bills of exchange to be credited against their import accounts in England. But wine was the chief article imported, and, together with fish and timber, it was soon to find an outlet in trade with the British West Indies.[109]

Of the Caribbean islands settled by the English in the seventeenth century— Barbados, the Leeward Islands (Montserrat, Antigua, Nevis, St. Kitts), and Jamaica—Barbados was by far the most important. Indeed, by the early 1640s more people lived on its 166 square miles of land than in all of the colonies of New England together. Settlement had begun in 1627, and the years between then and 1640 constituted the island's "tobacco age." Carribean tobacco was of poor quality, however, and no one made much money on it. At the end of the 1630s, therefore, the planters switched to cotton. The results were no better. Essentially the pioneers were engaged in subsistence agriculture while experimenting rather haplessly with the possibilities of one staple after another. They hit upon one with dramatic suddenness.[110]

Between 1640 and 1643 some Barbadian planters learned from the Dutch in Brazil how to process sugar cane, and the island switched with virtually explosive force from tobacco and cotton to sugar, a commodity that had always been a scarce luxury item in England. Between 1640 and 1660 the population climbed from ten thousand, mostly Irish, to forty thousand, half of it African slaves. Land changed hands rapidly, its price rising more than tenfold during a seven-year period in the 1640s. To make as much space available as possible for the raising of the new crop, the planters hacked down the massive locust, cedar, fiddlewood, mangrove, and other trees of the island's rain forest, and in consequence by the 1650s a timber shortage had developed. By the end of that decade about 80 percent of the land was covered with cane. Despite the fact that the population of the island was growing, planters sought to maximize their incomes by planting cane rather than provision crops. In consequence, Barbados became increasingly dependent on food supplies from England, Ireland, and North America. And upon North American timber and shipping as well.[111]

"It pleased the Lord," Governor Winthrop of Massachusetts announced in 1647, "to open to us a trade with Barbados and other Islands of the West

Indies."[112] The tie between New England and the sugar islands became an especially close one, and by the 1680s nearly half the ships serving the islands were from that region. Exports of timber, provisions, and other supplies mounted in response to the growing requirements of the Barbadian sugar planters. Red oak staves made excellent hogsheads, barrels, and tierces for sugar and molasses, almost all operating equipment was of wood, and the planters needed large numbers of building timbers, shingles, and boards for construction. Horsepower was utilized on some of the machinery, and hence expanded the market for Rhode Island and Massachusetts horses. Pork, salted beef, butter, cheese, flour, corn, and other provisions were also shipped, along with previously imported wine and English manufactures, reflecting the growing prosperity of the planters. Something else was reflected in the increasing exports of the cheapest and poorest grades of cod and mackerel, which New Englanders had hitherto found useful only as fertilizer. These were sold in Barbados to feed the slaves.[113]

New England's trade with Newfoundland and England was less important to the region's developing economy. By the 1620s coastal timber on Newfoundland had been cut down for firewood, casks, shanties, and other purposes by the twenty thousand fishermen from Bristol, Dartmouth, Plymouth, and other English ports who visited that island every season. Hence there was some demand—but not much—for the timber of New England, and for wine, tobacco, sugar, molasses, and other provisions as well. In addition, fishermen wanted increasing quantities of rum that had been distilled from West Indian molasses. Yet of the total tonnage of ships leaving Boston for overseas ports in a six-month period in 1661–62, only 3 percent went to Newfoundland. Trade continued to be small in the later years of the century as a result of a decline in the Newfoundland fishery. Permanent settlers on the island, numbering only 1,700 in 1679, increased merely to 2,159 by 1701, and in some years few visitors came to fish.[114]

Significantly more Boston tonnage—18 percent of the total in 1661–62— went to London. Little of this represented bulky timber products, however. Because of shipping costs, "neither New England nor any other region of America ever supplied a major portion of the timber used in England." Yet the possibility that an enemy nation might interfere with the flow of timber from northern Europe to England made it desirable to import from across the ocean some naval stores, especially masts hewn from white pine or spruce. New Englanders appear to have begun shipping naval stores to the mother country with some regularity after 1645. Although the number of vessels departing Boston for Great Britain was small, ten mast ships rated at four hundred tons each left Piscataqua for England almost every year in the 1680s.[115]

Of the various trades opened to New England during the seventeenth century, early primacy belongs to the region's commerce with the wine islands and southern Europe. That trade accounted for the largest share, 40 percent, of the tonnage departing Boston for overseas ports in 1661–62, and even in the 1670s it may have continued to dominate. Sometime between 1660 and 1685, however, New England merchants began sending a greater proportion of their tonnage to the West Indies than to the wine regions. Between 1686 and 1688 trade with the West Indies engaged from 57 to 66 percent of Boston's total tonnage, in contrast to the wine regions' 9 to 16 percent. The latter continued its relative decline, and in the early eighteenth century it accounted for an even smaller part of the total.[116]

The West Indian trade, on the other hand, still occupied more than half of New England's export tonnage in the early eighteenth century. Feeding an increasing demand for North American produce was growth in population and sugar output not only in Barbados but in the other English islands as well. By 1683 there were more than 70,000 persons in Barbados, 46,000 of whom were slaves. By 1678 the Leeward Islands had over 10,000 whites and 8,000 slaves, and by 1672 the population of Jamaica had reached 17,000 persons, about half of whom were slaves. Sugar production expanded rapidly in the Leeward Islands, and by 1672 Jamaica was producing over a million pounds a year. Indeed, exports of sugar to England from the British West Indies as a whole increased between 1669 and 1700 from 11,700 tons a year to 24,000 tons.[117]

By no means all the provisions carried to the islands in the ships of New England originated in that region. By 1661–62, 9 percent of the tonnage leaving Boston for overseas ports went first to other ports in continental America. Trade between Boston and the other mainland colonies grew very rapidly between the 1660s and the 1680s, and by the early eighteenth century (1714–1717) it accounted for 17.2 percent of the total. Behind this growth lay increases in total output that were largely made possible by rapid population growth and new patterns of settlement.[118]

Between 1670 and 1700 the numbers of people in provincial America more than doubled, rising from 112,000 to 250,000. Natural increase rather than immigration was mainly responsible for this growth, but the course of American history was not a little affected by population pressure in the English sugar islands, especially on Barbados, which, by dimming the prospects for younger children, induced several hundred people to migrate to South Carolina between 1670 and 1680. In the 1680s and 1690s, before the introduction of rice as a staple crop, the colony already had a sizable black labor force; many of the slaves had been brought by the emigrés themselves from the Caribbean. During the same two decades new settlements in North Carolina and Pennsylvania also raised agricultural output, especially in the case of Pennsylvania, whose population rose twenty-fivefold in those years. In addition, New Englanders were carrying tobacco from Virginia and Maryland by the 1680s while perhaps monopolizing the tobacco trade of North Carolina. And not only tobacco, for by that decade the agricultural output of Virginia, together with that of the newly opened lands of the middle colonies and South Carolina, was supplying the English sugar islands with most of the grain they needed. By the 1690s Virginia was helping supply New England itself with corn, wheat, rye, barley, oats, and peas![119]

In sum, the vessels of New England, called into being by expanding foreign markets, especially those of the wine regions, began in the seventeenth century the process of knitting the several market-producing areas of continental America into coordinated economic life. The process was as yet only in its initial stages, although the merchants and ships of New York and Philadelphia were soon to make notable contributions to its development. It was an age of sail, of slow-flowing information on prices and market conditions. Yet the coastal trade was less affected by this constraint than foreign trade, and the former was much larger than surviving statistics suggest. The reason is that customs agents recorded few vessels under ten tons. The dimensions of underreporting are suggested by contemporary testimony that several hundred vessels rated from six to ten tons were carrying goods between Boston and surrounding towns in 1676. Probably many of them visited the colonies to the south as well.[120]

Domestic exchanges were undoubtedly increasing with great rapidity in the second half of the century. To be sure, they were small scale, especially in retrospect, yet they were sufficient to generate demand for increases in the money supply. One response was the minting of the famous pine tree shilling at Boston from 1652 to 1684, another the issuances of paper bills of credit by Massachusetts in 1690. Neither did much to alleviate shortages of currency deriving fundamentally from persistently unfavorable balances of payments, whose origins and broader effects we shall later discuss. But in view of the central role played by Boston shipping in the burgeoning commerce of the period, it can hardly be surprising that Massachusetts should have been the scene of the only colonial attempt to coin money, and the first to issue bills of credit.[121]

Nor ought it be surprising that in Boston, in contrast to the situation in inland towns, a relatively small proportion of the taxpayers held a relatively large proportion of the town's property. In 1687 the top quarter of the taxable population was composed of merchants with large investments in England and West Indian trade and persons with interests in shipbuilding and distilling. This commercial group controlled 66 percent of the town's wealth. The profits of trade had not gone equally to all, however, but rather "had flowed to those whose daring initiative and initial resources had begun the exploitation of the lucrative colonial market." By 1687 the upper 15 percent of the property owners held 52 percent of the taxable assets of the town. The fifty individuals composing the highest 5 percent accounted for more than 25 percent of the wealth.[122]

Skewed distributions of income and wealth were not confined to urban centers but were found wherever commercial opportunities existed. The Chesapeake tobacco country was lacking in towns, not least because of the existence of numerous navigable rivers that permitted seagoing vessels to penetrate to the very wharves of the tidewater planters. The tradesmen here were the planters themselves, men like Colonel William Fitzhugh of Virginia, who maintained a correspondence with many English suppliers, ordered merchandise, and proceeded to retail it both from his two stores and via small boats permitting him to "trade . . . up the River." Taking tobacco in exchange, such men assembled it on their wharves together with their own and consigned it to England for sale.[123]

Fitzhugh had a good deal more than most of his neighbors to begin with, and his enterprise brought him still more. So it was in Maryland. At midcentury, as we have seen, the physical personal wealth of the poorest 30 percent of the farmers was appraised at only £11 sterling, and at century's end it had risen in value only to £13 sterling. The next group of 30 percent—the lower middle group—did substantially better, its wealth rising from £37 to £45 sterling. The 30 percent following them—the upper middle group—did better still, its wealth going up from £108 to £164 sterling. The wealth of the top 10 percent—the richest—increased from £349 to £630 sterling. Surprisingly, the lifestyles of the very wealthy differed but little from those in the less affluent middling groups. The differences were more a matter of degree than of substance, especially where food and clothing were concerned. But although the rich had more of everything, including bigger houses, their "preferences lay along the same lines: plain furniture and simple tableware, decent linens, some nice pieces of silver, perhaps, and good—really good—beds." They preferred getting a living to ornamenting it.[124]

The ways in which they got it, in Virginia as well as in Maryland, were the ways of the market. They planted broad acres in tobacco, cultivated them with growing numbers of slaves and servants, exported their tobacco, and, like Colonel Fitzhugh, also kept stores from which they sold dry goods, hardware, and other merchandise imported from England. Although a few owned shares in vessels and even engaged in foreign trade, the overwhelming majority did not, and those who did, did so rarely. These men were not merchants in the sense that the planters of Charleston were merchants, and even less did they resemble the merchants of New York, Philadelphia, and Boston, men who exported and imported, maintained commercial relationships with fellow merchants in many of the world's ports, sold primarily at wholesale, and owned shares in a number of ships. Rather, they were storekeepers, men who sold at retail, men whose horizons formed over the land rather than over the sea. For all that, they were businessmen still, and it was because of the success with which they exercised their talents as businessmen that their stock in life went up. Wealth in colonial America had been distributed unequally from the beginning. It is perhaps inevitable that men of enterprise should have widened the gap still more. Had they not been willing to embrace risk in the hope of reward, many other people, from urban artisans to farmers raising products for the market, would have been worse off than they actually were.

3

A Growing People

Pursuing essentially the same economic activities as before but improving somewhat their ways of doing them, the colonies continued to grow in size and wealth in the remaining years of the colonial period. Between 1700 and 1774 the population increased ninefold, rising from a quarter of a million to 2,354,000, and in the latter year the average net worth of the head of a free family[1]—calculated by subtracting debts from claims on others and including cash as well as the value of physical assets—amounted to an estimated £243 sterling, a sum which, in terms of the dollar in 1978, is equivalent to roughly $13,000.[2] It is an astonishingly high sum, one which testifies to the economic success of colonization in North America. Yet average wealth, like average income, tells us nothing about the way in which wealth or income is distributed in society. That is another story, and we shall turn to it in time.

The physical wealth of an overwhelmingly agricultural society mainly took the form of land—including houses, barns, and other structures—servants and slaves, livestock, farm tools, crops, and clothing. Naturally, the forms in which property was held differed from one region to the next. Southerners owned 95 percent of the value of slaves and servants, for example, whereas New Englanders were far stronger in maritime assets such as vessels and docks. Quantities and values also varied. In New England in 1774 the average net worth of a household head amounted to £138 sterling, a good deal less than the average of £207 sterling in the middle colonies. The figure for the South, £372 sterling, is almost startlingly higher. It is two and one-half times that of New England and 80 percent more than that of the middle colonies. In land (including structures and improvements), in producers' capital (farm tools and equipment, for example) and even in consumer goods, average wealth per free inhabitant was higher in the South than elsewhere in colonial America. Clearly, when markets widened for their products, southerners were able to obtain the necessary means of augmenting their supplies of the factors of production. Just as clearly, the other two regions met with less success in doing so.[3]

Above all it was the ability to command supplies of labor that mattered.

The reason is that existing factor proportions in agriculture generally discouraged the diffusion of techniques for raising the productivity of labor.
Given the relative abundance of fertile land, Americans tended to discount the
utility of applied new knowledge. Although improved equipment and techniques to raise output per worker were adopted to some extent, in the main
the colonists relied on additional land and workers to increase production.

The principal difference in the economic activity of the seventeenth and the
eighteenth centuries is that with the passage of time more people were present
to take part in it. Population growth in the earlier century had occurred at a
faster *rate*—rapid early growth from small numbers generates larger percentages than equally rapid growth from larger numbers later on—yet the rate of
increase even in the eighteenth century was about twice that of England. The
contrast between colonial experience and that of Great Britain and other parts
of Europe deeply impressed the Reverend Thomas Malthus; in his *Essay on
the Principle of Population,* first published in London in 1798, he expressed the
view that the rapidity of the colonial increase was "probably without parallel
in history." Indeed, it was directly from America's experience that Malthus
formulated his demographic law that "population, when unchecked, goes on
doubling itself every twenty-five years, or increases in geometrical ratio."[4]

The Malthusian law requires that a population double itself through reproduction—that is, through natural increase—at a decennial rate of 32 percent.
Although the statistical remains from the colonial period are fragmentary and
unreliable, at least one useful estimate of the size of the total population has
existed since the early twentieth century. The figures developed at that time
by the Bureau of the Census form the basis for the rates of decennial increase
by regions that are shown in Table 1. The table also gives the regional distribution of the population from 1700 to 1790 and makes it clear that the average
decennial rate of increase was 34.5 percent, well above that required by the
Malthusian formula. However, the figures include imported slaves and immigrants, and unless their numbers are deducted, the rate of natural increase
of the existing population cannot be determined.[5]

Fortunately, for more than a century American historians have tended to
agree on the number of slaves imported in the seventeenth and eighteenth
centuries. A recent estimate places the number at 250,000 for the period
between 1700 and 1790; once these have been allocated to the intervening
decades and their contribution to the growth of those decades taken into
account, the average decennial increase of the total population falls from 34.5
percent to 30.8 percent.[6]

The problem of estimating the volume of white immigration in the eighteenth century is of a different order of magnitude and, given the preponderance of whites in the population, of greater demographic significance. Scholars
have usually assumed that immigrants represented a declining proportion of
the population in the eighteenth century and that the flow varied over time,

Table 1. Characteristics of colonial population, 1700–1790.

Year	New England	Middle Atlantic	South Atlantic	Total
	Rate of decennial increase (percent)			
1700–1710	20	53	29	30
1710–1720	20	36	41	33
1720–1730	38	37	39	38
1730–1740	31	42	36	36
1740–1750	26	38	41	36
1750–1760	33	43	29	33
1760–1770	28	34	44	37
1770–1780	21	31	27	26
1780–1790	20	47	41	41
Average	28	40	35	34
	Distribution of population (percent)			
1700	39	19	42	100
1710	35	23	42	100
1720	32	23	45	100
1730	32	23	45	100
1740	31	24	45	100
1750	29	24	47	100
1760	29	26	45	100
1770	28	26	46	100
1780	26	27	47	100
1790	25	28	47	100

Source: Jim Potter, "The Growth of Population in America, 1700–1860," in *Population in History: Essays in Historical Demography,* ed. D. V. Glass and D. E. C. Eversley (Chicago: Aldine, 1965), p. 639. For the form in which this table appears, I am indebted to W. Elliot Brownlee, *Dynamics of Ascent: A History of the American Economy,* 2d ed. (New York: Alfred A. Knopf, 1974), p. 60. Used with permission.

being small during periods of war in Europe and swelling with the return of peace. But as a rule they have been unwilling to venture in the direction of quantitative assessments beyond general statements of these kinds.[7] Important recent exceptions include an estimate that English migration to America in the late-colonial period comprised 15,000 to 20,000 persons, and that of the Scots about 25,000. Other scholars estimate that from 100,000 to 125,000 Ulster Scots (the Scotch-Irish) entered the country between 1718 and 1775 and that total German immigration possibly amounted to 100,000.[8] These numbers suggest a somewhat smaller total volume of white immigration than one historian's conjecture of 350,000 persons between 1700 and 1790, but in view of the longer period for which he prepared his estimates, they may well be close to the truth. If that figure is accepted as reasonable, the rate of natural increase of the white population falls to slightly over 28 percent per decade.[9] Thus the final adjusted percentage is somewhat below the 32 percent required by the Malthusian formula for a doubling of the population every twenty-five years. Yet the rate achieved considerably exceeds that found in England in the eighteenth and nineteenth centuries and justifies close examination of the birthrates and death rates that made it possible.

Once again, we must resort to conjecture. One scholar has written that the number of babies added to the population in any one year is the most uncertain of all demographic data throughout the colonial period and beyond it as well.[10] Deaths too were probably extensively unregistered in the seventeenth and eighteenth centuries. Infant mortality appears to have been significantly underrecorded in both private and public documents in colonial New England.[11] Furthermore, it was the common practice of colonial newspaper editors to minimize or suppress news of death or disease in order to protect the economic well-being of their communities. In sum, the existing evidence on colonial mortality is so uncertain that "no conclusions connecting high or low decadal growth rates to periods of lesser or greater mortality can be made."[12] There is even disagreement on whether death rates in the eighteenth century were higher or lower than those of the preceding century.[13] The balance of probability, however, favors a birthrate of the white population of 45 to 50 per thousand and a death rate of 20 to 25. The contrast with Europe is striking, for there a birthrate of 28 per thousand and a death rate of no less than 40 per thousand were common.[14] Although the colonial figures are hypothetical, they illustrate the essential point: birthrates in colonial America were generally much higher and death rates much lower than those of contemporary Europe, and these trends combined to serve as the main source of the country's phenomenal population growth.

Accurate birthrates and death rates cannot yet be calculated, but recent research has improved our knowledge of the factors affecting them. It was once widely believed that marriage occurred at an early age in colonial America and that in consequence large families were the rule, with families of ten and twelve children being very common, and those of twenty to twenty-five "not rare enough to call forth expression of wonder."[15] This belief is probably unfounded. A recent broad sampling of twenty New England towns covering the years from 1720 to 1760 found very few teenage marriages and no family with more than sixteen births. The average number was seven. Were the older belief valid, high colonial birthrates alone would go far toward explaining the demographic differences between the Old World and the New. Recent scholarship does indeed suggest that average age at first marriage in the colonies was somewhat earlier than in Europe—from 20 to 23 for women and from 24 to 26 for men in the former, in contrast to 25 for women and from 26 to 28 for men in the latter—and as a result Americans did tend to have more children over the course of a marriage, and a larger percentage of the population was of child-bearing age. Births per family probably averaged six or seven, in contrast to four or five in Europe. These differences are modest, but their cumulative effects on a large population over a long period were undoubtedly substantial. In sum, age at first marriage and family size in England and America were more similar than dissimilar, but the modest differences contributed significantly to the rate of natural increase in the colonies.[16]

A lower colonial mortality rate, especially of infant mortality, appears to have made an even more important contribution. In contrast to a death rate of at least forty per thousand people in Europe, probably only twenty to twenty-five per thousand died in an average year in the colonies. The colonial American environment was an extraordinarily healthy one, although it was clearly less so in the growing cities of the eighteenth century than in the countryside. Cities were sites of outbreaks of disease such as smallpox in New York in 1731, yellow fever there in 1743, and scarlet fever in Boston in 1735–36. Epidemic mortality was sometimes heavy, as in Hartford in 1724–25, but probably never more so than in New England in the mid-1730s, when a terrible throat distemper (diphtheria) attacked the children, leaving nearly a thousand dead in New Hampshire alone. Serious though a number of these urban onslaughts were, it must be remembered that even at the end of the colonial period scarcely one person in ten lived in a city.[17]

The countryside and its small inland agricultural towns tell another story, although not one that is without change, especially in the towns. In Andover, Massachusetts, before the 1750s—when life expectancies somewhat dropped—people were remarkably healthy, lives unusually long, and women exceedingly fecund.[18] In Dedham, Massachusetts, as in New England generally after 1670, population was "increasing steadily while that of parts of Europe was not," so that "the conditions of life in this part of the New World must have been more favorable than in Europe."[19] Not only in New England but throughout rural America were those conditions more favorable. The widespread ownership of land, the fertility of the soil, and the substantial practice of subsistence farming guaranteed a sufficiency of food for almost everyone. Above all, perhaps, the plentiful supply of food sustained the health of pregnant and nursing women and thus kept low the infant mortality rate.[20] If the specter of famine was held in check, so too were the harsh effects of cold, for the abundant forest provided wood for heating, cooking, and construction. One scholar believes that over three-quarters of the adult married freemen in the colonies may well have had their own houses. This situation contrasts sharply to that in England, where ever since the early seventeenth century an acute shortage of wood even for fuel had existed. Finally, it is possible that a general improvement in climate took place around the middle of the eighteenth century. "Thus the primary factors that explain natural increase were those that bore more directly upon mortality; disease, diet, and climate were much less burdensome in North America than in contemporary England and northern Europe."[21]

This is not to suggest that favorable conditions were everywhere the same in colonial America. Undoubtedly they were not, although little can be said at present about regional variation in fertility and mortality rates. Recent research does indicate, however, that the birthrate in New England (around forty per thousand) was lower than in the colonies at large.[22] Other regional differences have long been assumed to exist, but they have not been carefully tested. One common assumption is that the age of marriage was lower in the South than in the North; another is that the severity of the climate in New England resulted in high infant mortality.[23] The old belief that death in childbirth was common in New England and that many women died between the ages of twenty and thirty from overwork and childbearing is probably accurate. One recent study, at least, concludes that somewhat less than one New England woman in six died from causes associated with childbearing.[24] By modern standards that proportion is frightfully high, and although colonial women generally lived longer than their European counterparts, the high mortality rates for those in childbirth accounts for the fact that women could expect to live only until their forties. Men did better, surviving into their sixties.[25]

Whatever the role of factors affecting natural increase, it is undeniable that population growth in New England lagged behind that of the rest of the country. The region's decennial growth rate of 27 or 28 percent was much lower than the colonial average (34 percent), and in consequence its proportion of the total population fell from 30 percent in 1700 to only 24 percent in 1790 (see Table 1). Helping to produce this result, besides the fact that New Englanders imported few slaves for their own use, was the relative unattractiveness of the region to immigrants in the eighteenth century. Harsh winters and poor soil not only reduced the interest of immigrants but also led to substantial out-migration as well. As early as the mid-1640s, leaders in Virginia and Maryland began actively to encourage New Englanders to move south. Indian hostility and the constant possibility of war with the French discouraged settlement of the northern part of the region in the first half of the eighteenth century. After the English victory over France in the Seven Years' War, large numbers of Massachusetts citizens migrated to the lands in Maine and New Hampshire that were no longer barred by the enemy. Despite the availability of land in the North, however, net migration appears to characterize the New England region as a whole in the last three decades of the century. The inhospitality which repelled immigrants throughout the century was not that of nature alone. In the closely knit Puritan communities of Massachusetts the cold was partly human. Not till after the Revolution were Jews permitted to live there.[26]

The middle colonies displayed remarkable growth in the eighteenth century, their decennial rate of increase of 40 percent markedly exceeding the colonial average (see Table 1). In 1700 their population was only about half that of New England, but by the time of the Revolution the two regions were almost equal—the middle region's share of the total population rising in that interval from 19 to 24 percent. By 1780 Pennsylvania was second in size to Virginia, and Philadelphia the largest city in North America. Immigration played an important part in the growth of the region. Philadelphia and New York City were favored ports of entry, and whereas the land system of New York discouraged voluntary migrants from settling in that province, Pennsylvania owed a good deal of its growth to immigration. Increasing agricultural prosperity and trade, William Penn's promise of complete religious freedom, and a humane criminal code combined to attract Europeans, many of whom came as indentured servants. Germans and Scotch Irish were prominent among the newcomers, and many of them settled not only along the frontiers of the middle colonies but in the Piedmont of North and South Carolina as well. Benjamin Franklin's observation that a third of the population was foreign born is untrue for the colonies as a whole but may well be true of Pennsylvania. Undoubtedly many of the immigrants brought skills essential to the increasing development of Philadelphia and its environs as a manufacturing center for a host of trades.[27] Recent analysis of lists of eighteenth-century Englishmen emigrating to America under contracts of indentured servitude indicates relative decline in agricultural occupations and significant increase in a wide variety of nonagricultural trades and crafts, particularly metalwork and construction.[28]

Whatever the findings of future scholarship about mortality and fertility rates in the South, the contribution of slaves to the region's growth will undoubtedly continue to be viewed as a significant one. While the number of slaves in America in 1700 is unknown, it is generally believed to be small, in the range of 5,000 to 20,000.[29] If the lesser figure is the appropriate one, blacks then made up only 2 percent of the population. By the time of the first federal census of 1790 they numbered 675,000 and accounted for 20 percent. The growth of the black population was thus more rapid than that of the whites, although it is improbable that a higher rate of reproduction accounts for this.[30] Rather, imports do. The inflow of roughly 275,000 slaves between 1700 and 1790 was an uneven one, with about 75,000 being imported in the 1760s alone. Primarily because of these large imports—the overwhelming majority of the slaves bought for use in the South—that region's population during the eighteenth century increased from 42 percent to 47 percent of the total and maintained a decennial rate of increase slightly exceeding the colonial average. The importance of nonfamily labor in the South is clear from recent estimates of the interregional distribution of servants and slaves on the eve of the Revolution. In New England merely 3.3 percent of the wealthholders possessed them, and in the middle colonies 16 percent did so. For the South the figure is 59.6 percent—nearly two out of three.[31]

Above all it was the labor requirements of expanding tobacco, rice, and indigo plantations, and the production of naval stores as well, that were responsible for rising imports of slaves in the eighteenth century. It was possible for tobacco to be grown without slave labor; indeed, a considerable part of the crop was produced by backwoods farmers largely lacking slaves or other help outside the family. But slaves produced the bulk of it. Tobacco required intensive and careful labor, from the preparation of the seedbed to hoeing, cutting, curing, sorting, packing, and marketing, the last often done by rolling the hogsheads to shipping centers. In North Carolina the distribution of slaves was related to the general location of the area within which the crop was grown, with perhaps 40 to 60 percent of the households in tobacco-growing counties owning slaves. Presumably the same was true in Virginia and Maryland, source of at least 95 percent of exported tobacco through the pre-Revolutionary period.[32]

Rice and indigo were also labor intensive. Preparation of the ground, planting, cultivation, and after-harvest tasks that had to be done before they could be marketed "were all so laborious and time consuming that both crops were notorious for the heavy strain they placed on available supplies of labor."[33] Both required for their cultivation the importation of vast numbers of African slaves,[34] a requirement that may explain why, during a five-year period (1768–1772) in which Virginia and Maryland together imported 6,056 slaves, South Carolina alone imported 15,561. Rice and indigo were complementary crops. Rice was grown on sites that could be flooded, and indigo was planted on adjacent dry lands. Because the growing and making of indigo ended with summer, whereas the rice harvest required threshing and cleaning in the winter months, a planter could switch a large labor force from one to the other and avoid periods of unprofitable employment. In addition, the possession of slaves was "almost a *sine qua non* for the large-scale production of naval stores. The making of tar, pitch, and turpentine was time-consuming and laborious, and without the labor of slaves the work could not be done efficiently enough to ensure a healthy margin of profit." And because naval stores, unlike field crops, could be produced at almost any time of year, slaves could be used efficiently when few other tasks required their attention.[35]

Tobacco was the leading export not only of the South but of all the continental colonies. An available list of articles shipped abroad in 1770 gives its value at more than £900,000 sterling, an amount nearly twice that of the next most important commodity, bread and flour.[36] Given the ease with which small farmers might enter tobacco production, the consequent large number of producers, and the frequent failure of efforts to raise prices by provincial laws restricting output, tobacco prices tended from time to time "to sink almost to starvation levels and remain at those levels for long periods" before the onset of "considerable periods when prices of moderate profitableness prevailed." Yet it was this very tendency toward lower prices that facilitated the gradual social and geographic diffusion of the practice of tobacco and snuff taking, a diffusion synonymous with rising demand for the weed.[37]

Indeed, before the 1680s the initial expansion of the industry in the region took place within a context of long-term falling prices. The cost of producing and marketing the crop, however, also fell sufficiently to encourage planters and merchants to maintain their investments. These costs were high at first because of the need to gain experience in the most efficient methods of growing, collecting, curing, transporting, packing, storing, and marketing the weed, and because of the serious threat to the survival of the English in Virginia posed by the thinness of early settlement, the inadequate food supply, and the dangers of Indian attack. In time these risks and uncertainties abated, followed by a decline in both production and marketing costs and the rates of return necessary to attract new capital to the industry.

During the middle decades of the century, for example, the amount of tobacco a man could make in a year approximately doubled as knowledge spread of improved transplanting and curing methods. Added to the price effects of this increase in per worker productivity were savings from improved packaging and lower freight charges, the latter due to a more efficient use of shipping space, improvements in market organization in the colonies, and declining risks associated with piracy and privateering. In sum, the tobacco industry grew before the 1690s because savings on the costs of producing and marketing the crop lowered the price to consumers and expanded the market for the staple. In the eighteenth century, in contrast, costs increased and were absorbed by higher prices. Thus a transition occurred between an early expansion induced by forces of supply and a later one encouraged by those of demand.[38]

Although the market dominated the longer run forces playing upon supply and demand, acts of government were sometimes influential as well. The political interest in tobacco touched the crop at many points. Determined to keep the profits of empire from the pockets of foreigners, the English government named tobacco an "enumerated" article in 1660, forbidding its direct shipment to non-English markets. A large proportion of the tobacco sent to England was reexported to continental markets in Spain and Portugal, Holland, the states of Germany and Italy, and France; indeed, except for a single year, no less than 50 percent, and usually much more than this, was reexported during the period from 1700 to 1775. Hence English shippers and insurers, as well as English workers engaged in cutting and rolling, grading, sorting, and repacking operations, benefited from the restriction. England also had a fiscal interest in the weed, although most of the customs duty assessed against imports was refunded upon reexportation. Other European states had a similar interest, and in the eighteenth century that of France in particular was to affect not only the price of tobacco but its production and marketing as well.[39]

In the early years of the trade, shipments from the Chesapeake rose very rapidly, increasing about tenfold from the 1630s to the 1660s. Expansion then slowed, and between 1668–69 and the end of the century exports merely doubled. The wars of 1689–1713 brought on relative stagnation. High freight and insurance rates discouraged the British from sending ships to the Chesapeake, and in consequence prices fell in the colonies and rose in Europe. The former tended to discourage further expansion of cultivation in Virginia and Maryland, while the latter greatly stimulated production in Europe. This period of relative stagnation lasted till the 1720s. Intent on widening continental markets for American tobacco, Sir Robert Walpole in 1723 had Parliament remove the last halfpenny per pound of the import duty retained (since 1660) at reexport. The price advantage of continental tobaccos was thus narrowed, and in the late 1720s and early 1730s colonial production trebled. Significantly, the slave population of Virginia grew more than sixfold between approximately 1730 and the Revolution, while that of Maryland rose threefold. Since there is little or no evidence of increased output of tobacco per man in the eighteenth century—although production on fertile, new land probably resulted in some increase in output per acre—the probability is strong that much of the rise in production was due to the greater number of slaves obtained through both natural increase and importation. A vast expansion in the amount of credit was mainly responsible for the latter—credit that came from the Scotch but was made possible by cash sales of tobacco to the United General Farms of France, the state importing monopoly.[40]

Scotland and France were comparative latecomers to the tobacco trade. Throughout the seventeenth and early eighteenth centuries most colonial exports were handled by English merchants on consignment.[41] The planter remained the owner of the tobacco till it was sold by the merchant to whom he had consigned it. The latter acted as the planter's agent and charged a commission for his services, which included unloading the vessel and paying customs duties, carting the tobacco to the warehouse, then sorting and grading it preparatory to selling it in the best obtainable market at home or on the Continent. The Act of Union of 1707 opened the empire and its trade to the Scots, but it was not till about 1740 that sharp increases occurred in the volume of colonial tobacco shipped to Glasgow and other Scotch ports. These increases coincide with a relative rise in the Scotch share of the French market. By the 1760s and 1770s the Scots were shipping to France about three times the amount of tobacco being shipped by the English, the French taking about 40 percent of Scotland's export and only 12 percent of England's.[42]

These rising sales to the French, contracted for in advance, had an important impact on production and marketing in the Chesapeake. Unlike other purchasers in tobacco resales markets, the French paid in cash, or in thirty—or sixty—day promissory notes that could easily be discounted for cash, as soon as the tobacco arrived in Glasgow. Aided by their ability to turn over their capital rapidly, the Scotch merchants in turn proceeded to expand tremendously the amount of credit extended to the planters of the Chesapeake, thus enabling the latter to purchase additional land and slaves and increase their production of tobacco.[43] Deliberately bypassing the large planters of the tidewater region, the Scots opened chains of stores in the interior to tap the supplies of smaller farmers.

The ideal was to establish a store capable of serving farmers residing within a distance of twelve to fourteen miles, from whom a purchase of at least three hundred hogsheads of tobacco a year could be made. William Cunningham & Company, for example, established headquarter stores near the heads of navigation at Petersburg and Richmond and at Fredericksburg and Falmouth on the Rappahannock River, and used the merchandise stocked in them to supply dependent stores farther inland, seven in Maryland and fourteen in Virginia.[44] Farmers brought their tobacco to these stores to exchange it for merchandise; the Scots then gathered up the tobacco and took it to warehouses and barns where it could be inventoried and, on the arrival of their vessels, quickly loaded and shipped to Glasgow for sale on their own account. Thus the older technique of consignment increasingly gave way to one of direct purchase, and by the time of the Revolution the latter probably accounted for the marketing of two-thirds of the annual crop of the Chesapeake. The newer system was more efficient. It is quite likely that port times in the Chesapeake were reduced, and this improvement, together with the shorter route north of Ireland traversed by Scotch vessels, enabled the Scots to make two voyages a year on the average rather than the single one that the English tobacco shipper typically made.[45]

The staples of the lower South were relatively late in their development as important export commodities. South Carolina's most valuable trade for twenty years after its settlement in 1670 consisted of the exchange of goods manufactured in Europe for deerskins and furs obtained from the Indians. Deerskins ranked as the colony's number one export, more than 317,000 being shipped to England during the seven-year period 1699–1705. However, the average annual value, estimated at between £15,000 and £25,000 for these years, was soon dwarfed by that of rice. The early years of rice culture had been marked by active experimentation with differing varieties to determine those best suited to Carolina conditions. Production increased rapidly after 1700, and along with it, the size of the slave population and the granting of land. A recent study concludes that the grant of more than 100,000 acres in South Carolina from 1698 through 1705 probably reflects headrights obtained for imported slaves.[46]

The story in North Carolina is a different one. The production and exportation of rice, and indigo as well, was undoubtedly small throughout the colonial period, chiefly because the colony lacked the large amounts of slave labor required.[47] Georgia's relaxation in 1749 of its initial ban on the use of slaves, together with the final abolition in 1750 of all restrictions on the buying, selling, and mortgaging of land, account for rising slave imports in the later colonial period and for rapid growth in the production of rice and indigo.[48] Clearly, slaves and the staples of the lower South, in particular, were as inseparable on the continent of North America as sugar and slaves in the Caribbean. As one influential scholar wrote long ago about the cultivation of rice, the area's most valuable crop, "it was the prevailing belief in the colonial period that white men could not endure the conditions of labor required by the industry—the necessity of working continually in the hot, pestilential swamps, the laborious process of clearing land, digging and cleaning ditches, preparing and cultivating land entirely by hand labor, and harvesting, threshing, and pounding rice." For black men toiling in the Carolina rice swamps, life was short, and it was not sweet.[49]

By 1705 rice had become sufficiently important as a staple to induce Parliament to place it on the list of enumerated commodities, which forbade its export to non-English ports. Much of the rice sent to England, however, was reshipped to the Continent, where one of the best markets comprised the ports of the Iberian Peninsula during the early spring months. Enumeration closed this trade to colonial merchants because of the impossibility of shipping the autumn's harvest to England in time for reexport to Spain and Portugal by early spring. Despite this abridgment of the market, exports of rice from Charleston to England nearly tripled between 1717 and 1724, with exports to all regions nearly doubling again between 1725 and 1729. The next year Parliament decided to allow direct shipments to ports south of Cape Finisterre, that is, to Spain and Portugal, on condition that vessels complete the voyage by sailing to England, where one-half the duty that would have been paid had the rice been landed first in England and then reexported was payable. Thus encouraged, rice exports from Charleston to countries south of Cape Finisterre increased from 6,397 barrels in 1731 to 25,136 barrels in 1766. Despite the concession, shipments to England remained far more important, averaging more than 60 percent of the total exported during these years. The total itself, which also included exports to Scotland and the British West Indies, to continental colonies and the foreign West Indies, approximately doubled during the period. In 1770 exports were worth £340,693 sterling, making rice the fourth most valuable export of British North America, just after fish.[50]

Both naval stores and indigo were beneficiaries of bounties offered by Parliament to encourage their production and exportation to England. Not only tar, pitch, and turpentine were wanted for the Royal Navy, but also hemp, masts, yards, and bowsprits, and the act of 1705 provided for bounties on these as well. The main source of naval stores proved to be the forests of the lower South rather than those of New England. The latter region had been settled earlier, and lumbering operations had reduced the supply of trees near the coast. Deep forests remained, but transportation to seaports was rendered uneconomic by the nearly complete lack of streams that were navigable for more than a few miles inland. The navigability of the rivers flowing down the wider coastal plain of the South made accessible millions of acres of the longleaf pine (*Pinus palustris*) that was native to the sand hills and flatlands of that area, and this was the tree sought after by tar burners and turpentine collectors. No evidence exists that naval stores were widely manufactured in South Carolina before 1705, and although the province supplied only a minor fraction of all exports of tar and pitch to Great Britain in the first decade after enactment of the bounty, annual exports from that province increased by about 85 percent by 1717–1720. Some of the exports may have been the product of North Carolina, and by 1768 about 60 percent of total colonial shipments of naval stores originated in that province.[51]

Like naval stores, indigo too was a latecomer to the list of staples of the lower South. Source of a purple dye needed for England's growing textile industries, the plant was introduced into South Carolina in the late 1730s and became an export of some importance after Parliament granted a bounty of six pence per pound on it in 1748. Mainly a product of that province, although also cultivated in Georgia and to a lesser extent in North Carolina, Virginia, and Maryland, indigo rose in value as an export crop from £79,000 to £209,000 between 1768 and 1772—with one-third of the rise attributable to increased quantities exported and the other two-thirds to higher prices.[52]

Clearly, the production and exportation of the southern staples were matters of keen interest to British businessmen and their government. Because of that interest the staples dominated colonial shipments to the mother country. Indeed, in the five-year period 1768-1772 they accounted for 86 percent of the value of those shipments. And because the value of all colonial products exported to Britain during the period exceeded that of shipments to all other regions combined, they also dominated the whole of American trade.[53]

It remains to inquire into the possible relationship between that interest and the low level of urban development that marks the colonial South. The tobacco colonies were the least urbanized. Despite the fact that tobacco was the leading export of colonial America, it was not till 1750 or 1760 that either Virginia or Maryland could boast a town with as many as three thousand people. Towns like Norfolk, Yorktown, Alexandria, Fredericksburg, Richmond, and Petersburg in Virginia and Georgetown and Port Deposit in Maryland were merely shipping points rather than collections of merchants, traders, and artisans. Was this because entrepreneurial decisions on tobacco were made in Europe by Englishmen and Scots rather than by merchants in the colonies? Did these ports fail to generate an "entrepreneurial headquarters effect," that is, a need for "a population of sailors, shipwrights, sailmakers, ship chandlers, and the like, as well as specialist brokers, insurance underwriters, and often a manufacturing population to process goods in transit"?[54]

It is difficult not to answer these questions affirmatively. Still, under the older consignment system larger planters like Colonel William Fitzhugh of Virginia did make entrepreneurial decisions to some extent by deciding whether to consign their tobacco to London or to an outport and by shifting from one English commission house to another in an effort to obtain better prices and services. In Fitzhugh's and similar cases, however, an important consideration was the location of most tobacco planting in a tidewater area rich in navigable rivers. The accessibility of the tobacco to oceangoing vessels made shipping points of planters' wharves throughout the seventeenth century. There was no need for "a compulsory point of trans-shipment as at Philadelphia where wholesale dealers and greater merchants might congregate and services usefully be centralized." In fact, planters like Fitzhugh were themselves essentially middlemen who retailed imported merchandise from their own stores or took them in small boats upriver to sell to lesser planters. The tobacco they accepted in exchange merged with the produce of their own plantation to form the outward cargoes to England. The facts of commercial geography, then, must also be taken into account.[55]

What about the Navigation Acts themselves, especially their enumerated-article provisions? To be sure, some smuggling occurred, but its importance in the export trade can be gauged by the fact that more than 99 percent of colonial tobacco was exported to England. Does this not mean that even after underlying conditions of commercial geography had changed with the movement of tobacco growing into the interior, the enumeration requirement ensured that "entrepreneurial headquarters" would be located in Europe rather than in America?[56] Possibly. But it must also be considered that the greater part of the tobacco of the Chesapeake continued to find its way to Britain even after the Revolution, and that as of 1790 Virginia and South Carolina were the only two states that still had more British than American ships entering their harbors. Of course, both situations were fading afterglows of long-engrained practices, but the essential question is whether the artificial requirements of the Navigation Acts or natural market conditions were responsible for them.[57]

Given the relative scarcity of short-term capital in a developing preindustrial economy and its relative abundance and cheapness in Britain; given the conjunction of British interest and American need for the generous credits, usually up to a year, that could be founded on that capital; and given, finally, the market expertise that enabled British mercantile houses to respond to the shadings of continental demand, there is something to be said for the role of the market. All three factors, then—geography, legislation, and the market—must be taken into account if we are to understand the convergence of policy and interest, colonial as well as British, that supplied the South with the capital it needed in the form of slaves, the shipping required to move the staples to market, and the numerous services needed in the marketplace itself. The region's dependence on Great Britain for these requirements weakened the urbanizing effects that domestically located entrepreneurial headquarters might have exerted.

At bottom, though, it is British policy and interest that are the decisive factors. The reason for concluding this is simply that significant towns *did* develop in the Chesapeake, at Norfolk and at Baltimore, "on the fringes of the tobacco regions but outside the grip of that staple trade."[58] They did so in response to the marketing requirements of wheat, an article which, like most other provisions, was not enumerated because of Britain's desire to protect the interests of its own farmers at home. Encouraged by the rise of wheat prices in Europe after 1750, Scotch-Irish and Germans from Pennsylvania pushed southward to take up lands in western Maryland that were better suited to wheat than to tobacco. Because of its convenient location with respect to these new wheat-producing areas, Baltimore became a principal center to which wheat and flour of backcountry origin were brought for exportation. The town began to grow, erect flour mills, siphon off wheat from adjacent parts of central Pennsylvania west of the Susquehanna River, build shipyards, and attract merchants to handle its exports of wheat and flour. By the end of the colonial period Virginia, too, had become an important producer of wheat, and of Indian corn as well.[59] By 1770 overseas wheat exports from Virginia and Maryland were worth £92,776 sterling, and on the eve of the Revolution both Baltimore and Norfolk had populations of approximately 6,000.[60]

At first glance, Charleston appears to form an exception to these conclusions. With a population of 4,500 as early as 1730, the city increased in numbers to 8,000 by 1760 and to 12,000 by 1775, when it became the fourth largest urban place in America. One important question, however, is why it did not become even larger. Charleston was a busier port than New York on the eve of the Revolution, yet it never developed a significant shipbuilding industry and did not have as large a native business community as the northern centers did. Surely the reason for the city's failure to develop into a true commercial center or general entrepot is that it offered commodities desired in England. English merchants were attracted there more than to the northern ports. For the most part, English or Scotch factors (commission merchants) were the great merchants of the city, and natives were either factors for English houses or retail traders. And for the most part, entrepreneurial decisions were "made in England, capital was raised there, ships were built or chartered there and outfitted there, [and] insurance was made there—all for the South Carolina trade."[61]

Yet Charleston, like the colony (and later the state) to which it belonged, is unique and difficult to characterize. Quinessentially southern, it was also influenced by the commercial cultures of both the northern United States and the Old World. If it is important to ask why the city did not become as large as northern cities, it is also important to ask why it became larger than any other southern city. Nor is size all that counts. Business conditions in Charleston were more like those in Philadelphia, New York, and Boston than like the conditions in Virginia or Maryland. Some of the city's greatest merchants bore Huguenot names, for in Charleston the Huguenots were finding a field for the exercise of those business talents that had made them important in

France out of all proportion to their numbers. To a greater extent than in the case of the tobacco colonies, business in South Carolina required middlemen, because the shoal channels of the streams did not permit oceangoing vessels to penetrate the country. Inland and coastal trade had to be organized in a more complicated way, and this afforded opportunities for natives as well as for the British factors attracted by rice and indigo. Charleston had more native businessmen than did any other southern city, and also a considerable group of shipmasters and seamen, ship builders and repairers, keepers of ropewalks, and fishermen. If larger planters of the upper South were sometimes retailers too, those of South Carolina were wholesale merchants. Even the Charleston factor "invested in lands and slaves and operated plantations to such an extent that it was often difficult to determine whether his dominant interest was planting or merchandising." Not as large as it might otherwise have been, Charleston was more a part of the great trading world of the Atlantic community than any other city of the colonial South.[62]

Of necessity, the colonies north of Maryland participated more widely in the exchanges of the Atlantic community than those to the south. This was because most northern products were usually unwanted in the mother country. Indeed, in the five-year period 1768–1772, they accounted for only 14 percent of the value of colonial exports to Great Britain.[63] Only in times of scarcity and high prices did the Corn Laws, designed to protect the British farmer against competition, permit the importation of grain. Meat and livestock were altogether excluded.[64] If, therefore, the inhabitants of the middle colonies and New England were to obtain the English merchandise they desired, they had no choice but to ship their commodities to other markets, either exchanging them for articles that were in demand in England or selling them for cash or bills of exchange which could be remitted to London to pay for imports. The principal markets were those of the West Indies and southern Europe. All regions shared in the West Indies trade, but New England and the middle colonies dominated it, together accounting for more than 70 percent of its value during 1768–1772. Wheat and bread and flour from the middle region primarily account for its leading role in the export trade with southern Europe.[65] However, shipments of wheat, Indian corn, and bread and flour from the upper South and rice from the lower South were almost as valuable, total exports from the South as a whole averaging £155,000 a year during the period, in comparison with £185,000 for the middle colonies.

The markets of both areas expanded vigorously in the eighteenth century. Behind the rising West Indian demand lay an ever-deepening commitment of resources to the production of sugar. As Brian Edwards wrote in his *History of Jamaica* in 1793, "It is true economy in the planter . . . to buy provisions from others . . . [for the] product of a single acre of his cane fields will purchase more Indian corn than can be raised in five times that extent of land, and pay besides the freight."[66] The official value of sugar exports to England

and Wales, rising consistently every decade before the Revolution, quadrupled between 1700–1709 and 1760–1769.[67] In response, the value of colonial exports to the West Indies, according to recent rough estimates, rose from £125,000–£150,000 annually in the 1720s and 1730s to £175,000–£200,000 in the 1750s and then soared to an average of £775,000 a year between 1768 and 1772. Although Indian corn from the upper South and rice from the lower South contributed to these rising values, their main source was an increase in the exportation of dried fish, livestock, and wood products from New England and bread and flour from the middle colonies. Connecticut alone supplied about two-thirds of the horses, three-fourths of the cattle, and 40 percent of the sheep and hogs. So popular was the pacer, bred by the Narragansett planters, that "excessive exportation has been assigned as a reason for the rapid decline of the breed, virtually extinct by 1800."[68]

West Indians evidently preferred to leave milling and baking to others, for although they imported only negligible quantities of wheat, they absorbed nearly half the average annual exportations of bread and flour between 1768 and 1773. The big market for wheat was Spain, Portugal, and the Mediterranean, which took 80 percent of the colonial wheat exportation during the period, and 35 percent of the bread and flour as well. Poor harvests at home were partly responsible, but change in underlying conditions may have been a factor in southern as well as northern Europe, where growth of population, urbanization, wealth, and, in the case of England, early industrialization gradually increased the area's dependence on foreign food supplies. England had long been an exporter of grain, its net foreign sales during the years 1742–1751 amounting to 38 million bushels, but between 1766 and 1775 England imported 11 million more bushels than it shipped abroad. A series of poor crops in the 1760s, however, induced exceptionally large importations of bread and flour in 1768 and 1769. Those were the forms in which most wheat was exported—indeed, two-thirds of it in 1770—because of the higher freight rates entailed by wheat, which is disproportionately bulky in relation to its value. So much bread and flour was sent abroad in the late colonial period that between 1768 and 1772 their average annual value of £412,000 ranked them second in importance to tobacco.[69]

Rising demand for wheat and its products affected colonial production and trade in a number of ways. In Massachusetts the legislature sought to encourage a revival of wheat in the older towns, and both that colony and Rhode Island enacted laws designed to eradicate barberry bushes, hosts to wheat rust. New England's main contribution to wheat production, however, seems to have been emigration. Jared Eliot remarked in 1749, "Our lands being thus worn out, I suppose to be one Reason why so many are inclined to remove to new Places that they may raise Wheat."[70] The main response was a striking expansion in the wheat belt after the mid-eighteenth century. By the Revolution, that belt, to define it roughly, included the Hudson Valley and the eastern end of the Mohawk, with an extension into eastern Vermont and western Connecticut; a sixth of land in New Jersey reaching from New York City to Philadelphia; the southeastern quarter of Pennsylvania; northern Delaware; the piedmont region of Maryland, Virginia, and North Carolina, and in Virginia and Maryland, a part of the tidewater too. Facilities for milling kept pace with the unfolding belt, both custom and merchant mills—the former serving local needs and the latter oriented toward the export trade—being erected in large numbers over a wide area. Like the cultivation of wheat itself, however, they were most numerous in Pennsylvania and New York, being concentrated especially on the streams near Philadelphia, the chief colonial market. Between 1759 and 1782 the number of mills in Chester County alone increased from 78 to 123.[71]

Philadelphia tapped a trading area that comprised not only all or parts of a half-dozen Pennsylvania counties, including northern and eastern Chester County, but also the three lower counties on the Delaware River, and a large section of West Jersey as well.[72] These ample sources enabled wheat, flour, and bread to form consistently more than half the total value of Philadelphia's exports. Wheat may have been more important than flour in the early eighteenth century, but in the years just before the Revolution the annual value of the city's flour shipments was usually ten times greater than that of wheat.[73] New York was the second most important flour market, and by the mid-eighteenth century the city was attracting wheat and flour not only from adjacent counties and the whole Hudson Valley, but also from the eastern end of the Mohawk Valley, western Vermont, and even Virginia and Maryland. Much came from eastern New Jersey, the province in which farmers may have succeeded in specializing in the cultivation of wheat to a greater degree than elsewhere, and where some of the best mills in the country were located.[74]

Despite the vigor of the colonial response, especially the growth in the area devoted to the cultivation of wheat and an extensive displacement of tobacco by wheat in Virginia and Maryland, wheat prices in Philadelphia rose from an average of 2.49s per bushel in 1744 to a high of 7.74s in 1772. The price of flour in port towns had been under $3 a barrel till about the mid-eighteenth century when it rose abruptly. From then till the Revolution it usually cost about $4 a barrel. This price behavior suggests strongly that supply was unable to keep up with demand. The average wheat planting per farm was "little more than 7 or 8 acres, which yielded a total of about 87 bushels, or a surplus above family consumption of about 42 bushels."[75] Evidently this was the yield of acres which had been under the plow for some time, for "abundant comment suggests that five to twelve bushels was all that could be expected on old land." From newer land, though, 20, 30, or even 40 bushels per acre were reported in southwestern Pennsylvania.[76] Farmers in the middle colonies made an effort to increase their productivity, for there is some evidence that agriculture was becoming more capital intensive in relation to land and labor. Yet a recent quantitative study concludes that resulting gains were only modest.[77] Scarcities of labor, especially seasonal labor, appear to have been the chief obstacle to specialization. Given the existence of a "sickle technology," a command of labor above the resources of the individual family was necessary if farmers were to be able to concentrate their resources on the production of wheat in order to take advantage of greatly improved markets for that commodity.[78] Thousands of Irish and German servants and redemptioners migrated to the middle colonies in the eighteenth century, but the region's labor shortage continued.

New England's main lack was not labor but agricultural resources. It is true that the inhabitants of the region sought to compensate for the thin promise of their hinterland by turning to the sea, forests, and pastures. Indeed, one historian, with the last in mind, has called grass the basis of New England agriculture. But most of it was unnutritious native grass. Nearly 90 percent of the land in four Massachusetts counties was devoted to pasture in 1767, but only 10 percent of it was planted to cultivate grass. A pasturage problem, already critical by 1750 because of increased population density and predominant reliance on native pasture, limited livestock expansion. Prices of meat and dairy products moved up strongly till after the French and Indian War, but it was Irishmen rather than New Englanders who reaped most of the benefits. Ireland was the leading supplier of beef, pork, and dairy products, finding its best market for beef and pork in the English colonies themselves, besides dominating the markets of the West Indies, especially those of the British islands. Rising corn prices after 1758, it is true, may have limited meat production by inducing farmers to sell their corn rather than use it for feed, but pork was often scarce and high in the 1740s, before corn prices rose. As for beef, exports "were not commensurate with the number of producers or the land utilized."[79]

The commodity exports of all thirteen colonies were insufficient to pay for their imports, and during 1768–1772 the annual deficit from their trade with Great Britain and Ireland is estimated to have averaged £1,331,000. The only commodity trade giving rise to a large surplus was that with southern Europe, the amount averaging £412,000 a year. Exports to Africa, mainly rum made in New England from West Indian molasses, probably exceeded the value of imports of goods, but certainly not that of slaves. Commodity trade to the West Indies gave rise to a small average annual deficit of £13,000. Overall, the imbalance between commodity exports and imports was much more severe for New England and the middle colonies than for the South. In all probability, the reason is not that the value of imports into the two northerly regions was larger than that of the South, but rather that their exports were less. In 1770, at any rate, the per capita value of exports from both regions was well below the average of £1.32 sterling for the thirteen colonies as a whole, while that of the South was well above it. (The figure for New England is £0.85

and for the middle region £1.10. Those for the lower and upper South are £1.55 and £1.80, respectively.) Thus, although all the colonies had to supplement their earnings from commodity exports, the need was especially keen in the two northerly regions.[80]

Fortunately, a concentration of ownership of vessels in those regions, especially in Philadelphia, New York, and Boston, enabled them to use their earnings from sales of vessels abroad,—estimated to have yielded to all the colonies between £12,000 and £18,000 sterling a year during 1763–1775[81]—and from shipping and other "invisible" sources to reduce the colonial deficit in the British commodity trade. Shipping earnings took the form of freights earned by colonial ships on each of the major trade routes. Surprisingly, earnings between foreign ports appear to have been insignificant, for colonial vessels did not typically traverse the famous "triangular" routes—for example, from Boston to Newfoundland to the West Indies and back—that historians have long emphasized. Rather, they engaged in to-and-fro shuttle voyages. Two other important sources of invisible earnings were insurance on vessels and cargoes obtained from colonial underwriters and mercantile profits. Recent estimates suggest that shipping earnings were large, on average £610,000 a year, ranking them second in value to the £766,000 realized from exports of tobacco. New England alone made 54 percent of the sum. The other "invisibles" averaged £222,000, and, together with earnings from shipping, they offset the deficit by 62 percent. The total had the effect of reducing the deficits of New England and the middle colonies and raising to a surplus position the balances of the southern colonies.[82]

The colonists also entered into other types of economic relationships with foreigners, some increasing and, others reducing the size of the remaining deficit—technically, the deficit on current account of the balance of payments. It may be helpful at this point to explain that a balance-of-payments statement is a record of the economic transactions—the exchanges of goods and services; governmental expenditures; immigrant remittances and other invisibles; gold shipments; and capital claims—between the residents of one country (the thirteen colonies) and those of all other areas during a given period. Goods, services, immigrant remittances, and government transfers are included in the "current account," and if, as a result of exports and imports and other transactions involving them, foreigners had larger claims on the colonists than the latter had on foreigners, then the thirteen colonies may be said to have run a deficit balance on current account. The function of two other main sections of the statement is to record how the deficit was financed. In part, investments by foreigners may have financed a part of the current account deficit. From the viewpoint of the recipient country, such investments are capital imports, and their effect is to increase that country's liabilities to foreigners. (In a sense, long-term debt is substituted for short-term debt.) Any remainder of the deficit on current account must be made up by monetary flows, by exports of gold or silver, either as coin or as bullion. The pertinent questions, then, are these: what additional items affected the balance on current account, and, assuming that a deficit remained, what was the probable size of the capital imports and gold shipments by which the colonies balanced that deficit?

Until recently, although numerous historians were aware of the existence of a deficit on current account, no one had tried to estimate the value of the invisible items in that account or the size of capital inflows. To do so is extremely difficult because of the lack of adequate evidence, and two scholars acknowledge that their estimates are very crude and probably subject to a large margin of error. Yet it is useful to have even an imperfect idea of the magnitudes involved, if only because of their implications for colonial economic development.

These scholars believe there were two principal kinds of transactions that increased the amount of the deficit on current account and two that reduced it. The former were expenditures on imported slaves and indentured servants, and the latter sales of ships to overseas buyers and expenditures made by the British government in the colonies, especially for purposes of defense. After taking these and some lesser transactions into account, they conclude that the average annual deficit between 1768 and 1772 was very small, perhaps in the range of £50,000 to £100,000 and perhaps even smaller; indeed, it is possible there was no deficit at all during this particular five-year period. If so, it follows that both foreign investments in the colonies and colonial exports of coin and bullion must have been small. Since the researchers are persuaded that these conclusions for 1768–1772 may well be applicable to the earlier years of the eighteenth century too, and especially that "long-term foreign investments in the thirteen colonies were nil,"[83] the former implies that the growing capital stock in the colonies must have been due almost entirely to colonial saving rather than to foreign investment. The latter suggests that earlier historians may be wrong in supposing that most or all of the specie imports from the West Indies and southern Europe went out the other end of the funnel as exports to discharge the unfavorable balance of trade with Great Britain. Even if much of the specie was retained, however, the question remains whether the colonists believed the amount of it sufficient to move their growing volume of trade.

Unquestionably, they believed it was not. The emphasis on belief is pertinent. It can be argued quite strongly that the colonists were acting in their own interest when they exported specie to reduce an unfavorable balance on current account; that they were better off using less expensive forms of money as media of domestic exchange and sending their gold and silver to Europe to buy the merchandise and capital goods essential to their economic progress. Benjamin Franklin, at least, came very close to seeing it that way in the 1760s.[84] But this was a somewhat sophisticated view of the matter, and it is probable that not many of his contemporaries would have agreed. The colonists, after all, lived in an age of mercantilism, and it would be surprising if they had not shared the reigning conviction that the nation's true treasure lay in its stock of gold and silver. The belief animated British policy, which was to attract and retain as much of the precious metal as possible. One English government after another prohibited the exportation of gold and silver, even to the colonies.[85] And because the colonies did not themselves mine the precious metals, it was only by a favorable balance of trade, and by policy, that they could hope to get any.

The most important silver coin imported into the colonies was the Spanish "piece of eight" (eight reals), superseded by the Spanish milled dollar, in 1728. The Spanish silver dollar was not only the chief element in the colonial specie supply but also the coin which Congress accepted as the monetary standard of the United States in 1786. There were several colonial varieties: the Peru, or light piece of eight, and the heavy pieces, Mexico, pillar, and Seville. Spanish fractional money—the four-real piece (half-dollar), the two-real piece (quarter dollar), the one-real piece, and two small coins valued, respectively, at one-half and one-fourth real—supplied small change. The principal gold coins were the Portugese johannes, or joe; the moidore; and the Spanish and French pistole. In addition, the circulating currency included Dutch and German coins.[86]

The quantity of these several coins available at any given time is unknown, as is the volume of business they facilitated as means of payment. It is likely, however, that because of the sparseness of the population, the coins did not change hands very rapidly, so that it took more money per person to make possible a given number of transactions than would be the case later. Even more surely, the use of the coins was attended by some risk and inconvenience. Coins were clipped, sweated, and otherwise made to yield some of their metallic content, common practices which made it necessary for merchants to weigh them to determine their value. Loss might be avoided, however, by the simple expedient of paying them out again.[87]

In an effort to lure the precious metals into their respective jurisdictions, the colonial assemblies competed with one another in enacting legislation raising the legal value of the Spanish piece of eight and of other coins in proportion. The mint value of gold and silver coins depended on the amount of pure metal they contained. For more than two centuries after 1600 the pound sterling contained 1,718.7 grains of fine silver, so that a shilling had 83.94 grains of pure metal. Since Newton's official assay at the English mint in 1704 gave the dollar a rating of 386.8 grains of fine metal, it followed that the Spanish dollar was worth 4s. 6d. of English money. Colonial assemblies proceeded to increase this value to 5s. and 6s., even to 7s. and 8s. In effect, they decreased the silver content of the shilling (since it would thereafter take fewer dollars to pay off a debt in shillings). Thus they overvalued colonial money and devalued English money.[88]

The device worked, but only briefly and not well. Some of the colonies temporarily enjoyed a small measure of success in attracting specie. (Pirates tended to bring the precious metal to ports where its legal value was highest.) But because the rates differed from one colony to the next, it was manifestly impossible for all to benefit at the same time. Furthermore, the inflow increased the money supply and tended to raise the general price level in proportion to the amount of the overvaluation. There was a second consequence: English merchants trading with the colonies complained that the increased shilling value of Spanish money was permitting the colonists to pay off their debts with fewer Spanish coins. In response, the Board of Trade obtained a royal proclamation in 1704, followed by an act of Parliament in 1708, which forbade the colonies to rate Spanish pieces of eight at more than six shillings, an overvaluation of 33.3 percent. The act was widely ignored, however, and many of the colonies pushed the legal value of foreign coins to even higher levels.[89]

In their continuing effort to cope with problems of exchange created by an inadequate and insufficient supply of money, the colonists were led to adopt numerous substitute ways of making payment for goods and services. Many staples were monetized, an act of assembly stating the value in pounds, shillings, and pence at which the articles would be received in public and private payments. As in the case of Virginia and Maryland, taxes were sometimes made payable and debts contracted in the commodity itself. The need for means of payment was less compelling in the slave-labor colonies than in the free-labor ones because of the directness of their exchange with England, essentially an arrangement in which tobacco, rice, or indigo was bartered for merchandise. Nevertheless, both parties to a transaction had to keep bookkeeping records of the values involved in the exchange, the unit of account serving in late-seventeenth-century Virginia (and in late-eighteenth-century Boston as well) as a standard of deferred payment. Thus "bookkeeping barter" facilitated trade even when money was not used as a means of payment. And since, on the one hand, the unit of account was usually sterling pounds, shillings, and pence, or the pounds, shillings, and pence as defined by law in a given colony—and which accordingly became known in Massachusetts, for example, as "Massachusetts curency" or the "lawful money" of that province— whereas, on the other hand, the means of payment were Spanish pieces of eight, commodities, or something else, the two most essential functions of money—to serve as a means of payment and to serve as a unit of account— were divided in colonial America as in so many other times and places in history. In addition to specie and designated commodities, the colonists also used various kinds of paper as means of payment. Among these were warehouse receipts or notes for tobacco inspected and stored in public warehouses in accordance with legislation in Virginia (1714, 1730) and Maryland (1747) designed to elevate the quality of the tobacco tendered in payment of public dues. Intended for local circulation, the notes were made a legal tender in all tobacco payments. Because taxes, duties, court fees, and the salaries of the clergy were all paid in tobacco, the holder of a note had only to present it at the warehouse to have it redeemed by the inspectors in tobacco of the kind called for by the note. Such tobacco was called "transfer tobacco," as distinct from "crop tobacco" deposited in a warehouse to await exportation. A recent authority believes that the system provided "a fairly satisfactory currency for the needs of Virginia's rural economy, although, since the value of the notes fluctuated with the price of tobacco, it did not provide a stable monetary medium."[90]

In the leading port cities, too, the idea of paper substitutes for money was a familiar one. But the paper circulating there was private paper: promissory notes and bills of exchange, commercial paper generated by business transactions which, when endorsed, passed from hand to hand in payment of debt. Probably the circle in which this paper moved was a small one, but so too were the business communities that created it. Their very smallness made it possible for businessmen to know one another's general affairs and reputation well enough to judge the value of paper and hence to impart currency to each other's promises and orders to pay. In all probability only part of the business community was involved, namely, merchants engaged in foreign trade, men who exported and imported, who sold primarily at wholesale. Retail storekeepers, whether urban or rural, probably only rarely required a formal IOU from those making purchases on credit, their daybooks and ledgers serving to record the debt and its repayment. Commercial paper was circulating debt, and since no commercial banks existed, merchants themselves probably made loans by discounting the paper, that is, by deducting an interest charge from the face value of the note or bill. Thus private paper served as a vehicle for loans as well as a means of payment. The colonists also discovered the usefulness of public paper. Indeed, the leading authority on the subject regards paper currency issued under governmental auspices as "the distinctive contribution of the American colonies to financial and monetary practice."[91] This favorable view, shared by other modern scholars, stands in stark contrast to that of numerous earlier writers. Until relatively recently U.S. monetary history was written for the most part by so-called sound-money men. Persuaded that money must be made of gold or silver if it is to be "sound," they deplored the use of paper and smothered the differences between one colony's practice and that of others beneath a blanket condemnation of all. The differences mattered very much, as they usually do. Carried to excess, paper money washed out values in an inflationary tide. Issued in more limited quantities and with adequate provision for its redemption—a matter of importance in young communities—colonial bills of credit served a number of purposes and served them well.[92]

The assemblies authorized the issuance of bills of credit on the basis of two distinct types of security. One was the security of land; the other, the credit of the colony supported by tax funds. In the former case the legislature established a loan office, struck off a sum in bills, and declared them legal tender. Commissioners of the loan office proceeded to lend the bills in limited sums, the loans usually being secured by a mortgage on landed property double the value of the sum lent. Borrowers were required to pay interest each year but were given a period of eight to ten years to repay the principal in annual installments. During that time the bills became a part of the circulating currency as borrowers spent them to buy and improve land or to pay off debt.[93] Thus these so-called "land banks"—not banks at all in the modern sense, but rather batches of paper money resting on the security of land—provided individuals with the long-term credit needed to expand their agricultural activities, government with a source of revenue in the form of interest payments, and the public at large with an increased supply of money.[94]

In the eighteenth century the colonies began to use land banks as monetary devices to combat depressions. New York did so in 1715 and 1737, Pennsylvania and Delaware in 1723 and 1729, New Jersey in 1723, and Maryland in 1733. After analyzing the effect of the currency issues of 1723 and 1729 on internal prices, foreign-exchange rates, foreign trade, and the domestic market, a modern economist reached the conclusion that the issues "did stimulate economic recovery from business depression, and did so without any detrimental effects later on."[95] The economist published his analysis during a period when the New Deal was searching for ways to end a far more severe depression in the 1930s, and his implied acceptance of an unmodified quantity-of-money theory of prices (including exchange rates) has recently been subjected to criticism. Yet, another scholar finds that, except in New England, "few contemporaries doubted that land banks stimulated the economic growth of the country."[96]

They were most successful in the middle colonies, where interest received by the government was sufficient to pay most of the ordinary cost of administration and served as a substitute for taxes.[97] In 1782 a contemporary historian, George Chalmers, attributed the "singular prosperity" of Pennsylvania in part to the "prudent policy of promoting enterprise by feeding circulation with loans of paper money, gradual yet moderate." That province managed a land bank so well for more than fifty years prior to the Revolution that the price level during that time exhibited more stability than the American price level has during any succeeding fifty–year period in U.S. history.[98] Experience in the South and in New England was different. Virginia never adopted a land bank, but in both Carolinas and in New England land-bank loans played a part in the decline of the currency's value. The excessive issues of currency in Rhode Island in particular helped bring on the first statutory regulation of paper money by Parliament in 1751.[99]

Bills issued on the credit of the colony came into being initially because of the difficulties in financing the costs of war. Their success then led legislatures to turn to the same means of meeting financial emergencies in peacetime. Given the relatively small tax base, the scarcity of specie, the lack of liquidity in property, the nonexistence of commercial banks and business corporations, and the urgency of need, especially in wartime, the colonies found themselves unable to depend on taxation or borrowing. As Robert Carter Nicholas, the treasurer of Virginia, observed after that colony had made its initial emission of paper, "the Sums required, from Time to Time, were so very considerable, that there was no prospect of borrowing them . . . . Hence arose an absolute necessity of having Recourse to a paper Currency."[100] Once authorized by the assembly, an issue was turned over to officials to pay out to the public creditors. Usually the authorizing act provided for calling in and retiring the bills by earmarking the proceeds of specific taxes for that purpose. For example, a tax would be levied for a five-year period and its proceeds used to redeem one-fifth of the bills annually. Essentially the system, aptly termed one of "currency finance," provided a way of anticipating tax revenues. It therefore partook of the character of a forced loan.[101]

What sustained the value of these bills? They were not convertible into specie, nor as a rule did they earn interest. Usually, however, they were made a legal tender in both public and private transactions, a feature which at the minimum promoted their utility. Unquestionably their value was also sustained in part by the tax fund earmarked for their redemption. Was this enough? One scholar believes that "since the money was created and upheld solely by political acts, confidence in the government was essential to its value." No doubt that is true. And probably the most essential prop to confidence was neither the redemption fund nor the legal tender provision. Rather, it was knowledge that the quantity issued did not overly exceed the amount of business transacted, the requirements of trade at existing levels.[102]

When excessive issues were authorized, depreciation followed in their wake. In New England and the Carolinas paper currency depreciated considerably, but in the middle colonies the success and good credit of government paper are indubitable. In fact, wholesale prices in New York and Philadelphia, and in New Jersey and Delaware—the economies of West Jersey and Delaware being closely tied up with that of Pennsylvania—were more stable in the colonial period than from the adoption of the Constitution to the Civil War.[103] Perhaps the greater volume of business transactions in Philadelphia and New York, which were outdistancing the population growth of Boston, helps account for interregional differences in degrees of success in avoiding high rates of inflation.

Yet other considerations must also be weighed. Massachusetts was in the difficult position of being inundated by loan office bills from Rhode Island, a little colony which "sported with land banks," issuing enormous sums on loan to preferred individuals, and Massachusetts' position was aggravated by its own large emissions to pay for its rather extensive participation in the Anglo-French wars of the period.[104] Differential rates of participation in war must have been a significant factor in comparative inflation, for when men are at war instead of at work, the number of things for sale falls in relation to the amount of available money. The paper money of the New England colonies did not begin to decline in value till large amounts were issued in 1713 to fight the French and Indians in Queen Ann's War, and the same thing occurred in South Carolina.[105]

A relatively small volume of business transactions appears to have contributed to inflation in the tobacco colonies. The apparent explanation for the depreciation of Maryland's first emission in 1733 is that "tobacco remained the primary medium of exchange." In sum, the extra money was not yet needed. But by 1764 that province's bills of credit were much in demand, and large emissions thereafter held their value. The explanation appears to be that the increasing shift of Maryland's farmers from tobacco to wheat and the rapid growth of Baltimore increased the volume of business transactions beyond the ability of tobacco and tobacco notes to mediate.[106]

Tobacco notes also served Virginia's currency needs till the colony's participation in the French and Indian War forced it to resort to a paper emission in 1755—the last colony to do so.[107] Had the war not occurred, Virginia might have continued indefinitely to meet its currency needs with tobacco notes. For although that province, like Maryland, was shifting some of its resources out of tobacco and into wheat, urban growth did not accompany that development. In sum, although the cost of war accounts for a general colonial resort to "currency finance," it was urban and business growth in the leading port cities that generated a continuing daily need for larger amounts of money to facilitate transactions.[108]

In the closing decades of the pre-Revolutionary period, four of the five largest cities experienced remarkable rates of population growth. Between 1743 and 1775 New York grew by 72 percent, Charleston by 66 percent, Philadelphia by approximately 60 percent, and Newport by 44 percent. Boston alone did not register an increase; indeed, the city's numbers appear to have fallen slightly during the interval. From the longer perspective of growth since 1700, Philadelphia's eightfold expansion overshadows all others, although Charleston's population grew sixfold and New York's fivefold in the same period. On the eve of the Revolution, Philadelphia stood preeminent among American cities, with an estimated population of 40,000. New York, with 25,000, ranked second, followed by Boston (16,000), Charleston (12,000), and Newport (11,000).

"The size of all towns in America," a discerning visitor, Isaac Weld, remarked in 1795, "has hitherto been proportionate to their trade, and particularly to that carried on with the back settlements."[109] The essential meaning of Weld's observation is that preindustrial port cities were marketing and

004

service mechanisms that grew with expansion in the demand and supply of goods. They were funnels through which the surplus produce of the countryside was poured to await exportation, as well as markets themselves for some of the produce. They were central gathering places, and the greater the quantity and diversity of the goods brought there, the more complex the facilities for servicing them and the larger and more occupationally diversified the population. All this was less true, however, where investment decisions relative to marketing were made for the most part in headquarters located overseas, where factors merely executed those decisions in return for commissions— a role debarring them from the potentially higher earnings associated with risk taking. The effect was to limit the number of native businessmen, and urban growth and development as well.

The reason is plain: within limits etched by capital need and availability, the wider the scope of investment opportunity, and of freedom of discretion with regard to investment, the larger the number of businessmen seeking to profit thereby. The more risk taking entrepreneurs there were, the greater the demand for vessels, crews, and a host of crafts, occupations, and services necessary for the sustenance of a vigorous, multichanneled commerce.[110] And the larger the market, too, for the products of numerous handicrafts pursued by artisans living in the city itself and in its surrounding countryside. The traditional explanation for the arrested development of the mechanical arts in colonial Charleston is that white mechanics emigrated to the northern colonies in order to avoid the social stigma attached to labor performed by hired-out black tradesmen.[111] It is more likely that those tradesmen were able to fill a demand for mechanics that was relatively small because of the constraints on the development of native enterprise in that urban funnel for enumerated rice and indigo.

The growth of the northern port cities accompanied the growth of trade, although it would be too much to claim that it did so in any precisely parallel fashion. Unfortunately, it is possible only to guess at the dimensions of the latter. Goods were sent not only to foreign markets but also to other American colonies and to the hinterland beyond the ports. We know a little about the foreign import-export trade, less about the coastal trade, and least about trade with the backcountry. In none of the three areas is it possible to specify total values, except for the first two trades during a brief part of the late colonial period. Yet it is certain that growth was the hallmark of all three in the eighteenth century.

As farmers moved west of the coastal plain in search of new or better lands, they were soon followed by retail merchants opening backcountry stores. Stores dotted the rural landscape of the middle and northern colonies as well as that of the South. Their essential function was to barter imported dry good and other merchandise for country produce. In the store in Lebanon, Connecticut, kept by Jonathan Trumbull in the 1730s and 1740s, an incredible variety of items, ranging from pepper, lace, gloves, gunpowder, drugs, pots and pans, needles, and knives, to molasses, rum, and copies of Watts's *Psalms*, were exchanged for hogs, oxen, sheep, pork, beef, deerskins, firewood, turkeys, potatoes, and numerous other forms of "country pay." Trumbull carted the latter to Norwich and Boston for sale and there obtained the merchandise for his retail shelves. His store was typical, except for the obscurity of the location in which some were to be found.[112] On a journey to the Ohio country in 1789 Colonel John May of Boston was surprised when he came upon "a settlement of five log huts, or cabins, & not more than fifty acres of land cleared," called Mingo Bottom. "Yet, small as the settlement is," the colonel confided to his journal, "here is a store, with a very good assortment of goods, to the value, as I suppose, of £1000." The average value of the merchandise in all stores at any time is unknown, but almost all goods were funneled to the backcountry from the leading ports.[113]

Merchants resident in those ports also dispatched their vessels on coastal voyages in order to distribute imported merchandise and colonial products, as well as to collect cargoes destined for foreign markets. A recent study enables us to see something of the typical patterns of trade and of their magnitude in relation to the value of foreign trade in the years 1768–1772. Coastal trade was more important to New England than to any other region. One reason for this was New England's dependence on imports of grain and flour— foodstuffs that came from the middle colonies and the upper South—to feed its population. Another followed from its leading role in overseas trade with the West Indies, for this led naturally to prominence in the coastal redistribution of imported molasses and New England rum. New England's ships also carried to other regions a number of goods of its own produce or manufacture, such as lumber products and spermaceti candles. Presumably they played a conspicuous part in the gathering of principal components of foreign cargoes such as lumber products, dried fish, furs, and flaxseed—the last for Ireland's expanding linen industry. So too did ships of the middle colonies, which joined New England in dominating the coastal trade. The region's main coastal exports were bread and flour, a few manufactured goods such as bar and pig iron, and wine and salt—the last two reflecting the middle colonies' leadership in trade with southern Europe. The importance of the coastal trade is often insufficiently appreciated. The estimated annual value of the coastal trade of the colonies as a whole from 1768 to 1772 averaged about 25 percent of the value of colonial shipments overseas. For the middle colonies the figure is nearly 40 percent, and for New England more than 60 percent. The trade must have contributed significantly to the development of the leading ports in those regions, for almost certainly the trade of New England was dominated by Boston and Newport, and that of the middle colonies by Philadelphia and New York. Had it not been for the limited capacity of its hinterland, Boston would probably have kept pace with the others.[114]

Available figures for foreign trade cover a longer period but are limited in the main to the colonial relationship with Great Britain. They include the official value of imports as well as of exports, both series testifying to impressive rates of growth. The annual average value of New England's exports between 1740–1744 and 1770–1774 increased twelvefold, that of imports nearly quadrupled. New York's exports approximately quintupled, and its imports tripled. Pennsylvania's exports more than tripled, while the value of its imports rose nearly sevenfold.[115]

Despite the dearth of export-import figures for other areas, there is every reason to believe that the volume and value of trade also increased over the course of the eighteenth century. A historian of the New York merchant on the eve of the Revolution believes that New York's trade with the West Indies was quite as fundamental as the trade with Great Britain and estimates that it accounted for fully half the city's annual exports and from 30 to 40 percent of its imports. Commerce with southern Europe and the wine islands was considerable and growing.[116] In the case of Philadelphia, newspaper shipping reports reveal an increase in the number of vessels leaving that port for the West Indies, from an annual average of 83 in the 1730s to 166 in the 1750s and to 262 in the early 1770s. Clearances to southern Europe and the wine islands rose from 18 or 19 a year between 1730 and 1734, to 36–37 between 1750 and 1754, and to 101 in the years just before the Revolution.[117]

These vessels, moreover, were largely built and owned by the colonists themselves. In the words of a recent historian: "The victory of the merchants of Boston, Newport, Philadelphia, and New York was complete. By the seventh decade of the century 95 percent of the ships trading between the Caribbean islands and New England and 82 percent of those serving the middle colonies were owned by the residents of those areas. By this time as well all the American coastal trade was in colonial hands, as was 75 percent of all direct trade between northern ports and the mother country." Moreover, by the eve of the Revolution a third of the entire British merchant fleet was composed of ships built in America. In sum, all signs point to buoyant growth, both in foreign and in domestic trade and, except for Boston between 1743 and 1775, in the size of the leading port towns.[118]

Does this mean that the per capita incomes of the colonists were rising too, that economic growth in this "intensive" sense accompanied the undeniable evidences of "extensive" growth? The question is a difficult one because of the lack of data on aggregate output over time. Yet recent studies by Alice Hanson Jones afford a remarkably clear view of the wealth of the American colonies on the eve of the Revolution. If we bear in mind that wealth implies saving (hence acquisition through theft or conquest can be ruled out); that saving implies the ability to produce more than is needed for purposes of immediate consumption; and that this, in turn, implies the possession and use of capital to augment the output from which savings may be drawn, we shall be better able to make a tentative judgment about the relationship between wealth in 1774 and growth of output previous to that time.

According to Jones's estimates, the aggregate value of privately owned physical wealth was roughly £110 million sterling, or about $5.25 billion in the dollars of 1976. Of this total, over one-half was held in the South, about one-fourth in the middle colonies, and the rest in New England. Average overall net worth per capita in the South was £51.6 sterling, compared with £46.4 sterling in the middle colonies and only £31.3 sterling in New England. Per free wealthholder—essentially the head of a free household—the figures are £372, £207, and £138, respectively, equivalent in 1978 dollars to approximately $13,000, $11,200, and $7,500.[119]

The South predominated to the extent that it did because it held 95 percent of the value of all indentured servants and slaves, forms of property that were worth nearly £21.5 million sterling in 1774. If this sum is subtracted from the aggregate value of physical wealth, the southern advantage is reduced but not eliminated. Nearly half the remaining £89.5 million sterling in nonhuman physical wealth is still to be found in the South, a little over a quarter in the middle colonies, and less than a quarter in New England. Surely part of the explanation is that some of the assets of the South—for example, improved lands and structures—owed their existence to the work of slaves. Were it possible to take fully into account and to deduct the contribution of slavery to the creation of the southern capital stock, the South's advantage in wealth-holding over the other regions would be reduced still more. Even as it is, the distribution of nonhuman physical wealth among the regions comes close to matching the distribution of the population itself. While the South held over half that wealth, it also held nearly half the population. The middle colonies had a little more than a quarter of the wealth and slightly more than a quarter of the population, and New England, the poorest of the regions, had less than a quarter of the wealth and a quarter of the population.[120]

Then why not exclude servants and slaves from the category of physical wealth? In fact, the distinguished nineteenth-century utilitarian philosopher John Stuart Mill explicitly urged that this be done. The ownership of slaves, Mill argued, tells us something about the distribution of a society's wealth but nothing about its productive capacity. For the latter is no greater whether the slaves are self-owned or owned by others. Modern economists are also aware of the distortion to which Mill called attention, and their solution to the problem is the suggestion that estimates be made of the value of free as well as of unfree human capital. Jones herself has made an admittedly crude calculation of this kind—by capitalizing the value of the expected lifetime earnings of the free population and deducting the costs of its rearing and maintenance. The very rough consequence is that the aggregate wealth of the thirteen colonies is nearly doubled, and the southern advantage over the northern regions greatly reduced, although not eliminated.[121]

But this is not history. The historical fact is that servants and slaves had market values and free whites did not. The historical fact, however painful it may be to recollect, is that whites in the South owned blacks and their labor and its product, and because the law and mores of southern whites confirmed that ownership, their wealth considerably exceeded that of white people in other regions. Southern slave capital alone was worth more than all forms of nonhuman producers' capital in all thirteen colonies together. Use of this capital in production goes far to explain why the per capita value of white-owned southern land, including structures and improvements, averaged £42.5 in 1774, in contrast to £27.3 in New England and £28.3 in the middle colonies. As far as the categories of material wealth are concerned, New England fared less well than its neighbors. Only in the average value of consumer goods and, more slightly, in equipment of nonfarm business did that region have an edge over the others, the per capita figures for the two categories being £2.2 (compared with £3.1 for the South and £4.0 for the middle colonies) and £0.4 (compared with £0.3 for the middle colonies and £0.1 for the South), respectively. Possessing less producers' capital than the other regions, New England was at a disadvantage in production. It had less capital per worker, and this meant less output, less savings, less capital formation, and so on about the circle. Did it also mean a lower rate of economic growth?[122]

Probably. Lack of data on output over time makes estimates of growth rates little better than fragile guesses. Yet interregional differences in wealthholding per capita may imply interregional differences in rates of growth of output per capita—without implying an unchanging degree of association between the two variables. Wealth is a stock and output a flow, and we cannot say that output in the South grew two and one-half times as fast as it did in New England merely because at a particular point in time—the year 1774—southern wealth per free household was two and one-half times as large. Many influences impinge upon the relationship between output and saving—for example, differences in propensities to consume—and we lack knowledge of these matters in colonial America. Since output was very largely agricultural in character, what ideally we should know is whether or not increases occurred in the quantities of land, labor, and capital used in farming, and whether the productivity of these factors of production was raised by inputs of knowledge that improved either their quality individually or the efficiency with which they were combined in use. And we should know too whether increases in output per unit of factor input exceeded the rate of population growth.

We are as yet unable to answer questions about changing quantities of factor inputs. Recent studies, however, suggest that the distribution of agricultural commodities was becoming more efficient in the eighteenth century. Productivity gains were realized in maritime shipping as increases in security from privateering and piracy made it possible to dismantle heavy guns from the decks of vessels, reduce the size of crews, and free up more space for cargo.

And the quickening of turnabout times made possible by the adoption of central warehousing arrangements for tobacco also contributed, as we have seen, to growth in efficiency by increasing the number of round-trip voyages a vessel might make. Although these sectoral gains took place on the narrow periphery of the economy, it may still be argued that they encouraged increases in agricultural output by improving the mechanism of distribution, thereby increasing the earnings of farmers.

So too did widening markets for colonial products. Indeed, by pulling unemployed or underemployed resources out of the subsistence sector and into the commercial portion of the economy, widening markets acted as the prime lever of colonial economic growth. The question, though, is how the lever worked, and this, basically, is a question concerning the elasticity of the supply response. Assuming that output grew in the same proportion as or greater than the increase in demand, were the variables at work long-term ones of a demographic nature or shorter-term technological ones? Widening markets and improved mechanisms of distribution may conceivably have encouraged immigration, marriage, and fecundity, as well as efforts to raise output per worker.

We know too little to respond to the former possibility. That of technological innovation, however, turns substantially on factor proportions in agriculture. Given the relative abundance and cheapness of land, incentives to improve the productivity of capital and labor tended to be blunted. Output could keep pace with growing demand by improving the quality of a single input—land. And quality was improved not as a rule by increasing the amount of relatively expensive capital and labor per acre but rather by buying new land. As Thomas Jefferson remarked to the English agricultural reformer Arthur Young, "We can buy an acre of new land cheaper than we can manure an old one."[123] In sum, technology cannot be assigned much weight as a source of increase in average efficiency, but movement onto new and fertile soil probably raised output per acre, especially in the middle colonies and in the South.

Perhaps this, together with somewhat greater intensity in the use of capital in relation to labor and land, largely accounts for the increase in total factor productivity (output per unit of capital and labor combined) recently found in the agriculture of Chester County, Pennsylvania. But the pace of increase was slow, almost glacially so, at 0.1 and 0.2 percent per year. Productivity gains in the tobacco industry, as we have seen, were largely confined to the seventeenth century. In addition, the movement of rice growing from relatively high lands to coastal marshes and tidelands brought improvements in the production of that crop. More broadly, it is possible that superior organization of the agricultural labor force under the southern plantation system yielded increases in output per unit of labor input in the eighteenth century.

These, then, appear to have been the chief sources of productivity gains in an agriculture which, slowly but increasingly commercialized in response to widening markets, led a slow upward movement in per capita output in the eighteenth century. It follows that much of the wealth of the American people on the eve of the Revolution must have been painfully accumulated over long stretches of time, and that the processes of capital formation and economic growth were slow. This does not mean that growth, at whatever level it occurred, was constant or that differentiation by region, subregion, or even smaller locality; by industry; and by occupation, did not take place. About the latter possibilities we as yet know little. One scholar, examining a sample of probated estates in New England, argues that average incomes in that region rose at an annual rate of between 1 percent and 1.6 percent between 1650 and 1709, only to be offset and slowed by a population boom in the eighteenth century.[124] Very recently, however, two scholars have found clear evidence of growing wealth, mainly in the form of land and buildings, in southern New England in the later years of the colonial period.[125] In the Chesapeake tobacco region, still another scholar finds that individual income rose rapidly in the 1630s and gradually from 1640 to 1670, and remained steady for the rest of the century. As in early New England, however, demographic change, in this case a steep rise in the number of people supported by males (wives, children and relatives), prevented per capita incomes from growing between 1670 and 1720.[126]

Other local studies find a per capita rate of growth in overall wealth of 4 percent per decade between 1704 and 1776 in Prince George's County, Maryland,[127] and an examination of the asset composition of estates in St. Mary's County in the same province confirms rising living standards there in the eighteenth century.[128] Estate records of personal wealth yield for another investigator a growth rate for all of Maryland that averages 0.8 percent for the approximately fifty-year period between 1670 and 1719.[129] These findings and the probings into local places at discrete time periods are difficult to generalize into all-colonial patterns of economic change. One effort to describe the latter, however, suggests that colonial living standards were elevated by an increase in agricultural productivity brought about by the introduction and use of the cradle scythe by at least some farmers after the mid-eighteenth century, in conjunction with a rise in export prices of agricultural products in relation to the costs of manufactured goods imported from England—a shift in the terms of trade in favor of the colonies after 1760. Even so, the small size of the export sector in relation to the economy as a whole must have limited the effects of these developments.[130] The tail was too small to wag the dog.

In sum, it is at present impossible to determine the overall rate of growth of the colonial economy. Perhaps the best-informed guess is one that rests on Alice Hanson Jones's careful examination of inventories of probated estates in all three major colonial regions. On the assumption that a ratio of 3.5 or 3.0 to 1 expresses the relationship between wealth and income, Jones extrapolates backward her wealth findings for 1774 and suggests that per capita income grew at the rate of 0.3 percent per year from 1650 to 1725, at 0.4 percent from 1725 to 1750, and at 0.5 percent from 1750 to 1774.[131] These are indeed slow rates of growth. Yet they are not slow in the context of the times, especially in view of the large absorption of population made possible by the resources of colonial America. Only in Holland and England were population and per capita incomes also rising simultaneously. Furthermore, if a rate as high as 0.6 percent a year was achieved—a modest rate still, and one conceived as possible by a leading economic historian[132]—its effect would have been to double colonial incomes in the 125 years between the mid-seventeenth century and the Revolution and to justify Jones's belief that the standard of living obtaining by then was "probably the highest achieved for the great bulk of the population in any country up to that time."

Once again, though, the processes of capital formation and economic growth varied by region, with New England lingering in the wake of advances realized in the middle colonies, and the latter in the wake of advances in the South. As we have seen, whereas New England's hinterland had relatively few natural resources, the middle colonies mainly lacked extrafamilial sources of labor. The South lacked neither; indeed, the suitability of the soil and climate for the production of staples in rising demand on world markets focused the interest of British businessmen and their government on that region. The former supplied the credit that enabled southern planters to increase their supplies of labor and land and thus to expand their output, and the latter enacted legislation requiring the funneling of that output into the hands of British businessmen. The planters benefited from the arrangement as well as the British, and their profits enabled them to increase still more their investments in land and slaves.

And live high off the hog as well:

> The Eighteenth century was the golden age of the Virginia slaveholders. It was then that they built the handsome homes once so numerous in the older counties, many of which still remain as interesting monuments of former days; it was then that they surrounded themselves with graceful furniture and costly silverware, in large part imported from Great Britain; it was then that they collected paintings and filled their libraries with the works of standard writers; it was then that they purchased coaches and berlins; it was then that men and women alike wore rich and expensive clothing.[133]

This was true not only in the tobacco colonies, of course. Charleston had its Laurenses, Manigaults, Brewtons, Gadsdens, and other wealthy families too. Indeed, the planters or "gentlemen" of Charleston were the richest southerners of all. Obviously wealth was not distributed equally, either in the South or anywhere else. It was distributed more unevenly in New England than elsewhere. In 1774 the net worth of the richest 10 percent of free householders in New England amounted to 56.8 percent of the total, in comparison with 42.1 percent in the middle colonies of New Jersey, Pennsylvania, and Delaware, and 48.8 percent in the South. The poor fared poorly everywhere. The net worth of the lower 50 percent of free families amounted to 9.4 percent of the total in the middle colonies and to 4.3 percent in the South. For New England the figure is a minus 1.6 percent! In that poorest of American regions, in short, wealth was more heavily concentrated than elsewhere, and the poor were worse off.[134]

Growth in total income or wealth, however, is not the only measure of improvement in living standards. A widening variety of inexpensive household or personal goods also tends to elevate the well-being of families. In recent years students have called attention to the importance to both England and its colonies of an increase in available kinds of consumption goods in the eighteenth century, an increase significant enough to deserve recognition as a "consumer revolution." Such a revolution appears to have taken place in the second half of the eighteenth century in southern New England. According to Gloria T. and Jackson T. Main, families who were only modestly well-off managed to acquire a greater variety of both personal and household items— for example, inexpensive amenities like cups and saucers, teapots, and forks.[135]

On the other hand, the greater one's purchasing power, the wider one's command of variety. The same applies to geographic regions, among which are found gross disparities in wealth. While this relationship is not easy to explain, it is probable that differences in degree of commercialization and in attendant complexity of the social structure, especially of occupational diversification, play an important part. In his pioneer analysis of the structure of America's economic and social classes in the period 1763–1788, Jackson Turner Main suggests a quadripartite categorization of developing communities. When first occupied, an area and its settlers belonged to the "frontier stage" of development, a level marked by a high degree of equality in the distribution of property and by minimal occupational differentiation. The changes that ensued depended on the quality of soils and, above all, on the accessibility of markets. Where soil was poor and settlement remote from markets, as in the New England uplands, the economy produced only a small surplus above subsistence needs. Such communities were largely, although never entirely, self-sufficient. Subsistence farm villages were "the most common type throughout New England and perhaps in the entire North." Society became more complex, more differentiated at the subsistence level, but nevertheless remained markedly egalitarian. In the town of Harvard, Massachusetts, for example, the 10 percent of the citizens who paid the largest tax in 1771 owned 26.5 percent of the taxable wealth, "a proportion which emphasizes the economic equality of the town."[136]

The commercial farm community was one which sold a much larger quantity of agricultural products than did subsistence farming areas. Such a community had good soil and was accessible to market, either because of its closeness to a major urban center or ocean harbor or because it was located on a navigable river. Towns rather than villages, they had greater average wealth, a greater concentration of wealth in the hands of large property holders, a somewhat higher proportion of laborers, and greater occupational diversification—more artisans, shopkeepers, and professional men. Most of the wealth was owned by large farmers. In towns in the vicinity of Boston such as Braintree, Cohasset, and Hull, the wealthiest 10 percent owned more than half the property.[137]

Persons of wealth in the northern cities, whether greater or lesser urban centers, were both richer and more numerous than elsewhere in the North. Whereas commercial farming areas had a larger proportion of persons with property valued at between £1,000 and £2,000, "cities contained a far larger percentage of residents who had fortunes of £2,000 and almost all of those owning [as much as] £5,000." Their wealth was gained primarily in foreign trade, although many rich urbanites also had substantial investments in real estate. Tax lists indicate high concentrations of wealth, with 10 percent of the taxpayers in the early 1770s owning nearly half the property in Portsmouth, New Hampshire; 45 percent of the property in Kittery, Maine; 43.5 percent in Waltham, Massachusetts; 57 percent in Boston; 44 percent in Albany, New York; and over 66 percent in Philadelphia. Diversified occupationally to a far greater degree than elsewhere, the social structure of the cities also included "an exceptionally high proportion of men at the bottom of the economic scale." In general, the more populous towns had the largest number of poor.[138]

Studies of eighteenth-century urban society by Gary B. Nash also emphasize "the parallel emergence of the fabulously wealthy and the desperately poor." By the 1740s Boston was "not only the commercial and intellectual center of New England Puritanism . . . but also . . . the New England center of mass indebtedness, widowhood, and poverty. By the end of the Seven Years' War in 1763 poverty on a scale that urban leaders found appalling had also appeared in New York and Philadelphia."[139] Nevertheless, Main finds the "very large proportion of substantial middle-class property owners" to have been the "outstanding feature of northern society."[140] And although Nash believes that people "measure the quality of their lives within their own locales and make comparisons primarily with the world of their parents," he also acknowledges that "the material circumstances of life" for colonists who were both white and free "were far more favorable than they had previously known."[141]

Other recent studies not only support Main's emphasis on the importance of commercialization and its attendant occupational changes but point out that, except for the cities, the degree of inequality in the distribution of wealth increased gradually throughout the eighteenth century. When the first provincial tax was levied in 1693, the upper tenth of the population in Chester County, Pennsylvania, commanded less than a quarter of the community's taxable wealth. Between then and 1760 the degree of concentration gradually increased to 29.9 percent. The gap between the rich and the relatively poor, however, widened more perceptibly, for the share of the lowest 30 percent of the taxpayers declined in the same interval from 17.4 percent to 6.3 percent.[142] In an analysis of long-range trends in New England communities, another scholar finds a constant tendency for the amount of relative wealth owned by the top 30 percent of society to increase, and for that owned by both the middle 40 percent and the bottom 30 percent to decrease. After the first forty years of their development, however, subsistence farm areas showed precisely the same degree of concentration of wealth in the top 30 percent of the wealth-holders as did commercial areas. But surely such areas were less devoted to subsistence farming than forty years before. To some extent, one suspects, such discrepancies may reflect difficulties in sharply distinguishing the amount of commercialization to be found in the two categories. The question at issue is the proportion of resources devoted to the production of salable goods rather than total amounts of goods offered for sale by a given community, for the latter often varied with the size of the community rather than with its location on what was essentially a continuum of commercialization. About urban centers there can be no doubt, and here the surprising finding is that stability rather than change was the rule. Wealth was highly concentrated in the cities in 1700 and continued at the same level through 1776 without significant change in patterns of distribution.[143] A similarly high degree of concentration also characterized New York City at the beginning of the eighteenth century, when property assessments on tax lists show that the most well-to-do 10 percent of the population controlled 47 percent of the wealth, with the top 20 percent possessing 69 percent of it.[144] In sum, it is perfectly clear that very wide inequalities in the distribution of wealth existed long before the advent of industrialization. Beginning first in the urban centers, inequalities developed in the countryside as various parts of the hinterland became linked to urban and foreign markets. Throughout the colonies the wealthiest groups in 1774 were, first, those designated as esquires and gentlemen, together with officials, and then the following occupations in descending order: merchants; farmers with ancillary income and fishermen; professionals; farmers and small planters with no outside income; shopkeepers and innkeepers; artisans and chandlers.[145] By the eve of the Revolution wealth was highly concentrated not only in the larger cities but also in the plantation South, with the well-to-do forming a social and political elite that was unlikely to welcome an abridgment of the economic freedom that had enabled it to achieve such a striking degree of material success.

4

Independence

Separated from the mother country by three thousand miles of wind and water, essentially in charge of most of the local concerns that mattered to them, and subject to imperial regulations complied with for so long that they no longer seemed burdensome—or that were not restrictive, because unenforced—the colonists enjoyed a substantial measure of independence long before feeling compelled to declare it.[1] Under the old colonial system which governed the empire before 1763, British law lightly touched the economic life of the colonies at a number of points. Acts of trade and navigation, first enacted in the mid-seventeenth century, provided that no goods could be either imported into the colonies or exported therefrom except in English or colonial ships, of which three-fourths of the sailors should be English or colonial, and the master also. The purpose of the law was to exclude foreign vessels, especially those of the archrival Dutch, from trade with the plantations. Naturally this would increase the demand for English and colonial ships; the merchant marine would expand in size, freight rates would tend to fall, and auxiliary vessels as well as seamen would be available for the needs of war. Although foreigners were not permitted to trade with the colonies, English and colonial ships could trade freely with the foreign plantations provided they did not export to them certain specially enumerated colonial commodities. The latter were required to be shipped only to England, Ireland, Wales, or Berwick-upon-Tweed (on the Scottish frontier), or to other colonial plantations. Tobacco and indigo and other dyes were the first commodities to be enumerated, but over the years the list swelled to include goods such as beaver and other skins, naval stores, and rice—the last being permitted to go directly to any European port south of Cape Finisterre, an exception which allowed direct colonial trade to the Iberian Peninsula and the Mediterranean. The objectives sought by enumeration were to increase customs revenues; to supply the needs of the royal navy (naval stores), textile industry (dyes), and consuming public (tobacco); and also to generate income for merchants and shippers handling reexports to continental markets. Finally, the Staple Act (1663) required that all European goods destined for the colonies be shipped from England, Wales, or Berwick-upon-Tweed in English or colonial vessels rather than from the country of origin. Salt (largely obtained from southern Europe) and wines from the Portuguese islands were later excepted from the operation of the law.

Besides passing acts affecting shipping and trade—and currency—Parliament sought to discourage the growth of manufactures that might compete with those of the mother country. The Woolens Act (1699) forbade the export of woolen yarn or woolen manufactures from one colony to another, and the Hat Act (1732) placed a similar ban or beaver hats. The Iron Act (1750) sought to encourage the production of pig iron and bar iron in the colonies by allowing their duty-free importation into England. By 1775 American output constituted nearly one-seventh of world production. However, the erection in the colonies of mills for slitting and rolling iron, of plating forges, or of furnaces for making steel was forbidden. In sum, the colonies were envisaged as sources of supply for raw materials and profitable reexport commodities and as markets for the finished manufactures of the mother country—expectations that were hardly unreasonable in view of the fact that English money and manpower had been expended in the founding of the colonies, as well as English military and naval power in protecting them and their shipping.[2]

Very probably the colonists would have imported the great bulk of their goods from Great Britain even in the absence of law. As Silas Deane remarked in a letter of June 1781 to Robert Morris:

> Every one who has had an opportunity of comparing the manufactures of one nation in Europe with another, of observing the different modes and principles of transacting business, will at once give England and her merchants the preference. All the more solid, substantial and useful articles are made better, and afforded cheaper there, than anywhere else, certain linens from Russia and Silesia excepted—and even those as well as the less important foreign articles, came to us, considering the drawbacks in England on exportation, nearly, if not quite as cheap, as we could have imported them directly.[3]

England served as a great warehouse for commodities from all over the world, and a vessel could obtain at London a diversified cargo without going to the expense and trouble of picking it up at numerous ports of origin. As for American exports, Deane continued, "if any part of the globe be dependent on us for our produce it must be the West Indies . . . Formerly as British subjects we had the right of supplying the British islands with whatever they wanted . . . [and] a right of carrying to the French, Dutch, and other foreign posessions in the West-Indies, all our productions, tobacco excepted."[4] In sum, it is difficult to believe that British legislation before 1763 had much if anything to do with the coming of the Revolution. Although some smuggling took place, most importing and exporting was conducted within the framework of law because, for the most part, the latter coincided with the natural conditions of trade. Where it did not, the law was easily evaded.[5]

It was not so much evasions of law as growth in the size, wealth, and political competency of the colonies that gradually engendered a fear in English political circles that the colonies might eventually be lost.[6] At the same time the increasing value of colonial trade made clear how serious that loss would be. Imports into England from the continental colonies rose by 165 percent in real terms in the seven decades ending in 1770, and during the same period the value of English exports rose more than twice that fast.[7] Ever since the Restoration, Britain had made periodic attempts to tighten the reins of empire, and in the late 1740s, prompted by a series of severe political and social disturbances in a number of the colonies, it determined to do so again. The outbreak of the Seven Years' War in 1756 forced a suspension of these efforts, but on its conclusion Britain renewed them.[8] The timing was particularly unpropitious: so long as France remained a power in North America, the mutual need of colonies and mother country for protection and military aid had tempered colonial attitudes toward Britain and British policy regarding the colonies. Now that France was defeated and Canada ceded to Britain, an ameliorative element in their relationship was gone.

The ministry's first step in a reinvigorated colonial policy took the form of the Proclamation of 1763, a royal decree which forbade the establishment of new settlements and restricted the confirmation of new grants of land west of a line drawn along the crest of the Appalachians. The purpose of the decree was to minimize contacts between settlers and Indians that might lead to wars and disrupt the fur trade, now a lucrative British activity.[9] With the French out of the way, land companies and settlers had looked forward to additional acquisitions and profitable sales in the farther reaches of the West. Whereas these were to be denied only temporarily by the Proclamation, passage of the Quebec Act (1774) invalidated colonial claims to the area northwest of the Ohio by incorporating the region into the province of Quebec. Not only did this act represent an extension southward into territory claimed by Virginia, Connecticut, and Massachusetts, but it also placed on the borders of New York, Pennsylvania, and Virginia a government conducted entirely without the consent of its subjects and in effect established the Roman Catholic church in that region. Neither the Proclamation nor the Quebec Act was executed with complete rigidity, but both helped check colonization projects and speculation in land.[10]

The Sugar Act (1764) inaugurated the new postwar policy of enforcing the acts of trade. This law, which amended and extended the Molasses Act of 1733, had an objective essentially different from that of the earlier act. The intent of the Molasses Act had been to protect British rum-distilling interests in the West Indies. Indeed, agitation for its passage had begun in Barbados and Antigua, the former of which in particular depended more on sales of rum in North America than in the English market. Rum distilled in New England from cheaper molasses imported from the French islands cut into these sales, and the British purpose was to make the molasses more expensive by laying on it a duty of six pence per gallon. It was hoped the colonists would then import more rum from the British islands and make less themselves. The Molasses Act was systematically violated, however, and with the passage of the Sugar Act the British objective shifted from the discouragement of imports of foreign molasses to the raising of money by taxing them.[11]

The Sugar Act reduced the duty to three pence per gallon and established elaborate machinery for its collection, including locating at Halifax, Nova Scotia, a new vice-admiralty court where offenders would be tried without benefit of the juries used in common law courts—which in the past had seldom convicted them. Americans were quick to see the threat posed by this invasion by Parliament of an area long controlled by local government. In Massachusetts the assembly protested "that we look upon those Duties as a tax, and which we humbly apprehend ought not to be laid without the Representatives of the People affected by them."[12] Two years later Parliament repealed the Sugar Act and placed a tax of one penny a gallon on all imported molasses, British as well as foreign. The degree to which the colonial merchants complied with the new law is indicated by tax collections exceeding those of any year since the passage of the Molasses Act.[13] Nevertheless, smuggling went on as before. In a continuing effort to increase colonial revenue yields, the British enacted the Stamp Act (1765), the Townshend Acts (1767), and other familiar legislation. One important law, however, had a different purpose. In the Currency Act of 1764, Parliament extended to all the colonies the prohibition against further issues of legal tender paper money which the act of 1751 had applied to New England alone.

Postwar British legislation thus affected not only the interests of merchants and traders but also those of settlers and land speculators. It is difficult not to believe that the cumulative grievances provoked by these laws led the colonists down the path to revolution. This is not to say that affronts to economic interests are alone sufficient to explain the movement toward independence. For one thing, it is clear in some cases, as in the protests against British policies in Philadelphia, that the merchants, at best, were unwilling partners of a group of popular or radical leaders.[14] In other cases, economic interest was not present at all. Throughout colonial history nonconformists had suspected the existence of an ecclesiastical conspiracy to stamp out religious liberty in America, and, in more recent times, this suspicion had been fanned into a fear that Britain intended to establish an American episcopate. Perhaps above all, though specific acts aroused the resentment of some Americans, it was necessary that colonial leaders discern the pattern inherent in multiple instances of British intervention and to extract from it an overall meaning of sufficient power to engage the minds and hearts of their countrymen.

Fortunately, they had at hand an ideology ready-made to the purpose. They interpreted events after 1763 in terms of a tradition of antiauthoritarianism reaching back to the English Civil War and then transmitted to them most directly by opposition politicians and radical publicists in England in the early eighteenth century.[15] It was this tradition that gave meaning to those events, that convinced the colonists that a deliberate and surreptitious assault was being launched against liberty both in England and in America, and that in the end the English constitution and all the rights and privileges embedded in it would be destroyed.[16] Few if any more precise statements of the relationship between the newly enforced commercial regulations and these more deepseated fears exist than one contained in Silas Deane's letter of June 1781 to Robert Morris: "The Parliamentary regulations and restrictions on our commerce were a principal cause of the unhappy contest between the two countries, and we were impatient under them because we were apprehensive, that they were part of a system to enslave us entirely." It was fear of this larger "system" that roused the colonists.[17]

Did anything else rouse them? Were the colonists predisposed to revolution by the existence of social and economic tensions within America itself? At one time there was widespread agreement that the answers to these questions were affirmative. Between 1900 and 1930 several historians depicted the Revolution as a struggle by the underprivileged against the political dominance and special privileges of the old colonial aristocracy. Some went so far as to hold that the Revolution was not merely a contest for home rule but also one over who should rule at home.[18] Few if any historians now share these views, for in the decades since the end of World War II, they have been discredited by detailed studies of virtually every colony. Recently, however, more subtle efforts to identify social tensions have been made. One historian in particular has suggested that the "frenzied rhetoric" and inflammatory words—such as "slavery," "conspiracy," and "corruption"—used by colonial pamphleteers seeking to explain and justify their cause could have sprung "only from the most severe sorts of social strain." While it would be mistaken to view internal tensions in terms of "coherent class conflict or overt social disruption," he suggests that the Americans were "deeply alienated from the existing sources of authority and vehemently involved in a basic reconstruction of their political and social order."[19]

Studies of older communities in eastern New England lend a degree of plausibility to some of these possibilities. Most of them tell essentially the same story of too many sons and too little land, of the pressure of growing population against limited resources. The typical early inhabitant of an eastern Massachusetts town had an estimated 150 acres at his disposal. By the end of the Revolution this area had shrunk by more than two-thirds: in 1786 the average holding per adult male in the whole of Suffolk County amounted to no more than 43 acres.[20] Greater cultivation of marginal lands, a tripling of land prices over the century 1660–1760, and probably rising food prices as well, all point to overcrowding, a phenomenon also discovered in the frontier town of Kent, Connecticut. By the third generation after 1780 lands which may have seemed inexhaustible to the first generation of settlers in 1740, and ample to the second generation in the 1750s and 1760s, appeared quite limited.[21] The shrinkage in average landholdings must certainly have reduced economic opportunity. It is even possible that alterations in the structure of society accompanied these developments. With the rich becoming richer and more numerous, and the poor becoming poorer and more numerous, society itself may have gradually become polarized between an agricultural proletariat and a rural gentry. These patterns, in turn, may have significantly affected the thinking of many of America's Revolutionary leaders. Although American society was not as stratified, oppressive, or corrupt as English society, a number of American politicians and clergymen were making plain their dissatisfaction with it.[22]

The thrust of these hypotheses is toward a society constrained, bulging against the narrowing agricultural framework containing it, and increasingly resembling the societies of the Old World—indeed, one which was saved from an even closer likeness by the great migration of Americans to the West after 1790.[23] Additional evidence implicit in the denial of the rights to issue legal tender paper money (Currency Act, 1764), and to purchase land or settle in the area west of the crest of the Alleghenies (Proclamation of 1763), as well as in the tightening of the conditions under which commerce was conducted, strengthens still more the hypothesis of constraint. Indeed, as we shall see, given continuing expansionist pressures against the values of the imperial system, it may be that the Revolution would have occurred a generation or so later if it had not broken out when it did. In that case, although Americans might have continued to speak in terms of the constitutional rights of Englishmen, their talk of slavery would have referred more pointedly to economic constraint than it did in 1776. In 1776, however, northern farmers, at least, were fairly prosperous and had been so for a dozen years.[24] Nor by any means was all westward migration delayed till the post-Revolutionary period. Indeed, an opposing hypothesis concerning the social origins of the Revolutionary impulse is also implicit in recent historical work.

In his already classic study of four generations of settlers in Andover, Massachusetts, Philip Greven shows how fathers used control of the land to maintain positions of authority in their families. By withholding title to land till late in their own lives, they delayed the maturity of their sons, who had to wait surprisingly long not only to marry but also to gain full economic independence. This pattern began to weaken in the third generation that grew to maturity between 1705 and 1735. In contrast to the earlier period, some fathers helped their sons gain autonomy relatively early by giving them deeds to land, by helping them emigrate to other places, or by settling them in trades for their livelihood. By the middle decades of the eighteenth century, the maturing fourth-generation sons were marrying significantly earlier than in previous generations and were able earlier and far more easily to establish independence from their fathers. For these sons, Greven suggests, "Thomas Paine's call for independence in 1776 from the mother-country and from the father-king might have been just what Paine claimed it to be—common sense. In their own lives, this generation had come to take for granted that young men ought also to be independent men." Thus political independence in 1776 may have been rooted in the changing character of many American families.[25]

There is no need to regard rival hypotheses as mutually exclusive. In any society, especially one marked by increasing differentiation, a diversity of interests and attitudes must be taken into account. Additional studies of older communities, especially outside New England, and more especially outside Massachusetts, will make it possible to fix the probable limits within which either pent-up or released forces were operative.[26] Above all, however, a stronger and more specific case than now exists needs to be made for the hypothesized relationship between changing social and family structures, on the one hand, and values and attitudes, on the other.[27] For the time being it seems reasonable to suggest that whatever the contribution of internal social change to the formation of revolutionary attitudes, in the absence of an intellectually coherent set of beliefs about the constitutional and political rights of Englishmen, there would have been no Revolution.[28]

The changes in property ownership and social structure which took place during the Revolutionary upheaval are another subject. To be sure, recent studies have severely challenged the belief of an older generation of scholars that "colonial aristocrats" were Loyalists whom the Revolution erased from American society. Although it is perhaps true that a "majority of the old aristocracy" emigrated from eastern Massachusetts, most respected families in the central and western parts of the state chose the Whig side and remained dominant in local affairs after independence.[29] Few outstanding persons can be identified in the Tory emigration from New Hampshire, a state in which, except for the region around Portsmouth, society was not highly stratified. The elite in Connecticut tended to be loyal to the Crown, but at least half the Tories never left that state. Perhaps the majority of the prominent merchants of New York and Philadelphia were Loyalist, or at least neutralist, but many stayed on in those centers of trade. In Maryland one group of planters, lawyers, and merchants struggled against another group of the same composition, with the plain people taking little part in the conflict. In the backcountry of North Carolina, though, the plain people were most stubbornly Loyalist. Probably Virginians came closest to unanimity in the patriot cause. At any rate, Loyalist claims for British compensation after the Revolution numbered only thirteen persons born in Virginia.[30]

Similarly, no wholesale redistribution of landed property appears to have taken place either during the Revolution or as a result of it. A far lesser degree of democratization of landownership than earlier scholars supposed followed upon the breakup of large landed estates and their sale in smaller parcels.[31] Although some of the land in the southern counties of New York seized by the Revolutionary government of that state went to former tenants and other landless persons, the bulk of it was bought by wealthy patriots. The same seems to have been true in Maryland, western Massachusetts, New Hampshire, and the Carolinas. Even in Pennsylvania, where the largest estate of all—the 21.5 million acres of the Penn family—was confiscated, the legislature "confirmed, ratified, and established for ever" the private manors of the Penns, amounting to more than 500,000 acres. Furthermore, the abolition of primogeniture and entail, to which Jefferson himself attached great significance, appears to have represented more a sweeping up of dead letters than a substantive legal reform. Neither operated to any important degree in Virginia, where most estates were not entailed and could be freely alienated. Primogeniture was mandatory only if a property owner died intestate, but most Virginia planters made wills. Furthermore, the conclusion that no radical change of custom in devising estates took place in Virginia as a result of abolishing primogeniture and entail may well apply to other colonies.[32] Certainly in New England the estate of an intestate parent was distributed equally to all the children from the beginning of settlement, and subsequent legislation merely confirmed this custom of partible descent, saving a double share for the eldest son. Pennsylvania adopted similar legislation in 1693.

Nevertheless, the Revolution appears to have exerted some effect. Not only was primogeniture outlawed in Georgia (1777), North Carolina (1784), Virginia (1785), Maryland and New York (1786), South Carolina (1791), and Rhode Island (1798), but in this same period New England and Pennsylvania dispensed with the Mosaic double portion for the eldest son, providing by statute for an equal division among all the children.[33] Whether or not large investments made by absentee landowners for the sake of income from leases and rentals, especially during the generation after 1725, deserve recognition as a form of "mercenary feudalism" to which the Revolution was required to put an end is a question worthy of additional thought and research.[34]

In contrast, changes in the ownership of more liquid assets appear to have been significant. No less an authority than Alexander Hamilton claimed that the Revolution had "destroyed a large proportion of the monied and mercantile capital of the country, and of personal property generally."[35] Loss and destruction may have been especially severe in the port cities of New York and Philadelphia. "You can have no idea," a New York correspondent wrote John Jay, "of the sufferings of many who from affluence are reduced to the most abject poverty." In Philadelphia, Pelatiah Webster testified to "the most pernicious shift to property," to "the many thousands of fortunes which are ruined."

But liquid wealth was not only destroyed in the war. It was also created by new opportunities in trade, privateering, and land speculation. Those who came into possession of it emerged as a nouveau riche class which rose to challenge the long social dominance of an older entrenched elite—with broad consequences that we shall later probe. As early as 1777 it seemed to Robert Treat Paine of Boston that the "course of the war has thrown property into channels, where before it never was, and has increased little streams to over-flowing rivers." From the same city James Bowdoin wrote in 1783: "When you come you will scarcely see any other than new faces . . . the change which in that respect has happened within the few years since the revolution is as remarkable as the revolution itself." "I sometimes almost lament that the Aristocracy in 1783 was suppressed," Stephen Higginson wrote four years later.

And so it went in city after city. In Charleston, David Ramsay asserted that new, bold traders had replaced the old and "rapidly advanced their own interests." "The men that had no money hardly, is now got the money," Dr. Joseph Orne said of society in Salem, Massachusetts, adding that they were called "the new Fangled Gentlemen." "Those who five years ago were the 'meaner people,' " declared an embittered Loyalist, Samuel Curwen, "are now, by a strange revolution, become almost the only men of power, riches and influence."[36]

Some twenty years ago the historian David Hackett Fischer observed that late-eighteenth-and early-nineteenth-century Americans "who analyzed the structure of their society sometimes divided it into two groups—the better sort and the meaner sort, the respectable and the ambitious." The distinction, he continued, was "not simply between wealth and poverty, but between attainment and aspiration, between those who had and those who hungered. The most hungry, the most ambitious, the most 'mean' from an elitist perspective were men who had much and wanted more—men who wished to add respectability to riches, or riches to popular influence." We shall see how representatives of the older elite, described by Fischer as "mature, static, homogeneous and ingrown,"—families who were inhabitants of dozens of counties in every state from Massachusetts to South Carolina—reacted to the challenge mounted by the nouveau riche to their economic, social, and political leadership by erecting in the American legal system protective bulwarks designed to secure vested property rights and maintain the status quo.[37]

Threats to property rights after the Revolution took the form both of social upheaval and of state laws enacted in an effort to cope with grievous economic problems. Not only urban communities but also farm families buying and selling on markets were affected by these problems. Although the important trade with England continued after the war on terms highly favorable to the United States—with tobacco, lumber, potash, pearlash, tar, pitch, pig iron, and bar iron, for example, being admitted either duty free or at tariff rates giving Americans a clear advantage over other countries in the competition for the British market—the important islands of the British West Indies were shut to American vessels. New Englanders dependent on these island markets for sale of their lumber, livestock, and other provisions were especially hard hit by the exclusion. One South Carolinian visitor to the region in the mid-1780s reported that Boston was "going fast to decay" and that the "ruin'd wharves of New-Port imply a melancholy truth," namely, that the "Northern and Eastern states are ruined [by the war] they were so anxious to bring about."[38] American ships had once dominated the trade with the islands, and while official figures do not fairly measure the effect of their postwar exclusion (because of smuggling), they reveal a decline in American exports by nearly one-half between 1771–1773 and 1793.[39]

Englishmen were by no means unanimously agreed on this policy. Indeed, the prime minister himself, William Pitt, had offered a bill in Parliament calling for the continued admission of American vessels. Unhappily, his bill encountered opposition stirred by the publication in 1783 of Lord Sheffield's influential "Observations on the Commerce of the American States." In this pamphlet Sheffield argued that England's "great national object is to raise as many sailors and as much shipping as possible." Parliament should endeavor to divert the whole Anglo-American trade to British ships.[40]

Sheffield also pointed out that the new American states lacked leverage in commercial bargaining with other countries. Their first constitution, the Articles of Confederation, adopted in 1781, had explicitly declared each state to be sovereign, free, and independent (article 2), and had withheld from the central government the power to pass laws regulating commerce. With individual states seeking commercial advantage over other states by lowering their tariff and tonnage duties, and with the Continental Congress powerless to stipulate uniform rates throughout the union, the fledgling republic could offer neither inducement nor threat to the nations of Europe whose trade it sought on favorable terms.[41]

The precocious Alexander Hamilton saw the situation clearly. "Suppose, for instance," he wrote in 1787, "we had a government in America, capable of excluding Great-Britain (with whom we have at present no treaty of commerce) from all our ports, what would be the probable operation of this step upon her politics? Would it not enable us to negotiate with the fairest prospect of success for commercial privileges of the most valuable and extensive kind in the dominions of that kingdom?"[42] But Lord Sheffield was no less clear-eyed. America had no such government. "No treaty can be made with the American States that can be binding on the whole of them." "It will not be an easy matter," he concluded, "to bring the American States to act as a nation; they are not to be feared as such by us." Pitt's bill was lost.[43]

The impact of British policy was by no means confined to the direct trade between America and the islands. One way in which merchants had been accustomed for many years to pay for their imports of goods from England was to order their ship captains to proceed from the islands to England with West Indian products and bills of exchange received from the sales of their outgoing cargoes. Such indirect remittances lessened the need to pay for an excess of imports over exports by shipping gold or silver to the mother country. After the war the burden on specie exports became very heavy, especially because American merchants had responded to a long pent-up wartime demand by ordering huge quantities of English goods. The loss of both specie and West Indian markets combined to exert strong downward pressure on prices, making the decade after 1782 a period of severe deflation.

Prices of American exports fell in relation to those of imported goods, the terms of trade declining each year between 1784 and 1789 from an index of 112 in the former year to 88 in the latter (see Table 2).[44] The resultant burden of debt was especially onerous in Massachusetts, where taxes which Hamilton said were the highest in the nation,[45] together with the execution of court orders for the sale of the property of delinquent taxpayers, created grave social tensions. Debtors importuned legislators to issue paper money to ease their tax payments and other obligations. Creditors, on the other hand, objected to being paid in paper that was worth less than specie.

To some extent the scenario was enacted in other states as well. When the paper-money forces won out in seven states—with four of the seven declaring the bills legal tender in private payments—alarmed creditors and other prop-

Table 2. Import-export prices and the terms of trade, 1770–1792.

Year	Index of import prices (1)	Index of export prices (2)	Terms of trade (2)/(1)
1770	110	69	63
1771	104	75	72
1772	102	83	81
1773	109	78	72
1774	108	73	68
1775	109	70	64
1784	103	115	112
1785	101	106	105
1786	101	97	96
1787	101	92	91
1788	99	87	88
1789	99	87	88
1790	100	100	100
1791	103	92	89
1792	110	86	78

Source: Gordon C. Bjork, "The Weaning of the American Economy: Independence, Market Changes, and Economic Development," *Journal of Economic History,* 24 (1964), 554. Used with the permission of Cambridge University Press.

Note: The year 1790 is taken as the base (100) in computing the indexes.

erty owners sought to defend their interests. In Rhode Island, for example, merchants refused to accept paper, some of them closed their stores, and would-be buyers resorted to force and rioting, with farmers pledging to withhold produce from townsmen refusing to accept paper at par with specie. In 1786 armed attacks on creditors and tax collectors took place in Maryland, and a large band of armed men imprisoned the legislature in New Hampshire. That same year unrest in Massachusetts culminated in Shays's Rebellion, the well-known affair in which a Revolutionary War captain led a group of farmers into revolt against the government of the state.[46]

In these circumstances, aggravated the more by state laws postponing the collection of debts or providing for their payment in installments or in commodities rather than in money, it is not surprising to find a growing concern over the insecurity of property rights. That concern began to dominate the criminal law of Massachusetts in the 1780s, especially after the end of the war, when the number of cases of prosecution for theft and similar offenses more than tripled those of the war years. In Middlesex County alone there were four prosecutions for rioting and five for attacks on tax collectors between 1780 and 1785, and in the western counties attempts were made to prevent the courts from sitting and to rescue prisoners. A recent study of the legal history of Massachusetts concludes that postwar violence "undoubtedly heightened the fear of social breakdown and disorder" in the state.[47]

Contemporaries saw clearly the connection between the commercial, political, and social situations and between these and the security of property. "Another unhappy effect of a continuance of the present anarchy of commerce," James Madison wrote in March 1786, "will be a continuance of the unfavorable balance on it, which, by draining us of our metals, furnishes pretexts for the pernicious substitution of paper money, for indulgences to debtors, for postponement of taxes. In fact, most of our political evils may be traced to our commercial ones."[48] Madison vigorously defended a constitutional revision which would transfer the power of coining money from the states to the federal government and forbid the states from emitting bills of credit (paper money). "A rage for paper money, or for any other improper or wicked object," he writes in *Federalist No. 10,* "will be less apt to pervade the whole body of the Union that a particular member of it."[49] The "Monied Interest will oppose the plan of Government," Gouveneur Morris said, "if paper emissions be not prohibited."[50] Not surprisingly, they were—the states in addition being forbidden to coin money, to make anything but gold and silver a tender in payment of debt, or to pass any law impairing the obligation of contract (article 1, section 10).

Years later Chief Justice John Marshall of the United States Supreme Court testified to the influence of the unsettled conditions of the 1780s on the inclusion of the contract clause. It was "the prevailing evil of the times," he wrote in *Ogden v Saunders* (1827), "which produced this clause in the constitution." Marshall defined the evil in terms of "the practice of emitting paper money, of making property which was useless to the creditor a discharge of his debt and changing the time of payment by authorizing distant installments." "The power of changing the relative situation of debtor and creditor, of interfering with contracts," he added, "[was used] to such an excess by the state legislatures as to break in upon the ordinary intercourse of society, and destroy all confidence between man and man."[51] Had he then been alive, Hamilton would have agreed, for in the era of the Constitutional Convention and later as well, he expressed the conviction that the "relaxed conduct of the State Governments [had] undermined the foundations of Property and credit."[52]

The concern of the founding fathers with the insecurity of property rights is easily explained. It is not that they were crass materialists, but rather that they were Lockeans. No philosopher exerted upon their values a stronger influence than John Locke, and to Locke the security of one's material wealth was intimately linked with one's freedom. Indeed, he defined "property" broadly to embrace one's life, liberty, and estate. The framers appear to have conceived property more narrowly, synonymously with estate, but the association with liberty was inseparable. "Property must be secured," John Adams wrote, "or liberty . . . [cannot] exist." Hamilton saw it the same way: "Adieu to the security of property[,] adieu to the security of liberty."[53]

Because the framers were endeavoring to erect and defend a structure of fundamental law, it is the more understandable that they should have emphasized fundamental relationships rooted in the law of nature and described for them so clearly by Locke. One of the most basic was the relationship between property and liberty, and since legislative majorities in the states had threatened that relationship, the framers decided that an increase in federal power was essential to its preservation. As a close student of our constitutional development once observed, "the problem of providing adequate safeguards for private rights and adequate powers for a national government were one and the same problem."[54] The Constitution met the problem head-on by granting the federal level of government sufficient power to restrain the activities of the states in the crucial area of property rights.

The security of property clearly depended on the preservation of a viable balance of power between the central government and the states. It no less clearly depended on the ability of government at the federal level to maintain its very existence. Constitutionally enfeebled from the beginning, central government under the Articles had died in childbirth. The same might happen under the Constitution if financial nutrients were denied it. The power to tax was essential, but something else was needed too, and this was the power to borrow. Both would come into play to meet the threat of war or other national emergency. But the ability to borrow depended on the nation's trustworthiness, on its good credit both at home and in the world's financial capitals.

Recognizing these things, and realizing also that national honor was involved, the framers stipulated explicitly that "all debts contracted and Engagements entered into, before the adoption of this Constitution, shall be valid against the United States under this Constitution as under the Confederation" (article 6), and they empowered the Congress "to lay and collect Taxes, Duties, Imposts and Excises, to pay the Debts . . . of the United States" (article 1, section 8).

The debts, contracted during the Revolution, were owed both abroad and at home.[55] France had supplied the only foreign loans until early 1782, when John Adams prevailed on a number of Dutch mercantile banking houses to underwrite a loan of about $2 million. As of August 1782 the debt to France was said by the comptroller of the Treasury to be "above five millions." Originally, the domestic part of the debt consisted only of loan-office certificates, the "war bonds of the Revolution," but bit by bit Congress assumed the responsibility for other obligations that added to its amount. In February 1782 Congress enacted a law providing for a systematic inspection of civilians claims, most of which had originated in supplies furnished the Quartermaster and Commissary departments, and in 1783 it added the claims of the Continental army. Finally, for a decade beginning in 1782 Congress settled the accounts of officials who had handled public money or property during the war. This consolidation of the domestic debt brought its total to more than $27 million, the sum being represented by securities originally sold to individuals or subsequently issued in settlement of their claims. By far the two largest components were war bonds and army claims, each of which amounted to approximately $11 million.

Up to 1783 only subscribers to war bonds received interest on their securities, but after the consolidation of the floating debt, Congress, in the words of the leading authority on the subject, E. James Ferguson, "considered itself bound to pay interest" on the entire debt. Yet just as the holders of war bonds had sometimes been obliged to receive not interest but written acknowledgments of their right to it (indents), so holders of claims for other services rendered had also to look to the future. The familiar difficulty was Congress' lack of authority under the articles to levy taxes. Its system of requisitioning sums upon the states, which the latter then tried with varying degrees of assiduity and success to levy on their respective citizens, proved a "failure . . . during the war" and was "still unproductive" afterward? "The financial plight of the country that confronted the Constitutional Convention," says Curtis Nettels, "is illustrated by the fact that in 1786 the total income of the central government was less than one-third of the annual charges on the national debt." During the whole of that year only two or three states made any contribution at all, yet the small sum collected— less than $200,000—was expected to support the civil establishment of the union and pay the necessary expense of maintaining guards and garrisons at public arsenals and on the frontier—to say nothing of the public debt, for the discharge of which there was no "surplus for paying any part . . . [whether] foreign or domestic, principal or interest." In the words of two financial historians, Paul Studenski and Herman E. Krooss, "The United States was bankrupt and no state seemed to care." The price of government bonds appears to have fallen as low as fifteen cents on the dollar.[56]

Named secretary of the Treasury by President Washington and called upon by the Congress to report to it on the state of the public credit, Hamilton made the elevation and maintenance of that credit the most important item on his agenda, one which far exceeded that of promoting the development of the manufacturing industry. Yet elevation of the public credit was only a means to other ends. Those ends were the security of property rights and the maintenance of the union. As Hamilton himself expressed it, his fiscal program had the support of men who were "not personally interested in the debt" but who nevertheless "considered the maxims of public credit as of the essence of good government, as intimately connected . . . with the security of property in general, and as forming an inseparable portion of the great system of political order."[57] In less elegant language, the strengthening and maintenance of the new constitutional union and the security of property were "intimately connected," and both depended on provisions for the payment of the public debt.

It was for these reasons that Hamilton urged Congress not only to fund the debt—to consolidate all its separate parts into a single sum and to earmark specific items of revenue for the payment of interest—but also to assume as a federal obligation the debts contracted by the states during the war. Why the latter? To be sure, the possibility of assumption had been mentioned in the Constitutional Convention and discussed in newspaper articles and correspondence, probably most persuasively by Oliver Wolcott, a future secretary of the Treasury, who in a significant letter to Hamilton outlined a plan for settling the accounts of the states and assuming their debts that was "similar in almost every respect to the plan suggested" by Hamilton in his Report.[58] The question does not concern Hamilton's originality, however, but rather his purposes, and it is a question that is especially important in view of Ferguson's opinion that the debts of the states (and the public debt too for that matter) might easily have been extinguished by continuing a practice which some states had begun to adopt as early as 1780, namely, that of accepting the securities in payment of taxes. It would have been a "cheap" method: had the states accepted them at their low market value in 1786, the principal, which was about $28 million, could have been retired for perhaps $5 million. Instead, assumption increased by about 50 percent the size of the domestic debt, which, with interest included, amounted to roughly $63 million at the beginning of 1790.[59]

Now Hamilton himself was aware that "certain States by vigorous efforts had considerably reduced particular [that is, state] debts while others had made little impression on them," but he countered the implication of unfairness by arguing that the former had enjoyed "adventitious advantages." New York, for example, had been able to absorb a "considerable proportion of her debt" because of that state's possession of a large acreage of disposable land and a great deal of confiscated property—and also because it had been able to keep the value of the debt low by avoiding the payment of interest on it. Connecticut, in contrast, had lacked these advantages, "though her citizens were burthened with a much more considerable effort in contributions." Was it therefore inequitable that Connecticut should find relief through assumption? Hamilton asked. His reply: "Surely it was not." In his view the "most simple and satisfactory notion of Justice was to secure that individuals of the same Nation who had contended in the same cause for the same object their common liberty should at the end of the contest find themselves on an equal footing as to burthens arising from the contest." "Nothing could be more revolting," he added, "than that the citizens of one state should live at ease from Taxes and the citizens of a neighbouring State be overburthened with taxes growing out of a war which had given equal political advantages to the Citizens of both states."

Justice among individuals, Hamilton went on, was "better promoted in another sense." The new Constitution had given the federal government an exclusive right to the duties on imposts, a branch of the revenue "which for a considerable time to come in this country is likely to be most productive." Had the national government obligated itself to pay only the national debt, those with claims against the several states would have been not only "in a very unequal but in a very bad situation . . . Men who had contributed their services and property to the support of the common cause at the instance of a State Government would have fared worse than those who [had] done the same thing at the instance of the General Government."

To Hamilton there appeared to be only one way of "untyeing or severing" what he called the "Gordian Knot of our political situation," and that was "to leave the states under as little necessity as possible of exercising the power of taxation." The field of taxation would be less encumbered by the states, and this would enable the federal government to enjoy a "more full & complete command of the resources of the Nation." Hamilton's choice of language here is revealing. The Gordian knot had to do with the *political* situation, which suggests that he desired to minimize conflict over available sources of revenue because he wished above all to minimize political challenge to the Constitutional settlement. Deprived by the Constitution itself of access to the impost, the states would have had to saddle burdensome excises on various forms of property.[60] Converting state debts into federal obligations and paying them out of federal revenues mainly touching taxpayers only indirectly and in the form of higher prices on imported goods lessened the likelihood of opposition from divisive forces of state particularism. Hamilton was fully aware that *"plenary* power" to tax "must ever be considered as the vital principle of government,"[61] and he wished to afford to the states the smallest possible need for concern with vital principle. In matters of taxation as well as of debt, his fiscal goals were subordinate to constitutional ones.[62]

And as always, the latter were intertwined with the objective of securing the rights of private property. The "public obligations in the hands of the public Creditors . . . were as much their property as their houses or their lands, their hats or their coats." The "assumption by uniting the interests of public Creditors of all descriptions was calculated to . . . fortify the public opinion in opposition to the efforts of faction and of the *antiproprietary* spirit." The "cause of credit and property is one and the same throughout the states. A blow to it in whatever state or in whatever form is a blow to it in every state and in every form." Providing for the public debt not only "manifest[ed] a due respect for property" but "preserve[d] the Government itself."[63]

Hamilton had still another reason for favoring assumption: the measure made it necessary for state creditors to look to the federal government rather than to the states for payment of their claims. "If all the public creditors receive their dues from one source, distributed with an equal hand, their interest will be the same. And having the same interests, they will unite in the support of the fiscal arrangements of the government . . . [U]nion and concert of view among the creditors . . . in every government is of great importance to their security, and to that of the public credit." Hamilton later discounted this consideration, saying in July 1795 that on the whole it was the one on which he least relied, but he did not deny that at the time of the assumption itself its tendency "to strengthen our infant Government by increasing the number of ligaments between the Government and the interests of Individuals" had "naturally occurred" to him. Hamilton himself believed a "large proportion" of the public creditors to have been "very influential," men who had had "a considerable agency in promoting the adoption of the new Constitution for this peculiar reason . . . among the many weighty reasons which were common to them as citizens and proprietors," namely, that "it exhibited the prospect of a Government able to do justice to their claims." Had it failed their expectations, their "disappointment and disgust quickened by the sensibility of private interest could [not] but have been extreme." Provision for the public debt in its entirety therefore had obviated a "possible subversion" of the government "and with it that of the Union" while at the same time parrying "a severe blow to the general security of property."[64]

Hamilton also believed that funding the debt would add to the infant republic's resources of "monied capital" and by relieving the scarcity of that "active wealth" promote the country's economic development. He conceived public securities as exercising a kind of multiplier effect. Creditors would purchase them, and government would disburse the purchase money in the

course of paying its bills. In the meantime, the bonds themselves would provide a separate source of "capital" because of the ease with which they could
be converted into money.[65]

The process he describes is akin to that of monetization of debt by the
banking system, but it cannot be proved that Hamilton had this process in
mind. He was explicitly aware, however, of the possibility of foreign capital
transfers through investment in public securities. Provided only that their
credit rating was high, foreigners would be likely to purchase government
securities and emigrate with their capital to the United States. Whether or not
they did, the value of their investments, when used as capital in developing
enterprises, would far exceed their cost in interest.[66]

Getting the credit rating up and keeping it there—that was what mattered.
Hence Hamilton opposed "discrimination": regardless of who proffered securities to government for redemption or of the circumstances in which they
had been acquired—and by no means could it be maintained that most present
holders had bought them for a speculative song from the fleeced and the
needy—both the honor and credit of the government and the security of
transfer were involved. Who in the future would buy a bond from another if
the government might not pay him or her the face value of its promise at
maturity? For similar reasons Hamilton wanted the public debt paid at par
and in specie. The price of a country's bonds was "the thermometre of its
credit."[67] Furthermore he wanted the debt funded at as low a rate of interest
as possible. Not only would a low rate reduce the burden on the government;
it would also, he probably believed, tend to reduce the market rate and hence
cheapen the cost of capital.[68]

For the domestic debt Hamilton chose an average rate of 4 percent, and
although this decision had an initially adverse effect on prices of government
securities, by July 1791 they had risen above par.[69] The president was jubilant.
"Our public credit," he wrote that month, "stands on that ground which three
years ago it would have been considered as a species of madness to have
foretold."[70] And having risen at home, it also rose abroad. From London later
that year a correspondent informed Hamilton that "the American Funds had
inspired no Confidence in this market 'till they had acquired a high price at
home & three months ago a sale of them must have been affected here with
the greatest difficulty. The Case is now so materially alter'd that one friend of
mine has bought & sold near a Million of dollars."[71] In May 1795 foreigners
held $20,288,637.71 of the funded domestic debt of the United States, and
by September 1801 the total had reached $33,041,135.59. This was exclusive
of the foreign debt, most of which Hamilton had refunded by floating new
loans in Amsterdam and Antwerp.[72]

The achievement was due not only to the government's decision to fund
the debt and pledge the revenues required for interest payments but also to
its efforts since August 1790 to retire part of the principal. Early that month

Hamilton had urged Congress to authorize "purchases of the public debt in the Market," pointing out that "very considerable savings to the nation will result from raising the price of Stock by this operation inasmuch as foreigners must pay a higher price for what they buy."[73] Subsequently named commissioners of the sinking fund proceeded to authorize the secretary of the Treasury to direct purchases of the public debt "at the market price, & in an open and public manner," at the rate of $50,000 a month, first in New York and then in Philadelphia. Later, additional sums were authorized.[74]

The sinking fund was to serve an unanticipated good purpose. During an early but typical stock market panic in New York ignited by the failure of the country's leading speculator, William Duer, Hamilton, with the support of the commissioners, used the fund for open market operations designed to maintain the price of government securities.[75] In his instructions to William Seton, cashier of the Bank of New York and purchasing agent for the government in that city, he sought to maximize the psychological effects of his intervention: "If six per Cents should sink below par, you may purchase on account of the United States at par to the extent of Fifty thousand Dollars." However, Seton was not to declare on whose account he was acting. Although it would probably be conjectured that he was appearing in the public interest, "the conjecture may be left to have its course without confession." He was to purchase either at auction or by another mode, and all at once or bit by bit, whichever would "best answer the purpose."

Furthermore, Seton was to announce the news, for the validity of which Hamilton pledged his honor, that the American minister in Amsterdam had "effected a loan for Three Millions of Florins at 4 P Cent Interest on account of the United States." Hamilton asked: "Why then so much despondency among the holders of our Stock? When Foreigners lend the United States at 4 P Cent will they not purchase here upon a similar scale making reasonable allowance for expence of Agency &c? Why then do Individuals part with so good a property so much below its value? Does Duers failure affect the solidity of the Government?"[76] Hamilton detested "undue" or "excessive" speculation and feared its effects on his efforts to raise the nation's credit and keep it on an even keel. Wild gyrations in the price of public stocks might well be regarded by European investors as evidence of the political instability of the new nation. "How vexatious that imprudent speculations of Individuals should lead to an alienation of the National property at such under rates as are now given!" he wrote Seton in April 1792.[77]

He detested most particularly increasing the means of speculation by an undue expansion in the number of banks. News in January 1792 that a new bank had "started up" in New York City caused Hamilton "infinite pain."

Its effects cannot but be in every view pernicious. These extravagant sallies of speculation do injury to the Government and to the whole system of public

Credit, by disgusting all sober Citizens and giving a wild air to every thing. It is impossible but that three banks in one City must raise such a mass of artificial Credit, as much endanger every one of them & do harm in every view.[78]

Imprudent, risky bank loans were not much better. "While I encourage due exertion in the Banks . . . ," he told Seton in March 1792, "I hope they will put nothing to risk . . . No calamity truly public can happen while these Institutions remain sound; they must therefore not yield too far to the impulse of circumstances."[79]

In all probability the needs of the Treasury effectively prevented the Bank of the United States, which Congress had chartered in 1791 for twenty years, not only from yielding too far to the impulse of circumstances but also from responding adequately to the business community's demand for loans. It is true that in his "Report on a National Bank" (1790) Hamilton had said forthrightly that "public utility is more truly the object of public banks than private profit." But he had also made an impassioned plea for private management, and done so explicitly to warn against the injury to the institution's credit which would follow upon excessive loans to the government. To attach full confidence to an institution of this nature, he had argued, it was essential that it be "under a *private* not a *public* Direction, under the guidance of *individual interest,* not of *public policy.*" Under the latter it was likely to be "too much influenced by *public necessity,*" the very suspicion of which would be damaging to the credit of the bank. "It would indeed be little less than a miracle, should the credit of the Bank be at the disposal of the Government, if in a long series of time, there was not experienced a calamitous abuse of it." While it was true that the real interest of government would be to avoid that abuse, what government, Hamilton asked, "ever uniformly consulted its true interest, in opposition to the temptations of momentary exigencies? What nation was ever blessed with a constant succession of upright and wise Administrators? . . . The keen, steady, and, as it were, magnetic sense, of their own interest, as proprietors, in the Directors of a Bank, pointing invariably to its true pole, the prosperity of the institution, is the only security, that can always be relied upon, for a careful and prudent administration."[80]

The logic was powerful but exigency proved more so. As secretary of the Treasury, Hamilton felt compelled to borrow sums from the Bank of the United States again and again. On at least one occasion, there is reason to believe, the board of directors displayed reluctance to comply with the secretary's requests. Hamilton's reaction contrasts strikingly with the managerial advice he had given in his *Report*. Pointing to the chartered privileges conferred by government grant and to the advantages enjoyed by the Bank in consequence of the *"vast deposits"* made in the institution by the Treasury, Hamilton argued that such advantages "could not easily be defended" if the

Bank failed to render "equivalent services" to the government. Concluding simply that the Bank "ought to make the loan," he summed the case by saying that "loans to Government stand on very different considerations from those to individuals." Exigency produced its own powerful logic, but it did so in the interests of a different client—the stability and credit rating of the government rather than the prosperity of the Bank. The loan was needed to pay an installment of a million guilders on the principal of the Dutch debt, together with 470,000 guilders in interest.[81]

Hamilton was unstinting in his appreciation of the Bank of the United States. It was "an indispensable engine in the administration of the finances."[82] "No man placed in the office of Secretary of the Treasury, whatever theoretic doubts he may have brought into it, would be a single month without surrendering those doubts to a full conviction, that banks are essential to the pecuniary operations of the government."[83] Their loans and their depository and transfer services were important to the government, but so too were their loans to merchants. This was so because of the dependence of the government on import duties, which at this period supplied 90 percent of its revenues.[84] Hamilton regarded "exact punctuality" in the payment of duties as "essential to the whole system of public Credit and Finance."[85] It took banks, however, to make possible that punctuality. This was because the merchants were not required to pay the duties right away; the revenue laws permitted them to sign customs bonds falling due at a later date, and in consequence "a considerable part of the duties [was] always outstanding."[86] In the absence of credit facilities enabling the secretary to make immediate use of sums collectible only in the future, the fiscal operations of the Treasury would have stalled. Doubtless, it was with relief that Hamilton was able to inform the officers of the branches that the Bank of the United States had agreed to discount the promissory notes of "such merchants as are endebted to the Custom house, for 30 days, for the respective sums that shall become payable."[87] That is to say, the Bank would discount the merchants' thirty-day notes for the amount of their bonds, crediting the proceeds to the account of the collector of customs, who would then draw them out for remittance to the Treasury.

The fiscal needs of the Treasury placed Hamilton in a position of dependence on state institutions as well as on the Bank of the United States. Before the chartering of the national bank in January 1790, he had no choice, of course. Even so, it was his confidence in the notes of prudently managed "public banks"—state-chartered institutions as well as the Bank of the United States—that led him soon after entering upon his duties in the fall of 1789 to place a broad administrative construction on section 30 of the act of July 31, 1789, regulating the collection of tariff and tonnage duties.[88] The section stipulated that duties and fees be received in gold and silver coin only, but Hamilton construed this to permit the payment of duties in the notes of specie-paying public banks. Later he explained to the House of Representatives that he interpreted section 30 "as having for object, the exclusion of payments in the paper emissions of the particular States, and the securing the immediate or ultimate collection of the duties in specie." The "receipt of the notes of public banks, issued on a specie fund," would permit "the eventual receipt of the duties in specie."[89]

The secretary did not discontinue relationships between the Treasury and the state banks, especially the Bank of New York, even after the establishment of the Bank of the United States and its branches. That he believed himself acting in the public interest in doing so is unquestionable. When the Bank of New York appeared threatened by a speculative "bankomania" in New York City at the beginning of 1792—speculation in $25 bank script or subscription certificates had sent their price soaring to $300 even before the Bank of the United States was organized—Hamilton told Seton: "I consider the public interest as materially involved in aiding a valuable institution like yours to withstand the attacks of a confederated host of frantic and I fear, in too many instances, unprincipled gamblers." He not only used the Bank of New York as a depository for duties and for the proceeds of foreign bills but also "explicitly directed the Treasurer to forbear drawing" on the institution "without special direction from me." His intention was to leave the bank "in possession of all the money you have or may receive till I am assured that the present storm is effectually weathered."[90] In March the threat came from the direction of a prospective branch in New York, but Hamilton advised Seton that his bank might "boldly accommodate" the merchants, who owed considerable sums in duties that month and next, "under an assurance that the public money shall in no event be drawn out of your hands in less than three Months, unless perfectly agreeable." If the branch failed to maintain the expected cooperation with the state bank, "I will decidedly aid your Institution so as to preserve it from harm." Seton replied that his bank would "do anything" to accommodate merchants with duties to pay.[91] Although the branch opened in April 1792, the Treasury kept a deposit in the Bank of New York till sometime between the middle and the end of 1793.[92]

The Bank of New York, it may well be argued, was a special case, and in no small part because Hamilton had himself drawn up its charter, been a member of its board of directors, and as secretary applied to it successfully for a loan of $5,000 in an instance in which "a direct public good" was said by him to be involved, namely, meeting the financial needs of the Society for Establishing Useful Manufactures.[93] (The bank agreed immediately to a loan of $10,000 and to an additional $35,000 soon afterward.)[94] But the secretary also relied on other state institutions for aid in meeting the exigencies of the Treasury. Except for the Bank of Providence, an institution Hamilton decided to utilize because of the absence of a nearby branch, all public monies were being kept in the Bank of the United States and its four branches by March 1794. Yet the secretary felt obliged to borrow $200,000 at 5 percent from the Bank of

New York in October 1794 and two months later an additional $100,000, the latter a one-year loan at 5 percent possessing the unusual feature of annual renewability for five years. The Bank of Pennsylvania, chartered in 1793, also granted the secretary a loan of $50,000 in December 1794. In the light of these evidences of the secretary's reliance on state banks, his advice in 1796 to his successor, Oliver Wolcott, takes on special significance: "It is very much the policy of the Treasury not to be exclusively dependent on one institution."[95]

Hamilton's dependence on bankers, merchants, and other businessmen is fundamentally attributable to his need for their aid in sustaining the fiscal props of national union. As early as 1783 it was clear to him that the men who were advocating "funding the public debt on solid securities" were attached to continental rather than to state politics.[96] Ten years later he told Washington that if the funding system were undone by "a formed [political] party deliberately bent upon the subversion of measures, which in its consequences would subvert the Government," not only would the honor and credit of the nation be prostrated, but the government would also be brought "into contempt with that description of Men, who are in every society the only firm supporters of government."[97] Informing the collector of customs at Providence that merchants had complained of his "too *punctilious,* and not sufficiently accommodating" administration of the revenue laws, Hamilton reminded him that "the good will of the Merchants is very important in many senses, and if it can be secured without any improper sacrifice or introducing a looseness of practice, it is desireable to do it."[98] On another occasion he referred to the "body of the Merchants" as an "enlightened class of citizens" which had manifested toward the national government "a supportive disposition" and "seconded its operations" with "alacrity."[99] He could not have put the matter more plainly than he did when informing the president of the Bank of North America of his appointment as secretary of the Treasury: "To the acceptance of this arduous trust, I have been not a little encouraged by the hope that my inviolable attachment to the principles which form the basis of public credit is so well and so generally understood as to insure me the confidence of those who have it most in their power to afford me support." In the next paragraph he asked for a loan of $50,000 to the government.[100]

In sum, Hamilton devoted a considerable part of his public career to efforts to solidify the union of the states, to bolster the nation's credit, and to increase the security of property rights. Upon the latter, once again, liberty itself depended: "Adieu to the security of property[,] adieu to the security of liberty."[101] As we have seen, it was a view close to that of the great jurist John Marshall, for as chief justice of the Supreme Court Marshall time and again was to invoke the preeminent power of the federal government, not for the purpose of justifying the enactment of legislation on the part of Congress, but rather to strike down as unconstitutional attacks on property rights implicit in state laws.[102] In providing a counterpart on the federal level to the preoccupation with the defense of existing property rights which characterized decisions by state courts in Massachusetts, Marshall was reflecting his generation's widespread concern over the insecurity of property, a concern deeply implicit both in the movement for constitutional reform and in Hamilton's fiscal program.

Embedding vested property rights in the security of the legal system, however, is hardly conducive to innovative challenges, to risk taking, to new types of investment paving the way to diversification and growth. But there is little reason to believe that these objectives were held in high priority by either Hamilton—despite his words—or Marshall. In his *Report on Manufactures,* submitted to Congress in 1791 at that body's request, Hamilton explicitly stated that "manufacturing establishments . . . occasion a positive augmentation of the Produce and Revenue of the Society" by promoting diversified investment, the division of labor, the use of machinery, immigration, and a wider market for agricultural produce.[103] But, as John R. Nelson, Jr., has suggested, both the *Report,* and the Society for Establishing Useful Manufactures (SEUM), which, with Hamilton's financial and other support, sought unsuccessfully to develop large-scale textile manufacturing in Paterson, New Jersey, in the early 1790s, "appear to have been geared as much toward the merchant-creditors and the securities market as toward manufacturers." Largely prompted by securities market problems, the SEUM represented an attempt not only to encourage manufacturing but also to draw mercantile capital away from speculation in the debt, its charter requiring that 50 percent of all subscriptions to its stock be payable in government securities.

The secretary's "priorities did not lie with manufacturers" but rather with sound public credit and the security of property. Duties on imports were the principal source of the revenues needed to operate the government and to service the debt. Hamilton therefore opposed the manufacturers in their efforts to induce the Congress to stem the flow of competing imports by enacting protective tariffs. In consequence, his "ties to manufacturers were first strained, then severed by conflicts between their interests and his program." "By the end of 1793 his pro-importer political economy was driving manufacturers from Boston to Charleston into opposition to the Federalists."[104]

Hamilton's actions are consistent with the hypothesis that he favored a world of slow or negative economic and social change rather than one of growth. Emphasis on vested property rights served the interests of an older elite whose patina was the more attractive to a man born out of wedlock and in a foreign country (the West Indies). The more keenly in need of acceptance and approval for these reasons, he married into one of the oldest and wealthiest colonial families, the Schuylers of New York. And, as we have seen, his policies as secretary of the Treasury were hardly encouraging to newer men in search of capital. His drafts on the funds of the Bank of the United States severely constrained the ability of that institution to make loans to the business community.[105] The Bank's balance sheets for the years 1792–1800, discovered a half-century ago by James O. Wettereau, prove the Bank's loan and discount policy to have been a highly conservative one. For most of those years the relationship between notes in circulation and specie reserves was close, ranging from a high of 4.93 to 1 in 1794 to a low of 0.96 to 1 in 1800. The average for the nine years was merely 1.95 to 1, less than two dollars in banknotes for every dollar in specie.[106] It is of course true that the Bank opened a total of eight branches in as many cities, so that the needs and convenience of the business community can hardly have been wholly ignored. But Hamilton was at first ignorant of the branch system, and when he learned about it, he opposed it.[107] As we have seen, the appearance of a third bank in New York City in 1792 brought him "infinite pain." In sum, Hamilton put first the need to cement the union and increase the security of property rights, and the consequent necessity for bolstering the nation's credit threw him into an alliance with public creditors and merchants rather than with those seeking to alter the structure of the economy and drive it at a faster pace.

Nevertheless, whether wittingly or not, his policies laid foundations for future growth. Without security of property rights, civil society can hardly exist, much less investment take place. The longer-term effects of those policies have never been, to my knowledge, better expressed than by a historian who wrote more than 150 years ago. Said Richard Hildreth:

> The great secret of the beneficial operation of the funding system was the reestablishment of confidence; for commercial confidence, though political economists may have omitted to enumerate it among the elements of production, is just as much one of those elements as labor, land, or capital—a due infusion of it increasing in a most remarkable degree the productive activity of those other elements, and the want of it paralyzing their power to a corresponding extent. By the restoration of confidence in the nation, confidence in the states, and confidence in individuals, the funding system actually added to the labor, land, and capital of the country a much greater value than the amount of the debt thereby charged upon them.[108]

Above all, policies which ensured the viability of the constitutional settlement—at least till 1861 when its embedded canker of slavery nearly rent it—contributed most to future growth. The Constitution laid the legal foundations of a national market—the nineteenth-century equivalent of the next century's European Common Market. The grant to Congress of authority over interstate commerce potentially deprived the states of the power to interpose obstacles to the free movement of people, products, and productive factors throughout the nation. Vehemently absolutist with regard to the contract clause's protection of vested property rights from impairment by the states, Marshall also exercised vigil, as did the Courts of his successors, over state laws placing local over national economic interests. Far more than he could have realized, his rulings helped preserve foundations on which an industrial empire would rise.

Even empires have less than imperial beginnings, however. Almost from the outset of settlement in the New World, governmental bodies in British America offered bounties, premiums, and subsidies to people willing to provide needed raw materials and manufactured goods. A Maryland law of 1671, for example, granted a bounty of one pound of tobacco for every pound of hemp raised in the province; it gave two pounds of tobacco for every pound of flax. In an effort to promote the manufacture of duck in America, the Massachusetts assembly in May 1726 granted to John Powell, a Boston merchant, a bounty of twenty shillings for every bolt of canvas of specified dimensions and quality made in the colony. In the northern colonies generally, public lands were granted to encourage new industries. Massachusetts granted John Winthrop three thousand acres of land in 1648 on condition that he set up salt works making one hundred tons annually. Town aid to mills was very common, especially for the purpose of encouraging the erection of gristmills, watermills, and sawmills.

Legislatures also offered public loans, that of Rhode Island, for example, tendering William Borden five hundred pounds in 1725 to assist him in establishing his sailcloth manufacture. The colonies granted hundreds of monopolies and patents to encourage invention or production of needed commodities. The first patent issued in America for a mechanical invention was given in 1646 by the colony of Massachusetts to Joseph Jenks for improved sawmills and scythes. Monopoly rights to manufacture soap, flax machines, cornmills, sawmills, duck, paper, glass, stoneware, pearl ash, linseed oil, potash, and other articles were granted by one colony or another at various times.[109]

Generally speaking, English governments showed a considerable tolerance for colonial legislation. From the outset of settlement the intent of the Crown and its ministers seems to have been to delegate the authority to cope with local needs, for there was no way of knowing what problems would arise in the new plantations. In the "charter colonies"—Massachusetts till 1684, Connecticut, and Rhode Island—powers of legislation rested fundamentally on the right of these colonies as corporations to pass bylaws for their better government. The charter of the Massachusetts Bay Company authorized it to make "Lawes and Ordinances for the Good and Welfare of the saide Companye, and for the Government and orderings of the saide Landes and Plantation, and the People inhabiting and to inhabite the same." Laws and ordinances, however, were not to be "contrarie or repugnant to the Lawes and Statutes of this our Realme of England."[110]

The significance of these reservations became clearer at the close of the seventeenth century when the English government adopted a new policy of "constructive imperialism." Smaller self-governing proprietary units were combined into larger units of administration, executive power was strengthened at the expense of the representative assemblies, and chartered colonies were replaced by royal governments. The new charters reserved to King in Council both the right to disallow colonial legislation and the right to hear cases on appeal from provincial courts. In the implementation of these provisions the Board of Trade, which made recommendations to the Privy Council for or against disallowance, continued to be widely tolerant of colonial experiments in legal engineering. The board realized the absurdity of applying English common law standards to situations in which local customs differed from those of England. But there were limits to toleration, and where the colonial law infringed upon the royal prerogative, conflicted with fundamental imperial policy, or worked harm to the economic interests of the mother country, it was generally disallowed. The number of laws disallowed was relatively small: only 469, or 5.5 percent, of 8,563 acts submitted for review.[111] However, the possibility of royal disallowance may well have discouraged the enactment of legislation. "Legislatures debating the bill, litigants pursuing lawsuits, may have been aware of the council's distant shadow; this awareness may have modified their action in real but unknowable ways."[112]

Certainly the British position was clear. Vetoing a Pennsylvania statute in 1706, the Board of Trade remarked, "It cannot be expected that encouragement should be given by law to the making any manufactures made in England in the plantations, it being against the advantage of England." It was also made clear by the extension to the colonies of the Bubble Act of 1720, which prohibited the erection of corporations without legal authority from Parliament or Crown. The occasion for the passage of this extending act in 1741 was the floating the year before of a "Land Bank or Manufactory Scheme" in Massachusetts. Whether the extension is explainable in terms of English opposition to land banks or, more likely, to manufacturing is unknown. One authority, however, believes that the significance of the extension may easily be exaggerated and finds no evidence that it was of any consequence in the colonies after 1750. He does acknowledge that the act "may possibly have hindered the development of colonial joint stock companies, corporate or unincorporate," and that resort to it certainly might have been had "if companies distinctly objectionable to the royal authorities had been formed."[113]

Although the Bubble Act and the possibility of disallowance of colonial legislation may have discouraged efforts to erect business corporations, the argument continues, it is not British opposition but primarily the relatively undeveloped nature of the economy that explains the paucity of business corporations formed in the colonial period. Businesses were generally small scale and local in character. No large supplies of capital or labor were seeking employment, and those which were found outlets in unincorporated joint stock companies—legally partnerships—which sometimes reached surprising size in mining, land speculation, and other areas of late colonial enterprise. Had capitalists sought incorporation, they would generally have found few legal obstacles in the way. Not only Parliament and Crown, but colonial proprietors, governors, and legislatures as well possessed "within limits which were not always clear but which were for the most part wide, the right to erect corporations for operation in America."[114]

Nevertheless, it does not follow that the mushroom growth of corporations in the early national period was unrelated to political change. During the entire colonial period only a half-dozen business corporations have been traced, two in the seventeenth century and four in the eighteenth. In contrast, more than three hundred business corporations received charters from state governments during the eleven-year period between 1789 and 1800. And during the first decade of the nineteenth century, the corporation law of at least one state (Massachusetts) witnessed the triumph of the doctrine of limited liability, a triumph which must certainly have encouraged both the security of investment and the transferability of property. To ascribe the startling growth in the number of business corporations to a greater degree of economic and social maturity in the post-Revolutionary period is not persuasive. Can that much maturity have come in so short a time? A distinct political element is present and deserves recognition.[115]

Most colonial corporations were erected by charters granted by royal governors in the name of the Crown, although usually with the consent of the provincial councils. That is to say, the sovereign was recognized as the source of legal authority, with parliamentary approval required after 1688 in the case of a grant of exclusive or monopoly privilege. In both royal and proprietary colonies the legal right of the assembly to incorporate was subject to the negative of the governor or of higher English authority. The Revolution brought an important change in this situation. Because of the fiction that the Revolution had been fought to free the colonists from the exactions of the Crown, a revulsion against executive authority became manifest in the early state constitutions, as well as in the Articles of Confederation. The power to incorporate, in sum, shifted from the executive to the legislative arm, where it was more sensitively responsive to community pressures on government to aid in the provision of community services. With the Revolution came a new view of the role of legislation in the legal system, a shift to the belief that law rested not on its conformity with past law and principle but rather on the power of a legislative majority.[116]

More than two-thirds of those three hundred corporations were organized to finance the costs of constructing inland navigation, turnpikes, and bridges. Even if it is true that the British authorities would not have hesitated to approve colonial requests for incorporation in general, is it not likely they would have frowned on the purposes served by most of these corporations? Given the values of the imperial system, can British governments have been expected to encourage wholesale movements of population to the West and the development of manufactures in the inland communities resulting therefrom? The Board of Trade was well aware of the connection between the two, for in a paper laid before it in 1768, manufacturing was viewed clearly as "a consequence which, experience shows, has constantly attended, in a greater or less degree, every inland settlement." On the eve of the Revolution itself, Benjamin Franklin learned at first hand how adamant the British had become on the subject of manufactures. Just before leaving England in 1775, Franklin was drawn into informal negotiations with men closely connected to the ministry and asked to write out a set of propositions he believed would lead to permanent union. One of them was that all acts restraining manufactures be repealed. This proposition, Franklin relates, "they apprehend would meet with difficulty. They said, that restraining manufacturers in the colonies was a favorite here; and therefore they wish'd that article to be omitted, as the proposing it would alarm and hinder perhaps the considering and granting others of more importance." The contrast between British policy and American public law could not be more clear. The former was far from being hospitable to the growth of manufacturing. Can it be shown, then, that British legislation hindered the development of a more diversified American economy?[117]

Almost certainly the answer is no, and the reason is that scarcities of capital, labor, and technological knowledge militated against the growth of manufacturing. These, rather than hostile laws, were the decisive counters. This is not to deny the existence of urban craft shops, of the domestic industry of rural households, of the manufacture of clothing, utensils, nails, furniture, and other products. One finds evidence of these things almost throughout the colonial period, as well as shipbuilding, lumber and flour milling, and other mill industries employing water power. Manufacturers used tools belonging to age-old craft traditions rather than machinery, and in general enterprises were small in scale. They were neighborhood industries, widely dispersed rather than geographically concentrated, local manufactures protected by high transport costs from the competition of distant producers. Furthermore, they were technologically backward. Most of the water wheels were undershot and utilized only a fraction of the water power applied to them. There was so little understanding of power transmission that it was generally necessary to employ a separate wheel for each piece of machinery. These characteristics endured until shortly before the Revolution. Even in England the great inventions that gave that nation its industrial eminence were not successfully applied to manufactures until about the same time. About the year 1790 manufacturing everywhere broke free from ancient technical constraints, and processes of production were revolutionized. In sum, although efforts made by colonial governments to encourage manufactures were confined to local and provincial bailiwicks—in contrast to British law, which was intercolonial in its reach—it is highly doubtful that manufacturing would have developed even if British hostility had been replaced by intercolonial encouragement. The "factor balance" would have remained decisive, just as it did in the early decades after the achievement of independence.[118]

Yet even if we acknowledge the primacy of both that balance and the private sector, it does not follow that action on the part of government is irrelevant to economic change. To see this we need only ask whether manufacturing growth would have been restrained by legal discouragement after the factor balance began to shift in its favor. Suppose the colonies had remained within the British Empire. Would continuation of a policy of discouragement have inhibited the development of manufacturing? There are some who would say that the question is not a historical one, that it is hypothetical or counterfactual in nature and ought not be asked. In truth, however, the intertwined filaments of a causal web can be separated in no other way. It may be granted that our answers to such questions are neither true nor false. At best, they represent historical judgments, not historical facts. What makes for uncertainty is the possibility of change in other important elements of a situation. It is possible, for example, that the British Empire would have given way to the British Commonwealth before in fact it did, in which case an industrialized United States might have continued its political connection as partner rather than tutelary. But that is not likely. The Revolution itself played an important role in a gradually evolving view of the need to restructure Britain's relationship with its dependencies. Had the Revolution not occurred, imperial change might have been much longer in coming. Till then, to express the thought in words written by Alexander Hamilton in February 1775, "Those things we manufacture among ourselves, may be disallowed. We should then be compelled to take the manufactures of Great-Britain, upon her own conditions."[119] History is fact chosen and explained by judging men and women. In my own opinion the breaking of the imperial connection was a necessary condition, although not a sufficient one, for the emergence of a modern industrial economy in America.

Perhaps it is not too much to suggest that a will to industrialize was another of the necessary conditions. Certainly there is much evidence of that will in influential quarters, and evidence too of its impact. In the wake of the Revolution, Matthew Carey's magazine *The American Museum* pushed vigorously for an extension of manufactures, and so too did Tench Coxe, Hamilton's assistant in Treasury, in numerous addresses, articles, and pamphlets. (Coxe, by the way, was probably the most knowledgeable person on the subject in the country. It was he, not Hamilton, who wrote the first draft of Hamilton's *Report on Manufactures*. Although Hamilton revised the draft and made some additions, in the judgment of Coxe's most recent biographer, Jacob Cooke, "when the lineage of the Report on Manufactures is traced, the main threads are found to lead to Tench Coxe.")[120]

In 1789 George Washington observed that more "substantial improvements to manufactures" had recently been made "than were ever known in

America." Hamilton identified some of these in his *Report,* which contains references to the "complete success, which has rewarded manufacturing enterprises in some valuable branches"; to "several branches [that] have grown up with a rapidity which surprises"; to achievements with skins, iron, wood, flax and hemp, bricks and tiles, brewing, printing, hats, sugar, oils and soap, copper and brass, tinwares, and other "regular Trades" and with textiles; to a "flourishing" sailcloth manufactory at Boston; to New Jersey's chartering of the Society for Establishing Useful Manufactures; to new cotton manufactories at Beverly, Massachusetts, and Providence, Rhode Island, the latter having "the merit of being the first in introducing into the United States the celebrated cotton mill" (Arkwright's); and to "a promising essay, towards the fabrication of cloths, cassimers, and other woolen goods, . . . likewise going on at Hartford, in Connecticut."[121]

Three years later Henry Wansey, a well-informed traveler with thirty years of successful experience as a manufacturer in western England's textile trades, recorded in his *Journal* (published in 1796) some remarkably accurate observations on the state of numerous American manufactures. The most technologically advanced establishment visited by Wansey was a cotton factory near New York City. His *Journal* entry of May 31, 1794, records his observations in detail:

> Went with a party to see Dickson's cotton manufactory at Hell Gates, about five miles from New York. It is worked by a breast water wheel, twenty foot diameter. There are two large buildings four story high, and eighty feet long. In one shop I saw twenty-six looms at work, weaving fustians, calicoes, nankeens, nankinets, dimities, etc. and there are ten other looms in the neighbourhood. They have the new-invented spring shuttle [that is, fly shuttle]. They also spin by water, using all the new improvements of Arkwright and others. Twelve or fourteen workmen from Manchester. All the machinery in wood, steel, and brass, were made on the spot from models brought from England and Scotland. They are training up women and children to the business, of whom I saw twenty or thirty at work; they give the women two dollars a week, and find them in board and lodging; the children are bound apprentice till twenty-one years of age, with an engagement to board, clothe and educate them. They have the machine called the mule, at which they have spun cotton yarn so fine as twenty-one hundred scains to the pound, and they purpose making muslins.[122]

It is thus evident that in the decade 1785–1795 not only a euphoric burst of enthusiasm for manufactures but also the beginnings of large-scale industry itself were visible in the United States. Before we ask what happened to those beginnings, we should note that here, once again, economic change in America was a reflection of earlier change elsewhere in the Atlantic community. In the present case the originating locus of change is clear from Wansey's references to workmen from Manchester, to the new improvements of Richard Arkwright, and to "the machine called the mule." England was of course the home of the first Industrial Revolution, and despite the existence of statutes prohibiting the export of machinery and the emigration of men who understood the new manufacturing processes, it proved impossible to contain the outward thrust of a power destined to transform the world—the power of technological knowledge.

5

The Early American Industrial Revolution

History has seen many examples of a sudden spurt in levels of human welfare deriving from the luck of the harvest; the spoils of war; or recovery from protracted desolation, such as Western Europe's resurgence in the second half of the fifteenth century after the devastation of bubonic plague. During such times particular cities or regions have flourished—in medieval Italy and Flanders, for example—and as always, and under almost all conceivable conditions, particular individuals have been enriched. But the advances have been localized and short-lived, receding beneath the waves of people whose numbers they have often done so much to encourage. It was the Reverend Thomas Malthus who taught the grim lesson that population growth, unless checked by war or disease, will tend to swallow up increases in the output of goods, and that people will be no better off later than before. What makes the Industrial Revolution a turning point in history is that people for the first time began to learn how to make production grow at a faster pace than population itself, so that output per capita could rise as well as numbers of people. Setbacks have occurred; distribution of the fruits of achievement has often been frightfully skewed, advance has been dangerously slow over much of Africa, Asia, South America, and the Near East; and environmental damage has sometimes threatened the continuation of progress. Yet the Industrial Revolution is the most significant "event" ever to have affected the material welfare of humankind. Occurring first in England in the eighteenth century, spreading from there to the Continent, and then moving over more and more of the earth's surface, it has made possible sustained increases in real income per capita and enabled humanity to overcome the specter of Malthusian stagnation. Since it has laid foundations on which for the first time in history the hopes of humankind for a decent livelihood may rest, we could well call it the Industrial Renaissance.[1]

Undeniably more pessimistic views exist. Although the term *Industrial Revolution* is of French coinage and dates from the early nineteenth century, when it was created in conscious parallel to the term *French Revolution,* it was the English historian Arnold Toynbee who most eloquently fixed in the literature of industrial history a conception of the evil consequences of this apparently sudden and dramatic economic change. Lecturing at Oxford University a century ago, he depicted an England which, before 1760, had been a country of "scarcely perceptible movement," a quiet and contented world. Upon this green and joyous landscape burst a series of inventions in spinning and weaving and in the production of power; within about twenty years industry came to be overrun by steam and machinery. Factory smoke now blackened the sky and blighted the lives of exploited men, women, and children. A new world of rapid change, of dislocated and miserable people, replaced the quiet security of the old agricultural order. The Industrial Revolution had been born.[2] Toynbee, however, was unaware of an estimate of the population and wealth of England and Wales in the year 1688 made by Gregory King, secretary to the commissioners for the public accounts. Highly regarded by both his contemporaries and later investigators, King's estimates reveal dimensions of preindustrial poverty that would have stunned Toynbee: over half the total population of England and Wales had been unable to live by its income alone and had to be aided by private charity and poor relief.[3]

Toynbee's notion that the Industrial Revolution had come with the virtual suddenness of a coup d'état has run an interesting course. All bodies of historical knowledge have tails, and historians are fond of debating their length. Not surprisingly, studies have emphasized the contributions to industrial change made by longer-term agricultural improvement, commercial and urban growth, accumulated savings, population increase, and a stream of scientific thought "issuing from the teaching of Francis Bacon and enlarged by the genius of Boyle and Newton." The Industrial Revolution was indeed served by many tributaries, some of which began their rise in distant hills. Large-scale industry and technological innovation could be traced to the sixteenth and seventeenth centuries, and the process of mechanical change itself ran unbrokenly to the Middle Ages. The tail was long indeed—but what of the rapidity of the wiggle?[4]

Recent patterning of the evidence on the issue of acceleration tends to fall on Toynbee's side of the debate. To be sure, some historians see "the beginning of rapid, cumulative, structural change, with the onset of rates of growth of up to 2 per cent per annum," as early as the period between the 1740s and 1780s.[5] Others emphasize the importance of the final two decades of the century, when the "curves of imports and exports, and tonnage cleared from British ports rise almost vertically," when "almost every available statistical series of industrial output reveals a sharp upward turn," when "the rate of growth in national product effectively out-stripped the rate of growth of population." In one scholar's opinion, the years 1783-1802 form "the great watershed in the life of modern societies," the period of the British economy's "take-off into sustained growth."[6] It is unlikely that any historian would deny the relevance of both the long run and the short, a position nicely encapsulated in the suggestion that "significant discontinuities" sometimes occur in the "seamless web" of history—which is a way of saying that the web is always seamless, except sometimes![7] The accelerated rate of change in the relatively brief gathering years of the Industrial Revolution marks off those years as such a time.

What lay at the heart of the transition was an interdependent process of technological innovation in which change begot further change. Perhaps no single innovation contributed more to the development of interdependence than Henry Cort's discovery (1783–84) of an improved way to remove carbon and other impurities from pig iron. Considered "one of the outstanding events in the history of technology," the process resulted in vast increases in the output of iron. In consequence, metal began to replace timber and stone in construction; the hardware industries expanded their range of products; and numerous other activities, from agriculture to shipbuilding and from engineering to weaving, also experienced the animating effects of cheap iron. More fundamentally, the manufacture of machines from iron instead of from wood had revolutionary effects on industries producing capital goods, that is, durable goods for producers rather than products for consumers. Iron machinery was long lasting and could be run continuously with little wear. Its use ensured more accurate results than the eye of the skilled craftsman could effect. Applied to machine tools—machines that make machines—"it made precision work possible for the first time, and this was susceptible of infinite development." In a word, cheap iron ushered in the engineering industry and the beginnings of the machine age.[8]

Many technical improvements, moreover, became feasible only after advances had been made in associated fields. An improved steam engine, for example, depended on an effective condensing engine, but the latter required accurate cylinders, which could not be made till better methods of metal working had been devised. Productivity gains made possible by one innovation then proceeded to exert pressure on related industrial operations:

> The demand for coal pushed mines deeper until water seepage became a serious hazard; the answer was the creation of a more efficient pump, the atmospheric steam engine. A cheap supply of coal proved a godsend to the iron industry, which was stifling for lack of fuel. In the meantime, the invention and diffusion of machinery in the textile manufacture and other industries created a new demand for energy, hence for coal and steam engines; and these engines, and the machines themselves, had a voracious appetite for iron, which called for further coal and power.

Thus innovations almost too various and abundant for compilation mutually reinforced one another, resulting in further gains on an ever-widening front.[9]

The improvements sought by the English bore a close relationship to their available supplies of fuel. Indeed, their concentration on the technology of the iron industry comes close to having been a matter of historical necessity. For centuries they had depended on wood as their major source of fuel, as a building material, as an industrial raw material, and as a source of chemical inputs (for example, potash, used in the production of alkalis). Eventually their supplies of timber began to run out. By the Age of Queen Elizabeth wood fuel prices were rising three times as rapidly as prices generally, and the scarcity of wood had become a matter of national concern.

Why then not substitute coal for wood fuel? Unfortunately, a deleterious chemical interchange frequently occured between the mineral fuel and the final product, most importantly, iron. Repeated experimentation encouraged by the critical nature of the need finally made it possible to shift from the use of charcoal in the blast furnace to coke, and by the end of the eighteenth century the use of mineral fuel was widespread. Thus the "Industrial Revolution in Britain essentially substituted cheap coal for wood as the source of fuel and power, and cheap and abundant iron for vanishing timber supplies."[10]

In the early decades of the nineteenth century the situation in the United States was quite different from that in England. Vast supplies of timber adjacent to population concentrations made it unnecessary for Americans to adopt the new iron technology, and they were slow to do so. In 1840 almost all pig iron produced in the country was made with charcoal. As late as 1860 only 13 percent of American pig iron "was being smelted with the 'modern' fuel—coke."[11] But just as England's need to take advantage of its abundant coal led to innovations in the iron and machine tool industries, so America's similar need to make the most of its rich timber resources encouraged its people to bring to "an advanced stage of perfection a whole range of woodworking machines for sawing, planing, mortising, tenoning, shaping and boring, in addition to innumerable other specialized machines."[12] In the more mature industrial economy of the later nineteenth century, specialized machines, now made of metal and each producing a uniform, standardized part capable—although not yet perfectly so—of being used interchangeably with any other similar part in the production of an end product, would make possible mass production. Even as late as the mid-nineteenth century specialized machines like those in widespread use in the United States were "entirely unknown" in England, as were other quite surprising products of an extraordinarily versatile American ingenuity. At the famous Crystal Palace Exhibition in London in 1851, some of these products proved sensational, among them the McCormick reaper and a remarkable lock, assembled by Alfred C. Hobbs from rigidly standardized, uniform, and interchangeable parts. The American exhibit which "exceeded all others in capturing the fascinated attention of visitors" was Samuel Colt's repeating pistols, also assembled from uniform interchangeable parts. Somewhat less spectacular were exhibits of rifles, "the various parts made to interchange," which had been manufactured by Robbins and Lawrence of Windsor, Vermont. Deeply impressed by the firearms exhibits, and not least by the wooden gunstocks which, despite their irregular shape, had almost incredibly been made by machinery (namely, by the famous Blanchard lathe, invented by Thomas Blanchard in 1818),[13] the English dispatched a team of technical experts to the United States in 1853 to study the "American System of Manufactures." The subsequent reports of two of the commissioners, John Whitworth and George Wallis, provide a detailed and reliable account of American manufacturing methods in the middle of the nineteenth century.[14]

Compared with England's economy, capital and labor in the United States were scarce, and timber supplies and other resources abundant. Not surprisingly, therefore, both Whitworth and Wallis "emphasize that the scarcity and therefore high cost of labour in a bountiful resource environment was responsible for the invention as well as the ready adoption of labour-saving techniques."[15] In essence, America compensated for the relative scarcity and high cost of capital and labor by substituting its abundant and relatively cheap natural resources in production. The nation developed and adopted a "resource-intensive technology."[16]

In contrast, labor abundance in England appears to have led English workers to be relatively unreceptive to innovation. In Wallis' words, "With the comparatively superabundant supply of hands in this country, and therefore a proportionate difficulty in obtaining remunerative employment, the working classes have less sympathy with the progress of invention." In remarks made about the same time at a meeting of the English Society of Arts the American locksmith Alfred Hobbs was even more pointed. An English employer, he said, "had more to contend with in the workmen than in the want of capital. In America they might set to work to invent a machine, and all the workmen in the establishment would, if possible, lend a helping hand. If they saw any error they would mention it, and in every possible way they would aid in carrying out the idea. But in England it was quite the reverse. If the workmen could do anything to make a machine go wrong, they would do it."[17] Obviously such contentions must have exaggerated. Were they literally true, would it not be difficult to account for Britain's technological leadership in the forces underlying the Industrial Revolution?

Whitworth and Wallis had another point to make, however, in their effort to throw light on conditions in America that were favorable to innovation. They attributed to the "free and beneficent play of market forces" in the United States, to the absence of common European arrangements such as "the organization of labour along craft skill lines and the ossifying impact of apprenticeship systems," the initiative, independence, and self-reliance of the American worker. The American environment "placed no obstacles of traditions, attitudes, or institutions" in the workers's way. These favorable conditions nurtured his "ingenuity, . . . indomitable energy and perserverance."[18]

America's successful search for labor-saving innovations would continue in the later nineteenth century to mark the path of its technological progress. U.S. entry onto that path in the early decades of the century, as had been true in England, was by way of mechanical efforts to increase the output of textiles. It is instructive to examine briefly England's efforts, not only because they define the beginning stages of the classic Industrial Revolution, but also because their success established an interdependence between England, with its demand for cotton, and the American South, which supplied the raw fiber.

Textiles of course are cloths produced by weaving, by the interlacing of yarns or threads, one set of which is vertical (the warp) and the other horizontal (the weft). The industry's origins in Britain date from the early eighteenth century, when parliamentary legislation was enacted to protect the native woolen industry from the competition of printed cotton fabrics imported from the Far East. So fashionable were cottons, however, that the effect of the ban on importation was to encourage their manufacture in Britain itself! In 1719 Parliament tried to stop that too, but the effort was unavailing, and what is known as the fustian industry (fustian is a textile with a linen warp and a cotton weft) gradually developed in Lancastershire, especially in Manchester. The rising demand for cotton to provide the weft in fustian was met by an increase in imports from the Levant and the West Indies, but total imports of raw cotton never reached as much as 7 million pounds in any of the first eighty years of the eighteenth century. Imports became sizable in the final two decades because of a series of technological innovations which made it possible to manufacture textiles entirely out of cotton, warp as well as weft.

The first of these innovations was the fly shuttle, invented in 1733 by John Kay. A small device for automatically shooting the thread of the weft from one edge of the cloth to the other between the threads of the warp, the fly shuttle allowed clothiers to weave wider cloths without employing extra workmen. (The width of the material which a single workman could make by throwing the shuttle from one hand to the other had previously been limited, of course, by the length of his arms.) Weaving could also be done more quickly; indeed, a weaver could double his output. This did not happen right away, however. Kay's invention not only encountered opposition from Lancastershire weavers; it also had mechanical difficulties that were only slowly overcome. Not till after 1760 did the fly shuttle come into general use. When it did so, it immediately created a new problem, one for the spinners of yarn. Since the weaving process could now be speeded up, a way had to be found to increase the output of yarn. Inventions in spinning associated with the names of Hargreaves, Arkwright, and Crompton were not long in coming.

Sometime between 1764 and 1767 James Hargreaves devised a simple hand machine called the jenny. With it a woman could spin at first six or seven threads at once, and later as many as eighty. The jenny was adopted with enthusiasm. By 1788 about twenty thousand of the machines were at work in England. The jenny-spun yarn, however, was soft and therefore suitable only for weft. The warp still had to be spun on the hand wheel—until, that is, the invention associated with the name of Richard Arkwright, namely, the water frame. (Arkwright was not really the inventor; he was an astute and somewhat indelicate businessman who knew how to exploit the inventions of others.) The crucial contribution of the water frame was to produce a yarn of sufficient strength to serve as warp as well as weft. But although the warp spun on the water frame was strong, it was also coarse. Samuel Crompton's mule, invented in 1779, combined features of both the jenny and the water frame (which is why it was called the mule). The mule produced a yarn that was both strong and fine. Suitable for both warp and weft, it made possible the manufacture of the fine muslins which had been imported as luxury goods from the East. The mule was subsequently enlarged and made automatic. These varied inventions in spinning put pressure, in turn, on weaving. The response was the invention of the power loom by Edmund Cartwright in 1785. Unlike the spinning devices, however, the power loom made slow progress. Many improvements had to be achieved before it could be an effective instrument of factory production. Even as late as 1813 it was estimated that no more than 2,400 power looms existed in Britain. By 1820, however, there were about 14,000, and by 1833 about 100,000. Before the "bugs" had been ironed out of that invention, hand-loom weavers enjoyed the unusual opportunity for good earnings stemming from the disparity between spinning and weaving technology.

Hargreave's jenny had been small enough to be use in a cottage; it was cheap to build and required little strength to operate. But power greater than that of human muscle was needed to work an Arkwright water frame, and from the beginning it was installed in mills or factories. Horses supplied the initial power, then water, and finally the steam engine. First built in 1775 by James Watt and subsequently improved, the steam engine, even in the early nineteenth century, transformed the spinning process from a hand-operated system to one of power-driven mechanization.[19] But weaving was unaffected; indeed, except for English cotton spinning, manufacturers in leading industries such as textiles, iron smelting, and flour milling, in both England and the United States, much preferred water wheels to engines as late as the 1830s. Only in the 1840s did steam begin to take hold where water was unavailable or noncompetitive, as in the American Midwest.[20] Nevertheless, the contribution of steam power to the rise of the Cotton Kingdom in the American South was very great. Its dominance in English cotton spinning served to enlarge demand for the fiber, and its role in American transportation, first in the steamboat and then the railroad, helped to increase supply.

As we have seen, then, the immediate effect of the English textile innovations was to generate enthusiasm for a similar kind of industrial renaissance in the United States, and a number of textile and other enterprises were launched, some of them on a surprisingly large scale. The obstacles in the way of early success, however, were formidable, and the visiting textile expert Henry Wansey took due note of them in his journal of 1794. Despite the fact that the manufactory at "Hell Gates," New York, was mechanically equal to the latest English innovations, Wansey did not think it would endure. The enterprisers had "sunk a vast deal of money in buildings and machinery unnecessarily, which is a heavy tax on the undertaking, so that the interest of the money will eat up almost all the profit." Moreover, the workmen were "dissatisfied, and ready to leave the factory as soon as they have saved up a few pounds, in order to become landholders up the country, and arrive at independence." The latter was Wansey's general observation: millions of unsettled acres in America militated against success in manufacturing, and so too did generally inadequate technical knowledge. Wansey found manufactories poorly sited and machinery poorly constructed. He thought it would be at least half a century before American manufacturing could supply the needs of the growing population.[21]

Wansey's timetable proved unduly pessimistic, for coarser fabrics at least, but the difficulties to which he pointed were real. In the main, these early ventures, like Hamilton's overtures, proved premature. For all its advanced technology, the cotton manufactory at "Hell Gates" closed its doors within a year of Wansey's visit. Despite Hamilton's detailed advice and the financial support of the Society for Establishing Useful Manufactures, the most ambitious industrial corporation in America to that time, the project collapsed for lack of mechanical and engineering experience, skilled workers, and, especially, managerial competence. Hamilton's *Report on Manufactures,* sent to the Congress only a month after the chartering, was pigeonholed by the House. The early start proved a false start on the path of industrialization. But this consequence was due, in some part at least, to a diversion of capital funds to far more profitable opportunities in foreign trade opened up by European war. As a contemporary, Adam Seybert, observed in 1818, the "brilliant prospects held out by commerce, caused our citizens to neglect the mechanical and manufacturing branches of industry."[22]

Just one year before, Timothy Pitkin, an early compiler of statistics on American foreign trade, astutely noted that "since the establishment of the present government, the progress of national, as well as individual wealth has kept pace with the increase of population; and until the commencement of commercial restrictions in December 1807, and the declaration of war against Great Britain, in 1812, no nation, it is believed, had ever increased so rapidly in wealth as the United States."[23] The main source of this progress in wealth was growth in foreign trade, especially in the reexport and carrying trades following the outbreak of the wars of the French Revolution in 1793. Interestingly enough, a modern scholar reaches a similar conclusion, calling these trades "main sources of expansion in the economy during the boom years prior to the Embargo." During these "years of unparallelled prosperity," he adds, "the economic development of the United States was tied to international trade and shipping."[24] Thus commentators separated from each other by more than a century and a half are agreed on the importance of foreign trade to the welfare of the American people during a protracted period of European war. Trade came to a virtual halt with the passage of the Embargo Act in December 1807 and revived only fitfully after substitution of a policy of nonintercourse with England and France in March 1809. Declaration of war against Great Britain in June 1812 brought to a definitive end "an era of growth based on American neutrality in a world at war."[25]

The story of American foreign trade during these years of unique opportunity must begin with the fact that the colonial empires of most of the European powers were normally closed in peacetime to the ships of other nations. As we have seen, after the Revolution England excluded American ships from its ports in the West Indies, and although in the Jay Treaty of 1794 England conceded entry to small vessels of forty tons or less, an indignant Senate struck the article from the treaty before ratifying it. In 1784 France had opened seven of its West Indian ports to American ships, but on condition that they carry only rum, molasses, and French merchandise. The Spanish Empire was locked tight as a drum, at least insofar as law could succeed in doing so. (Bribery of colonial officials was a not unknown device for prying open the gates.) With the outbreak of war between England and France in 1793, this situation began to change. France realized immediately that English naval superiority would interdict French shipping between its colonies and Europe, and so by a decree of February 1793 France opened the doors of its colonial empire, including the East Indies and the Isle of France and Bourbon as well as the West Indies, to American vessels. Spain did the same in 1797 under a special licensing system. Wartime conditions also resulted in the reopening of the British West Indies ports to American ships. In general, the war made such demands on British shipping that England's prohibitions against American vessels entering its West Indian ports were simply not enforced. Thus by accident of war nearly the entire commercial world was thrown open to neutral American shipping.

Not right away, however, and not without exceptions. England's reaction to the war-born generosity of France was to invoke a regulation it had adopted during the Seven Years' War (1756–1763)—the so-called Rule of 1756. According to this rule, in time of war no neutral nation might engage in a trade denied it in time of peace. England, after all, was the world's greatest sea power. It wished to bring that power to bear upon its enemies, to destroy their commerce and shipping. England also wished to achieve an economic blockade of France. The strategy, therefore, was to capture the French West Indian islands. England would also seize neutral vessels attempting to enter the blockaded ports. Finally, it would take from neutral vessels any French goods found on board and any contraband, that is, goods, such as munitions, which nations agree at various peacetime conferences are such as aid enemy countries in time of war and which therefore cannot be supplied those countries by a neutral vessel. (The difficulty, of course, is that in wartime great naval powers trying to starve their enemies into submission tended to stretch the list of contraband goods to include even food.)

England's first impulse, therefore, was to construe narrowly the so-called rights of neutrals. During 1793 many American vessels were both seized and condemned by British admiralty courts. But in January 1794 came a British order-in-council which was to change the situation dramatically, and in America's favor. The British decided to permit neutral vessels to buy goods from England's enemies so long as they carried them to their own neutral ports. England expected that Americans would buy French goods in Haiti, for example, bring them to an American port, pay duty on them, and unload and sell them. Some of them would no doubt be bought for American consumption, and some bought by merchants intent upon reexporting them to Europe. What often happened in practice was quite different. American ships carried goods from Haiti and then, after touching at an American port, set sail for Europe without even the formality of unloading them! They paid duties on the imports, but American law permitted a refund of all except 1 percent. Still, the Americans could argue that calling at an American port broke the voyage. It was not a *continuous* voyage between enemy colony and enemy homeland, and hence it was legal. The British agreed. In 1800 a British admiralty court ruled in the case of the ship *Polly* that the practice of breaking the voyage by calling at an American port legalized the voyage. Americans, then, were importing foreign goods and then reexporting them. When they did so for others rather than on their own account, they were engaging in what is known as the carrying trade.[26]

Timothy Pitkin's statistics on the reexport trade clearly show the result. In 1793 reexports were worth only $2 million. The next year they tripled in value. In 1796 they amounted to $26 million, a thirteenfold increase in a period of three years. Then in 1797 the value of these reexported foreign goods exceeded that of domestic exports, an unusual phenomenon which continued every year from then on (except during the Peace of Amiens in 1802–03) until the embargo virtually put an end to foreign trade in 1808.[27] (American merchants imported goods such as coffee, cocoa and other tropical products from the West Indies, or textiles, dyestuffs, coffee, and other goods from the East Indies, and then transshipped the bulk of them to Europe. From Europe, in turn, came return cargoes of clothing, hardware, and other goods for both colonial and American consumption. American merchants did not simply charge commissions—that is, a percentage of the value of the goods carried— for handling this trade. They also earned profits. That is to say, they purchased and sold both colonial and European products on their own account as well as on the account of some plantation owner, European merchant, or manufacturer. Precisely how high their profits were nobody knows, although we do know the results of shipments made by a few men. Others risked too much and failed—when values crashed during the Peace of Amiens, for example. But some grew rich.

The French Revolution and the Napoleonic wars (1793–1815) created the first American millionaires. During the colonial period there had been merchants who were better off than other members of their respective communities. A seaboard elite of wealth and social position existed in America from at least the end of the seventeenth century, and probably before. Colonel William Pepperell of Piscataqua, New Hampshire, was pretty well off in the 1690s and he made his money in trade. In the eighteenth century the Browns of "Providence Plantations" made significant earnings from foreign trade, rum distilling, iron making, and a variety of other enterprises. Other wealthy colonists might also be mentioned, such as the Carrolls and the Ridgelys of Maryland, as well as Thomas Boylston of Salem, the richest man in colonial Massachusetts, whose wealth amounted to around $400,000. But not a single colonial millionaire seems to have existed. At least three millionaires, however, emerged from the period of the Napoleonic wars. Elias Hasket Derby of Salem, Massachusetts, was one. In 1799 he was worth a million and was reputed to be the richest man in America. Ten years later Robert Oliver, a Baltimore merchant, was worth somewhat over a million, and by the end of the wars Stephen Girard of Philadelphia had perhaps between seven and nine million, which made him by all odds the richest man of his day. Around 1815 there may have been a half-dozen millionaires in the country. But there were many men whose capital funds had been increased significantly by profits from neutral shipping and trade.[28]

Although the story of profits is not necessarily the story of economic growth, abundant evidence shows that these were flourishing times, that the level of welfare of numerous economic groups was rising. In the first place, hundreds of merchants in the leading seaboard cities of the North and East appear to have taken advantage of the "brilliant prospects held out by commerce." "The great number of new and elegant buildings which have been erected in this town within the last ten years," a former Bostonian wrote in 1808 after returning for a visit, "strikes the eye with astonishment, and proves the rapid manner in which the people have been acquiring wealth."[29] Much of the wealth came from shipping earnings, for although gross registered tonnage in foreign trade little more than doubled during these years, earnings from vessels rose sevenfold. In part, an increased utilization of ships was responsible for this surge, but mainly it was due to the very substantial rise in ocean freight rates. Shipping earnings played a major role in financing imports of goods which exceeded exports in value throughout the period. Moreover, the terms of trade, with only a minor interruption in 1797, became increasingly favorable until 1799–1800, when they declined, dropping sharply in 1808 and once again in 1810–1814. Given quantities of American goods, that is to say, commanded generally rising quantities of foreign goods. Both producers of the former and consumers of the latter, therefore, must have benefitted.

Flourishing shipping and trade also promoted urban and economic development in the northeastern states. The percentage of the population living in urban places rose from 5.1 percent in 1790 to 7.3 percent in 1810, with most of the increase occurring in the four major ports of Boston, New York, Baltimore, and Philadelphia. Growth was particularly impressive in New York and Baltimore, which nearly tripled in numbers between 1790 and 1810; Philadelphia more than doubled in size, while Boston did not quite do so. Expansion in shipbuilding followed the rising curve of freight rates, while ship-fitting industries, particularly ropeworks and sail making, developed and prospered around the shipbuilding areas. Other business organizations and institutions also grew in numbers to accommodate the needs of the reexport and carrying trades. Among these were bill brokers and commission houses, marine insurance companies and commercial banks, the latter then being incorporated in increasing numbers because of the ease with which charters could be secured from state legislatures. Facilities for warehousing and docking expanded and so too did retail shops of many kinds. Finally, the growing urban population widened the market for food and agricultural products and generated pressures to develop turnpikes in order to reduce transport costs between the agricultural hinterland and the seaboard.

One additional development is worthy of notice. Once more, as in the decade 1785–1795, textile and other manufactures flourished. They were enabled to do so both because of the idling of commercial investment by embargo and war, which induced numerous merchants to transfer capital to industrial enterprises, and because of the protection afforded by these events to domestic industry. The development was short-lived: with the cessation of hostilities many of these industrial firms disappeared, unable to compete with the production economies available to more experienced British manufacturers. Whether or not this renewal of the industrial impulse between 1807 and 1815 owed anything to the knowledge and experience gained in the earlier period is difficult to say. And it is equally hard to tell whether the renewal itself transmitted techniques which would gradually be picked up once again, and this time more permanently, in the 1820s and 1830s. Surely the thirty-year period 1785–1815 witnessed the first advance of the Industrial Revolution in America, but in any comparative sense it was feeble and unenduring.[30]

The 1820s begin the telling of a different story, one whose principal theme—gradually accelerating industrialization—continues to develop in all the subsequent decades before the Civil War. Let us begin with the reminder that families almost everywhere, from early on in the colonial period, had made in their own homes, and for their own use rather than for sale, a wide variety of products, including soap and candles, leather and maple sugar, and especially wearing apparel. Indeed, as late as 1820 an estimated two-thirds of the clothing worn in the United States were products of household manufacture. Commercial sources of goods and services also existed. Particularly in the more populous East, household manufacturing was supplemented by the labors of craftsmen such as cobblers, blacksmiths, curriers, coopers, hatters, tailors, and weavers working in their little shops, often in their own homes, making hats, shoes, clothing, and other goods to order. In addition, gristmills, sawmills, and other neighborhood industries such as ironworks, paper mills, wool carding and fulling mills, potash plants, breweries, tanneries, and brickyards continued to be commonplace, especially in older, more settled communities. This "household-handicraft-mill complex" accounted for a large portion of American manufacturing at the end of the War of 1812. In frontier areas, and in communities lacking in improved transportation facilities, the complex continued to be visible deep into the nineteenth century, with mills and furnaces producing largely for local or nearby consumption. Elsewhere it began to break up, most markedly wherever canals, steamboats, or railroads made easily available the products of domestic or foreign factories. Household manufacturing appears to have reached a peak about 1815, after which decline was so rapid that the transfer from homemade to shop- and factory-made goods was generally complete before 1830.[31]

In contrast to this decline, especially pronounced in the 1820s, a number of leading manufacturing industries grew at decade rates far exceeding the 35 percent increase in population. The cotton textile industry was one of the most important. In 1807 the fifteen or twenty mills in existence employed a total of approximately 8,000 spindles. By 1811, according to Albert Gallatin's report to Congress of the preceding year, an estimated eighty-seven firms were expected to have ten times this number of spindles in operation. By 1820 the spindle total had risen from 80,000 to 191,000. These increases pale before those of the 1820s: in 1831 spindles in use numbered nearly 1.25 million. Cotton textiles had become a very substantial industry. In New England alone the output of cotton cloth is estimated to have risen from less than 4 million yards in 1817 to 323 million in 1840. During the same years, textile prices fell substantially more than those of other commodities—that of ordinary sheeting, for example, falling to about one-fourth its former level. A combination of factors led to the price declines: better textile machinery (which cut wage costs), a fall in the price of raw cotton, and growth in the number of skilled technicians.[32]

These developments not only go far to explain the decline of household manufacturing, the rapid substitution of store-bought fabrics for homespun. They also help to explain why daughters of farming families, deprived of their former domestic occupation, were receptive to efforts made by textile manufacturers to recruit them.

As in cotton textiles, so also in the production of woolen goods, carpets, paper, flint glass, lead, sugar and molasses, salt, iron, and steam engines. Factory consumption of wool rose from 400,000 pounds in 1810 to 15 million in 1830, with fully half the increase occurring between 1816 and 1830. Carpet production grew from an output of 9,984 yards in 1810 to 1,147,500 in 1834, with most of the increase occurring during a four- or- five-year period beginning in 1827. Production of the steam engine, first manufactured in the United States in 1805, was stimulated especially after 1815 by the development of steamboats. During the 1820s, 359 engines were required for this purpose alone. In 1830 Pittsburgh produced 100 engines, and Cincinnati 150.[33]

Had engines destined for steamboats plying the western rivers been manufactured in the East and then shipped west, shipping costs would obviously have been prohibitive. They are exceptions to the rule that most manufactured goods were made in the East, an area embracing New England and the Middle Atlantic states, extending from Maine to Maryland and west to the Appalachian Mountains. Not only did supply originate mainly in the East: so too did demand. Indeed, the region created its own demand. Precisely because it allocated increasing proportions of its resources to manufacturing, finance, and commerce—in contrast to the West and South, which devoted most of their resources to the production of agricultural goods—per capita income growth in the East was the highest in the nation, specifically, 25 percent higher in 1840. Most of the trade in the manufactured products of the East was therefore an intraregional trade. Foreign markets and those of other American regions took only limited quantities, the North-South trade, for example, being estimated at between 20 and 25 percent of northern manufacturing output in 1840.[34]

The techniques by which these goods were produced varied in part with the kind of product involved and the locus of manufacturing, but in general three methods were employed: enlarged shop or handicraft production, the domestic or putting-out system, and the factory system. The financial resources and managerial expertise of wholesale merchants were often crucial to the first two. As in colonial years, a master craftsman continued to direct the work of journeymen and apprentices in his shop, but the numbers of those workers increased in consonance with rising demand. Instead of making goods on order for local customers, he sold his output to a wholesale merchant for distribution in more distant markets. The putting-out system was largely confined to the production of shoes, textiles, and wearing apparel, with the merchant supplying leather, for example, to men who worked in their own homes and with their own tools. As the volume of demand continued to mount, these dispersed workers were often gathered into a central shop, where tasks were carefully differentiated and production was supervised.[35]

In the boot and shoe industry in Massachusetts, for example, workmen in central shops specialized in tasks such as the cutting of leather and the lining or stitching and binding of uppers, lasting, and soling, all manual operations in which they employed their own tools. With the introduction of mechanical devices for cutting and rolling leather, and then of pegging machines and sewing machines between 1840 and 1860, machinery displaced these tools. Power to drive the machines, however, began to be utilized only after the outbreak of the Civil War. It is the use of power, together with the performance of all tasks of production under the same roof, so to speak—rather than partially in the central shop and partially elsewhere—that defines the factory.[36]

Factories made their first appearance in the textile industries, a development favored by the circumstance that much the largest segment of American demand was for uniform coarse fabrics that were more dependent on machinery, and hence on centralized production, than fine goods requiring the skills of the artisan. Cotton textiles showed the way—the Boston Manufacturing Company erected the first modern factory at Waltham, Massachusetts, in 1813—and almost immediately displaced what had been the leading homespun occupation of the colonies, namely, the making of linen cloth. Unlike flax, wool met no similar rivalry from competing fibers, and although carding mills sustained homespun and household industries longer than in the case of cotton, the largest textile factories in America before 1860 made woolen goods. Except for carpet manufacturing, which grew rapidly in the 1820s, and the anthracite furnaces and rolling mills of eastern Pennsylvania and western New Jersey, which were rapidly becoming major factory operations by the later 1840s, factory organization appears to have made its way gradually into the structure of industry. It was not till shortly before the Civil War that it was extended to branches of wood and metal manufacturing requiring the mechanical production of uniform and interchangeable parts—a process tracing its American origins to the experimental methods of Eli Whitney and Simeon North in the 1790s. Both the ability to compose end products by putting together standardized, interchangeable parts and the use of the assembly line, a technique which dates from Oliver Evans' introduction of the principle of continuous process production in a flour mill built by him in 1782, were to become principal marks of distinction between American mass-production methods and those of most other countries, including Great Britain. In the waning antebellum years, establishments for making firearms, agricultural implements, sewing machines, clocks and watches, and still other products, more and more resembled textile factories in their wide use of power-driven automatic machinery, interchangeability, systematization of processes, and administration of labor. By 1860 the factory system was "rapidly becoming important in practically every industrial field and the stage was set for its phenomenal development in postwar years."[37]

Factories, mills devoted (usually) to a single process, and the putting-out system together wrought an enormous increase in the volume of manufactured goods. According to a recent estimate, between the years 1809 and 1839 manufacturing output climbed an average of 59 percent per decade, soaring by 153 percent in the 1840s before settling back to a more modest 60 percent in the 1850s. By 1860 the American manufacturing sector ranked second or third among the nations of the world.[38]

Table 3 exhibits the ten leading manufacturing industries in 1860 in the order of their importance. One noteworthy feature is the evidence it provides of the overwhelming presence of industries specializing in the processing of raw materials, with cotton, lumber, leather, and grain leading the way.[39]

Perhaps not surprisingly, publication of the census of 1870, the first to record horsepower, revealed the milling industry to be the largest single industrial user of power in the United States, consuming nearly 25 percent of the total. Milling utilized four times the steam power used by the cotton industry, in this respect exceeding the power used by the iron industry as well. Steam, as we have seen, entered manufacturing slowly before the Civil War. Even in 1850 all American factories together probably generated merely some 181,000 horsepower from steam, at a time when inanimate sources supplied 2.5 million, and the total horsepower from all sources, including human muscle, reached 8.5 million. Only in 1870 was the turning point reached, when steam-generated horsepower of 1,215,711 in manufacturing barely edged out water-generated horsepower of 1,130,431. Waterpower, just as much a natural resource as were the raw materials produced by the rich American land, had the disadvantage of confining manufacturing to sites where it was available, particularly in New England. Steam enabled industry to decentralize and thus to expand, as it was to do in a subsequently more mature phase of the American Industrial Revolution.[40]

A fundamental part of any explanation of the advance of industry during these years was the relative scarcity of labor in the United States. Although both capital and labor were in shorter supply in the United States than in Great Britain—and this was especially true of unskilled labor—labor was the scarcer factor of production, particularly from about the mid-1830s. Its relative dearness gave manufacturers an economic incentive to save on that factor by investing in capital-using innovations, the more so because skilled machinery makers were more plentifully available. Although heavy machinery tools were imported from England, skilled American labor built the machinery used in most industries and adapted it to specialized needs as well.

In the textile industry, for example, the largest New England firms constructed the first machine shops in the United States in order to supply their own requirements. The more manufacturers sought to mechanize, however, the wider the market for machines. The textile machine shops responded at first by making machines for other industries as well as their own. They then split off from their parent firms and became independent, after about 1840 becoming highly specialized in response to mounting demand. By the 1850s visiting English technicians could observe that "in the adaptation of special

Table 3. United States manufactures, 1860.

Item	Cost of raw material	Number of employees	Value of product	Value added by manufacture	Rank by value added
Cotton goods	$52,666,701	114,955	$107,337,783	$54,671,082	1
Lumber	51,358,400	75,595	104,928,342	53,569,942	2
Boots and shoes	42,728,174	123,026	91,889,298	49,161,124	3
Flour and meal	208,497,309	27,682	248,580,365	40,083,056	4
Men's clothing	44,149,752	114,800	80,830,555	36,680,803	5
Iron (cast, forged, rolled, and wrought)	37,486,056	48,975	73,175,332	35,689,286	6
Machinery	19,444,533	41,223	52,010,376	32,565,843	7
Woolen goods	35,652,701	40,597	60,685,190	25,032,489	8
Carriages, wagons, and carts	11,898,282	37,102	35,552,842	23,654,560	9
Leather	44,520,737	22,679	67,306,452	22,785,715	10

Source: George Rogers Taylor, *The Transportation Revolution, 1815–1860* (New York: Holt, Rinehart & Winston, 1951), p. 243 (computed by Taylor from *Eighth Census of the United States: Manufactures*, pp. 733–742). Used with permission.

apparatus to a single operation in almost all branches of industry, the Americans display an amount of ingenuity, combined with undaunted energy, which as a nation we should do well to imitate."[41]

They had begun to display that ingenuity in the manufacture of textiles as early as the decade 1814–1824. By 1818 the chief mechanic of the Boston Manufacturing Company, Paul Moody, had developed warping and dressing machines and had modified the spinning frame to enable it to spin filling yarn directly onto bobbins for use in the subsequent weaving process. Other important American adaptations and inventions were the ring spindle, the Goulding automatic roving machine, the self-acting temple, and various self-stopping devices in case of breakage. The mechanization of weaving proceeded rapidly after Francis Cabot Lowell designed his power loom in 1813. The power loom was then soon adapted to the weaving of woolens and worsteds, industries in which Americans also made important advances in carding and in the finishing processes.

In sum, Americans radically improved many of the processes involved in the manufacture of textiles. But their ingenuity was by no means confined to that industry. Viewing the progress of technology throughout the economy generally, the commissioner of patents observed in 1843, "The advancement of the arts, from year to year, taxes our credulity, and seems to presage the arrival of that period when human improvement must end." Although the number of patents issued each year has many faults as a statistical series, it is not without interest that the average annual number increases from 535 between 1820 and 1830, to 646 between 1841 and 1850, and to 2,525 the following decade.[42]

The level of literacy in the United States during these years was generally high, and perhaps nowhere higher than in New England, so that the question arises whether or not there was a connection between this fact and the undoubted progress of industrialization. If so, the relationship was not a simple one. Surely the organizers and managers of manufacturing firms may safely be assumed to have been able to read and write. Just as surely, unskilled workers did not require that ability. But what of the skilled? What of the men who built machines and adapted them to new uses? Careful inquiry may well reveal that literacy, as ordinarily defined, was no indispensable prerequisite. What was required was the "literacy" of experience, and this was obtained by work itself. How else, save through experience, could a boy of thirteen who had been a cotton mill operative for seven years have learned enough to be entrusted with the responsibility for repairing and setting in operation the machinery of a cotton mill in Tiverton, Rhode Island? How else could a lad of nineteen, after eleven years of on-the-job training, have become superintendent of the Pawtucket Thread Mill in 1826? More generally, even if skilled mechanics were able to read and write, the assumption that they learned most by doing, by on-the-job experience is particularly attractive in application to

a technological age in which innovation was empirically rather than scientifically based.[43]

The chances are that mechanical ability among males was almost as widespread as literacy itself. In his *Report on Manufactures,* Hamilton notes that "a
remark often to be met with" was that "there is, in the genius of the people of
this country, a peculiar aptitude for mechanical improvements." A distinguished English machine tool inventor, James Nasmyth, makes a similar observation in the mid-nineteenth century: "The American working boy develops
rapidly into a skilled artisan . . . ; there is not a working boy of average ability
in the New England states . . . who has not an idea of some mechanical
invention or improvement in manufactures, by which, in good times, he hopes
to better his position, or rise to fortune and social distinction."[44]

To suggest that literacy or, more broadly, education may not have been a
necessary condition for early industrialization is not to say that it hindered the
process. Just the opposite is true: in regions where literacy was widespread, it
no doubt helped, and in those where the resources devoted to it were nig-
gardly, it can hardly have done so. New England illustrates the former, the
South the latter. Literacy among New England males was nearly universal by
the end of the eighteenth century (and, in addition, nearly half the women
were literate), probably because of the Puritan emphasis on its indispensability
to the practice of religion, especially reading the Bible. In contrast, while the
white population of the slaveholding states was nearly half that of the northern
states in 1850, the region, in part because of the dispersal of its inhabitants,
had less than one-third as many public schools, one-fourth as many pupils,
and one-twentieth as many public libraries, with the latter containing one-
sixth as many volumes. Education was largely confined to wealthier people,
whose sons were sent to colleges in the North and abroad. Among the slaves,
illiteracy was an almost universal condition. Although the West greatly exceeded the South in numbers of schools per one hundred square miles and in
tax monies devoted to public education, in thinly settled parts of the region a
large proportion of the people were illiterate. Overall, even if one adds direct
expenditures on schooling to earnings forgone by enrolled students, the total
American investment in education in 1860 was 1.5 percent of the national
product.[45]

Many recent studies of educational development in antebellum America
have concentrated on quantitative measures of change such as numbers of
schools and pupils, attendance rates, length of the school day and year, and
amount of money spent. For example, in Massachusetts, the most studied
state, the length of the public school year increased from 146 days in 1840 to
177 days in 1877. More generally, in the 1850s an older system under which
parents contributed to the costs of providing an elementary education for their
children began increasingly to be replaced by the free public school system.
Public secondary institutions also increased in number, and by 1860 some

320 high schools were in existence, more than half of them located in Massachusetts, New York, and Ohio. The generation attending school in 1800 had received on average a lifetime total of 210 days of education, but by midcentury this number had more than doubled. Educational change is also evidenced by the existence of mechanics institutes, which appeared in many of the large cities in the 1820s, and of academies, both incorporated and nonincorporated private secondary institutions, which also experienced rapid growth before the Civil War. (By 1860, 1,261 incorporated academies existed, but the unchartered ones were far more numerous at all times.)[46]

Numbers are important, and so too is the sobering fact that the rise of mass education before the Civil War was due more to the expansion of school attendance in the rapidly growing agricultural states of the North Central and South Central regions than to changes in the older industrialized areas of the Northeast. More specifically, it was in the younger regions that the largest increases in school enrollment rates occurred between 1840 and 1860. New England, meanwhile, experienced a slight decline.[47]

What then was the causal relationship between formal, institutional education and the development of industrialization? The answer must be that we do not know as yet. Nor can we know until qualitative considerations are brought into the account. We need answers to questions such as: What courses were taught, and what standards were applied to adjudge their successful completion? What texts were used, and what methods of instruction employed? What variations in these matters are to be found in urban and rural schools, in schools differing in immigrant, native, and ethnic composition? And precisely by what explanatory hypotheses do we relate these variables to aptitude and expertise in business and in "mechanics"? Perhaps above all, how do we distinguish between the knowledge and interest imparted by familial emphasis, by experience, and by educational institutions? In short, "education" needs to be defined more rigorously and divided by its component sources. It may well prove that definitive answers to these questions, or to some of them, lie beyond our available sources of information. Pending their exhumation and scrutiny, in sum, we may remain confident that there exists a causal relationship between education and industrialization, while acknowledging both the need for careful definition and further exploration of the nature of the linkages.

The process of industrialization itself contributed to the diffusion of knowledge through its impact on urbanization, for cities decreased space and time separation between their inhabitants and facilitated the circulation of news about alternative and improved ways of making and doing things. The amount of urban growth during these decades is impressive. Despite a tripling of the land area between 1790 and 1860, population grew even more rapidly and increased in density from 4.5 to 10.6 per square mile. Urbanization accounts for a major part of this growth, and while the share of the population living in cities (defined by the census as consisting of 2,500 or more people) grew in every decade from 1790 save one, 1810–1820, it was not till the 1820s, the decade of rapid manufacturing development, that sustained growth commenced. All the eastern states experienced "urban take-offs" in the 1820s, reaching peak acceleration rates in the 1840s and 1850s.[48]

Much of this growth had its source in manufacturing development. In the first place, the great eastern ports continued to expand as they attracted manufacturing because of their "large markets, ample supplies of labor, raw and semi-manufactured material inputs, access to low-cost transport whether by natural water, canal, or railroad and with their efficient commercial and financial sectors." Philadelphia, for example, had owed most of its colonial development to its shipping and commerce, but in the early nineteenth century the city's foreign trade deteriorated. Growth thereafter came "primarily from the expansion and transformation of its manufacturing sector." Long distinguished for the variety and excellence of its handicrafts, the city once again prospered with the expansion of the textile, machinery, metal, chemical, and drug industries.[49]

The founding of new towns served as the second way in which manufacturing contributed to urban growth. The mushroom growth of many of these towns, such as Lowell, which was transformed in a few years from a farming district to a city of 20,000 people and then went on to become the largest of the mill towns of the antebellum years and the nation's leading center of textile production, can only be called astonishing. Lawrence, Massachusetts, founded in 1845, had a population of 17,639 only fifteen years later. Manchester, New Hampshire, went from 3,235 in 1840 to 20,107 in 1860. New Bedford, Massachusetts, whose population was 4,361 in 1800 and only 12,087 forty years later, rose to 22,300 in the next twenty years as textile manufacturing there began an expansion that was destined to be sensational following the Civil War. Newburyport, Massachusetts, a seaport city in decline, possessing fewer people in 1840 than it had boasted thirty years before, doubled its population because of textile manufacturing between 1840 and 1860.[50]

As early as 1820, two-thirds of Philadelphia's labor force was engaged in manufactures and trades. Even in the adjacent counties of the eastern hinterland one worker in five was so employed. Fortunately, the new mills and factories that undermined the primary economic activities of farmers' daughters—the spinning of yarn and weaving of cloth at home—also offered employment opportunities which many found impossible to resist. The consequence was a mass movement of women into the early mills. By 1860 the cotton textile industry in New England alone employed more than sixty thousand women.[51]

Studies of the origins and composition of the labor force in the Lowell mills shows conclusively that sheer economic need did not drive these young women to work, at least not the needs of their families. Rather, they wished to earn wages in order to provide for a dowry, buy clothes, further their education, or achieve other personal objectives. Their earnings in the mid-1830s amounted merely to about $3.25 for a seventy-three-hour work week, but room and board in company boarding houses cost only $1.25, leaving them a surplus of of about $2.00 a week. These wages compare favorably with earnings in domestic service, teaching, and sewing, three of the main alternative occupations open to women in these years. Men fared better: their daily earnings were more than twice those paid to women. Unlike males, whose wages reflected the going rate in New England for each trade or skill group, piece rates offered females were not subject to market constraint. Since no well-developed market for female industrial workers existed, at least in the earlier years, the lower limit of female wages had to be set just high enough to attract young women from farms and away from such competing female employments as household manufacturing and domestic service. All the supervisory positions in the Lowell mills, it should be added, were reserved for men.[52]

Reductions in wage rates, lengthening of the workday, or resort to the "speed-up" and "stretch-out" (respectively, increasing the operating speed of machinery and assigning additional machines to be tended by each operative) provoked sporadic strikes by female operatives in the 1820s and 1830s before giving way in the next decade to a more coordinated and organized form of struggle—the Ten Hour movement. Occasionally the struggles resulted in some gains for women, but in the long run protests failed to halt the deterioration of earlier standards. Then, with the arrival in Boston of tens of thousands of Irish immigrants and a stepped-up inflow from Quebec, the visible protests ceased. In dire economic need as they often were, the Irish were in no position to complain about wage reductions or the increasing pace of work. And the mills offered steady and relatively well-paid jobs, certainly in comparison with domestic service or outdoor labor. In consequence, although the textile corporations took advantage of the opportunity to reduce piece rates and increase the pace of work for immigrant and native alike, the 1850s stand out as a period of industrial peace. Yet, if the great availability of immigrants was to pave the way for more onerous conditions of work, immigrant women were soon to benefit from a change in the composition of the workforce. The departure of native women in large numbers enabled the immigrants to move up to higher-paying jobs in the weaving and dressing rooms.[53]

Female operatives in Massachusetts were by no means alone in protesting the often harsh working conditions attending industrialization. The 1830s were a decade of deep unrest in the ranks of American labor, and many labor organizations rose to protest some of the consequences of the transformation of an older system of production based on close relationships between master craftsmen, journeymen, and apprentices. Now that the urban craft shops had lost their independence and become mere links in a production and distribution chain managed by wholesale merchants, a widening gulf separated employer and worker. To defend their wages, hours, and skilled positions, skilled workers organized local trade societies within individual crafts, urban central labor groupings—or trades unions—and even national unions. Although a strike by male artisans for the ten–hour day initially failed in Boston in 1825, within a decade numerous trades in Philadelphia, New York, and elsewhere had achieved the desired reduction in the hours of labor. At times their efforts even won governmental support, as in 1835 when the Philadelphia common council agreed to a ten–hour limit on local public works. With the signing of an executive order by President Van Buren in 1840 making ten hours the legal length of the working day for federal employees, the early labor movement achieved its crowning success.[54]

Early labor organizations at the national level expired with the coming of depression in 1837. Nor did labor organizations enjoy much success in the political arena in the form of Workingmen's parties. These parties were not really made up of laboring men but consisted of merchants, lawyers, and other professionals as well. The Workingmen's movement in New York in the 1830s, for example, included large elements of the middle class.[55]

Early trade unionism failed partly because, although economic and class differences certainly existed, class lines fell lightly over the contours of an essentially fluid society. Even on the eve of the Civil War, individual proprietorships and partnerships rather than corporations predominated as forms of business enterprise, which suggests that for most purposes the sums required as investment capital to enter business were within the capacities of many individuals. Not until the 1850s did incorporation and the factory system take their sharp rise, and even then much machinery remained light, wooden, and inexpensive. Perhaps not surprisingly, therefore, it is only in the 1850s that the industrial worker came to regard himself as a permanent wage earner— probably because of the rising capital requirements of machinery powered by steam.[56]

Till then, many workers were aspiring entrepreneurs hoping to use their savings to establish their own small businesses—with the aid, perhaps, of investments or loans from extended-family members or friends. In Paterson, New Jersey, for example, the typical manufacturer in the new locomotive, machinery, and tool industries had been a skilled craftsman or had served an apprenticeship and founded his business as a small proprietorship or partnership. And in Newark, New Jersey, the leading industrial city in the nation on the eve of the Civil War, it was artisans who, by amassing the necessary capital, developing new processes, utilizing the labor of male immigrants from northern Europe, and locating new markets, were the architects of growth. Such firms could expand the volume of production per worker by teaching new skills to semiskilled workers and pouring their funds into materials. Small businesses flourished—in the making of shoes, hats, saddles, jewelry, trunks, and leather—perhaps nearly a third of them representing capital investments of $1,000 or less in 1850.[57]

If we add to this scenario of opportunity for small businessmen in manufacturing the reality of comparable openings in the nonindustrial sector (for example, in retail and wholesale storekeeping) and in the rapidly growing urban service sector (for example, for lawyers, real estate agents, employment bureaus, innkeepers, and teachers of bookkeeping), the buoyantly confident and entrepreneurial cast of the national mood of the antebellum years becomes an understandable phenomenon. Of course, other circumstances also worked to sustain that mood. The ending of the second war with England had seen independence preserved and the nation poised to begin one of the greatest economic conquests of history. Before the American people stretched an agricultural domain of imperial dimensions. Indeed, the acquisition of the Louisiana Territory from France in 1803, which more than doubled the size of the national domain, had prompted President Jefferson to remark that there was now room enough for a thousand generations. Merchant vessels, so recently caught in a crossfire of British orders-in-council and Napoleonic responses under the Continental system, to say nothing of the wartime pincers of the British fleet itself, now stood ready once again to turn their cargoes in the world's ports. Prices of American staples, responding to a series of poor crops in Europe and to a mounting English demand for cotton, were beginning to rise on world markets and to generate increases in land sales, rapid movement to the West, and demand for "internal improvements" to weld the newer sections of the country onto the older ones along the Atlantic coast. Standing on the threshold of what John Higham has aptly termed an age of boundlessness,[58] the American people put their faith in the power of individual initiative to enrich themselves and the nation as well. Perhaps above all, they wished to root the political independence of their fledgling republic in the soil of economic growth.

If so, to what extent were they successful? Did the long-term rate of economic growth accelerate in the years between the achievement of independence and the outbreak of the Civil War? If it did, was the average person better off than before because of a more equitable distribution of income? These are questions that have no definitive answers. Although federal censuses began in 1790, they have little to say about agriculture or manufacturing before 1840. Indeed, early censuses are so poor in these respects as to have been termed almost worthless. In consequence, historians at work in a statistical half-light have had to make what use they could of surviving fragmentary materials, to extrapolate backward from later periods, and to indulge in bold assumptions. But they have also been quick to emphasize the "deficiencies in the available evidence" and to advise the reader to "use the results derived . . . with great caution."[59]

Statements about the earlier years are especially vulnerable. The volume of shipping and trade in the first ten years after the Revolution was substantially greater than before the war, but since population growth in the South exceeded exports by a wide margin, while only approximately keeping abreast of both exports and shipping in the North, per capita trade declined. If, therefore, the ratio between exports and total output remained constant—an assumption of uncertain legitimacy since the ratio has varied historically both in the long run and in the short—per capita product was lower in the 1780s and early 1790s than before the war for independence. Other evidence tends to confirm this impression. A comparison of estimates of per capita nonhuman wealth (that is, excluding the value of slaves) for the years 1774 and 1805 indicates drastic deterioration not only during the Revolution itself but perhaps in the 1780s as well.[60]

Historians differ in their interpretation of the evidence available for the period between the early 1790s and the Civil War. One suggests that three distinct "long swings" or growth cycles—intervals of fifteen to twenty years' duration in which growth at an accelerated rate (the "surge") is followed by continued growth at a declining rate—are identifiable. The first surge occurred during the years 1793–1806 and is associated with the expansion of shipping and trade made possible by American neutrality during the wars of the French Revolution and Napoleon. The second lasted from the early 1820s to about 1834 and appears to have been connected with early manufacturing development. The surge of the third growth cycle, also apparently associated with continuing industrialization, commenced in the latter half of the 1840s and ran its course before the firing on Fort Sumter. None of the surges, it should be emphasized, involved a break in the secular growth rate. Acceleration occurred within three separate cycles and faded in each of them rather than developing an increased momentum over time. There was near-term but not long-term acceleration.[61]

In contrast, others believe that a gradual secular acceleration did take place.[62] One vigorously debated thesis maintains that the angle of transition between relatively slower and faster rates of growth was so abrupt in the late 1840s as to justify use of the term *take-off* to describe it.[63] However, most students of U.S. economic history, indeed of history generally, find it difficult to accept the existence of discontinuous shifts. They believe the terminology of take-off misleading in its implications that an economy moves from one discrete stage to another and that the defining characteristics of a given stage are readily identifiable and separable from those of another. They emphasize the overlapping of past and present and the gradualness with which economic and social structures undergo fundamental change. Furthermore, they recognize that the effects of developments which enhance the efficiency of productive effort are not felt everywhere at once. These developments make their way with varying rates of speed and degrees of success through the geographic regions, economic sectors, industries, and firms of which an economy is composed. Sometimes they encounter opposition from firms desiring to protect older techniques embedded in investment. Sometimes mere slowness of entrepreneurial imagination or failure of entrepreneurial nerve is at work. And sometimes insufficient or inadequate printed media for the dissemination of information on new techniques slow the process of diffusion. Change in the rate of growth reflects substantial change in the quantity or quality of productive inputs, and this process takes time.

The third point of view holds that a gradual acceleration in the secular growth rate took place during the antebellum period and that quantitative evidence in support of the hypothesis is clearest from about the mid-1830s to the late 1850s. Reasonably comprehensive federal censuses in 1840, 1850, and 1860, together with nine industrial censuses and data published annually by a number of states, make it possible to build up national product estimates covering the entire period 1834–1859. These estimates reveal very high rates of change of both real national product and real product *per capita*. The former rose at a rate of about 5 percent a year, the latter at 1.8 percent.

> The former rate compounds to 63% per decade and, if sustained for a century, would result in a value 132 *times* as large as the initial value in the series. No other country has achieved a sustained rate so high and only in the post Civil War decades has the U.S. economy subsequently grown so fast. The per capita rate of growth compounds to a 20% decade increase and, over a century, to a figure six times as large as the initial figure. This is well within the range of performance of modernizing economies.

In sum, the estimates "display most of the earmarks of modern economic growth."[64]

This conclusion is sustained by changes in the structure of the economy which help to account for the high rates of economic growth achieved. In the first place, a pronounced regional reallocation of resources occurred, reflecting changing economic opportunities as population shifted to the West. Note particularly in Table 4 the high rates of growth in the West South Central and North Central states between 1839 and 1859. All regions, however, exhibit significant advances in both total output and in output per capita. In the second place, significant sectoral changes occurred. Value added by commodity output in agriculture continued its historic relative decline, whereas its counterpart in industry, trade, and transportation increased by measures displayed in Table 5. Corresponding shifts occurred in the structure of the labor force, the agricultural portion declining from 63.4 percent of the whole to 53.2 percent, the numbers engaged in factory production and in construction rising from 13.9 percent to 18.5 percent. These sectoral changes go far to explain the high growth rates of the period, real net national product per capita rising from an estimated annual rate of 1.0–1.5 percent between 1799 and 1838 to 1.7 percent between 1839 and 1854. Labor productivity in agriculture was probably considerably lower than it was in manufacturing—income per worker in agriculture amounted to merely 45 percent of national income per worker between 1839 and 1859, while in manufacturing and mining the

Table 4. The regional distribution of national product and the rates of growth of regional product and regional product per capita, 1838–1859.

Region	Distribution of national product		Rates of growth	
	1839	1859	Regional product	Regional product per capita
Northeast	58%	52%	4.0%	1.7%
North Central	13	21	7.0	1.6
South Atlantic	14	9	2.5	1.2
East South Central	11	9	3.8	1.3
West South Central	4	8	8.5	1.0

Source: Draft version of Stanley L. Engerman and Robert E. Gallman, "Economic Growth, 1783–1860," in *Research in Economic History,* vol. 8, ed. Paul Uselding (Greenwich, Conn.: JAI Press, 1983). Used with permission.

Table 5. The sectoral distribution of value added: 1839, 1849, 1859 (percent).

Sector	1839	1849	1859
Agriculture	42	35	35
Industry, trade, and transportation	37	44	46
Mining and manufacturing	15	30	20
Construction	4	5	5
Transportation and public utilities	6	4	6
Trade	12	15	15
Shelter and services	20	21	19

Source: Stanley L. Engerman and Robert E. Gallman, "Economic Growth, 1783–1860," in *Research in Economic History,* ed. Paul Uselding (Greenwich, Conn.: JAI Press, 1983), VIII, 12. Used with permission.

percentage was 113 percent—so that the structural shifts, by decreasing the proportion of the workforce in the sector of relatively low productivity, contributed significantly to the productivity of the labor force as a whole.[65]

In sum, it seems clear that the rise of manufacturing industry supplied the cutting edge of a gradual acceleration in the long-term rate of economic growth in the closing decades before the Civil War. Surprisingly, industry during these years was not, in general, fixed-capital intensive. Analysis of the information on northeastern manufacturing firms collected by the Treasury Department in 1832 (the McLane Report) reveals that working capital—inventories and accounts receivable (credit extended to customers)—attracted a substantial share of the investments made by manufacturing firms. In only a few industries—cotton and woolen textiles and the manufacturing of paper—did fixed-capital shares heavily outweigh working capital, and only in cotton textiles was the capital invested in machinery and in taxes a large fraction (nearly 30 percent) of total investment. In all other industries the value of the buildings, land, and fixtures far outweighed that of machinery and tools.[66]

More generally, and even more surprisingly, industrialization did not increase the ratio between the value of capital and that of output (the capital/output ratio). Even early in the century the percentage of net national product devoted to capital formation was already high—between 6.2 and 7.0 percent in the years 1805–1840–and whereas this percentage rose to 9.5 percent between 1834 and 1843, to 10.2 percent between 1839 and 1848, to 11.4 percent between 1844 and 1853, and to 12.1 percent between 1849 and 1858 (thus nearly doubling over the final two decades before the war) the capital/output ratio performed much more modestly, increasing from 1.625 to 1 in 1840 to only 1.8 to 1 a decade later. (Unfortunately, figures for the year 1860 are unavailable.) Once again, industrial output during these years of early modernization rose at a more rapid pace than did the fraction of real net national product devoted to investment in manufacturing capital. The capital/output ratios in heavy industries were not generally higher than those in the light industries. Capital deepening in American manufacturing requiring masses of investment was a phenomenon of the decades following the Civil War.[67]

One consequence of the relatively low capital/output ratios of earlier years was the ability of partnerships and proprietorships to raise most of the capital sums required by antebellum industry. While incorporation underwent significant expansion in the final decades before the war, its utility as a mechanism for raising large sums of capital for industry naturally increased after the war in tandem with the capital-deepening process itself. Before the war commercial banks were primarily attuned to the financial requirements of merchants, but, as we shall see, they also had a hand in the financing of early industrialization.[68]

6

Money and Banking
before the Civil War

The relationships between money, bank credit, and economic growth raise a host of intriguing questions which historians have only recently begun to explore. The long delay in entertaining them has probably been due, in part, to a preoccupation with the politics of banking, especially with federal politics in relation to the Second Bank of the United States, but also in part to the long reign of classical economic theory. According to the latter, the world of finance must be distinguished from the world of "real" economic variables, from supplies of land, labor, and capital and the technological innovation that heightens their productivity. Growth required increases in real variables. The rate of investment (physical capital formation) was determined by the supply of savings, referring not to money but to unconsumed current output. Money was a "veil": its expansion could induce a higher general level of prices; its contraction, deflation. But it could not cause output to rise or fall, certainly not in the long run.

A resurgent interest in monetary theory in recent years has moderated the astringency of these views. While the difference between finance and capital remains a real one, it is clear that the former, given the existence of full employment, can impart a command over resources sufficient to transfer them from consumption to investment. A bank loan to an entrepreneur wishing to finance an innovation enables the borrower to offer higher prices to attract resources from their current employment in producing consumption goods, the output of the latter will fall, their prices will rise, and the real buying power of consumers will be reduced. Inflation will thus "force" consumers to save, the released resources being transferred from the production of consumer goods to investment. In the nineteenth century the nation's commercial banks were an important source of the finance needed to sustain entrepreneurial innovation. It is true that available price statistics show deflation to be a more abiding reality than inflation in the years before the Civil War. Yet the substantial volume of involuntary savings generated by the commercial banks kept prices from falling as rapidly as they otherwise would have, given the impact on them of productivity growth.[1]

The effect of bank loans on prices highlights the dual role of commercial banks. In the very process of extending credit, they created money, and this duality made for monetary instability. This then was their dilemma: the public wanted abundant credit, but at the same time it wanted money whose value could be counted on. It was difficult for the banks to fill both needs simultaneously. Of course, the "public" had multifaceted interests. As always, for example, creditors stood to lose and debtors to gain by cheapening the value of money. More germane to the years before the 1850s is a suggested association between the "credit creation effect" of commercial banking, on the one hand, and the spatial expansion of the economy, on the other, and from mid-century on, between the "fund concentration effect" and growth in both capital intensity and the scale of enterprise. We can see these relationships more clearly if we begin at the beginning and build the structure of commercial banking brick by brick.[2]

A commercial bank performs four basic functions. It transfers sums from one account to another when ordered to do so by check; it issues banknotes, makes loans, and accepts deposits. All these functions, except that of issue, had been performed in the colonial period by merchants, who served also as exporters, importers, wholesalers, retailers, and in other diverse ways. With the growth of population, output, and trade, widening demand for services enabled people to specialize in single functions, and incorporated commercial banks rose as institutional intermediaries between those who had money to lend (depositors) and those who wished to borrow it. This centralization or pooling of loanable funds must have enhanced their productivity by creating economies of scale in lending; at the same time it reduced the risk of loss on loans by formalizing the process by which credit-worthiness was ascertained. The signature of a known and respected businessman on an IOU (promissory note) was often sufficient, even without collateral security, for a loan to be granted. Bills of exchange—orders to pay specific sums 30 to 120 days after sight, which exporters drew on importers abroad and then sold to a bank—could similarly be "discounted" for cash or credit on the bank's books. To discount, of course, was to deduct in advance an interest charge which the bank earned by its willingness (and ability) to wait till the note or bill matured before presenting it for payment. Interest charges were the principal and often sole source of a bank's earnings.

When a bank lent money, it did so either by issuing banknotes or by opening an account in the name of the borrower and crediting the sum to that account. (When a depositor brought coin to the bank for safekeeping, a similar credit would be entered to his account, which may explain why loans made in this form were called deposits.) Borrowers were then given a supply of checks, each of which ordered the bank to pay the sum designated on its face to a specified recipient. (If that recipient had an account at the same bank, the check was in effect an order to pay by transferring the sum from the account of the drawer to that of the payee.) The extent to which banks made loans in this fashion in the early antebellum years is debated—and probably long will be because of the impossibility of deciding what proportion of the deposits listed on surviving bank balance sheets represents "lodged" deposits and what proportion "created" deposits. Yet the commonly held view that the use of checks was unimportant until just after the Civil War is surely mistaken.[3] Indeed, there is good reason for believing that checks drawn on created deposits were important from an early date in the United States, certainly in the great commercial cities. Pelatiah Webster testified in 1791 that the practice of withdrawing sums by check instead of in the form of banknotes was almost universal in the Bank of North America in the 1780s, but the evidence is clearer that customers were withdrawing their own lodged deposits of cash rather than deposits created by the bank in making a loan.[4]

The testimony of Alexander Hamilton, however, is unambiguous. In his "Report on a National Bank" (1790) Hamilton remarks that every loan which a bank makes is, in its first shape, a book credit which is often merely transferred to different creditors, "circulating as such and performing the office of money until someone, into whose possession it has come, decides to use it in cancellation of his debt to the bank, or to call for its conversion into coin or notes."[5] And in 1810 Eric Bollman observed that most large payments were made not in specie (coined gold or silver) but in "bank credit, rendered portable, transferable, and divisible into exact sums, by the contrivance of checks." These credits the bank "creates and multiplies at pleasure," becoming a "mine and a mint."[6] As early as the 1790s the Baltimore merchant Robert Oliver drew checks on Maryland banks about one of every three times he made payments of any kind. So long as both drawer and payee had accounts at the same bank—common in the relatively small communities of the early nineteenth century—the bank itself served as "clearing house." It simply debited (charged) the drawer's account—a page in a ledger across the top of which the name of a person or institution, or another title, was written—and credited the payee's account. The drawer then had less and the payee more funds to his credit. These accounts, like those of merchants, were kept by the rules of double-entry bookkeeping, which signified nothing of legerdemain and everything of good housekeeping. Recall that the basic principle of double entry is simply this: because every business transaction has a dual aspect, with something being given and something else received, the record keeping of the transaction must also be dual in nature. The account for the asset given must be credited and the account for the asset received debited. In this way the businessman might keep track of the changes in the forms of his property wrought by daily transactions. Thus if, for example, a bank discounted a merchant's $100 IOU for banknotes, it credited the cash account $94 and debited the notes receivable account $100. The different of $6 between the two sums it entered as a credit to its interest account.[7]

Most bank loans took the form of banknotes.[8] These were institutional IOUs, promises on the part of the bank to pay in specie, to a named individual or to the bearer on demand, the sum specified on the face of the banknote. Because of that promise, banks had to keep in their vaults some proportion of their total liabilities in the form of specie. But what proportion? And were bankers generally aware that deposits, like banknotes, were also liabilities? Indeed, they could readily be converted to banknotes by anyone cashing a check or receiving a credit on the bank's books permitting a subsequent withdrawal of banknotes. As to deposits, the evidence is unclear. Apparently not till 1842 did a state (namely, Louisiana) require the keeping of specified specie reserves against both forms of liability. Bankers were none too clear about reserves either. Experience soon taught what the average day's demand for specie was likely to be, and except in the case of banks on which a heavy demand for silver was likely to fall for use in the trade to the East Indies or China or for other export purposes, or banks whose reputability had been jeopardized by hesitancy or failure to keep the commitment to redeem notes on demand, those demands were readily calculable and guarded against. Lodged deposits of specie also augmented reserves, especially when rates of dollar exchange abroad were favorable to the dollar, and specie imports came in. But specie could also go out when the exchange rate rose above the specie export point. The trading nations of the nineteenth century operated on the basis of *fixed exchange rates,* and it is better to be clear about the meaning of this term too.[9]

The precious metal content not only of the dollar but also of the pound, franc, and other national monetary units was stipulated by the laws of the countries involved. In the case of the United States, the Coinage Act of 1792 defined the dollar as consisting of 371.25 grams of pure silver and 24.75 grams of pure gold. (Following Hamilton's advice in his *Report on the Establishment of a Mint* that "to annul the use of either of the metals, as money, is to abridge the quantity of circulating medium," Congress adopted a bimetallic standard.)[10] Since British law defined the pound sterling to consist of 1718.7 grams of pure silver, it followed that, in terms of the law, or mint par, one pound sterling equaled $4.63. This mint par of exchange, however, necessarily differed from the market rate of exchange, which was determined not by law but rather by the supply and demand for pounds sterling by Americans. The supply of sterling exchange—that is, bills of exchange drawn by Americans on the British—was largely determined by exports of goods and services to Great Britain and to other parts of the commercial world whose importers had credit balances on which Americans might be instructed to draw for payments of goods, or in payment for services such as freights earned by American vessels or insurance provided by American companies. The demand for sterling exchange, on the other hand, was largely determined by the needs of American merchants to pay for imports of goods and services. Like any other price, the exchange rate was thus determined by the relationship between supply and demand. If supply exceeded demand, the market rate tended to fall beneath the mint par of exchange; if demand exceeded supply, the rate tended to rise above mint par. But there was a point beyond which it was unlikely to rise. This was the "gold export point," the level at which it became cheaper to procure gold (or silver) coin and to insure and ship it abroad than to buy a bill of exchange. The specie was obtained from commercial banks by the simple procedure of presenting banknotes for redemption, and the greater the loss of specie, the more a bank had to curtail its loans and discounts. For obvious reasons, merchants withdrawing specie were not popular with bankers. Nevertheless, the system was an automatic, self-regulating one, with the supply of banknotes and deposits rising and falling in accordance with the demands of business.[11] At least in theory.

In practice, numerous banks, either from ignorance of proper reserve ratios or from lack of proper restraint on the penchant for profit, sometimes over-expanded their volume of credit, especially in times of rising prices and profit expectations on the part of farmers and planters as well as of merchants. Prudent bankers tended to guide their credit operations in accordance with the "real bills" doctrine, which called for short-term loans that would be liquidated by the sale of goods whose purchase had been financed by the loans. But most discounted "accommodation" paper from time to time, paper arising from an accommodating exchange of IOUs between two businessmen rather than from a genuine commercial transaction, and some also converted short-term loans into long-term ones by frequent renewals. Prudence tended to favor the interests of merchants in the eastern commercial centers, long-term loans those of agriculturalists in the South and West as well. Some of the latter, however, were also made to industrialists.[12]

Conservatism appears to have been the hallmark of the earliest banks. When the new government under the Constitution went into effect in 1789, there were only three commercial banks in the country. The Bank of North America, chartered by the Continental Congress in 1781, and the banks of New York and Massachusetts. Apparently the thinking of the time favored the establishment of a single quasi-governmental bank in each state, an institution that would operate under private management in the public interest.[13] Hamilton formulated his defense of the First Bank of the United States in precisely these terms. The overriding fear of political leaders was that a multiplicity of banks would swamp the channels of trade with depreciated paper, repeating the inflationary experience of the 1780s with continental and state bills of credit, hobbling the functions of government. This is why Robert Morris asked Congress to grant a monopoly for thirty years to the Bank of North America, and why the Congress obliged, stipulating that "no other bank, public or private, [be] permitted during that period."[14]

The conservative character of the bank's loan and discount policy is clearly revealed in a statement made by Thomas Willing, its president, to Hamilton in October 1789. The capital of the Bank of North America, Willing said, "is exactly 728.400 dollars . . . "our paper in Circulation has never been much above half this Sum." "We are all of us Stockholders," he added, "and have a character to support and Shall never pass our paper into Circulation without having what we deem good Security for it."[15] The Constitutionalist majority in Pennsylvania's Council of Censors warned in September 1784 that the Bank of North America might become "a monster of weight and influence, and be able to counteract and overrule our legislative proceedings," but a modern student finds that the leadership of the anti-Bank Constitutionalists consisted mainly of merchants, manufacturers, lawyers, speculators, and professionals. "Entrepreneurial opportunity, not agrarianism," he notes, "was the mainspring of their democracy." In the spring of 1784 they had unsuccessfully tried to launch a competitor, the Bank of Pennsylvania.[16]

From this evidence it seems clear that the ultraconservative policies of the Bank of North America were failing to meet the credit needs of a significant portion of the business community of Philadelphia and its environs. A similar situation appears to have obtained in New York, for by the beginning of 1792 a third bank was operating in that city. The conservative policies followed by the administrators of the First Bank of the United States, chartered by Congress in January 1790, were even more serious because of the broad reach afforded by that institution's eventual eight branches. In part, that conservatism, as we have seen, was a product of the fiscal needs of the Treasury. So severe was the drain on the Bank's funds that the institution was simply incapable of fully servicing the legitimate needs of commerce and manufacture. By 1796 the Bank's steadily increasing loans to the government totaled $6 million, so depriving the institution of operating capital that it was obliged between 1793 and 1795 to borrow almost three-quarters of a million dollars in Amsterdam. On the day of Hamilton's resignation, loans to the government amounted to $4.7 million, virtually half the Bank's authorized capital.[17]

The extent to which the Bank of the United States was an integral part of government has been insufficiently appreciated. It is of course well known that three-fifths of the Bank's capital stock of $10 million was made up of government securities, that the government subscribed one-fifth of the stock, and that the Bank served government as an agent in the payment of interest on the funded domestic debt, received subscriptions to new government loans, paid the salaries of government officials, and conducted sinking fund operations. The Bank also helped the Treasury in its foreign-exchange dealings and in the collection of customs bonds. It made loans to government, provided a depository for federal funds, and transferred them from place to place without charge. The Bank served indeed, as Hamilton said, as "an indispensable engine in the administration of the finances."[18]

It came close to being an arm of government. Two of its eight branches, those in New Orleans and Washington, were established at the request of the government. The Bank's officers appear to have regarded themselves as government officials. At any rate, the cashier of the New York branch—in those days the cashier was the chief operating officer—in requesting in 1800 that the parent board increase his salary, pointed out that it had been fixed in 1792 and that "all the officers of Government have had a considerable augmentation of Salary since that period."[19] Certainly there can be no mistaking the parent board's awareness, to cite its own language, of "how intimately the Bank of the United States is connected with the Government of the Union, by forming an essential Link in the Chain of its monied Operations, which constitutes the Foundation of the Public Credit."[20]

The relationship to government would alone have imposed a conservative loan and discount policy on the Bank even in the absence of the received wisdom of the real bills doctrine. Fragmentary remains from the minutes of the Board of Directors[21] disclose that by 1795, at least, the parent bank was aware of its power and duty to keep the supply of bank credit within careful limits. In an important policy statement of October 1795, the board made it clear that it regarded itself as guardian of the "System of Bank Credit." That month it made two significant recommendations to the branches: first, that a branch accept only the notes of banks located in the same city as itself, and second, that the branches expand their discounts with great caution. The board deplored "the recent Institution of so many Banks," especially what it called "the inferior order of them." Because of their small capitals and limited resources, such banks became vulnerable when mismanaged, when trade stagnated, or when prices fell. "Unfortunately, the Derangement of any one Institution," the board said, "would create an Alarm & a serious Crisis; which would deeply injure the reputation of all."

An excessive number of banks overexpanded the supply of credit. In the words of the board, "It must be Strikingly evident to those who have contemplated the Business of Banking, that its Resources & Advantages have their Limits." In 1795 the board believed these limits to be defined "by the Extent & Value of the alienable & active Property of the Country."

> If Bank Credits far exceed the Sum that is necessary to furnish the Means of Transfer for the Same, they degenerate into an Evil of a very alarming Nature, for by being too great and disproportionate to their Object, they tend to raise to an undue Value, every Article they represent, & at the same time force into Circulation More Paper than it can possibly retain;—the redundancy of which, as it cannot be usefully employed, will return upon the Bank, & extract Specie in Exchange therefore, to be sent abroad as an active & productive Capital.

Implicit in the board's statement, it should be stressed, is the concept of a fixed amount of wealth; the proper function of bank credit was apparently not to increase that amount but to facilitate its transfer. The emphasis on the importance of safeguarding specie reserves ought also be noted. Available balance sheets for the period 1792–1800 suggest a generally high degree of success in this regard. The ratio of banknotes in circulation to specie holdings was generally quite small (see Table 6). While part of the deposits probably arose from Bank loans rather than from sums lodged in the Bank for reasons of safety, the conclusion that the Bank followed a markedly conservative policy with regard to credit expansion is well supported by the evidence.

The parent board also sought to prevent excessive drains of specie abroad. In February 1805, for example, the board, "after duly considering the present scarcity of specie and the continued drain thereof in aid of commercial pursuits," decided that it was their "indispensable duty . . . to prevent, *at this time,* the exportation of the precious metals, on which the safety of our monied institutions principally depend[s]."[22]

In May 1806 Samuel Breck, the board's most influential member after the retirement of William Bingham of Philadelphia in 1801, suggested that a rise in the exchange rate above par serve as a signal for restraint. Such a rise, he urged, "ought always govern our discounts." His reasons are compelling: "altho' there may be a sufficient sum of Specie in our Vaults for Bank operations, yet it is well known that the Balance in favor of England against this country, is little short . . . of *Eighteen Millions of Dollars Annually,* which with our East India Trade[,] would not fail, if any material Branch of our foreign Commerce should be checked, of producing the exportation of the precious metals to an amount that might embarrass our Banks"—"an event," Breck added, "that must by all means, be avoided."[23]

Bingham had an alternative criterion for the proper volume of loans and discounts. "Experience will soon convince you," he wrote on behalf of the board in April 1800 to the new branch at Norfolk, "that the average amount of your Deposits, forms the essential Basis of Bank Business, enabling you to extend, or compelling you to contract, the Sphere of your operations." In this context Bingham was surely thinking of lodged deposits. (What is interesting in the remark is the modernity of its substitution of deposits for capital as the basis for ascertaining the proper volume of loans and discounts.)[24]

But a growing population and trade created a need for comparable growth in the volume of credit, for a policy of accommodation rather than of conservative constraint, by the Bank of the United States. Sharp increases in the number of state banks and in their capital stock represented a response to this need. During the life of the First Bank (1791–1811), banks chartered by the states increased in number from 5 to 117, their combined capital stock from $4,600,000 to $66,290,000. Most of the increase took place in the Middle Atlantic and New England states. The number of banks in the latter region rose more rapidly than elsewhere, increasing from 2 to 54, but the growth in the region's capital stock, which rose from $1,300,000 to $19,285,000, was

Table 6. The volume of business of the First Bank of the United States and its branches:[a] financial position at or near[b] year's end, 1792–1800 (rounded to nearest dollar).

Year	Bills and notes discounted	Specie	Circulation	Ratio of specie to circulation (Specie) (notes)	Circulation (percent increase over 1792) (1792 = 100%)	Deposits[c]	Deposits (percent increase over 1792 (1792 = 100%)
1792	5,430,689	976,910	1,689,486	1 to 1.73		2,657,359	
1793	5,343,712	1,201,884	2,022,501	1 to 1.68	19.7	3,301,587	24.2
1794	6,383,315	745,735	3,677,805	1 to 4.93	117.7	2,966,819	11.6
1795	7,019,117	1,436,780	3,653,715	1 to 2.54	116.3	2,764,370	4.0
1796	7,902,070	1,579,407	3,383,136	1 to 2.14	100.2	3,742,688	40.8
1797	8,509,501	2,707,596	3,126,149	1 to 1.15	85.0	5,659,155	113.0
1798	9,434,097	3,075,303	4,079,391	1 to 1.33	141.5	5,201,030	95.7
1799	11,278,251	4,001,358	4,276,685	1 to 1.07	153.1	7,412,940	179.0
1800	11,498,179	5,671,949	5,469,063	1 to 0.96	223.7	9,869,732	271.4

Source: Consolidated balance sheets prepared by James O. Wettereau.

a. Boston, New York, Baltimore, and Charleston. A small volume of business at the Norfolk branch is included in the figure for 1800.

b. The year-end figures for 1800 are taken from balance sheets ranging in date from August 23 to November 11. The widest variation in any of the other years is December 1 to January 1.

c. Deposits include those made by the federal government and by individuals. They include bank loans and sums deposited for safekeeping, although the proportions of each are unknown.

considerably less than that which occurred in the Middle Atlantic states. In that region the number of banks rose from 3 to 41, but the capitalization increased from $3,300,000 in 1791 to $34,155,000 in 1811. By then the southern states, which had no state bank at all till 1801, had a total of 10 banks, their combined capital amounting to $7,850,000. In the southwestern states the number rose from 1 in 1804 to 6 in 1811, and the capital from $600,000 to $1,300,000. The western states had a single bank capitalized at $500,000 in 1803 and 5 capitalized at $2,200,000 in 1811.[25]

The expiration of the First Bank's charter in 1811 removed external restraints on the expansion of credit; thus encouraged, state banks quickly multiplied in numbers and in the volume of their loans and discounts. Between 1811 and 1816 they doubled in both numbers and authorized capital stock. More significantly, total note issues more than tripled during those years, reaching a level in 1816–1818 that was not to be attained again for fifteen years. Not even the specie brake was on. Runs on banks induced by the British raid on Washington in August 1814 quickly spread to Baltimore, Philadelphia, and New York, and soon suspension of specie payments was general throughout the country, except in New England. The banknote currency circulated at a variety of discounts from place to place, and since the government was compelled to accept it in order to collect the taxes and imposts due— there being no other money to accept—the public finances became so disordered as to threaten all the operations of the federal government. It was in this context of nationwide inflation and governmental derangement that Congress decided to charter a Second Bank of the United States in the expectation that the institution would be able to force the state banks to resume specie payments and restore soundness to the currency. After concessions granted the state banks at the insistence of the secretary of Treasury, who was "more interested in a nominal return to specie payments and the immediate convenience of the Treasury" than in a sound currency, resumption occurred in 1817.[26]

Historians critical of the judgment and managerial competence of the first president of the newly chartered Bank, William Jones, have many just grounds for indictment, but they should not overlook how difficult it would have been for him to refuse to comply with the demands of the Treasury. At best Jones was pedestrian in his stewardship, and he profited financially from fraudulent operations by the Baltimore branch. He is universally condemned for his failure to check an extravagant overexpansion of note issues on the part of the Bank's branches in the South and West and to curb the excesses of the state banks in those regions. Both catered to and stimulated still more a wildly speculative demand for land that had been initiated by poor European crops and rising prices of American agricultural staples after the War of 1812. In merely three years, from 1816 to 1818, the amount of state bank capital nearly quadrupled in the Southwest, while in the West the number of banks tripled. According to Ralph Catterall, the early-twentieth-century historian of the

Second Bank of the United States, that institution's "entire capital" of $35 million "was rapidly being shifted to the South and West" during the same period. The eastern branches were being drained of their specie to redeem the notes issued by the branches in the South and West. This was because the Bank had decided to allow the branches to redeem all notes, regardless of which branch had issued them, and because the normal flow of notes was from the South and West to the East.[27]

The reckoning was not long in coming. Prices of agricultural products began to fall on international markets in the first quarter of 1818, credit contraction followed suit, and in the final quarter of 1818 foreign demand declined precipitously. The wholesale price index number of United States exports, which was dominated by the prices of agricultural raw materials, fell from approximately 212 at the end of 1818 to 125 in the middle of 1819. Exports themselves fell from $73,854,437 in 1818 to $50,976,838 in 1819. International price movements, in a word, were the fundamental cause of the domestic contraction that soon occurred.

Its precise timing, however, was influenced and probably determined by the Bank's fiscal responsibilities. The first big share of the Louisiana bonds issued by the federal government fell due on October 21, 1818, with $3.5 million of the $4.5 million to be redeemed in foreign hands. The Bank faced the problem of making these large remittances to foreign bondholders at a time when its specie reserves were dangerously low. On July 20, 1818, specie stocks totaled $3,357,000, and demand liabilities amounted to $22,372,000. The Bank had been borrowing specie abroad—more than $7 million between July 1817 and July 1818—in a hopeless effort to ride out the tremendous inflation and maintain specie payments. Furthermore, it had been demanding in vain the collection of balances due from state banks in the South and West. When therefore it decided to curtail operations, it did the only thing possible in the situation. Once more, however, we must take note of the important part in monetary contraction that was played by the fiscal policy of the government.[28]

The ensuing depression of 1818–1820 was a severe one, characterized by great contraction in the money supply, falling prices, unemployment, business and farm bankruptcies, and severe human distress. Catterall's assessment of fundamental fault has the ring of moral fervor:

> The keenest distress fell upon the West. In that section there never existed the slightest justification for the preposterously large loans of the bank, and, as the state banks had been equally generous, the inflation and over-trading were unparalleled. Worse yet, much of the indebtedness had been created by loans to farmers, who had no security to offer excepting mortgages on real estate, absurdly overvalued, and absolutely unsalable during a commercial crisis. A moment's reflection should have convinced anyone that these new and insignificant towns of the West could not possibly pay debts as vast as those contracted in New York and Boston, and should never have been per-

mitted to borrow such enormous sums. *Of course, the money had been mostly expended on permanent improvements, and could not be repaid on demand.* The borrowers never expected to pay when the notes came due, the usual custom being to renew over and over again.

The historian is addressing the situation in the West in these remarks, but he clearly means to characterize the South in essentially the same terms, for he adds that "in the South there were difficulties of like nature."[29]

I have with good reason italicized this identification of the main use to which the borrowed funds were put. A more recent study of cyclical patterns in the sale of public lands makes the important point that the high level of sales in 1818–19 "is to be attributed almost wholly to the course of activity in the newer areas, especially in Alabama," where receipts soared from $1,718,000 in 1817 to $8,676,000 in 1818 before subsiding to $4,148,000 in 1819.[30] The westward movement of the cotton belt and its surging output hardly hesitated in the face of foreclosed mortgages, losses, and bank failures. Production climbed steadily during these years, increasing from 262,000 bales in 1818 to 349,000 in 1819, and then, after dipping slightly to 335,000 in 1820, reaching 377,000 in 1821 and 439,000 in 1822. It would not be the last time that the more fundamental motions of the economy would continue despite financial disaster. Is it possible that an econometric exercise in socio-economic cost accounting might reveal that the losses incurred by government, banks, and business firms were more than compensated by a more rapid and extensive development of the economy—and all that this entailed?[31]

Whether or not this should prove to be the case, implicit in this account are the peculiar problems faced by growing frontier areas in their need for capital. The older sectors and regions of the country appear to have experienced little difficulty in raising the capital required for expansion. This was particularly true of foreign trade, but even nascent manufacturing enterprise in New England and the Middle Atlantic states was able to tap the resources of commercial banks, frequently obtaining renewals of short-term loans. Some of the manufacturers bore names once familiar in trade, especially in New England, and an older reputability doubtless stood them well in their time of new need. But older reputability alone cannot explain the finding that about 55 percent of the loans obtained from all sources by eight New England cotton textile mill firms between 1837 and 1860 came from commercial banks. From 1847 to 1860 the firms obtained an average of $1 million a year in bank loans. Something more is needed, namely, the superior information which investors had of resources and opportunities available in areas close to home. Frontiers were far away, in time as well as in space.[32]

A national market in information did not yet exist. Even when distant opportunities were perceived, it was difficult to exploit them, for a developed system of financial intermediaries was not yet in existence either. Loanable funds were far more abundant and available in Europe and on the East Coast than in the West and South. At the end of the War of 1812 the capital stock of the commercial banks in the Middle Atlantic states amounted to $67,140,000; in New England, $24,495,000. In contrast, the southern states had $13,797,000, the southwestern states $3,400,000, and the western states $6,400,000. Albert Gallatin reveals his customary perspicacity in the way he calls attention in 1831 to "the newly settled parts of the country, which present a state of things, different from that found in any other part of the civilized world, and to which, therefore, even the most generally admitted principles of political economy will not always apply."

> Within a very short time, our numerous new settlements, which in a few years have extended from the Mohawk to the great western lakes, and from the Allegheny to the Mississippi and beyond it, afford the spectacle of a large population, with the knowledge, the intelligence and the habits which belong to civilized life, amply supplied with the means of subsistence, but without any other active capital, but agricultural products, for which, in many instances, they have no market.[33]

Scarcity of "active capital" and lack of markets were basic conditions of early frontier life. Since capital did not as a rule flow from wealthier areas of the United States or from Europe "to finance transportation and other improvements necessary to make markets for the resources and products at a speed sufficient to equalize rates of return all around," bank credit creation "became a substitute for a developed system of intermediaries."[34] Between 1819 and 1837 the share of the nation's authorized capital stock possessed by commercial banks in the New England and Middle Atlantic regions declined from 64.1 percent to 49.6 percent, whereas the share of the South and West rose from 35.9 percent to 50.4 percent. The percentile change in the southwestern states far exceeded that of any other region, rising from 8.7 percent to 26.5 percent. That of the West declined from 16.7 percent to 10.5 percent. In both regions, however, states issued charters of incorporation to special kinds of banks. "Property banks" in the South, particularly, helped meet the need for rural credit. A historian of banking in Louisiana explains the arrangements made for putting into operation that state's first property bank, chartered by the legislature in 1827 as the Consolidated Association of the Planters of Louisiana. "The planters were to exchange $2.5 million in mortgages on their own property for the bank's $2 million of capital stock. The bank would then use the mortgages as collateral for $2 million of bonds which would be sold abroad to raise a specie reserve."[35]

The relationship of the Second Bank of the United States to the credit needs of the South and West following the administration of William Jones is an intriguing one. Under the presidency of Langdon Cheves, who succeeded Jones in 1819, contact was decidedly minimal. Cheves "clearly perceived that the essential cause of the bank's embarrassment" lay in the business done by the southern and western branches, and the latter were immediately directed not to issue their notes. The parent bank in Philadelphia itself ceased to purchase and collect exchange on the South and West. In sum, under Cheves "the Bank of the United States might almost as well have been non-existent, so far as the West and Southwest were concerned."[36] The initial impulse of Nicholas Biddle, who replaced Cheves in 1823, was to continue in this policy. "We have had enough, and more than enough," Biddle says in one of his first official letters as president, "of banking in the interior. We have been crippled and almost destroyed by it. It is time to concentrate our business—to bank where there is some use and profit in it . . . to make at present the large commercial cities the principal scene of our operations."[37]

Although Biddle's policy called for an end to the discounting of promissory notes on personal security in the South and West, he soon adopted a plan to increase the currency and credit available there. The essence of the plan was to have the branches in those regions purchase inland (domestic) bills of exchange and issue the branch's own banknotes in payment. When sold, the proceeds of the bills provided a fund for the redemption of the banknotes, an arrangement which "made possible extensive loans in those sections without incurring the danger of transferring the capital thither from other offices."[38]

Nevertheless, the loans were short-term ones. Even the New York office was instructed to discount paper at only 60 and 90 days, although it might take notes at 120 days if "beyond all exception, and for a good customer." A rare exception to Biddle's concentration on short-term loans was an authorization by the Board of directors to discount six-month paper during a period of business slack in 1827. Loans on real estate or stock security were forbidden. Foreign exchange was of little consequence till 1826; by 1827–28 it was an important source of earnings to the Bank as well as of convenience—and savings—to southern factors and planters and northern importers. Factors or planters exporting cotton and other produce drew bills on foreign importers and sold them to the branches of the Bank in the South and West, whence they were remitted to the northern and eastern branches for sale to importers desiring a means of payment abroad. Existence of a bill market in the southern branches resulted in favorable prices for southerners, while the available supply in the North tended to lower bill prices in that region. Thus the system tended to stabilize both domestic and foreign rates of exchange. By 1828 Biddle had extended the dealings of the Bank in the Southwest and West "out of all proportion, and in doing so had returned to that policy of extensive interior loans of which, in 1823, he felt sure that the bank had had "enough and more than enough." An even larger extension lay just ahead.[39]

Total purchases of inland bills in those regions had amounted to only $2,540,000 in 1824. In 1828 the total was $8,140,000; in 1831, $27,000,000; and in 1832, $40,900,000. The volume of purchases of domestic exchange in the West and Southwest thus trebled from 1824 to 1828, was more than ten times greater in 1831 than in 1824, and was sixteen times greater in 1832. That mounting volume represented increasingly large proportions of the Bank's entire inland exchange business, rising from about 29 percent of the whole in 1824 to 32 percent in 1827, 46 percent in 1829, 56 percent in 1830, and 60 percent in 1832. Small wonder that the widespread hatred accorded the Bank in these regions in 1818–1820 changed to widespread appreciation and support by 1832![40]

The standard biography of Biddle emphasizes the nationalist cast of his mind by pointing out his early advocacy of a protective tariff, internal improvements, and the Bank of the United States. As a member of the Pennsylvania legislature in 1810 Biddle had unsuccessfully sought to interest that body in supporting internal improvements, and in 1824 he had joined with Matthew Carey in organizing the Pennsylvania Society for the Promotion of Internal Improvements. According to his biographer, Biddle's "willingness as president of the Bank to aid the financing [of the railroad] was one of the contributing reasons for its rapid introduction into the country." He quotes with evident approval, but does not otherwise document, a statement by the editor of *Niles Register* in 1832 that two-thirds of the loans of the Bank had been made for the "direct encouragement and extension of agriculture and the mechanic arts, the promotion of internal improvements, and erection of all sorts of buildings," and remarks that after President Andrew Jackson's veto of the Maysville Road bill in 1830, "the Bank, through direct and indirect aid to private companies and states . . . tried to take the place of the national government." What a pity it is that the ledgers, journals, and other accounting records of the institution do not appear to have survived, for they would permit us to specify the length, number, and value of long-term loans for nonmercantile purposes. But we do know that in 1829 Biddle offered a loan of $8.5 million to Pennsylvania at 5 percent and that in September 1830 he was "eagerly inquiring as to the chances of getting Louisiana and Mississippi stocks." These efforts, though unsuccessful, reveal his views as president on the proper uses of the Bank's resources. Another index is his willingness, following the defeat of his attempt to win renewal of the Bank's charter, to lend to Pennsylvania in return for a charter from that state (granted in 1836) up to $6 million for the completion of its canal and railroad, to subscribe a total of $675,000 to the stock of any private railroad or canal company that the legislature wished to encourage, and to pay a bonus of $2 million.[41]

These facts, together with the very substantial loans to the West and Southwest, suggest a frame of values somewhat removed from that of a banker originally intent on concentrating the resources of his institution on self-liquidating loans to merchants in foreign trade. In addition, Biddle's developing values can be seen in a letter written to the cashier of the Baltimore branch of the Bank on March 3, 1828:

For some months past the importations from France & England have been very excessive, and without great caution the results may prove highly disastrous. The low price of our exported articles and the tardiness with which the crop of Exchange from the south comes into the market this year have diminished the means for paying for these importations, and resort has of course been had to the exportation of coin. The natural corrective of this evil—for beyond a certain point it is an evil—is the diminution of the business of those institutions which are the depositories of the coin, which by rendering Bank credits less easy makes them more valuable, & by depriving the importers of the artificial facilities to obtain money, diminishes the means & the temptation to continue these importations, and of course lessens the demand for & the price of, exchange. This course which all prudent Banking companies should adopt, is the only true & ultimate restraint on excessive importations . . . The whole evil therefore lies in an overbanking which occasions an overtrading, and the whole remedy lies in preventing this overbanking. One of our most respectable & extensive merchants trading to France assured me a few days ago that he was alarmed at these excessive importations & had written to France to send no more, as he anticipated a great glut of French goods with all its train of ruinous consequences. Agai.ist these it is the business of the Bank of the U. States to guard. It has accordingly placed itself in an attitude of security & strength, so as to interpose whenever it may be necessary to protect the community.[42]

Certainly Biddle makes clear in this letter that in his view "overbanking" by the state banks leads to "overtrading," to excessive importations, which in turn lead to a diminution of the specie reserves of the banking system; that not only is this something to be avoided, but also that it is the proper business of the Bank to take steps to avoid it in order to "protect the community." The language is that of a central banker, but for the moment that is not my point. Can one legitimately infer from this language that Biddle has taken a stand in opposition to the interests of import merchants in order to safeguard the reserves of the banks for other uses? If so, does the evidence of his interest in the domestic economy support the speculation that the other uses he has in mind are, in part at least, internal and developmental, rather than external and exploitative of resources already in being? One may speculate, of course, but that is all the evidence permits us to do. The possibility, however, is an intriguing one. The least we can say is that Biddle thought it a proper function of the Bank to limit the outflow of specie to foreign shores, to protect the nation's specie reserves. Were a central banker today to operate within a similar system of international settlements characterized by fixed exchange rates, he or she would almost certainly approve Biddle's views.

Does this mean that Biddle's bank was a central bank, a bank that assumed responsibility for the success of the banking system as a whole by acting as lender of last resort in time of crisis? The answer is that Biddle sometimes acted as we would expect a central banker to have acted, and sometimes in opposite ways. In 1825 his decisions increased the severity of a credit crunch instead of relieving it. He sold government bonds instead of purchasing them on the open market, and thus sucked up purchasing power when he should have pumped more in. The sales strengthened the reserves of the Bank at a time when the correct central banking policy would have been to reduce them somewhat in the interest of increasing the money in circulation and easing the crisis. The result was that "a sharp drop occurred in the total of Bank credit outstanding in November, 1825, just when the business community would have been most grateful for an expansive policy."[43] In 1828, on the other hand, and despite his advocacy of limitation on facilities granted to New York importers, Biddle did not fail to give reasonable aid to the business community at a time of emergency. That year the Bank increased its total discounts and bills from 33.7 million to 39.2 million, and its notes in circulation by about 1.3 million. Biddle's behavior during the course of the "Bank War" with President Jackson is surely no ordinary case by which to judge whether his actions narrowly served the stockholders of his own institution or the larger interests of the nation. Persuaded of the Bank's importance to the latter, he deliberately curtailed credit from August 1833 to September 1834 in an effort to convince the administration and the country that it would be folly not to renew the Bank's charter. The upshot was "a crisis which in 1834 forced discount rates as high as 18 to 36 percent and brought great distress to the business community."[44]

Despite this unhappy dénouement, the Bank probably came as close as any institution of its day to being a central bank.[45] Certainly it succeeded in maintaining a sound national currency. The mechanism by which it did so was a simple one.[46] The currency was very largely made up of banknotes, most of which were placed in circulation by the state banks. This being the case, payments made to the federal government— for example, by purchasers of public land or by merchants owing customs duties—were likely to be made in that form. And far more payments were made to the federal government than to any other transactor of business in the nation. In consequence, the government deposited large quantities of state banknotes in the Bank of the United States and its branches. Of course the state banks also received deposits of banknotes which the Bank of the United States and its branches had issued. But as a rule they had far fewer of the Bank's than the Bank had of theirs. The Bank and its branches were usually the creditors of the state banks, after exchanging notes, a process which Biddle described as follows: "Every morning the clerks from this Bank [that is, the parent bank in Philadelphia] and the State Banks meet and interchange the notes received on the preceding day. The balances are struck accordingly."[47] In the smaller towns settlements were made weekly rather than daily. As creditors of the state banks, the Bank of the United States and its branches could insist on payment in specie, and it was the threat to do so or its implementation that induced the state banks to keep their loans and discounts in bounds, and this in turn enabled them to redeem their notes in specie at par.

How important was this achievement? Our answer must be that it was important indeed if we look at it from the point of view of the federal government. Congress had chartered the Bank of the United States in 1816 for that specific purpose—to restore specie payments and a sound currency. In essence, the law made the Bank a monetary means to a fiscal objective, that of restoring order in federal receipts and payments. It was expected to serve as the fiscal agent of the government in a number of other ways as well, and its charter made this plain. The Bank and its branches were to furnish depositories for federal monies and transfer them free of charge from place to place when ordered to do so by the secretary of the Treasury. It was to serve as the agency through which payments were to be made to public creditors. Not least, it was to lend money to the federal government, the charter stipulating that no loan should exceed $500,000.[48] In sum, as Secretary of the Treasury A. J. Dallas observed in December 1815 to John C. Calhoun, it was not "an institution created for the purposes of commerce and profit alone, but more for the purposes of national policy, as an auxiliary in the exercise of some of the highest powers of Government."[49] That was precisely accurate—and precisely the problem. The Bank could not succeed equally well in both its fiscal and its monetary functions. If, as a great commercial bank, larger than any other and a receiver of the government's deposits as well, it could succeed in maintaining sound money, it could not at the same time make available to the expanding population and economy the credit they needed. The objective of sound money forced it to curb not only the loans and discounts of the state banks, but its own volume of business as well. Had it not done so, it would have put in the hands of the state banks the very means they needed to increase their business, namely the notes of the Bank, and this would have entailed surrender of the creditor status essential for the maintenance of sound money.

The money was good but there was not enough of it. The evidence for this is seen in the behavior of prices. Table 7 displays wholesale price indexes for all commodities from 1790 to 1860. Note the rise that occurred in 1793 with the outbreak of the wars of the French Revolution and continued not only through the end of the War of 1812 but for another five years as well, till 1820. Note the downward long-term drift that commences then and lasts till the outbreak of the Civil War, a drift that is interrupted only by speculative surges in the mid-1830s and mid-1850s. The surprising thing about this price behavior is that it took place *despite* large increases in the number of commercial banks and in their note issues and deposits (see Table 8). And that is not all. Even when we add the coined money supplied by the government and talk in terms of the *total* money supply, the conclusion remains unchanged. According to recent estimates, the nominal money supply—demand deposits

Table 7.   Wholesale price indexes for all commodities, 1790–1860
            (1910–1914 = 100).

Year	Index	Year	Index	Year	Index
1790	90	1814	182	1837	115
1791	85	1815	170	1838	110
1792	n.a.	1816	151	1839	112
1793	102	1817	151	1840	95
1794	108	1818	147	1841	92
1795	131	1819	125	1842	82
1796	146	1820	106	1843	75
1797	131	1821	102	1844	77
1798	122	1822	106	1845	83
1799	126	1823	103	1846	83
1800	129	1824	98	1847	90
1801	142	1825	103	1848	82
1802	117	1826	99	1849	82
1803	118	1827	98	1850	84
1804	126	1828	97	1851	83
1805	141	1829	96	1852	88
1806	134	1830	91	1853	97
1807	130	1831	94	1854	108
1808	115	1832	95	1855	110
1809	130	1833	95	1856	105
1810	131	1834	90	1857	111
1811	126	1835	100	1858	93
1812	131	1836	114	1859	95
1813	162			1860	93

Source: Bureau of the Census, *Historical Statistics of the United States, Colonial Times to 1970*
(Washington, D.C.: Government Printing Office, 1976),I, 201–202.

together with currency outside banks (coin and banknotes)—increased from
$0.08 billion in 1819 to $0.58 billion in 1859, or more than sevenfold.[50] Yet
in this same interval the price level *fell*—from an annual average wholesale
index of 131.0 between 1790 and 1819 to an annual average of 96.0 between
1820 and 1859. (If we measure the fall within the period 1820–1859 itself,
the decline, in terms of annual averages per decade, is as follows: 1820–1829
(100.8); 1830–1839 (101.6); 1840–1849 (84.1); 1850–1859 (97.4). The
fact that prices fell during a period in which the nominal supply of money rose
points unmistakably to the real need of a growing population and expanding
economy for increased means of transacting a swelling volume of business.
The growth of the money supply fell short of that need. That being the case,
it is difficult not to conclude that the policy of restraining credit expansion in
the interests of monetary stability was the wrong policy for the times.

Table 8. Banking statistics for selected years, 1815–1860.

Year	Number of state banks	Banknotes issued (millions of dollars)	Deposits (millions of dollars)
1815	208	45	—
1820	307	45	—
1830	330	61	—
1834	506	95	76
1835	704	104	83
1840	901	107	76
1845	707	90	88
1850	824	131	110
1855	1,307	87	190
1860	1,562	207	254

Source: William M. Gouge, *A Short History of Paper-Money and Banking* (New York: B. & S. Collins, 1835), p. 61; and Board of Governors of the Federal Reserve System, *Banking Studies* (Washington, D.C.: Federal Reserve System, 1941), pp. 417–418.

It must be acknowledged, however, that the power of monetary policy to affect the price level was limited by the operation of the international specie standard.[51] Even so, policy was effective within these limits, and there can be but little doubt that the Bank's influence was deflationary. Despite the fact that Nicholas Biddle was a man of broadly national developmental views, he was prevented from implementing them more than he did by his fundamental responsibility for the soundness of the nation's currency. Were the currents of opposition set in motion by his policies responsible for the "Bank War"? Or were other forces involved? Does that "war" deserve the emphasis it has long received in U.S. history?

Historians have long been convinced that the Bank War of the 1830s belongs among the major domestic conflicts of American history, that the struggle between President Jackson and Nicholas Biddle, president of the Bank of the United States, had profound repercussions on social, economic, and political life. To Frederick Jackson Turner, the Bank was an engine of aristocracy, and the contest between Jackson and Biddle one that pitted the capitalist against the pioneer, the few against the democratic majority. Arthur Schlesinger, Jr., accepted Turner's interpretation of the Bank War as a class struggle, but added to Turner's western pioneers the farmers of the South and the workingmen of the East. To Richard Hofstadter neither interpretation made sense. The fundamental struggle of the 1830s took place not between classes but within the capitalist, entrepreneurial class itself, and its antagonists were an older elitist group in possession of exclusive legal privileges and a newer and more numerous younger group demanding legal equality in order to gain its fair share of corporate franchises.[52]

For Hofstadter, the Bank War took on a symbolic significance, the Bank standing for an older privileged order, for inequality before the law. Bray Hammond agreed with Hofstadter that the Bank War was the by-product of an expanding economy, and he pictured the institution as a central bank thwarting the path of multitudes of new businessmen brandishing an agrarian rhetoric, but really intent on easy credit. In Marvin Meyers' sensitively drawn psychological vignette we see schizophrenic, tension-torn Jacksonians with one eye on the main chance and the other on the simple bucolic virtues of their Jeffersonian past, clawing at the Bank as a guilt symbol of all the elements in society which threatened the values of the Old Republic. The Bank War, according to Meyers, was "the great specific mission of Jacksonian Democracy . . . Here the party formed, or found its character. Here was the issue which stood for all issues."[53]

Thus, like a gathering of the curious at the scene of a crime, scholars continue to revisit the dramatic events of the early 1830s, agreed indeed that crime there was, while differing on the identity of the victim, or on the question of whose knife it was that felled mighty Caesar—perhaps we should say Frankenstein, for the word *monster* was the favorite epithet hurled by the Jacksonians at the Bank. "The government will not bow to the monster . . . Andrew Jackson yet lives to put his foot upon the head of the monster and crush him to the dust." Those are the words of Jackson himself, spoken in 1834. "Andrew Jackson," he added, "would never recharter that monster of corruption. Sooner than live in a country where such a power prevailed, he would seek an asylum in the wilds of Arabia."[54]

From all signs that were outward and public, it must be said, the people who elected Jackson president in 1828 must have been at least mildly surprised to learn his real views on the Bank. For the presidential campaign of 1828, like that of 1824, was based on personalities. The Bank was not mentioned in the campaign by either Jackson or John Quincy Adams or by their supporters. After Jackson's election, however, some of the members of his party thought that their political victory entitled them to control the Bank and its branches. They raised the false charge that two of the branches in Kentucky—those at Lexington and Louisville—had tried to influence the election by refusing loans to Jacksonians. That is to say, the charge was that the members of the board of directors at these branches, whose function it was to approve or disapprove loan applications, had rejected applications from supporters of Jackson. Members of Kentucky's delegation in Congress wanted these directors removed and friends of General Jackson installed in their place.[55]

Biddle's first reaction was one of incredulity. "There is no one principle better understood by every officer in the Bank," he wrote Senator Samuel Smith of Maryland in December 1828, "than that he must abstain from politics."[56] He added that he did not know of a single violation of this rule in any part of the Union. Nevertheless, he ordered an investigation of the charge;

the result was that it was refuted by the testimony of board directors of both political parties at the two branch banks in question.

Biddle felt sure that Jackson was not involved in this attempt by Kentucky congressmen to subject the branches to political control. All the superficial evidence confirmed his view. None of the leaders of the coalition that supported Jackson opposed the Bank. John C. Calhoun was the leader of one major faction, and he had been mainly responsible for the passage of the bill chartering the Bank. The nominal leader of the other major faction, William H. Crawford of Georgia, was a consistent advocate of the Bank while secretary of the Treasury. Crawford was ill and enfeebled, and Martin Van Buren had taken over real leadership of the Crawford group, but Van Buren was then a personal friend of Biddle's and not regarded as an enemy of the Bank. Most of the men chosen by Jackson as his personal and political advisers were friends of the Bank.

Biddle did not know Jackson. Jackson and his motives were an enigma to even his closest associates. In reality, his silence concerning the Bank during the campaign masked a determined and relentless opposition to all banks which made loans and issued banknotes. Jackson was "an uncritical Republican in the Jeffersonian tradition."[57] He opposed all debt, governmental or private. He was against all banks, state banks as well as the Bank of the United States. "Everyone that knows me," he wrote in 1833, "does know that I have been always opposed to the United States Bank, nay all banks."[58]

Indeed, Jackson wanted to announce his opposition to the Bank in his inaugural address. His political advisers dissuaded him from doing so, perhaps in the hope that his experience in office would prove to him the usefulness of the institution. But the charges of politics levied against the Kentucky branches, and later against the branch at New Orleans—even when impartial investigation revealed them to be without foundation—only confirmed what really needed no confirming in Jackson's mind, namely, that banks were cesspools of corruption, or "hydra of corruption," to use his favorite phrase. Jackson's mind was one of agrarian simplicity. How could a bank create money simply by opening an account in some borrower's name, giving him credit and checks for use in drawing on it? How could a bank print more paper dollars than it had gold dollars or silver dollars in its vault to back up? There must be something corrupt in the mysterious legerdemain of banking.

Had he not experienced the corruption of the paper system at first hand? In the 1790s he had been a merchant and wanted to buy goods for his store in Tennessee. So he sold some land he owned and took the promissory note of the purchaser of the land in payment. This note he in turn gave in payment for the store goods he bought. Then the buyer of his land failed. His note was no longer worth anything, and the storekeeper to whom Jackson had given it insisted that Jackson make it good. He spent years in the effort. The whole paper system was corrupt. The only good money was *hard* money. The only honest dollar was the dollar earned by the sweat of one's brow—not the borrowed dollar. Borrowed money came too easily and led to spendthrift, wastrel, corrupt habits. Jackson's real opposition to the Bank arose from his "hard-money views."[59]

The hard-money views themselves, however, stemmed from something even more basic: Jackson's stern, flintlike Presbyterian morality. This is the Jackson that emerges so clearly from his letters. "I loathe the corruption of human nature," he wrote in 1833, "and long for retirement and repose at the Hermitage. But until I can strangle this hydra of corruption, the Bank, I will not shrink from my duty." Jackson was engaged in a moral crusade dictated by his conscience and by his concern for what he called "the safety and purity of our free institutions." Compromise is impossible for the man who crusades for something he believes to be morally right. How can one compromise with evil? "The bank, Mr. Van Buren, is trying to kill me, *but I will kill it.*" If two words can sum up Jackson, they are *duty* and *will*.[60]

Charges of political corruption were therefore grist for Jackson's mill. He wanted to believe the Bank guilty of improper political activities. Biddle, of course, reacted in a precisely opposite manner. When charges of the Bank's corruption continued to be repeated even after he considered them successfully refuted, the flash-fire of his indignation exploded in these words: "I will not give way one inch in what concerns the independence of the Bank, to please all the administrations, past, present, or future. The bigots of the past reproached me with not being for them, the bigots of the present will be annoyed that the Bank will not support them. Be it so, I care nothing for either class of partisans and mean to disregard both."[61]

That was said in private, to a friend and confidant. What he said in public was, if possible, even worse. The Bank would *not* submit to partisan control. It would not appoint directors because they were good Jacksonians or good Whigs. To the secretary of the Treasury Biddle wrote in September 1829: "I deem it my duty to state to you in a manner perfectly respectable to your official and personal character, yet so clear as to leave no possibility of misconception, that the board of directors of the Bank of the United States . . . acknowledge not the slightest responsibility of any description whatsoever to the Secretary of the Treasury touching the political opinions and conduct of their officers, that being a subject on which they never consult and never desire to know the views of any administration."[62]

It was typical Biddle. In 1811, at the age of twenty-five, he had opened an important speech in the lower house of the Pennsylvania legislature with these words: "[Since the] first virtues are frankness and candour . . . I mean to tell you plainly and simply that you are wrong."[63] Later, as Roger B. Taney recalled it, "in a letter of . . . Biddle to the chairman of a committee of the Senate written some time before the question of [the Bank's] recharter was brought before Congress, [Biddle stated] with great confidence, that it had always been in the power of the Bank of the United States to break any state bank it pleased"; and the tone of his letter, Taney said, "seemed to imply that he thought himself entitled to credit for his forbearance!" "This statement of the power of the bank," Taney continued, "ought in my opinion to have been of itself sufficient to prevent the renewal of the charter. It certainly would have been a most dangerous experiment to continue the existence of a monster admitted to be capable of swallowing up the whole of the state banks."[64] Brilliance, even genius, does not equate with wisdom. Most scholars have had little difficulty in finding in the character of Biddle himself an important part of the explanation for his failure in the Bank War. They have variously attributed to him abuse of power; vanity and absence of self-criticism; excessive fluency; and errors of judgment, temper, and calculation. The evidence supports all these accusations.[65]

In his first annual message to Congress, delivered at the end of 1829, Jackson opened his attack on the Bank. The Bank's charter, he said, would expire in 1836, and it was not too soon to begin considering whether to renew it. "Both the constitutionality and the expediency of the law creating this Bank are well-questioned by a large part of our fellow citizens; and it must be admitted by all that it has failed in the great end of establishing a uniform and sound currency." To question the Bank's constitutionality and expediency is one thing; to say that they were "well-questioned" is another. Especially when one considers that James Madison, the foremost authority on the Constitution, had signed the bill which established the Bank, and that the Supreme Court had affirmed its constitutionality. As for the claim that the Bank had failed to establish a uniform and sound currency—that was preposterous.[66] It was Jackson himself, rather than his party or any interested group, who made the rechartering of the Bank a political issue. The reason for his action is not to be found in any act of commission or omission by the Bank itself, or in any widespread discontent with it. Rather, Jackson followed his own view of what was moral, constitutional, and proper. All his political advisers had sought unsuccessfully to dissuade him from this cause. But as he told the son of Alexander Hamilton, who tried to restrain him, "My friend, I am pledged against the Bank."[67]

Long before Jackson's message to Congress at the end of 1829, Biddle had wanted Jackson to approve the proposal to recharter the Bank. But in view of Jackson's opposition, he bided his time till he believed public opinion was strongly in favor of the proposal. The time seemed ripe in 1832, the year of the presidential election. Madison had, the previous July, published a letter in which he defended the constitutionality of the Bank, and this letter had had great influence. So too had letters released to the press by James Monroe and William H. Crawford—two Old Republicans who favored the Bank. Biddle was almost entirely sure that Jackson would veto a bill to renew the charter, that this would cost him the election, and that Henry Clay would be the successful candidate.[68]

Jackson vetoed the bill on July 10, 1832. Three weeks later, on August 1, Biddle wrote Clay and said, "You are destined to be the instrument of . . . deliverance." He added," The President . . . must pay the penalty for his own rashness." Biddle badly miscalculated.[69] The recharter bill was introduced in Congress. It passed in the spring of 1832 by a Senate vote of 28 to 20 and a House vote of 107 to 85. As expected, Jackson vetoed it; thus the Bank became the great political issue of the 1832 election. The result is familiar. Jackson won decisively against Clay by 219 electoral votes to 49. The South and West rallied in support of the Old Hero, New England in support of Clay.

Jackson interpreted his decisive victory in the election as a popular mandate against the Bank. He decided to destroy the institution by removing the government's deposits from it and placing them in selected state banks instead. (These were called pet banks by the opponents of the measure; actually no money was removed, except in the ordinary course of the government's business. But future deposits were made in the pet banks.) Removal of the deposits destroyed the Bank's power to maintain a sound currency. In 1836, after its federal charter had expired, it was given a charter by the state of Pennsylvania. Biddle remained its president till his retirement in 1839. In 1841 the bank fell victim to the currents set in motion by the Panic of 1837, and failed.

Thus the Bank of the United States passed out of existence, setting back the cause of central banking till 1913, when the Federal Reserve System was enacted into law.

What defeated the Bank? We may determine sectional attitudes toward the Bank by examining the combined votes of both houses of Congress on the recharter bill of 1832. New England (Maine, New Hampshire, Vermont, Massachusetts, Connecticut, and Rhode Island) supported recharter by a combined vote of 35 to 12, and the Middle Atlantic states (New York, New Jersey, Pennsylvania, and Delaware) also did so, by 48 to 23 (New York voting against recharter 21 to 12). The Southeast (Maryland, Virginia, North Carolina, South Carolina, and Georgia) opposed recharter, 41 to 19, as did the Southwest (Tennessee, Alabama, Mississippi, and Louisiana), 9 to 17. On the other hand, the Northwest (Ohio, Kentucky, Indiana, Illinois, and Missouri) favored recharter by a vote of 25 to 13. Writing many years ago, in 1903, Ralph Catterall concluded that the "determined opposition was from the South and Southwest."[70] But Catterall reached this conclusion by ignoring the vote in the House. Furthermore, if we discount the nine votes cast in opposition to the Bank in Tennessee, the home state of President Jackson, arch-opponent of the Bank, the strength of pro-Bank forces in the Southwest exceeds that of the opposition by a margin of 9 to 8. The "determined opposition," then, came from the Southeast, a region which opposed the westward expansion of the cotton belt because of the effect of increases in the supply of cotton on the price of that commodity. The generous aid given by the Bank to the planters of the Southwest helped sustain that expansion and generated the political hostility of the Southeast.[71]

In part, then, the defeat of the Bank was due to economic opposition. Other evidence of economic opposition is seen in the attitude of some of the state banks, which resented the restraints which the Bank imposed on their profit-making opportunities; in that of some merchants, for example, Alexander Brown and Sons of Baltimore, who resented the domination of the foreign-exchange business by the Bank (and their inability at times to obtain specie for export); and in that of bill brokers, who resented the dominant role of the Bank in the domestic-exchange market.[72]

But the extent of economic opposition is easily exaggerated. Rather, the emphasis belongs on the personal opposition of President Jackson himself, and on the Old Republican views which lay behind it. As Biddle said in 1830, opposition to recharter was "not . . . a cabinet measure, nor a party measure, but a personal measure." Yet Jackson had key supporters who also opposed the Bank, men like Amos Kendall, his postmaster general, and Roger B. Taney, first his attorney general, then secretary of the Treasury, and finally chief justice of the Supreme Court. And throughout the nation there was considerable support for the president. The "big" question is: can this support be interpreted as opposition to the Bank?[73]

Probably not. Such was Jackson's enormous popularity that the issue of the Bank may have had little to do with his great victory in 1832. This view finds added support in the outcome of the voting for members of the House of Representatives in 1832. One hundred and seven members had voted *in favor of* recharter. Yet 50 of the 107 were returned to the House by the electorate— just about every other one. The same result obtained in the case of the 85 House members who voted *against* the recharter bill. Forty-one of the 85 were returned to the House in the 1832 election.[74]

Do these results not suggest an even balance of public sentiment—half for the Bank, half against it? Surely they indicate that the nation was by no means overwhelmingly behind Jackson in his war against the Bank. They suggest the possibility that the electorate was not unduly excited either in favor of or against the Bank. In other words, Jackson's landslide victory in 1832 may well have reflected a personal popularity that had little or nothing to do with the feelings of the electorate in regard to the Bank War.

Additional considerations support this view. For one thing, the formation of the Democratic and Whig parties between the years 1824 and 1840 owed nothing at all to public issues and everything to the gradual revival of contests for the presidency in the majority of states during these years. This "second American party system" was an artificial system that was based on a tacit agreement by political leaders to keep out of the arena of partisan politics issues that were sectionally divisive—above all, the issue of slavery. Apparently it was safe enough to debate such sectionally innocuous issues of fiscal policy as those centering on the Bank of the United States.[75]

Then there is the evidence of the widespread support which the Bank enjoyed. In 1832, before the veto of the recharter bill in July, a majority in both houses of Congress, most state legislatures, and an impressive number of state banks supported the institution. Among the people at large, one finds more direct expressions of pro-Bank than of anti-Bank sentiment. Citizens' memorials, some containing hundreds, others thousands of signatures, favored the Bank 118 to 8. The strongest support came from the West, very probably because the Bank made currency available to a region which would otherwise have had an insufficient supply of it.

So far as state banks were concerned, only in Georgia, Connecticut, and New York is there evidence of positive hostility. A majority of those in North Carolina and Alabama strongly supported the Bank, and this was also true of Louisiana and Mississippi. Virginia gave some support. For the most part, then, state banks in the South and Southwest rallied in favor of the institution. In New England, the banks of Vermont and New Hampshire were strong in their support, but not those in Massachusetts, probably because the Bank's notes represented a very small proportion of those issued by the state's banks. In sum, Biddle was right in his claim that "the state banks in the main are friendly."[76]

It is also essential to bring into the account long-held but erroneous views concerning the economic consequences of Jackson's veto of the recharter bill. Historians once believed that the veto and the subsequent removal of the government's deposits from the Bank in 1834 unleashed a series of drastic economic changes. The number of state banks soared from 506 in 1834 to 901 in 1840, with those in the Southwest and West, particularly, proceeding to initiate an unsound credit expansion and an inflation characterized by unprecedented speculation in public lands. Jackson's reaction was to issue a specie circular in 1836 putting an end to the financing of land purchases by banknotes and in the following year distributing to the states the surplus revenues collected from sales. Together these policies produced the Panic of 1837, after which the boom collapsed and the economy settled into one of the worst depressions it has known.[77]

In fact, it was a rapid rise in the specie reserves of the state banks in the 1830s that was responsible for the boom. The obligations of those institutions did not rise faster than their receipt of new reserves. The boom, therefore, did not have its origins in the Bank War, but rather in a combination of large capital imports from England and in a change, initially begun by Biddle in 1825, from an older trading method of exporting silver to China to pay for return cargoes to one using bills of exchange drawn on English houses. The result was not only a rapid increase of silver in the United States but also an enhanced ability to retain it as reserves in the banking system. Not Jacksonian policies, but diminution in this inflow of capital from England led to the Panic of 1837. Finally, the depression of the early 1840s, as was also true of its predecessor in 1819-1822, was essentially marked by price deflation rather than by a decline in output.[78]

In sum, the Bank of the United States was widely supported and was not a sectionally divisive issue. For these reasons it was an institution whose life chances could be freely debated, essentially because it did not matter that much—a hypothesis also strengthened by the nearly equal split in the voting for members of the House in 1832. Recent correction of older views on the causes of the speculative land boom of the postveto years should also give us pause. At the least, we have to ask ourselves whether the Bank War was the important phenomenon that historians have long believed it to be. Is it not possible that we have mistaken the sound of words for the substance of things?

Sound and substance, or smoke and fire: the degree of closeness between the pairs often defines the very essence of the problem of historical reconstruction. But if the political and literary polemics of the Bank War seem some distance removed from underlying political and economic realities, we shall see that "sound" in the form of public and private exhortation to believe in the future of the country and to work hard to get ahead affected both public and private values and the development of the legal system, helped generate capital outlays by governmental bodies, and shaped private incentives governing the intensity of the labor input of free men and women. Admittedly, these dimensions of resource inputs are difficult to quantify, but they are not on that account to suffer deemphasis in an inquiry into the forming of conditions hospitable to economic growth.

7

Values, Law, and
the Developing Economy

E conomists teach us that economic growth takes place when an increase occurs in the factors of production—land, labor, and capital—or in the efficiency with which these factors are combined in use. In recent years they have also pointed to the fact that capital is not homogeneous—that it includes a human as well as a physical dimension—and they have emphasized the contribution which education makes to the formation of this human capital. Skills imparted by education raise the productivity of labor, increasing its output per unit of input. In a word, skill alters the quality of capital. But what of will? Surely there is a difference between the performances of a willing and of an unwilling worker, and there are different degrees of willingness itself. Ideally, all other things being equal, we would be able to measure these degrees of willingness and to associate changes in output with changes in the intensity of effort. Ideally too we would be able to identify and weigh the complex factors of personality and environment which play upon the will to work. The difficulty is that real life is too complicated to allow us to be convincing when we abstract from its complexity, try to hold "everything else" constant, and perform a mental experiment designed to explain change. Always, out of the corner of the most disciplined eye, the experimenter sees the protestant squirming of reality.[1]

Fortunately, a professor of psychology has charted a path through this difficult terrain. In his analysis of *The Achieving Society,* David C. McClelland tells of experiments conducted with male college students that were designed to test the strength of the subjects' need for achievement ("*n* Achievement"). In one of the experiments the students were divided into two groups, one of which was indoctrinated beforehand by being told that their reactions to a series of pictures thrown upon a screen would serve as indexes of their general intelligence and capacity for leadership. For purposes of comparison, the second group was subjected to "normal conditions" and told nothing of the sort. The results were striking. The language of the imaginative "stories" written by the members of the indoctrinated group "contained more references to 'standards of excellence' and to doing well, or wanting to do well, with respect to the standards" than did those of the control group.

For example, in response to a scene depicting a student sitting at a desk with an open book before him, the latter group described the student as daydreaming. Most of the indoctrinated group, in contrast, described him in terms of "the need for achievement, anticipations of success or failure, affective states associated with succeeding and failing, blocks in the way of achieving, and help from other persons in the direction of achievement." Since similar results were obtained in experiments involving high school students with more random socioeconomic backgrounds, from widely divergent groups such as Navajo Indians and Brazilian students, McClelland concluded that it "would not be at all surprising to imagine that an increase in n Achievement should promote economic or cultural growth." One may go further: given other favorable conditions, incentives to invest one's time, effort, and capital, to work to the best of one's ability, and to improve one's situation—in short, a determination to get ahead—may well be in the most important single factor in economic growth.[2]

In the experiments just described, it was McClelland and his assistants who introduced the psychological factor that led the subjects to emphasize achievement. In the far more diffuse and uncontrolled laboratory of early-nineteenth-century America, a number of forces presented psychological factors sufficiently different from those of the past to affect both the way in which the American people viewed their environment and the nature and intensity of their responses to the challenges and opportunities it posed. No one, of course, can know enough to characterize the "mind" of the American people, for, like other large and complex social organisms, American society, even in the early nineteenth century, was composed of communities which varied in ethnic background, customs, and traditions; in race, economic class, and social status; as well as in cultural and other ways. We can, however, cite the opinions of men and women who were then alive and, where appropriate, say why we think their testimony deserves notice. Even though the views are those of an educated and articulate minority, they emanate from so many distinct parts of the social system and ring with such a high degree of internal consistency as to convince us that they represent widely shared values bound to have influenced not only economic and political behavior but the legal system as well.

According to the publisher of *Niles Register* in December 1815, "ambition to get forward" was "almost universal" among Americans.[3] "Getting forward" meant succeeding; it meant making money. To be sure, it had meant the same thing long before this. Cadwallader Colden could assert of New York City in 1748 that the "only principle of Life propagated among the young People is to get Money, and men are only esteemed according to what they are worth— that is, the Money they are possessed of."[4] The prosperity maxims ("Time is money") published by Benjamin Franklin in *Poor Richard's Almanack* (1732– 1757) are believed by one student of American culture to have "probably exerted as much practical influence on Americans as the combined teachings of all the formal philosophers."[5] It is hardly surprising that a "worship of wealth" should have appeared in a country where "so little else existed on which men could exercise the impulse to make distinctions or establish a standard by which to define and imitate success."[6] Yet, if it is true that this criterion was easily adopted in American experience, it is also true that it was heavily reinforced by the spread of markets and opportunities for business success in the antebellum period. Accordingly, a new generation of success propagandists revived Franklin's self-help themes in the 1820s.

During the years 1815–1845 the cult of the "self-made man" was universally accepted in America. Although it is not without irony that Henry Clay should be credited with having coined the phrase in a speech on behalf of a protective tariff, the age believed that the key to success lay within. American institutions created a fair field for all white men, at least; success was up to the individual. Man was the master of his fate; whether he "made it" or failed was determined neither by heredity nor by environment but by character and personal determination alone. The conviction was a source of national pride. "The character of the American people," said a Fourth of July orator in 1831, "has been the sole cause of their growth and prosperity. Natural advantages have been elsewhere wasted."[7] Whatever else he does, the orator shows the way in which his age established a link between private success and the nation's economic growth.[8]

In view of McClelland's emphasis on "achievement motivation" in fostering economic growth, it is significant that the fundamental responsibility for inculcating the beliefs and values we have been discussing fell to the family. According to an article published in *Harper's New Monthly Magazine* in 1853, the "idea instilled into the minds of most boys, from early life, is that of 'getting on.' The parents test themselves by their own success in this respect; and they impart the same notion to their children."[9] To the vast majority of Americans, the article added, success had long since come to mean achievement in business and making money. Successful businessmen urged upon poor nephews the importance of practicing industry, sobriety, and frugality and repeated the same thought at commencement exercises, in newspaper interviews, and in books. The antebellum press characteristically explained entrepreneurial success in terms of the possession of the same personal qualities.

Protestant clergymen were also among the leaders of the cult of self-help. Men such as Henry Ward Beecher and Lyman Abbott preached that "godliness was in league with riches" and "put the sanction of the church on the get-ahead values of the business community." Abbott used the parable of the talents to justify his claim that Jesus approved the building of great fortunes. Jesus did not condemn wealth, Abbott declared. "On the contrary, he approved of the use of accumulated wealth to accumulate more wealth." Others said similar things in books. The Reverend Thomas P. Hunt summarized the case for riches in the title of a work he published in 1836: *The Book of Wealth:*

In Which It Is Proved from the Bible That It is the Duty of Every Man to Become Rich.[10]

Not only the family, church, press, lyceums, and reading rooms of mercantile library associations but elementary schools as well served as institutional channels for the self-help theme. The famous readers of William Holmes McGuffey extolled the glories of labor to several generations of American youth. One scholar believes that as many as half the schoolchildren in America may have learned industry, frugality, and sobriety from him from 1836 to the end of the century.[11] The McGuffey readers "contained the same synthesis of Christian and middle-class virtues that could be found in the leading manuals on success." For example:

> Work, Work, my boy, be not afraid;
> Look labor boldly in the face;
> Take up the hammer or the spade,
> And blush not for your humble place.

However poor or unfortunate, no boy had reason to despair as long as he was willing to work. "Persevering industry will enable one to accomplish almost anything," said a New England common-school textbook. "Any man's son may become the equal of any other man's son," Frances Trollope added after completing a three-and-a-half year visit to the United States in the early 1830s, "and the consciousness of this is certainly a spur to exertion."[12]

Such sentiments cannot be dismissed as mere hypocritical rationalizations on the part of employers, as expressions designed to encourage effort in a society whose supplies of labor were scarce in relation to the demand for it. For one thing, employers themselves appear to have practiced what they preached. Although evidence on the intensity of work effort is extremely hard to come by or to measure, we do know that foreigners sometimes commented that an intense work psychology embraced not only the business community but the entire nation as well. "America seemed to be the only country where a man felt ashamed if he had nothing to do." "You have no right to complain of laboring like a slave," a Baltimore merchant admonished a young man in 1832, "as every man should and generally do [*sic;*]." Clearly, a secularized Protestant ethic, particularly the doctrine of the calling, promoted this psychology. (The merchant just quoted, Robert Oliver, was himself a Presbyterian who paid his "Rent for the Pew.") And the labor shortage also helped.[13]

But more than rationalization of self-interest is involved. An intriguing study of the "intellectual origins" of New England's textile industry suggests a second reason for not questioning the sincerity of the work ethic on the part of employers. It is plain that these men faced a twofold problem: that of reducing imports of competing European textiles, and that of recruiting a labor supply. They addressed themselves to the problem of competition by petitioning Congress in 1815 to protect American "consumers" from foreign goods, which they said were deceitfully made from "very inferior materials." They also patriotically contrasted American morals and European manners, making things such as "fashionable dress, intellectuality, leisure, and often art into foppish instruments of the devil," while at the same time elevating "the ascetic virtues of simplicity of dress and manner, plainness of speech and thought, modesty, sobriety, manliness, and industry."

As we have seen, the farm daughters of New England provided the answer to industry's need for labor. As the cotton textile manufacturer Nathan Appleton later recalled, "There was little demand for female labor, as household manufacture was superseded by the improvements of machinery. Here was in New England a fund of labor, well educated and virtuous." All that was necessary was to convince the girls and their parents that work in the mills was not morally degrading. This the manufacturers did in two ways: they depicted European manufacturing as "presided over by a devilish class of aristocrats," with its urban workforce underpaid and degraded. And "for moral as well as economic reasons," they established their mills in rural areas where, in many cases, they provided family plots of land, forbade grog shops and taverns, and erected attractive boardinghouses, schools, and churches.

Their efforts were successful: they obtained tariff protection in 1816 and later, and, as Appleton put it, "the daughters of respectable farmers were readily induced to come into these mills for a temporary period."[14]

This may appear to have been a coldly calculated program. Indeed, the manufacturers "exalted the virtues of sobriety, industry, and the like, not merely because they had inherited these as part of the Protestant business ethic, but because these virtues were from the beginning opposed to the urban vices of indolence, drunkenness, and lewdness, which, in turn, were considered vices of a leisured aristocracy." Nevertheless, there is every reason to think that American manufacturers believed their own propaganda. Their letters and journals reveal how deeply they held in private the views they expressed in public. For example, when immediate members of the family or business associates took trips to Europe, they were warned by those at home to be wary of the corrosive seductions of foreign cities. And letters from the travelers described spectacles of "pomp and iniquity, extravagance and wretchedness." "Bring home no foreign fancies which are inapplicable to our state of society," Amos Lawrence admonished his son in Paris. There must be no corrupting of the Garden of Eden.

It is clear that these men conceived themselves as leaders in a great moral crusade to free Americans from a contaminating dependence on European manufactures. They were "frequently explicit, almost poetic, about their divine mission in America." "God has given us a good land and many blessings," Amos Lawrence wrote his son. "We shall be called to a strict account." Describing his part in the Industrial Revolution, Nathan Appleton wrote: "Ours is a great novel experiment . . . Whatever the result, it is our destiny to make

it. It is our mission—our care should be to understand it and make it succeed."
Looking upon themselves as "servants of the Lord who were setting a national
example of manufacturing morality and skill," the textile manufacturers of
New England were often generous in encouraging the establishment of rival
factories. Abbott Lawrence wrote to the southerner William C. Rives, "We
have not [*sic*] jealousy, whatever, concerning the establishment of manufactories in all parts of the country." George Cabot expected that New England
operatives would "diffuse their knowledge and skill through all the States in
the Union where manufactories can be carried on." Francis Cabot Lowell
fostered the growth of manufacturing elsewhere by letting out his patents for
the power loom on easy terms. Noted for their philanthropy, these men were
yet stern with themselves and with others. "It is on account of so much leisure,
that so many fine youths are ruined in this town," Amos Lawrence once told
a young Bostonian. Young Baltimoreans fared no better. "You are wasting
your means," Robert Oliver admonished one of them, "and . . . it is absolutely necessary to commence some kind of industry—you appear to have no
turn for any kind of business, and it is difficult to say what a person of your
Indolence can, or should do."[15]

Sons of the well-to-do were exceptions. Whether moved by a sense of mission, by the profit motive, or by a desire to get ahead, the antebellum generations, employers and employees alike, were a "people in motion." Theirs was
a striving society, one in which people pushed themselves to make the most
of the opportunities opening up in their developing economy, one in which
people worked hard, relying on their ancient faith in the value of industry and
sobriety to provide the moral justification for the pace at which they worked.
In the early 1830s Alexis de Tocqueville, perhaps the most acute of all foreign
observers of American institutions, witnessed and found "difficult to describe
the rapacity with which the American rushes forward to secure this immense
booty that fortune proffers to him . . . Before him lies a boundless continent,
and he urges onward as if time pressed and he was afraid of finding no room
for his exertions." Wealth circulated "with inconceivable rapidity, and experience shows that it is rare to find two succeeding generations in the full
enjoyment of it." The "commercial activity" of Americans he could only describe as "prodigious," including that of farmers, for "most of them make
agriculture itself a trade."[16]

Of course no mood of exhilaration is indefinitely sustainable. Moods move
in cycles, like business itself—to which they are doubtlessly closely related—
and one need not maintain that the people of antebellum America endlessly
rang the changes on ambition, self-help, and money as the measure of success.
They need not have done so to support the conviction that such values are not
only consonant with economic development but also conducive to it. And if
success in business, including that of farming, was a paramount value of the
age, development of the country's resources was a widely accepted goal of

public policy and of law. The two sets of values were mutually supportive, and in the nation's earlier years both depended to a surprising extent on the legal system—on active, interventionist government and on law.

Sparsely settled, ever-enlarging, yet underdeveloped, the United States in the early nineteenth century required a more efficient transportation system to marshall its resources for growth. How to make progress in that direction was the question. In earlier legislation admitting Ohio to the Union, the federal government had already taken steps which would culminate in its construction of the National Road, and in 1806 the Congress followed up by passing an "Act to Regulate the Laying Out and Making of a Road from Cumberland, in the State of Maryland." That same year, President Thomas Jefferson in his annual message invited Congress to consider the application of surplus revenues "to the improvement of roads, canals, rivers, education, and other great foundations of prosperity and union, under the powers which Congress may already possess, or such amendment of the constitution as may be approved by the states." The Senate responded by directing Secretary of the Treasury Albert Gallatin to draw up "a plan for the application of such means as are within the power of Congress, to the purposes of opening roads and making canals, together with a statement of the undertakings of that nature, which, as objects of public improvement, may require and deserve the aid of Government."[17]

Complying with the congressional directive in 1808, Gallatin pointed out in his *Report on Roads and Canals* that "good roads and canals will shorten distances, facilitate commercial and personal intercourse, and unite, by a still more intimate community of interests, the most remote quarters of the United States. No other single operation, within the power of Government, can more effectually tend to strengthen and perpetuate that Union which secures external independence, domestic peace, and internal liberty." Improved transportation, in a word, would "cement the union."

Gallatin's plan called for improving communications between North and South by building a turnpike from Maine to Georgia that would pass through all principal seaport cities, and by digging one hundred miles of canals through the four necks of land which, beginning with Cape Cod and ending with the marshy tract dividing Chesapeake Bay from Albemarle Sound, prevented safe tidewater shipping. Even more important, indeed the leading object of Gallatin's report, was the devising of means to breach or skirt the Appalachian Barrier to the West. It was useless "in the present state of science" to think of crossing the mountains by canals, so Gallatin suggested making use of four pairs of east-west rivers—the Allegheny and the Susquehanna (or the Juniata), the Monongahela and the Potomac, the Kanawha and the James, and the Tennessee and the Santee (or the Savannah). The navigation of the eastern rivers should be improved, he suggested, and roads built to connect them with the western streams. Finally, the geography of the North should be taken advantage of: since the Hudson was the only river which "breaks through or turns all the mountains," a canal should be constructed to connect it with the Great Lakes. Such a canal—the Erie—was indeed constructed, between 1817 and 1825, but by the state of New York rather than by the federal government.

Projected internal improvements at federal expense constantly encountered difficulties. True, the National Road pushed on into the wilderness, reaching the Ohio River at Wheeling, Ohio, in 1818 and at Vandalia, Illinois, by midcentury. But this was the exception, "the one major developmental enterprise of the time to be constructed directly by the federal government." No less a figure than John C. Calhoun tried to induce Congress to implement the Gallatin plan after the end of the War of 1812: "Let us then, said Mr. C."— as the *Annals of Congress* reported—"bind the Republic together with a perfect system of roads and canals." Subsequently the major constitutional theorist of southern sectionalism, Calhoun was then a foremost nationalist, a leading advocate not only of federally financed improvements but also of the chartering of a Second Bank of the United States. He proposed that the government's bonus from the charter and its future income from the Bank be set aside as a fund for internal improvements. But President James Madison vetoed the bonus bill on the ground that it exceeded the power of the federal government.

Madison's successor, James Monroe, gave early signs of following in the constitutional footsteps of his predecessor, for in 1822 he vetoed a measure authorizing the government to establish toll gates and collect revenue for the maintenance of the National Road. In 1824, however, he approved a general survey bill which instructed the president to arrange for surveys of the routes of canals and roads of national importance. And on his last day in office he approved a governmental subscription to the stock of the Chesapeake and Delaware Canal. According to Monroe's most recent biographer, he favored internal improvements at federal expense but preferred to avoid head-on constitutional conflict by stretching as far as possible the authority given Congress in article 1, section 8, to construct military and post roads.[18]

John Quincy Adams was even more positive about the government's constitutional authority and during his administration signed into law bills calling for federal subscriptions to the stock of three canal companies—the Louisville and Portland Canal (around the falls of the Ohio River at Louisville), the Dismal Swamp Canal, and the Chesapeake and Ohio Canal, the latter being the main beneficiary of $3 million in appropriations. Furthermore, federal public works were authorized by the passage in 1824 of the first river and harbor improvement bill, merged two years later in a long series of "rivers and harbors" measures. With the election of Andrew Jackson, this constitutional movement reversed its course. Although Congress approved appropriations for the extension of the National Road, the completed portions were turned over to the states in which they lay, and a further appropriation for the Louisville and Portland Canal received a pocket veto. In his farewell address Jackson boasted that he had "finally overthrown . . . this plan of unconstitutional expenditure for the purpose of corrupt influence."

The existence of constitutional and other obstacles for the use of federal funds for internal improvements suggested the use of federal lands instead. (Many men, however, especially the Old Republicans of the South, opposed the use of lands as well as of money. But they were in a minority.)[19] Enabling acts, passed when states were admitted to the Union, sought to encourage road construction by giving the states 5 percent of the net proceeds from the sale of public lands lying within their boundaries. The Ohio Enabling Act of 1802 set the precedent that was to be followed with the subsequent admission of Indiana, Mississippi, Alabama, and Missouri. Other legislation was even more generous. To ease the burden of construction costs, the federal government began in 1823 to make public lands available to the states for specific internal improvements. States could sell the land or use it as collateral for loans to fund their projects. The grants were extensive: between 1823 and 1866, when the program ended, states received 4.5 million acres to help in the building of canals, 3.5 million acres for roads, and 1.7 million acres for river improvements.

Additional public lands became available to the states under other programs. Under the Internal Improvements Act of 1841, not repealed till 1889, each public land state received 500,000 acres for general improvement purposes rather than for specific construction projects. The Swamplands Act of 1850 sought to make use of low-lying public lands unfit for cultivation. States in which they lay were authorized to sell them, to use part of the proceeds of sale to drain them, and to apply the balance to internal improvements. Combined with the Internal Improvements Act, the swamplands legislation brought a total of 65 million acres to various states.

Another measure of 1850, the Illinois Central Land Grant Bill, was the first to aid in railroad construction. By 1872, when the law was repealed, a total of 131 million acres had been turned over to the states. Between 1850 and 1862 the grants were made to the states, and by the latter to railroad companies. Those made between 1862 and 1872 went directly to the railroads, which were extending their lines through unorganized territories. The grants before 1862 provided for a right-of-way two hundred feet wide (that is, the path of the railroad) and also alternate sections of land—a section being one square mile—on both sides of the right-of-way, to a depth of six square miles. The pattern was like that of a checker board: for every mile of track laid, the government granted to the railroad company every other square mile of land on both sides of the track to a depth of six miles (the reds), while retaining ownership of the bypassed square mile (the blacks) for itself. In theory, the railroads would be better able to market their bonds because of the landed collateral behind them, while the government would be enabled to sell the retained acres at double the minimum price because of the enhancement of their value by the very existence of the railroad. (In addition, the railroads were required to carry government traffic free of charge and mails at rates set by federal authority.) The theory was fine, but in practice the railroads found it so hard to raise the funds required for construction that in 1864 Congress raised the ante from a depth of six to ten square miles on either side of the right-of-way.

Land grants were not the only federal aids to railroads. Under a law that was on the statute books between 1824 and 1838 federal engineers were authorized to make railroad surveys at government expense, that is, to survey the land before the laying of track or the building of bridges. Finally, between 1830 and 1843 Congress lowered the duties on iron used for railroad construction, saving the railroads an estimated $6 million—until domestic iron manufacturers succeeded in convincing Congress that it ought to protect iron manufacturers instead of railroads!

All in all, the federal government made substantial contributions to the developing transportation system. Yet its promotional role tended to be a declining one in the later decades of the antebellum period. Democratic administrations predominated after 1829, and in these later years, if not during the first quarter of the century, Democrats adhered somewhat more closely to the Jeffersonian ideal of limited government. With respect to river and harbor improvements, Presidents Van Buren, Tyler, Polk, Pierce, and Buchanan were stricter constructionists than even Jackson had been. Although it would be a mistake to discount the force of Old Republican values, especially in the case of Jackson, it is not primarily a growth in political idealism that explains this phenomenon, but the maturation of conflicting sectional, state, and occupational interests. The sharpness of these differences made it difficult to reach agreements covering any wide area of national life. In short, a diversity of local interests militated against decisive action on the part of the central government.[20]

Two other strands enter into this developing centrifugal pattern. First, with increasing accumulation of stocks of private capital, men and groups lacking the advantages bestowed by law upon older corporate groups turned in the name of egalitarian opportunity against privilege sanctioned by the legal system. Second, as slavery edged ever closer to the center of the national stage, southern leaders were determined to contain federal authority within narrow bounds. As John Randolph of Roanoke, Virginia, observed during a debate on internal improvements during the 1820s, "If Congress possesses the power to do what is proposed by this bill they may emancipate every slave in the United States."[21] In a basic sense, therefore, leading public issues which involved the constitutional power of the federal government also involved slavery. But questions concerning federally financed internal improvements—like those concerning land policy, the tariff, and the Bank of the United States—

are also important. The fear of emancipation cannot explain all presidential vetoes of internal improvements bills or public pronouncements of the unconstitutionality of direct federal action in this area. Opposition to logrolling, waste, local bickering, and corrupt use of patronage also played a part.

The South nearly always opposed internal improvements at federal expense. Not only was the region well supplied with rivers for carrying western produce to the South and southern cotton to the sea, but the construction costs would reduce federal funds and make necessary an increase in the tariff level to replenish them. In the earlier years of the century, furthermore, the greatest of the improvements were those designed to overcome the barrier of the Appalachian Mountains. But improved trade connections between East and West brought little benefit to the southern states, and to the lower South, none at all. Henry Clay's "American System," which called for tariff protection for the East and internal improvements for the West, posed the possibility of an East-West alliance that would threaten the political position of the South. Presiding over the Memphis Convention in 1845, John C. Calhoun, however, bespoke southern anxiety over the effects on southern wealth of the great rise in direct shipments of western produce to the East, and called upon the federal government to improve the navigability of the western rivers. The West favored rapid settlement not only for its effects on land values, general business, and access to eastern markets, but also for the greater security its growing population provided against Indian attack. For the same reasons the region's spokesmen in Congress generally approved liberal land policies.

A constitutional amendment clarifying federal authority in the field of internal improvements therefore would not have addressed the underlying differences which impeded action at that level. Undoubtedly this helps explain why compelling popular pressure on behalf of a national program was lacking. It was also lacking, in part, because of a belief that the states were themselves well equipped to carry out the essential improvements. A writer in the *North American Review* argues well this point of view:

> The compass of each state is sufficiently narrow, and its legislative power sufficiently diffused, to render knowledge of its internal condition, wants, and resources easily attained . . . Scarce any object of public utility is beyond the grasp of the resources of the single states; so that, after all, the care of individual objects of public improvement is put into the hands of those most sure to be benefited by them.[22]

Even within the smaller arena of the state, however, distinct geographic and other interests made statewide agreements difficult, and they were often achieved only by the grant of costly or wasteful concessions to disaffected areas or groups. Intrastate conflicts were nevertheless more easily harmonized than differences between national regions, and in consequence the promotional activities of state and local governments far exceeded those of the federal government. With the decline in the role of the latter, advocates of roads and canals, and soon thereafter of railroads, pushed their projects in every state and in almost every locality. Some states, as the case of Virginia illustrates, institutionalized procedures for choosing between proposed projects.

"There never has existed a doubt but that it is a duty, as well as the interest of every good government to facilitate the necessary communication between its citizens. Next perhaps to the enjoyment of civil liberty itself are the blessings which governments can secure to the people by good roads, navigable rivers and canals."[23] Justifying the details of its report in these words, the Virginia Assembly's Committee on Roads and Navigation recommended at the end of 1815 that the state contribute to the capital funds required for projects by subscribing to the stock of private companies—but only in such quantities and on such terms as would encourage private investment. Management of the projects should remain in private hands, the committee believed, with the state's only responsibility being that of preventing or correcting abuses.

The legislature responded in 1816 to this report by creating a fund for internal improvements and placing it under the control of a newly established Board of Public Works. The latter was composed of prestigious figures such as the governor, treasurer and attorney general of the state, together with ten citizens. So that the varying needs of different parts of the state would find representation on the board, three of the ten were to be selected from west of the Alleghenies, two from the Shenandoah Valley, three from the Piedmont, and two from the Tidewater. The board was authorized to employ a principal engineer and with his aid to examine all proposals laid before it. Those approved for state aid were to be so recommended to the Assembly. The law required the sponsors of each project approved by the Assembly to raise by private subscription three-fifths of the amount needed for construction, the state then subscribing the other two-fifths and appointing its proportional share of directors on the board of the corporation chartered to build the project. Thus there existed no overall master plan for the state similar to that which Gallatin had drawn up for the nation in his report of 1808.

The system established by law in 1816 remained in effect, with some changes in its outline (for example, regional members of the board were dropped in 1831, and the state's subscription later rose to three-fifths), until the military operations of the Civil War put an end to it. In the main, the state raised the money it needed by borrowing, by issuing bonds, the proceeds of which it then used to purchase the stocks of the improvement companies. (Thus loans were based on the state's ability to tax rather than on a corporation's ability to earn profits.) Sometimes the state turned the bonds over to the companies to sell; usually it sold the bonds itself and turned over the money. In the late 1830s the state was turning over about $1 million a year to various companies engaged on approved construction projects. During the 1850s the amounts averaged $2 million a year. Remarkable results were accomplished under the system.

In 1851 the board reported that Virginia possessed 872 miles of "the most capacious and substantially constructed canals in the union," and about 3,000 miles of turnpikes. In 1860 the state owned an interest in twelve canals, ten plank road companies, and fourteen bridge companies. Twenty-five roads had been built entirely from state funds. Virginia also owned an interest in sixteen railroads in 1860. Miles of operation had risen from 147 in 1840 to 1,350 in 1860.

Virginia was by no means alone. Very few states failed to participate in the drive for internal improvements. Sometimes the state built and operated a project entirely with state funds, as New York did in the case of the Erie Canal. Indeed, "in no other period of American history has the government been so active in financing and actually promoting, owning, and controlling banks and public works, including turnpikes, bridges, canals, and railroads."[24] Pennsylvania, for example, not only invested more than $6 million in some 150 "mixed" corporations but also spent over $100 million on the construction and operation of the Main Line canal and railroad system. By 1860 Massachusetts had invested more than $8 million in eight railroads, and by the same date Missouri had pledged some $23 million for a number of improvement projects. The states raised most of these sums by borrowing, with foreign lenders providing a large proportion of them. State governments could sell their bonds abroad because of the great prestige and strength given American public credit by the rapid payment of the national debt and its final extinction in 1832. "No other country had ever paid off a national debt, and it was felt that there could be little risk in lending money to a people whose resources were so great and whose disposition so frugal."[25]

Thus state governments frequently used the private business corporation as an agency of the state for accomplishing public purposes. In doing so, they continued a practice that had begun soon after the Revolution. Of course, incorporation itself had been used long before then as a device for giving legal life to public or quasi-public associations. During the colonial period it had been used to establish towns, boroughs, and cities as well as organizations devoted to charitable, educational, and ecclesiastical purposes. But in all those years incorporation had been employed only a half-dozen times for business organizations. In contrast, state governments created more than three hundred business corporations between the end of the Revolution and 1801. A brief examination will disclose their semipublic character.

Fully two-thirds of the corporations were established to provide inland navigation, turnpikes, and toll bridges. Thirty-two were empowered to underwrite insurance policies, a need deriving from expansion of the geographic area and the volume of foreign commerce, especially after 1793, when the outbreak of war in Europe opened the commercial world to American neutral vessels, increasing their risks of loss. At the same time, the increased volume of trade gave rise to a need for the short-term credit facilities of commercial banks, with the result that no less than thirty-four were incorporated between

1781 and 1801 (twenty-seven of them between 1790 and 1801). Commercial expansion, by increasing the size of urban populations, also increased the need for other services, so that thirty-two corporations for the supply of water and four for the erection of docks were created in the six-year interval between 1795 and 1801. The greater need of urban communities for protection against fire losses was reflected in the organization of nearly a dozen mutual insurance companies between 1786 and 1800. Most insurance companies, however, were permitted to underwrite both fire and marine risks.[26]

The experience of Pennsylvania suggests that these early objectives of incorporation continued to predominate in the antebellum period. Of 2,333 business corporations chartered by special act between 1790 and 1860, 64.17 percent were in the field of transport, 11.14 percent in insurance, 7.72 percent in manufacturing, 7.2 percent in banking, 3.21 percent in gas production, 2.79 percent water supply, and 3.77 percent in miscellaneous categories. It is not difficult to visualize the semipublic character of early manufacturing corporations. Certainly in the troubled years preceding and during the War of 1812, some state governments appear to have adopted the view that the chartering of domestic manufacturing concerns was required by patriotism. Between 1808 and 1815 New York issued more charters (165) to joint stock companies engaged in manufacturing than to all public utilities combined (164), a phenomenon that appears not to have recurred in any other period before the Civil War. But the larger truth is that, given the strengths of the American desire for economic development, the scarcities of capital funds in the early years following independence, and the sharpness of competition from foreign suppliers, manufacturing was endowed with a quasi-public rather than private character and given numerous encouragements by the state.[27]

It is not only the functions of the corporations but also the language of the laws creating them, the powers of government in which they were sometimes clothed, and their subsequent relation to the state that reveal their unmistakable semipublic nature. "Be it enacted by the Senate and House of Representatives in General Court assembled," reads a Massachusetts statute of 1818, that the following named individuals "hereby are constituted a corporation and body politic" for the purpose of erecting a flour mill. As bodies politic, corporations were accorded certain exclusive privileges to encourage the devotion of scarce private capital to public ends. Among these privileges were monopoly rights of way, tax exemption, the right of eminent domain, and the right granted to many nonbanking corporations to engage in banking and to hold lotteries in order to raise needed capital more easily. Many states established state-owned banks or invested in bank stock to provide funds or sources of credit for public enterprises. Sometimes the enterprises were private. Western and southwestern states issued millions in bonds to provide capital for "property banks" specializing in loans to cotton planters. In Pennsylvania it was legislative practice to include in bank charters a requirement which specified that transportation companies be given financial assistance.[28]

Corporate charters also provided for strict regulation by the state, including, for example, detailed specifications relative to the size and power of boards of directors, the liability of officers and stockholders, the nature of capital structures, and the operations to be undertaken. In addition, bank charters specified maximum interest rates, dividends were controlled by law, and public utilities were subjected to rate regulation. In this connection it should be noted that the significance of Chief Justice John Marshall's decision in the *Dartmouth College* case (1819) is sometimes misapprehended. That decision, holding a corporate charter to be a contract, did not place such charters beyond the control of the state issuing them. It did not alter the established practice of including elaborate regulations in original charter acts, and even insofar as subsequent regulations were concerned, "the inclusion of reservation clauses in charters and the pursuit of a strict construction policy by the state judiciary severely limited the effect of the anti-state barrier erected by Marshall."[29]

The dominant role of state governments began to falter two years after the beginning of the Panic of 1837. Overextension, corruption, maladministration, and other factors accentuated a crisis in which five states temporarily defaulted on their interest payments and one partially repudiated the principal of its debt. A wave of revulsion against state participation in internal improvements swept over the Old Northwest, and between 1842 and 1851 all six of its states bound themselves constitutionally not to make loans to improvements enterprises. In addition, Michigan, Indiana, Ohio, and Iowa also prohibited stock ownership; Maryland, Michigan, and Wisconsin prohibited state works; and Ohio, Michigan, and Illinois abandoned their extensive programs of state construction. Pennsylvania sold part of its state stock in 1843, Tennessee virtually abandoned its improvements program, and in the early 1840s even Virginia reduced its expenditures. The check to state enterprise was to prove only a temporary one, with a second wave of revulsion following in the 1870s, but it was sufficient to induce promoters of improvements projects to turn increasingly to local governments for aid. Their efforts were extraordinarily successful.[30]

Municipal governments participated in improvements projects to an even greater extent than did the states, especially in the decade following the Civil War. No fewer than twenty-two hundred laws passed by thirty-six states between 1830 and 1890 authorized the giving of local aid. In New York, 315 municipalities pledged approximately $37 million toward the construction of the state's roads between 1827 and 1875. Large as were the pre–Civil War commitments of Pennsylvania, state investment at its height was "of minor significance compared with investments by cities and counties." In Missouri during the 1850s it was the cities and counties along the routes of the railroads that bought most of the stocks of the state-aided railroads. In the antebellum South, cities and counties gave $45.6 million of total southern contributions of $144.1 million. Baltimore, Cincinnati, Milwaukee, and other cities also made generous contributions, subscribing to stock, purchasing railroad bonds, guaranteeing the credit of railroad companies, and even making donations. By 1879 outright gifts totaled nearly $30 million![31]

A contemporary historian has observed that "a persistent theme in the nation's economic development" has been "the incorrigible willingness of American public officials to seek the public good through private negotiations." One need add to this rich suggestion only its obverse: the equally incorrigible insistence of private citizens that government encourage or entirely provide those services and utilities either too costly or too risky to attract unaided private capital. It was especially on the underdeveloped frontiers of the nation that capital needs and development needs conjoined most pressingly. Social overhead capital, especially in transport, was a frontier need and both a sign of economic development and a prerequisite for further growth. As these frontiers receded, private investment could flow in larger relative proportions into areas properly scoured of risk by community action. Government, therefore, typically played the part of pioneer. Because of wide popular demand that it do so, the roles of political man and private citizen are difficult to distinguish. Hence if waste and lack of scruple, political and private, sometimes appeared onstage, and if one also finds such subordinate elements as "glib promoters reaching eagerly for public funds" or hopeful administrators seeking state investments so profitable that taxes could be reduced, the play itself was in large part written by community consensus.

In the closing decades of the antebellum period there occurred a noticeable rise in hostility to the state, only part of which is explicable in terms of reaction to economic depression and governmental defalcation. Perhaps basically the new attitude reflects the fact that as supplies of capital accumulated through profits won in internal and foreign commerce and in manufacturing, new groups rose to challenge the privileged positions of vested corporations. The note of egalitarianism is struck again and again in the political discourse of the time, and there is little reason to doubt that an increasingly active electorate and a professionalization of politics contributed importantly to a newly forming system of values. Some historians have attributed to this egalitarian impulse the general incorporation movement that marks the thirties. Studies of that movement in Massachusetts, New Jersey, Pennsylvania, and Missouri, however, "reveal it to be something other than a Jacksonian extension of privileges to all comers." In these states general laws were "rigid and unwelcome rules written by men who wanted to restrict corporate power and growth." Enterprisers sought to avoid them, and their success in doing so may be measured by the fact that incorporation by the traditional means of special legislation remained dominant until 1875.[32]

The future, however, was to belong not to hostility to incorporation per se but rather hostility to the privileged corporation possessing exclusive rights entrenched in law. It was to belong to the corporate values of Roger B. Taney, who deserves appreciation as the jurist of what has well been called the egalitarian age.[33] Taney took his stand on the premise that the interests of the community override all special interests. To promote those interests, the state charters corporations and gives them "peculiar privileges." But the gift must be carefully scrutinized to make sure that public interest really justifies those privileges. And charter grants must be narrowly construed thereafter to prevent vested property rights from interfering with the right of the state to create additional corporations in the public interest. Corporate egalitarianism is the phrase which appears best to describe Taney's ideal of publicly sponsored free competition in the interest of community welfare. His essential contribution was to adjust constitutional law to the needs of the corporation so as greatly to stimulate its use in business.

Taney gave clear expression to his corporate egalitarianism even before his appointment as chief justice of the Supreme Court in 1836. A former director on the boards of Maryland banks, he spoke from knowledge when he declared, "There is perhaps no business which yields a profit so certain and liberal as the business of banking and exchange; and it is proper that it should be open, as far as practicable, to the most free competition and its advantages shared by all classes of Society."[34] Believing that Nicholas Biddle's Bank of the United States restrained free enterprise in banking, he played, as Jackson's secretary of the Treasury, a well-known key role in the "war" against that institution. Although it is impossible to impute the subsequent increase in the number of state-chartered banks alone to the Jacksonian victory over the Second Bank, that event does help explain why the number of banks rose from 506 in 1834 (the year in which federal deposits ceased to be made in the Bank) to 901 in 1840. (See Table 8.)[35]

In one of his first statements as chief justice, an analysis written in June 1836 of an act providing for the rechartering of the banks in the District of Columbia, Taney vigorously stated his conviction that the power of the state must not be used to grant special privileges to any corporate group except for the purpose of promoting the public interest:

Every charter granted by a state or by the United States, to a bank or to any other company for the purpose of trade or manufacture, is a grant of peculiar privileges, and gives to the individuals who compose the corporation, rights and privileges which are not possessed by other members of the community. It would be against the spirit of our free institutions, by which equal rights are intended to be secured to all, to grant peculiar franchises and privileges to a body of individuals merely for the purpose of enabling them more conveniently and effectually to advance their own private interests. No charter could rightfully be granted on that ground. The consideration upon which alone, such peculiar privileges can be granted is the expectation and prospect of promoting thereby some public interest, and it follows from these principles that in every case where it is proposed to grant or to renew a charter the interests or wishes of the individuals who desire to be incorporated, ought

not to influence the decision of the government. The only inquiry which the
constituted authorities can properly make on such an application, is whether
the charter applied for is likely to produce any real benefit to the community,
and whether that benefit is sufficient to justify the grant.[36]

These principles inform Taney's decision in the *Charles River Bridge* case
(1837), wherein he refused to uphold the claim that the bridge company's
charter of incorporation gave it exclusive, monopolistic rights by implication.
Were this precedent established, modern improvements would be at the mercy
of old corporations. The country would be "thrown back to the improvements
of the last century, and obliged to stand still, until the claims of the old turnpike corporations shall be satisfied; and they shall consent to permit these
states to avail themselves of the lights of modern science, and to partake of the
benefit of those improvements which are now adding to the wealth and prosperity, and the convenience and comfort, of every other part of the civilized
world."[37] The effect of Taney's decision was to free new businesses from the
fear of monopolistic claims by older corporations with ambiguously worded
charters. In 1851 he applied the same principle to railroads in *Richmond Railroad v. Louisa Railroad* and served the public interest by opening another area
of enterprise to free competition.

Other decisions of the Taney Court also stimulated corporate development.
In *Bank of Augusta v. Earle* (1839) he held that a corporation might do business through its agents in states other than the one from which it had received
its charter, provided those states permitted it to do so. In *Louisville, Cincinnati
and Charleston Railroad Co. v. Letson* (1844) the Taney Court extended to
corporations the legal fiction of citizenship, thereby assuring them the protection of federal judicial review of assaults upon them by the states. In *Briscoe
v. Bank of Kentucky* (1837) the Court upheld the constitutionality of banknotes. Finally, to abbreviate the list of instances that might be cited, in *Woodruff v. Trapnall* (1851) and *Curran v. Arkansas* (1853) Taney opposed attempts
of banks or states to circumvent their legal obligations, thus increasing men's
sense of security in transactions involving corporations and their instrumentalities.[38]

Not only corporations but partnerships and proprietorships as well looked
to the legal system for the adjudication and enforcement of claims and obligations arising out of contracts, bills of exchange, promissory notes, agency
relationships, and other elements of private business transactions. Had not
the law responded to the businessman's need for predictability in these matters, the development of national markets would surely have been obstructed.
The problem was this: while rules for the settlement of claims and obligations
had long been features of mercantile practice, and indeed had been incorporated in part in the common law, their interpretation by the courts varied from
one state to another. What was required was uniformity, and this the Supreme

Court provided in 1842. In *Swift v. Tyson* the Court established the principle that, in private suits arising between citizens of different states, federal judges possessed the power to determine which common law rule should decide the case—regardless of state law. The doctrine laid down in *Swift* remained the law of the land until 1938 and supplied the basis for "an enlarged national jurisprudence that was virtually a body of federal common law."[39]

In sum, judicial interpretation at the federal level, together with state governments and their corporate agents, played major roles in the marshaling of the resources required by the developing economy. The importance of the federal judiciary deserves emphasis. In the earlier years of the century the rulings of the Marshall Court had fallen on the side of vested property rights. A vehement absolutist with respect to contractual obligations, Marshall moved well beyond the intent of the founding fathers, which was to confine contract impairment to private engagements. A legislative grant of land is an executory contract, he stated in his majority opinion in *Fletcher v. Peck* (1810), and it cannot be impaired by the rescinding act of a subsequent legislature. A corporate charter granted to individuals by government is also a contract, he ruled in the *Dartmouth College* case (1819), and its terms cannot be impaired by later legislation. Marshall was so adamant on the obligation to honor one's agreements that in *Ogden v. Saunders* (1827) he argued in dissent from the majority opinion—the only instance in his thirty-four years on the bench when his reasoning failed to win a majority—that the Court ought to hold unconstitutional not only state bankruptcy laws freeing debtors from contractual obligations assumed *prior* to the enactment of those laws, but even those releasing debtors from contractual obligations entered into *after* their passage.[40]

It is unquestionably true, as Associate Justice Joseph Story wrote after the death of Marshall, that his revered master's doctrine was essential if individuals rather than governments were to be expected to provide capital for society in the form of roads, bridges, and other structures. The difficulty was that the same doctrine which secured investment from impairment by state legislatures also tended to preserve the status quo—unless the charter grant reserved to the legislature the right to change its terms. The preservation of attractive privileges, even of monopoly rights, was justifiable when savings were limited and the risk of loss a pronounced one, for otherwise private individuals would not have been willing to invest their money and government would have been forced to resort to taxation, then as now a highly unpopular alternative, to raise the funds required. But although we have no figures to prove it, savings per capita were surely far more abundant by the time of Taney than they had been in the later colonial years. And the people doing the saving were far more numerous than earlier wealthholders. Their numbers and affluence had increased not only with the opening of opportunities in trade, privateering, and land speculation during the Revolution, but probably even more as a result of those created during the wars of the French Revolution and Napoleon (1793–1815) and, after their conclusion, those in banking, early industry, and agriculture, especially the growing of cotton. By the mid-thirties new entrepreneurs were beating on the doors of legal privilege and demanding equal investment opportunity before the law.

The legal historian Morton Horwitz believes that "the *Charles River Bridge* case represented the last great contest in America between two different models of economic development. For . . . Justice Story of the Supreme Court, the essential elements for economic progress were certainty of expectations and predictability of legal consequences."[41] The other model, that of the Taney Court majority, was that of a public policy promotive of free, fair, and open competition. Another possible view of the matter, however, is that the contest was not between two different models of economic development at all, but rather between a model of development and an effort by an older elite to hold back the forces of change in the interest of preserving its place in a more stable society.

This older elite of original investors wanted the legal system to protect its exclusive monopoly rights to income from public utilities, and where exclusivity was not granted explicitly by the corporate charter, they maintained it was implied. Taney, on the other hand, wanted to apply brakes to exclusivity to prevent it from running over and crushing competition. Once again, exclusivity was essential in earlier years if infrastructure was to be provided by private investment rather than by the tax system. Now that population growth and increase in urban density had made investment in bridge construction and other public utilities potentially profitable, the heavy hand of an older elite must be struck away whenever the grant of monopoly was not explicit. When it *was* explicit, the government could use its power of eminent domain, the power to take private property—in the case of the Charles River Bridge, property in the form of tolls—and to accord a just compensation to the proprietors for the taking.

The Taney Court provided the legal foundation for a democratized capitalism. Not only did it rule in favor of new and innovative investment while preserving the property rights of original investors. It also elaborated a constitutional basis on which the corporation as "citizen" could both sue in federal court and have standing in contract cases, rulings which paved the way for wider use of that increasingly essential mechanism for raising capital. State legislation would not be permitted to protect local business interests from outside competition by barring the activities of corporations chartered in other states. The battle against state protectionist policies was not a new one, nor would it end with the decisions of the Taney Court. Later in the century, as we shall see, Justice Stephen J. Field would continue the judicial effort to keep uncluttered the channels of activity essential to the development of a national market whose geographic bounds paralleled the territorial limits of the United States.

Federal constitutional exegesis by no means provided the only body of law to work in the direction of economic progress. Quieter and until recently hardly noticed by historians, was the role played by judge-made law at the state level, especially in the settlement of private suits over property rights. In a recent influential publication, Morton Horwitz maintains that the process of economic development in the United States "necessarily involved a drastic transformation in common law doctrines," and that this, in turn, "required a willingness on the part of the judiciary to sacrifice "old" property for the benefit of the "new."[42] The latter implies a redistribution of property, and the most potent legal weapon used to effect it was the power of eminent domain. Eminent domain had arisen only infrequently in the eighteenth century, and in consequence the principle that the state should compensate individuals for property taken for public use had little opportunity to develop. By 1820, however, "the influence of Blackstone's strict views about the necessity of providing compensation, reinforced by the antistatist bias of prevailing natural law thinking," had led every state in the Union except South Carolina to make statutory provisions for compensation. Nevertheless the principle admitted of shadings and qualifications which tended to be defined in ways favorable to the state as the cost of internal improvements mounted.

As late as 1800 an influential and perhaps dominant body of opinion continued to maintain that individuals held their property at the sufferance of the state—an opinion from which an easy transition was made to the view that a provision for compensation was a gratuitous limitation on an otherwise unrestrained sovereign power. The view enabled its proponents to confine the scope of the protection given, and throughout the first half of the nineteenth century this limiting disposition accompanied a trend toward providing for compensation in state constitutions. Behind the view, indeed the "basic source" of the resistance to the compensation principle in the earlier decades of the nineteenth century, were "those entrepreneurial groups who regarded it as a threat to low cost economic development." By about mid-1850 they had changed their minds and come to look upon uncompensated undertakings as egalitarian redistributions of wealth. By then, "many of the important benefits of cheap economic development had already been achieved."

The burden of damage judgments also had to be lessened if the costs of internal improvements were to be kept in bound. The experience of New York with damage claims arising out of the diversion of large upstate freshwater rivers into the Erie Canal illustrates the compulsion which judges in state courts were under to adapt the English common law to American circumstances. The unaltered common law had long held that title to the bed of rivers not subject to the ebb and flow of the tide vested in the owners of the adjoining banks, for such rivers were regarded as nonnavigable. But while this test of navigability fit the English situation, it did not fit that of America, where there were many navigable freshwater rivers in which the tide did not ebb and flow. If the English test were upheld, New York would have to compensate numerous owners of mills on the banks of upstate freshwater rivers. New York courts turned first this way and then that in confronting this question for nearly two decades after the completion of the Erie Canal in 1825, "finally ending up with an inconclusive *ad hoc* test of whether in particular cases there was an original intent by prior owners to grant title to the stream along with adjoining land." The result was that the state was relieved of a considerable portion, although not all, of potential damage claims. Similar problems in other states were also in some instances relieved by the courts, for example those of the proprietors of the Middlesex Canal in Massachusetts, who by 1807 had already devoted $58,000 of total expenditures of $536,000 to compensate for impaired water rights and land values.

Another source of increased costs for internal improvements was the traditional legal doctrine which held that trespasses or nuisances to land could not be justified by the social utility of the actor's conduct. Nor could the absence of negligence limit legal liability for injury to person or property. Since inevitably many improvements either directly injured or indirectly reduced the value of portions of neighboring land "common law doctrines appeared to present a major cost barrier to social change." Courts therefore had a strong incentive "not only to change the theory of legal liability but also to reconsider the nature of legal injury." If damage judgments could be eliminated or reduced, and juries sympathetic to injured parties replaced by state-appointed commissions charged with the task of assessing damages, landowners whose property values were impaired could essentially be compelled to underwrite some part of the cost of economic development. Here then was a potential source of "forced investment," an opportunity not to be lost, given the scarcity of capital for development.

American courts responded to the pressure of damage judgments by changing the legal rules. Distinguishing between immediate injuries and consequential ones, judges began to exempt the latter from liability, especially when actions by government were involved. For example, in a case in which New York undertook various public works to improve navigation on public rivers, the supreme court of that state held that neither the overflowing of riparian lands nor obstruction of access to private docks was a compensable injury. "Every great public improvement must, almost of necessity," the court explained, "more or less affect individual convenience and property; and where the injury sustained is remote and consequential, it is . . . to be borne as part of the price to be paid for the advantages of the social condition. This is founded upon the principle that the general good is to prevail over partial individual convenience." After 1825 courts usually defended this doctrine of consequential damages as a vindication of the general good, although as a rule extending it only to the state.

Another application of the same doctrine provided a similar immunity to private companies. Public works sometimes impeded access to private property and water privileges or gave rise to injuries to property in the form of odors and noises, all of them sources of a host of nuisance actions. On the face of things, American courts before the Civil War did not challenge an older principle of law which held that even a lawful use of one's own property which caused injury to the land of another could be enjoined as a nuisance. Most judges, however, shared the partiality toward economic development of the Kentucky Court of Appeals, which asserted in 1839:

> The onward spirit of the age must, to a reasonable extent, have its way. The law is made for the times, and will be made or modified by them. The expanded and still expanding genius of the *common law* should adapt it here, as elsewhere, to the improved and improving conditions of our country and our countrymen. And therefore, railroads and locomotive steam cars—the offsprings, as they will also be the parents, of progressive improvement—should not, in themselves, be considered as *nuisances,* although in ages that are gone, they might have been so held, because they would have been comparatively useless, and therefore more mischievous.

While most judges did not openly adapt the law of nuisance to the needs of economic development in the manner of the Kentucky court, they did work out a number of variations in the application of the older law which "eventually transformed the substantive doctrine itself."

One of the more pervasive of these was resort to an old distinction between public and private nuisances according to which a public or common nuisance could be reached only through indictment instituted by public authorities. This "public nuisance doctrine . . . enabled courts to extend to private companies virtually the same immunity from lawsuits that the state received under the theory of consequential damages." Even when the proximity of a particular property to the locus of an improvement brought a greater injury than that suffered by owners of more remote property, the "common and public" nature of the improvement might immunize it from private damage suits or injunctions. Railroads proved to be the most frequent beneficiaries of this doctrine. In short, after 1840 state courts held that private companies authorized by law to undertake works of public improvement were immune from nuisance actions as long as their conduct was not negligent.

The "negligence principle" itself enjoyed a significant rise in prominence during the pre–Civil War years. In 1800 the general presumption of private law was that a man using his property in an otherwise lawful way was still liable for nuisance if he caused injury to the land of another. It was incumbent on him, the eminent English jurist William Blackstone held, to "find some other place to do the act, where it will be less offensive." At the beginning of the nineteenth century virtually all injuries were conceived of as nuisances, but by the time of the Civil War many types of injury had been reclassified by the courts as "negligence," substantially reducing entrepreneurial liability. The rise of the negligence principle thus "led to a radical transformation not only in the theory of legal liability but in the underlying conception of property on which it was based."

Legal writers contributed substantially to the developing theory of legal liability. In the 1830s and 1840s Theron Metcalf, Simon Greenleaf, and Theodore Sedgwick participated in a significant debate on the question of punitive damages. In the past, violations of the tort law had been regarded universally as unjustified and unsocial acts, and there was little moral pressure to "calibrate damage judgments to the precise level of the injury." These writers helped adapt the earlier moralistic and penal conception of damages to the needs of a developing economy in which damage judgments were themselves among the costs of development. In doing so, they responded to a "widely shared need in the first half of the nineteenth century to import greater certainty and predictability into the law of damages, so that entrepreneurs could more accurately estimate the costs of economic improvements." By midcentury the proposition that the question of damages was an issue of law and that judges, if necessary, could set aside jury verdicts that were excessive, was gaining in general acceptance. So too was the momentum of a movement to have damages assessed by commissions rather than by juries. Juries were suspected of partiality toward the interests of small landowners whose property had been damaged by the activities of large transportation companies. It was a commonplace that their damage awards tended to be large. The impact of commissions on the size of damage judgments proved of particular importance to many railroad corporations during and after the 1830s. Movement to eliminate juries thus supplemented reduction in the likelihood of punitive damages to lessen the financial risks of entrepreneurship.

In sum, especially in the final two decades before the Civil War, American courts increasingly abandoned an earlier principle of strict liability and its associated principle of just compensation in favor of a negligence doctrine which held both governments and their chartered offspring not liable for damages unless caused by carelessness. Significantly, this tendency to extend the negligence standard to all actions in tort became manifest earliest in New York, Pennsylvania, and Massachusetts, states whose canal and railroad investments put them in the vanguard of modernization. The law of negligence thus

> became a leading means by which the dynamic and growing forces in American society were able to challenge and eventually overwhelm the weak and relatively powerless segments of the American economy. After 1840 the principle that one could not be held liable for socially useful activity exercised with due care became a commonplace of American law. In the process, the conception of property gradually changed from the eighteenth century view that dominion over land above all conferred the power to prevent others from interfering with one's quiet enjoyment of property to the nineteenth-century

assumption that the essential attribute of property ownership was the power to develop one's property regardless of the injurious consequence to others.

In essence, these years witnessed a transformation of common law doctrines, the effect of which was to create immunities from legal liability. The upshot was that the legal system, rather than the tax system, provided "substantial subsidies for those who undertook schemes of economic development."

The explanation offered for this choice of instrumentalities is straightforward. Change brought about through technical legal doctrine could more easily disguise underlying political choices. Had taxes been increased for the purpose of providing the subsidies, political conflict would have been difficult to avoid. And besides, widespread hostility to taxation existed. State budgetary expenditures in the first several decades of the nineteenth century were extraordinarily low and taxes generally light. The state budget in Massachusetts remained constant at roughly $133,000 between 1795 and 1820, the state using legal instruments such as monopolies and franchises as alternatives to cash outlays. In the early twenties about half of the state's revenues were derived from property and poll taxes and half from a tax on banks. New York amassed an enormous debt in building the Erie Canal, but the state looked upon its financial arrangement as means of facilitating profitable investments rather than as cash subsidies out of the tax system. New York had a general property tax from 1815 through 1826 but thereafter, despite very large increases in its debt, did not impose one again till 1843. Pennsylvania did not initiate a vigorous tax program till 1842. Investment in canals had simply "supplemented [a] strong anti-tax bias" with "the idea of positive profit-making state—a state in which taxes were abolished." The southern and western states depended chiefly on property taxes but rates were generally low. In Georgia there existed an "ever-present desire to find a substitute for taxes." In short, "every bit as significant as overt forms of direct financial encouragement of enterprise were the enormous, but hidden, legal subsidies and resulting redistributions of wealth brought about through changes in common law doctrines."

Furthermore, it is "quite likely," the argument continues, that legal subsidies contributed to "an increase in inequality by throwing a disproportionate share of the burdens of economic growth on the weakest and least organized groups in American society." Significantly, when state taxation did increase dramatically in the 1840s, it was accompanied by a no less dramatic upsurge in explicit laissez-faire ideology. The implication is clear: the state was actively interventionist in providing the social overhead capital required by a developing society so long as it could be financed by profitable investments or concealed subsidy. But the depression of 1839–1843 brought an end to hopes for expected returns from state investments. Instead of receiving a major part of their income from them, the states were suddenly faced with the necessity of taxing their citizens to meet interest payments on the debts incurred to finance the improvements. The ideological response was one of insistence that the state withdraw from the field.

These powerful suggestions deserve close scrutiny. Transformation of the common law did permit some portion of the cost of internal improvements to be financed by those who were injured in person or property by that process. But we need to have a clearer idea of the size of that portion in relation to the total cost, and also a profile of the land-owning group whom the law failed to protect. However, we surely do not need to add to these tasks of research that of identifying "entrepreneurial groups" bringing pressure upon the legal system on behalf of their interests in development. Belief in the importance of economic development was so widely held that courts and judges as well as lawmakers shared with a large public this key element of the antebellum value system.

We *do* have to ask whether the burden of the cost borne by the relatively weak and powerless would have been a lesser one if damages for injuries had been allowed them and then recouped via higher tolls. In that event, their cost would have been borne by users of the service and consumers of the products carried by canals and railroads. If we assume the demand for those services and products to have been elastic, that is to say, if we assume that an increase in toll charges or product prices would have resulted in a disproportionately larger decrease in demand, then there would have been fewer users, and smaller economic growth—consequences which strengthen the argument that these options were chosen to expedite growth. Yet a far larger number of individuals would have been called upon to bear a portion of its cost, and some farmers would have been pressed back to subsistence levels of well-being.

We need also inquire into the effect of the choices actually made on the interests of the relatively weak and powerless who benefited by those choices. In all probability the individuals whose property was damaged by a work of internal improvement were far fewer in number than those who benefited from higher land values, improved terms of trade, and an eventually widened tax base permitting additional public services to be provided. In short, a form of social cost-benefit analysis is required, one that takes into account the credits as well as the debits of society's decisions, before we can hazard a reliable estimate of their historical impact. One final suggestion may be advanced: the supply of capital was often less than the demand for it in antebellum America not because it did not exist absolutely but rather because those who possessed it chose alternative investments of lesser risk. This being the case, knowledge that large damage claims would not be allowed may well have had the effect of loosening the purse strings of investment.

Thus far we have stressed that the widespread demand for economic development in antebellum America found expression in legal activism at federal, state, and municipal levels, and in private as well as public law. We now have to ask what difference it all made. What was the total investment by government in relation to private investment? In the absence of the former, would the latter have been forthcoming anyway, perhaps at a somewhat later time? If so, what value, if any, attaches to the speedier development made possible by governmental encouragement? Were there costs as well as benefits of speed?

Some of these questions are extremely difficult to answer; but not all of them are. Recent researches into the role of state governments in the nineteenth-century economy show that from the outset of the quantitative record in 1820 to the end of the 1840s, investment in social overhead capital dominated aggregate expenditures. Furthermore, expenditures for transportation were the major component of that investment, as is clear from Table 9, which gives estimated data for overlapping decades.[43]

One school of thought explains this widespread governmental activism in terms of shortages of private stocks of capital, together with a natural disinclination on the part of holders of such supplies as did exist to venture them in enterprises of high risk. The Erie Canal, for example, cost $7 million, a sum fourteen times the largest private-canal investment (namely, in the Middlesex Canal) and ten times the largest authorized capital of any manufacturing corporation in existence (in 1817). "It is impossible to believe," one scholar writes, "that American business was ready for such a quantum leap."[44]

Scarcities of private capital particularly affected needs for transport, in which returns on investment were apt not only to be long deferred but to take the diffused form of enhanced land values, increased employment and business opportunities, and other external gains. In other words, public funds were needed most when what economists call the social rate of return on investment promised to be higher than the private rate of return. This was likely to be the

Table 9. Expenditures by state governments on social overhead and transportation, 1820–1860 (overlapping decades).

Decade	Social overhead (% of aggregate expenditures)	Transportation (% of social overhead)
1820–1829	47.8	42.8
1825–1834	60.3	58.1
1830–1839	64.0	59.7
1835–1844	59.1	52.6
1840–1849	46.7	38.6
1845–1854	30.6	16.3
1850–1859	31.0	14.3
1855–1864	16.7	6.2

Source: Adapted from Charles F. Holt, *The Role of State Government in the Nineteenth-Century American Economy, 1820–1902: A Quantitative Study* (New York: Arno Press, 1977), p. 50 (reissued by The Ayer Company, Salem, N.H.). Used with permission.

case when canals and railroads were not projected as links between settled points. Lack of sufficient population density meant that opportunities for gain did not yet exist and would have to be created by the transport facilities themselves. This they would do by affording ease of movement at reduced costs for people and products. Projectors of most canals and railroads found themselves in this situation. The facilities they hoped to build were "developmental" rather than "exploitative" in character. Public assistance, by lessening risks of loss, helped attract private funds, foreign as well as domestic, to ventures they might otherwise not have supported.

The conquest of the Appalachian Barrier, the argument continues, is a case in point. Of the total government investment in internal improvements before the Civil War, well over half was spent in the seven states that faced or included the Appalachian Mountains. By the early 1850s five major improvements had reached the Midwest by crossing or by-passing this barrier, namely, the Erie Canal, and four trunkline railroads—the New York Central, the Erie, the Pennsylvania, and the Baltimore & Ohio. Of these, the Erie was a public work of the state of New York. On the other hand, the New York Central was built almost entirely with private funds. Each of the other three made its way to Lake Erie or the Ohio River by means of an investment that came almost equally from public and private sources. The Pennsylvania Railroad and the Baltimore & Ohio Railroad were mixed enterprises, with government subscriptions largely from the cities of Philadelphia and Baltimore, respectively, while the Erie Railroad received a substantial donation from the state of New York.[45]

Critics reply to these arguments by distinguishing between internal improvements projects. Construction ahead of demand and in the face of scarcities of private capital cannot justify every decision taken by public bodies. Some projects were failures, the Pennsylvania Main Line notoriously so. Indeed, despite the massive intervention of government in the financing of canal construction, it is probable that most of the canals were unsuccessful, in the sense that their private rates of return proved smaller than those obtainable from alternative investment opportunities. One scholar calculates that probably only about 20 percent of total construction costs were devoted to canals which, like the Erie, succeeded. Another points out that, in contrast to the dismal history of many canals, most of the railroads built in the Midwest in the 1850s were financially successful ventures built in response to existing demand from settlements already in place and largely financed by local private capital. Apparently the market was a better judge of need than was government.[46]

If so, the market would almost certainly have yielded the funds needed to cross the Appalachian Barrier later in the century. To be sure, settlement of the interior would have been delayed, and the chances are that the Midwest in the 1850s would not have contained a large enough population to have induced private entrepreneurs to construct railroads with private funds. The railroads would have had to wait. So what would have been the consequences? Although the economic consequences, to say nothing of the social and political ones, are beyond the bounds of measurement, it may be reasonably conjectured that when construction decisions were well taken, the process of economic development in fact got under way sooner than it would otherwise have done. Spatially separated markets were extended and integrated, commercialized agriculture made greater inroads on the subsistence sector, land values rose, and prices of commodities shipped over long distances declined along with freight costs. In all probability, savings increased, interest rates went down, and capital was formed in the major sectors more quickly. But once again, we can only speculate on the consequences of delay. Fortunately, the growing transport net affected not only the world of the subjunctive, but also of historic actuality, principally in the form of population movements to the West and the shape of the nation's number one enterprise, agriculture.

8

The Agricultural Republic

Pouring through the Cumberland Gap in the Appalachians, beating their way over rough roads and Indian trails through dense wilderness, floating on flatboats down the Ohio, thronging onto horse-drawn barges along the Erie Canal, or following a number of other routes, early nineteenth-century Americans began a process which sent the frontier reeling westward, till by 1890 the census taker was obliged to report that the frontier was so broken into that it no longer could be said to form a continuous line. It was one of the great movements of human history, and one made at substantial human cost, not least to the native Indian tribes swept aside by the avalanche. It was of course not a continuous movement, and at any time the numbers of people involved varied with considerations such as land prices and farm commodity prices, the latter in foreign as well as eastern markets; availability and cost of transportation, and farm-making costs in the West, including the cost of getting there. Why they went seems pretty obvious. People who are able to do so usually get up and go because they are not doing well where they are or think they can do better elsewhere. But while economic motivation can rarely be dismissed, neither can the restless challenge of new experience, especially in the eyes of adventurous young men and women.

Whatever the motivation, it would be difficult to exaggerate the importance of the westward movement and of the vast stretches of accessible land which sustained it. Together, they continually restocked the resources available to the American people, and did so at a lesser cost in factor inputs once the tide of settlement reached the treeless plains. They also sustained agriculture as the dominant economic pursuit, graduating the process of industrialization over a longer span of time than we are accustomed to believe. Land also occupied an important place in public policy and law. Most of it was public domain owned by the federal government. Obviously, therefore, laws governing the terms of its disposal also belong among influences on the timing and size of the westward movement.

The public domain originated in the surrender of western land claims held by seven of the original thirteen states on the basis of their colonial charters.

At first these states—Massachusetts, Connecticut, New York, Virginia, North Carolina, South Carolina, and Georgia—were reluctant to give up their claims to the lands lying between the Allegheny Mountains and the Mississippi River. Possession would enable them to raise needed public revenues from land sales rather than from taxation. Residents of states lacking similar claims, however, realized that people and their enterprises would be tempted to migrate to areas of low taxation, and, with Maryland representatives serving as spokesmen in the Continental Congress, they argued that lands which "had been secured by the blood and treasure of all, ought, in reason, justice and policy, to be considered a common stock, to be parcelled out by Congress into free, convenient, and independent republics." Maryland refused to ratify the Articles of Confederation till the privileged states surrendered their claims to the Union. New York did so on March 1, 1781, and Maryland ratified the Articles the same day. The other claimant states followed suit in the years from 1784 to 1802, giving up to the Union some 233 million acres in all.

Title to Florida and to the remaining area west of the Mississippi (except for Texas) passed to the federal government at the time of their incorporation into the national domain. Table 10 lists the acquisitions made before the Civil War and the number of acres involved in each. All told, the federal government acquired title to well over a billion acres, nearly three of every four acres of land in the United States.[1]

The framing of policies to govern the alienation of the public lands involved conflicting private and public interests from the outset. At the beginning not only Hamilton but also Jefferson, Gallatin, and nearly all other political leaders agreed that the public domain should be sold to raise revenue, especially for the purpose of retiring the public debt. Opinion divided, however, not only

Table 10. Acquisition of public domain, 1784–1853.

Means of acquisition	Number of acres
Ceded by seven states to the U.S. (1784–1802)	233,415,680
Louisiana Purchase (1803)	523,446,400
Florida (1819)	43,342,720
Oregon Compromise (1846)	180,644,480
Treaty of Guadalupe Hidalgo (Mexican cession) (1848)	344,479,360
Purchase from Texas (1850)	78,842,880
Gadsden Purchase (1853)	18,961,920
	1,413,133,440
Private land claims confirmed and patented	− 34,000,000
Total	1,379,133,440

Source: Bureau of the Census, *Historical Statistics of the United States, Colonial Times to 1970* (Washington, D.C.: Government Printing Office, 1976), I, 22-23.

on whether sales to speculators or settlers would maximize those revenues, but even on whether a high or low price per acre would appeal to the former! Both Gallatin and Hamilton, political opposites, disapproved of speculation, but Gallatin believed a sales price of two dollars an acre would discourage it, whereas Hamilton thought a low price of twenty or thirty cents would do so.[2]

As it turned out, neither settler nor speculator showed much interest in the terms finally settled on by a congressional statute of 1796. The law required a minimum purchase of 640 acres at a price of two dollars an acre and offered the following credit terms: 5 percent down, with half the balance due in thirty days, the other half in a year. The terms were not nearly so generous as those commonly offered by landholding states and private owners. In effect, they favored the interests of eastern landholders, who feared the depressing influence of widespread emigration on land values in the older states. It was in these states that the great bulk of the people lived, the first federal census of 1790 showing them distributed almost entirely along the Atlantic seaboard between Maine and Florida. Only 3 percent of the population lived west of the Appalachian Mountains. The southeastern edge of the Allegheny plateau marked the general limit of continuous settlement, the most populous areas being found in eastern Massachusetts, Rhode Island, Connecticut, and around New York City.[3]

Despite the unattractiveness of federal sales terms, the movement west picked up between 1790 and 1800, presumably under the stimulus of rival state and private terms, and by 1800 residents in the western states and territories made up 7 percent of the total population. At many points during the decade, however, settlements were retarded by opposition from the Indians, especially in Georgia, where powerful tribes of Creeks and Cherokees resisted the encroachment of the white man.[4]

After 1800 the movement west became more rapid still, certainly in part because Congress, disappointed with the results of the act of 1796, proceeded to respond to spokesmen for the frontier and liberalized the land laws. The act of 1800 made no concession on price, which remained at two dollars an acre, but it reduced the minimum purchase to 320 acres and made major changes in credit terms. Buyers were permitted to pay one-twentieth at the time of purchase, one-fourth of the balance in forty days, a second fourth in two years, and the third and fourth installments in three and four years. The year 1804 brought further liberalization, the minimum plot being halved to 160 acres; by 1810, 15 percent of the population of 7,224,000, or 1,048,000 people, resided in the western states and territories.[5]

By that year the federal government had extinguished Indian titles to the unsecured portions of the Western Reserve and to great tracts of Indiana, along the Ohio River and up the Wabash Valley, thus, in the words of Frederick Jackson Turner, "protecting the Ohio highway from the Indians, and opening new lands to settlement." New Englanders had already begun to cross

Pennsylvania on their way to Ohio; after the discouraging economic effects of the embargo, their emigrant wagons, precursors of the "prairie schooner," greatly increased in number. Migration from New England and the Middle Atlantic states constituted the northern wing of the westward movement. There was also a southern wing, and, as in the case of its counterpart, accommodations with Indian tribes facilitated settlement.[6]

Despite the fact that settlement generally followed the course of the rivers on which people depended to carry their surplus produce to market—areas between the rivers being lightly occupied—and despite the impressive early peopling of the West, the region was of limited economic significance to the rest of the nation. Large numbers lived at the level of subsistence or close to it. Although some were able to produce more than was required for consumption needs and to exchange the surplus for goods provided by wandering peddlers or nearby stores—often floating stores on midwestern rivers—many represented an underemployed economic resource.[7]

As Congressman Peter B. Porter of New York remarked in a speech to Congress in 1810, the "great evil . . . under which the inhabitants of the western country labor, arises from the want of a market." Western soils were so fertile that farmers had to spend only half their time in labor to fill their consumption needs. And since there was "nothing to incite them to produce more," they were "naturally led to spend the other part of their time in idleness and dissipation."[8] The value of produce received at New Orleans, the port through which most of the trade of the West passed, was $5,370,000 in 1807, and by 1816 it had risen to only $8,773,000. Other evidences of expanding trade—flourishing towns and cities—were conspicuously few. In 1810 New Orleans, with a population of 24,562, was the only city of any considerable size in the West. Pittsburgh had 4,768 inhabitants, Lexington 4,326, and Cincinnati 2,540. Louisville, St. Louis, Nashville, and Natchez each had fewer than 1,000.[9]

A principal deterrent to the growth of the West before the end of the War of 1812 was the high cost of transportation for the commodities of the region. The wheat, flour, butter, pork, tobacco, hemp, lead, and other products of the rich agricultural lands of the Ohio Valley were of low value in relation to their bulk. Because of this it was cheaper to ship them more than three thousand miles by water—down the Ohio and Mississippi rivers to New Orleans, then up the Atlantic coast to Philadelphia, New York, or Boston—than three hundred miles overland across the Appalachian highlands to Philadelphia or Baltimore. Traffic, moreover, was for the most part a one-way flow—downriver—for shipments upriver against the current were almost prohibitively expensive. Textiles, hardware, hats, tea, and other commodities of high value relative to their bulk were imported from across the Appalachians rather than brought up the river. This was in the main another one-way flow of goods (one of the chief exceptions being cattle driven on foot over the mountains to the East Coast). This difficult pattern of interregional trade encouraged subsistence rather than commercial agriculture, and it depressed farm incomes in the West, as well as making western food and raw materials more expensive in the East.[10]

The appearance of steamboats on the rivers of the West after the War of 1812 marked the beginning of significant change in the region's pattern of economic life. In 1817 only 17 steamboats plied the western rivers, and the total volume of freight carried amounted to only 3,290 tons; by 1855 these figures had increased phenomenally to 727 vessels and 170,000 tons. Steamboats made possible much more upriver traffic and reduced shipping costs both upstream and downstream. The reduction in upriver freight rates, far greater than in downstream charges, lowered the costs of imported merchandise. Just before the Civil War downstream rates averaged 25 to 30 percent of their level in the years from 1815 to 1819, but upstream rates had fallen to 5 or 10 percent of those charged in the earlier period. The latter decline shifted the "terms of trade" in favor of the farmer—that is to say, it lowered the prices of goods farmers bought relative to the prices of those they sold. The net effect was to increase western farm income substantially and to encourage both an increase in the settlement of the West and a shift from subsistence to commercial agriculture. Lowered freight rates promoted the rapid development of the trans-Appalachian frontier. Most of the decline took place in the early 1820s—it was in 1823 that the terms of trade began a long-term rise in the farmer's favor—and in 1828 and 1829 public land sales jumped from an annual average of 814,000 acres (1823–1827) to an average of 1,587,500 acres.[11]

The steamboat was not the only transport innovation contributing to this result. Turnpikes, canals, and railroads also improved the facilities of the country and made the West more attractive to settlers. Yet a leading scholar's opinion that the steamboat was "the most important agency of internal transportation in the country" until the 1850s is surely justified.[12] The amount of traffic carried by railroads before 1840 was negligible in comparison with that moving on all inland waterways. And the direct influence of turnpikes was lessened by their inability to provide a cheap means of transportation over considerable distances. Some turnpikes were important as avenues of movement to the West—the Cumberland Road, for example, which by 1818 was opened to traffic as far as Wheeling on the Ohio River, afforded easy access into southern Ohio and southern Indiana—but they were much less useful for shipping bulky commodities to the East. Like the canals, they proved to be feeders rather than competitors of steamboats.[13]

Nevertheless canals exerted a significant impact on the volume of agricultural production even when serving as feeders. They did so by lowering the overland freight charges made by wagon transport, their most direct competitor. The rate for carriage by wagon appears to have varied between $.30 and

$.70 a ton from 1800 to 1819, rates which discouraged the long-distance shipment of bulky agricultural commodities of low value. By the 1850s, $.15 per ton-mile appears to have been the usual rate on ordinary highways. Particular canals effected even more dramatic reductions. In 1817 the average rate for freight shipments between Buffalo and New York, via overland wagon and the Hudson River, was $.19 per ton-mile. After the completed Erie Canal linked these two cities in 1825, the rate fell to an average of only $.02 per ton-mile during the years 1830–1850, a decline of more than 90 percent.[14]

While the importance of transport improvements cannot be denied, market changes provide the most fundamental explanation for the development of the West. Rising international prices for American commodities led not only to migration westward but also to a growing insistence on internal improvements, both on the part of eastern seaboard interests desiring to serve as export funnels for western produce and on the part of the West itself. The coming of peace after the War of 1812 brought a large European demand for American wheat, flour, tobacco, rice, and especially cotton, which reached the highest price it would ever attain. Selling at an average annual price of $.14 per pound in the New York market during the years 1809–1814, the price of "middling Upland" rose to $.21 in 1815, then soared to $.30 the next year. Such prices, together with an anticipation of still higher ones, induced farmers and planters in Virginia, the Carolinas, and other southern states to abandon their over-cropped and worn-out lands and move west, first to Kentucky and Tennessee and then to "Mississippi Territory." During the same intervals the price of wheat in the Philadelphia market rose from an annual average of $1.63 per bushel (1809–1814) to $1.94 in 1816 and $2.41 in 1817. North of the Ohio River—the geographic boundary between freedom and slavery—sales from the public domain increased from 1,093,000 acres in 1815 to approximately twice that number in 1819, but in Mississippi and Alabama the increase was spectacular in its proportions: from 27,000 acres in 1815 to 2,278,000 four years later. Sales west of the Mississippi River also underwent large increases, 1,133,424 acres being sold in Missouri in the single year 1819.[15]

It was cotton that led the southern wing of the western movement. Cotton's rise to commercial prominence was a supply response to demands set in motion by the beginnings of the Industrial Revolution in England. As we have seen, during the eighteenth and early nineteenth centuries a series of technological innovations in spinning and weaving and in the generation of power (the steam engine) transformed the manufacture of cotton textiles. Although power spinning and weaving were only rarely brought together under the same roof to constitute factory production—in contrast to subsequent American methods—mechanization did enlarge greatly both the output of yarn and cloth and the demand for the raw cotton essential to their production. The result was an increase in the production and export of cotton to England from the numerous countries whose climatic and other conditions were favorable to its growth. India, Brazil, and other nations increased their cotton output, but the American South emerged as the principal source of supply.[16]

Though not unknown in the colonial period, cotton had been cultivated on a comparatively small scale before the final decades of the eighteenth century. The extent to which it figured among American exports as late as 1784 may be gauged by the reputed seizure of eight bags of American cotton by the customs officers in Liverpool on the ground that so much cotton could not possibly be the produce of the United States! (The customs officers were sure it must have originated in the West Indies, the produce of which was forbidden by the Navigation Act to be imported into England under a foreign flag.)[17] How dramatically this situation was to change in the course of a few years is clearly revealed by the figures for cotton exports during and after the 1790s (see Table 11).

First to respond to the British demand was the production of Sea Island cotton. Of the two varieties of cotton grown in the United States, Upland and Sea Island, the second was a late-comer. Not until about 1786 did some planters, after having acquired seed from the Bahama Islands, introduce its culture along the Georgia and South Carolina coast. The English market promptly placed a high premium on the silky, long-fibered, but strong cotton from America. Before the end of the century prices in Liverpool rose to a high of five shillings per pound, and American production responded accordingly. By 1805 exports of the Sea Island staple amounted to nearly 9 million pounds. Unlike the "Upland," Sea Island fibers were easily detached from the seed by squeezing the cotton between a pair of simple rollers. Climatic requirements, however, confined the culture of Sea Island cotton to within a strip thirty or forty miles wide along the coast of South Carolina and Georgia, and in consequence exports never amounted to as much as 16 million pounds in any year prior to 1860. The small size of this figure in relation to the nation's total cotton exports each year is evident from the figures presented in Table 11. In sum, a pound of Sea Island cotton was worth a good deal more than a pound of "middling Upland" (which was second-grade cotton), but the overwhelming bulk of the cotton exported by the United States during the period was nevertheless of the latter variety.[18]

What made possible the massive export of Upland cotton was Eli Whitney's invention of the cotton gin. Rarely, if ever, does an invention so clearly appear to have been the child of economic necessity. Given the rising British demand and a supply response that was potentially vast, provided only that some mechanical way was found to reduce the labor cost of separating the sticky short fibers from the green seeds, Whitney was by no means the only American trying to solve the problem. His gin was a simple device—so simple as to lend credence to the belief that someone else would have soon developed it if Whitney had not. The gin consisted of a cylinder fitted with wire teeth. The latter drew the seed cotton through a wire screen that separated the seed from

Table 11. United States cotton exports, 1784–1860.

Year ending August 31	Exports (thousands of pounds)	Year ending August 31	Exports (thousands of pounds)
1784	1	1823	173,723
1785	2	1824	142,370
1786	1	1825	176,440
1787	16	1826	204,535
1788	58	1827	294,310
1789	126	1828	210,590
1790	12	1829	264,847
1791	189	1830	298,459
1792	138	1831	270,980
1793	488	1832	322,215
1794	1,602	1833	303,609
1795	6,276	1834	372,946
1796	6,107	1835	375,638
1797	3,788	1836	415,493
1798	9,360	1837	442,833
1799	9,532	1838	597,063
1800	17,790	1839	412,681
1801	20,911	1840	718,509
1802	27,501	1841	517,628
1803	41,106	1842	581,703
1804	38,118	1843	822,146
1805	40,383	1844	671,350
1806	37,491	1845	864,759
1807	66,213	1846	685,042
1808	12,064	1847	534,967
1809	53,210	1848	774,895
1810	93,874	1849	971,340
1811	62,186	1850	681,176
1812	28,953	1851	827,303
1813	19,400	1852	1,045,880
1814	17,806	1853	1,107,439
1815	82,999	1854	997,234
1816	81,747	1855	973,987
1817	85,649	1856	1,240,935
1818	92,471	1857	1,000,180
1819	87,997	1858	1,586,981
1820	127,860	1859	1,350,567
1821	124,893	1860	1,739,893
1822	144,675		

Source: Adapted from Stuart Bruchey, ed., *Cotton and the Growth of the American Economy, 1790–1860: Sources and Readings* (New York: Harcourt, Brace & World), table 3A. Used with permission.

the lint, and a revolving brush then removed the lint from the teeth of the cylinder. Before its invention, a good hand took a day to clean one pound of cotton. The gin enabled him to increase his output by fifty times. Because it was easily imitable—particularly after the shed in which Whitney had stored his model was broken into and the machine stolen—several models soon appeared in the South, with the result that Whitney and his partner, Phineas Miller, found themselves entangled in a maze of virtually fruitless litigation. Had they been able to secure their patent and the monopoly prices this would have made possible, the spread of cotton culture would surely have been de- layed. Their inability to do so meant that the gin became available at a com- petitive price.[19]

In possession of a favorable climate, abundant supplies of cheap and richly productive land, and an expandable plantation-labor system with which to work it, the South soon saw cotton establish a comparative advantage over most alternative crops in the regions suited to its growth. Sugar, tobacco, and rice continued to be important crops in local areas on the fringes of the Cotton Kingdom, but neither they nor any other crop succeeded in challenging the sway of the ruling staple. The cultivation of rice could not be greatly expanded, because it was confined to the marshlands along the Carolina and Georgia coasts that could be drained, diked, and flooded. Requirements of soil and climate confined sugar to a small area. Wheat did not do well in the lower South. The indigo industry of the Carolinas and Georgia all but died out when the Revolution ended the bounty of six pence per pound that the British had paid. As for tobacco, that industry was entering in 1783 "upon a half century of such wellnigh constant low prices that the opening of each new tract for culture was offset by the abandonment of an old one, and the export remained stationary at a little less than half a million hogsheads."[20]

In contrast to these other commercial crops, cotton became the great staple of an ever-widening portion of the southern landscape. In 1790 its growth was largely confined to a few islands off the South Carolina and Georgia coast and a few favored areas on the mainland within a few miles of the sea. With the invention of the gin, cultivation moved into the backcountry of Georgia, where, with Augusta as center and chief market, it soon covered the upland parts of that state and South Carolina. For more than a quarter of a century this was the principal cotton-producing area of the nation. Indeed, as late as 1821 more than one-half of the entire cotton crop was grown in these two states alone. (see Table 12).[21]

The first shift from its original center took the cotton belt north into North Carolina and Virginia and west over the mountains into southwestern Ten- nessee. Following the War of 1812, the decisive movement was to the South- west, with the tide of cultivation flowing first into Alabama, Mississippi, and Louisiana and eventually into Arkansas and Texas. By the mid-1820s South Carolina and Georgia had begun to lose their original dominant position; by

Table 12. Percentage share of individual states in United States cotton production, 1791–1859.

Year		N.C.	S.C.	Ga.	Fla.	Ala.	Miss.	La.	Tex.	Ark.	Tenn.	All other states
							State					
1791:	% of total	—	75.0	25.0	—	—	—	—	—	—	—	—
1801:	% of total	10.0	50.0	25.0	—	—	—	—	—	—	2.5	12.5
	% increase	—	1233.3	200.0	—	—	—	—	—	—	—	—
1811:	% of total	8.7	50.0	25.0	—	—	—	2.5	—	—	3.8	10.0
	% increase	75.0	100.0	100.0	—	—	—	—	—	—	200.0	60.0
1821:	% of total	5.7	28.2	25.4	—	11.3	5.7	5.7	—	—	11.3	6.7
	% increase	42.8	25.0	125.0	—	—	—	400.0	—	—	566.6	50.0
1826:	% of total	3.1	21.2	22.7	0.6	13.6	6.0	11.5	—	0.1	13.6	7.6
	% increase	0.0	40.0	66.7	—	125.0	100.0	250.0	—	—	125.0	108.5
1833:	% of total	2.3	16.7	20.0	3.4	14.8	15.9	12.5	—	0.1	11.3	3.0
	% increase	0.0	4.3	17.3	650.0	44.4	250.0	44.7	—	60.0	11.1	−48.0
1834:	% of total	2.1	14.3	16.4	4.4	18.6	18.6	13.5	—	0.1	9.8	2.2
	% increase	−5.0	−10.3	−17.3	−33.3	30.8	21.4	12.7	—	−37.5	−10.0	−23.1
1839:	% of total	6.5	7.8	20.7	1.6	14.8	24.3	19.5	—	0.8	3.5	0.5
	% increase	46.3	−5.8	17.9	39.5	37.8	27.3	48.2	—	00.0	38.5	55.0
1849:	% of total	3.0	12.2	20.2	1.8	22.9	19.7	7.2	2.3	2.6	7.8	0.2
	% increase	−43.2	94.5	22.1	48.8	92.4	0.4	−53.6	—	330.0	180.9	−64.5
1859:	% of total	3.2	6.9	15.4	1.5	21.7	26.4	15.4	1.0	0.8	6.5	1.2
	% increase	119.0	17.5	56.5	66.1	65.3	175.8	335.5	727.5	524.5	69.6	1443.8

Source: Adapted from Ernst von Halle, *Baumwollproduktion und Pflanzungwirtschaft in den Nordamerikan Sudstaaten*, vol. 1, *Die Skalvenzeit* (Leipzig: Duncker & Humblot, 1897), pp. 169–170. Used with permission.

the time of the Civil War they accounted for less than a quarter of the nation's cotton output. Mississippi and Alabama had become the leading states, with Louisiana not far behind. New Orleans—the great central market for the cotton of the western region—had received only 37,000 bales in 1816; but in 1822 the number was 161,000, in 1830, 428,000, and in 1840, 923,000 bales. Expressed in terms of changing proportions, the states and territories from Alabama and Tennessee westward increased their share of the nation's total output from one-sixteenth in 1811 to one-third in 1820, one-half before 1830, and nearly two-thirds in 1840. In 1791 cotton production in the United States had represented less than one-half of one percent of world output. By 1840, 62.6 percent, or nearly two of every three bales produced in the world, originated in this country.[22]

Again and again, the lodestar promise inherent in the rising prices of cotton and agricultural commodities led farm families to push against the periphery of settled communities. By 1820 the frontier line extended from southeastern Michigan into Missouri territory, from which point, after making a great semicircle to the east, it swept west again around a body of population in Louisiana and ended along the Gulf coast in that state. Settlements in Alabama, previously held back by the Creeks, were rapidly reinforced in consequence of the victory of General Jackson over that tribe and its subsequent cession of portions of its territory. Overall, more than 2 million people, or 23 percent of the total population of 9,618,000, lived in the West in 1820.[23] In that year the federal government cut the price of public land to $1.25 an acre—while requiring full payment on the day of purchase—and in 1832 it reduced to forty acres the minimum plot that had to be bought. Continued liberalization of the land laws undoubtedly helped many families reach the decision to go west, and they did so in ever-increasing numbers. During the 1820s they tended to concentrate within the existing frontier line rather than to extend it. In consequence, by 1830, when the population stood at 12,901,000—with 29 percent, or nearly 4 million persons, living in the West—its average density of 7.4 persons per square mile of land area exceeded that of any earlier decade after 1790. In other words, those parts of the country that were already relatively densely settled became even more so. Outside the body of continuous settlement large groups of people were no longer to be found, although small patches of population existed in Ohio, Indiana, Illinois, and Michigan territory.[24]

By 1840 the American people numbered 17,120,000, and of these, 37 percent, or 6,334,400 persons, resided in the West. While the frontier line resumed its outward push during the decade, average density increased once again, and in 1840 it stood at 9.8 persons per square mile of land area. Comparatively dense settlement characterized the large areas of Georgia, Alabama, and Mississippi from which the Cherokees, Creeks, Choctaws, and Chickasaws had been removed to Indian territory, constituted by an act of June 30,

1834. A similar removal of the Sac, Fox, and Patawatomi tribes from their country in northern Illinois resulted in prompt settlement of nearly all of Indiana, Illinois, and other regions across Michigan and Wisconsin as far north as the forty-third parallel. Population crossed the Mississippi River into Iowa Territory, while in Missouri, settlements spread north from the Missouri River almost to the boundary of the state and south until they covered most of the southern portion and connected on both right and left with the settlements of Arkansas. The latter remained sparse but had spread widely away from the streams, covering much of the prairie regions of the state. Table 13 shows the geographic distribution of the population by major regions from 1790 to 1860. As the table makes clear, the population living in the East North Central states (Ohio, Indiana, Illinois, Michigan, and Wisconsin) increased more rapidly than that of any other region. As we shall see, the rate of per capita income growth in that region was to be the highest in the nation from 1840 till the end of the century.[25]

In the last twenty years of the pre–Civil War period, as before, the most important source of agricultural change was the western movement. In 1790 almost all the American people had lived on the East Coast; by 1860 precisely half of them inhabited either the East Central region (35 percent), the West Central region (13 percent), or the Far West (2 percent) (see Table 13). Massive shifts of these dimensions altered not only the economic prospects of the people who moved but also the prospects of those who remained behind. Given the comparative advantage of prairie soils such as those in Illinois, Wisconsin, and Iowa—three states whose output accounted for 45 percent of

Table 13. Regional distribution of population as percentage of total United States population, 1790–1860.

Region	1790	1800	1810	1820	1830	1840	1850	1860
East Coast	97	93	85	77	71	63	57	50
New England	26	23	20	17	15	13	12	10
Middle Atlantic	24	27	28	28	28	30	25	26
South Atlantic	47	43	37	32	28	20	20	14
East Central	3	7	14	20	26	32	34	35
North	0	1	4	8	12	17	19	22
South	0	6	10	12	14	15	15	13
West Central	0	0	1	3	3	5	8	13
North	0	0	0	1	1	2	4	7
South	0	0	1	2	2	3	4	6
Far West	0	0	0	0	0	0	1	2
Total U.S.	100	100	100	100	100	100	100	100

Source: Bureau of the Census, *Historical Statistics of the United States, Colonial Times to 1957* (Washington, D.C.: Government Printing Office, 1960), pp. 12–13.

the increase in the American wheat crop between 1849 and 1859—farmers in eastern and southern states tended to abandon wheat as a major cash crop. Some left their overcropped farms and went west; others took up cattle raising, dairy farming, and cheese making or went into diversified types of farming. Similar phenomena were to be found in the South. In the upland areas from Virginia to Georgia, the expansion of cotton and tobacco left soil exhaustion in its wake. By 1850 a large proportion of Virginia and Maryland east of the Blue Ridge Mountains was a waste of old fields and abandoned lands. The impact of the westward movement on individuals thus varied from crop to crop and place to place, depending on the vagaries of nature, past history, markets, and technology.[26]

Undoubtedly, the main way in which that movement influenced the growth of the economy was through the creation and development of the resources of newer agricultural regions. Abetted by transport changes and other developments to be discussed, output gradually increased and altered regional shares of the nation's personal income per capita (Table 14). Again, note that the table reveals relative rather than absolute changes in income in the United States as a whole. I shall illustrate the process by which the western movement in this period brought about these changes in income shares by focusing on the development of agriculture in the western prairies, especially in the West North Central region. Although this region's rate of income growth was somewhat lower than the national average, its population, in response to the lessening of difficulties in prairie farming, was increasing very rapidly in the 1850s (see Table 13). Furthermore, the rate of income growth in the 1860

Table 14.   Personal income per capita in each region as percentage of United States average income, 1840 and 1860.

Region	1840	1860
United States	100	100
Northeast	135	139
New England	132	143
Middle Atlantic	136	137
North Central States	68	68
East North Central	67	69
West North Central	75	66
South	76	72
South Atlantic	70	65
East South Central	73	68
West South Central	144	115

Source: Richard A. Easterlin, in *American Economic History,* ed. Seymour E. Harris (New York: McGraw-Hill, 1961), p. 528. Copyright 1961 by McGraw-Hill Book Company; used with permission.

estimate reflects the inclusion of the new frontier states of Kansas, Nebraska, and Minnesota. If the rate of growth had been computed only for the states of 1840 (Missouri and Iowa), it might have compared more favorably with the national trend.

By 1860 the northern part of the western domain stretched irregularly between the Appalachian Mountains and a region of diminishing rainfall marked by the hundredth meridian. Bounded on the north by the Great Lakes and on the south by the border states, the area was principally one of lake plains or prairie plains. The former clustered about the Great Lakes; the latter began in a small way in Ohio and Michigan before marching to the horizon as they penetrated northern Indiana, central Illinois, Missouri, Iowa, and eastern Kansas. Treeless except for groves of oak, hickory, and walnut on the morainal ridges and stands of timber along the streams, the prairies were an area of extremely high fertility. The glacial ice cap had pulverized rocks into a deep and finely powdered soil rich in phosphorous, potassium, magnesium, and other chemical constituents. The rotting of the coarse, thick, and deeply penetrating root structure of the bluestem grass that covered the prairies with a luxurious growth added valuable humus to the soil. The contrast with the thin forest soils of upland New England and New York could hardly have been more marked. Blessed with an abundance of rainfall and sunshine, the area was potentially one of the richest agricultural regions of the world.

A number of obstacles, however, impeded the settlement of the prairies before the 1850s. Among these were the absence of natural drainage; the lack of timber for buildings, fences, and fuel; and the resistance of the coarse root structure of the soil to wooden moldboard and cast iron plows. Moreover, the damp and heavy prairie soils clung to the plowshare of the common sorts of plow used by the early settlers in the area. By the 1850s cast steel plows imported from England were introduced, and these combined greater smoothness in the moldboard with lightness and strength. Tiling and the construction of ditches made better drainage possible, although both were costly operations beyond the resources of men of small means. The coming of the railroad to the prairie states, finally, made it possible to bring in lumber from other regions, while the introduction of wire fencing provided material for enclosing the fields.

Partly in response to these developments, an exceptionally large amount of new land was improved for agricultural use during the 1850s. Indeed, if we compare the amount of land improved during a given decade with the amount of improved farmland in existence at the beginning of the decade, we obtain a ratio of 0.33 for the decade ending 1849 and an increase in that ratio to 0.44 for the ten years ending in 1859. That the prairie states figured substantially in this development is suggested by the fact that, aside from the Far West, where population change was relatively small, the West North Central region was the fastest growing part of the nation in the 1850s (see Table 13), with population gains in Minnesota, Iowa, Missouri, and Kansas particularly impressive.[27] The contribution of improved means of transport to this growth and, more generally, to the economic growth of the whole country deserves emphasis. Nineteenth-century Americans chose the railroad from the platter of choices tendered them by the available technology. To be sure, they might have chosen to increase canal and turnpike mileage and to make other adjustments required by a different menu. For some purposes those alternatives would have made reasonably good substitutes for the fabled iron horse. But not for all. Surely the railroad provided a faster and more comfortable means of travel, inducing more people to travel and to go farther than they would otherwise have gone. Surely the railroad increased the speed of information flows on which business decisions were made, and for a long time provided the only available institutional experience in the management of large-scale organizations. In short, although the relative importance of the railroad, or the causal significance of any other historical event, can be assessed only by positing its absence from the historical scene and by judging the consequences of that absence, railroads were "indispensable" to American economic growth in the same sense in which that word must be applied to any other historical event: they were indispensable means for achieving the precise results associated with their existence.[28]

Sparked by federal and state land grants to the Illinois Central and other prairie railroads, and encouraged by the absence of engineering difficulties on the level land, a major railroad construction boom got under way in the 1850s. During that decade mileage in Indiana, Illinois, Missouri, and Iowa increased from 339 to 6,635 miles. Settlers did not wait upon the railroads but entered the region in anticipation of their coming, in anticipation of rising land and commodity prices. Initial levels of agricultural production were low except for those enjoying access to markets by water. Completion of railroad construction resulted in immediate increases in the volume of output in these areas and spread a thicker blanket of settlement and production as well. The advent of efficient transportation thus made a major contribution to the development of prairie agriculture.[29]

In enabling prairie land to be cleared, the railroad also made possible a significant saving of the nation's resources. If the prairie states had not been settled, additional acres of the forested land of the East would have had to be cleared. The difference in cost emerges from estimates that whereas eleven dollars per acre was expended in the 1850s in preparing for the cultivation of 5 million acres of treeless land, the same extension on the forested land of the East would have cost twenty-four dollars an acre. Actual cultivation in the West saved not only money but labor as well. Recent research has shown that both corn and wheat could be grown on western soil with smaller inputs of labor. The preharvest and harvest operations on the corn crop of the West required only 1.81 man-hours per bushel. This compares with a national average of 3.51. For wheat, the difference is smaller—2.84 man-hours, in contrast to 3.17 nationally. These measurements reflect only the smaller number of man-hours required on each acre of western soil. But there is also reason to believe that yields per acre increased as one moved west onto virgin soils with the accumulated fertility of centuries.[30]

In sum, agricultural productivity increased in the prairie states because of the advent of the railroad, the lower cost of readying open lands for cultivation, and the somewhat superior yields of western soils. To these sources of greater efficiency we must now add the contribution made not only to prairie farming but to agriculture generally by better machinery. The chances are that between 1800 and 1850 the contribution was slight in old areas of settlement—that is, in the states in production in 1800—but both there and in the newer areas the story appears to change dramatically in the final prewar decade and thereafter.[31]

The beginnings of technological improvement in agriculture go back to the early nineteenth century; but such innovations as Jethro Wood's iron plow (1819), steel plows adapted to tough prairie soils (1830s), harrows and seed drills (1840s), and corn planters (1850s) exerted only limited impact because relatively few of these farm implements were manufactured and sold commercially. In the 1850s, however, real farm gross output increased considerably, and in the decade 1855–1865 the annual rate of real investment in implements and farm machinery rose to $23 million, more than double that of the preceding decade. By 1857 John Deere was turning out ten thousand plows a year, and as early as 1851 Cyrus McCormick was making a thousand mechanical reapers a year in his Chicago factory. The contribution of the reaper to labor productivity may be seen in the following estimate: a man with a sickle could cut one-half to three-quarters of an acre of wheat in a day; with a cradle he could cut two to three acres a day; and with a self-rake reaper he could cut ten to twelve acres a day.[32]

The adoption of the reaper had a tremendous effect on the agriculture of the Northwest. Farmers turned from corn to wheat, and wheat acreage more than doubled. A major wheat-producing center came into existence in northern Illinois and southern Wisconsin. In the years 1849–1857 eleven counties in northern Illinois purchased approximately one-fourth the total number of McCormick reapers sold. By the eve of the Civil War northern agriculture stood poised on the threshold of the first U.S. agricultural revolution. What made for revolution was the rapidity of change from manpower to horsepower. By 1860 every stage in the growing of grain was amenable to the use of horse-drawn machines.[33]

What of the South? of slavery? of cotton? To what extent did this region and its people and products participate in the expansion that characterized northern agriculture between 1840 and 1860? The answers to these questions may be surprising. In the first place, in the South as well as the North, the rate of population increase was greater in the western parts than in the older areas. In the states of the South Atlantic region, the number of people increased by less than 50 percent, and in those of the East South Central region, by less than 60 percent. In contrast, the increase in the West South Central states exceeded 300 percent. As in population growth, so also in output growth. Percentage increases in cotton production in the three West South Central states between 1849 and 1859 far exceeded those of any other state. The output of Arkansas rose by 524.5 percent, that of Louisiana by 335.5 percent, and that of Texas by a whopping 727.5 percent (see Table 12). Shifts in the composition of agricultural output favoring cotton had a major impact on the value of that output before 1850, and hence on the productivity of land.

We must not permit the figures for output growth in the West South Central states to mislead us, however. Although they are truly indicative of rapid growth, we must not confuse percentage *increases* in output, which are typically high in early stages of growth, with percentages of *total* output. In 1859 the cotton crop of Texas was only 1 percent of United States production, that of Arkansas 0.8 percent, and that of Louisiana 15.4 percent. Nearly half the total output—48.1 percent—was the product of two states of the East South Central region, Mississippi and Alabama. Georgia, an older state of the South Atlantic region, contributed an additional 15.4 percent (see Table 12). These are sufficient reasons for not confining our search for sources of productivity advance to any one part of the antebellum South. Rather, we must examine the Cotton Kingdom as a whole.

When we look away to Dixieland we are apt to see only vast plantations on which hundreds of slaves toiled "from day clean to first dark" to produce the South's cotton crop. To be sure, the large plantation was an essential part of the picture, but the part must not be mistaken for the whole. In 1860 there were in the South 1,516,000 free families, of whom only 385,000 were owners of slaves; nearly three-fourths of all free southern families owned no slaves at all. The typical white southerner was not only a small farmer but also a nonslaveholder. A large majority of the slave-owning families, moreover, owned only a few slaves. In 1850, as Table 15 reveals, 89 percent of the owners held fewer than 20 slaves; 71 percent, fewer than 10; and almost 50 percent, fewer than 5. If we accept the usual definition of a planter as a man who owned at least 20 slaves, these proportions make it clear not only that the typical slaveholder was not a planter, but also that the typical planter worked only a moderate-sized gang of 20 to 50 slaves. The planter aristocracy was made up of some ten thousand families living off the labor of gangs of more than 50 slaves. Yet it was on the large agricultural units that most of the slaves were to be found. Ownership was so highly concentrated that only one-fourth the slaves belonged to masters holding fewer than 10; considerably more than half lived on plantations holding more than 20; and approximately a quarter belonged to masters owning more than 50.[34]

Table 15.   Distribution of slaveholding families according to number of slaves held, 1790 and 1850 (percentage of total families).

Number of slaves	Percentage of families	
	1790	1850
1	24.5	17.4
2 to 4	30.5	29.5
5 to 9	22.0	24.4
10 to 19	14.3	17.4
20 to 49	6.4	9.1
50 to 99	1.0	1.7
100 to 199	0.2	0.4
200 to 299	a	0.1
300 or more	a	a
Unknown	1.0	0.0

Source: *Compendium of the Seventh Census* (Washington, D.C.: A. O. P. Nicholson, Public Printer, 1854), table xc, p. 95.
a. Less than .001 percent.

As is suggested by the fact that a large majority of the owners held only a few slaves, cotton was the crop of the little man as well as the big. Indeed, its cultivation required no slave labor at all, and it was accordingly grown on small farms without slaves—or with only a few—and on middling-to-large-sized farms as well as on plantations. Unlike rice and sugar cane, which required large investments of capital for processing machinery, cotton was cheap to grow. A small farmer could cultivate it with the assistance of his wife and children, and he had little trouble getting it ginned and prepared for market. As a rule, the value of cotton in relation to its bulk was sufficiently high to bear the costs of transport over considerable distances without jeopardizing the chance for profit. Cotton stood abuse much better than many other farm commodities; it was nonperishable and hence suffered relatively little from rough handling, exposure, long delays, and poor warehousing while in transit to market. Smaller agricultural units were thus enabled to make some contribution to each year's crop. Nevertheless, the great bulk of the crop came from the plantations, where most of the slaves were concentrated.[35]

Modes of operation and management, which varied with the size of the agricultural units, may well have been more efficient on large plantations. On small farms—the great majority of the units in the South—masters usually gave close personal supervision to the unspecialized labor of a few slaves. Many were obliged to work in the fields alongside their hands, although those owning as few as a half dozen slaves sought a more elevated social status by refraining from such labor. Small slave forces lacked skilled craftsmen, and their masters found it necessary to repair tools, do carpentry work, and perform other specialized tasks. At picking time in the fall the master usually supplemented his small force with his own labor.

Substantial farmers and small planters who owned ten to thirty slaves normally lived on their own land and devoted their full time to the management of their enterprise. They did not as a rule employ overseers, although they might have the aid of a slave foreman or driver, whose essential function was to urge on the slave gangs by word or whip. Agricultural units of this size usually benefited from some labor specialization. Besides the field hands and driver, a few slaves might exercise manual skills or perform domestic work. Even so, the unit was too small for full-time carpenters or cooks, so that the latter often had to work in the fields as well.

Maximum specialization was possible for those planters who owned thirty or more slaves, although no more than one-third of them used overseers. The latter were generally retained on a year-to-year basis under a written contract that could be terminated at will by either party, and as a rule each overseer made use of one or more drivers in working the slave gang. The gang system was one of two basic methods of labor management. Under the other—the less frequently used task system—each hand was given a specific daily assignment and could quit work when the task was completed. The planter who hired a full-time overseer was able to devote his own attention to problems of marketing, finance, and general plantation administration. He also enjoyed sufficient leisure to be able to absent himself from his plantation more or less at his own discretion. But absentee ownership was not characteristic on plantations of any size.

Plantations containing thirty or more slaves enjoyed a considerable degree of labor specialization. Household servants and field hands were clearly distinguished from each other, and the latter were divided into plow gangs and hoe gangs. On the larger plantations slaves were able to devote their full time to occupations such as ditching, tending livestock, driving wagons, and taking care of vegetable gardens. In 1854 one Virginia planter had 8 plowmen, 10 hoe hands, 2 wagoners, 4 oxcart drivers, a carriage driver, a hostler, a stable boy, a shepherd, a cowherd, a swineherd, 2 carpenters, 5 masons, 2 smiths, a miller, 2 shoemakers, 5 spinners, a weaver, a butler, 2 waitresses, 4 maids, a nurse, a laundress, a seamstress, a dairymaid, a gardener, and 2 cooks attached to the field service. The owner of a very large establishment employed a general manager or steward to help him run the estate. If several plantations were involved, he might run one himself, but as a rule he hired an overseer for each of them.

In sum, the ability to employ specialized labor was one of the sources of the economies of scale that may have been possible on large plantations. Since scale economies develop when inputs of land, labor, and capital result in a more-than-proportionate increase in output, proponents of the scale hypothesis associate such increases with big plantations manned by disciplined labor gangs working rhythmically as teams in consonance with orders given by drivers; in short, with superior management. The specialization, or more precisely defined division of tasks facilitated by large numbers, they add, may well have raised output by increasing the input of practiced, knowledgeable, and hence more effective labor; in short, by raising the intensity of labor input per hour. If scale economies were indeed realized, it would follow that the westward movement, by making available cheaper land to be organized into large agricultural units, must be included among the sources of productivity growth in the Cotton Kingdom.[36]

Efforts to measure these economies, however, have not won universal scholarly approval. It seems evident that large plantations also gave rise to diseconomies, partly in the form of losses of time in getting about, and perhaps partly also in the form of an increase in the ratio of drivers to overseers. Certainly it is plausible to assume that the larger the number of drivers, the greater the problem of supervising them and, in consequence, the greater the opportunity for slave gangs to relax the intensity of their labor. But there is some evidence that slaves worked more days per year and perhaps more hours per day than free farmers. Indeed, the necessity of keeping slaves fully employed in all seasons made for an intensity of labor input that helps explains the economic performance of the antebellum South. Although it is difficult to measure the contribution made by intensity, of one thing we can be sure: labor productivity—in the production of grains as well as cotton—was the dominant source of total factor productivity in antebellum agriculture. This recent finding raises a number of interesting questions, the first of which has been debated for more than a century: was slavery profitable?[37]

In October 1808 John Steele, a North Carolina planter, wrote as follows to one David Anderson: "Having abundance of prime cotton land, I can make three or four times as much annual income by vesting capital in Negroes, as I can by any Stock annuities."[38] The concern with profit, the implicit interest in maximizing it, and Steele's awareness of an alternative investment opportunity are revealing. Were this the single surviving piece of testimony on the profitability of antebellum slavery—and of course it is not—delighted historians would presumably make as much of it as their confreres are obliged to make of the only pipe roll on royal finances to survive the reign of England's Henry I! At the least, it supports a presumption about one planter's experience at a given time and place under one specified condition, namely, possession of a plentiful supply of fertile land. For all we know, however, the relatively greater profitability of Steele's investment may have depended also on the cost of slaves and other inputs, the number of slaves he owned and the uses to which he put them, the number of acres planted in cotton, the farm price of the staple, the quality of management, and the price of stocks! Without information on these other variables, it would be as difficult to generalize from

Steele's statement as it is from the relatively few surviving sets of plantation financial accounts, even when standardized accounting procedures are employed to determine profit or loss.

Of course, historians have not confined themselves to the testimony of individuals and to plantation records in their efforts to judge whether or not slavery was profitable. It was on the basis of the rising differential between the cost of slaves and the price of cotton in the 1850s, a differential which he believed could not be fully explained by the "lessening of cost" in production, that the leading authority on American slavery in the early decades of the twentieth century, Ulrich B. Phillips, reached his conclusion that the institution was unprofitable. To his modern successor, Kenneth Stampp, the testimony of business records and reports prepared by masters for southern periodicals constituted important evidence to the contrary. But the "best and most direct" evidence of continued profitability was the high valuation of black labor in the 1850s when hired out for work in agriculture, in factories, and mines, on riverboats, or on internal improvements projects.[39]

In his close scrutiny of the sources of profitability, Stampp emphasized the small cost of maintaining the slave labor force, the significant contribution to profits made by its natural increase, the earnings from the sale of slaves, and the capital gains from increases in their value. The "market value of a young slave," he suggested, "far exceeded the small expense of raising him." In fine, Stampp had no difficulty in reaching the conclusion that, although the owners of a large slave gang earned proportionately higher returns than the owner of a small gang, "on both large and small estates, none but the most hopelessly inefficient masters failed to profit from the ownership of slaves." Their returns ranged from the "fabulous profits" earned even during the 1850s in the Mississippi delta, the Louisiana bayous, the Red River and Arkansas River valleys, and the Texas prairies, to common returns of 7 to 10 percent on capital investment in the older cotton, sugar, and rice areas of the Deep South. The rewards from agriculture in South Carolina and Georgia were, on average, less than in the Southwest, "but this does not mean that slavery had ceased to be profitable." Even in the upper South "slavery was amply rewarding to those who took pains to preserve or restore the fertility of their soil and who directed their enterprises with reasonable efficiency." The crucial fact of the 1850s was that the high sales prices of slaves were "based on a solid foundation: the slave was earning for his owner a substantial, though varying, surplus above the cost of maintenance." In his insights into the sources of profitability, and in his recognition that the purchase price of a slave involved the capitalization of future income from his labor, Stampp anticipated approaches adopted by two young economists soon after the appearance of his book—and some subsequent investigations as well.[40]

In what is now widely regarded as a classic economic analysis, Alfred Conrad and John Meyer divided the slave economy into two sectors. Male slaves were assumed to have been a form of capital goods used to produce cotton. Female slave capital, however, produced not only cotton but additional slaves as well. Profits (or losses) from the ownership of slaves therefore depended on total production costs in each sector in relation to revenues received from the sale of both cotton and slaves during the lifetime of the labor force.

Taking first the males, the economists consulted traditional historical sources for information enabling them to calculate the average cost of a prime field hand in the period 1830–1860, together with the average amount of equipment, animals, and land assigned him for use in cultivating cotton. Recognizing that land varied in quality, they made separate cost estimates for four different grades, and in consequence concluded that the total investment per male slave ranged between $1,250 and $1,650.

The annual gross income derived from the employment of this capital depended on the average number of bales of cotton produced on each grade of land, multiplied by the farm price per bale. "The maximum," they found, "seems to have been 7–8 bales on the best lands," and the minimum 2–3 bales "on the poorest land." Net income was what was left after subtracting an allowance for food and clothing, medical care, supervision and other costs of maintaining the slaves. To determine the value of the capital investment, it was then necessary to multiply the annual net income by the number of years in which this income could be expected to be received. This of course depended on the average length of time a field hand lived and worked. Mortality tables for the 1850s suggested that a life expectancy of thirty years for twenty-year-old slaves working as prime cotton hands was plausible for the period 1830–1850. The upshot of all the calculations, then, was a figure for a stream of earnings that could be expected on the average to flow for thirty years. The two economists found that the present value of that income stream exceeded the cost of the investment and yielded a rate of return on capital which varied on the average between 4.5 and 6.5 percent. This was the most typical return. But on land of the poorest quality, such as that of upland pine country or the exhausted eastern seaboard, rates ranged from 2.2 to 5.4 percent. On the "best lands of the new Southwest, the Mississippi alluvium and the better South Carolina and Alabama plantations," the range of rates ran as high as 12 and 13 percent.

Computing the rate of return on the female slaves was more complex: in addition to her own productivity in the field, that of her children had also to be evaluated and estimates made of the returns realized from the sale of the latter. The extra cost of maintaining the children had to be counted, and maternity and nursery costs as well. Assuming that each prime female field hand produced five to ten marketable children during her lifetime, that she worked land of about average fertility yielding 3.75 bales of cotton per hand, and that the net farm price was $.75 per pound, the economists calculated a rate of return on the streams of net income flowing from sales of cotton and children amounting to 7.1 percent for a female with five children, and to 8.1 percent for one with ten.

Thus planters in the upper South who earned only 4 or 5 percent on male slaves were able to increase their income by selling the offspring of females to planters in the Southwest. For evidence that a specialized breeding area indeed existed, the economists relied principally on analysis of the age structure of slave populations in the slave-breeding and slave-importing areas. In 1850 and 1860 selling states had a large proportion of slaves under age fifteen and over fifty, whereas buying states had a predominance of slaves of prime working age. In sum, investments made in slaves between 1830 and 1860 were profitable investments, with a return of 6 percent being the most probable rate on all except the poorest land. This rate of return compared favorably with rates yielded by alternative assets such as New England municipal bonds, New York Stock Exchange call loans, and railroad debentures.[41]

Although Conrad and Meyer were the first modern economists to examine the economics of slavery, they were certainly not the last. The ink on their study was hardly dry before other economists challenged their figures on average cotton output and market price per slave, their failure to take into account the difference in value between the output of the slave who died before the expiration of his thirty–year working life and that of the slave who lived and worked longer than that, and their contention that rates of return on slave investments were competitive with those obtainable on alternatives. The correct competitive rate, one critic held, cannot be identified without knowledge of the relative risks of different investments. Their demographic and actuarial assumptions were especially hard hit: a 4 percent growth rate of the slave population was implicit in their estimates of life expectancy and fertility— approximately double the rate actually recorded by the census. Historians also joined the fray, one suggesting that their estimate of the cost of animals was peculiarly unfortunate in that it was based on a mule population of a given size and the assumption that the population was thereafter self-reproducing. "What the hell," Conrad replied, "we're city boys and we didn't know about such things."[42]

These and other criticisms did not mean that Conrad and Meyer were wrong in their essential conclusion that slavery had been profitable. Indeed, further critical studies indicated either that they had underestimated the productivity of slave labor, and hence the average rate of return on investments in slaves, or that they had ignored the evidence for profitability implicit in slave rental rates. One pointed out that the capital gains from merely holding slaves were so great in the 1850s that an owner could have made a rate of return competitive with alternative investments with no marketable crop surplus at all! In consequence, while a firm average rate of return cannot yet be stipulated, the consensus of modern scholarship is that returns were positive even in relation to the high slave prices of that decade.[43]

Granted that slavery was profitable, was it also economically viable? This question, an even more fundamental one, has to do with the relationship of returns to the cost of reproducing the slave labor force. Even if the rate of return on slave purchases were positive, the long-term viability of the system depended on whether owners had an incentive to keep the slaves they already owned and to allow them to reproduce.

All the profitability studies answer the first part of this requirement in the affirmative. Clearly, slave owners were able to capture a sufficient portion of the difference between the cost of caring for a slave (the subsistence cost) and the value arising from the difference between this cost and the slave's productivity. As for the second part, slaveowners had an incentive to allow their slaves to reproduce as long as the market value (price) of a working slave exceeded costs of reproduction such as the mother's lost working time during pregnancy and nursing and subsistence during the early childhood years. Economists speak of the difference between these rearing costs and market value at maturity as "capitalized economic rent." The discovery that this rent was positive—indeed, that it never fell below 50 percent of a young adult slave's market value at any time between 1820 and 1860—answered in the affirmative the question of the viability of the "peculiar institution."[44]

Slavery was both profitable and viable, but the most successful owners did not confine their investments to it. "They were also mining magnates, builders and promoters of transportation facilities, bankers, factory owners, speculators in urban real estate and merchants."[45] Evidence of this kind certainly supports the assumption that, whatever the varying degree to which slaveowners were also motivated by such noneconomic considerations as desire for status and power, some of them were, at heart, profit maximizers. And it may be that "some" should read "many." The antebellum South does not resemble the land of moonlight and roses depicted in tales of romance.

But this does not mean that typical large plantations and small farms sank all their resources into the great export staple and relied on their ability to purchase supplies of food from the West. Some studies of the interregional trade flows do suggest modest imports of western corn and flour in the 1840s, and significantly larger ones in the last few years before the war. On the whole, however, while the antebellum South specialized in cotton, it was also self-sufficient with respect to its human and animal requirements for food. Far from being dependent on external sources, southern cotton farms were in a position to supply food to outsiders on an impressive scale.[46]

Yet, if at least some cotton farmers sought to maximize their profits and cotton was more profitable to grow than corn, why did they not devote all their acres to the great staple? The explanation is simple: labor demand, which peaked at the time of the cotton harvest in the fall, was far more slack in other seasons. Putting the slaves to work growing corn, beans, and sweet potatoes and raising pigs into hogs not only saved expenditures on outside food supplies but kept the labor force more fully employed in off-seasons than it would have been otherwise. And since land was cheap and outside rental demand for slaves thin, planters could grow corn without reducing cotton capacity, that is, at little real cost in terms of opportunities forgone. In sum, a substantial corn crop was not inconsistent with the largest cotton crop.

The "output mix," however, varied with the size of the farm and the number of slaves. The largest slaveholding cotton plantations devoted three-fifths or more of their resources to cotton, whereas the typical slaveless farm confined its investment to about one-fourth. Large planters could afford to run risks which small farmers, with or without slaves, preferred to avoid. They knew from experience that unpredictable variations in cotton yields and prices rendered their decisions highly uncertain. In this context of uncertainty, "only a fool or a rich man could safely maximize expected profits in the Cotton South." In other words, abandoning self-sufficiency was risky, because households had to eat regardless of the outcome of the season's yields and prices.[47]

In following a strategy of safety first, in refusing to jeopardize their independence and freedom of choice as owners, small farmers in the South acted like their counterparts in the North. The words of a New England farmer in the 1850s testify to the similarity: "As a general rule, however, it is better that the farmer should produce what he needs for home consumption . . . . He may obtain more money from tobacco or broom corn than from breadstuffs, but taking all things into consideration, will he be better off?"[48]

The weighing of the crop mix decision more heavily on the subsistence side of output may have been perfectly rational for the small farmer, but does it not also follow that he was less efficient than the larger planter? Clearly, the answer depends on whether large-scale operations made for economies unrealizable on small farms, an issue which remains unsettled. One critic has found that increases in the size of farms did not result in measured increases of output, either per worker or per acre. It remains possible, though, that the ability of wealthy planters to take risks by allocating larger percentages of their resources to cotton enabled them to generate more output value from a given quantity of factor inputs.[49]

Nevertheless, large slaveholding plantations, as we have seen, also sought self-sufficiency in foodstuffs. Did slaves benefit from the ready availability of fresh vegetables and other foods grown on the master's land? Some did, of course. Martin W. Phillips of South Carolina, for example, furnished his plantation cook twenty-two to twenty-four pounds of fat bacon daily and unlimited meal, vegetables, and buttermilk to feed fifty-six slaves. "I have no 'poor starved niggers,'" he wrote in June 1854. "So far from it, I guess they dine on as nice bacon, cabbage heads, beans and Irish potatoes as any other man white or black."[50]

Exceptions do not rule. Certainly it was in the interest of slaveholders to protect their investments in slaves by providing a diet for them with ample calories and, to the best of their knowledge, ample nutrients for good health. Furthermore, it is true that the rate of growth of the slave population in the United States far exceeded that of other slave populations in the Western hemisphere, with growth through natural increase between 1810 and 1860 far outdistancing estimated imports of about one thousand blacks a year, imports which occurred despite legal prohibition after 1808. This demographic fact, taken together with the relatively high life expectancy of slaves, persuasively suggests a tolerable standard of health. Finally, no contemporary critic of the diet of slaves described them as malnourished. They were not. "There is no question that the slave diet was sufficient to maintain the slave's body weight and general health."[51]

The real issue, however, is whether the typical slave diet was anything but monotonous, coarse, and crude. And the scholarly consensus that the standard food ration for an adult field hand was three and one-half pounds of salt pork or bacon and one peck of corn meal per week suggests strongly that it was not. Indeed, the extraordinarily high caloric intake of a carbohydrate-intensive diet also suggests food-energy needs associated with hard labor. Slave diets were also nutritionally suspect. There are only scattered references to pellagra, beriberi, and other diseases caused by nutritional deficiencies, so that it is possible that ignorance on the part of slaveowners, rather than miserliness was responsible. On the other hand, it remains true that the profit motive drove most masters to feed their slaves as cheaply as possible.[52]

The same motive dictated parsimony in the provision of clothing and living space. The most frequently encountered clothing allowance is two or three pairs of pants and shirts a year; the typical slave cabin was fifteen feet square. With an eight-foot-high ceiling, the resulting cubic feet of air volume suggest that the slave and his family were housed at a level commensurate with absolute necessity and that plantation resources were not used to improve his dwelling much beyond this. Finally, black infants died at a rate twice that of white infants, a difference apparently due to extreme poverty, low birth weights, and poor postnatal care. It is difficult not to conclude that owners sought to maximize returns from slavery "by using force to extract the maximum amount of work from the slaves while providing them only with sufficient food, shelter, clothing, and health care to keep them healthy and hardworking."[53]

The slave trade offered owners another method of maximizing returns. Slaves were sold both locally and to distant owners. Sales continually broke up slave families, separating children from parents and husbands from wives. In one of the rare instances in which the cries of the victims of slavery have come to us in their own voices, a slave mother speaks of the loss of her son: "Dear Husband," Maria Perkins writes to Richard Perkins from Charlottesville, Virginia, in October 1852, "I write you a letter to know my distress my master has sold albert to a trader on Monday court day and myself and other child is for sale also." The extent to which sales were responsible for the great forced interstate migration of an estimated 1 million slaves between 1790 and 1860 is a question requiring more research for its answer.[54]

The migration followed the westward movement of the cotton belt from the Old South to the New South. It is estimated that in the 1850s the eastern states of Delaware, Maryland, Virginia, North Carolina, and South Carolina supplied 68 percent of the migrants, and that the southwestern states of Mississippi, Louisiana, Arkansas, and Texas received 89 percent of them. Since the new lands were more fertile than the overcropped eastern soils, planters in the Southwest enjoyed a productivity advantage which contributed, along with profits earned by Louisiana sugar refiners and those arising from trade down the Mississippi River to New Orleans, to an extraordinarily high rate of per capita income growth between 1840 and 1860. But since the impact of the new lands on slave productivity was offset by the lower cotton prices resulting from the increased supply, slaveowners in the Southeast failed to benefit from the great migration. Indeed, till the late 1850s congressional representatives from the South Atlantic states persistently opposed proposals to accelerate the distribution of the public lands. Undoubtedly, the revenue impact on that sector of the South prevented the region as a whole from registering a higher rate of income growth than it did in the closing decades before the war.[55]

Available measures of income growth depict an average annual rate of 1.7 percent per capita between 1840 and 1860, even with the slaves included in the population count. This exceeds not only the rate of growth in the North Central states, but the national average of 1.3 percent as well. With the slaves excluded from the population and treated as "intermediate goods," the relative advantage of the South over the West appears even more striking. The average income of free southerners exceeds that of free westerners by nearly 70 percent. And the southern growth rate becomes 1.8 percent more than a third larger than the national average.[56]

When looked at more closely, however, the numbers are seen to support a somewhat less exuberant view of southern growth. The rate between 1840 and 1860 is "probably increased by the particular state of demand during the two census years involved." Econometric estimates of the cotton demand curve indicate that demand was well above its trend value in 1859–60—that the price of cotton was above the level predicted on the basis of production and trend by 7.6 percent to 15.9 percent. Similar estimates for 1839–40 show the cotton price to have been between 4 percent and 11.5 percent below its predicted value. The choice of endpoints dictated by available census data clearly gives an extra upward tilt to the path of southern income growth.[57]

Even if we accept at face value the figures in Table 16 for southern income growth between 1840 and 1860, it will be evident at a glance that the growth is wholly attributable to the extraordinary performance of the West South Central subregion. The other two subregions, the South Atlantic and the East

Table 16. Per capita income by region, 1840 and 1860 (given in 1860 dollars).

Region	Total population		Free population	
	1840	1860	1840	1860
National average	$ 96	$128[a]	$109	$144
North	*109*	*141*	*110*	*142*
Northeast	129	181	130	183
North Central	65	89	66	90
South	*74*	*103*[b]	*105*	*150*
South Atlantic	66	84	96	124
East South Central	69	89	92	124
West South Central	161	184	238	274

Source: Robert W. Fogel and Stanley L. Engerman, *The Reinterpretation of American Economic History* (New York: Harper & Row, 1971), p. 335. Used with permission.

a. Growth in level of income = 33 percent.

b. Growth in level of income = 39 percent.

South Central, grew at rates substantially below the national average. The problem, therefore, is that of explaining why the West South Central area did so well. The answer is straightforward: incomes in that region were bolstered substantially by profits from sugar refining in Louisiana and from earnings in New Orleans derived from the huge shipments of the products of midwestern farms and mines down the Mississippi River. But that is not all. The redistribution of population from the Old South to the New, from overcropped and outworn fields to the fertile lands of Texas and the other West South Central states, also deserves part of the credit. Yet migration as such would have exerted a far lesser impact on incomes in the absence of the demand for cotton. It is the latter, then, that must be stressed. Even so, the element of time deserves even greater emphasis, for the fact is that the growth in world demand for cotton which provided the fundamental underpinning for most of the income growth was essentially a temporary phenomenon. In sum, southern income growth was less substantial than the figures imply, and what there was of it was not destined to last very long.[58]

World demand for cotton had grown at the rate of 5 percent a year between 1830 and 1860, but in the 1860s it collapsed catastrophically. Output of the British textile industry began to decline in the early 1860s, and in consequence cotton demand had barely recovered its 1860 peak by the late 1870s. Between 1866 and 1895 demand ran at an enfeebled rate of less than 1.5 percent per year. Measured from the peak year, the growth in demand was little more than 1 percent per year to the turn of the century.[59]

What this means is that the economy of the prewar South was hitched to a falling star. The high prices of cotton and slaves in the late 1850s would almost certainly have declined drastically even if the Civil War had not occurred, dragging down land values and the profits of the planters with them. Ulrich B. Phillips was surely right when he called attention in the following words to the implications of the overpricing of slaves by the close of the fifties: "Indeed the peak of this [slave] price movement was evidently cut off by the intervention of war. How great an altitude it might have reached, and what shape its downward slope would have taken had peace continued, it is idle to conjecture. But that a crash must have come is beyond a reasonable doubt."[60] And there would have been no early recovery.

Does this impending long-term collapse in values imply that the Civil War was an unnecessary war, that the institution of slavery would have fallen of its own economic deadweight had the politicians of the 1850s found ways of avoiding headlong confrontation? No one can say for sure, but it is doubtful this would have happened. The planters would have had to make severe, even cruel, adjustments in their living styles and material satisfactions. But it is arguable that they would have made an effort to hold on indefinitely to an institution bringing them other kinds of satisfactions. Eugene Genovese calls attention to deeper truths when he depicts the plantation system and slave-master relationship not so much as a way of organizing labor, investing wealth, or managing race relations but as the basis for a regional social order and special way of life. Ownership of slaves imbued the master class with a "special set of values and interests incapable of being compromised." The master's "slaveholding psychology, habit of command, race pride, rural lordship, aristocratic pretensions, political domination, and economic strength militated in defense of the status quo."[61] The weakening of the element of economic strength would have frayed most of the other categories, but it might also have concentrated southern energies more fully on the necessity of economic diversification—on manufacturing, and not merely on the growing of foodstuffs and export staples. After all, it was the *dependence* of the South on an ever-rising long-term demand curve for its major crop that made for the impermanence of its economic situation.

This is not to say that manufacturing and its concomitant, urbanization, were entirely absent from the antebellum South. They were not, but as Tables 17 and 18 make clear, they were present on a much smaller scale than in the North. The per capita value of the manufactures in New England in 1860 was more than eight times that of the South. And whereas in the former region every third person lived in a city, about one in ten did so in the South. The principle of comparative advantage heads the list of explanations offered for these contrasts: The South concentrated its resources on cotton because the region's total command of goods and services was greater than it would have been otherwise. But although the South's terms of trade did improve during the years before the war—its consumption potential expanding more rapidly than its production—the existence of slavery was probably more fundamental.

Table 17.   Manufacturing investment and output by region, 1850 and 1860 (in dollars per capita).

Region	Manufacturing capital		Manufacturing value	
	1850	1860	1850	1860
New England	57.96	82.13	100.71	149.47
Middle states	33.50	52.21	71.42	96.28
South	7.60	10.54	10.88	17.09
Cotton South	5.11	7.20	6.83	10.47
United States	22.73	32.12	43.69	59.98

Source: Eighth and Ninth Census of Manufactures, cited in Gavin Wright, *The Political Economy of the Cotton South* (New York: W. W. Norton, 1978), p. 110. Used with permission.

Table 18.   Percentage of population living in urban areas, 1820–1860.

Region	1820	1830	1840	1850	1860
New England	10.5	14.0	19.4	28.8	36.6
Middle Atlantic	11.3	14.2	18.1	25.5	35.4
East North Central	1.2	2.5	3.9	9.0	14.1
West North Central	—	3.5	3.9	10.3	13.4
South	5.5	6.2	7.7	9.8	11.5
East South Central	0.8	1.5	2.1	4.2	5.9

Source: Douglass C. North, *The Economic Growth of the United States, 1790–1860* (Englewood Cliffs, N.J.: Prentice-Hall, 1961), p. 258. Used with permission.

The use of rented slaves in southern urban manufacturing was bitterly opposed by white artisans, tradesmen, and even unskilled workers who stood to lose economically by the presence of close substitutes. Not only did slaves tend to depress wages, but they were also commonly used as strike breakers. Urban slavery therefore goes far to account for the low level of immigration of free white workers into southern cities. Slaveowners also had interests at odds with greater free-labor immigration. Any increase in southern labor might conceivably lower slave property values. More important, those values might be threatened by an influx of nonslaveholding outsiders whose antislavery political views might jeopardize the region's strength and unity in national politics.[62]

Despite the opposition to slave workers on the part of white artisans, demand for them rose in most southern cities in the 1850s. The supply response, however, fell short, as slaves were pulled out of the cities by strong agricultural demand—rather than pushed out by disruption and fear. The urban demand for slaves was much more price elastic (price sensitive) than the rural demand:

a small increase in slave hiring rates induced employers to switch to free work-ers. But because free labor was unwilling to work in gangs in the cotton fields, slave labor was unique in the rural sector and had no close substitutes. In short, it was the cotton boom of the 1850s which resulted in the pulling of urban slaves back into the countryside because of the impact of increasing demand for cotton and slaves on slave rental prices.[63]

Slavery, in sum, was hostile to the growth of a labor supply in southern manufacturing. But if enough slaveholders had had an incentive to encourage a more diversified development of their region—and of course some did—efforts to obtain labor-saving machinery would have been systematically made. At bottom, then, satisfactory returns from investments in slaves, together with fear of the disruptive influence of development on a highly valued way of life, stayed the regional hand. Lacking in a vigorous urban-industrial sector, the South was also deficient in its supply of innovation and native entrepreneur-ship. Its businessmen in the Atlantic and Gulf ports were either seasonal so-journers from the North and from Europe or local agents of distant mercantile houses which provided the shipping and financial services required by the cotton trade. In sum, it was outsiders who organized the exports to Liverpool or Boston, gave the planters credit in the form of advances on those shipments, and supplied the vessels to carry them. The South was a semicolonial appanage of England and the North, and the penalties for its undernourished develop-ment were to be severe, not only in the imminent Civil War but also in its long aftermath. Long before a twentieth-century president declared it to be so, the South was the nation's number one economic problem.[64]

Southerners can hardly be faulted for their failure to envisage what lay in store for them. The outward and visible signs were far from discomfiting. While their section of the nation fell behind others, particularly New England, in its rate of growth in income per capita between 1840 and 1860, it exceeded both the national average and the growth rate of the North Central states. And the wealth of the free families in the cotton-, sugar-, and rice-growing areas averaged four times the wealth of those in the rest of the country ($12,000 to $3,000). The range of individual landholdings in the South was probably wider than in the North, and the distribution of property among free men more unequal. But the basic reason for a highly unequal wealth distribution was the existence of slavery. "The average slaveowner was more than five times as wealthy as the average Northerner, more than ten times as wealthy as the average nonslaveholding Southern farmer."[65] Since most slaves held little wealth, the bottom of the wealth pyramid in the South was distended by a very large group of propertyless families.[66]

The South was not the only place where the distribution of wealth was highly unequal. It was also true of the cities. Here young workers owning no capital of their own—the urban equivalent of landless northern farm work-ers—resided in large numbers. Undoubtedly many were immigrants. Their lot was a hard one and their material rewards relatively meager. A study of unskilled immigrant Irish labor in Newburyport, Massachusetts, between 1850 and 1880 reveals a modest degree of property mobility, but it was painfully eked out of earnings by the practice of "ruthless underconsumption." In general, the average wealth of the native born was three or four times that of the foreign born in 1860. Had the American dream failed in the eyes of the dreamer?[67]

For some it had not. As we have seen, there were perhaps a half-dozen millionaires in the country in 1815. By 1840 the number of millionaire families is roughly estimated to have risen to 60, then to 100 in 1850, and to 150 in 1860. More generally, "the richest 5 percent of families probably received between 25 and 35 percent of the national income." The average incomes of this 5 percent were from six to ten times as large as the average incomes of the remaining 95 percent of American families.[68]

This degree of concentration, while surprisingly high for so early a period in U.S. history, does not appear to be markedly different from that exhibited in other large societies in Europe in the nineteeth and early-twentieth centuries. The bright, the vigorous, the well-born and well-endowed probably have accumulated material possessions far greater than those of the ordinary run of humankind, and done so at most times and places in history. What is remarkable about the American case is that the high concentration of wealth was accompanied by decent standards of living for the large majority of other people as well—even the slaves, at least on plantations in the Southwest. "Were anyone perverse enough to bother," a historian of slavery has written, "he might easily find that the living conditions of a large minority or even a majority of the world's population during the twentieth century might not compare in comfort with those of the slaves of Mississippi a century earlier."[69] He believes that the more favorable economic conditions of the Southwest meant that planters and farmers did not have to skimp on food and clothing, that slaves there enjoyed a higher degree of comfort than they did back east. We have seen how the lands of the fertile West also contributed significantly to economic growth by increasing the output of labor on those lands. In the end, then, the rich resources of an abundant continent underlay the increasing well-being of the American people. We shall now inquire into the impact of the Civil War on that well-being and on the economy which sustained it.

9

In the Wake of the Civil War

It is not easy to assess the impact of war on an economy. To begin with, one must distinguish between short- and long-run effects, between those occurring during wartime and those arising later. Destruction of plant, equipment, and other resources obviously slows the pace of current output, but it may also, as in the case of Western Europe and Japan in World War II, lead to a postwar reconstruction in which older technologies are replaced by newer ones on a scale less likely to have occurred in peacetime. Any attempt to estimate the impact of war must therefore take into account the value of postwar increases in productivity originating in plant renewal above the average rate of peacetime replacement. In wartime itself, of course, labor shortages may lead to a substitution of capital for labor, especially in plants producing munitions and other materiel. As for policies and laws, those adopted during wartime bear varying degrees of relevance to the circumstance of war itself—some might have won acceptance in peacetime, although perhaps less readily—so that care must be taken in any causal analysis not to ascribe to war everything that takes place during that period. Finally, the tracing of lines of effect radiating out from war related actions must confront perplexing uncertainties when these lines meet and cross others whose points of origin began before or after the war. And this is to say nothing of the problem of determining the endpoints of the lines. How indeed does one determine when the effects of war have run their course? . . . Not all of these considerations are relevant to an inquiry into the economic consequences of the American Civil War, but they do serve to illustrate the analytical difficulties of the problem. They also help explain why scholars have confronted that problem again and again and must continue to do so. Simple things may rest in peace.

Not so many years ago historians looked upon the Civil War as a great divide separating modern America from its preindustrial past. To Charles and Mary Beard, for example, the war was a "second American Revolution" which ended in "the unquestioned establishment of a new power in the government, making vast changes in the arrangement of classes, in the accumulation and distribution of wealth, in the course of industrial development, and in the

Constitution inherited from the Fathers."[1] It seemed reasonable to believe that the federal government's contracts for guns, munitions, army uniforms, and other supplies must have created a massive set of demands which, given the acute shortage of labor in wartime, could not have been filled without a widespread mechanization of industry. It seemed self-evident that with the political power of the agrarian South gone from the Union, nothing could block the enactment of legislation favorable to northern industrial interests. In the words of Louis Hacker, the "industrial capitalists, through their political spokesmen, the Republicans . . . succeeded in capturing the state and using it as an instrument to strengthen their economic system."[2] Citing issuance of greenbacks, tariff increases, founding of the National Banking System, adoption of the Homestead Act, grants of land and other subsidies to the transcontinental railroads, passage of the Morrill Land Grant College Act, and enactment of contract labor laws, historians argued that federal legislation, together with wartime demand, accelerated the process of industrialization and paved the way for postwar growth in national income.

The argument was a plausible one—indeed, one must acknowledge that the policies "undoubtedly pushed in the right direction"—but it fails to find support in evidence that has since become available.[3] Recent statistical studies show that the rate of economic growth probably failed to accelerate during the decade in which the war was fought. Increases in commodity output averaged only 2 percent per year between 1860 and 1870, the lowest growth rate of any decade in the nineteenth century. If we look at particular industries, the story is much the same: output continued to grow during the war years, but at declining rates. Annual production of pig iron increased 24 percent from 1850 to 1855, 17 percent from 1855 to 1860, 1 percent from 1860 to 1865, and 100 percent from 1865 to 1870. The number of bales of cotton consumed in United States manufacturing rose 143 percent from 1840 to 1850 and 47 percent from 1850 to 1860, only to fall to 6 percent from 1860 to 1870. New railroad track laid from 1851 to 1855 totaled 11,627 miles; from 1856 to 1860, only 8,721 miles; and from 1861 through 1865, only 4,076 miles. Although we do not know the rate of increase of output as a whole during the war years—total output data are available for the census years 1860 and 1870 but not for the years 1861–1865—-the ground would appear firm for the presumption that the war had a retardative effect on that rate.

When we take into account the changing share of manufacturing in commodity output, the presumption is only reinforced. That share was larger before the war than afterward. This follows from two considerations: (1) whereas the increase was equally as large—not larger—in the twenty years before the war as in the twenty years after it, (2) commodity output itself increased at a greater annual rate before the war (4.6 percent between 1840 and 1860) than afterward (4.4 percent between 1870 and 1900). If we shift the focus to value added in manufacturing, the conclusion is strengthened still more: growth between 1840 and 1860 proceeded at an annual rate of 7.8 percent, in contrast to a rate of 6 percent between 1870 and 1900. The results are even more conclusive when we look at the decade of the Civil War itself. Between 1860 and 1870 value added by manufacturing increased at an annual rate of 2.3 percent, the lowest rate of increase of any decade in the nineteenth century; the manufacturing share in commodity output rose only from 32 to 33 percent; and labor productivity in manufacturing *fell* by 13 percent, a unique occurrence for the nineteenth century.[4]

What accounts for these rather surprising results? The answer is to be found in the nature of the Civil War itself. Far from being the first modern war, it was the last of the great preindustrial conflicts. It was unmechanized and fought by men on foot or horseback armed with rifles, bayonets, and sabers. The consumption of iron attributable to small-arms production amounted merely to 1 percent of the total output of iron between 1861 and 1865. Although artillery was used, it too was a minor consumer of iron and steel.

The effect of the war on the agricultural implement industry is an unsettled question. One available set of figures shows increases in production of farm machinery of 110 percent from 1850 to 1860, 140 percent from 1860 to 1870, and 95 percent from 1870 to 1880. But the biographer of Cyrus McCormick, commenting on a survey of agricultural equipment manufacturers made in 1864, observes that "it is significant that very few of them increased their annual output since 1861." Moreover, production figures need to be offset by unavailable statistics on wartime destruction of agricultural machinery and placed in the context of a rise in the number of farms by about one-third during the 1860s. The latter helps explain why the average value of machinery per farm *fell* nearly 25 percent in the decade of the war. More research is needed, however, because of the possibility that the machinery was concentrated on farms of larger size; that is, larger agricultural units may have undergone an increase in capital-intensive modes of production. Thus wartime labor scarcity in agriculture may have had a greater effect on the rate of growth in output per capita than wartime labor scarcity in manufacturing.[5]

Output per capita did rise at a more rapid rate after the war. In contrast to an annual rate of only 1.45 percent between 1840 and 1860, it measured 2.1 percent between 1870 and 1900. Does this mean that the Civil War accelerated the rate of growth in the later years of the postwar period? Probably not. Since per capita commodity output declined during the decade of the Civil War, the higher postwar rate may merely represent a catching-up process. The possibility is suggested by the fact that the immediate postwar years show the highest growth rate, and by the fact that the growth rate of per capita commodity output was the same between 1860 and 1900 as it had been between 1840 and 1860. The same reasoning explains why the share of capital goods in commodity output rose in the decade of the Civil War, reaching a nineteenth-century peak in 1870. The rise, that is to say, is best understood in the light of probable declines in the earlier years of the 1860s, for the rate of growth in the stock of fixed capital fell from 8.5 percent in the 1850s to 4.1 percent in the 1860s. Finally, the stock of fixed capital in manufacturing grew more rapidly in the postwar years, at an annual rate of 6.8 percent, in comparison with a prewar rate of 6.3 percent. Had earlier historians known of this statistical finding, they undoubtedly would have maintained that the higher postwar rate rested upon the shift toward mechanization they presumed to have occurred during the Civil War. As we have just seen, however, the chances are that the increased rate of growth in the capital stock came after the war.[6]

The plausible connection between political and economic change thus turns out to be an improbable one. And there are additional reasons of a nonstatistical nature for so regarding it. No such monolithic entity as a "northern business class" existed. Rather, the community of interest once supposed to have been represented by the Republican party was riven by conflict. Furthermore, simple comparisons erode one's confidence in the economic effectiveness of Civil War legislation. Both economic growth and an acceleration of manufacturing enterprise have occurred during periods of low tariffs as well as during periods of high ones; in times of monetary stringency and of monetary plenty; under land-disposal policies of many kinds; and in the face of generally high labor costs. One scholar maintains that the Civil War tariff legislation "persisted as a key influence on subsequent development." Yet he acknowledges that "forces other than the tariff were at work" and that protectionist policies antedated the war. But if the latter is so, the question arises why those earlier protectionist policies did not exert the influence claimed for the wartime legislation.[7]

They evidently did not do so because forces other than the tariff were not then favorable to development. That being the case, the emphasis would appear properly placed on those other forces, on the totality of the causal complex in which the tariff appeared, rather than on the tariff itself. An unloaded gun will not fire. To demonstrate the effects of a tariff requires a rare kind of economic ingenuity. With just one exception, its impact on a single industry, let alone on the manufacturing sector as a whole, is still unknown.[8] Finally, that the development of industry did not require a prior development of railroads is conclusively shown by the growth of textile manufacturing in New England before the beginning of the railroad era in the 1830s. This is not to say that railroads did not encourage the further growth of industry. Whether or not the industrialization that took place after the war was particularly dependent on cheap or inland transportation is an issue we shall consider later.

In sum, the available evidence suggests strongly that the Civil War inhibited America's economic growth. We are left to wonder why an opposing point of view remained unchallenged for so long. The answer may simply be that potential countervailing evidence was not marshaled before the recent work to which I have referred. Yet one suspects the presence of a contributing factor. The older view of the effects of the Civil War has an interesting pedigree. In the later years of the nineteenth century the belief was widely shared that the war had unlocked the energies of the nation for a glorious period of national growth. One finds this view expressed in late nineteenth-century-memoirs, for example, those of Grenville M. Dodge, chief engineer in charge of the construction of the Union Pacific Railroad, and those of the eminent lawyer Ralph D. Ingersoll, as well as in the writings of Mark Twain. As Twain put it, America "had just completed its youth, its ennobling WAR—strong, pure, clean, ambitious, impressionable—[and was] ready to make choice of a life-course and move with a rush." That historians should have perpetuated the myth is not surprising. As Thomas C. Cochran has suggested, given the great cost and human losses of the war, it was natural for Americans, who like to see their history in terms of optimism and progress, to believe that the war had the beneficent effects of achieving both freedom for blacks and industrial progress.[9] Industrial progress there was indeed. But it cannot be attributed to war.

The Civil War does not deserve to be known as a second American Revolution, nor were the economic changes that followed it simple and direct products of wartime legislation. Yet it does not follow that actions taken during the war were without effect on the subsequent economy. For one thing, the validation of the Emancipation Proclamation by the victory of the North had important effects, as we shall see, on agricultural output in the postwar South. For another, the methods used by the North to finance the war almost certainly accelerated capital formation and growth in that region after Appomatox.

If an economy is fully employed or nearly so, as was the case in the United States in 1860, mobilization for war requires that measures be taken that will transfer real resources from individuals to the government. Resources can be released from civilian uses by reducing personal consumption, by reducing private domestic capital formation, and by borrowing abroad. Taxation, conscription, and confiscation are direct and obvious means of gaining command of the goods and services needed for war, but on the whole democratic governments have not placed their main reliance on them. So it was in the Civil War. Although the federal government raised the tariff and imposed a wide variety of excise (consumption) and other taxes, including an income tax, it resorted in the main to the less transparent method of issuing debt (bonds and money). It issued long-term bonds of varying maturities, short-term treasury notes, non-interest-bearing demand notes, evidences of temporary deposit, and certificates of indebtedness. And it printed and circulated paper currency (greenbacks).

Table 19 shows both the deficits incurred by the federal government during

Table 19.   U.S. federal government deficit and financing, 1861–1865.

Item	1861	1862	1863	1864	1865	Total
			(millions of 1860 dollars)			
Total expenditures	63.4	382.1	503.6	511.9	674.6	2,135.6
Receipts	38.0	42.4	96.1	172.9	198.2	547.6
Deficits	25.4	339.7	407.5	339.0	476.4	1,588.0
Price index	103	114	136	170	193	
			(percentage of deficit financed)			
Bonds	92.5	14.4	29.2	77.8	35.0	38.9
Liquid assets	−1.2	51.4	28.8	−4.5	52.4	33.3
Interest-bearing currency	—	—	—	35.4	2.8	8.3
Other currency	—	38.1	40.2	7.3	0.3	20.4
Change in treasury balance	8.7	−3.8	1.8	−16.0	9.5	−0.8

Source: Stephen J. DeCanio and Joel Mokyr, "Inflation and the Wage Lag during the American Civil War," *Explorations in Economic History,* 14 (1977), 315. Used with permission.

the war years (that is, the difference between total expenditures and receipts) and the percentages of the deficits financed by diverse means. The category "liquid assets" deserves particular notice, not least because most of the debt issued by the government over the period 1861–1865 was of the short-term or liquid kind. Indeed, only 39 percent of the total wartime deficit was financed by long-term bonds, whereas 62 percent was financed by "liquid assets," "interest-bearing currency," and greenbacks. Composed of short-term securities—that is, temporary loan deposits, some treasury notes, bonds, and certificates of indebtedness—liquid assets served in many instances the purposes of currency, replacing idle cash balances in the portfolios of wealthholders. The inflation resulting from the issuance of so much short-term liquid debt was rapid and its cumulative impact large. From an index level of 100 in 1860, consumer prices rose to 196 in 1865, an annual average rate of increase of 13 percent. In 1863 and 1864 the rate reached 25 percent.[10]

Wartime inflation affected the distribution of income. Money wages lagged behind prices—according to a recent estimate, the real income of wage earners declined a total of $317 from its level in 1860, with half the decline attributed to the wage lag—and in consequence income was redistributed from workers to entrepreneurs (money lenders and profit recipients with a higher propensity to save). The total contribution of this mechanism to the financing of the Civil War, however, was not great, mainly because the labor force was much larger than the northern segment subject to the lag.[11]

Nevertheless, this does not exhaust the effects of federal debt creation and management. The use of excise taxes to finance debt payments after the war also transferred income to savers and investors. Furthermore, by rapidly retiring the debt, the government increased the supply of funds available for long-term investment, an increase which exerted downward pressure on long-term interest rates and encouraged investment. Finally, the promotional campaigns of the banker Jay Cooke, on whom the federal government relied heavily for the sale of its bonds during the war, encouraged the public to save more of its earnings. Cooke's improved marketing techniques, when institutionalized, would later bring together investors and capital seekers on an unprecedented scale.[12]

Fundamentally, the needs of capital seekers arose out of opportunities created by the growth, movement, and increasing well-being of the American people. During the forty years from 1870 to 1910, the population of the United States more than doubled, its annual average growth rate of 20.5 per thousand increasing its numbers from just under 40 million to nearly 92 million people. Examination of the contributions made by demographic forces behind this rate of growth show how it was achieved. The annual birthrate, much the largest of the three forces involved, amounted to 34.7 per thousand. When the death rate, averaging 20 per thousand, is deducted, the resultant rate of natural increase—14.7 per thousand—is seen to be more than twice as large as the contribution of 5.8 per thousand made by net immigration.[13]

Little is at present understood about the factors underlying fertility and mortality in this period. The time patterns of declining birthrates, for example, vary from one country to another, and this makes it difficult to find an explanation that is both simple and universally applicable.[14] We do know that both rates continued their historic declines, the birthrate falling from an annual average of 40.8 during 1870–1875 to 29.6 for the years 1905–1910. Presumably, increasing urbanization and per capita incomes played important parts in this result. Certainly numbers of children under five years of age per thousand women twenty to forty-four years old have been larger in rural than in urban areas throughout the nation since at least 1800 and probably long before. Indeed, the fertility ratio of native white women living in rural areas was twice that of their urban counterparts between 1885 and 1909. There may well exist an inverse relationship between population density and fertility that would help explain these results, but the conditions under which the association appears have not yet been sufficiently explored to warrant generalization. Rising incomes and standards of health care may well have contributed to a decline in the death rate from 21.8 per thousand to 16.6 per thousand between 1870 and 1910. Approved medical and basic science schools increased in number from 75 to 131 during those years, their graduates rising from 7,988 to 39,997. Professional nursing schools numbered 15 in 1880 and 1,129 in 1910, their graduates rising from a mere 157 to 8,140. It is unlikely that the American population shared equally the benefits of these developments. Around 1900 expectation of life at birth in rural areas is estimated to have been ten years above that in urban areas. And life expectation of 33.8 years for nonwhites was sixteen years less than that of whites.[15]

The overwhelmingly predominant white population—88 percent of the total in 1890—was composed of foreign and native stocks. The former—immigrants plus the first generation of their descendants, that is, native-born persons of foreign or mixed parentage--accounted for 33 percent and the latter for 55 percent of the population in 1890. The median age of the population had been less than 19 years in the mid-nineteenth century, lower than in any of fourteen European countries, where median ages mostly clustered around 23 to 25 years. By 1910 it had risen to 22.8 years—24.5 for whites and 21.1 for nonwhites. The youthfulness of the population did not reflect the decline in mortality nearly so much as it did the unusually high birthrate. In consequence, as that rate declined in the course of the century, the median age gradually rose. The rise in average age was accelerated for whites by an influx of immigrants. Relatively few of the latter were under 15 years of age; two of three were between 15 and 40. Indeed, despite a substantial shift in the average age of the population, the age structure of nineteenth-century immigration was responsible for the maintenance of a highly stable proportion of young adults aged 20 to 29 right down to World War I.[16]

Although immigration played a lesser role than natural increase in generating population growth, a stunning total of nearly 20 million foreigners were attracted to the United States between 1870 and 1910 (see Table 20).[17] Each postbellum decade registered far higher numbers of foreign arrivals than any earlier one, except for the wartime decade of the 1860s, which exceeded the

Table 20. Immigration into the United States, 1870–1910.

Decade	Number of arrivals	Departures		Net immigration
		Number	Percent of arrivals	
1870–1879	2,714	651	24	2,063
1880–1889	5,247	944	18	4,303
1890–1899	3,695	1,441	39	2,254
1900–1909	8,203	3,691	45	4,512
Total	19,859	6,727	31.5[a]	13,132

Source: Bureau of the Census, *Historical Statistics of the United States, Colonial Times to 1970* (Washington, D.C.: Government Printing Office, 1976), I, 106–107; Simon Kuznets and Ernest Rubin, *Immigration and the Foreign Born* (Washington, D.C.: National Bureau of Economic Research, 1954), Occasional Paper 46, pp. 17, 95. Used with permission.
   a. Average.

immigration total of the 1860s by merely 100,000 people. Of course, not all of these people stayed, the purpose of many young unmarried men, or men who came without their families, being to acquire savings that would enable them to elevate levels of living in their homelands. As before in our past, the predominance of Europeans was overwhelming, although the nationalities of other continents contributed significantly in particular years, for example, Canadians in 1880–1883 and Chinese in 1873, 1876 and 1882. Within Europe, the British and Irish continued to send large, although relatively declining, numbers of their peoples: from the end of the Civil War till the mid-nineties the Germans were almost always more numerous then either group. Scandinavians were an important element throughout, but in the nineties, and even more so in the first decade of the twentieth century, emigrants from eastern and southern Europe, particularly Russians and Italians, became especially prominent.[18]

This great migrant stream, like all other flows of peoples between geographic areas, was placed in motion by a variety of factors at its points of origin and destination. Not only economic conditions and prospects at home, together with expected opportunities abroad and the cost of getting there, but also war, political conditions, culture, language, and other noneconomic considerations played a role in determining the level of migration at a given time. Not all of these factors need fluctuate, however, to generate periodic swings in the amount of migration over time, swings from a relatively light to a relatively heavy movement of people. Indeed, changing conditions in the United States rather than in the countries of origin were responsible for initiating them. Among these conditions, the most important by far were corresponding movements in the demand for labor.

Decline in the rate of growth of the native labor force in the late nineteenth century tended to raise real wages in the United States and to attract European migrants in larger numbers. Typically, a rising rate of immigration was preceded by a rising rate of growth in hourly wages and by evidence of a decline in unemployment. Conversely, a falling rate of immigration tended to follow a decline in the growth rate of hourly wages and a rise in unemployment. In sum, since immigrant waves were formed by peoples living under a diversity of conditions in different parts of Europe, Canada, and Asia, the ground is strong for the belief that they formed in response to a common external stimulus, namely, changes in unemployment conditions in the United States.[19]

Later we shall examine the contribution made by immigrants to the growth of the labor force and to American economic growth as well. It is appropriate to observe here, however, that the latter contribution was intimately related to the part immigrants played in the process of urbanization. While thousands of the foreign born settled on farms in Minnesota, Wisconsin, and elsewhere, no less than 61 percent of net foreign born migration between 1870 and 1910 increased the populations of Massachusetts, New York, New Jersey, Pennsylvania, Ohio, Illinois, and Michigan, the area of major industrial and commercial concentration in the United States. Over the period as a whole, an even larger proportion, 71 percent, chose the states of the Northeast. In the first two decades of the period some 288,000 more foreigners moved to the North Central area than to the Northeast, but between 1890 and 1910 the Northeast predominated overwhelmingly by 1,790,000 persons. New York, Pennsylvania, Massachusetts, and New Jersey received most of the northeastern migrants, and Illinois, Michigan, Minnesota, Wisconsin, and Ohio most of those who moved to the North Central states. Except for an upsurge of migration to California between 1900 and 1910, foreign born movement to the West was numerically unimpressive, and to the relatively unurbanized South least of all. Not only foreign born whites, but the first generation of natives of foreign or mixed parentage continued to register their preference for urban life and occupations. In 1890, 1900, and 1910 the peoples of foreign white stock accounted for more than half the urban population of the United States. Their role in the growth of American cities was thus a very important one.[20]

Immigrants imparted momentum to the process of urbanization, but they did not initiate it. From the beginning of the United States as an independent nation, the urban population has increased at a higher rate than either the rural or the total population (except for the decade 1810–1820, a period of early settlement of some of the midwestern and southern states). It was not until the 1860s, however, that the absolute numbers of persons added to the urban segment exceeded those added to the rural segment. Thereafter, except for the decade 1870–1880, urban increase was invariably greater in cities (defined by the census as incorporated places of 2,500 or more inhabitants), which increased in both number and size (see Table 21). Cities in most class sizes tripled and quadrupled in number over the forty-year period, but as Table

Table 21. Number of United States cities, by size, 1870–1910.

Population size	1870	1880	1890	1900	1910
1,000,000 or more	—	1	3	3	3
500,000 to 999,999	2	3	1	3	5
250,000 to 499,999	5	4	7	9	11
100,000 to 249,999	7	12	17	23	31
50,000 to 99,999	11	15	30	40	59
25,000 to 49,999	27	42	66	82	119
10,000 to 24,999	116	146	230	280	369
5,000 to 9,999	186	249	340	465	605
2,500 to 4,999	309	467	654	832	1,060

Source: Bureau of the Census, *Historical Statistics of the United States, Colonial Times to 1970* (Washington, D.C.: Government Printing Office, 1976), I, 11.

22 reveals, people living in rural areas continued to form a precarious majority, one that dwindled from 74.3 to 54.3 percent between 1870 and 1910. The table also gives the percentage of the total population living in cities of various sizes. The very largest—1 million or more—and the very smallest—2,500 to 10,000—housed minority portions of the urban population in all four decades. The rate of growth in the former, however, exceeded that of any other size of city.

The Northeast was the most highly urbanized of the major regions (see Table 23). By 1880 it was more than 50 percent urban, and thirty years later, nearly 71 percent. The most urban of the states in the region were those of southern New England and the Middle Atlantic. Indeed, Massachusetts and Rhode Island were more than 50 percent urban by 1850. New York became so by 1870, New Jersey by 1880, and Connecticut by 1890. While the growth of cities was relatively slow in the South, in both the North Central and western regions urbanization was approaching the 50 percent mark by 1910. In the former, it was the industrial states of the Middle West, especially Ohio, Illinois, and Michigan, that conferred an urban character on the region as a whole. In the West, it was the Pacific states, particularly California, that urbanized most rapidly. Already in 1870 the population of that state was 37.2 percent urban; by 1910 the proportion was 61.8 percent, and in Oregon and

Table 22. Percentage of total United States population living in urban places of various sizes, 1870–1910.

Year	Total population	Urban places with populations of —				Rural areas
		1,000,000 or more	100,000 to 1,000,000	10,000 to 100,000	2,500 to 10,000	
		Population (in thousands)				
1870	38,558	—	4,130	3,408	2,364	28,656
1880	50,156	1,206	5,005	4,584	3,335	36,026
1890	62,948	3,662	6,036	7,748	4,661	40,841
1900	75,995	6,429	7,779	9,848	6,103	45,835
1910	91,972	8,501	11,801	13,751	7,946	49,973
		Percent of total				
1870	100.0	—	10.7	8.8	6.1	74.3
1880	100.0	2.4	10.0	9.1	6.6	71.8
1890	100.0	5.8	9.6	12.3	7.4	64.9
1900	100.0	8.5	10.2	13.0	8.0	60.3
1910	100.0	9.2	12.8	15.0	8.6	54.3

Source: Hope T. Eldridge and Dorothy Swaine Thomas, *Population Redistribution and Economic Growth, United States, 1870–1950* (Philadelphia: American Philosophical Society, 1964), vol. 3, *Demographic Analyses and Interrelations,* pp. 3–5. Used with permission.

Table 23.   Regional percentages of urban population in the United States, 1870–1910.

Year	United States	Northeast	South	North Central	West
1870	25.7	44.2	9.3	20.8	25.8
1880	28.2	50.5	9.4	24.2	30.8
1890	35.1	58.7	13.3	33.1	37.4
1900	39.7	65.5	15.2	38.6	40.6
1910	45.7	70.9	20.1	45.1	48.7

Source: Hope T. Eldridge and Dorothy Swaine Thomas, *Population Redistribution and Economic Growth, United States, 1870–1950* (Philadelphia: American Philosophical Society, 1964), vol. 3, *Demographic Analyses and Interrelations,* pp. 3–5. Used with permission.

Washington it was 45.6 percent and 53 percent, respectively. The western movement increased both the urban and the rural populations of the region, but the growth of cities far outstripped that of rural areas. Above all, it was the rise of manufacturing that spurred the growth of cities and sent the process of urbanization tumbling to the west on the heels of the process of industrialization. As we have seen in the case of Philadelphia, even in the early nineteenth century, industrial development, rather than mere commercial expansion, played a primary role in urban growth. Thereafter, the spatial redistribution of the population increasingly nationalized the process.

The course of urbanization differed not only between regions but also between race and nativity groups. Table 24, which discloses the proportions of each group living in cities in each of the major regions, makes it clear that the foreign born were more urban than native-born whites or Negroes throughout the period. While the urban percentages of both the latter groups doubled between 1870 and 1910, the former from 22.4 to 43.5 percent and the latter from 13.4 to 27.3 percent, already in 1870 a majority of foreign-born whites were city dwellers, a preference registered by seven of ten of them by 1910. Those living in the Northeast favored city life by a large margin throughout, but by the end of the period this was true of the majority in every region except the South. Table 25 gives the percentage of each group living in urban and rural areas in the major regions and reveals the steady preference of foreign-born white urban dwellers for the cities of the Northeast. The same was true of native-born whites, although to a declining extent. Urban blacks preferred the South, their rural counterparts overwhelmingly so. No less conspicuous, however, are the generally rising percentages of all three racial and nativity groups in both urban and rural locations of the North Central and western regions as time passed. All were participants, as we shall soon see, in a wavelike motion of peoples washing over the resource-rich American West.

The postwar urban movement represents merely a later chapter of a storied

Table 24. Percent urban of the native white, foreign-born white, and black
population in the United States, by region, 1870–1910.

Region	1870	1880	1890	1900	1910
Native white	22.4	25.8	32.7	37.8	43.5
Northeast	37.9	44.6	53.3	60.8	66.5
South	7.7	8.3	12.0	14.2	19.5
North Central	16.8	20.9	29.5	35.5	41.7
West	21.0	25.0	35.6	39.4	47.9
Foreign-born white	53.6	55.5	60.5	65.5	71.2
Northeast	68.9	75.1	77.6	81.7	84.1
South	55.0	47.1	48.9	44.7	46.1
North Central	37.0	37.6	47.1	51.9	60.3
West	45.6	49.8	46.1	48.2	54.0
Black	13.4	14.3	19.7	22.6	27.3
Northeast	43.7	50.5	59.8	66.1	71.1
South	8.8	9.0	13.5	15.5	19.7
North Central	37.1	42.6	55.8	64.4	72.6
West	45.7	51.5	54.1	67.4	78.4

Source: Hope T. Eldridge and Dorothy Swaine Thomas, *Population Redistribution and
Economic Growth, United States, 1870–1950* (Philadelphia: American Philosophical Society,
1964), vol. 3, *Demographic Analyses and Interrelations,* p. 204. with permission.

search for betterment which reaches back to the beginnings of American colonization. Our forefathers moved wherever land was to be had that was better than the land they were plowing, or wherever gold, iron, or other riches of the earth were to be taken. And they moved too in search of better jobs, to the East and North as well as to the West. Indeed, as Stanley Lebergott has suggested, there have been many "Wests" in American history, so that West is merely a symbol of our mobility.[21] In this sense there were two major westward movements of the nineteenth century, one involving concentration, the other dispersion of the population. In the first, as we have seen, the foreign born played a prominent role in developing the nation's cities, especially in the Northeast and Midwest. The second was composed mainly of native-born Americans pushing out the frontiers of available natural resources farther west. The spatial redistribution of the American people in the nineteenth century was a composite of these two movements. That of the twentieth century was to be dominated by urbanization and by its variant, suburbanization—at least till its closing decades.

The redistribution of the population exerted profound effects on the structure of the American economy. It shifted components of the labor force to employment in new areas, generated or increased pressures for transport improvements, helped move centers of manufacturing off long-familiar bases,

Table 25. Regional distribution of urban and rural population of the United States as a whole and of the native white, foreign-born white, and black populations, 1870–1910.

Region	1870	1880	1890	1900	1910
Urban					
United States	100.0	100.0	100.0	100.0	100.0
Northeast	59.5	56.3	50.0	49.3	46.8
South	10.6	10.1	11.1	11.5	13.2
North Central	27.3	29.7	33.6	33.7	32.1
West	2.6	3.9	5.3	5.5	7.9
Native white	100.0	100.0	100.0	100.0	100.0
Northeast	61.9	57.8	50.5	48.5	44.8
South	8.3	8.1	9.3	9.8	12.2
North Central	27.6	30.9	35.0	35.9	34.5
West	2.2	3.2	5.2	5.7	8.5
Foreign-born white	100.0	100.0	100.0	100.0	100.0
Northeast	61.5	60.2	56.3	59.4	60.1
South	5.4	4.3	3.5	2.9	2.8
North Central	29.3	30.1	34.6	32.2	29.7
West	3.9	5.4	5.6	5.5	7.4
Black	100.0	100.0	100.0	100.0	100.0
Northeast	28.1	28.1	23.8	24.4	22.3
South	56.0	53.8	58.8	58.6	61.5
North Central	15.5	17.4	16.3	16.0	14.7
West	0.4	0.6	1.0	1.0	1.5
Rural					
United States	100.0	100.0	100.0	100.0	100.0
Northeast	26.0	21.7	19.1	17.1	16.1
South	35.6	38.4	39.5	42.3	44.1
North Central	35.9	36.5	36.7	35.3	32.8
West	2.6	3.4	4.8	5.3	7.0
Native white	100.0	100.0	100.0	100.0	100.0
Northeast	29.3	25.0	21.5	19.0	17.4
South	28.7	31.1	33.2	36.1	38.5
North Central	39.6	40.6	40.7	39.6	37.1
West	2.4	3.3	4.6	5.4	7.1
Foreign-born white	100.0	100.0	100.0	100.0	100.0
Northeast	32.0	24.9	24.8	25.2	28.0
South	5.1	6.0	5.6	6.9	8.1
North Central	57.6	62.3	59.5	56.7	48.3
West	5.3	6.8	10.0	11.2	15.5
Black	100.0	100.0	100.0	100.0	100.0
Northeast	5.6	4.6	3.9	3.7	3.4
South	90.2	91.4	92.7	93.6	94.4
North Central	4.1	3.9	3.2	2.6	2.1
West	0.1	0.1	0.2	0.1	0.2

Source: Hope T. Eldridge and Dorothy Swaine Thomas, *Population Redistribution and Economic Growth, United States, 1870–1950* (Philadelphia: American Philosophical Society, 1964), vol. 3, *Demographic Analyses and Interrelations,* p. 202. Used with permission.

pushed the process of urbanization from coast to coast, effected a reordering of the locales specializing in the production of particular crops, and created institutional pipelines in which capital could flow to fill new investment needs. All in all, it quickened the pace at which a national economy was emerging. Local and regional markets would long survive the period of our present concern, but prices of increasing proportions of the nation's output would be determined by forces affecting supply and demand not only in the nation as a whole but abroad as well, including the price of capital.

In one sense, a "national market" was an old and familiar phenomenon of American history rather than a development first apparent in the late nineteenth century. Even in the seventeenth century, when most settlements were within fifty miles of the Atlantic coast, price signals from food-deficit areas gave rise to intercolonial coastal shipments from regions of surplus. In the eighteenth century there is evidence, too, of arbitraging dispatches of bills from coastal cities where exchange rates were low to others where they were higher—a phenomenon that was to become common with the establishment of branches of the Second Bank of the United States in the next century. Such shipments tended to weld the separated communities into a single market area and to dampen differentials in price.

This early "national market" was disrupted by massive population movements to the West, especially after 1815, only to be restored once more by the construction of turnpikes, canals, and railroads linking western farms with eastern cities and foreign markets. The discovery of gold in California in 1848 was a principal source of disruption once more as tens of thousands of people migrated to the Far West in search of easy fortunes. And once again the national market was restored, this time by the extension of the great transcontinental railroads to California. In this physical or geographic sense, therefore, a national market repeatedly formed, only to be disrupted by population movements, before being restored once again through mechanisms of transportation—and, after the commercial development of the telegraph in the late 1840s, also of communication.

In the legal sense, however, we shall see that a national market was potential rather than actual before the railroad knit together the entire continental domain into a source of demand so buoyant in its prospects as to generate techniques of mass production and distribution. Before then almost all shipments of manufactured goods were local or regional, and the license fees and taxes imposed on them by states enjoying a concurrent jurisdiction over interstate commerce in the absence of congressional legislation were not sufficiently burdensome to generate legal protest. With an enlarged volume of output and distribution, however, devices adopted by the states to protect local manufacturers and merchants became too costly to tolerate.

It was the railroad, exaggerated in its economic importance by some scholars and underappreciated by others, which knit together into a single market area the disparate regions composing the continental domain.[22] Surely the railroad was a major dynamic force in American economic development. The first rapid and efficient overland transport innovation, the railroad contributed to development in a number of ways. In common with earlier innovations, especially the canal and steamboat, but in a more pronounced fashion, the railroad reduced the quantity of resources required to produce a given amount of transport service, its relatively greater efficiency in this respect resulting in a relatively larger saving of society's scarce resources. This saving, amounting to more than 10 percent of the gross national product in 1890, made a significant contribution to the nation's economic growth.

The lower cost of total input per unit of output led, in turn, to a correspondingly lower real price for railroad transport services. This lowered price naturally influenced the decisions of consumers of railroad services because the lessened cost of inputs made their current level of activity more profitable. The chief beneficiary was agriculture. Because transport charges form a large part of the total cost of bulk commodities, and because the export demand for those commodities was elastic, the railroad accelerated the geographic extension of agriculture and encouraged both commercialization and regional specialization. It enabled commercial agriculture to move farther west than would have been possible in the absence of comparable transport efficiencies from some alternative means of transport. This is not to say that the extension of the railroad was indispensable, merely that it occurred. It occurred because contemporaries implicitly decided that the savings in long-distance shipping costs via railway exceeded the opportunity costs of the capital sums required for railroad construction, maintenance, and replacement, sums that were greater than those required by the next best alternative method of shipment.

Nor is this all: there are also "backward linkages" to be considered, for railroad construction and maintenance reallocated resources of materials, manpower, and capital. Already by 1860 the railroad's consumption of iron for rails absorbed more than 40 percent of all rolled iron. Moreover, rail mills were not only the largest mills in the country but also leading sources of technological innovation. Between 1867 and 1891 more than 50 percent of the annual output of Bessemer steel went into rails, the average ratio exceeding 80 percent until 1880. The railroad's impact on the coal industry was also impressive, for between 1880 and 1910 locomotives consumed close to one-fifth of total production. Perhaps even more significant from the point of view of the industrializing economy, the development of elaborate repair facilities by the railroad industry in Detroit, Cleveland, Chicago, and other cities disseminated industrial skills over a wide geographic area. In 1860 only 1 percent of the labor force was employed by railroads; in 1900 the figure was 5 percent. Gross capital formation by railroads also rose from an antebellum peak of 15 percent of investment in the 1850s to 18 percent in the 1880s. These shares, exceeded only by residential construction, are far larger than claims on savings by other industries. By 1910 railroads were a 10-billion-dollar industry, the amount of capital invested in railroad track, the most important component, and in bridges, stations, shops, and rolling stock having quintupled in real terms in the forty years since 1870. A huge sum, it represented perhaps one-sixth of the nation's reproducible wealth in the early 1900s.

Between 1870 and 1910 the capital/output ratio declined by 60 percent— that is to say, because of the realization of economies of scale, less capital per unit of output of transport service was required. If the services of capital were proportional to output, which increased during the period at an annual rate of 7 percent—faster than national income, total commodity production, or any other single major sector—then these scale economies explain approximately half the productivity advance achieved by the sector. Technological innovations embedded, so to speak, in the capital stock explain most of the remaining half. Two innovations, the air brake and automatic coupler, were of minor economic significance from this point of view, although both were important because of the contribution they made to increased safety in travel. Two others, steel rails and enlarged equipment capacity, contributed most to the productivity gains. The replacement of strap iron rails by ones of steel was of fundamental importance. Steel rails not only wore longer but bore heavier loads without breakage. They made possible heavier locomotives and more capacious freight cars. By 1909 the primitive ten–ton locomotives of the 1830s had given way to the greater tractive power of behemoths weighing seventy-two tons—with almost half the increase coming after the 1870s.

Although a fuller accounting of the sources of productivity gains would require not only continued refinement of the analysis of technical progress but also inclusion of factors such as the increasing educational level of railway employees, the value of an experienced labor force, and savings made possible by improvements in railroad organization and management, the sources already identified largely explain why "it cost little more than one-tenth as much to purchase a ton-mile of transportation in 1910 as in 1839, and about two-fifths as much for a far more comfortable passenger mile." Not all regions, industries, and firms benefited equally from these cost reductions, as we shall see, but the overall contribution of the railroad to the development of the economy cannot be persuasively doubted.

The 30,000-mile railway network of 1860 represented half the world total, but even this impressive achievement was to pale before that of the postwar decades. By 1890, 140,000 additional miles were available, and while new track continued to be laid thereafter, although in smaller annual increments, the network was practically completed by the time of the depression which began in 1893. Nevertheless, double tracking and other additions were still required by an expanding economy, as we shall see. The network not only spanned the continent—the first of the great transcontinentals having been completed with the juncture of the Central Pacific and the Union Pacific in

Ogden, Utah, in 1869—but embraced all the major commercial centers of the nation, both east and west. In fact, an intensification of rivalry between the major systems took the form of competition for access to these centers in the 1880s, and in consequence that decade saw the construction of more railway mileage than any other in American history. The linking of important cities to producing centers and export markets is a foremost achievement of postwar railroad construction. And since an increasing number of those producing centers lay in the West, the railroad served as both cause and consequence of the westward movement.

It was cause to the extent that the railroad was built in advance of major population shifts, ahead of the demand for their services by communities already settled and in commercial production. But while demand constraints largely justified federal subsidization of the transcontinentals by land grants and loan guarantees, total mileage constructed in the least-settled areas under these programs was limited between 1868 and 1873. Kansas, Nebraska, Minnesota, and Texas had more than twice the mileage of Colorado, Utah, Nevada, Wyoming, and the Dakotas. In short, the attraction of a ready market proved an influence whose importance must not be discounted.[23] Railroads leading to areas of lesser population density were obliged to charge proportionately higher rates to compensate for the smaller demand.

It was otherwise when construction resumed after the severe depression of 1873–1879. Investment in the five years 1879–1883 took place largely in the less-developed regions of the Northwest and Southwest, where new mileage amounted to around 50 percent of the nation's total construction during those years. Even so, demand—for example, for wheat and for precious metals—was so buoyant that the time lapse between settlement and commercialization was reduced. In sum, despite the undoubted occasional importance of governmental subsidies, despite the fact that the timeliness rather than the amount of aid offered by all levels of government was sometimes significantly helpful in scouring an area of investment of initial risks associated with unfamiliarity and uncertainty, private capital, both foreign and domestic, but chiefly the latter, accounted for the bulk of the funds required for the completion of the American railway net. Prospects of profit from serving rural and urban producers and urban consumers and middlemen thus induced market forces to respond to the growing need of the American people for more efficient transportation. Above all, it was the westward movement over a vast continental domain which sped the development of the railroad net. The West would have been settled and its resources exploited without the railroad, but the process would have been much slower, with impacts on demographic, social, and economic change—to say nothing of politics—which are fundamentally immeasurable, despite a leading economist's heroic effort to quantify some of them.[24]

The railroad and the resources of the West which it did so much to open up belong among the forces underlying the growth of the postwar economy, and in the next chapter I shall tell the story of the pulsating push of millions of Americans against an ever-receding western frontier. But first let us look southward once again, to a region whose prospects for advance were anything but promising.

The economic history of the post–Civil War South must begin with one bedrock fact: poverty. By any standard of measurement the South was poor. It was poorer after the war than it had been before, and it was poorer than the rest of the country. In 1880 its per capita output was only about 80 percent of what it had been in 1860. Twenty years later, after a rate of per capita income growth that equaled the national average, its incomes were still merely 51 percent of that average. The region's incomes continued thereafter, except for the 1920s, to converge upon the average—by 1920 they had risen from 51 to 62 percent—but it was not till around 1950 that the South was able to regain the relative standing it had achieved on the eve of the Civil War. What explains the persistence of southern poverty in a nation undergoing rapid economic growth?[25]

It is tempting to blame it all on the Civil War, on the destruction of the physical capital of the South, and to attribute lingering low incomes to that destruction.[26] It is certainly true that many miles of railroad were wrecked or kept in repair only with great difficulty; that the region's manufacturing plant was crippled and its farms devastated, its barns, fences, farm equipment, crops, houses, and livestock laid waste by General William T. Sherman's marauding soldiers in Georgia and South Carolina; that destruction was widespread in Virginia and Alabama; and that heavy losses were reported for Louisiana after General Benjamin F. Butler ordered the sequestering of all rebel property west of the Mississippi.[27] Yet it is by no means certain that much of the region's subsequent poverty and lagging growth can be attributed to these conditions.

The railroads were restored to operating order by 1870. Manufacturing, too, displayed a surprising postwar resilience: by 1869 total output, value added, and capital investment greatly exceeded their prewar levels. Between that year and the end of the century, manufacturing activity in the five cotton-producing states of South Carolina, Georgia, Alabama, Mississippi, and Louisiana expanded impressively, output and value added rising more than sixfold even when evaluated in terms of gold. Indeed, the number of manufacturing establishments rose by 64 percent in the decade 1860–1870 alone. Yet the manufacturing sector occupied only a small part of the southern economy, accounting for the employment of only 6.5 percent of the labor force even at the end of the century. As it had before the war, agriculture continued to dominate the economic life of the South. Did agriculture lay in ruins in 1865?[28]

Surely the soil itself did not. What then of the working stock, the most important form of agricultural capital? Wartime losses were substantial, yet the price in gold of mules in the mule-raising states of Kentucky, Missouri, and Tennessee in 1870 was markedly lower than it had been in 1859—just the opposite of what we should expect if there had been a shortage of mules in relation to demand. And the same phenomenon of price decline was also seen in the five cotton states in the early postwar years. Farm implements such as plows, wagons, harrows, and hoes may have suffered more from neglect than from direct destruction, but in any case their replacement was not costly. Twenty-five dollars is a liberal estimate of the value of the required implements per working hand on a large prewar plantation. And though depreciation may have necessitated replacement or repair of wagons, fences, and farm buildings, it was possible to have repaired this form of capital during the first year of operation.[29]

Since no inventories exist of the South's agricultural capacity or physical capital at the end of the war, historians have generally relied on differences in values contained in the federal censuses of 1860 and 1870. Comparison of the two suggests that by the latter date the cash value of farms in the eleven states of the Confederacy had declined by over 50 percent, there were fewer improved acres in farms, the real value of farm implements had declined by over 50 percent, and the real value of livestock had fallen by more than 45 percent. The census of 1870, however, was deficient in many respects. Not only were the population and agricultural output of the South substantially undercounted. So too were things such as tilled acreage, value of farms and implements, and number and value of livestock, including mules. In a word, a more substantial recovery of agricultural capital was achieved in the early postwar years than historians have traditionally believed.[30]

Yet "recovery" was insufficient, not only in agriculture but in the economy as a whole. The pace at which the economy would grow depended fundamentally on the ability of the South to add to its capital stock, on its ability to form capital at a more rapid rate than that at which its population was growing. But capital depends on savings, and they were meager, partly because the region lacked adequate institutional means for channeling them. More fundamentally, however, savings were meager because of the low productivity of labor in agriculture, the overwhelmingly dominant sector. This was not the fault of the workers. Rather, it was due to the persistence of age-old labor-intensive methods of cultivating the soil and harvesting the cotton crop. Mechanical harvesting methods need not have awaited the mid-twentieth century for their introduction: they were technologically feasible in the late nineteenth. Old methods persisted because an abundant population made them cheaper. Improved productivity in agriculture would have freed workers for industrial pursuits either in the South or elsewhere. Sufficient emigration would have raised the cost of labor and encouraged industrialization, bringing even greater savings, capital formation, productivity advances, and growth. All these changes were to happen in the course of the twentieth century, beginning with the opening of alternative employment opportunities for blacks in the North during World War I. When they did, the specter of poverty began to fade, and though there were setbacks, by midcentury a rapidly industrializing South had regained the position in the nation it had held a century before.[31]

One additional reason why savings were meager is suggested by the South's colonial status in the nation after the Civil War. It was the agents of the Morgans, Mellons, Rockefellers, and other northeastern business interests who took charge of the region's railroads, mines, furnaces, financial corporations, and eventually its distributive institutions.

> Southern counterparts of the Northeastern masters, however, failed to appear. The number of Southern businessmen increased steadily, and some of them waxed in fortune. But the new men, as well as many of the old, acted as agents, retainers, and executives—rarely as principals. The economy over which they presided was increasingly coming to be one of branch plants, branch banks, captive mines, and chain stores.[32]

Southerners earned salaries and commissions, but residual profits found their way to the North, adding to an unfavorable interregional balance of payments originating principally in the South's postwar loss of self-sufficiency in the production of foodstuffs. Had the region's industries and resources attracted sufficient loans and investments to right the balance, the South would have been better able to diversify into manufacturing and been less dependent on cotton exports for that purpose. But even in the late 1860s northern businessmen, especially those interested in investment in the South, believed the policies of Reconstruction governments to be inimical to business enterprise. "No one," a New Yorker wrote Governor James L. Orr of South Carolina, "will invest or emigrate, so long as . . . stay laws are made to prevent the collection of debts." Other northerners insisted that capital would boycott the South as long as ignorant blacks had a dominant voice in southern public affairs. Although this situation presumably changed substantially with the end of Reconstruction in 1877, subsequent investment continued to be insufficient.[33]

Cotton had provided the raw material for the first Industrial Revolution, and after the invention of the gin near the end of the eighteenth century it had become the inveterate habit of the South, well suited to its soil and climate, molding its culture and its values, its politics and social structure. Cotton would have become the South's leading postwar commercial crop in any case—the land could produce little else commercially—but a sharp rise in price right after the war guaranteed the immediacy of its resuscitation—provided a labor force could be recruited to grow and harvest it. The planter elite had survived the war and so too had the plantations, but the slaves who had previously worked them were now free men and women. Therein lay the quintessential problem of economic Reconstruction: how to convert masters into employers, and slaves—and former self-sufficient white yeoman farmers—into free workers. It was an extraordinarily difficult problem. The former masters were unaccustomed to bargaining with employees as equals, and the freedmen were inexperienced in allocating time between work and leisure. "It seems humiliating," wrote one Georgian, "to be compelled to bargain and haggle with our servants about wages." A North Carolina farmer said he was willing to pay wages "where I thought them earned, but this must be left to me." On the other hand, the freedmen, as one planter complained, did not respond to marketplace incentives for steady labor: "released from the discipline of slavery, unappreciative of the value of money, and but little desirous of comfort, his efforts [were] capricious." New institutions would have to be worked out by methods of trial and error, and the legal system renovated to accord, as usual, with the perceived needs of the dominant property interests.[34]

During the war the year-long written contract for wage labor had been instituted by the army in occupied areas, and this procedure was continued with the support of the Freedmen's Bureau after the war. Accordingly, large landowners entered into contracts with freedmen right away in an attempt to revive the work-gang system of the prewar plantation. These contracts contained an agreement to pay wages in cash, rations, and housing, and sometimes an additional reward—perhaps a suit of clothes—for superior work. Success, however, was brief, in part because of an almost total lack of circulating currency in 1865–66. Landowners proceeded to substitute a share of the crop for cash wages, the shares initially being as small as one-twelfth. From the landlord's point of view, the new method had distinct advantages. For one thing, his need for working capital was lessened because cash payments did not have to be made until the crop was sold. This condition guaranteed that his workforce would remain with him throughout the crop year. In the first few years of freedom, the system of work for wages was universally adopted, both by the plantations and by those smaller farms that required a hired hand or two.[35]

The disadvantages to the freedmen were no less obvious, most notably the uneasy resemblance between the wage system of the large landowner and the work gangs, slave headquarters, overseers, and corporal punishment of slavery. They soon had additional reason for disillusionment. Planters colluded to lower wages and keep dissatisfied freedmen from quitting the plantation before the harvest. Their power over state legislatures undiminished since antebellum days, they also sought to protect themselves from the competition of other employers through the passage of laws that restricted freedmen's mobility. The infamous Black Codes, enacted by all the cotton states, were the result. A typical example is a law passed by Alabama in February 1866 which made it unlawful "for any person to interfere with, hire, employ, or entice away, or induce to leave the service of another, any laborer or servant who

shall have stipulated or contracted, in writing, to serve for any given period."
Vagrancy statutes, subjecting to arrest and fine any freedperson unable to
prove in writing that he or she was employed, were also universally adopted.
With good reason for wondering whether they had really escaped the bonds
of slavery, the freedmen wanted out from the system of gang labor in favor of
work in a particular area and pay in the form of a share of the particular crop
they had cultivated and gathered.[36]

Over the years a bewildering array of land-tenure arrangements emerged,
but two of them, tenancy and sharecropping, proved of fundamental importance. Under tenancy rent was often paid in the form of a share of the crop,
but despite this superficial resemblance to sharecropping, the two kinds of
tenure were very different. Usually as early as the 1870s the law in every
southern state sharply distinguished the relationship between landlord and
tenant from that of landlord and cropper. Court decisions made it clear that
the cropper was a wage laborer who was paid a certain *proportion* of the crop
as wages. The tenant, on the other hand, paid a *fixed amount* of rent, either in
money or in crop, to the landlord. Other differences were even more basic.
Under tenancy, the tenant had possession and control of the entire crop and
paid his rent either in kind or in cash. Under sharecropping, the landlord had
possession and control until he made the division. The difference significantly
affected the credit status of the two in the eyes of the law.[37]

Both croppers and most tenants required credit for food and clothing as
well as for farm equipment and supplies over the long period during which
the crops were planted, cultivated, and harvested. But because the landlord
retained ownership of the crop until it was divided, the cropper was unable
to provide security for the supplies he received on credit from a nearby storekeeper ("furnishing merchant"). Crop lien laws were designed to provide the
necessary security to the merchant. It soon became evident, however, that if
the lien was on the worker's entire production, the landlord might be left
without security, that is, his portion of the crop as well as the worker's might
be taken by the merchant. The law soon provided the landlord, if not the
worker and merchant, with the protection he needed. In one court decision
after another it was made clear that a lien given by a worker to a merchant
could not become operative until the landlord took his share of the crop and
gave the employee his share. And in the many instances in which landlords
rather than merchants supplied the workers, landlords were assured of protection by laws passed by every southern state legislature making the landlord's
lien for rent and advances superior to all other liens and mortgages. These
laws gave the landlord the desired control over his labor force, increasing his
power in the black belt and limiting that of the merchant.[38]

Thereafter many merchants shifted toward the white-yeoman areas in the
hill country, for these former subsistence farmers also needed credit as they
turned after the war to commercial farming. At the same time, ample oppor-

tunities remained for black belt merchants, many of whom supplied the land-lords; the latter, in turn, passed on the supplies to their tenants and croppers. Differences between landlord and merchant, however, were minor disputes within the new landlord-merchant business class which came to dominate southern agriculture by the end of the nineteenth century. They were easily settled under new laws providing the legal basis for the defense of the interests of that class.

The same system of law which created a business class out of former slave-owners and country storekeepers also transformed former slaves into free workers and self-sufficient yeomen into commercial tenant farmers. Yet nei-ther worker nor tenant found it easy to be free from debt and its consequences. Although the laws of each state provided explicitly that liens for advances were valid only against the particular crop for which they were made, the courts construed this limitation virtually out of existence. In Alabama, for example, the courts ruled in 1888 that "when the tenant fails to pay any part of such rent or advances, and continues his tenancy under the same landlord, on the same or other lands, the balance due therefor shall be held and treated as advances to him by the landlord for the next succeeding year."[39]

Since other southern courts adhered to the same or similar positions, land-lord-merchants "could easily keep their borrowers in debt and preserve their lien to cover old as well as new debts." Movement to another landlord offered little hope of release.

> A tenant or cropper whose old debts fell under the new year's lien would be unable to bargain for better terms elsewhere because a new lender would have an inferior lien and therefore scant security for his loans. The old lender, without fear of competition from others, could then apportion new loans in a manner best designed to secure himself from loss. A tenant or cropper without cash or an alternative source of loans had no choice but to accept the terms as offered.

But that is not all. The lender's power to grant or deny applications for credit enabled him to dictate production decisions. Indeed, his domination also extended to the personal lives of his borrowers when the latter needed loans for food, clothing, medical attention, or even luxury items. The courts com-pleted the circle of control by ruling that these personal loans were necessary for production and thus covered by the liens. In sum, the new planter-mer-chant class exercised "a degree of control over their work force far beyond that available to employers elsewhere in the nation."[40]

Before the war labor was wealth; it was like a fixed cost, and masters "strove to raise the output of each slave by spreading the labor across as many acres as possible, and by finding ways to use the young, the old, and the women as well as the men." After emancipation, however, the former masters "were primarily *landlords*, whose concern was to raise the value of output per acre,

treating labor as a variable cost." One way in which they did so was to concentrate their crop acreage on cotton, the output value per acre of which was
two or three times that of corn. But labor had its own reasons for supporting
the economic interests of landlords. By 1880 the plantation system was gone,
and the typical family farm, dwindling in size under the pressure of population, measured from thirty to fifty acres. Subserviency to debt, coupled with
the small size of the farms, made it extremely difficult for the debtor, whether
tenant or cropper, to avoid putting most of his acreage in cotton. Only in this
way could he hope to reduce his indebtedness.[41]

It is thus possible to view the farmer as moved by his own self-interest to
specialize in cotton. Essentially, he was a gambler pursuing the main chance,
concentrating on cotton in the hope that a good year would clear his debts
and leave him a surplus. Unhappily, and unknown to him, he was taking this
action at a time when the world demand for cotton was declining. Economic
progress based on cotton could not be restored because of the weakness of
the forces governing market demand. The individual farmer could not win,
nor could the South. Overproduction of cotton had the underside of under-
production of corn and other food crops. The postwar South quit its historic
path of agricultural diversification and self-sufficiency, an abandonment which
made the region a substantial net importer of food. Not just slavery, "but the
self-sufficient prosperity of 1860, was gone with the wind forever."[42]

The farmer's self-interest in cotton received powerful support from that of
his creditors, especially the furnishing merchant. The sharecroppers who dominated the cotton counties were in a parlous position. Their only asset was
their labor and that of their families. This they exchanged for the use of land
and a house, as well as for fuel, working stock, feed for the stock, farming
implements, and seed. It must often have been true, however, that the landlord's own limited assets did not permit him to supply all these items of working capital. In that case, the cropper had to obtain them, together with food,
clothing, and any other supplies he might need, from a furnishing merchant,
and he had to obtain them as advances, on credit. Whether tenant or cropper,
credit was an absolute necessity for most small farmers. But the merchant
refused to grant credit unless the farmer was willing to make cotton his principal crop. The farmer was thus locked into the production of cotton. Because
he was not self-sufficient, he was obliged to seek credit year after year, and the
terms on which he obtained it ensured that the farm could not become self-
sufficient. The farmer was caught in the "trap of debt peonage."[43]

Outrageously extortionate charges for credit—credit prices averaged 60
percent above the level of cash prices in the 1880s--tightened the grip of the
trap. And so too did the downright cheating of illiterate freedmen, who had
to accept the merchant's statement of the balance of his account or the merchant's evaluation of his cotton, as well as the prices set on the supplies he

purchased. The farmer could not escape. The merchant exercised a "territorial monopoly" of the supply of short-term credit in the immediate neighborhood of his store, and this permitted him to employ a monopolistic pricing system for the goods he sold.[44]

Is there no ray of light in this dark picture of exploitation? Were 4.5 million blacks set free by the victory of Northern arms only to fall victim to a legal system which afforded them no protection, to a political system in which they did not count, and to racist oppression and brutality on the part of private persons determined that blacks should not become owners of land, educated, or accorded an elemental recognition of their humanity? Yes, there is a ray of light. Despite the great odds against them, southern blacks managed some notable achievements. Virtually illiterate at the end of the Civil War, more than half could read and write by 1910. Many acquired skills—not least, expertise in farm management. And many owned land, tools, buildings, and work stock. The postwar story must be told in terms not only of coercion but of competition as well, indeed of an intense competition for labor, and due emphasis placed on the black man's mobility, "the most precious jewel of emancipation, his ultimate reliance in resisting oppression."[45]

These reminders, together with the suggestion that concentration on cotton reflected the farmer's personal interest as well as mercantile oppression, lighten somewhat the burden of guilt whose weight no historian can escape the need to assess. But they do not, in my judgment, remove it. It is not only fair but also important to point out the element of risk involved in agricultural credit, the scarcity of capital in the South, and the high interest rates paid by merchants themselves in borrowing money in Charleston or New York, rates which ranged from 12 to 36 percent, and occasionally went even higher. But 60 percent? It is true that "many" freedmen "did flee from their creditors." The black man's ability to flee was "an action that could succeed after 1865 on a scale quite impossible under the slave regime," but the number who did so in relation to those who could not, whether because of ignorance, moving costs, or oppression, must remain in doubt. Surely most did not.[46]

As for competition between landowners for labor services, the case appears stronger for the market power of scarce workers in the earlier postwar years when the ex-slave for the first time enjoyed the freedom to lighten his burden and reserve a portion of his time for himself. Withdrawing his wife and children from labor in the fields, he also reduced the hours of his own workday. In these circumstances, landowners were compelled to offer increasingly better terms for labor, and by the early 1870s a sharecropping contract had become standardized which gave half the crop, or its value after sale by the landlord, to the cropper. Surely this was a culmination to which competition provided the driving force. There is evidence, too, at least from the early postwar years, that farm-to-farm turnover among sharecroppers was high, and that both black and white farm laborers moved from state to state and from employer to employer. But given the surplus agricultural population of later years and the declining size of farms in response thereto, it is easier to believe that in the longer view of half a century competition played a bit part rather than a major role in the drama of struggling black farmers.

A sensitive scholarly analysis of difficult, contradictory evidence reached the final conclusion that "competitive forces and the forces of ignorance and discrimination were so inextricably entangled that a clear portrait of the rural labor market is difficult to paint." The most recent effort to do so suggests that that market was a dual one. There was a local and a long-distance market. The local market was that of sharecropping families dependent on credit, families which exchanged advances on their subsistence needs and the promise of family autonomy for the landlord's assurance of a year's labor. The long-distance market was a competitive wage-labor market which unattached males could resort to if they were "willing to travel long distances and take their chances." Unfortunately, the two markets were poorly integrated. Attachments to families, combined with the hope of rising from wage labor, sharecropping, and tenancy to farm ownership, "limited the ability of sharecroppers to take advantage of the competitive labor market." In fine, competition would appear to deserve a lesser weight than factors conducive to coercion.[47]

10

Three Frontiers

The distribution of the American people over the western reaches of the continent represents one of the three great population movements of the nineteenth century, the other two being urbanization and immigration. Although the West was much the least populated area of the country between 1870 and 1910, its rate of growth far exceeded that of any other region, doubling that achieved by the next fastest growing section between 1870 and 1890, and tripling it, from 1900 to 1910 (see Tables 26 and 27).

By the eve of the Civil War the frontier along the farms of the western prairies had followed an irregular line of settlement from St. Paul, Minnesota, to Fort Worth, Texas. Between that line and other settlements on the Pacific coast lay half of the continental domain, a vast area of nearly 1.25 billion acres of land awaiting exploitation and containing merely 1 percent of the nation's population. Some of this land was rich in minerals, notably gold and silver, and over most of the Far West prospectors and miners pioneered innumerable pockets of settlement, many of them as ephemeral as the metallic mirages that drew them on.

Between the Rocky Mountains and a transition zone in the vicinity of the hundredth meridian lay the Great Plains, stretching 1,300 miles from Canada to Texas and varying in width from 200 to 700 miles. Although containing islands of timber on the mountain tops in Colorado, Wyoming, and elsewhere, this vast, flat region was in the main a treeless area with a subhumid or arid climate. Home of the prairie dog, the jack rabbit, and above all the buffalo, or American bison, the rich grasslands of the plains supplied the physical basis for the rise of the Cattle Kingdom. Although the Great West was potentially rich agriculturally, only in Minnesota, Kansas, Texas, and California had a substantial number of farms been established by the eve of the Civil War: 18,181; 10,400; 42,891; and 18,716 farms, respectively. The rest of the West contained found only 19,098 farms, with a mere 7,437,819 improved acres of a total of more than 1 billion acres.[1] The story of these developing frontiers throws much light on the ways in which new resources essential to economic growth were made available to the American people.[2]

Table 26. United States population by region, 1870–1910 (thousands).

Region	1870	1880	1890	1900	1910
United States	39,818	50,156	62,948	75,995	91,972
Northeast	13,336	15,767	18,848	22,698	27,697
South	12,510	12,527	18,587	22,872	27,561
North Central	12,981	17,364	22,410	26,333	29,889
West	991	1,768	3,102	4,091	6,826

Source: Adapted from Hope T. Eldridge and Dorothy Swaine Thomas, *Population Redistribution and Economic Growth, United States, 1870–1950*, vol. 3, *Demographic Analyses and Interrelations* (Philadelphia: American Philosophical Society, 1964), p. 10. Used with permission.

Table 27. Changes in United States population, by region, 1870–1910 (percent).

Region	1870 to 1880	1880 to 1890	1890 to 1900	1900 to 1910
United States	26.0	25.5	20.7	21.0
Northeast	18.2	19.5	20.4	22.0
South	22.0	21.8	23.1	20.5
North Central	33.8	29.1	17.5	13.5
West	78.5	75.5	31.9	66.8

Source: Adapted from Hope T. Eldridge and Dorothy Swaine Thomas, *Population Redistribution and Economic Growth, United States, 1870–1950*, vol. 3, *Demographic Analyses and Interpretations* (Philadelphia: American Philosophical Society, 1964), p. 11. Used with permission.

Aside from explorers, hunters, and trappers who had been crossing the Far West for decades, it was prospectors and miners who pioneered the distant reaches of cordilleran America. Colorado lay 600 or 700 miles from the Missouri frontier, California 2,000, with the intervening Great Plains essentially untenanted prior to the completion of the Pacific Railroad in 1869. The first of the mining frontiers opened in the Sierra Nevada region of northern California following the discovery of gold at Sutter's Mill in 1848, with silver mines in Colorado and Nevada defining new frontiers for a number of years beginning in 1859. Then in the 1870s came surges of population into Arizona, New Mexico, and the Black Hills of South Dakota. In consequence, California's population, excluding Indians, expanded from an estimated 14,000 in 1848 to 380,000 by 1860, and that of Colorado grew from 40,000 in 1870 to 194,000 a decade later. By no means had all these people come in search of precious metals. The census of 1870 found only 36,339 "miners" in California and only 8,241 in Nevada. Most settlers formed part of a service community called into being by the needs of the miners. This community included storekeepers, innkeepers, saloon keepers, traders, teamsters, bankers, and farmers, among others—not to mention gamblers and other desperate men. It was the output of precious metals that sustained them, and diffused mineral wealth that raised per capita incomes in the mountain states to the second highest level among the nation's regions in 1880.[3]

For those successful in their search for gold, the metal was easily come by in the early years. Virgin deposits on the western slopes of the Sierra Nevada were so rich that all the prospector had to do was to use his knife, hornspoon, or shovel to dig out the gold and then "wash" it by swirling it around in a pan or bowl to separate it from foreign matter. These shallow placer deposits had been formed by fast-moving streams which, after eroding subsurface mineral deposits on the hillsides, had slowed on reaching the canyon floors and dropped their burdens of heavy gold onto the gravel beds. By the mid-1850s a more scientific and capitalized kind of mining had developed from river mining: deep-gravel and quartz mining. To river mine for gold one had first to dam and divert the stream in order to dig out the exposed bed, a speculative type of enterprise requiring the labor of a large number of men organized in co-operative companies. Deep gravels required more than labor-intensive techniques. Costly tunnels, many as long as two thousand feet, had to be dug to reach placer deposits laid down by prehistoric streams and subsequently buried by layers of dirt, rocks, or lava. An even more effective way to attack deep gravel was by hydraulic mining, which involved bringing in water under high pressure and playing it upon a hill believed to be underlain by the auriferous channel of an ancient river. Requiring a heavy initial capital investment, hydraulic mining eventually became the most important single method of mining gold. Quartz, or deep-vein, mining—tracing a vein, sinking a shaft, breaking loose the ore, hoisting it to the surface, crushing it, and extracting the gold from the mass of ground-up material—was the most technical of all kinds of mining. It appears also to have been the least successful way to mine gold. Placer mines, including those worked by hydraulic-mining techniques, yielded almost all the gold obtained between 1848 and 1860.

If controversial estimates of output are to be believed, the gold mines of California yielded an astounding total of $81,294,700 in 1852, and nearly $70 million in each of the next two years. After that the trend was steadily downward. For nearly twenty years after 1865 California produced between $15 million and $20 million a year, with output never falling below $11.2 million in any year in the remainder of the century.

Although quartz mining may have been the least successful way to mine gold it was from the quartz mines of California that came the knowledge, machinery, and experienced hands needed to begin the exploitation of the rich silver and gold deposits of Nevada's Comstock Lode after 1859–60. But the past was merely prelude. When the dip of the vein plunged beneath 175 feet, totally unfamiliar problems had to be confronted. Miners at Comstock already knew how to install stream-pumping machinery to rid a mine of flooding underground water, and they had used hoisting equipment to lift out the ore. But at the greater depths veins were forty-five to sixty-five feet in width and soft and crumbling in composition. Even the strongest timbers used as pillars broke under the load, with the result that miners worked under a constant threat of cave-ins. Philip Deidesheimer, an able young German engineer with previous experience in California, solved the problem by inventing the square-set method of timbering. Timbers were "mortised and tenoned at the ends so that they could be fitted together to form hollow cubes, each cube interlocked with the next in endless series." The device became standard practice throughout the Comstock, with engineers from all over the world coming there to study and copy this important innovation in underground-mining practice. Other innovations, especially Almarin Paul's invention of the technique of "panamalgamation" to extract precious metal from crushed ore, proved essential to the mining of the Comstock riches.

Those riches were of spectacular proportions and included both silver (57 percent) and gold (43 percent). The initial probes had proved relatively unpromising. Between 1861 and 1863 output more than doubled each year, slowed to $16 million the next year, and then gradually declined to less than $7 million in 1869. Subsequent exploration by daring entrepreneurs who cut drifts, tunnels, and crosscuts far underground and installed costly surface machinery led by the mid-1870s to the discovery of "the greatest bonanza of all time." Between 1873 and 1882 two mines joined together as the Consolidated Virginia produced a total of $105,168,859. The yield of sixty principal Comstock mines between 1859 and 1882 amounted in all to $292,726,310. The role of rising capital inputs in producing these results is suggested by a calculation that the ratio of total capital to product in the production of precious metals rose from 2.55 to 3.15 between 1870 and 1880, and to 5.41 in 1890.[4]

Eastern and European investors supplying these mounting capital inputs could do so in complete confidence that the legal system would respond to the pressure of their interests and, by protecting their property "rights," lower the risks of investment. Initially they had, in strict legal terms, no property rights at all, for they were trespassers on the public domain and therefore merely tenants-at-will. Ever since 1785 the policy of the federal government had been to "retain title to public mineral lands in order to extract rents from them for the 'public purpose.'" A great variety of public-land acts had been passed which reserved mineral lands, preventing their sale. Even the Preemption Act of 1841, which allowed squatters on surveyed but not-yet-offered lands of the public domain to purchase them at the minimum price fixed by law, expressly excluded the public mineral lands.

Instead of selling these lands, the government experimented with a leasing system after lead and copper deposits were discovered in the Midwest. High enforcement costs and a host of other problems, from fraudulent administration to widespread local resentment, led to abandonment of the effort and to the transfer of legal title to private claimants. According to President James Polk, the leasing system had yielded rents amounting to less than one-fourth the cost of administration. But although laws passed in 1846 and 1847 permitted the sale of lead and copper mines in Illinois, Michigan, Wisconsin, Iowa, and Arkansas, the as-yet-undiscovered mineral lands of the Far West continued to be reserved with no provision for transfer to private holders.[5]

  This remained the situation for twelve and a half years after the discovery of gold in California. Officially the national government retained title to the gold fields, the act admitting California to the union reaffirming federal ownership of the mines. But no real attempt was made to enforce the national title, a failure which led the California supreme court to rule that the federal government tacitly approved private ownership. Enforcement, however, would have been extremely costly in view of the remoteness of the West Coast and the state of communication and transportation technology. In addition, the very nature of placer mining made the assertion of congressional authority difficult. To have apprehended and evicted thousands of highly mobile miners from an extensive area covering 250 miles along the edge of the Sacramento and San Joaquin river valleys would have required federal officials patrolling every gully and gulch.

  Since the federal government could provide security to neither persons nor property rights in the remote reaches of the Far West, the famed mining camps developed their own unofficial local systems of protection. Collective action leading to the establishment of customary law was rooted in an American tradition as old as the Mayflower Compact and as recent as the claims clubs organized by nineteenth-century midwestern farmers to prevent others from outbidding them at public auctions and wresting from them lands which they had occupied and improved prior to public sale. The mining camps administered their own criminal laws, backed primarily by a hemp rope, and established mining codes containing rules for acquiring and maintaining claims. Some of the provisions related to initial discovery, others to the size and marking of claims and the amount of work required to hold the land from other claimants. The basic principle of prior discovery was the order of the day: preemption not only underlay the formation of claims clubs; it figured prominently in the public laws as well. And the doctrine of prior appropriation of water, essential to both early mining methods and later hydraulic techniques, was a natural concomitant of the customary mining law.[6]

  Early Comstock was a repetition of California's experience. Five months after the first major strike in January 1859, a group of miners collectively organized the Gold Hill Mining District and drew up the "first written rules prescribing claim location procedures, claim sizes, conditions for maintaining mining rights, and arbitration procedures." Additional strikes in the Comstock region later that year and the next were soon followed by the organization of other mining districts and the adoption of similar sets of rules and regulations. By obeying the district's rules, individuals obtained private ownership rights to public lands. When in 1865 and 1866 the federal government for the first time recognized the existence of possessory rights in mining property and opened the mineral lands, it expressly provided that occupation was to be subject to local rules. In so doing, federal law placed the legislative and judicial support of the government behind the resource allocation system established by the mining district rules and regulations, behind private owners of mineral rights.[7]

The mining codes remained at the core of a growing body of mineral law at the local level as well. After Congress granted territorial status to Nevada in 1861 and authorized the establishment of executive, legislative, and judicial authority, the territorial legislature declared in its first session that in all actions respecting mining claims, "proof shall be admitted of the customs, usages or regulations established and in force in the Mining District embracing such claim; and such customs, usages, or regulations when not in conflict with the laws of this territory, shall govern the decision of the action in regard to all questions of location, possession and abandonment." Through the territory period (1861-1864) the courts refined private rights by applying these general mining district rules to specific cases, and after Nevada achieved statehood, its courts continued to assert the legality of local district rules.[8]

The early rules at Comstock were well suited to the relatively simple problems of shallow placer mining and, not surprisingly, they bear striking resemblances to the mining codes of California. By 1861, however, the superficial deposits had been removed and the remainder of the ore found to be far below the surface and to contain not only gold but also silver in complex compounds. "Extraction required deep, underground mining and elaborate milling processes to separate the bullion from the captive elements." The consequent need for shafts, tunnels, and custom mills to refine the ore entailed the replacement of early labor-intensive operations by capital-intensive ones. The financial requirements of the latter, in turn, led to a corresponding replacement of early general mining rules implemented by part-time enforcement officials, by laws that were more precise and more rigorously enforced. The precise rights of individuals and corporations in staking, working, and selling mine claims could be determined only by legal battle and judicial determination of controversies such as those over procedures for establishing claims, the boundaries of claims, actions taken by a claimant to protect his holdings from trespass, and provisions for the transfer of ownership. More rigorous enforcement of the law required legislative and judicial definition of taxes due the state and of the duties of sheriffs, surveyors, recorders of claims and mine records, notaries, commissioners of deeds, juries, and judges in enforcing mineral rights.

In addition, jails had to be provided for the punishment of violators of the law.[9]

It was above all the growing value of mineral output and mineral lands which generated these improvements in the law and in its enforcement. Increasing specificity brought greater clarity and precision to the definition of individual mining rights and consequently enhanced the security of ownership. By decreasing uncertainty with respect to title to valuable claims, the law reduced the risk of investment and encouraged the higher levels of capital input required to work the deep veins of precious metal at Comstock—and to mill the ore. The specificity of mineral law rose rapidly along with increases in output through 1868. By that year, however, most questions of ownership of the Comstock Lode were largely resolved, rights were strictly defined and enforced, titles were secure, and pressure for further refinements declined. As a result, after 1869 there was a fall-off in adjustments to mining law. The mineral rights structure was well established and supported at both the state and federal levels.[10]

California's gold and Nevada's silver and gold are perhaps the most famous of the mining frontiers of the Far West, but they were not the only ones. Discoveries of silver, copper, and zinc in Colorado; gold and silver in Idaho and Montana; gold and lead in Utah; gold, silver, and copper in Arizona; gold and copper in New Mexico; and gold in the Black Hills of South Dakota opened new mining frontiers in both the Northwest and Southwest between 1860 and 1880. Some of the consequences of these developments were local, others regional and national. Mining camps and towns sprang into life, attracting crowds of lawyers, small tradesmen, and mechanics besides encouraging hotels, restaurants, brothels, and hurdy-gurdy houses, only to decline and die off with the petering out of deposits that could be mined with the available technology or of yields that were economically infeasible given the discouraging trends in world silver prices. Regional service towns and cities fared better than the local ghost towns and camps because their tributaries of supply and demand were larger and more diversified. San Francisco became the queen city of the California gold region almost from the beginning, "the great port where goods from the outside world were landed, bought and sold by merchants, and then loaded onto steamboats or small sailboats for carriage up the Sacramento and San Joaquin rivers to the principal commercial centers of the great interior valley." Food, clothing, hardware, mining supplies, heavy mining equipment, whiskey, books, and newspapers were among common items dispatched to leading interior distributing points such as Sacramento, Stockton, and Marysville. From there supplies were hauled by pack trains and wagons to the larger mining towns or to the hundreds of ephemeral camps. Under the stimulus of this trade San Francisco flourished, expanding from a population of less than a thousand in 1848 to 56,802 in 1860. The opening of the Comstock Lode refreshed the boom by opening a huge new market for the iron foundries and machine shops of the Queen City. Demand for mining machinery made San Francisco into an industrial town, with about two-thirds of California's manufacturing concentrated there before the end of the 1860s. By 1868 its population numbered about 133,000.[11]

On the national level, the significance of large increases in supplies of precious metals lay mainly in their influence on price levels as the metals were converted into coin and added to the reserves of the banking system. There was also a change in the relationship between the relative values of the metals as, first, increased supplies of gold coins augmented the value of their silver counterparts, only to be followed by the reverse of this situation as Comstock poured forth its hordes of silver. But changes in the balance of payments and worldwide demonetization of silver also contributed to this result. Some political consequences must also be noted, from the so-called Crime of '73 to the formation of the Populist party and splinter movements in the major parties. These were not without influence on developments in an increasingly national political economy.

The second of the three western frontiers to be opened to settlement was the cattlemen's frontier of the Great Plains. An area of devastating blizzards, hailstorms, and high winds sweeping uninterruptedly over the treeless grasslands, the threat was ever present of economic ruin to man, beast, and crop. The presence of no fewer than eleven Indian tribes, including the Comanche, Arapaho, Blackfoot, Crow, and Cheyenne, added immeasurably to problems of settlement and use. Some of these tribes, like the robber barons of feudal Europe, demanded tribute in the form of cattle before they would allow a herd to pass on to the grasslands. Nomadic and nonagricultural, they depended for their existence on the nearly countless numbers of bison which roamed the plains.[12]

The foundations of the Cattle Kingdom lay in Mexican herds which were the offspring of Andalusian cattle brought to the New World by Spanish conquerors. These herds gradually spread through the vast pampas regions of Texas. By 1860, 3.5 million cattle were listed in that state for assessment purposes. As early as 1842 drovers had delivered cattle to New Orleans, and subsequent drives to Ohio, Chicago, the territory of Colorado, and California all took place before the Civil War. By 1866 railway construction was pushing into the grazing areas of Kansas and connecting them with the great markets of St. Louis, Chicago, and the Atlantic seaboard. The arrival of thirty-five thousand Texas cattle in Abilene the following year marked the beginning of the northbound Texas cattle trail. Millions of steers were to be driven over that trail in the next two decades and dispersed over the natural feeding grounds of the Great Plains.

The Texas Trail was no mere cow path; rather, it consisted of numerous paths and trails converging toward the northern part of the state before branching out into the grazing grounds of the western plains. Abilene, where J. G. McCoy, an Illinois entrepreneur engaged in a large livestock-shipping business, had built stockyards, pens, and loading chutes, was the original point where the north-south cattle trail intersected the east-west railroad, but the trail end shifted westward as the railroads advanced. For about ten years after the Atchinson, Topeka, and Santa Fe reached Dodge City, Kansas, that town was the greatest cattle market in the world. Abilene, Dodge City, and other shipping points were more than loading points or stations where cattle would be held until a suitable eastern market could be found. They were also entry points for cattle used to stock the great ranges of the northern plains.[13]

Between 1866 and 1880 nearly 5 million cattle were driven north from the plains of southwest Texas to Abilene and northern and western ranges. In addition, other herds were turned directly west to the ranges of New Mexico, Arizona, and Colorado, while still others went to Montana, Wyoming, and the Dakotas. Thus, in the space of fifteen years the range and ranch cattle industry spread over the Great Plains, an empire of grass whose formal proprietor was the federal government. As Table 28 discloses, although the percentage of cattle produced on the Great Plains was always small when compared to cattle production in the rest of the country, the increase in their number on the plains was much greater than in the rest of the United States. From 1860 to 1890 these percentages rose from less than 1 percent of the total in 1860 to about 3 percent in 1870, 10 percent in 1880, and 21 percent in 1890. In the East many farmers had a few head of cattle and their aggregate numbers were large. In the West both the ranches and the numbers of cattle on each were huge, although such ranches were not numerous. One large ranch on the Great Plains might produce as many cattle as a thousand eastern or midwestern farms.

Although cowboys, rodeos, frisky horses, chuck wagons, branding, and the

Table 28.   Number of beef cattle in the United States as a whole and in the Great Plains region, 1860–1890.

Year	U.S.	Great Plains[a]
1860	14,779,373	107,086
1870	13,566,005	410,443
1880	22,488,550	2,870,029
1890	33,734,128	7,791,285

Source: George W. Rollins, *The Struggle of the Cattleman, Sheepman and Settler for Control of Lands in Wyoming, 1867–1910* (New York: Arno Press, 1979), p. 43.

a. Rollins defines the Great Plains region as excluding Texas and the Pacific Coast states. Used with permission.

romance of the "long drive" north from Texas enrich the folklore of the Cattle
Kingdom, an important economic distinction between the rancher and the
eastern farmer lay in the former's specialization of investment in livestock,
which often included sheep as well as cattle. Specialization might yield substantial profits in a rising market, but it also exposed cattlemen to heavy losses
when prices fell. Before 1880 the cattle business of the plains was largely a
frontier industry. The open-range system of ranching held full sway, so that,
aside from the money needed for the purchase of cattle, the investment was
slight.

> The usual procedure was for a stockman to select a site along some stream or
> water hole and secure perhaps 160 acres, either by pre-emption or homestead,
> as a ranch headquarters. On this site he might construct a rude dwelling,
> perhaps only a dugout on a hillside or a rude log or frame building. A small
> stable for his horses or at least a corral was also constructed. He might also
> fence in a small tract of meadow land on which he cut hay for winter feed for
> his horses. The new operator would then purchase a suitable herd of cattle
> and graze them on the public domain. The cattle were allowed to run loose
> and were rounded up in the spring for branding and marketing and in the
> fall for shipment to market.[14]

During the summer months the cattle were usually allowed to roam at will
over the range, and even during the winter they received only slight attention.
Since winter winds generally blew away the light snow and exposed nutritious
bunch grasses, very few cattlemen fed their herds during the winter.

Under the open-range system, in which stock belonging to various ranches
often became mixed, any attempt to improve the breed of cattle was almost
futile. Rising prices for beef around 1880, however, brought important changes
in the conduct of the cattle industry of the plains. Prices had fallen to a low of
$1.50 cwt. on the hoof at the Chicago market in 1874 but by 1880 had
climbed to $6.50. Cattlemen began building up their herds by buying more
heifers and fewer two-year-old steers. The ranges were becoming increasingly
well stocked, and stockmen began to see the need for gaining control over
more land instead of depending exclusively on the open range. They began
not only buying or leasing as much land as possible but also, thanks to Joseph
F. Glidden's invention of barbed wire in 1874, fencing it in—in the process
often illegally including many acres of the public domain along streams or
around water holes, which gave them control of the surrounding uplands. In
sum, the livestock industry, like the manufacturing industry, was undergoing
change around 1880 from small business to big business, from a regime in
which herds were small and investments in land almost nil to one in which
vast land areas, huge herds, and large amounts of capital were necessary. And
as in manufacturing, these beginnings of an era of consolidation in the livestock industry, in which small cattlemen were compelled to sell their herds

and ranches to larger, incorporated companies, reflected the advent of a national market and the technological, transport, and legal changes required for the working of that market.[15]

Beef prices continued to rise in the early 1880s, to highs in Chicago of $7.50 cwt. in 1881 and to $9.35 the next year, in the process spawning reports of fabulous profits. Walter Baron von Richtofen, a German who had been in the cattle business in Colorado, gave many examples of profitable investments in his book *Cattle Raising on the Plains of North America* (1885). A Denver banker, for example, was reported to have earned a net profit of $120,000 on investments in cattle over a six-year period. In testimony before a House committee in 1885 E. V. Smalley, an experienced livestock buyer of Minneapolis, Minnesota, reported that "an average yearly profit of twenty to thirty per cent could ordinarily be expected on capital invested in the cattle business in Wyoming and Montana." Such accounts did not go unheeded. From 1880 to 1885 the ranges became stocked to capacity, the trend toward large companies increased, and capital flowed in from eastern and European investors, especially English and Scotch. According to a statement published in the *London Economist* in March 1886, eleven English and Scotch corporations operating in the western states from 1883 to 1885 "owned" 2,016,883 acres as well as 672,013 cattle and, on a capital stock of 3,947,089 pounds, paid dividends ranging from 10.5 to 6.7 percent. Unfortunately, many of the companies purchasing cattle in the early eighties were counting the increased value of the herds as profits rather than as income earned from operations. When beef prices fell after 1887 and herds decreased in value, these purported gains were converted into losses.[16]

As the declining dividend rates of these illustrative English and Scotch firms suggest, the bonanza in cattle began to fizzle out after 1883, when beef prices fell from $4.25 cwt. for the lower grades to as low as $1.00 in 1887. Growth in demand for beef did not keep up with an even more rapid growth in supply. Not only were the ranges being overstocked and cattle marketed too soon, but cattlemen found themselves contesting more and more bitterly with sheepmen and settlers for access to the grasses of the open range. The growth in the number of sheep on the Great Plains was almost as rapid as that of cattle. According to the census of 1890, the plains region held nearly 3 million more sheep than cattle that year, their number having increased by nearly 300 percent between 1870 and 1890. During the same interval the number of farms on the plains grew from 49,424 to 145,878 and the number of acres devoted to farming from 16,219,086 to 47,282,233. The unusually harsh winter of 1886–87 dealt a lethal blow to the open-range livestock business, with thousands of cattle perishing in severe and prolonged blizzards. Numerous firms went to the wall, among them many of the largest. Like the South Sea Bubble and Dutch tulip craze of earlier centuries, the Cattle Kingdom, built by men attracted by the promise of tremendous profits and the myth of limitless free grass, fell into ruin and whimpered into history. But not without a legacy of betterment. Meat-packing centers in cities such as Chicago, St. Louis, Kansas City, and Omaha had developed to minimize the cost of transporting cattle and meat products from the ranges to the consumers. And with the decline of the open range and the accompanying growth of barbed-wire fencing and winter feeding, it became possible to improve the quality of meat products. The era of longhorns grazing on the public domain gave way to an era of stocking with improved European breeds such as Herefords, shorthorns, and Anguses. By 1900 the livestock industry of the post–Civil War West was producing nearly 50 percent of the nation's cattle, 56 percent of its sheep, and about 25 percent of its hogs.[17]

These achievements were not without their costs. Thousands of acres of the public domain were illegally fenced by stockmen in an effort to keep out competing sheep herders or farmers. In addition, grazing interests resorted to fraud and perjury in order to obtain sufficient amounts of land for pasture. It is difficult to condemn them: the Preemption Act, Homestead Act, and other land laws had been drawn up in the interests of farm families and on the basis of experience with the humid regions of the country. But the 160 acres of land allowable under these laws were too few for graziers, and, furthermore, most of the mesa and tablelands of the Great Plains could not be utilized for agricultural purposes. In a celebrated report to Congress in 1879, Major John W. Powell of the United States Geological Service recommended grazing homesteads of 2,560 acres as the amount of land necessary for the support of a family in the arid region of the United States. But Congress failed to act; nor did it respond to criticism of the land laws by the Public Land Commission, which pointed out in a report in 1880 that the "homestead and pre-emption laws are not suited under the old conditions attached to them for securing the settlement of more than an insignificant portion" of the arid regions. The "people of those regions," the commission added, "have to a certain extent framed customs which take the place of laws. In other words they are a law unto themselves."[18]

In sum, stockmen grazing their herds on the public domain found themselves in a situation somewhat similar to that of the miners. But whereas in the latter case Congress took no action at all for many years, in the case of the land laws legislation had been framed with eastern conditions in mind. Until Congress responded to the differing needs of the arid West, graziers had little choice but to ignore the letter of formal law and draw up their own sets of rules for the recognition and enforcement of "grazing rights" on the public domain. And so, in the spirit of the miners they established "range rights," rights secured by prior discovery and utilization, possessory rights due to occupation. In the spirit of the miners? Perhaps it would be truer to speak of the American spirit.

The advent of barbed wire did more to hasten the decline of the Cattle

Kingdom by changing the dominant occupation on the Great Plains from ranching to stock farming. It also made it possible for farmers to accelerate their march across the prairies and onto the plains. But although cheap fencing enabled the homesteader to protect his agricultural unit from the grazing herds of cattlemen, this was not the only necessary condition for successful farming on the arid plains. The farmer also needed access to water, for in the Great Plains region west of the ninety-eighth meridian rainfall is spasmodic, varying from thirty to less than ten inches a year. In consequence, the runoff is large. In addition, there is much sunshine and great wind movement. Altogether, these conditions make the area even drier than the small amount of precipitation itself would suggest. Aside from dry farming, a technique for making crops with a minimum of rainfall, main reliance had to be placed on irrigation, either via artesian wells utilizing underground water or via windmills to raise ground water to the surface. Neither method proved universally successful, but of the two, the windmill, first used extensively by the transcontinental railroads, contributed most to the advance of the agricultural frontier into the subhumid West.[19]

That advance was slow before 1900 except for an important wheat belt of bonanza farming in the Red River Valley of the North. Yet without local markets provided by miners, freighters, and army posts, the advance would have been slower still. To be sure, land and agricultural booms, promoted by railroads with lands to sell and by land companies, town-site promoters, and a host of land speculators of many kinds, periodically encouraged a rush of settlers, for example, into eastern Dakota between 1878 and 1887, an advance which raised the population of Dakota from 135,177 to 511,527 in ten years and increased the number of farms from 17,435 to 95,204—or, at the same time, into western Nebraska and Kansas and eastern Colorado. Many of these settlers, as on other frontiers, arrived with little equipment or capital, erected a sod house or cheap frame house, and with a team of horses or oxen, a wagon, and a plow, began to farm. Fortunately in the case of Dakota, a series of good years during the decade before 1887 converted thousands of nearly penniless farmers into established operators. Many did well, with bumper wheat yields of twenty-five to forty bushels an acre realized in one Dakota county in 1882. But by 1887 the wheat and land boom in Dakota was over, destroyed by droughts so terrible that fields throughout the territory averaged between eight and nine bushels per acre that year. By the winter of 1889–90 many families were in dire want. During the next seven or eight years periodic crop failures and low prices following the Panic of 1893 left many farmers in debt and barely able to make a living. By the late 1890s better crops and higher prices generated a new boom, and thousands of farmers settled on land west of the hundredth meridian. But rainfall was meager and uncertain, and this made crop farming under current agricultural practices a highly risky business. Thousands succeeded in establishing decent homes, but few got rich.[20]

Much the same story could be told of farming on other western frontiers, for example, on the central plains frontier represented by western Kansas and Nebraska and by eastern Colorado between 1878 and 1896. Boom periods were cut short by severe droughts only to be followed by renewals of the same alternating developments in the same or more western locales. Most of the settlers on the eastern Colorado frontier, like many on all the agricultural frontiers of the Great Plains, were poor and lacking in knowledge of the true geographic character of the region. Perhaps at best they survived on their traditional homesteads of 160 acres, "raised a few acres of corn or wheat, or both, owned a few head of livestock and sold meager quantities of dairy or poultry products." At worst, they failed, victims of nature and lack of understanding of the limitations and requirements for successful dry farming. In sum, the farmers who settled on the Great Plains in the 1880s endured tremendous hardships, "but out of their experience came a more accurate and realistic view of the region's true nature and a recognition of the type of agriculture that could succeed there." As a result, a more stable and prosperous farming economy developed in the twentieth century.[21]

The story of the bonanza wheat farms in the Red River Valley of North Dakota and Minnesota has a similar ending, but its intervening chapters are dramatically different. Large farms of a thousand acres or more were nothing new in American history, nor were they by any means confined in the later nineteenth century to the Red River Valley of the North. What is striking about the latter phenomena, however, is not only their rapid growth in the 1870s—from 2 to 145 in Minnesota and from none to 74 in Dakota Territory—but the fact that they were an agricultural reflection of contemporaneous developments in manufacturing industry. Often incorporated, owned, and financed by eastern and foreign investors but managed in the West, their extensive acreages required not only the employment of seasonal gangs of migratory workers, especially for harvesting operations, but also a degree of mechanization not found anywhere else in the United States, except in the Central Valley of California.[22]

Probably the best known of the farm managers was a Minnesota wheat grower named Oliver Dalrymple, who was hired in 1875 by officers of the Northern Pacific Railroad to establish a model large-scale farm so successful in its operations as to demonstrate the productivity of the region and encourage sales of the railroad's land. Dalrymple was given full managerial control. It was he who decided how much land to plow and plant, what wages to pay, whether to store or sell the crop, and what machinery to purchase. In 1877 Dalrymple had 26 breaking plows, 40 plows for the turning of the broken sod, 21 seeders, 60 harrows, 30 self-binding harvesters, and 5 steam-powered threshers, each of the latter capable of threshing a thousand bushels of wheat a day. Fifty men were employed during spring planting to operate the machinery, and they sowed 220 acres of wheat a day. Harvest time required the hiring of 80 to 100 men. All this in only his second year! The planting of additional acres required additional machinery and labor. By 1880 Dalrymple had 25,000 acres under crop, divided into farms of about 6,000 acres of plowland, each of them under the control of a superintendent. The farms, in turn, were again divided into parcels of about 2,000 acres. Each farm had its own buildings, boarding houses, stables, blacksmith shops, and so on, managed by a foreman. The 2,000-acre units were considered sufficiently large for systematic management, yet not so large as to make it necessary for the men to travel far to and from work—and invite diseconomies of scale. Eventually the Dalrymple interests amounted to about 100,000 acres.

Other notable bonanzas in North Dakota, which generally adopted the organizational and managerial practices used by Dalrymple, included the Hillsboro Farm, 40,000 acres; the Cooper Farms, 34,000; the Amenia and Sharon Land Company, 28,350; the Spiritwood Farms, 19,700; the Mosher Farms, 19,000; and the Antelope Farm, 17,300. These and other bonanza farms accounted for a substantial proportion of the wheat output of Dakota Territory. In 1879 Caso County, center of Dalrymple's operations, averaged nearly twenty bushels an acre and produced more than a third of all the wheat grown in Dakota that year. But the bonanza operators made up only a minor portion of the population. Thousands of small farmers rushed into the valley after 1875, seeking both railroad and government land—under the Homestead Act and Timber Culture law—on which to establish wheat farms. Their combined output catapulted the Red River Valley of the North into the nation's leading wheat region. Between 1879 and 1884 wheat acreage in the six Minnesota counties and nine North Dakota counties, which were all or partially in the valley, leaped from 130,877 to 2,450,658 acres. Production rose from only 2,498,642 bushels to 29,340,512 bushels in the same decade.[23]

By the late 1880s bonanza farming was on the decline, with large tracts being broken up into small farms and leased or sold. Despite the efficiencies achieved by specialization and large-scale production, farmers were fundamentally at the mercy of two uncontrollable forces—nature and the market. They could determine neither their output nor the prices of the things they bought and sold. Indeed, as we shall see, the price of wheat was determined by supply and demand in a worldwide market. Anticipated large profits, therefore, proved ephemeral, partly because they were not based on genuine cost-accounting calculations. They loomed large in prospect in 1879 and 1880, when a crop of around twenty bushels an acre brought from $.80 to $1.00 a bushel. After 1881 wheat never again brought $1.00 a bushel in the nineteenth century. In 1884 in Dakota the price fell to less than $.50 under the weight of a large crop, but rust, insects, drought, floods, and other natural phenomena brought partial crop failures in numerous subsequent years. Wheat growers did make large profits during some years, but these were probably the exception rather than the rule. The big operators "made their real money by selling both wild and improved land to small farmers." Large, medium-sized, and small farmers had been doing the same thing for a long time. Capital gains from the sale of improved real estate probably have contributed substantially to the creation of agricultural wealth throughout American history.[24]

But there was another capital gain yielded by the Red River Valley, namely, the demonstration effect of the utility of new horse-drawn equipment. Smaller farmers who witnessed or read in the *Prairie Farmer* and other farm journals about the highly mechanized operations of the bonanza farms were encouraged, within the limits of their financial capability, to acquire postwar horse-drawn innovations or improvements such as the gang plow, sulky, disc harrow, self-binding reaper, twine binder, and "combine" reaper-thresher. One index of the extent to which they did so is the rise in the number of farm horses from 7.1 million in 1870 to 16.9 million in 1900. Another is the rise in the annual value of American manufactures of agricultural implements from $21 million in 1860 to $101 million in 1900, a nearly fivefold increase in total annual sales despite declining prices for many of these implements. Mechanization was the main direct source of improved productivity in the output of wheat, corn, and oats, accounting for 56 percent of the gain in output per farm worker calculated to have occurred between 1840 and 1910. The other main source was the westward expansion of agriculture onto millions of acres of newly opened fertile land. The availability of the new machines, especially the reaper and thresher, enabled the farmer to place more acres under cultivation and thresh many more bushels of grain than had previously been possible with hand implements. This was particularly true in the West, on whose great expanse of level land machinery could most successfully be employed in plowing, harrowing, and planting.[25]

The westward migration of agriculture accounts in substantial part for the fact that between 1870 and 1900 farmers settled and placed under cultivation more land than in all the previous years of American history. Between 1607 and 1870 about 407 million acres were occupied and 189 million improved, but between 1870 and 1900 another 430 million acres were peopled and 225 million brought into production. The part played by the westward movement in this astonishing achievement is suggested by the fact that cleared agricultural land in the five prairie states of North and South Dakota, Iowa, Nebraska, and Kansas alone accounted for 28 percent, 46 percent, 30 percent, and 27 percent of the nation's total improved land in the decades 1870-1879, 1880–1889, 1890–1899, and 1900–1909, respectively. Furthermore, since lands of the prairies and plains were relatively treeless, they could be placed in production at a far lower labor cost than elsewhere. In none of the decades between 1870 and 1910 did the number of man-years devoted to the clearing of land in the five prairie states amount to more than 2 percent of the national total.[26]

A number of economic and institutional consequences may be attributed to the rise of the western agricultural and livestock industries, although it must be emphasized that similar and earlier change is implicit in the fact that westward migration, transport innovation, market stimulus, and the need of farmers to make many small adaptations to new soils and climates have been nearly constant features of American history since at least the late eighteenth century—and in the case of adjustment to the environment, from the very beginnings of the American experience. For one thing, agriculture continued the steady continuity of its challenge to subsistence farming, which clung to its ancient ways only in inhospitable circumstances. And within the enlarging circle of commercial production, farmers increasingly specialized in particular crops, and so too did geographic regions.

These regions shifted with migration to the West and accompanying transport and market development. On the eve of the Civil War, Illinois, Indiana, Wisconsin, and Ohio led the nation in wheat production, but by the end of the century these states had given way to Minnesota, North Dakota, Ohio, and South Dakota. With the exception of Illinois, the leading corn producer in both 1859 and 1899, the corn belt also moved west, with Ohio, Missouri, and Indiana being displaced by Iowa, Kansas, and Nebraska. And except for Iowa, which had more beef cattle than any of the Great Plains states in 1899, the center of beef production moved to the realm of the Cattle Kingdom. In sum, specialization in agriculture was considerably greater in the plains states— and as we shall see, also in the South—than elsewhere in the country.[27]

Older areas, once dominant, lost the comparative advantages they had once enjoyed. Upper New York State, the leading producer of wheat earlier in the century, turned to the truck gardening and orchard industries, producing potatoes, cabbage, spinach, and other vegetables and fruits destined for the tables of urban New York and other nearby growing cities whose backyard gardens were rapidly disappearing. By the end of the century, the value of New York's truck and small fruits sold in the East was nearly twice that of its nearest competitor, New Jersey. It held a similar predominance over Pennsylvania in the value of orchard fruits sold or consumed in the North.[28]

The nature of agricultural change in New England, more particularly in northern New England—which is more representative of the rural character of the region than the southern parts—appears in the light of recent study to have been misunderstood. The area has been traditionally depicted as a scene of agricultural ruin between 1870 and 1900, with widespread desertion of farms and a pronounced decline in rural population. The reassessment confirms a reduction in rural population and in the agricultural labor force but finds no evidence of a widespread abandonment of farms or farming. Despite the competitive superiority of the Midwest in wheat and corn production, income per farm worker in New Hampshire, the focal state of the reexamination, increased by nearly one-half, while income per acre rose 17 percent

during the period. The state's farmers readjusted the allocation of their resources and concentrated on the production of commodities that were effectively isolated from western competition because they were destined for local
and regional markets protected by lower transport costs. Hay for city horses
was particularly important, along with dairy products (specifically fluid milk),
eggs, vegetables, and forest products.[29]

The fortunes of cities and farms have almost always been intertwined in
American history. Farm workers displaced by urban-made machinery and
equipment, together with some of the sons and daughters of farm families,
have moved to the cities and found jobs, not only in New England but also
in the Midwest and elsewhere. These linkages are displayed with particular
clarity in the prairie states after the Civil War. From the edge of the prairies
near Chicago, railroads ran out to the Mississippi River, bent northward to
the Missouri, and pushed west to the Great Plains and beyond. With ready
access to the rapidly developing agricultural West, factories making the bulk
of the machines for western farms sought the locational advantages of Chicago
and other cities along the southwestern shore of Lake Michigan and on the
middle stretches of the Mississippi River.

Second only to Chicago in the manufacture of agricultural implements was
the industrial center of Rock Island and Moline in Illinois and Davenport in
Iowa. Already by 1860 three great trunklines—the Erie, the Pennsylvania,
and the Baltimore & Ohio—connected Chicago with the East Coast. Chicago
was also the natural geographic center for the stockyards which, following the
construction of the transcontinental railroads and the invention of the refrig-
erator car in the 1880s, fed the products of that city's meat packing industry
to major urban markets throughout the country. Local slaughterhouse monopolies bitterly resisted the competition and temporarily had their way when
the Supreme Court, in an effort to restore the federal balance after its disruption by the growing power of the national government during the Civil War,
ruled in the *Slaughter-House Cases* in 1873 that Louisiana's grant of exclusive
slaughtering rights to a privileged local group in New Orleans lay within the
bounds of the police powers of the state. But, as we shall see later in more
detail, when Minnesota and other states enacted a law in 1889 requiring the
inspection of livestock by the state within twenty-four hours before slaughter,
a requirement clearly designed to protect local packing interests rather than
the health of local consumers, the Supreme Court in *Minnesota v. Barber*
(1890) held that the law represented an unconstitutional regulation of interstate commerce. Here, as in other instances to be observed, the high Court
kept open the channels in which commodities of all kinds might flow throughout the national market.[30]

No commodity in that flow was more important than wheat, and two cities
of the prairie states emerged as world capitals because of the nature of their
relation to that grain. Minneapolis became the capital of the flour-milling

industry and Chicago of the internal grain trade. Annually, railroads which penetrated the grainfields of the West brought to Chicago tens of thousands of carloads of three to four hundred bushels each, but since the city itself was never a great consuming center, almost all of the wheat was shipped on to the East via lake navigation and railroad. Shipments nearly doubled between 1870 and 1890, rising from 77,105,740 to 150,515,761 bushels. Elevators were necessary adjuncts of railroads, which built many of them, for they enabled cars from the West to unload and carriers from the East to obtain loads without delay. As late as 1880, 80 percent of the wheat received from the West went into storage, but the rapid development of through service reduced the proportion to 54 percent by 1890. In 1888 the storage space provided by Chicago's elevators totaled 30 million bushels, the amount having doubled in each of the three preceding decades.

Elevators were huge skyscraper warehouses holding 500,000 to 5 million bushels each. Long, slender, perpendicular bins enabled cars and boats to be loaded by gravity. Grain was carried from the bottom to the top of the building and delivered to the proper bin by a long, endless, power-driven belt equipped with buckets. Each bin held grain of a designated grade, with the grain being mixed by grade instead of separated by ownership. The owner or his agent was given a warehouse receipt entitling the bearer to withdraw a certain portion of a specified grade of grain. The development of standard grading and of warehouse receipts enabled trading in grain to proceed rapidly and easily on an exchange, merely by the transfer of receipts. By about 1880 Chicago grades had become standard throughout the commercial world. Chicago's vast store of grain functioned like a gold reserve, for the huge issues of warehouse receipts based thereon served as collateral for advances from local banks, eastern investors, and grain merchants, the resulting credit being used to buy more grain and eastern goods and even to build railroads. Thus the grain trade served as a prime source for midwestern growth. Grading and warehouse receipts, together with the durability and constantly flowing supply of grain facilitated by the elevator system, also enabled futures trading to develop in Chicago. In the absence of these preconditions, extensive short selling—that is, operations in which a dealer seeks to profit by selling for future delivery at one price and by making delivery with grain bought later at a lower price—could not have occurred. Despite the almost universal condemnation of grain speculators, the trading of futures reduced many of the risks inherent in a free market. "By protecting millers, dealers, and exporters from losses, they helped narrow the difference between the average price paid to farmers and the average price charged to the ultimate consumer."[31]

The production of American wheat and flour was responsive not only to domestic demand but to the stimulus of foreign markets as well, especially that of England, whose dependence on American breadstuffs increased markedly in the decades following the repeal of the British Corn Laws in 1846.

Between 1870 and the turn of the century Britain purchased about half of its
annual imports from the United States. Indeed, by the 1870s "the American
supplies had come to be regarded as the principal factor in the international
wheat trade." The American trade became so highly developed and tightly
organized, its techniques of assembling, handling, financing, and transporting
grain so vastly superior to those of any other nation, that other countries,
hoping to emulate the efficiency of American operations, sent numerous mis-
sions to the United States to study the technology involved, especially Chicago's grain elevators and its systems of grading and inspection. In the main,
however, they failed to appreciate the role of futures trading, which was of
fundamental importance to the whole system.[32]

Britain's dependence on American wheat was so substantial before the 1880s
that the volume and price of American exports were primarily influenced by
the size and condition of British harvests. Other countries, however, especially
Argentina, Australia, and Canada, were also beginning to emerge as major
producers and exporters. Increasingly, therefore, the export price of American
wheat was determined in the international market centered in England by
total world supply and demand. American farmers accustomed by poor British
yields to count on good prices for their own crops now found prices unexpectedly lower because of bumper crops in distant parts of the world. Although this was not the first time in American history that the expectations
of farmers were unmet because of distant factors of demand or supply beyond
their control, it is nevertheless reasonable to believe that the consequences of
the development of the international wheat market played some part in the
growth of agrarian protest organizations and political movements, especially
their espousal of populism in the early 1890s. But the organization of postwar
farm protest began in the late 1860s and early 1870s and multiplied for many
reasons that historians far from fully understand.[33] Before roughly the end of
the World War II historians tended to echo the protests of midwestern farmers
themselves against what they regarded as unfair treatment by railroads, money
lenders, manufacturers and retailers of farm equipment, banks, and other
"middlemen" "who by virtue of monopolistic position and undue influence
on government policy were able to deprive the farmer of what should have
been his share in rising American income." More explicitly, farmers accused
railroads of bribing legislators and subsidizing the press, of charging more for
a short haul than for a long one, of discriminating against some persons and
places in favor of others, and, along with other elevator owners or managers,
of cheating them by grading their wheat falsely, charging too much for storage, and practicing other abuses. It was difficult to distinguish between railroad managers and warehousemen in these respects, for the former built their
own elevators (warehouses) or leased land on their right-of-way to warehousemen with whom they worked very closely. Livestock shippers had their
own set of complaints, accusing the railroads of taking poor care of their cattle,

of putting them in inadequate cars crowded with animals improperly fed and watered, cars in which they were sometimes trampled and killed, and often bruised, with the consequence that the survivors brought lower prices. Banks, mortgage associations, and other money lenders, both east and west, were accused of demanding extortionate interest rates on mortgages. Historians depicted farmers as bowed beneath burdens of debt, emphasizing that the rapid expansion of agriculture into the plains states in the 1870s and 1880s and the resulting heavy capital requirements for establishing new farms and financing railroads led to a large burden of debt and taxation. They also pointed to the long secular decline in the level of farm prices between 1869 and 1896. They therefore defended both agrarian support of the Greenback party's opposition to further withdrawal of greenbacks from an already too scarce money supply and subsequent support by farmers of the silverite demand that free coinage of silver dollars be resumed by the United States Treasury. Finally, they charged that short-term loans needed for carrying on farm operations were hindered by inadequate banking facilities. These, then, were the principal reasons assigned to explain the myriad forms of collective action by farmers, from the organization of the Grange in 1867; Farmers Alliances in the 1870s and 1880s; cooperative organizations for the marketing of wheat, dairy products, livestock, and fruits; and mutual insurance companies, to political action, particularly in support of the Greenback and Populist parties. Collective action also generated pressure on legislatures in Illinois, Iowa, Wisconsin, and Minnesota to place the railroads under closer public supervision.[34]

Morre recent studies by economic historians cast doubt on the validity of some of these views. For one thing, although the prices of farm commodities underwent a long-term decline between 1869 and 1896, the prices of the goods which farmers bought declined still more, if only slightly so. The farmer's real terms of trade, therefore—the quantity of goods which his output would buy—trended in his favor during the period. Additional support for this position, and a partial refutation of the charge of monopoly pricing of farm equipment, is provided by a study made in 1901 by the Department of Agriculture. This study shows that of fifteen "typical machines" used on farms, the prices of seven rose, while those of eight declined or remained the same between 1895 and 1900. If 1880 is selected as the earlier of the two dates, none of the fifteen items is disclosed as having risen in price by 1900, two remaining the same and the other thirteen declining, some by more than half.[35]

Recent scholarship challenges other charges. One historian has shown that interest rates were falling rapidly with the secular deflation of the period and that credit was easily available. Another suggests that the short life of mortgages in the Midwest allowed rapid adjustment at lower rates of interest. And still others maintain that "the low average size of debt relative to equity indicates that most farmers in most regions of the country could not have experienced a heavy real burden of debt in the agricultural conditions of the late 19th century." As for freight rates, both earlier and later historians agree that railroad rates fell faster than farm product prices.[36]

And that is not all. The most recent study of the relationship between economic conditions and farm protest movements denies the very existence of a general depression in agriculture in the last decades of the nineteenth century. On the contrary, it finds that "agricultural gross product per worker rose in every one of the thirty states examined [New England and the mountain states were excluded] over the course of the 1870–1890 period." Rates of growth varied considerably from one region to another, however. Increases were greatest in the Northwest Central states, especially in the plains states, and least in the South, with the eastern and Middle Atlantic states holding intermediate positions. Agricultural depressions were not always general either. Although all states were hard hit in the early nineties, depression struck the southern states with particular severity in the early 1870s. Interstate differences in agrarian protest movements and movements in support of Greenback and Populist party candidates partially reflected interstate and interregional variations in degrees of economic decline. And they partially reflected the broad social and political impact of industrialization, urbanization, and the expansion of a complex market system into previously semi-self-sufficient and frontier areas. Developments of these kinds altered the relative political power and status of different social groups.[37]

These modern studies enrich our understanding of the economic and social forces behind movements of protest in the later nineteenth century, but they by no means reduce to irrelevancy the specific counts on the indictment drawn up by farmers and other small businessmen at the time. Take, for example, the complaint that the railroads charged more for a short haul than for a long one, even when the goods being shipped were traveling the same line and going in the same direction. The classic case is one which played a key part in the Supreme Court's decision in *Wabash, St. Louis & Pacific Railway Company v. Illinois* (1886). Gilman, Illinois, was eighty-six miles closer to New York City than was Peoria, Illinois, yet the Wabash charged more for shipments from Gilman. In 1877, to cite another instance, freight rates on the Burlington Railroad west of the Missouri River were almost four times as high as those east of the river, then half as high down to 1900. In general, rates were lower between Chicago and the East Coast than for comparable mileages west to Chicago.

Farmers and other local producers rightly believed that their interests mattered less to the railroads than broad regional concerns. It had not always been so. Before the 1850s, the early railroads had been financed in the main by local businessmen, usually with supplemental aid from state or local governments in the form of bond subscriptions or other loans. Their objective was improved access to markets, with all its attendant advantages, for example, increases in population and in real estate values, economic diversification, and an enlarged tax base. The identity between the interests of the owners of the railroad and the businessmen and producers of a given area had been close.

This relationship began to change as railroads came to be viewed as worthwhile investments in themselves, as outside investors bought into strategically located companies for speculative purposes. The value of railway properties became measured more and more by their ability to produce dividends. Without the infusion of outside capital, most American railroads, particularly those in the West, would not have been completed. But the growth of absentee ownership led to a sharp division between the interests of the new proprietors and those of local businessmen and governments. Frequently, the former sought to develop regional transportation and marketing systems, and in doing so they were not inhibited by state boundaries or by local concerns.[38]

Operating as they did in broad regional markets, the railroads were naturally sensitive to competition from other carriers. The Northern Pacific Railroad charged almost twice the rate on wheat shipments from Fargo, North Dakota, to Duluth, Minnesota, than from Minneapolis to Chicago, although the latter distance was twice the former. Why? Because Minneapolis shippers had a choice of railroads on which to ship, whereas shippers in Fargo did not. And why were freights cheaper east of Chicago than west of the city? Because of the competition provided by the Great Lakes and the Erie Canal. Moreover, once a shipment of freight was loaded, the cost of transporting it a hundred miles was only a little less than carrying it several times that far. If long-distance traffic had to be carried at the same rates as those charged for short hauls, many bulky products like corn and wheat, whose value is low in proportion to their weight, could not have paid the freight charges.[39]

The economic discrimination in favor of long hauls, however clear and defensible, could hardly appease farmers and other local interests injured by it. Nor could smaller producers be expected to tolerate the economic leverage of big shippers, that is, their ability to obtain volume discounts in return for their patronage of a particular line in competitive situations. Wheat growers in the Northwest, for example, complained that the James J. Hill railroads would haul no grain from elevators of less than thirty-thousand-bushel capacity.

Rate wars between competing railroads in the sixties, seventies, and eighties were no less unsettling, and small businessmen as well as farmers complained about the fluctuating and uncertain departures from established rates.[40] When asked whether the railroads had given lower rates to any of his competitors, Gideon Holmes, treasurer of the Plymouth Cordage Company, replied, "We do not know that they have, but there is a feeling of unrest when we have to run around to see whether we can get any special advantages, and sometimes succeed." Holmes added, "All that we ask for is at all times to know that none of our competitors get a lower rate of freight than we are getting. We should be better satisfied if we knew that every one of our competitors had to pay the same rate of freight; whether it is 20 cents or 50 cents, we do not care."[41] Vacillating and uncertain rates challenged a quest for certainty and calculability that marks the business mind of the era.[42]

Finally, the complaint that the charges levied by the grain elevators of Chicago were too high; that railroads and warehousemen cheated on weights and tampered with grain in store, keeping the best for themselves; and that warehouse receipts were not accurate and reliable is clearly sustained by the evidence. During the almost continuous fight for cheaper transportation in the 1860s and 1870s, it was a powerful Chicago elevator ring that seemed to contemporary merchant associations and farm groups the logical point of attack. As one historian has expressed it, "it is quite certain that the Chicago elevator industry of the 1860's and 1870's was a virtual, if not a virtuous monopoly."[43] In 1869–70 a whirlwind of discontent gathered force. Backed by farm sentiment but also by outraged grain dealers, other businessmen, and people concerned for the reputation of the city, the constitutional convention of 1870 inserted articles in the Illinois constitution not only prescribing governance of grain elevators but also directing the legislature to "pass laws to correct abuses and to prevent unjust discrimination and extortion in the rates of freight and passenger tariffs on the different railroads in this state." The following year the legislature set maximum passenger fares, stipulated that freight charges be based entirely on distance traversed, and established a board of railroad and warehouse commissioners to enforce the laws.[44]

Illinois was not alone. Three other midwestern states—Minnesota, Wisconsin, and Iowa—also enacted so-called Granger laws in the early 1870s. The railroads fought back, either by obeying them in such a way as to make them appear obnoxious to the public or by lodging lawsuits in state courts. On and on dragged the suits, in appeal after appeal.[45] Finally they were settled—for the time being—by the Supreme Court. In *Munn v. Illinois* (1876) the Court found in favor of the state regulatory laws. In the words of Chief Justice Morrison Waite, "When private property is devoted to a public use, it is subject to public regulation." More prophetic of the future was the dissenting opinion of Justice Stephen Field. Citing the Fourteenth Amendment's provision that no state can deprive any person of life, liberty, or property without due process of law, Field argued that if a state legislature were to determine the prices which the owner of property should receive for its use, this behavior would "deprive him of the property as completely as by a special Act for its confiscation or destruction." "If this be sound law," he said of the ruling in *Munn*, "if there be no protection, either in the principles upon which our republican government is founded, or in the prohibitions of the Constitution against such invasion of private rights, all property and all businesses in the State are held at the mercy of a majority of its Legislature."[46] Historically, "due process of law" had referred to procedural safeguards, to the right of the accused to be confronted in court by his accuser, for example. Field converted procedural safeguards into substantive ones, arguing that the very substance of a state law, its specification of a maximum rate chargeable for the provision of a service, deprived a company of its property without due process of law.

In *Chicago, Milwaukee and St. Paul Railway Company v. Minnesota* (1890) the Court majority adopted Field's position, declaring, furthermore, that the reasonableness of rates was a matter for the courts to decide, rather than the legislature.[47] In essence, the Court overturned *Munn.* But we need not follow the course of the law into the nooks and crannies of judicial interpretation of the Fourteenth Amendment. More arresting is the reflection that, a century before, agrarian pressures on the legal system in Massachusetts and other New England states had brought forth stay laws, moratoria on debt collection, commodity payment laws, and other provisions designed by the states to relieve the distress of farmers. Such laws had helped generate the contract clause of the Constitution which Chief Justice John Marshall soon thereafter employed to protect property rights from assault by state legislatures. A century later a Court in which Associate Justice Stephen J. Field was a most influential member was to do the same thing, this time utilizing the new doctrine of substantive due process to protect property rights in railway and grain elevator investment from laws such as those of Illinois, Iowa, Wisconsin, and Minnesota which, by prescribing maximum rates (or by authorizing commissions to do so) were so low in the eyes of the companies concerned as to deprive them of their property without due process. Thus had history come full circle. The causes of agrarian discontent were multiple in the 1780s and no less so one hundred years later. How important was each count on the agrarian indictment? Who can say?

The Supreme Court's disallowance of state efforts to regulate commerce whose origin or destination lay beyond the state's boundaries—including even that part of the transportation lying entirely within the state and despite the absence of federal action—meant that railroads would not be regulated at all unless the Congress acted.[48] In view of the acute grievances we have discussed, this was a step Congress could not avoid taking. It did so when it passed the Act to Regulate Commerce—more familiarly known as the Interstate Commerce Act—in 1887. The act prohibited discriminating between persons, commodities, or localities; pooling; and charging more for a short haul than a long haul. It also set up a five-man commission to enforce the law.

Support for the legislation was widespread among farmers and businessmen.[49] It is even possible that some railroad executives also applauded the act, preferring federal authority to the unpredictable threat of control by the various states. As Charles E. Perkins, president of the Chicago, Burlington & Quincy Railroad, remarked in 1886, "The only point with the people is that in the State courts the railroads cannot get justice, and therefore they want to put us there."[50] Did they expect the Court in this heyday of laissez faire at the federal level to pull the act's teeth, as the Court was indeed soon to do,[51] and soon to do also to the second piece of major federal regulatory legislation passed in this era, the Sherman Antitrust Act of 1890? We do not know. Railroad executives did want protection from their competitors and from large shippers demanding expensive rebates. They had been seeking protection by consolidating their lines and forming pools, especially in efforts to avoid the losses incurred in competitively cutthroat rate wars—as we shall see in the next chapter. Pools were illegal at common law, and many executives favored a law which would legalize them. But the act forbade them, and the presidents of most of the nation's railroads opposed the law, indeed worked for its defeat by exerting pressure on senators and representatives.[52]

Not till 1903, when Congress tightened the ban against rebating and personal discrimination by passing the Elkins Act, and especially not till 1906, when in the Hepburn Act it amended the original law, did it become clear that the railroads were going to be subjected to effective federal control. The Hepburn Act expressly delegated to the Interstate Commerce Commission (ICC) the power to determine and prescribe just and reasonable maximum rates and, in addition, authorized new procedures to insure prompt enforcement of the commission's orders. Still other deficiencies in the commission's authority were remedied by the Mann-Elkins Act of 1910. Finally, the Supreme Court itself contributed to the revitalization of the commission by shifting its position to one which attributed to ICC findings of a greater measure of finality than it had previously been willing to vouchsafe.[53]

Armed after 1906 with the authority essential to effective regulation, the members of the commission proceeded to react negatively to railroad requests for general increases in rates. In the light of railroad history and the unfavorable climate of public opinion which that history had engendered, it would have been difficult for them to do otherwise. Nevertheless, the fact is regrettable. Times had changed. Most of the abuses of the past, especially rebating and the various forms of discrimination—in favor of particular persons and places, and in favor of long hauls over short ones—were products of the rate wars of the 1860s, 1870s, and 1880s, products of bitter, cutthroat competition. In the 1890s railroads as well as manufacturing concerns combined their interests to lower the costs of competition.[54]

The congressional reaction was to forbid combination, to insist on the economic and other benefits of competition. While this was a valid stance with respect to manufacturing, its application to railroads, especially to the interstate lines, is questionable. Essentially, railroads were public utilities. Their construction had been subsidized in part by government money or land, and because they were public utilities, government was right in requiring them to be regulated in the public interest. The fundamental problem was that the ICC, overreacting to the historical events which had led to its creation, was unable to see clearly what the public interest was.

That interest lay in an expanded, modernized, and technologically improved system rather than the spindly legged product of competitive, overrapid nineteenth-century construction. Nearly everything required improvement and enlargement, from motive power, rolling stock, signal systems, terminals, and other essentials of railroading, including regrading and bridging, right down to the tracks themselves. The railroads were certainly making an effort to meet the huge needs of a new century. "During the enormous development of the last four years," President Edward H. Harriman of the Union Pacific Railroad wrote to President Theodore Roosevelt in 1904, "the railroads have found it very difficult to keep pace with the requirements imposed upon them, and the so-called surplus earnings, as well as additional capital, have been devoted to providing additional facilities . . . This work . . . must go on [and] during the next decade every single-track railroad in the country will have to be double-tracked, and provide enlarged terminal and other facilities."[55]

Modernization, as Harriman made plain, cost money, and since the federal government was not itself disposed to nationalize the roads and provide the necessary capital through public appropriations, the need had to be met by private investors. From 1898, at the end of a severe four-year depression, till 1907, annual investment in railroad plant kept pace with the economy's growing demands on the system. After that it faltered, turning downward almost as consistently as investors lost interest with the advent of the ICC's repressive denials of general rate increases. The profitability of railroad operations shriveled after 1911, and by the outbreak of World War I in 1914 the system was showing "unmistakable signs of distress owing to capital undernourishment." In another two years it nearly collapsed under the weight of wartime demands, and was at last taken over by the government. Entrepreneurial and managerial ability followed the flight of capital to more attractive growing sectors of the economy.

For the railroads the story is a sad one. For the public too. And not least for the farmers, producers, and shippers whose very real grievances had so much to do with the writing of the story in the first place. The grievances of factory workers were real too, as we shall see, but they were not unalloyed with material benefits and opportunities opened up by the more rapid industrialization of the economy.

11

The Maturing of American Industry

B etween the Civil War and World War I the United States emerged as
the leading industrial nation in the world. As industry advanced, agriculture retreated—shifts in relative position traced everywhere by economies
undergoing processes of modernization. Calculations of the value added by
the two sectors show manufacturing rising from 43 percent to 65 percent
between 1870 and 1900 and agriculture falling from 57 percent to 35 percent.
Changing shares in commodity output measure the same phenomenon, that
of manufacture increasing from 33 percent to 53 percent and that of agriculture declining in exactly reverse proportions, from 53 percent to 33 percent.
Finally, between 1870 and 1910 workers in agriculture fell from 52.5 percent
to 31.4 percent of the labor force—from more than one-half to less than a
third—whereas those in manufacturing rose from 19.1 percent to 22.2 percent.[1]

The process of industrialization did not await the ending of the Civil War
before beginning to unfold. The Industrial Revolution was not an economic
coup d'état. As we have seen, the American economy had begun to embark
on the path of industrialization as early as the 1820s, if not before. That early
decade had witnessed a rapid rise in the manufacturing share of commodity
output and the virtual completion of the transfer from the use of homemade
goods to those made in shops and factories. The number of immigrants tripled
in the 1820s, and that many of them settled in the cities to work in growing
industries is suggested by the fact that the rate of increase of the urban population doubled that of the population as a whole. Indeed, most leading manufactures grew at decade rates far exceeding the 35 percent increase in
population. Recent research, however, discloses a surprising amount of industrial activity in rural towns and villages.[2]

The advance continued in the remaining years before the Civil War. Although manufacturing accelerated throughout the Northeast during the 1830s,
the sector's output increased by an astonishing 152 percent in the following
decade. Growth took place at the more modest rate of 76 percent in the 1850s,
a decade in which railroad mileage, however, more than tripled. The process

of industrialization imposed increasingly heavy demands on saving and investment, and the rising capital requirements are reflected in the growing numbers of corporate charters issued by the states. Three "long swings" of incorporation are implicit in the data, the first from 1800 to 1821, the other two from 1821 to 1843 and from 1843 to 1861. They bespeak the rising needs not only of the transport sector but also of manufacturing and financial institutions. From the 1840s on, machines made of iron tended to replace those made of wood, and in all probability the scale of output in some industries also rose, particularly in transport and paper, as well as in cotton and woolen textiles. The acceleration of output described a slow upward path throughout rather than bunching in a posture of "take-off" at some particular time. The Civil War interrupted the march of industry, but during the years that followed, the pace quickened as industrialization leaped over its local and regional boundaries and began pouring its products into markets whose dimensions were becoming national in their continental scope.[3]

As it did so, however, industrialists soon encountered obstacles to national flows in the form of state laws enacted in the interests of local tradesmen and manufacturers. Laws designed to protect local markets from outside competition were familiar American—and European—devices, and indeed had been one of the principal reasons for the calling of the Constitutional Convention of 1787 and for the inclusion of a clause in the Constitution empowering the Congress to regulate interstate and foreign trade. In that earlier era the spokesmen for national interests had been public men—politicians—but in the 1870s they were private business firms, as the story of the leadership role of the I. M. Singer Company makes clear.

In 1873 the Singer Company, already foremost among manufacturers of sewing machines, faced a substantial problem. Its new factory at Elizabethsport, New Jersey—by far the largest in the world—was nearing completion, but the firm was still dependent on commission agents to sell the great bulk of its machines. Merchants who sold on commission had no special incentive to push the sales of any one manufacturer's product; worse, they did not know how to demonstrate the machines, lacked both the knowledge and the facilities necessary for their maintenance and repair, and were unable to provide potential buyers with consumer credit. Since sewing machines were relatively new, complex, and expensive products, the Singer Company had decided even before the Civil War to open its own branch stores, each with a female demonstrator, a mechanic, a salesman, and a manager. But these outlets entailed high overhead costs, and as late as 1872 the firm had fewer than a hundred of them. Still, there was little point in enlarging the volume of production unless sales could also be increased. The next year the firm's central office therefore committed itself to a policy of expanding its own outlets over the entire domestic market. By 1879 its distribution network consisted of 530 retail stores, and it had severed its relations with all independent merchants.

What finally enabled the firm to break free was the successful outcome of its determined challenge to inhibiting state laws. The leading case in what Charles W. McCurdy has well called a crucial doctrinal transformation came up in Missouri in 1875. Missouri had passed a discriminatory revenue measure thirty years before which defined peddlers as persons selling commodities "not the growth, produce, or manufacture of th[is] state" and required them to pay a license fee for the privilege of engaging in local business. An agent of the Singer Company, M. M. Welton, had been convicted under the statute, and the law had been sustained by the state's highest court. Singer's counsel thereupon appealed the case to the Supreme Court, and in an extraordinarily important decision handed down in *Welton v. Missouri* in 1876, Justice Stephen Field held the state law in violation of the commerce clause of the Constitution, the protective power of which "continues until the commodity has ceased to be the subject of discriminating legislation by reason of its foreign [or out-of-state] character."[4] Justice Field's ruling that "inter-state commerce shall be free and untrammelled," together with subsequent Supreme Court decisions in *Webber v. Virginia* (1880) and *Minnesota v. Barber* (1890), was "of immediate importance to large-scale manufacturers and had an enduring influence on American economic growth." Had state legislation succeeded in balkanizing the American continent, had it prevented the emergence of the great American common market of the nineteenth century, the scale on which goods were produced, distributed, and consumed would have been abridged by higher unit costs and prices. Thus economies of scale and lowered transaction costs depended on the constitutional allocation of power over interstate and foreign commerce to the Congress, on the willingness of the Supreme Court to defend that allocation in the interests of free trade, and on the emergence of firms with sufficient financial resources and interests to press for improvement in the efficiency of the legal system, that is to say, for the adoption of legal rules minimizing transaction costs. While most legal change reflects the interests of one or more powerful constituencies, can there be any doubt that in this case there was close correspondence between those interests and the needs of the nation?

Those needs were being generated by continuing population and urban growth and by businessmen's confidence that they could convert this growth into effective consumer demand by increasing the productivity of labor, thereby raising the rate of growth of output to levels higher than that at which population was increasing. They succeeded in doing so. Unlike the case of India or China, where mounting population in these years brought greater starvation, disease, and death, population growth in the United States was accompanied by even larger gains in incomes.

Per capita incomes had increased at an average rate of 1.45 percent per year between 1840 and 1860, but from 1870 to 1910 the rate rose to 2.1 percent. More broadly, "between the first and second halves of the century the long-term per capita output growth rate accelerated, increasing by roughly 0.5 percentage points to the 1.7–1.9 percent level per annum which has been maintained in the United States economy throughout the last hundred years."[5] Between 1870 and the outbreak of World War I net national product (which is exactly equivalent to national income) rose fivefold, and real per capita income nearly tripled. It is during this period, therefore, that we may speak for the first time of the mass demand of a mass market, a national urban market being knit together by the railroads, protected as a free trade area by constitutional law, and sustained by rising per capita incomes. Thus the later postbellum years witnessed a quantum leap in the scale of demand for goods and services. Had the supply response to this demand faltered, rising levels of material well-being would have been checked. Mass demand therefore called for mass production and distribution. The American economy responded.[6]

Mass production held out the promise of economies of scale, of reduced unit costs over a wide range of output, and mass distribution promised a reduction in unit transaction costs. To achieve production and distribution in high volume, however, required substantially enlarged investment in plant and equipment, in producers' durables, and in branch offices and other facilities. In sum, what was needed was massive capital deepening. But not of physical capital alone. Knowledge and experience were also required. Economists refer to the acquisition of knowledge and experience as human capital formation. But we may usefully distinguish the kind of knowledge and experience that result in technical improvement in machinery and equipment, together with skill in their use by the labor force, from the kind that enables the business firm to improve its control over the uses of the factors of production. The latter include not only spatial realignment of productive processes and time-and-motion studies of those processes, but also organizational and administrative changes, as well as developments in accounting which improve the flows of information on which business decisions are based. Innovations of these kinds are comparable to the embedding of knowledge in management and deserve recognition as business capital formation. We cannot assume, however, that firms of all sizes and degrees of entrepreneurial perceptivity will at all times be equally motivated to invest in business capital. We shall see that Big Business had other priorities for a generation after its rise at the turn of the century.[7]

What made possible the required deepening of physical capital was a marked rise in the rate at which Americans were saving—diverting current income from expenditure on consumer goods, or, expressed in "real" terms, diverting current net national product from consumption to capital formation. Even before the Civil War, it is true, Americans had devoted a substantial portion of their output to capital formation. In the first four decades of the nineteenth century that portion amounted to "perhaps 6 or 7 percent," and in the final two antebellum decades to "between 10 and 12 percent." In contrast, between the Civil War and World War I the savings rate rose to between 18 and 20 percent of output.[8]

Historians differ on when the upturn began. One scholar stresses the unprecedented increase between the 1850s and 1870s, estimating the savings proportion of total output to have amounted to 7 percentage points during the decade of the Civil War. To another, the 1850s and the postwar decades are of particular importance, at least insofar as savings by the corporate sector are concerned. The 1850s saw the culmination of a third antebellum surge in numbers of charters issued by the states, and from the late 1870s till the mid-1880s incorporation took place at an extremely rapid rate. By the end of the century two-thirds of the nation's industrial output was the product of incorporated enterprise. Corporations tended to save larger proportions of their income than unincorporated businesses. Individual funds were the major source of savings, however—changes in the government sector not appearing to contribute significantly to the increase in the savings rate—and the rise in the median age of the population, a reflection of the increasing proportion of males in the age group forty to eighty, was the likely source of an increase in the ratio between savings and income.[9]

In all probability, the transfer of funds from the East to the West, from a region of relative capital surplus and inelastic investment demand to one in which the opposite of these conditions obtained, was also an important factor in shifting the saving rate upward in the postbellum period. Nor can we overlook the contribution to income inequality made during and after the Civil War by the debt management policies previously discussed; nor the simple fact that with more people and workers there was every inducement to accumulate more capital to supply workers with tools, households with residences, businesses with buildings, and society as a whole with more hospitals, inventories, improved transport and communication facilities, and other "infrastructure."

There was indeed every inducement to accumulate capital, yet had it not been for the development of financial institutions whose function it was to mediate between saving and investment, capital accumulation would have been much more modest. It is true that surpluses of capital existed in the maturer economies of western Europe, where returns were less attractive than in areas of capital deficit such as the developing American economy. In consequence, net capital flows into the United States, set in motion primarily by English investors, amounted to $1.5 billion between 1870 and 1895. Most of the investment went into municipal and other local bonds and into railroads and public utilities, although a few manufacturing firms were among the beneficiaries. Domestic savings substantially outstripped foreign investment. Even when we select the low rate of 25 percent to represent the portion of gross national product saved, total savings by governments, businesses, and households during these decades (1869–1895) amount to $4.6 billion (current prices). It is just for this reason that domestic financial institutions are so important. Indeed, one authority attributes to their development most of the substantial increase in the savings/income ratio that took place in the decades 1830–1880.[10] If we add to this scenario the fact that interest rates during these years were declining substantially, it becomes even more clear that financial considerations posed no obstacle to rapid development. Long-term capital needs were supplied in part by financial intermediaries such as mutual savings banks, building and loan associations, life insurance companies, and mortgage companies, all of which grew rapidly and played significant roles in the mobilization and transfer of long-term capital from surplus to deficit areas. In part, too, they were supplied by the rapid growth of an open market for funds in the late nineteenth century, especially the New York stock and bond markets, and by the rise of investment banking. In contrast to the variety of institutions instrumental in developing the long-term capital market, the market in short-term capital (that is, loans and investments running less than a year) was primarily the province of the commercial banking system. The performance of the banking system in these years has received severe criticism from both contemporaries and scholars, but a recent thorough analysis shows the opposite to be deserved.[11]

Critics fastened on the legal and theoretical constraints under which banks operated instead of examining closely the actual workings of the financial system. Regnant banking theory continued to hold to the "real bills" doctrine, calling for self-liquidating short-term loans stemming from actual business transactions. If banks restricted their loans and discounts to real business paper originating in the need to finance the production, storage, or shipment of goods, they would in effect be bridging the gap between shipment and receipt, seedtime and harvest, purchase of raw materials and sale of finished products. All were short-term transactions which, when completed, would yield the revenues out of which the loans could be repaid. Loans would therefore be confined to the "real needs" of business, bank liabilities would automatically be limited, banks liquid, and the currency elastic. Long-term loans to finance the purchase of capital by business firms were clearly not self-liquidating and were to be avoided. The theory was logically consistent and dominated banking in the nineteenth century. But substantial numbers of banks did not trim the sails of their loans. To a considerable extent commercial loans were made to meet needs for working capital rather than to finance self-liquidating operations. Well-informed bankers estimated that at least 40 or 50 percent of unsecured loans in large cities were renewed at maturity. And in the early twentieth century a leading scholar estimated that at least 20 percent of noncollateral loans were used for financing fixed capital.[12] The practice of rolling over short-term loans to finance long-term investments was characteristic of continental European banking in the nineteenth century. It was also followed in the United States to an extent that is not negligible.

Legal constraints on banking also provide unreliable guides to banking practice. Under the national banking system established by Congress in 1863, national banks were forbidden to make real estate loans (until 1913; some, however, did so illegally). They were subjected besides to minimum capital requirements, the amounts of which varied with the size of the population in the towns and cities in which they functioned. Banks chartered by the federal government under the act were only required to have a minimum capital of $50,000 if they did business in towns with fewer than 6,000 inhabitants; but those operating in cities under 50,000 needed $100,000, while those in cities of 50,000 or more people had to have $200,000. Strict rules required that capital subscriptions be fully paid in, and that reserves in lawful money (specie, United States notes, gold and silver certificates, and clearing house certificates) be maintained against both banknote and deposit liabilities.[13] Big-city banks, classified as "central reserve city" banks, had to keep all of their required reserves of 25 percent in their own vaults. (At first only New York City was so classified, but in 1887 Chicago and St. Louis were added.) "Reserve city" banks were allowed to keep half of their required reserves of 25 percent in national banks located in central reserve cities, whereas "country" banks might keep three-fifths of their lesser requirement of 15 percent in national banks in reserve cities. These concessions regarding the location of reserves implicitly acknowledged the need of all banks for correspondent relationships with banks in other regions to facilitate nonlocal business and payments. Banks chartered under state laws (that is, state banks) also maintained correspondent relationships.

The growth of the new national banking system, slow at first, speeded up after Congress voted in 1865 to impose a prohibitive tax of 10 percent on the banknote issues of state banks. By the end of 1866 more than sixteen hundred banks were functioning under the system, and by the late 1860s the system covered about three-fourths of the nation's banking resources. However, this situation was not destined to endure. As early as 1871 the deposits of state banks roughly equaled national bank resources, and from then till the present the two classes of banks have remained roughly equal in the size of their deposits. Indeed, national banks have more frequently had the smaller total.

The growth in the *number* of state banks was of even greater significance for the emergence of a national market in short-term capital. After the early 1890s state banks both outnumbered and grew more rapidly than national banks, the latter declining from 32.1 percent of total commercial banks (11,474) in 1896 to 29.1 percent of the total (24,514) in 1910. What spurred this growth, in large part, was the freedom which state banks enjoyed from the restrictions under which national banks were compelled to operate. For a decade or so after the Civil War the expansion of state banks was retarded by their loss of the power of note issue, but this did not prove a handicap for long. The composition of the money stock changed dramatically in the postbellum era, with deposits increasing rapidly in relation to currency, especially in the South and West. Already by the mid-1860s deposits made up nearly 60 percent of the money stock, and by 1914 the proportion had grown to over 88 percent. Encouraged by the ability to charter banks under general incorporation laws, by state laws lowering the minimum capital requirements of rural banks to about $10,000-$15,000 between 1895 and 1909, and by the freedom to make loans on real estate, state banks proliferated between 1879 and 1909, especially in the South, Midwest, and western and Pacific states.

In consequence, interregional differences in interest rates on short-term capital narrowed substantially. Average Middle Atlantic country bank rates were very close to those in New England, and the North Central states narrowed the gap with New England significantly in the late 1890s. Rates in the latter two regions were virtually equal by 1900. Although differentials were larger farther west, the decreases were dramatic. The differential decreased from over 5 percent to less than 4 percent in the Great Plains and Rocky Mountain states, a fall of nearly 40 percent. The fall in the mountain and Pacific states amounted to around 25 percent; the southern states registered a more modest decline of 15 percent. In part this narrowing of interregional rates was due to decreases in the riskiness of southern and western loans and probably also, although to a lesser extent, to declining transaction and information costs. In the main, however, the explanation for this gradual evolution of a national market in short-term capital is simply that the increased number of state banks eroded the power of local monopolies to charge what segmented local and regional markets would bear.

In the absence of other institutional developments, however, the capital funds which permitted this wide efflorescence of state banking would not have been available. Competitive business in areas which had been settled earlier and had developed numerous and diversified economic enterprises tended to lower interest rates in those areas and send capitalists in search of more profitable outlets on developing frontiers where funds were more scarce, rates of return more attractive, and investment opportunities more elastic. The correspondent banking system and a national market for commercial paper that was expanding rapidly in the late nineteenth century served as the principal instrumentalities for the interregional transfer of funds. Although the law permitted national banks to keep stipulated proportions of their required reserves in central reserve and reserve city banks it was interest—in the sense of interest paid on deposits—that helped induce them to do so.

Critics of the national banking system pointed out that this pyramiding of reserves, whose apex rose in New York City, where national banks made the most of their opportunities by lending out the funds on the call loan market, tended to increase the severity of many financial panics, especially those of 1873, 1884, 1890, and 1907. Farmers would require loans in the fall to finance crop moving activities, country banks would draw back their balances from the New York banks, and the latter would call in loans which had financed purchases on the stock market. Stock values would fall, New York banks would suspend payments, and banks in the interior would follow suit. All would come tumbling down like dominoes, and panic would be upon the land. The system *did* exacerbate financial panics, but the underlying source of weakness was the inelasticity of reserves and the absence of a lender of last resort, a central bank which could come to the aid of other banks in a state of liquidity crisis. After 1914 the Federal Reserve System would provide an institutional framework for the needed sustenance. Unfortunately its decisions were not always wisely taken, as we shall see.

Meanwhile, it was not only national banks which sent idle balances to New York and other cities; private banks, trust companies, and state banks did likewise, and this was particularly true of country banks, which have traditionally been depicted by critics as operating as units in isolation from other institutions. In fact, the correspondent banking system enabled them to enjoy large numbers of connections, especially in New York, but by no means there alone. There was a constant flow of goods and funds between New York and the interior, and most interior bankers found it convenient to keep funds on deposit in that great American city of the nineteenth century. By 1900 deposits from interior banks amounted to a third of the total assets of New York national banks. Interior bankers also maintained accounts with Boston and other cities in order to provide customers with domestic exchange, facilitate out-of-town collections, secure answers to credit inquiries, and obtain other services, the most important of which were loans, either on the borrowing bank's own note or through the rediscounting of paper of the borrowing bank's customers. Reserve city banks as well as country banks availed themselves of these services, and intraregional city banks, notably in the South and Great Plains, also provided loans and other services to country banks in their regions; but the leading role was played by the New York banks, and the principal beneficiaries were the country banks, especially those in the South, which had significantly fewer banks per capita than any other region. Between 1897 and 1914 almost half of the total borrowing by banks was made by southern banks.

In sum, the correspondent banking system provided an effective channel for the transfer of short-term funds from West to East via deposits of required reserves or idle balances, and for a return flow from East to West and South, and from city banks to country banks, via interbank borrowing. The commercial paper market offered another important channel for the interregional flow of funds. Unlike the interbank borrowing market, which functioned within the correspondent banking system, the commercial paper market was an open, impersonal market which expanded rapidly in the late nineteenth and early twentieth centuries, both in volume and in geographic extent. Business firms chose not to offer their paper or notes to local banks for discounting in part because the National Banking Act limited loans to a single borrower to one-tenth of the capital and surplus of the bank. With the growth of large-scale industry after the Civil War, increasing numbers of firms may have experienced difficulty in obtaining adequate financing from local banks, with the result that they had to look elsewhere.[14]

But businessmen also wished to escape the monopoly power and high interest charges of local banks, and this is probably a more important reason why they turned to the open market. A large number of firms in the South and West did so, offering their paper to commercial banks in other localities and regions, which looked upon such investments not only as attractive earning assets but also as secondary reserves, six months being by far the most common duration of the paper. In all probability the commercial paper market was national in scope; a list of offerings of a Boston house as early as 1873, for example, included paper from firms in Cincinnati, Oshkosh, Memphis, St. Louis, and Louisville as well as the East Coast. The house in question was a commercial paper house, which, unlike the note and bill brokers of the antebellum period, purchased paper and then resold it. Commercial paper houses expanded considerably both in numbers and in their area of operations in the postbellum period, but commercial banks were by far the leading purchasers of commercial paper. Both were mechanisms permitting the commercial paper market to continue its inexorable westward march, which, by the turn of the century, reached the Pacific Coast. The spread of the commercial paper market may well have joined hands with the multiplication of state banks to erode local monopoly and promote the lowering of local interest rates for short-term capital.[15]

Obviously, New York banks did not dominate the commercial paper market as they did the flows of the correspondent banking system. But they did play a role in the development of the market for long-term capital. In essence, their call loans converted short-term into long-term capital. Such loans financed equity purchases, which in turn financed capital expenditures by firms in the rapidly industrializing Midwest as well as elsewhere. Indeed, any firm anywhere could have issued or sold securities purchased on the basis of call loans.[16] As late as the 1880s, however, an investor interested in purchasing industrial issues would have been more likely to turn to Boston than to the New York market, and even in Boston the market was very thin. Securities markets throughout much of the nineteenth century had aided the interregional mobilization of funds for the public sector and for the growing transportation industries, but they had made little direct contribution to western or southern manufacturing. In 1885, however, the New York Stock Exchange organized a department of unlisted securities, and this enabled a number of distant manufacturing companies to reach the "big board." Even then it was their preferred stock rather than their common stock that was offered for sale. Not till a decade later did the endorsement of J. P. Morgan, the enormously prestigious investment banker, make it possible to raise large sums through the sale of common stock. Only Morgan's firm (and perhaps Kuhn, Loeb) could have marketed successfully a main industrial issue in 1900. By the 1920s, however, several others were able to do so.[17]

While New York functioned as a financial intermediary, returning short-term deposits to the West via loans and purchases of commercial paper and converting other short-term funds into long-term investments, a broader regional view reveals that the New England states as well as those of the Middle Atlantic were strong exporters of long-term capital in the period 1890–1910. Furthermore, the larger part of the funds exported originated in eastern savings rather than in western short-term flows. The Midwest was a fairly substantial capital importer throughout, but the South, already a significant importer between 1890 and 1900, became a very strong one after 1900, net imports during that decade almost doubling. The Great Plains and mountain states were strong importers until 1900, and after the turn of the century the Pacific states themselves became exporters of capital. A sense of the relative magnitudes involved is provided by estimates, in current dollars, of net interregional long-term capital flows over the period 1897–1913. In round figures, the East was a net exporter of $12.8 billion, and other regions net importers of the following sums: South, $4.75 billion; Midwest, $7.6 billion; and West, $490 million.[18]

The export role of the Northeast and the importance of savings in that region to interregional long-term capital flow suggest a broader institutional participation in capital mobilization and transfer than we have thus far noted. Of contributing institutions, we may single out for brief discussion insurance companies and mortgage companies. In the period after the Civil War life insurance companies emerged as the most important nonbank intermediary for the mobilization and interregional transfer of capital. Indeed, their assets increased more than twentyfold between 1869 and 1914. Rapid growth came with the innovation of tontine and industrial contracts after 1870. In the final quarter of the century their resources quadrupled, rising from $403 million to $1.7 billion; by 1900 eighty-four companies had more than $7.5 billion of life insurance in force. Collecting premiums from savers in many parts of the country, these companies proceeded to invest their funds in enterprises whose nature and geographic scope widened with the development of professional management and the easing of restrictive legal regulations. In the late 1860s only four states permitted insurance companies to invest in corporate securities, and most states imposed restrictions of one kind or another in the interest of safety. Many of these laws were altered in the last third of the century to allow investment in out-of-state mortgages and corporate securities. A parallel development of brokerage agencies to handle distant investments enabled the companies to become important forces in the interregional mobilization of capital.

They also contributed to transport development and intraregional industrialization. In the early 1880s leading firms began to invest heavily in railroad bonds, and by 1904 these issues accounted for one-third of their total assets. The case of the Massachusetts Hospital Life Insurance Company illustrates how insurance companies aided regional industrialization. Before 1830 this company had concentrated its investments in farm mortgages in western Massachusetts. In the 1830s securities and business loans became more important in its portfolio, and the locus shifted to the neighborhood of Boston and to the textile industry. In the 1840s the company played a singularly important role in the textile capital market as a source of long-term loans. By 1890 more than half of its loans went to textile companies in Massachusetts, New Hampshire, and Maine—companies whose combined capital represented more than one-fourth of the textile capital of those states.[19]

Mortgage companies played a very significant role in the interregional mobilization of capital for a short two-decade period in the 1870s and 1880s. At first the companies merely acted as middlemen, making mortgage loans in the West and selling the mortgages in the East. With the increase of competition, however, they began guaranteeing the mortgages they sold, then took the step in the mid-1880s of issuing general debenture bonds against portfolios of mortgages. At least 167 mortgage companies were in operation about 1890. The activities of the J. B. Watkins Land Mortgage Company of Lawrence, Kansas, illustrates how they did business. Organized in 1870, the company began as a middleman and then shifted first into guaranteed mortgages and then into debentures. To sell his mortgages and bonds quickly, Watkins set up a branch office in New York City and employed sales agents in Buffalo, Albion, Batavia, Rochester, Syracuse, Rome, and Johnstown, New York; in Wilmington, Delaware; in Boston; in Warner, New Hampshire; and in Ferrisburg, Vermont. In 1878 he opened a second branch in London in his search for still more investors. An analysis of Watkins' customers provides considerable evidence about the sources of eastern capital that flowed into western farmlands. Less than 1 percent of them were institutional investors; men and women were about equal in number; and of the men, about 15 percent were ministers, teachers, and doctors. Over a quarter of his customers were English, with most of the rest living in New England and the Middle Atlantic states.[20]

In sum, a number of institutions emerged or developed as instrumentalities of capital mobilization. Some of them—for example, the correspondent banking system and the commercial paper market—are significant for their roles in the interregional mobilization of short-term capital. Others—for example, insurance companies and mortgage companies—mobilized long-term capital. Some of the capital came from abroad, but much the larger part of the total originated in American savings. Still other institutions assisted in the process of mobilizing savings within a particular region, for example, mutual savings banks, which by 1900 had more than 6 million depositors and total deposits just short of $2.5 billion, almost wholly within the Northeast. Although savings banks commonly made mortgage loans, sometimes invested in railroads and canals, and even made direct loans to transportation companies and industrialists, their far closer association with commercial banks makes their role in capital formation somewhat indistinct. Many redeposited their own deposits in commercial banks and invested in their stock, their trustees often forming interlocking directorates with the officials of commercial banks. In New England, many were virtually savings departments of the commercial banks. Still, it is important to bear in mind that commercial banks themselves sometimes ignored their assigned roles as followers of the real bills doctrine and rolled over their short-term loans. What proportion of the nearly $7 billion in deposits created by some twelve thousand commercial banks in 1900 represented financing of agriculture, transportation, and industrial development seems impossible to know. But of this we can be sure: institutional innovation and development enabled American capital markets to respond to the huge demands engendered by the massive growth and structural change of the postbellum economy. Whether that response was an altogether efficient one, whether, that is to say, the long-term capital market was enabled by institutional developments facilitating interregional transfers to become a true national market in the sense of significant convergence of interregional differentials in interest rates, is a question that must await further research. But surely interest rates everywhere were lower than they would have been in the absence of these institutional aids to saving.[21]

The remarkable rise in the savings rate shifted the relative prices of the factors of production, with the price of capital declining relative to that of labor and land. This shift reinforced the intrinsic bias of late-nineteenth-century technological change toward capital and created incentives for adopting labor-saving techniques. It also facilitated a heavier use of landed resources, such as iron ore and coal, which capital-intensive methods of production often required. Evidence of growing capital intensity in the manufacturing industry is provided in Table 29, which shows capital investment per plant in more than a dozen manufacturing industries between 1870 and 1900. Investments rose nearly fivefold in iron and steel, more than sixfold in electrical machinery, and twelvefold in the production of agricultural implements. The figures in the table are expressed in current rather than constant dollars, but in view of the secular decline in prices during most of these years, the expenditures represent real increases in capital. Together with investments in railroads and the growing requirements of cities for transit lines, road systems, water and sewerage systems, lighting systems, and bridges and buildings, they are indicative of the massive capital deepening that was taking place. The average worker was being provided with additional capital to work with, and this enabled him to increase his output per manhour.

The rising stock of capital per worker was the main source of the produc-

Table 29.   Capital investment per plant in the United States, 1870–1900
(thousands of dollars).

Product	1870	1880	1890	1900	Percent of inventory
Iron and steel	150	265	576	882	4.88
Coke		38	80	151	2.97
Shipbuilding	12	10	27	70	4.83
Electrical machinery		20	101	144	6.20
Petroleum refining		318	824	1,423	3.47
Clay products	7	5	17	23	2.28
Glass	70	111	139	173	1.47
Lumber and timber products	6	7	18	17	1.83
Paper and wood pulp	52	65	138	220	3.23
Agricultural implements	17	32	160	221	12.00
Tobacco	5	5	8	7	0.40
Slaughtering and meat packing	32	57	105	214	5.69
Boots and shoes		22	46	62	1.80
Cotton goods	147	276	391	474	2.22
Wool manufactories	38	62	145	219	4.76

Source: Charles R. Van Hise, *Concentration and Control, A Solution of the Trust Problem in the United States* (New York: Arno Press, 1973), pp. 37–54 (orig. pub. 1912). Figures originally from the Census of Manufactures, 1905. Used with permission.

tivity gains generating higher per capita incomes. But it was not the only source. The quality of the labor force also went up. Workers were healthier, fitter, longer-lived, and hence better able to adapt to the changing industrial order. The improvement in health came largely from a decline in the incidence of infectious disease. For one thing, rising incomes made for better diets and housing. For another, new public health measures adopted by the cities resulted in the installation of sanitary sewers and the provision of central supplies of pure drinking water. These measures responded to a sanitation movement which, well under way in Europe in the 1870s, began in the United States around 1880. The discovery in the 1880s that several diseases were water-borne appears to have stimulated interest both in filtering water and in providing initially pure supplies. In 1875 fewer than 30,000 city dwellers had filtered water, but by 1910 over 10 million enjoyed it. In 1880 most American cities appear to have lacked sanitary sewers, but by 1907 nearly all urban dwellers were served by them. In consequence, life expectancy at birth for males rose dramatically, from thirty-seven in Boston in 1880 to forty-six in 1910, and from twenty-nine in New York City in 1880 to forty-five in 1910. Obvious economic consequences include not only longer work lives but also less absence for reasons of health.[22]

The labor force was also increasingly better educated. One measure of this is provided by recent estimates of expenditures for formal education, displayed in Table 30, which shows large increases in both total expenditures and in their public components in the second half of the nineteenth century. The latter reflects widening support by local communities of common schools and the rise of public secondary and higher education. In 1850 the country boasted a hundred high schools at most, with academies many times more numerous satisfying the appetites of those who wished and could afford further education. By 1900 there were more public than private high school students.[23] Nevertheless, many, many families, almost universally those living in rural areas, continued to depend on the labor of children, and over the period 1870–1900 children aged ten to fifteen represented 6 percent of the total labor force. As late as 1900 almost a fifth of the youths in that age group worked instead of attending school. As the commissioner of education commented in 1910, "It is noticeable that a much larger proportion of children from well-to-do

Table 30.   United States expenditures for formal education,[a] 1840–1900 (millions of current dollars).

Fiscal year	Public expenditure[b]	Total expenditure[c]	Ratio of public to total
1840	n.a.	9.2	—
1850	7.6	16.2	0.47
1860	19.9	34.7	0.57
1870	61.7	95.4	0.65
1880	81.5	106.4	0.77
1890	147.4	187.3	0.79
1900	229.6	289.6	0.79

Source: For 1840: income per pupil in 1850 multiplied by number of pupils in 1840. For 1850–1870: *U.S. Census of Schools,* relevant issues. For 1880–1900: *U.S. Commissioner of Education, Reports.* Private elementary expenditure and private secondary expenditure per pupil were estimated respectively at 1.3 and 4.0 times public elementary expenditure per pupil. Normal school expenditures per pupil were taken at 7 times the public elementary level; university, college, and professional schools at 15; and private commercial schools at 2.5. Private elementary attendance also had to be estimated for 1880. Information available for the given years affirms the validity of such weights, which have their basis in the 1911 *Report of the U.S. Commissioner of Education,* II, xxxvii. The table is from Albert Fishlow, "Levels of Nineteenth-Century American Investment in Education," *Journal of Economic History,* 26 (1966), 420. Used with permission.

a. Includes public and private elementary, secondary, and higher educational institutions as well as commercial schools, special schools for the blind, and so forth. Does not include reform schools, orphanages, and similar institutions.

b. For 1850–1870, defined as all public sources of funds, including receipts from permanent school funds for common schools; for 1880–1900, includes all public school expenditures.

c. Total for years 1840–1870 is income; therefore, expenditures.

families than those of more moderate circumstances or from the families of the poor are found in our high schools."[24] But a similar unbalance is unlikely to have characterized enrollments in public elementary schools. In part, rising incomes and the concomitant lesser need to have children work reversed the downward trend in enrollment rates. But this development was largely due to the enactment of compulsory education and child-labor legislation by the states.[25]

The two went hand in hand, and public elementary school enrollment rose from about 12.5 million in 1900 to about 16 million in 1910, with the average number of days per pupil per semester climbing in that decade from 86.3 to 113. Yet it was not enough to get the child out of the factory and into the school. Ways must be found to keep him there, for the expansion in school population was offset by a high dropout rate. Contemporaries estimated that only 40 to 50 percent of the children finished the eight grades of elementary school, and that only 8 to 10 percent finished high school. Between the ages of thirteen and fifteen more than half dropped out of school, most of them in the sixth and seventh grades. Public school reformers were surprisingly unanimous that the blame lay not with poverty, with unsympathetic or incompetent teachers, or with ineffective compulsory education laws. The problem was that the curriculum was not meeting the interests or needs of children. What the children needed, progressive reformers agreed, was vocational education.[26]

A demand for manual training in the elementary grades had launched an industrial education movement in the late 1870s. Then in the 1880s and 1890s a few vocational or manual training high schools had been established. Many public high schools had begun to add vocational courses to their programs, and elementary schools had begun a gradual expansion of their offerings in manual training. The nineties, in contrast, "brought a nationwide torrent of criticism, innovation, and reform that soon took on all the earmarks of a social movement."[27] Urban settlement workers, rural publicists, businessmen's associations, labor unions, and avant-garde pedagogues pushed the movement for vocational training, and in less than two generations the character of the American school was transformed.[28]

A movement so broad was bound to reflect diverse motivations and goals. Some, like Calvin M. Woodward of Washington University (St. Louis), criticized the public schools for adhering to outmoded ideals of gentlemanliness and culture. Woodward contended that those schools "trained a handful of children for the 'so-called learned professions' but cared little for the 'productive, toiling classes.' " The Manual Training School established by Woodward at Washington University in 1879 was the first of its kind in the United States. Its object was to provide a secondary program equally divided between mental and manual labor. "Mathematics, drawing, science, languages, history and literature were to be combined with instruction in carpentry, wood turning, pattern making, iron chipping and filing, forge work, brazing and soldering, and bench and machine work in metals." The goal was liberal rather than vocational.[29]

By the nineties American school reformers had begun to notice an element in the public schools which would surely come to dominate that population. The children of "the masses," they were convinced, were destined to follow manual pursuits. John Dewey explained why this was so, proclaiming in 1899 that "in the great majority of human beings the distinctively intellectual interest is not dominant. They have the so-called practical impulse and disposition." In his extremely influential *Laggards in Our Schools,* Leonard Ayres concluded in 1908 that the courses of study in city school systems "are adjusted to the power of the brighter pupils. They are beyond the powers of the average pupils, and far beyond those of the slower ones." Yet the concerns of the school reformers were not the only force behind curricular change. Those concerns coincided with the needs and interests of American industrial society in vocational education.[30]

With the emergence of the United States as the world's foremost industrial nation in the last years of the nineteenth century, powerfully rivaling England and Germany in world trade, Europeans began to speak of the "American peril" or "American menace" in describing the new giant. Advocates of vocational education were among many Americans taking pride in such epithets. The "rewards offered in this world trade are beyond comprehension," observed the Commission on National Aid to Vocational Education in 1915. If rivalry in trade was destined to be the warfare of the future, Americans could carry off the victor's share of the spoils by recruiting and training a new-style army, an industrial army. The new industrial order needed " 'recruits for our leading mechanical industries,' the services of an army of semiskilled workers who would 'adjust nicely [to] the industrial machine.' "

> What the schools had to provide, therefore, was an education with a vocational bias—one which would predispose the children to enter the factories and manual trades, impress them with the "dignity of labor," and equip them with "industrial intelligence"; some facility with handling tools and machines, basic literacy to enable them to read and understand directions, and discipline enough to enable them to conform to the requirements of large-scale rationalized factory routine. The privates, the rank and file, would have to be recruited and drilled in the public schools.[31]

Twenty-nine states had made provisions for some form of industrial education by 1910. Of these, 10 had provided for technical high schools, 18 for manual training, 11 for domestic science, 19 for agricultural training, and 11 for industrial and trade courses. With the passage of the Smith-Hughes Act of 1917 federal aid was extended to schools offering vocational training to persons over fourteen years of age who had acquired the foundation of a general education in the elementary school. This was a good deal less than many advocates had hoped for, particularly those who looked to vocational guidance and to differentiation of type of education by the socioeconomic status of the neighborhood as ways of assuring that "the masses" would begin to receive an industrial education at the elementary school level. Yet it was sufficient to speed up the process of transforming the public school, a process many of whose movers, it is necessary to add, were progressive intellectuals engaged in an effort to democratize American culture.[32]

Other forces were also promoting transformation of the educational process. A "long-term trend toward specialization and technical refinement in intellectual life" culminated in a "fundamental reorganization . . . of the major sources of formal knowledge."[33] In colleges and universities new departments were set up and manned by specialists. New universities introduced graduate schools of arts and sciences and also increased the number and vitality of the nation's professional schools. It was to the professional schools of engineering, science, and business that advocates of vocational education looked for the recruitment of the officer corps of the "industrial army." Meanwhile, the professions themselves—for example, engineering—split into a number of subdisciplines, "each with its own organization, elite, modes of communication, and special body of knowledge." Associations appeared in almost all fields of cultural endeavor, for example, in law, history, economics, philology, and education. In the 1870s at least 79 learned societies were organized; in the 1880s, 121. The objective of this "age of consolidation" was the definition of standards and goals by authoritative bodies of experts. The number of practitioners increased sharply, as did the degree of specialization. So too did journals devoted to the emerging specialties, and expenditures, for example, for physics laboratories. In consequence, the "transformation during these years was of such magnitude that the existence of a secular, upward trend in the output of formal knowledge seems beyond question." The transformation was particularly strong in science and technology.[34]

The growth in systematized knowledge and understanding of the forces of nature and of the physical universe has increasingly shifted the composition of inventive activity away from the older empirically based industries characterizing most of the nineteenth century to the newer science-based industries of the twentieth. Throughout the nineteenth century, although decreasingly toward its end, inventions were the product of a crude empiricism, of a trial-and-error use of problem-solving skills that were heavily concentrated in metallurgy, machine tools, steam power, and engineering. Nineteenth century industrialization focused strongly on the development of a machine technology. "The invention of new machines or machine-made products—cotton gin, reaper, thresher, cultivator, typewriter, barbed wire, revolver, sewing machine, bicycle, and later the automobile—involved the solution of problems which required mechanical skill, ingenuity and versatility but not, typically, a recourse to scientific knowledge or elaborate experimental methods."[35] With the dramatic growth of the chemistry-based, electrical- and electronics-based, and biology-based industries of the twentieth century, technological change has been growing more rapidly than the labor force as a whole ever since 1870. Table 31 shows the proportion of engineers and chemists in the labor force from 1890 to 1950.

Nevertheless, important, even epoch-making, innovations were sometimes achieved by the crude empirical methods of earlier times, although at the cost of a wasteful, inefficient search process. A long series of attempts by British ironmasters to smelt iron with a mineral fuel instead of charcoal preceded Abraham Darby's successful substitution of coke for charcoal in his Shropshire blast furnace in 1709. "The advance of metallurgical technique ahead of scientific understanding" culminated in 1856 when Henry Bessemer reported on his successful attempts to control the quantity of carbon in molten pig iron while it was still liquid—by blowing air through the molten iron and thus turning it into steel. Bessemer had conducted his experiments with phosphorous-free Swedish charcoal iron, but his emulators—and Bessemer himself—discovered to their dismay that his technique would not work with ores containing even slight traces of phosphorous. It was these failures which led to systematic study of the chemical processes involved in the production of iron and steel. The next major innovation, the "basic" process developed in 1878

Table 31. Proportion of engineers and chemists[a] in the labor force, 1890–1950.

Year	Number of individuals (thousands)	Percentage of labor force
1890	33	0.14
1900	52	0.18
1910	105	0.28
1920	169	0.40
1930	273	0.56
1930	277	0.58
1940	338	0.63
1940	363	0.68
1950	636	1.08

Source: John W. Kendrick, *Productivity Trends in the United States,* National Bureau of Economic Research, General Series, no. 71 (Princeton: Princeton University Press, 1961), table 12, p. 90. "The overlap in 1930 represents an adjustment of 1930 'gainful workers' to the labor force concept. The overlap in 1940 represents reconciliation of 1940 and 1950 Census counts of engineers." Kendrick's original source is David M. Blank and George J. Stigler, *The Demand and Supply of Scientific Personnel* (New York: NBER, 1957), tables B-1, B-2, pp. 144–147.

a. Chemists include metallurgists, and engineers include surveyors (who cannot be segregated before 1930). Used with permission.

by the chemists Sidney Gilchrist Thomas and Thomas Gilchrist, was a direct outcome of this study.[36]

The beginning of modern metallurgical science dates from studies undertaken in the immediate post-Bessemer period. The discovery of the basic process was soon followed by the advent of the Siemens-Martin or open hearth process for avoiding brittleness in steel by removing nitrogen from molten iron. Yet it was the introduction of the Bessemer process which transformed the pre–Civil War iron industry into the postwar iron and steel industry. The output of steel grew spectacularly in the 1870s and 1880s, rising from less than 70,000 gross tons in 1870 to 1,247,000 tons ten years later. Associated with this growth in output was the increase in plant size that we have already noted. Early in the century iron had been made deep in the Appalachian forests in small charcoal furnaces and forges. By 1900 blast furnaces one hundred feet high were integrated with the giant steel mills that rose above the Monongahela River, Lake Erie, and Lake Michigan.[37]

The name of one industrialist in particular stands out among those who were responsible for this transformation. Often told, the story of Andrew Carnegie's remarkable achievements will be retold again and again. "Tormented by ambition," seizing every opportunity to forge ahead—"Whatever I engage in I must push inordinately," he once confided to a private memorandum intended only for himself—he rose from an impoverished childhood in Dunfermline, Scotland, to become the multi-multimillionaire described by J. P. Morgan in 1901 as "the richest man in the world" (despite having written in that same private memo at the age of thirty-three: "Man must have an idol—The amassing of wealth is one of the worst species of idolitary [*sic*]. No idol more debasing than the worship of money"). If during his active career he seemed to have forgotten those words in his determination to win out in the competitive jungle of business, he remembered them in the end. Before he died, he lived up to the creed expressed in his "Gospel of Wealth" and gave away most of his fortune.

We need not trace Carnegie's ascent up the ladder other than to note that it had a large number of rungs. His first job in America was working as bobbin boy in a textile mill at $1.20 a week; his second, running a steam engine and firing a factory boiler. He became a messenger boy and then a telegraph operator, first for the public and later for the superintendent of the Western Division of the Pennsylvania Railroad; soon he himself became the division superintendent. Then he invested in oil, coal, sleeping cars, and other enterprises so numerous as to defy characterization of his activity by any other term than the generic one of *capitalist*. At the end of 1863 his compliance with the filing requirements of the recently enacted federal income tax law revealed that he had earned an income that year of $42,260.67, almost as much as a millionaire could have claimed as interest on his principal. He was just twenty-eight years old.

Carnegie's optimistic faith in the country's economic growth and development was unwavering. He moved as investor and partner into the manufacture of wooden and iron bridges during the Civil War because he saw the key part which his company, and his sleeping car company as well, could play in the construction of the great transcontinental railroad that awaited only the end of the war to be launched. While his Keystone Bridge Company built iron bridges over the Ohio, Mississippi, and Missouri rivers—the most spectacular being the great St. Louis bridge over the Mississippi designed by James B. Eads—his Union Mills furnished the beams, plates, and posts for the bridges— an early beginning of the vertical integration for which his steel company would be famous. Profits on iron for the bridge parts represented a kind of corollary business integration, which also included the bridge contracts themselves, shares in the railroad companies that would use the bridges, and commissions earned on the sales of the bonds—by Carnegie himself—in the financial centers of Europe and the United States.

In the year after Appomattox, Carnegie added the word *steel* to his Freedom Iron Company and began the slow process of converting it into a Bessemer steel plant. The process was a slow one for several reasons, the most important being the unavailability in 1860 of iron ore in the United States that was free of phosphorous, or nearly so. True, the vast iron ore fields of the Upper Peninsula of Michigan had been discovered in the 1840s. But it was not yet known what kind of ore this was or how it could be gotten to the furnaces and mills of Pennsylvania. Solution of the latter problem began with the building of a canal to circumvent the rapids at Sault Ste. Marie and a railroad line from the mine fields to Marquette, Michigan, on Lake Superior. Then in 1868 came the first tests of the ore. They showed it to be nearly free of phosphorous, and with this announcement eastern capital poured into the enterprise, providing the funds to expand the railroad and develop the port facilities at Marquette. These improvements made it possible to direct a large flow of ore down Lake Huron and across Lake Erie, then by canal and river along an all-water route to the railroad terminals of Ohio, Pennsylvania, and New York.

Since 1866 Carnegie had been experimenting with substitutes for the Bessemer process and trying to secure the American patent rights to a pair of English inventions that would enable him to put a steel facing on an iron rail. It was just as well that he failed to win the rights, for neither process worked. But with the removal of the obstacles to the production of Bessemer steel, and with the advent of official sanction to use that process, which the United States Patent Office granted in 1866, he was ready to lead American manufacturers into the Age of Steel. A tour of the Bessemer plants in England in 1872 convinced him that his earlier plans for the expansion of the small Freedom Iron & Steel Company were much too modest. He decided to build an entirely new mill with the most up-to-date equipment available.

To supervise construction, he hired Alexander L. Holley, "the greatest authority on Bessemer mills in America, if not in the world," and between 1873 and 1875, years of deep depression (which enabled Carnegie to save an estimated 25 percent on construction costs), the Edgar Thompson Steel Works was built. When completed at a total cost of approximately $1.25 million, including real estate and housing for workers, Carnegie had the most modern and efficient Bessemer steel plant in America. Alert to the possibility of technical progress, Carnegie also included two Siemens furnaces. Serving as experimental laboratories, they eventually proved the practicality of the open hearth process for the mass production of steel.

Later in life Carnegie was fond of saying that "pioneering don't pay," but few American manufacturers were more eager than he to break with tradition and embrace the new. According to Carnegie himself, he was "the first to employ a chemist at blast furnaces," an innovation which broke the grip of rule-of-thumb methods in the manufacture of iron. Another early innovation was the introduction of accounting in his shops in order to determine the cost of each individual process in ironmaking. Carnegie continued to innovate and grow till what became the Carnegie Steel Company ranked as the largest such firm in the world, and in terms of capitalization one of the biggest businesses in all American industry. By 1901, the year in which Carnegie's sale of his interests to J. P. Morgan enabled the latter to found U.S. Steel, Carnegie Steel alone was producing nearly one-fourth of the entire steel output of the United States.[38]

Before 1880 almost all Bessemer steel was used for rails, but the demand for other iron and steel products rose even more rapidly thereafter. Especially prominent was the demand for steel plates, sheets, and structural shapes to build heavy machinery, transport facilities of all kinds, and the steel skeletons of the new skyscrapers. In 1890 steel production rose to 4,277,000 tons, in 1900 to 10,188,000, and in 1910 to 26,095,000 tons. Until 1890 Bessemer steel accounted for at least 85 percent of total annual output, but with the passing of the peak demand for rails, its relative importance declined. By 1910 its proportion of output had fallen to 36 percent and the primacy of the open hearth process was firmly established. Unlike the Bessemer process, the open hearth technique could utilize a wide spectrum of the abundant phosphoric ores of the United States. In 1910 the open hearth proportion of output stood at 63 percent.[39]

The economic impact of technological change in the production of iron and steel was delivered in the main to industries using iron and steel products, and of such industries by far the most important were those making producers' goods. On the eve of the Civil War the three largest industries in terms of the value added to raw materials by manufacturing processes made goods for consumers, namely, cotton goods, lumber, and boots and shoes. By 1910 the top three were making goods for the producers of consumer goods, and of these machinery ranked first. In industry after industry machines were becoming larger and more complex. At the beginning of the century a skilled weaver had made one pick a second with his hand loom, but by 1900 a factory worker could look after twenty Northrop automatic looms that together made sixty picks a second—looms that lowered labor requirements by permitting an automatic replacement of empty bobbins and automatic stoppage of the loom when threads broke.[40]

In the cotton industry, the ring spindle, adapted to coarse rather than fine yarns, to ordinary rather than quality goods, gradually replaced the mule spindle. Together with the use of higher-speed sewing machines and cutting machines able to slice through several thicknesses of cloth, the ring spindle and automatic loom made possible the rise and expansion of a clothing industry mass-producing standardized garments. As Adam Smith observed, it is mass demand which leads to specialization, the high degree of which in the shoe-making industry in the years just after the Civil War is amusingly illustrated by the case of a shoemaker of Marblehead, Massachusetts, who went from shoemaking to the study of law and then, following the outbreak of the depression of 1873, back to shoes. Such was the advance in the division of labor in the interim that he found himself one of sixty-four men working on successive phases of the production of a single shoe. Not surprisingly, he described himself as "one 64th of a shoemaker." By the end of the century a variety of machines had assumed nearly all of the basic tasks of shoe production.[41]

And so it went in field after field. The more machines replaced people, the greater the demand for metal-shaping machine tools—lathes, planers, boring machines, milling machines, precision grinders—to make those machines. The machine tool industry played a role of fundamental importance in the process of industrialization. The production of goods by machines requires great skill and highly specialized knowledge of the technological problems involved. Solution of these problems enables the development of machine tools capable of making the goods-producing machines. How quickly an economy becomes industrialized depends to no little extent on the speed with which this technical knowledge is diffused from its point of origin in one industry to other industries.[42]

Technical knowledge originated in successful efforts by machine-making firms to meet the needs of specific customers. At first, in the early decades of the nineteenth century, these firms did not specialize in making machines. There was then insufficient demand for machines to induce them to do so. These firms were either ones which, because they made metal or wooden products, also possessed the skills and facilities necessary to make machines, or they were ones which made textiles and set up their own shops to make the machinery they needed. The more successful of these shops proceeded not only to manufacture textile machinery for sale to other firms but also to produce a range of other machines as well, for example, steam engines, mill machinery, and machine tools. Simply by expanding their output, then, producers at this early stage transferred to other industries skills acquired in the production of one kind of machine.[43]

With the growth of a market for a widening array of specialized machines, machine tool production emerged as a separate industry. Most of its member firms specialized in a narrow range of products, often making only one type of machine tool, although in different sizes or with auxiliary attachments or components. Responding to the machinery needs of a succession of industries—textiles, railroads, firearms, sewing machines, bicycles, and, in the early decades of the twentieth century, automobiles—the machine tool industry served not only as the point of origin of technical knowledge and skill but also as a means for diffusing that knowledge throughout the machine-using sector of the economy. It could do this because the technical skills acquired in the industry of origin had direct applications to production problems in other industries.[44]

A historian of technological change explains why this was so:

> The use of machinery in the cutting of metal into precise shapes involves, to begin with, a relatively small number of operations (and therefore machine types): turning, boring, drilling, milling, planing, grinding, polishing, etc. Moreover, all machines performing such operations confront a similar collection of technical problems, dealing with such matters as power transmission (gearing, belting, shafting), control devices, feed mechanisms, friction reduction, and a broad array of problems connected with the properties of metals (such as ability to withstand stresses and heat resistance). It is because these processes and problems became common to the production of a wide range of disparate commodities that industries which were apparently unrelated from the point of view of the nature and uses of the final product became very closely related (technologically convergent) on a technological basis—for example, firearms, sewing machines, and bicycles.[45]

Thus the crucial role in industrialization played by the machine tool industry as both reservoir and conveyor belt for technical knowledge follows from the fact that industrialization essentially involved "the introduction of a relatively small number of broadly similar productive processes to a large number of industries." And from the further factor that nineteenth century industrialization "involved the growing adoption of a metal-shaping technology which relied increasingly upon decentralized sources of power."[46]

Those sources changed dramatically in both quantity and kind during these years. Primary power capacity in manufacturing—the work done by prime movers such as the water wheel, steam engine, steam turbine, internal combustion engine, and electric motor to convert the energy of nature directly into the energy of motion—expanded substantially over the course of the later nineteenth and early twentieth centuries, rising from 2,346,000 horsepower in 1869 to 29,410,000 horsepower in 1919. Water continued to be the major source of power well past the middle of the nineteenth century, but thereafter the relative position of steam improved at water's expense. By 1899 steam accounted for over four-fifths of the total power utilized by industry. The dominance of steam was precarious, however, and by 1919 it was being challenged by electricity.

It is not alone the increasing quantity but also the changing industrial distribution of power that testifies to the essential nature of the industrialization process in these years. In 1869 the lumber and food industries had almost 60 percent of total capacity. By 1919 their combined share had fallen to 22 percent, while primary metals, continuously increasing its share after 1869, emerged as the group with the largest capacity. The group was dominated by iron and steel.[47]

Except in New England, which was much slower than other regions to reduce its dependence on water power, coal was the source of the energy which powered the machines of the later nineteenth century. It was coal, specifically the opening up of the anthracite fields in eastern Pennsylvania, which had permitted the beginnings of factory production in industries other than textiles in the final two decades before the Civil War. Unlike many bituminous deposits, anthracite contains no sulphur, source of a deleterious chemical interchange in the blast furnace that resulted in the production of inferior iron. But neither does it contain gas, and for this reason it was very difficult to ignite. Fortunately, the problem was overcome in the late 1820s by an English innovation, the hot blast, which preheated the blast before it entered the furnace. A decade later anthracite in quantities essential for industrial purposes became available, making it possible to shift the site of production away from homes and small shops.[48]

By 1880 the manufacture of goods by machinery was concentrated in factories. According to the compiler of the census for that year, Carrol D. Wright, "of the nearly three millions of people employed in the mechanical industries of this country at least four-fifths are working under the factory system."[49] The triumph of anthracite, however, was to be a short-lived one. By 1880 45 percent of the nation's pig iron was being smelted with coke made from bituminous coal, a proportion which rose to 69 percent in 1890 and to over 90 percent in the first years of the twentieth century.

> Along with the Westward movement of the population and the more intensive exploration of the trans-Appalachian west came the discovery of high-quality coking coal in the Connellsville region of Pennsylvania. The physical structure of the coal and the absence of sulphur made it possible to produce pig iron of high quality. This, together with the development of a low-cost transportation network and further technical developments favorable to coke, assured the eventual domination of this fuel in the blast furnace.[50]

Yet the availability of coal and machines alone does not explain why the factory system expanded as rapidly as it did. Even more important were the reliability and speed made possible by the advent of the railroad and telegraph. It would have been difficult for manufacturers to maintain a permanent work-force or to keep expensive machinery in profitable operation machinery without a steady, all-weather flow of goods into and out of their factories.[51]

In an increasing number of industries manufacturers were making use of two techniques of production essential to output in high volume: the use of standardized interchangeable parts and continuous processing. Both innovations antedate by many years periods of rapid industrialization, but as in the case of skills honed in the machine tool industry, it is not so much the initial appearance of an innovation as it is its diffusion that increases productivity and economic growth.

Interchangeability is "a method of producing mechanisms possessing closely fitting and interacting components in such a way that a given component of any of the mechanisms [will fit] and perform equally well, *with no adjustments,* in any of the other mechanisms." The method requires a high degree of standardization and precision manufacture of component parts, features greatly facilitating mass production at lesser unit costs—by eliminating or substantially reducing costly fitting activities—while at the same time resulting in products far easier to maintain and repair than predecessor products requiring high degrees of skill on the part of craftsmen. Originating in firearms production, interchangeability came to dominate the light-metal-working industries and then spread to a wider range of products in the course of the nineteenth and twentieth centuries, to clocks and watches, sewing machines, agricultural implements, bicycles, and automobiles.[52] With the notable exception of firearms, however, true interchangeability continued to encounter problems requiring hand fitting and custom machining of component parts till the advent of Henry Ford and the automobile industry.[53] Continuous process manufacturing, or the handling of material by mechanical means with minimal human intervention, had its origins in a flour mill built by Oliver Evans of Philadelphia in 1782. From beginning to end the entire process, once commenced, proceeded automatically, the grain being moved horizontally from one machine to another by a conveyor and vertically from floor to floor, much as automobile bodies were to be moved in Henry Ford's plant of 1914. The next major advance in mechanical materials handling was taken at least by 1860 if not before, and not inappropriately for a country still primarily agricultural, it also facilitated the processing of food.

In the slaughterhouses of Cincinnati the "disassembly" of pigs was carried out by a technique involving workmen at fixed stations while a system of overhead rails suspended from the ceiling moved the carcass, hanging from a hook, at a carefully predetermined rate, from one phase to the next. Each man performed a single operation: one split the animal, the next removed its entrails, another removed specific organs—heart, liver, etc.—and the last man washed down the carcass with a hose. Although it was impossible to eliminate the reliance upon the human eye and human skill in the slaughter-house, the skillful handling of materials, the rationalized positioning of the workers, the elimination of time loss between operations, the minimization of energy expended by the workers in handling heavy carcasses, and the minute subdivision of labor brought about very substantial increases in the productivity of labor.[54]

Similar productivity-enhancing principles were implicit in the post–Civil War application of continuous process machinery and nearly continuous process factories to the production of tobacco, grain products, soap, film, and canned foodstuffs. By the mid-1880s, for example, continuous line canning operations included the preparation of the product, washing, peeling, grading, filling, cooking, cooling, and warehousing. Such innovations greatly raised the volume of output while at the same time sharply decreasing the labor force required in processing.[55] We shall see how, after the turn of the century, Henry Ford integrated the principle of manufacture by the use of interchangeable parts with that of the assembly line. The combining of the two principles was to become the most distinguishable feature of American methods of mass production in the twentieth century.[56]

Rationalization of the work process helped quicken what some contemporaries called the "throughput," or flow of materials through the plant or system of plants. The economic significance of speeding up the velocity of throughput deserves emphasis. Large increases in the daily use of equipment and personnel raised the volume of output and created economies of scale. Essentially, the increased intensity of use represented additional inputs of capital and labor, and since the former was undoubtedly the greater of the two, the consequence, even without technological change, was an even larger increase in output per unit of labor input. These economies of speed depended, however, on the development of new machinery, better raw materials, and more intense applications of energy, as well as on the creation of organizational designs and procedures to coordinate high-volume flows through the several processes of production.[57]

The major seedbed for modern factory technology and organization came to be located in the metal-working industries after declining demand and unused capacity attributable to the prolonged depression of the 1870s induced manufacturers to seek ways to reduce costs. In addresses before annual meetings of the recently formed American Society of Mechanical Engineers, business executives emphasized the need for better shop management and accounting practices, the former to improve coordination and control of the flow of work, the latter to enable a more precise determination of the relationship between time and wages, and of various costs and expenses. Herein lay the beginnings of what came to be known as "scientific factory management," a phrase indelibly associated with the name of Frederick W. Taylor.[58]

An engineer, industrial manager, publicist, and inventor—he made a fortune from his discovery of high-speed tool steel in 1899---Taylor is generally regarded as the father of the scientific management movement. First foreman and then chief engineer at the Midvale Steel Company in the 1880s, he standardized belting, maintenance, and other procedures and introduced stopwatch time study and an incentive wage plan which he hoped would induce workers to meet his "scientifically" determined production standards. In the nineties Taylor introduced improvements in accounting, especially standardized forms and procedures and a monthly balance of accounts, but these accounting suggestions were never widely adopted. Believing output restriction and low productivity the fault of management, he adopted a system of production planning and systematic management which eliminated the traditional foreman. He replaced him with a planning office, which directed all activities in the shop and coordinated the work of supervisors, and with "functional foremen," each of whom performed part of the traditional foreman's job. "A 'gang boss' coordinated the movement of materials, a 'speed boss' prepared the work, an 'inspector' insured the quality of the product, a 'repair' boss maintained the machinery, and a 'disciplinarian' hired and fired." Finally, in the first decade of the twentieth century Taylor devoted much attention in his popular writings to systematic motion study. By the time of his death in 1915 his ideas were widely diffused among manufacturers and engineers. He had published his *Principles of Scientific Management* in 1911, a Taylor Society had formed, and his disciples were giving wide currency not only to Taylor's ideas but also to their own improvements on them. After Louis D. Brandeis popularized the new method in the *Eastern Rate* case of 1910-1911, an efficiency craze hit the United States.[59]

There was much talk indeed. Less impressive is the record of adoption. Between 1901 and 1917 at least forty-six industrial firms and two governmental manufacturing plants introduced scientific management, but these were small and middle-sized companies rather than large ones.[60] Before the 1920s large corporations were mainly preoccupied with problems of administrative consolidation and with efforts to stabilize their companies' positions in their respective markets. The limited diffusion of productivity-enhancing practices surely goes a long way to explain why average annual rates of change in total factor productivity in the manufacturing sector were relatively unimpressive. Between 1899 and 1909 the rate was 0.7 percent, and between 1909 and 1919 it fell to 0.3 percent. In contrast, the "pre-1899" (apparently 1889–1899) rate was 1.4 percent. Evidently the initial impact of Big Business on the country's economic growth was not a favorable one.[61]

Big Business was the product of a vast merger wave that swept over the manufacturing sector between 1897 and 1903. Before then most firms in most industries, though increasing their capitalization to accommodate the need for larger individual plants, were relatively small. In some industries, however—for example, in meat packing and oil, in transportation and the electrical industry—a few corporate giants had carved out secure economic positions. Seminal studies by Alfred D. Chandler, Jr., show how they did so.[62] Some, particularly firms whose produce tended to be somewhat new in kind and especially fitted for the urban market, followed the path of vertical integration taken by the Swift brothers in meat packing, who first built their own nation-wide marketing organization and then created one for purchasing as well. Aware that demand in Boston, New York, Philadelphia, and other cities was outrunning local sources of meat supply, while at the same time great herds of cattle were gathering on the western plains, Gustavus F. Swift saw the possibility of using the refrigerated railroad car to connect the new supply and the growing demand, and in 1878 he formed a partnership with his brother Edwin for that purpose.

> For the next decade, Swift struggled hard to carry out his plans, the essence of which was the creation, during the 1880s, of the nation-wide distributing and marketing organization built around a network of branch houses. Each "house" had its storage plant and its own marketing organization. The latter included outlets in major towns and cities, often managed by Swift's own salaried representatives.[63]

The growing distributing organization soon required an increase in supply, especially after the partners began to market lamb, mutton, and pork as well as beef. So the Swifts set up meat-packing establishments, first in Kansas City, Omaha, and St. Louis, and after the depression of the 1890s, also in St. Joseph, St. Paul, and Fort Worth. They also systematized the purchasing of cattle at the stockyards. Before the end of the 1890s Swift had established a "great, vertically integrated organization, with major departments for marketing, processing, purchasing, and accounting tightly controlled from the central office in Chicago."[64] The Swifts' techniques proved so successful that other leading meatpackers had to build up similar integrated organizations in order to compete effectively. Before long the "Big Four" among them would contest yet another effort on the part of local interests to find shelter from the competition of national firms behind walls erected by state legislation.

From the beginning Swift had had to contend with prejudice against eating meat killed more than a thousand miles away and many weeks earlier. He did so by advertising "and other means." He also had to combat boycotts of local butchers and the concerted efforts of the National Butchers' Protective Association to prevent the sale of his meat in local markets. The association was confident it could do this by inducing various state legislatures to pass a law prohibiting the sale of dressed beef, mutton, or pork unless it had been inspected by state officials twenty-four hours before slaughter. The requirement would effectively banish the Big Four from all but the Chicago market. In 1884 the association persuaded lawmakers in Minnesota, Indiana, and Colorado to enact such a law, and within a year the leading case of *Minnesota v.*

Barber (1890) was on the docket of the Supreme Court. Counsel for Minnesota and Indiana argued that inspection laws "had long been used by the states to improve their producers' competitive position" and that these laws, furthermore, were essential to protect the health of citizens. Counsel for the defendant, an Armour agent, countered that unless the principles laid down in *Welton v. Missouri* were extended, the idea of a national free-trade unit "would necessarily be sacrificed at the altar of plenary state inspection power."

> If the State [of Minnesota] can prohibit interstate commerce in beef, unless the livestock is first inspected [t]here, it may in fish unless they are first inspected when caught. It may in butter and cheese and milk and leather, unless the cow from which they are drawn is first inspected [t]here. It may in wool and all clothing made from it, unless the sheep is first inspected [t]here. It may in cotton and clothing made from it, unless the cotton and the ground that produces it is inspected in Minnesota before the cotton is picked; and there is no product of the agriculture or manufacture of other States that this State may not thus exclude; none of this State that every other may not exclude.[65]

A unanimous Court agreed. "We cannot shut our eyes," Justice John Marshall Harlan declared, "to the fact that the act, by its necessary operation . . . directly tends to restrict the slaughter of animals . . . to those engaged in such business in that State."[66] In sum, the propositions formulated in *Welton* by Justice Field, rather than previous cases involving inspection laws, controlled the decision. Once again, the Court exhibited its determination to strike down state laws inhibiting the flow of goods throughout the national market.

The resulting competition between large distant and small local producers induced many of the latter, especially firms making established staple items, to take a second path leading to bigness, namely, that of horizontal combination. In the 1880s and early 1890s firms did so in the petroleum, leather, rubber boot and glove, linseed and cotton oil, distilling and other corn products, sugar and salt, biscuit, and fertilizer industries. These were difficult times for many firms in these and other industries. At one end, capital costs per unit of output were rising with the adoption of new technologies; at the other, price competition was cutting into revenues. To make matters worse, these were years punctuated by reiterated periods of stagnant demand. In terms of real output the depression of 1873–1879 was mild; yet it was the longest on record, in monetary statistics second in severity only to the contraction of 1929–1933 among post–Civil War business cycles, and marked by numerous bankruptcies, with their attendant impact on business confidence.[67]

The years 1881–1883 brought another downturn, with 1882 regarded by contemporaries as particularly unsatisfactory with respect to profits. During 1883 business grew steadily worse; *Bankers' Magazine* commented as early as

February, "That there should be such an increase of late in the number of failures, in view of the general prosperity of the country, is a very unpleasant fact."[68] Gathering momentum, the downswing continued till 1885, prompting a careful contemporary observer, Carroll D. Wright, to remark that "margins of profits [were] carried to the minimum range."[69] Soon after came the "recession" of 1887–88, another downturn in the second half of 1890—with price weakening and inventory accumulation in pig iron indicating "that output might be growing more rapidly than demand"—and intermittent "severe contraction" once more between 1893 and 1897 "characterized by failures, notably failures of railroads, iron and steel companies, and banks."[70]

The effect of these periodic setbacks was to compound for businessmen a major problem set in secular motion by the new national competition and by technological change—namely, how to cope with declining prices. From 1869 to 1896 wholesale prices fell, and they fell still more in years of depression and contraction. For example, *Bankers' Magazine* reported that in "January, 1880, steel rails were worth $71 per ton; in December, 1883, large contracts for steel rails were placed at $33 to $35 per ton. American pig iron was worth at the earlier date $35 per ton, and about January, 1884, it sold at $20 per ton."[71] Competitive reductions were a major reason why prices fell further in some industries than in others. In the iron and steel industry, for example, and in petroleum, the competitive tactic of lowering prices to expand sales made sense as a short-run action because of the nature of their cost structures during a period of rapid, capital-intensive technological change. A firm's plant and machinery—its fixed assets—represented fixed or "overhead" costs such as interest on the bonds or bank loans that financed their purchase. (Depreciation was not then regarded as a fixed cost. Until well into the twentieth century nearly all industrial firms used "replacement accounting," treating repairs and renewals of capital assets as expenses to be deducted from earnings, rather than charging depreciation to their capital account.)[72] A firm's direct or variable costs represented expenditures for wages and materials. These were by far the larger part of total costs, and the firm could cut down on them by curtailing production. It could stop them altogether by stopping production. But even if it did, the overhead costs would continue. Andrew Carnegie spoke for many industrialists when he commented in 1889:

> As manufacturing is carried on today, in enormous establishments with five or ten millions of dollars of capital invested and with thousands of workers, it costs the manufacturer much less to run at a loss per ton or per yard than to check his production. Stoppage would be serious indeed. The condition of cheap manufacture is running full. Twenty sources of expense are fixed charges, many of which stoppage would only increase . . . While continuing to produce may be costly, the manufacturer knows too well that stoppage would be ruin.[73]

The higher the ratio between a firm's investment in fixed assets and its output—the greater its capital/output ratio—the more severe the pressure it was under to expand its sales by cutting its prices. In this way, its overhead costs could be spread over a larger volume, its capital/output ratio lowered. As long as the revenue received more than covered the direct costs of production, at least some part of the overhead costs could be met. Obviously, no firm could continue to price its goods in this way indefinitely, selling its output at prices below its long-run average total costs. It would become bankrupt if it did, or forced to sell out to a competitor. In sum, price cutting might work as a short-run tactic, but as a long-run strategy it courted disaster. It was a situation well calculated to induce businessmen to look for some way to put an end to their bitter and costly price competition. "Combinations, syndicates, trusts," Carnegie frankly admitted, "they are willing to try anything. The manufacturers are in the position of patients that have tried in vain every doctor of the regular school for years, and are now liable to become the victim of any quack that appears."[74]

Initially, business managers sought to dull the blade of competition by loose, informal arrangements, such as the "gentlemen's agreement" and the pool. In the main, the former was a verbal pact to set and maintain prices, and its principal disadvantage was the early discovery that not everyone was a gentleman. Pools fared somewhat better. In the 1880s and 1890s they were widely used, mainly as a device to restrict output, by makers of meat products, explosives, whiskey, salt, steel rails, structural steel, cast iron pipe, and tobacco products. Here, too, there were disadvantages. To the degree that pools were effective in maintaining prices, they encouraged new entrants into a business. And when they broke down because of some participant's unwillingness in a time of business decline to adhere to his agreement not to encroach on the sales territory of another member of the pool, or not to exceed his assigned output limits, there was nothing that could be done about it. Under the English common law, enforceable in every American state except Louisiana, the pool was regarded as an illegal and hence unenforceable restraint of trade. To achieve the ends they sought obviously required devices ensuring tighter managerial controls over the centrifugal tendencies of independent firms, and a number of firms soon turned to more closely knit arrangements.[75]

The first and most famous of these—the trust—was the brainchild of S. C. T. Dodd, a lawyer attached to John D. Rockefeller's Standard Oil Company. Trusteeship is an ancient fiduciary device for managing property in the interest of another. In the depression-ridden years of the 1870s Dodd thought of a new use for it. Employing ruthlessly competitive business practices, Rockefeller and his associates had succeeded during that decade in gaining control of over 90 percent of the oil-refining capacity of the country. In 1882, three years after the formation of the Standard Oil trust under the laws of Ohio, they induced the stockholders of forty oil companies to turn their shares over to nine trustees. The latter thus acquired voting control of the forty companies. (This is why the "trust" as a technical form of business organization is sometimes called a "voting trust," to distinguish it from the generic name "trust" that was popularly applied during the period to all big businesses.) In place of stock, the former owners received "trust certificates" entitling them to dividends. So profitable did the device prove to be, and so successful as a means of centralizing control of an entire industry, that it was soon widely imitated. During the 1880s trusts were formed to control production in the tobacco, sugar, whiskey, cotton oil, linseed oil, and lead industries.

The fatal defect of the trust form of combination was that it was a matter of public record. And since an agreement to restrain trade or an attempt to gain a monopoly was illegal in the eyes of the common law, trusts were soon attacked in the state courts. In consequence of one such suit, the supreme court of Ohio ordered the Standard Oil Company to withdraw from the trust on the ground that it was attempting to create a monopoly. Clearly, some other form of combination would have to be used in place of the trust, and the solution to the problem became the holding company.

Holding companies do not make or sell anything. Their sole function is to manage operating companies that do these things, by purchasing and holding the securities of one or more subsidiary companies. The device is thus one which enables a corporation, formed for that purpose alone, to bring under unified control a number of previously independent firms. Some states had created holding companies by special acts of incorporation. What is new about the period of consolidation in American business is New Jersey's revision of its *general* incorporation laws in 1888–89 in such a way as to allow corporations to purchase and hold the securities of other corporations. It proved unnecessary even to consult nonvoting preferred stockholders or bondholders. Indeed, the common stock itself was often so widely distributed that it was possible to exercise effective control by purchasing less than 50 percent of it. New Jersey's holding company act proved so successful in bolstering that state's finances with revenues from incorporation fees that other states soon "liberalized" their corporation laws in an effort to induce businesses to seek charters from them. The word *liberalized* is deliberately quoted. Most state corporation laws were highly conservative at that time. Few of them required corporations to divulge significant information to the investing public. It was only after much mulcting of unprotected investors, stock watering, and other abuses by large corporations that the states, at about the turn of the century, abandoned their excessively liberal attitudes and began requiring increased publicity.

The holding company played the principal role in a giant merger wave that rolled over American industry between 1895 and 1904, figuring in 86 percent of the mergers. Holding companies were incorporated, recall, for the sole purpose of consolidating a number of previously independent firms, which, after the consolidation, retained their firm names as the operating parts of the corporate structure. As a rule, a holding company was created when the size of the companies to be consolidated was large, for then a large capital sum was required to purchase control of their stock. In contrast, a company already in existence would acquire control of small firms, which disappeared into the merger and lost their individual names. "Acquisition," as distinguished from "consolidation," figured in 14 percent of the mergers of the 1895–1904 period.

Mergers took place in all major manufacturing and mining industries, but most were concentrated in eight of them: primary metals, food products, petroleum products, chemicals, transportation equipment, fabricated metal products, machinery, and bituminous coal. The wave gathered strength slowly, merely 5 consolidations being effected in both 1895 and 1896. In 1897 that number suddenly doubled, then rose to 26 in 1898. The next year it soared to 106 before beginning an irregular tapering off to 42 in 1900, 53 in 1901, 48 in 1902, 15 in 1903, and 9 in 1904. Altogether, between 1895 and 1904, 319 consolidations took place, with 1898–1902 being the five peak years. The total capitalization involved was $6 billion 300 million, with 40 percent of that total accounted for by only 29 of the 319 consolidations. Each of the 29 had an authorized capitalization of $50 million or more. One, United States Steel, had a capitalization of $1 billion 370 million—the first billion-dollar corporation in history (it alone accounted for 23 percent of the total).

While the number of consolidations taking place affords one view of the great wave, another is presented by the number of firms disappearing into mergers. In the period 1895-1904 the average annual number was 301. In the five peak years of 1898–1902, however, merger activity reached heights never exceeded in United States history, with 1,028 firms disappearing in the year 1899 alone. The huge turn-of-the-century wave produced U.S. Steel, American Tobacco, International Harvester, DuPont, Corn Products, Anaconda Copper, and American Smelting and Refining, to name only a few of the well-known firms of the twentieth century. Of the largest corporations in the country in 1955, twenty were born during the period 1895–1904. The effect of the merger wave on American industry was therefore widespread and enduring.[76]

According to a conservative estimate, 318 firms had come into possession of 40 percent of all manufacturing assets by 1904. The absolute size of many of the new companies was a disturbing feature to many contemporary critics. But it was not the only one. More disturbing still was their size in relation to the markets they served. As a result of the merger wave between 1895 and 1904, a single firm came to account for 60 percent or more of total output in at least fifty industries. DuPont, General Electric, Westinghouse, Pullman, and American Tobacco were among sixteen companies controlling 85 percent or more of their respective markets. Surely the principal result, and probably also the principal purpose of the mergers, was the control of output and price. Only thus could cutthroat competition be brought to an end.[77] The same kind of competition had beset the nation's railroads too, for while traffic increased consistently throughout the nineteenth century, railroad mileage grew even faster. More and more virulent rate wars during the hectic years between the two great depressions of 1873 and 1893 drove down the revenues of even well-managed companies and forced others into bankruptcy. In the decade 1882–1891 no fewer than 279 railroad companies went into receivership, the bankruptcies involving nearly $2 billion in capital and thirty-eight thousand miles of track. The primary cause, says an early-twentieth-century historian of railroad finance and organization, was "over-expansion or excessive competition."[78]

Like the heads of manufacturing firms, railroad presidents also resorted to mergers. Their most distinctive, and also most important, technique for dulling the blade of competition was to form a "community of interest." One way to achieve this was for a railroad to purchase stock in other railroads, thereby gaining representation on their boards of directors. Such arrangements, which originated among eastern railroads in the mid-1880s, accelerated rapidly following a massive defaulting on bonds during the great shakeout brought on by the depression of 1893-1897. The president of the Pennsylvania Railroad Company, Alexander J. Cassatt, explained their advantages in an annual report to his stockholders:

> The only alternative [to indefinite cost reduction] is to arrest the reduction in revenue, which has been largely brought about by apparently uncontrollable conflicts between the railroad companies . . . To establish closer relations between the managers of the trunk lines, it seemed wise to your Board to acquire an interest in some of the railways reaching the seaboard and to unite with the other shareholders who control these properties in supporting a conservative policy.[79]

By 1902 the Pennsylvania Railroad owned $52 million of Baltimore & Ohio common stock, $26 million of Norfolk & Western, and $10 million of Chesapeake & Ohio, and President Cassatt reported that the community of interest was working well. Presumably it was also working well for the New York Central and other roads which had followed suit. By 1906 the greater part of the nation's railroad mileage and an even larger share of its traffic was accounted for by communities of interest. From a list containing merely thirty-nine names, it would have been possible to make up a majority on the board of directors of all the important railroads east of the Mississippi, railroads which controlled all access by land to the ports of New York, Philadelphia, and Boston.[80]

One of these communities—by 1906 there were eight in all—was the southeastern system of "Morgan roads." The group included eleven companies with almost nineteen thousand miles of track, besides a Morgan ownership interest in two other major groups, the Vanderbilt and Hill lines, which together amounted to nearly another thirty thousand miles. The influence of John Pierpont Morgan and his investment banking house was thus not confined to a single region of the country. The most outstanding private figure in the history of American finance, Morgan had assumed leadership of the forces attempting to stabilize American railroads since at least the 1880s, when he brought about harmony between the New York Central and the Pennsylvania.

Morgan had good reason for his concern that business relations among the railroads be orderly and harmonious, that the railroads abandon rate cutting and other competitive practices that threatened earnings, security values, and the financial stability of the industry. The railroads needed huge loans to upgrade their properties, and his banking house provided many of these loans by marketing their bonds. Indeed, Morgan & Company managed, comanaged, or participated in underwriting most of the major railroad loans of the Progressive Era. Morgan also sometimes gave his blessing to issues of common stock, which induced investors to buy what was then a relatively unfamiliar kind of security. To protect the interests of investors, Morgan men sat on the boards of corporations whose securities they issued. According to the 1912 report of the Pujo Committee, appointed by the Senate to investigate the activities of an alleged "money trust," Morgan or his partners held 721 directorships in 112 of the country's largest financial, transportation, industrial, and public utility companies. About half of the firm's total deposits of $162.5 million belonged to seventy-eight interstate corporations, and of these thirty-two included one or more Morgan men on their board. Between 1902 and 1912 Morgan & Company's public security offerings reached a total of $1.95 billion.

In sum, Morgan & Company and other investment banking firms reorganized the nation's railroads in the 1890s. They rehabilitated numerous bankrupt or financially weak roads and then proceeded to regulate competition. They did so by restructuring and rationalizing the systems and managements of the troubled companies through consolidations and by arranging for rival lines to buy stock in each other's properties. Finally, Morgan & Company partners served on many railroad boards and finance committees for the purpose of influencing investment and vetoing unwise expenditures in the interests of corporate stability and profitability. One of those partners, George W. Perkins—he was also a vice-president of the New York Life Insurance Company—unquestionably gave voice to the philosophy not only of Morgan but also of many of the nation's business leaders when in his testimony before the Armstrong Commission of New York, charged with investigating the insurance industry of that state, he said in 1905: "The old idea that we were raised under, that competition is the life of trade, is exploded. Competition is no longer the life of trade, it is cooperation."[81]

To put an end to competition, however, was to do violence to one of the deepest of American traditions. Indeed, hatred of monopoly sinks its roots in English as well as American soil. The tradition has found expression in different ways at different times. At first it took the form of opposition to special legal privileges granted by the state, for example, those bestowed on early-nineteenth-century corporations, including the First and Second Banks of the United States. Later, monopoly more often came to mean the exclusive control that a few persons achieved by their own efforts. Always, however, it meant unjustified power of one kind or another, especially when it got in the way of equality of opportunity.[82]

As the latter implies, antimonopoly is something more than an economic tradition. It is also political, social, and moral. Nineteenth-century Americans were neither the first nor last to look upon the discipline of competition as a mechanism for the development of character. They also believed that there was a close connection between a competitive economy and the whole democratic way of life, and they looked to the legal system to block private accumulations of power that might threaten democratic government.[83]

By the end of the 1880s public opposition to the "trusts," a term that soon came to stand for Big Business, was so strong that Congress had no choice but to respond. As Senator John Sherman told the Senate in March 1890, "I did not originally intend to make any extended argument on this trust bill, because I supposed that the public facts upon which it is founded and the general necessity of some legislation were so manifest that no debate was necessary to bring those facts to the attention of the Senate."[84]

Despite this acknowledgment of well-understood public facts, scholars remain uncertain why Congress cast a nearly unanimous vote—the Senate vote was 52 to 1, the House 242 to 0—in favor of the Sherman Antitrust Act of 1890. This was a conservative legislature, indeed one whose membership was so representative of the interests of Big Business as to have won the sobriquet the Billion-Dollars Congress. Yet the Stanfords, Platts, Paynes, Aldriches, and others condemned in sweeping language "every" contract or combination in restraint of interstate or foreign trade and "every" person who should monopolize any part of that trade, attempt to do so, or combine or conspire with any other person or persons to do so. Did they mean what they said? Intimately aware, as many unquestionably were, of the national market imperatives stimulating production in large volume by large firms, can they have meant to outlaw *every* combination by which size was achieved?

Big Business itself regarded the Sherman Act as unpractical, unenforceable, and hence innocuous. Some members of the fifty-first Congress felt much the same way. If the act were "strictly and literally enforced," said Senator Shelly M. Cullom of Illinois, "the business of the country would come to standstill." Senator Orville H. Platt of Connecticut accused his colleagues of playing politics: "The conduct of the Senate . . . has not been in the line of honest preparation of a bill to prohibit and punish trusts. It has been in the line of getting some bill with that title that we might go to the country with. The questions of whether the bill would be operative, of how it would operate . . . have been whistled down the wind in this Senate as idle talk, and the whole effort has been to get some bill headed 'A Bill to Punish Trusts' with which to go to the country." "Mr. Dooley," the Will Rogers of his day, quietly observed that "what looks like a stone-wall to a lay man is a triumphal arch to a corporation lawyer."[85]

Complex questions of motivation do not yield final answers; their solutions are judgment calls. In my view, there is something to be said for the suggestion that the main attention of the Congress during the years 1888–1890 was fixed on the tariff, that discussion of trusts was frequently intertwined with it, and that since some opponents of the tariff had raised the cry that the tariff was the "mother of the trusts," Congress enacted an antitrust bill to weaken opposition to the tariff. Yet the circumstance that talk about trusts was often intermixed with tariff talk does not mean that the latter was essential to the former. Such was the public concern over the trusts that political address of the question was probably inescapable.[86]

In the end it may be that the social and cultural context in which the law was enacted played a subtly significant role. If one commences with an awareness of the postbellum era as one of rapid and almost tumultuous change, as a period of unprecedented population increase and movement, of quickening urbanization and industrialization, it will not be difficult to appreciate the sense of uncertainty, of unsettlement, indeed of frustration and loss of identity, that must have accompanied the impact of these changes on once-secure values. Viewed in these terms, monopoly takes on a symbolic significance, a significance not unlike that vested by the Age of Jackson in the Monster Bank. Antimonopoly becomes a cry of protest on the part of individuals increasingly depersonalized and lost in corporate anonymity, of small towns increasingly invaded by the railroad, of small businesses and small farmers increasingly menaced by large-scale and distant competition. It may well be that Congress heard this outcry and responded to it. If so, that response was not fraudulent, but one of moral affirmation. Viewed in this light, the Sherman Act becomes not so much law as resolution. Speaking for the nation, Congress affirmed the validity of a traditional value—the belief in competition, a value closely linked with the political, social, and moral values of democratic government.

At the same time, one must not rule out the possibility that a conservative Congress "passed the buck" to the administration and to the federal courts in confident expectation that the Sherman Act would not be enforced or interpreted in ways hostile to the interests of Big Business. If so, the early history of the law justified the expectation. To discuss this history in detail, however, would be inappropriate here, the more so because the record is well worn from the playing of it. Suffice it to say that the resources at the command of the attorney general were so meager that any effort to prosecute antitrust cases would have been seriously hampered. The Department of Justice was under-staffed and overworked, and Congress made no move either to strengthen it or to provide special funds for enforcing the act. Perhaps this was because Congress, given the strength of the laissez-faire tradition, expected enforcement to be provided in the main by suits brought by injured private parties.[87]

The administrations of William Harrison, who had signed the bill into law, and of Grover Cleveland and William McKinley showed little more enthusiasm for the act than did Congress. Between 1890 and 1903 only eighteen antitrust actions were brought under the Sherman Act, many of them by federal attorneys in the field, with little support from Washington. From 1898 to 1901, when new combinations were being formed at an unprecedented rate, the only suit instituted by the government involved a relatively minor coke-and-coal pool.

Until recently, it was generally believed that the Supreme Court all but made the act a dead letter by its ruling in the *E. C. Knight* case (1895). Despite the fact that the American Sugar Refining Company had acquired a virtual monopoly (98 percent) of the manufacture of refined sugar in the United States, the Court did not find that a monopoly in manufacturing also entailed control of supply and price and hence interfered with interstate commerce. "Commerce," the Court ruled, "succeeds to manufacture, and is not a part of it."[88]

Unquestionably, the government's case was badly presented by the attorney general, Richard Olney, a circumstance that is hardly surprising in view of his previous effort to have the Sherman Act repealed. After the government lost the case, Olney wrote his secretary: "You will observe that the government has been defeated . . . I have always supposed it would, and have taken the responsibility of not prosecuting [other possible cases] under a law I believed to be no good."[89] Yet there is more to be said about this case than traditional accounts allow. It was the understanding of the Congress which passed the Sherman Act and of national administrations in the 1890s that the powers of the states were adequate to dismantle structural inhibitions to trade implicit in great size. Corporations were chartered under state laws which defined their powers. If a corporation exceeded these powers by acquiring stock in other firms—a structural change—state attorneys general could institute proceedings leading to its dissolution. State courts, moreover, had long sustained these actions. In sum, the Supreme Court was intent in the later nineteenth century on preventing state laws from inhibiting freedom of trade between the states. It left to the states' police powers the authority to determine the structure of the corporate enterprises doing business in their jurisdictions, an authority to limit capitalizations and prohibit mergers which the states had been employing for generations.[90]

The Court's determination to use the judicial power to keep open the channels of interstate trade was manifested once more in 1899 when it held a pooling agreement between manufacturers of cast iron pipe to apportion the market between them to be unlawful under the Sherman Act (*Addyston Pipe & Steel Co. v. U.S.*). The decision seemed to point to the probability that loose-knit combinations—gentlemen's agreements and pools—would be held illegal, but that close-knit combinations via mergers would be allowed. The financial promoters who ushered in the great turn-of-the-century merger wave acted under this belief. The principal instrumentality of those mergers, we have seen, was the holding company, so that the business community was shocked by the Court's decision ordering the dissolution of the Northern Securities Company in 1904. Apparently no form of business organization was safe, not even the holding company. But the Court ordered dissolution not because the Northern Securities Company was a holding company, but because it had been formed for the purpose of putting an end to railroad competition west of the Mississippi. The attempt to monopolize the traffic was obvious to the Court.[91] President Theodore Roosevelt is said to have regarded the successful prosecution of the Northern Securities Company as a notable victory. Yet fundamentally Roosevelt did not believe in breaking up Big Business. Why try to turn back the clock to the early nineteenth century, to a world of small, inefficient producers? he once asked. Rather than break up the big corporations, Roosevelt preferred efforts to discourage unfair business practices. In the earlier years of his administration he thought that publicity would go a long way toward accomplishing this, and in 1903 he induced Congress to set up the Bureau of Corporations and to empower it to investigate the conduct of any corporation, if necessary subpoenaing its officers and records for the purpose. Later in his administration he popularized a distinction between "good" and "bad" trusts. Good trusts gained their position through economies of large-scale operation, and they took no unfair advantage of competitors or consumers. Bad trusts competed unfairly and abused their monopoly power. Before long, both the Supreme Court and Congress would adopt a highly similar point of view.[92]

The point of view itself had long been an essential ingredient of the common law, although the members of the Congress which passed the Sherman Act do not seem to have been aware of this. The common law recognized the reasonableness of what are known as ancillary agreements to contracts, even when the agreements were in restraint of trade, so long as they were limited in scope and duration. A storekeeper who sold his store and agreed not to open a competing store in the same neighborhood would not have been able to sell his "good will" if this ancillary agreement had been unlawful. Some combinations in restraint of trade were therefore reasonable, and in 1911 the Supreme Court recognized this in its decisions in two cases, one involving the Standard Oil Company, the other the American Tobacco Company.[93]

The Standard Oil Company case had begun in 1906 after the Bureau of Corporations reported that the company controlled about 91 percent of the refining capacity of the United States. The American Tobacco Company by 1900 produced 50 to 90 percent of every kind of tobacco product except cigars (so little capital was required for cigar making that independent competition was indestructible). Yet the Court made no effort to decide whether these high percentages of control constituted monopoly. Indeed, it disregarded completely the market position of the firms. The only thing in which it was interested was company conduct, practices, behavior. Why? Because "good" behavior was considered to be evidence that there was no intent to monopolize; "bad" behavior argued the opposite. Just as Roosevelt had urged, if a company grew big through superior efficiency—the way Carnegie did in steel—it was safe under the Sherman Act. But if its behavior was like that of Standard Oil, which, among other things, sometimes hired thugs to beat up an independent refiner reluctant to sell out to Standard, the Court would order it dissolved. And the Court so ordered, in both cases.[94]

In its ruling, the Court virtually amended the Sherman Act. That act had outlawed every combination in restraint of trade. But this the Court refused to do. Regardless of the market position of a combination, regardless of what percentage of production it controlled, regardless of the extent to which it restrained trade, a corporation would be outlawed only if its restraint were unreasonable. And the Court would judge reasonableness by examining the practices pursued by the corporate giant in achieving and maintaining its position in the market. But if the Court in these two "rule-of-reason" decisions amended the Sherman Act, it also did something more. It returned to an important doctrine long embedded in the common law. In essence, its ruling brought statutory law more closely into harmony with common law.

All of this, however, applied only to close-knit combinations, to firms which had grown big through mergers. It did not apply to loose-knit combinations, to gentlemen's agreements or pools. Why not? Because the evidence of *their* intent to monopolize was the pooling agreement itself! Such an agreement was a conspiracy to restrain trade, illegal per se. Competition by such means was unfair. Like Theodore Roosevelt, the Court did not believe in trying to enforce the principle of pure competition—only that of fair competition. And if fair competition led to restraint of trade, to a near-monopoly control of an industry, this was acceptable. A firm that won such a dominant position by fair means was a "good" trust. One could not say that he believed in competition and at the same time penalize a firm which had been successful because of its diligent pursuit of fair competitive practices.

Yet it was far from clear where to draw the line between fair and unfair. Obviously, unless Congress gave some guidance in the matter, the Supreme Court would make antitrust policy by its decisions in particular cases. This Congress proceeded to do in 1914, by passing the Clayton Act and the Federal Trade Commission Act. The former designated certain practices, for example, tying-in sales and interlocking directorates, as unfair and hence illegal. The latter set up a federal trade commission to enforce the Clayton Act. We shall inquire later into the impact of this legislation on the American business community.

12

Workers in Industry

The "modernization" of the American economy was a multifaceted process involving massive population movements, regional and industrial reallocations of capital, technological innovation, and institutional adjustments of many kinds in fields ranging from banking and education to the law. What were the effects of these changes on the men, women, and children who composed the nation's workforce? What was it like where they lived and worked? How long was the workday in the manufacturing industry? What was the average take-home pay for a week's work? For a year's? Were earnings sufficient to enable working-class families to move up a notch or two in the social scale? What impact did immigration have on wages? Finally, what was the attitude of the law toward labor? Definitive answers to some of these questions are not possible. Perhaps they will never be. And if this should prove so, it will be the more understandable if compassion for the hard lot of the less fortunate tilts the balance of judgment about what it was like in those days to be a working man—or woman or child. A distinguished historian, Sir John Clapham, once described how he had taught his classes from marked passages in Arthur Young's *Travels in France*. Going through the volume twenty-five years later, he noted that "whenever Young spoke of a wretched Frenchman," he had marked the passage, but that many of his references to happy or prosperous Frenchmen had remained unmarked. "Sympathy with wretchedness," he observed, "is the sign of a generous mind. Let us hope that the attempt to record other things, in their due proportion, does not denote an ageing heart hardened by statistics." To which one can only say amen.[1]

A case in point is the question of living conditions. Here is the reaction of one "middle-class visitor" to a city slum in the late nineteenth century: "Look up, look down, turn this way, turn that—here is no prospect but the unkempt and disorderly, the slovenly and the grim; filth everywhere, trampled on the sidewalks, lying in windows, collected in the eddies of doorsteps."[2] In the slums of New York City, home for thousands of European immigrants, Jacob Riis in 1890 found tenements densely packed with families for whom long hours of work for meager earnings were standard daily fare. The Jewish child, he wrote in his classic *How the Other Half Lives,* "works unchallenged from the day he is old enough to pull a thread. There is no such thing as a dinner hour; men and women eat while they work, and the 'day' is lengthened at both ends far into the night. Factory hands take their work with them at the close of the lawful day to eke out their scanty earnings by working overtime at home."[3]

Other industrial cities yield up similar pitiable tales. Investigators in Chicago in 1892 "described case after case of men, women, and children working in dark, crowded, ill-ventilated hovels, surrounded by filth and laboring for a pittance." A "typical instance": a family of eight living and working in a three-room rear tenement. According to the investigators' report: "The father, mother, two daughters and a cousin work together making trousers at 65 cents a dozen pairs . . . They work 7 days a week . . . Their destitution is very great." In Wisconsin a factory inspector "reported twenty-four Italian miners living in one-half of a fourteen-by-twenty-four-foot shanty" in 1889.[4]

How representative are these pictures of bleak urban ghettos and drab mining villages? It is difficult to know. One scholar points out that Jacob Riis's observations of living conditions among New York City's immigrants, though accurate, were "systematically biased" by Riis's interest in improving those conditions in the tenement districts.[5] Other historians call attention to the existence of an upper as well as under side of life in the immigrant ghettos, to family and kinship networks, ethnic societies, saloons, music halls, and other institutions which preserved the cultural traditions and sense of community among Italians, Jews, Slavs, and Finns. Standards of judgment necessarily vary. Middle-class observers were appalled by what they saw, but that was not necessarily what the immigrants who lived there saw. "Even the slums of the days were beautiful to me compared to the living quarters of Lithuania," one of them testified. "Even though the toilet was in the hall, and the whole floor used it, yet it was a toilet. There was no such thing in Lithuania."[6] And there was running water besides. Had conditions in the eyes of immigrants been as bad as they were in the eyes of native middle-class Americans, it would be difficult to understand why so many thousands of immigrants wrote home to urge friends and relatives to come to America, often sending them the passage money from their savings.

The question of the impact of industrialization on the labor force also requires attention to underlying considerations, of which the following may well be the most important. Although industrialization so increased the demand for labor as to attract additional supplies from the countryside and from abroad and to induce participation in larger numbers by women and children, these responses fell short of demand. Labor, of course, is not a homogeneous factor of production, and there is every reason to believe that there was a greater demand for skilled than for unskilled workers in the early stages of rapid industrialization and that the consequence of the higher average price which employers had to pay for skill led them to seek to lower their unit costs of production by substituting capital for labor. The capital not only permitted economies in expenditures on skilled labor. It also made possible a more minute subdivision of production processes and enabled those processes to be handled by cheaper semiskilled and unskilled labor. But while unit production costs went down, output per unit of labor input rose with the increased scale of production which the capital inputs made possible. This advance in productivity was the source of gains in wages and improvements in hours.

But men and women did not share equally in these gains, nor did natives and foreigners, or whites and blacks. The extent to which wage differentials were measures of differences in skills, were products of discrimination, or were attributable to other phenomena is an important question to examine.

Between 1870 and 1910 the number of gainful workers ten years of age or older increased from 12,505,900 to 38,167,300. Most of these workers were white adult males, but the number of immigrant and native women joining the labor force also rose smartly during the period, from 1,836,300 to 8,075,800.[7] Women who worked for wages represented a small but growing minority—14.8 percent of all females over sixteen in 1870, 24 percent in 1910. The great majority of those who worked were young, single girls whose families depended on their earnings. After marriage most withdrew from the labor force, only reentering it when family income fell because of a husband's loss of a job, illness, work accident, or desertion. Working wives nevertheless made up a growing portion of the female labor force. In 1890 they constituted only 13.9 percent of the total, but by 1910 the ratio was nearly twice that, 24.7 percent. Although census enumerators did not count them as gainful workers, an unknown, but probably not large, number of housewives supplemented family budgets through piecework employment at home rolling cigars, binding shoes, or sewing garments.[8]

Agriculture and manufacturing continued to be major employers of women during these years, but changes in manufacturing and among service occupations substantially affected female employment. So too did numerous crosscurrents of opinion and social pressure. Within manufacturing, the mechanization of industrial processes to facilitate large-scale output led to an increasing specialization of work, the effect of which was a gradual dilution of the skilled trades. Tasks were subdivided, and their component parts assigned to men and women with no prior training or familiarity with machine operations.[9] The resulting growth of opportunities for the unskilled in food processing and canning; in the manufacture of paper and cardboard boxes; in the production of small parts for incandescent lamps, electric fans, irons, heaters, and other products of the new electric industry; and in other industries is reflected in the employment figures shown in Table 32.

In certain manufacturing industries women made up a large, sometimes dominant share of the total workforce. In the manufacture of clothing, for

Table 32. Number of women employed in selected industries, 1870–1910.

Year	Industry					
	Chemical	Electrical	Paper	Printing	Food	Metal
1870	403	—	6,242	4,397	2,460	5,217
1880	862	—	14,126	9,322	4,503	7,668
1890	2,140	—	22,444	24,640	10,169	15,232
1900	3,427	—	27,261	32,938	19,713	21,335
1910	15,198	12,093	33,419	47,640	48,099	56,208

Source: U.S. Department of Labor, Women's Bureau, *Women's Occupations through Seven Decades*, Bulletin no. 218, (Washington, D.C.: Government Printing Office, 1947), pp. 95, 120, 121, 123, 130, 133.

example, they constituted 58 percent of all employees in 1870 and 58.4 percent in 1910. In the same interval their proportion in the manufacture of tobacco rose from 16.3 percent to 46.5 percent, of boots and shoes from 19.8 percent to 33.3 percent, and of woolen textiles from 37.3 percent to 38.7 percent. Nevertheless, while manufacturing and agriculture remained large employers of women throughout the period, the share of both sectors in total female employment declined.[10]

The decline was a relatively modest one in these years and was compensated by growth in service occupations, which rose rapidly from 5.8 percent of female employment in 1890 to 10 percent in 1900. Job opportunities in sales and office work grew most rapidly of all. This was probably because the Victorian definition of domesticity attributed the role of consumer specialist to women. To sell the increasingly abundant products of the nation's factories to the middle-class urban woman, managers of department stores used young, attractive women as salesclerks. At the same time the rise and bureaucratization of large corporations created many opportunities for clerks, typists, stenographers, and bookkeepers. In 1890 two of every three high school graduates were women. Young, bright, articulate, and personable, they were in great demand. Besides, they could be hired more cheaply than men.[11]

That was equally true of factory employment. Women do not appear to have been paid less than men when they did the same work.[12] But they rarely did. As a rule, they worked in a narrower range of occupations and in less skilled positions than men.

Women concentrated in low-paying, unskilled and semiskilled jobs in textile mills, apparel centers, food-processing plants, tobacco factories, and commercial laundries. Men dominated mining, construction, transportation, and heavy industrial production. Even when men and women worked in the same field, they performed different tasks. In canneries, men cooked and preserved the fruit, shipped the goods, and managed sales and other aspects of plant operations. Women cannery workers washed bottles, scrubbed floors, sorted food, bottled, labeled, and filled jars. In the needle trades the women sewed garments which men cut and pressed. In the metal trades women produced small cores, armatures, and coils, tasks which required speed rather than skill.[13]

In sum, the market for labor was segmented by sex. The labor force had two separate work and wage tracks, one for men and one for women. Men were more than twice as likely as women to land jobs as professionals, managers, foremen, or skilled laborers—or to become proprietors. Moreover, certain jobs became stereotyped as women's work.[14] While domestic service declined as an employer of women—particularly after an array of consumer durable goods such as washing machines, wringers, iron clothes pressers, egg beaters, and sewing machines became increasingly available in and after the 1870s to lighten household chores—more than eight of every ten domestic servants throughout the period 1870–1910 were women. During the same interval female teachers as a percentage of all teachers rose from 66.2 percent to 80.2 percent. Women increasingly replaced men in office work. Merely 2.6 percent of all office workers in 1870, they constituted 37.7 percent in 1910. And in sales occupations it was much the same: 3.7 percent in 1870, 25.2 percent forty years later.[15]

Debarred by public opinion on proper spheres for "women's work" and by some labor unions—in the metal-working industries, for example—from apprenticeship programs leading to better-paying positions, women crowded in such numbers into the occupations open to them that employers were able to hire them at rates of pay that were less than those justified by their productivity. Recall, however, that most women who worked were "either young, unmarried, and simply pursuing short-term employment, or married and seeking to supplement the inadequate income of their husbands," considerations which themselves led to their concentration in lower-skilled jobs. All of these factors eased the path of discrimination against native-born women. But many immigrants faced even more difficult problems. Barriers of language, dress, custom, and sheer racism blocked the entry of immigrant families from southern and eastern Europe into the ranks of salesclerks and office workers. In consequence, needlecraft sweatshops proliferated because of this abundant source of cheap female and child labor.[16]

The labor of children was nothing new to an economy long dominated by agriculture and a scarcity of workers. Farmers had always trained their children to do the milking, haying, plowing, planting, hauling, and other chores, and throughout the period of our concern agriculture continued to be the greatest field of their employment.[17] Children had also been employed in large numbers in industry, notably in the early New England textile mills. In Rhode

Island, southern Massachusetts, and Connecticut employers solved the problem of obtaining an adequate labor supply by hiring entire families, with men doing the heavy work of operating spinning mules, and women and children assigned lighter tasks. Contemporary opinion looked with favor on the employment of women and children, not only to increase family income but also to keep children from falling into habits of idleness and vice. By 1820 about 45 percent of the cotton mill workers in Massachusetts were children, while in Rhode Island the comparable figure was 55 percent. In her history *The Early New England Cotton Manufacture,* Caroline Ware tells of a boy who, at the ripe age of thirteen, was entrusted to repair and set in operation the machinery of a cotton mill in Tiverton, Rhode Island. He had at the time been a cotton mill operative for seven years. Another, nineteen years of age, became superintendent of the Pawtucket Thread Mill in 1826. He qualified for this responsible position by no less than eleven years' experience in the business.[18]

Nevertheless, we have the judgment of the leading authority on manpower in American economic growth that "child labor never became a really substantial source of labor in America—not even in farming or homework." As early as 1833, he points out, it was on the wane in the industry in which it had probably been most important, namely cotton textiles.[19] By 1900 children between the ages of ten and thirteen still constituted 13 percent of the total number of wage earners in that industry. By then, though, the employment of children in the manufacturing industry was everywhere on the wane. Those under sixteen years of age numbered 114,628 in 1870, reached a peak ten years later at 181,921, and declined by the end of the century to 168,583.[20] Undoubtedly, children of foreign-born parents figured more substantially in these numbers than those of natives. In 1890, at any rate, they constituted one of every four gainfully employed children between the ages of ten and fourteen. At the same time the ratio for children of the native born was only one in ten.[21]

As Table 33 shows, immigrant men, women, and children made an extremely important contribution to the growth of the American labor force. In the table, column 1 displays the the total contribution made by three major sourrces of change between 1870 and 1910. These three sources were net immigration (column 2), aging and mortality (column 3), and change in participation rates, that is, alteration in the number of people entering and leaving the labor force (column 4). Comparison of columns 2 and 1 discloses the importance of immigration to increases in the size of the workforce during the period. Approximately one in three new workers was an immigrant.

While dependent women and children, persons without occupations, and those whose occupations were not stated on arrival in this country made up a large proportion of the immigrants—varying from about half before 1899 to about a third thereafter—census returns enable us to form some idea, albeit a

Table 33. Average growth rate of labor force by component of change, 1870–1910 (percent per decade).

| | Source of labor force growth | | | |
Decade	All sources	Net immigration	Aging and mortality	Change in participation rates
1870–1880	29.3	6.2	16.0	7.1
1880–1890	29.2	9.9	15.9	3.4
1890–1900	21.8	5.9	13.7	2.2
1900–1910	22.8	9.5	13.1	0.2
Average	25.8	7.9	14.7	3.2

Source: Adapted from Richard A. Easterlin, *Population, Labor Force, and Long Swings in Economic Growth: The American Experience,* National Bureau of Economic Research (New York: Columbia University Press, 1968), p. 190. Used with permission.

Note: Where the source indicates a range, I have averaged the two figures.

rough one, of the main occupational classes into which the immigrants fell. Of those who stated an occupation, unskilled "laborers" were the largest group, composing 41.4 percent of the total during the 1870s. "Skilled" workers averaged 23.8 percent, and farmers 17.8 percent. Comparison with average figures for the final decade of the period, 1900–1910, is difficult because of a change in census categories after 1898. Nevertheless, if we assume that the classification "laborers, including farm and mine" corresponds to the "laborers" of the earlier period, the unskilled, forming 38.9 percent of the total, remains the largest single group. Somewhat surprisingly, the percentage of farmers (assuming the legitimacy of adding relatively small numbers of "farmers and farm managers" to much larger numbers of "farm laborers and foremen") rises to 23.7 percent, while the category of skilled ("craftsmen, foremen, operatives, and kindred workers") declines to 17.8 percent—evidence, perhaps, of a lesser need for craftsmen as large-scale manufacturing developed. Despite residual uncertainties, it is clear that unskilled labor persistently responded to American employment opportunities in far larger numbers than the skilled, and that other "professional," "commercial," or "clerical, sales and kindred workers" entered the country in relatively small numbers. Indeed, if we assume the presence of unskilled workers among those without occupations to state—excluding dependent women and children—the unskilled must have formed half or more of all immigrants.

Numerous young women found their first opportunities in urban domestic employment. Already in the 1870s household servants represented 7.3 percent of all known immigrant occupations. In the first decade of the twentieth century that average nearly doubled, rising to 13.8 percent, in the process

affording evidence of rising affluence on the part of the native families employing them. We do not know the precise niches filled by the technically
trained, whose contributions to the development of particular industries may
well have been of greater significance than their declining numbers. The decline, after all, was a relative one, and even in the first decade of the twentieth
century their numbers averaged almost 110,000 a year. In the main, however,
immigrants found employment in the great public works of the early nation—
canal, road, and railroad construction—and in mining, service, and factory
trades in the later decades of the nineteenth century. Over the years they filled
a disproportionately large share of domestic service jobs and unskilled jobs in
cities and mines. "In the end foreign labor . . . provided most of all a supply
of those who would hew wood and fetch water for the industries of city and
town." Census reports show that 34.4 percent of the foreign born were employed in manufacturing and mechanical industries in 1870 and that 30.9
percent were so employed in 1890.[22]

Did their contributions to those industries, together with those made by
the skilled and nonskilled to agriculture, trade, and other productive processes,
help speed the pace of the country's economic growth? The chances are good
that they did. In the first place males, the overwhelmingly dominant sex in
the labor force of the time, outnumbered females among arrivals every year
between 1870 and 1910, a circumstance likely to have increased the labor
participation rate of foreigners. Perhaps even more important, only a small
proportion of the immigrants—15 percent or less—was forty-five years of
age or older. Fully two-thirds of them were between the ages of 15 and 40.
Presumably a large proportion was unskilled, and presumably once again some
of the skilled were among those returning to their homelands with savings
from their temporary labor in America. Still, the contribution they made,
though limited in time, was a real one. In the case of the skilled workers who
remained, we may say even more forcefully that younger people with a large
part of their working lives before them had been trained in Europe for jobs in
America. Undoubtedly some on-the-job retraining was often required, particularly in language skills but also in the internalization of values favorable to
productivity growth, such as regularity of work routines, but the fact remains
that much the larger part of the cost of this "human capital formation" was
borne by European countries. The latter thus contributed a significant, though
hidden, capital input to American production processes. As for the far deeper
pool of unskilled labor, the least we can say is that Europeans bore the cost of
nurturing to vigorous maturity a host of willing workers whose ability is
attested to by successful production in dozens of manufacturing firms. Recent
econometric work concludes that increases in capital resulting from the higher
labor force participation rate of immigrants generated economies of scale which
raised the per capita income of the native-born population by 21.9 percent
over the long period from 1824 to 1920.[23]

There is a second way in which immigrant industrial workers contributed to economic growth. Surely in the short run, immigration suppressed real wage improvement. Real wages did rise during the period, as we shall see, but the point is that they would have risen even more in the absence of immigration. One calculation concludes that if had there been no immigration at all after 1870, "real annual earnings in Eastern industries would have been higher by some 11 percent in 1910." Immigration increased the supply of workers and this, at a given level of demand, tended to drive the wage rate down. In addition, one must take into account the influence of the lower standards of living to which Europeans were accustomed.[24]

Immigration may have tended to depress the general level of wages, but this does not mean employers discriminated in favor of native workers and paid them more than immigrants. On the contrary, there is strong evidence that variations in earnings between native Americans and immigrants were significantly related to the length of time workers had lived in the United States. As length of residence increased, so too did the worker's mastery of the English language and level of literacy and probably other skills as well. Variations in these linguistic factors go far to explain differences in wage payments not only between natives and immigrants but also between ethnic groups among the latter.

This is clear from a recent analysis of a study originally made in 1909 by the United States Immigration Commission. The study disclosed the average weekly earnings of over 125,000 adult foreign-born workers in mining and manufacturing and of over 40,000 native-born white employees in the same fields. While the difference between the average earnings of the thirty-five ethnic groups shown in Table 34 ($11.69) and those of natives ($14.37) points to a first-glance possibility of discrimination, there exists in fact a strong correlation between a group's earnings and the percentage of the group either literate in its own language or able to speak English.[25]

With the level of literacy held constant, the analysis finds an increase of 10 percent in the proportion of a group speaking English to be associated with an increase of about $.38 per week in the group's average earnings; with the level of English-speaking ability held constant, a 10 percent increase in the literate proportion of a group is found to be correlated with an increase of almost $.80 per week. On the assumption that literacy and the ability to speak English are indexes of skill, the conclusion is difficult to resist that the differences between one group's average earnings and those of another group are principally attributable to their possession of different average amounts of useful skills.

The case for discrimination, particularly against the "new immigration" from southern and eastern Europe in the early years of the twentieth century, is therefore weak. Not only did participants in that wave of newcomers have less command of English than those who had resided for a longer time in the

Table 34. Characteristics of adult male foreign-born workers in mining and manufacturing occupations, 1909.

Ethnic group	Number reporting earnings	Average weekly earnings (dollars)	Percentage speaking English	Percentage literate	Percentage residing in U.S. 5 years or more
Armenian	594	9.73	54.9	92.1	54.6
Bohemian and Moravian	1,353	13.07	66.0	96.8	71.2
Bulgarian	403	10.31	20.3	78.2	8.5
Canadian, French	8,164	10.62	79.4	84.1	86.7
Canadian, other	1,323	14.15	100.0	99.0	90.8
Croatian	4,890	11.37	50.9	70.7	38.9
Danish	377	14.32	96.5	99.2	85.4
Dutch	1,026	12.04	86.1	97.9	81.9
English	9,408	14.13	100.0	98.9	80.6
Finnish	3,334	13.27	50.3	99.1	53.6
Flemish	125	11.07	45.6	92.1	32.9
French	896	12.92	86.6	94.3	70.1
German	11,380	13.63	87.5	98.0	86.4
Greek	4,154	8.41	33.5	84.2	18.0
Hebrew, Russian	3,177	12.71	74.7	93.3	57.1
Hebrew, other	1,158	14.37	79.5	92.8	73.8
Irish	7,596	13.01	100.0	96.0	90.6
Italian, north	5,343	11.28	58.8	85.0	55.2
Italian, south	7,821	9.61	48.7	69.3	47.8
Lithuanian	4,661	11.03	51.3	78.5	53.8
Macedonian	479	8.95	21.1	69.4	2.0
Magyar	5,331	11.65	46.4	90.9	44.1
Norwegian	420	15.28	96.9	99.7	79.3
Polish	24,223	11.06	43.5	80.1	54.1
Portuguese	3,125	8.10	45.2	47.8	57.5
Rumanian	1,026	10.90	33.3	83.3	12.0
Russian	3,311	11.01	43.6	74.6	38.0
Ruthenian	385	9.92	36.8	65.9	39.6
Scotch	1,711	15.24	100.0	99.6	83.6
Servian	1,016	10.75	41.2	71.5	31.4
Slovak	10,775	11.95	55.6	84.5	60.0
Slovenian	2,334	12.15	51.7	87.3	49.9
Swedish	3,984	15.36	94.7	99.8	87.4
Syrian	812	8.12	54.6	75.1	45.3
Turkish	240	7.65	22.5	56.5	10.0

Source: U.S. Immigration Commission, *Report* (Washington, D.C.: Government Printing Office, 1911), I, 352, 367, 439, 474. In this table "literate" means "able to read." Table compiled by Robert Higgs, *Transformation of the American Economy* (New York: John Wiley, 1971), pp. 116, 117. Used with permission.

United States, they were also less literate, and, in general, this probably implies they were less skilled. They came in on the lower rungs of the economic ladder, like other groups of immigrants before them, and as they learned English and developed other skills, their earnings rose. In sum, each group followed in the footsteps of those who had preceded it, and ethnic discrimination had little or no impact on wage levels. Had some employers discriminated by offering immigrants a wage lower than the value of their services to the firm, other employers could have increased their profits by hiring them at a slightly higher wage. Soon the competition for workers would push up the wage to a level at which it equaled the value of the worker's labor to the firm.[26] In industries marked by a high degree of concentration, however, the competitive blade was undoubtedly dulled.

Other recent analyses—for example, of the sixth (1890), seventh (1891), and eighteenth (1903) *Annual Reports of the [United States] Commissioner of Labor*—strengthen these expectations. Comparison of native- and foreign-born workers' earnings, by state, for various skill levels in the iron, steel, coal, coke, cotton, woolen, and glass industries in 1890–91 shows that in nearly all occupations immigrants earned virtually the same as natives for the same work. Foreign-born glassblowers and coal miners earned substantially more.[27]

Most of these immigrants, however, were established foreign-born workers. Representative of the "new" immigration of the 1890s and early 1900s from eastern and southern Europe—in this particular case from Russia, Italy, and Austro-Hungary—are clearly shown to have earned approximately 10 to 20 percent less than native-born Americans in a separate analysis of new immigrant workers in Illinois, New York, Pennsylvania, and the United States as a whole (1901). But the "new" also earned about 6 to 18 percent less than did the "old" immigrants. Once again, length of residence in the United States, literacy, and command of English appear to have been the governing factors in wage differences.

Other forms of discrimination, however, are not ruled out by these findings. Foreign-born workers faced discrimination in employment security: they were the first to be fired in periods of reduced industrial activity, and they also faced discriminatory practices in gaining access to employment relief. It is also possible that the real earnings of immigrants were less than those of natives, that prices (for example, rents paid by new immigrants), rather than wages, were discriminatory. Other areas of possible discrimination that remain to be investigated include educational facilities, intergenerational social mobility, and entry into trade unions. Union strength was greatest in the crafts, in the skilled trades, and it is possible that union opposition to the hiring or retention of skilled immigrant workers may have had the effect of crowding the latter into unskilled jobs, especially in periods of slack. Yet the evidence on the comparability of wage payments argues against any widespread impact from this source. So too does the general weakness of the labor unions of the period.[28]

If indeed the real earnings of immigrants were lower than those of native workers, those incomes, together with the lower rates paid women and children, surely must have tended to sustain the high degree of inequality in the distribution of income and wealth which existed between the Civil War and 1890. Even before the Civil War, as we have seen, the distribution of wealth was strikingly unequal, especially in the plantation South and in the larger cities of the North. Samples drawn from the 1860 manuscript census show that the top 10 percent of wealthholders then controlled more than 70 percent of the wealth. In the postwar decades, all authorities agree, inequality accelerated. By 1890 the wealth held by the superrich—the top .031 percent of American families—represented between 9 and 14 percent of total national assets. It is evident, as one analyst suggests, that "there were forces at work in the American economy during the nineteenth century that tended to produce greater inequality in the distribution of wealth over time."[29] It is less evident, but no less true, that most saving and investment originate in the higher income brackets, so that the maldistribution of income and wealth was favorable to capital formation in a critically important period of mechanization and capital deepening. And the effect of the latter was to raise labor productivity. Once more, however, despite rising productivity, heavy increases in the flow of immigrants tended to depress wage increases below the level they might otherwise have reached.

In the short run, but not the long. In any economy, mobility of labor—and capital— is essential if the allocation of these factors of production is to be adjusted in response to new market demands and changing resource availabilities. In the United States, the immense labor force of immigrants newly provided each decade, together with the high mobility of the native born, had the long-run effect of inducing a large, continuing increase in productivity and thereby wages.[30] An influx of unskilled workers was precisely suited to the needs of industrialization, for manufacturing firms were enlarging their scale of operation in the very northeastern and midwestern cities in which immigrants largely settled. In the short run, then, an industrializing America widened the opportunities open to immigrants, while tending to lower the wages of workers in manufacturing generally. In the long run the wages of all went up as a result of the additional mobility they imparted to the American labor force.

The record on the score of wages is clear: between 1860 and 1890 the average daily money wage in manufacturing rose 50 percent, with annual money earnings rising at nearly the same rate. Use of a consumer price index to gauge average expenditures for food, rent, fuel, light, clothing, and miscellaneous items shows that for the thirty-year period the net rise in real wages was about the same as the rise in money wages, approximately 50 percent.

Viewed by decades, however, the pace of the rise was uneven. Because of inflation during the Civil War, real wages in 1870 were only 3 to 7 percent above those in 1860. The cost of living declined greatly during the depressed 1870s, but the decline in money wages kept close pace, so that by 1880 real wages were only an additional 10 to 19 percent higher. Most of the overall gain occurred during the third decade, when a substantial increase in money wages, together with a substantial decrease in living costs, combined to raise real wages by 25 to 28 percent for the ten-year period, more than in the previous two decades combined.[31]

Between 1890 and 1899 average hourly earnings in manufacturing changed very little in money terms but then rose markedly between 1900 and 1914. Real wages, however, rose 37 percent throughout the period 1890–1914. This rate of growth was less rapid than the increase in output per man-hour in manufacturing. An economist suggests that the failure of wages to keep pace with productivity advances is explicable in terms of the high capital/output ratios of the industries: "The costs of using more capital per unit of output had to be covered before real wages could rise if the influx of capital was to be sustained."[32] However, the accounting records of manufacturing firms present no evidence to show that these costs were not covered. The wage lag is also compatible with the hypothesis that an oversupply of immigrant workers permitted employers in concentrated industries to pay lower wages than those justified by the value of their labor. The same hypothesis may help explain why the rate of increase in real wages during the period (37 percent) was less than that achieved earlier (50 percent). It is true, however, that a lower degree of literacy and skill on the part of the "new" immigrants from southern and eastern Europe would have tended to retard the growth of productivity.

Increases in hourly, weekly, or annual wages, needless to say, bring more take-home pay only to the employed. Unhappily, unemployment, sometimes prolonged, punctuated this period. The years 1873–1879 were ones of continuous depression. According to the American Iron and Steel Institute, as of November 1874 there were "at least a million" unemployed workers. A labor historian calculates that average unemployment ranged from 6 to 8 percent of the labor force in 1875 and had risen to at least 13 percent by 1879, with unemployment at 2 million and possibly more. A lesser rate of perhaps 7.5 percent characterized the depression year 1885, with an estimated 3,305,000, or 13.4 percent of the labor force, unemployed at the end of 1893; the proportion rose to 18.4 percent the next year.[33]

These figures and percentages apply to the total labor force and not to industrial workers alone. Because rates of joblessness in manufacturing were much higher than in agriculture, they understate the impact of unemployment on industrial workers. In addition, reductions in hours to effect economies during periods of slack demand also reduced wages. In general, though, almost all workers in the manufacturing industry benefited from a reduction in the numbers of hours worked, from about 65 hours per week in 1860, to 60 in 1890, and to 56.6 in 1910.[34] In essence, the average worker took part of his income in the form of leisure.[35] In some industries, hours were longer or shorter than average. As late as 1920 steelworkers labored an average of 63.1 hours per week. Some basic processes required a 12–hour day and a 7–day week, including the dreaded "long turn" of one 24-hour continuous shift, with one day off every two weeks.[36] On the other hand, the hours of some skilled workers—for example, miners and those in the construction industry— declined below the average. And, not surprisingly, their rates of pay were higher than those of the unskilled. In sum, although the possibility of discrimination—certainly against women and, in some forms, against immigrants— cannot be firmly overruled, most workers enjoyed increased wages and reduced hours during these years of rapid industrialization—significant evidence that labor was not "exploited."

Yet "exploitation" is only a word, and like any other word, it has to be defined, or would have to be if it were really an issue. But it is not. The real issue is whether labor could have done better than it did. Its productivity suggests that it should have, and voices were not wanting in support of that view. The opinion of a leading contemporary labor leader, Samuel Gompers, might well be discounted as partisan. Gompers conceded that the "laborer's share of the production of wealth" had "largely increased per dollar of the worth" between the end of the Civil War and the turn of the century. It had not, though, he added, "increased in the ratio that I think labor is entitled to."[37] The opinion of the leading authority on the course of wages between 1860 and 1890 is that of a scholar who is not partisan. To him, "the pace of wages and earnings during these three decades of almost unparalled economic advance must, by present standards, be regarded as moderate, a walk followed by a trot, allegretto rather than allegro."[38] In a word, the improvement, while real, was modest—but by present standards rather than by those of the age I am describing.

By present standards the age of America's first Industrial Revolution must be regarded as callous in its relative indifference to the welfare and safety of workers. The unemployed worker was cast adrift. As a rule, there was no such thing as public relief, and private charity was either insufficient or offered only on demeaning terms. The risks of injury or death on the job were grievously high. The United States had one of the highest industrial accident rates in the Western industrial world.[39] Yet we need to know far more than we now do about rates of mortality, injury, and illness experienced by different age groups, sexes, and occupations, nonindustrial as well as industrial, if we are to succeed in evaluating the impact of the industrial environment on workers. Unhappily, the amount of available information is limited. There are only four censuses between 1890 and 1950—those for 1890, 1900, 1930, and 1950—whose results were tabulated in a form immediately useful for occupational mortality injuries. As late as 1885, deaths were registered in only a few states, containing 28 percent of the total U.S. population. Studies in the field of industrial medicine were late in coming too, particularly in comparison with France and Germany, where such investigation began to be made soon after 1840. In the United States it was not till 1903 that Dr. C. F. W. Doering's inquiry into "Factory Sanitation and Labor Protection" was published by the United States Bureau of Labor, which had sponsored it. Doering's pioneering work was followed by that of Alice Hamilton, whose study of the white lead and lead-oxide industries in the United States, published in 1911, was largely responsible for establishing the field of industrial toxicology as the first branch of industrial medicine. Despite the existence of these inquiries and a few other comparable ones launched in this period—inquiries which would contribute in the twentieth century to a reduction in occupationally related mortality—we are still insufficiently informed for a judgment on the full effects of the industrial work environment on human health and economic welfare.[40]

One careful study of the surviving mortality statistics for males of various ages and occupations in a number of so-called registration states (ranging from nine to sixteen between 1890 and 1908) leads to a number of conclusions which, at first blush, are surprising (see Table 35). In every age group in 1890 death rates among workers in the "laboring and servant" category exceeded those in any other, including factory workers ("manufacturing and mechanical"). The same was true in 1900 and 1910, except for workers age sixty-five or older in the latter year. Indeed, in all age groups and years, deaths among employees in several nonindustrial categories exceeded those among factory workers. Accidental deaths in the coal mining and railroad industries appear to have been incredibly high, but it is difficult to form a balanced judgment on this kind of evidence without knowledge of accident frequency and severity rates over time for various categories of employment.[41]

This valuable analysis was conducted for the specific purpose of evaluating condemnations of the dangers of factory work made by early-twentieth-century writers (the "muckrakers"). But a somewhat wider assessment of the human costs of rapid industrialization would seem to be required. Railroad construction and coal mining are essential to the production and distribution of the steel needed in the industrial and urban utility sectors and as much a part of the process of industrialization as factory work itself. Occupational mortality and morbidity in all these sectors need to be compared with those in agriculture if we are to obtain one important measure of the human impact of industrialization. We also need to remind ourselves of the impact of industrialization on the whole population of a country rather than on its individual economic or other segments. Comparative studies have yielded the undisputed demographic finding that mortality rates in the entire population declined not only during the initial years of industrialization but also, for the

Table 35. Death rates per 1,000 by occupational class and age interval in registration states (males only), 1890, 1900, and 1910.

Occupation	Age 15–24			Age 25–44			Age 45–64			Age 65 and over			Total		
	1890	1900	1910	1890	1900	1910	1890	1900	1910	1890	1900	1910	1890	1900	1910
Professional	5.05	4.39	3.72	8.47	7.36	5.80	19.11	20.08	18.56	79.28	104.06	85.87	15.72	14.74	11.95
Clerical and official	6.16	7.00	7.30	9.15	10.99	7.27	13.65	19.65	15.64	38.54	55.42	40.88	9.88	13.32	10.75
Mercantile and trade	3.52	2.66	1.76	7.43	6.71	4.36	18.33	19.76	13.52	73.59	93.22	51.77	12.32	12.29	7.80
Entertainment, personal service, police, and military	7.31	5.05	3.15	11.88	9.20	7.82	21.02	20.82	33.11	61.93	63.71	49.69	15.12	13.18	11.21
Laboring and servant	9.73	8.99	7.65	16.96	16.28	12.29	33.20	35.59	30.58	114.87	133.14	70.21	23.12	23.43	17.01
Manufacturing and mechanical	5.02	3.97	4.25	9.18	7.69	6.99	20.13	18.89	21.17	77.67	100.72	95.80	13.13	12.79	13.03
Agriculture	2.38	4.02	4.88	3.43	5.36	5.92	9.64	13.86	15.08	57.81	97.16	72.38	12.11	18.36	15.32
Forestry and fishing	3.16	4.42	3.62	5.53	5.17	3.90	10.91	12.82	12.50	44.58	60.91	42.89	8.37	10.14	7.53
Mining	3.65	5.44	4.95	5.30	8.12	6.14	14.61	14.47	16.14	55.84	140.21	100.92	7.80	10.09	8.95
Transportation and communication	7.99	5.43	6.72	10.29	8.50	8.34	19.39	18.19	19.37	85.28	103.38	67.91	13.51	11.67	11.53
Total	5.58	5.08	4.98	9.29	8.70	7.22	18.40	19.79	18.71	70.07	98.11	72.49	13.98*	15.06*	12.73*

Source: Paul Uselding, "In Dispraise of the Muckrakers: U.S. Occupational Mortality, 1890–1910," in *Research in Economic History*, ed. Paul Uselding (Greenwich, Conn.: JAI Press, 1976), I, 343. Uselding cites his own tables A.13, A.14, and A.15 as sources. Used with permission.

(*) Crude death rates of the population as a whole.

most part, subsequently as well. Finally, we need to know more precisely how many, if any, unskilled workers are included in the category "manufacturing and mechanical." Listings of the industries in that category, it is true, specify "iron and steel workers," "mill and factory operatives (textiles)," "boot and shoe makers," and perhaps several others which may have included unskilled workers. But these are few in relation to a far larger number of occupations—carpenters and joiners, wheelwrights, coopers, and compositors, for example (forty-one of them in 1890)—which clearly designate craftsmen. If most unskilled labor was designed by census takers for inclusion among "manufacturing and mechanical" industries, the question may be raised why they established a separate category for "laboring and servant" ("laborers, messenger boys, and servants"). If indeed this category does embrace a substantial number of unskilled factory workers, the high mortality rates it consistently displays are understandable.[42]

Comparative death rates per thousand provide one legitimate view of the human costs of industrialization, but the sheer numbers themselves are even more arresting.

> From 1880 to 1900, 35,000 workers were killed annually and another 536,000 were injured. In Allegheny County, Pennsylvania (the Pittsburgh district) in one calendar year alone (1906–07) 526 workers died on the job, of whom 80 percent were under forty years of age and 60 percent were under thirty. Between 1905 and 1920, no year passed in the coal mines without at least 2000 fatal work-related injuries. A similar sort of human destructiveness existed on the railroads. Among railroad men in the year 1901, one of every 399 was killed; one of every twenty-six injured; among operating trainmen, one of every 137 was killed, and one of every eleven injured.[43]

According to estimates made by the Bureau of Labor Statistics in 1921, each year there occurred in the United States 2,453,418 industrial accidents in which the injury resulted in loss of time beyond the day on which the accident took place. Of these, 21,232 were fatal; 1.728 resulted in permanent total disability; 105,629 in permanent partial disability; and the remainder in temporary disability. Roughly 227 million man-days a year were lost, at a cost of slightly over $1 billion in lost wages.[44] By then numerous workers were covered by workmen's compensation laws. Railroad workers were so covered after 1909, and after 1914 several states enacted even broader legislation that was acceptable to the courts. Before then, however, workers suffering injury on the job could expect no compensation. Few could afford insurance, and the common law continued, as in the early nineteenth century, to reflect a developing economy's need for capital formation.

In the 1842 case of *Farwell v. The Boston and Worcester Railroad Corporation,* Chief Justice Lemuel Shaw of the Massachusetts Supreme Judicial Court laid down a principle of common law with respect to the responsibility of an employer for accidents which governed the course of law for much of the remainder of the nineteenth century. The principle was this: an employee could not sue his employer for injuries caused by the negligence of another employee (the "fellow servant" rule). Rejecting the ancient doctrine of *respondeat superior,* which held a master liable for the tortious acts of his servants, Justice Shaw adopted a contractarian view of the relationship between employer and employee. He held that a worker had entered into an implied contract to assume the "natural and ordinary risks and perils incident to the performance of [his] services" and that these were perils which he was "as likely to know, and against which he [could] as effectually guard, as the master." His wage included a premium for the risks he assumed. To be sure, a worker retained the right to sue his employer for injuries, provided they were caused by the personal misconduct of the employer himself. But the factory system and corporate ownership of industry made this right virtually meaningless. In all likelihood the owner of the factory was a corporation, a "soulless" legal entity, and even if the owner was an individual proprietor, the chances were that he did not have anything to do with the operation of machinery and equipment. If an employee were injured, then, legal fault would be ascribed to a fellow worker, if to anyone. And fellow workers were men without wealth or insurance. Thus the fellow-servant rule was an instrument capable of relieving employers from nearly all the legal consequences of industrial injuries.[45]

By compelling workers themselves to bear the costs of those injuries, the fellow-servant rule unquestionably relieved employers of large sums in compensatory payments, thus encouraging investment in industrial enterprises. When Shaw wrote in the early 1840s, the human consequences of rapid technological change were unforeseeable. By the last decades of the century, though, the quickened pace of industrialization was bringing in its train thousands of deaths and perhaps as many as 2 million injuries every year. In the seventeen years between 1889 and 1906 the railway injury rate doubled. In these circumstances, the fellow-servant rule was increasingly challenged, particularly by lawyers in large numbers willing to represent poor men on the basis of fees contingent upon successful suits. Plaintiffs won many of their lawsuits and in the process weakened the fellow-servant rule by encouraging still more attorneys to make a living from personal injury cases. The doctrine itself began to be modified at the appellate court level as judges adopted modifications such as the so-called vice-principal rule, which allowed an injured worker to sue his employer when the negligent employee occupied a supervisory position. In such cases, the latter could more properly be said to be an alter ego of the principal rather than a mere fellow servant. Many other exceptions developed, among them, the idea that employers had certain duties that could not be delegated, the most important being the duty to furnish a safe place to work, safe tools, and safe appliances. The upshot was that workers won so many suits that employers began to throw their weight behind workmen's compensation laws. Businessmen preferred a guaranteed, insurable cost that could be computed in advance on the basis of accident experience, for this promised to be less costly in the long run than the existing system.[46]

> Between 1910 and 1920 the method of compensating employees injured on the job was fundamentally altered in the United States. In brief, workmen's compensation statutes eliminated (or tried to eliminate) the process of fixing civil liability for industrial accidents through litigation in common law courts. Under the statutes, compensation was based on statutory schedules, and the responsibility for initial determination of employee claim was taken from the courts and given to an administrative agency. Finally, the statutes abolished the fellow-servant rule and the defenses of assumption of risk and contributory negligence.[47]

Early statutes of these kinds were disallowed by the courts, the New York Court of Appeals, for example, unanimously declaring the nation's first workmen's compensation statute unconstitutional in 1911. That same year, however, Wisconsin framed the first general compensation law to succeed in passing a court test. Other states followed, and in 1948 Mississippi finally enacted a compensation law. It was the last state in the union to do so.[48]

Labor fared poorly at the hands of the legal system in other respects as well during the age of rapid industrialization. From the late 1880s on, strikes, picket lines, and boycotts were easily broken up by the use of the labor injunction. Even before a trial to determine whether or not a formal injunction was to be issued judges usually granted restraining orders on request, frequently in the absence of anyone representing the persons to be enjoined, and frequently without even identifying the individuals who were the objects of the order. Judges behaved in the same casual manner after the trial held between the two parties to determine whether or not a permanent injunction was to be granted, for many of them made findings of actual or threatened violence or other unlawful conduct where nothing of the kind had occurred or was imminent. In fact, many judges believed that economic coercion exerted by labor unions was itself enjoinable and, by implication, illegal. Union leaders were in a quandary. Unable to predict how judges would react to specific actions taken by workers, they were unable to provide guidance to their followers on what constituted the area of permissible economic conduct. Thus they stood "under the shadow of a brooding and undefined judicial power" involving an almost certain suppression of most of organized labor's bargaining and organizational program, and this without any legislative declaration of policy, "or, indeed, of any rules of the game that might be called law."[49]

In 1895 the Supreme Court of the United States for the first time in its history passed on the scope and validity of an injunction in a labor controversy, affirming the validity of one ordering Eugene V. Debs and other leaders of the American Railway Union to desist from interfering with the business of a number of railroads. Thus was the famous Pullman strike of 1894 brought to an end. In Debs's words, "the ranks were broken, and the strike was broken up . . . not by the Army, and not by any other power, but simply and solely by the action of the United States Courts in restraining us from discharging our duties as officers and representatives of the employees."[50] In this case the Court's affirmation rested on a statutory provision forbidding anyone to obstruct or retard the passage of the mail. The Interstate Commerce Act of 1887 was subsequently to be far more important as a vehicle for federal jurisdiction over labor controversies. But of even greater importance for the time being was the Sherman Antitrust Act of 1890.

The first interpretation of the Sherman Act came from the lower courts when, in 1893, a district court held that Congress "made the interdiction include combinations of labor, as well as of capital." Succeeding decisions, with only a single exception, accumulated to the same effect, and in 1908 the view received the sanction of the Supreme Court itself in *Loewe v. Lawlor*. Three years later the Supreme Court gave its most definite exposition of the Sherman law in the *Gompers* case: "It [the Sherman Act] covered any illegal means by which interstate commerce is restrained, whether by unlawful combinations of capital, or . . . of labor; and we think also whether the restraint be occasioned by unlawful contracts, trusts, pooling arrangements, blacklists, boycotts, coercion, threats, intimidation, and whether these be made effective, in whole or in part, by acts, words or printed matter." These exuberances of judicial interpretation induced Congress in 1914 to pass the Clayton Act, section 6 of which reads: "The labor of a human being is not a commodity or article of commerce. Nothing contained in the antitrust laws should be construed to forbid the existence and operation of labor . . . organizations from lawfully carrying out the legitimate object thereof; nor shall such organizations, or the members thereof, be held or construed to be illegal combinations or conspiracies in restraint of trade, under the antitrust laws."[51] Decisive as was the language of Congress, the Supreme Court was soon to render it a nullity in 1921 in the case of *Duplex Printing Press Co. v. Deering,* and a few weeks later, *American Steel Foundries v. Tri-City Central Trades Council.* Not till the 1930s was labor to receive the benefit of a new deal, from the judiciary as well as from Congress and the executive.[52]

Yet the relationship of the legal system to the interests of labor during the era of rapid industrialization was complex, one involving variable actions by state legislatures and courts, as well as by the federal judiciary. Labor was strongest in the industrial Northeast and Great Lakes regions, and states in those regions enacted an increasing volume of protective laws. Some forbade the blacklist, some outlawed the "yellow-dog" contract, which exacted from workers as a condition for employment their promise not to join a union;

some required employers to pay their workers in cash (instead of in goods at the company store) or to pay them weekly or biweekly; and some even punished infringement of the union label. But these laws were poorly drafted, administered, and enforced. In court tests, their fate varied from state to state. Nevertheless, despite the fact that historians have been attracted by the more spectacular and reactionary cases, labor laws on the whole were upheld; indeed, most were never even questioned.[53]

Successful state enactments were those "where conscience and passion could join hands with some strong self-interest," and where a strong civil service, enforceable laws, and money were available to support programs of reform.[54] The labor of children and of women are cases in point. In the eyes of organized labor, both depressed wage rates, and accordingly the unions supported laws abolishing child labor and setting maximum hours and minimum wages for women. For similar reasons, labor successfully opposed the wage effects of unrestricted immigration, and in 1882 Congress suspended Chinese immigration for ten years and, after renewing the suspension, excluded the Chinese indefinitely by statute in 1902. Earlier, in 1885, Congress had also acted to rescind the importation of contract labor, first authorized in 1864 as a way of coping with the labor shortage of the Civil War years.[55]

Labor's wishes with regard to women workers were at least partially realized when in 1908 the Supreme Court sustained the right of the state to limit their hours of work to ten a day (*Muller v. Oregon*). The "future well-being of the race," the Court explained, required that women be protected "from the greed as well as the passion of man."[56] Before then, similar state laws had met a varying fate at the hands of state courts—for example, being upheld in Massachusetts in 1876 and disapproved in Illinois in 1895. Although the South lagged behind badly, numerous states in other regions enacted child-labor laws. But it was one thing to limit the labor of children in factories to ten hours a day or sixty a week, or to forbid it altogether, and another thing to enforce it. As we have seen, it was the enactment of compulsory education laws that put some life into child-labor laws. Even so, when Congress in 1916 required that goods shipped in interstate commerce be produced by the observance of specified standards with regard to child labor, the Supreme Court, in *Hammer v. Dagenhart* (1918), declared the law unconstitutional. And in 1922 it did the same with another congressional statute enacted in 1918.[57]

State laws imposing maximum hours for the labor of men met an uneven, but largely negative, response from the Supreme Court. In *Holden v. Hardy* (1898) the Court approved a Utah statute limiting to eight hours a day the working period for employees of underground mines and smelters. The statute was challenged on the ground that it abridged the privileges and immunities of the worker, deprived him of his property and liberty without due process of law, and, furthermore, deprived employers as well as workers of the equal protection of the laws. The Court, however, rejected this argument, declaring that "the right of contract . . . is itself subject to certain limitations which the State may lawfully impose in the exercise of its police powers . . . These employments when too long pursued, the legislature has judged to be detrimental to the health of the employees, and, so long as there are reasonable grounds for believing that this is so, its decision upon this subject can not be reviewed by the Federal courts." Justice Henry B. Brown concluded his opinion by concurring in the following observation of the supreme court of Utah concerning the employer's allegations:

> His defence is not so much that his right to contract has been infringed upon, but that the act works a peculiar hardship to his employees, whose right to labor as long as they please is alleged to be thereby violated. The argument would certainly come with better grace and greater cogency from the latter class. But the fact that both parties are of full age and competent to contract does not necessarily deprive the State of the power to interfere where the parties do not stand upon an equality, or where the public health demands that one party to the contract shall be protected against himself. "The State still retains an interest in his welfare, however reckless he may be. The whole is no greater than the sum of all the parts, and when the individual health, safety and welfare are sacrificed or neglected, the State must suffer."[58]

Seven years later, however, in *Lochner v. New York,* the Court struck down a New York law prohibiting the employment of bakery workers for more than ten hours a day or sixty hours a week. On the surface, the essential question of the case, so far as the majority was concerned, was whether or not bakery work was sufficiently deleterious to health as to justify denying to employers and employees the right to contract for more than sixty hours of work a week. "We think," said Justice Rufus Peckham for the Court, "that there can be no fair doubt that the trade of a baker, in and of itself, is not an unhealthy one to that degree which would authorize the legislature to interfere with the right to labor, and with the right of free contract on the part of the individual, either as employer or employee." To Justice John Marshal Harlan and two other justices joining him in dissent, however, it was important enough that the people of New York believed that labor in excess of sixty hours a week in bakeries might prove injurious to health. Furthermore, the testimony of expert witnesses—for example, Professor Hirt's treatise "Diseases of the Workers"— could be cited in support of that belief. Whatever the fact of the matter, a reasonable doubt existed, and this should have been the end of the case, for "legislative enactments should be recognized and enforced by the courts as embodying the will of the people, unless they are plainly and palpably beyond all question in violation of the fundamental law of the constitution."[59]

Disagreement on the question of the impact of long hours of bakery work on health, however, was not the basic question which the Court was confronting in this case. The real issue was the extent to which the Fourteenth Amendment, which forbade the states to deprive any citizen of his life, liberty, or property without due process of law and guaranteed him equality before the law, should be used to hem in the reserved police powers of the state to enact legislation in the interests of the health, safety, and welfare of its citizens. To Justice Harlan, a "decision that the New York statute is void under the Fourteenth Amendment will, in my opinion, involve consequences of a far-reaching and mischievous character; for such a decision would seriously cripple the inherent power of the states to care for the lives, health and well-being of their citizens. These are matters which can be best controlled by the states." "I think," wrote Justice Oliver Wendell Holmes in a separate dissent, "that the word 'liberty' in the 14th Amendment is perverted when it is held to prevent the natural outcome of a dominant opinion, unless it can be said that a rational and fair man necessarily would admit that the statute proposed would infringe fundamental principles as they have been understood by the traditions of our people and our law." Justice Peckham, however, speaking for the Court, argued that it "must, of course, be conceded that there is a limit to the valid exercise of the police power by the state. . . . Otherwise the 14th Amendment would have no efficacy and the legislatures of the states would have unbounded power, and it would be enough to say that any piece of legislation was enacted to conserve the morals, the health or the safety of the people; such legislation would be valid, no matter how absolutely without foundation the claim might be. The claim of the police power would be a mere pretext— become another and delusive name for the supreme sovereignty of the state to be exercised free from constitutional restraint."[60]

On the surface, once again, the basic issue here would appear to be that of federalism, an issue both old and, under the American political system, forever new, namely, the issue of where to draw the line between the powers of local governments and those of the central government. The question involves the freedom of the individual and therefore belongs to political science, philosophy, and ethics. But it also belongs to economics and economic history, not least because of the Supreme Court's unanimous opinion in 1886 that the Fourteenth Amendment, "which forbids a State to deny to any person within its jurisdiction the equal protection of the laws, applies to . . . corporations" as well.[61] At heart, the question of federalism reduces to a contest, repeatedly enacted, between those who defend the legal and historical legitimacy of the Court's exercise of judicial review to protect minority rights, particularly property rights, against the political will expressed by the majority in state legislatures, and those who defend the rights of the majority. A "fear of popular majorities," Edward S. Corwin once wrote, "lies at the very basis of the whole system of judicial review, and indeed of our entire constitutional system."[62]

"It is unfortunately true that labor, even in any department, may possibly carry with it the seeds of unhealthiness," wrote Justice Peckham in *Lochner*. "But are we all, on that account, at the mercy of legislative majorities?" To which Justice Holmes replied in dissent: "I strongly believe that my agreement or disagreement [with the "economic theory" on which the Court's decision was based] has nothing to do with the right of a majority to embody their opinions in law."[63]

From the beginnings of the American constitutional experiment the Supreme Court has enacted a role similar to that envisioned by the founding fathers for the Senate, namely, that of institutional defender of last resort of minority rights threatened by legislative majorities in the states. In the antebellum period, the Court's main concern in this area was the security of property rights, including those in slaves. Under Chief Justice John Marshall, as we have seen, the Court used the constitutional mechanism of the contract clause to defend those rights (*Fletcher v. Peck,* 1810). They were no less precious to his successor, Roger B. Taney, who ruled only that property rights cannot be read by implication into corporate charters (*Charles River Bridge,* 1837). After the Civil War, the favored constitutional mechanism came to be the due process clause of the Fourteenth Amendment. Historically, as we have seen, due process had denoted procedural guarantees such as the right of a defendant to be confronted by his accuser in open court, his right to counsel, to a fair trial, and so forth. In the post-Civil War decades, however, procedural due process became substantive due process: the very substance of a state law stipulating maximum rates which railroads or grain elevators might charge their users was arguably a deprivation of property "without due process of law" and forbidden by the Fourteenth Amendment.

Once again, substantive due process entered the mainstream of constitutional law by way of powerful dissents registered by Justice Stephen Field in the *Slaughter-House cases* (1873) and in *Munn v. Illinois* (1876). For a dozen or more years after the Civil War the Supreme Court sought to restore national harmony by righting a federal balance which had tilted during and immediately after the war to the side of central power. It did so by acknowledging the right of the state of Louisiana to exercise its police powers in the interests of the health of its citizens by granting to a chartered corporation the "sole and exclusive" privilege of slaughtering animals in specified parts of New Orleans. And soon after, it acknowledged the right of Illinois and other "Granger states" to fix by law maximum rates to be charged by railroads and grain elevators—on the ground that these were public utilities with elements of monopoly present which justified regulation in the public interest.[64]

The slaughtering monopoly, Field argued, by depriving other butchers of the right to pursue a lawful employment, abridged the equality of privileges and immunities guaranteed to all citizens by the Fourteenth Amendment. The majority decision validating that monopoly, he added, violated "the right of free labor, one of the most sacred and imprescriptible rights of man." The "property which every man has in his own labor," he said, quoting Adam Smith, "is the original foundation of all other property," and the "most sacred and inviolable." The Court's holding in *Munn* was also "subversive of the rights of private property." The fact that the public used grain elevators did not convert them from private to public buildings. The "public has no greater interest in the use of buildings for the storage of grain than it has in the buildings for the residences of families," and therefore the setting of prices which elevator owners might charge deprived the owners of their property "as completely as by a special act for its confiscation and destruction." If the Court's decision be "sound law . . . all property and all business in the State are held at the mercy of a majority of its legislature."[65]

The view that the question of the reasonableness of legislative rates was a judicial one under the Fourteenth Amendment's guarantee of due process of law became majority opinion with the Court's decision in the decisive case of *Chicago, Milwaukee and St. Paul Railroad v. Minnesota* in 1890. That decision, together with the development of the labor injunction as an antistrike weapon, the near-emasculation of the Sherman Antitrust Act in the *E.C. Knight* case, and the overthrow of the federal income tax in the *Pollock* case were related aspects of a massive judicial entry into the socioeconomic scene. They mark the beginnings of what one scholar has called "laissez-faire constitutionalism," a "conservative-oriented revolution" which "vastly expanded the scope of judicial supremacy."[66] But revolutions occur first in the minds of men and women. The revolution in American constitutionalism that took place in the 1890s was no exception, and its antecedents are to be seen in influential writings by learned men and in fears for the security of property generated by events of that decade.

In his *Constitutional Limitations,* (1868), Thomas M. Cooley brought together the scattered constitutional law of the various states and organized it in such a way as to enable it to serve as a principal source for citation in the state courts. In full sympathy with the restraints which the founding fathers had imposed on government, Cooley also made a contribution of considerable importance to laissez-faire constitutionalism by his discussion of "law of the land" and "due process of law." Lawyers and judges frequently quoted these and other passages as authority for judicial invalidation of state regulatory acts. So too did the dissenting opinions of Justice Field. Field's assertion that the Declaration of Independence guaranteed "the right of men to pursue their happiness, by which is meant the right to pursue any lawful business or vocation in any manner not inconsistent with the equal rights of others which may increase their prosperity or develop their faculties," became a standard quotation in freedom-of-contract decisions.[67]

The idea of freedom of contract received its most notable affirmation in *Godcharles v. Wigeman* in 1886. Before the Court was the Pennsylvania Store-Order Act of 1881 prohibiting manufacturing and mining companies from paying wages in other than lawful money. Boldly limiting state legislative power in the area of labor, Judge Isaac M. Gordom declared for the Court:

The Act is an infringement alike of the right of the employer and the employee; more than this, it is an insulting attempt to put the laborer under legislative tutelage, which is not only degrading to his manhood, but subversive of his rights as a citizen of the United States. He may sell his labor for what he thinks best, whether money or goods, just as his employer may sell his iron or coal, and any and every law that proposes to prevent him from doing so is an infringment of his constitutional privileges; and consequently vicious and void.[68]

One other book, Christopher G. Tiedeman's *Limitations of Police Power,* also became a rich source of citations justifying judicial invalidation of state regulation. Gathering together the latest judicial precedents and emphasizing throughout the book the narrowness of police power, Tiedeman formalized the current state of laissez-faire constitutionalism. Astonishingly forthright, he denounced "government interference," as a "panacea for every social evil which threatens the prosperity of society." The conservative classes, he declared "now stand in constant fear of the advent of an absolutism more tyrannical and more unreasoning than any before experienced by man, the absolutism of a democratic majority . . . If the author succeeds in any measure in his attempt to awaken the public mind to a full appreciation of the power of constitutional limitations to protect private rights against the radical experimentations of social reformers, he will feel that he has been amply requited for his labors in the cause of social order and personal liberty."[69]

The threats to "social order" that punctuated the years between 1886 and 1896, from the Haymarket riot to the William Jennings Bryan election campaign, took many forms:

Widespread outbreaks of labor militancy, agrarian crusades for free silver, demands for progressive taxation of large incomes, and incessant agitation against the "trusts" troubled the times. An economic depression that began in 1893 intensified social protest, creating an atmosphere of class antagonism. The growth of Populism, the Coxey "armies," the Pullman strike, the enactment of a graduated income tax—all seemed to portend a serious challenge to prevailing economic relationships. American industrial capitalism, raw and not yet really respectable, was experiencing a major crisis.[70]

In this atmosphere of social tension, the leading cases establishing the new judicialism were widely discussed by lawyers and judges before bar associations, in articles in law journals, and in speeches at commencement exercises, a ferment from which two main streams of legal conservative thought emerged. One emphasized laissez faire, vehemently opposed activist legislatures, and drew comfort from the "antipaternalism doctrines" of the English philosopher Herbert Spencer. The other's brand of conservatism was more traditional in its association of the protection of private property with the maintenance of liberty in an ordered society. As in the days of John Adams and Alexander

Hamilton, conservative fears for the insecurity of both property and liberty mounted in a context of social unrest.[71]

Conservative thought also reflected a widespread fear and suspicion of labor unions, feelings that were especially acute among businessmen.

> Few businessmen objected in principle to labor unions so long as they functioned only as fraternal organizations or mutual-benefit societies; but most refused to engage in collective bargaining. They equated labor organizers with labor agitators, and thought that unions made workingmen inefficient, discontented, and unenterprising. They appreciated the advantages of combination and centralization for management, but would not concede that labor might also find combination attractive, and for essentially the same reasons.[72]

"Labor organizations," N. F. Thompson, secretary of the Southern Industrial Convention, told the Industrial Commission in 1900, "are today the greatest menace to this Government that exists . . . Their influence for disruption . . . is far more dangerous to the perpetuation of our Government in its purity and power than would be the hostile array on our borders of the army of the entire world combined."[73] Newspaper publisher Joseph Medill believed that the "chief cause of the impecunious condition of millions of the wage classes of this country is due to their own improvidence and misdirected efforts."[74] Perhaps, at best, workers might hope for the benign insensibility of a William H. Vanderbilt, the railroad magnate: "Our men feel that, although I . . . may have my millions and they the rewards of their daily toil, still we are about equal in the end. If they suffer, I suffer, and if I suffer they cannot escape."[75] Some men are easily consoled. Some require a Protestant Ethic, others the assurances provided by Social Darwinism, by the law of supply and demand, or by the iron law of wages, to rationalize their feelings of guilt, to justify man's ways to man. Still others, like Vanderbilt, did not require much in the way of rationalization because they had so little human compassion to begin with.

The era was hardly conducive to flourishing successes on the part of organized labor, and not least because of repeated recessions. Unions recruit members more easily and bargain with employers more successfully during the years of upturn in the business cycle, when full employment tightens labor markets and employers can pass on to consumers higher wage costs in the form of higher prices. But when employers cut wages and jobs, the sheer need for survival induces many union members to disregard union rules and to work for less than "scale," or to drop out of the union altogether, all but destroying the union's bargaining power. The marvel is that a few unions were able to organize nationally and endure. Most did not.[76]

During the Civil War the pinch of inflation, in combination with labor scarcity, proved hospitable to the formation of national unions. By 1873 they were to be found in construction, among skilled railroad workers (conductor, engineers, and firemen formed brotherhoods), among cigar makers, telegraphers, iron and steel workers (the Sons of Vulcan), and shoemakers. The latter, organized as the Knights of St. Crispin, made up the largest of these unions. In 1870 it claimed fifty thousand members, but by 1878 it was gone, a victim of the great depression of 1873–1879. Workers in the Pennsylvania coalfields traversed a similar path. By 1873 between fifty thousand and sixty thousand miners were enrolled in the Workingmen's Benevolent Association. Two years later the union waged a six-month strike to protest a wage cut. The effort met with complete defeat, and by 1876 membership in the Pennsylvania fields was down to almost nothing.[77]

One of the most interesting of the evanescent national unions was the Noble and Holy Order of the Knights of Labor. Originating in 1869 as an ordinary trade union of Philadelphia garment cutters, it became, under its founder Uriah S. Stephens, a secret order with an elaborate ritual. Believing trade unions "too narrow in their ideas and too circumscribed in their field of operation," Stephens advocated the amalgamation of all workers in one great brotherhood. His appeal met little response till the great railroad strike of 1877, after which many workers, finding the idea of a brotherhood of labor appealing, joined the Knights. By 1879 the union had 9,000 members, by 1882 more than 42,000, and by 1885 over 110,000.[78]

Thr success of the union's strike against one of Jay Gould's railroads in 1885 had a startling impact on membership. Gould was one of the most powerful business figures of the era and well despised, then and now, as a notorious robber baron. News of his agreement to recognize the union—although the wage cut which had sparked the strike remained in force—zoomed membership almost overnight to over 700,000. A second strike in the spring of 1886, this time against Gould's Southwestern system, had a different result, and by May it was crushed. The failure of this strike, even more than the general obloquy which undeservedly fell upon labor following the well-known affair that month in Haymarket Square—an incident in which the police were induced to fire on participants in a rally organized by the Knights after someone threw a bomb—marked the turning point in the Knight's history.[79]

Nevertheless, the union would probably have begun to crumble soon anyway because of the inability of its officers to control rank-and-file members and, more significantly, to explain to them the purposes of the organization. Terence V. Powderly, "part idealist, part politician, part mountebank," had replaced Stephens as head of the Knights in 1879, and although Powderly discarded "secrecy and mumbo-jumbo," he had no deeper understanding than Stephens of what steps might be taken to improve the lot of workingmen.[80] Deploring the "wage system"—and opposing collective bargaining and even strikes!—he paid little attention to the importance to workers of short-run gains in wages and hours, looking ahead, instead, to the achievement of the millennium through "cooperation." At the same time he and other leading Knights denounced "soulless" monopolies and declared that there was no mutuality of interests between capital and labor. Not least, his union was a chaotic mixture of unions of skilled craftsmen and of semiskilled and unskilled workers. The bargaining power of skilled workers was greater than that of the unskilled, and they had little to gain from a dilution of that power by the unskilled. And so in 1886 the craft unions withdrew from the Knights and formed the American Federation of Labor (AFL). By 1900 the Knights were all but dead.[81]

One of the Knights who withdrew was Samuel Gompers, a founder of the Cigar-makers' International Union. Elected the first president of the AFL, he served every year but one (1894) from 1886 till his death in 1924. As a professional union man, if not in his personal philosophy, Gompers believed in business unionism, in "pure and simple unionism," in concentrating on the bread-and butter issues—improvement in wages, hours, and working conditions.[82] (Once when asked what the goals of the federation were, he is said simply to have replied, "More.") Shunning vast and vague programs of social reform, he accepted the American economic system and concentrated his efforts on winning a bigger slice of the pie for his union. People would not go to bed one night, start a revolution in the morning, and the next day organize heaven on earth. Gompers declared: "We are solving the problem day after day. As we get an hour's more leisure every day it means millions of golden hours of opportunities to the human family. As we get 25 cents a day wages increase, it means another solution, another problem solved, and brings us nearer the time when a greater degree of justice and fair dealing will obtain among men."[83]

Adviser and reconciler rather than autocratic executive, Gompers displayed an exceptional ability in solving jurisdictional disputes between the craft unions that composed the AFL. He also secured the formation of several new national unions in the 1890s, among them the Electrical Workers, the Building Laborers, the Teamsters, and the Musicians. Constantly urging the craft unions to recruit as many workers as possible in their trades, he gradually built up the membership of the organization.[84] The number rose slowly at first and then much more rapidly during the years of rising prices and prosperity after the depression of 1893–1897. By 1898 the original 140,000 members had doubled, and by 1904 they numbered 1,676,000. On the eve of World War I the AFL boasted 2,020,000 members.[85]

Even so, not even 8 percent of the American labor force was unionized at any time before 1914.[86] The ethnic heterogeneity of the urban workforce militated against labor unity. Indeed, to a large extent occupation was determined by national origins:

The most highly skilled workers—railroad engineers and printers for instance—tend to be predominantly American-born. The older immigrants,
Irish and German, dominated the building trades, and the Germans were well
established in cigar-making, brewing, and furniture work. The lake seamen
of Chicago were Scandinavian, the apartment janitors Flemish . . . The
Czechs, the Poles, and the Italians also crowded into the big cities and were
available for all types of unskilled work. Because they found it difficult to
communicate with earlier immigrants or with the native Americans, they
could readily be used as strikebreakers.

Although feelings of class solidarity permitted urban workers to unite for a
brief period, ethnic rivalries soon reasserted themselves.[87]

Labor's failure to profit to the extent it might have from the gains in productivity made possible by technological innovation can thus be ascribed variously to divisions in its own ranks, to the discordant tongues in which it
defined its objectives, to employer hostility to unions—as evidenced by the
use of spies, blacklists, Pinkerton detectives, strikebreakers, lockouts, and yellow-dog contracts—and to an unsympathetic legal system undoubtedly re-
flective of the values of articulate public opinion. Some of the men who helped
shape that opinion believed that many unions were dominated by foreign
influences and were a threat to "the American system." They were right about
the foreigners, but wrong about the nature of their impact.

It is true that voices were to be heard in advocacy of social revolution, of
the abolition of capitalism, but these voices were few, and in the main they
arose from the anarchistic or other fringes of the labor movement.[88] The
dominant tone was that of moderation, largely because of the leadership role
in union affairs played by immigrants from Europe, especially from the British
Isles. Many American workers and almost all their leaders fell under the influence of British and Irish ideas and men who had been active before their
migration to America in older labor movements abroad. "In key American
industries, crafts and shops they won positions of leadership; in mines and
factories throughout the country they organized new unions and new cooperatives, or revitalized and resuscitated old ones. Every major union or cooperative order from 1860 to the mid-nineties felt their impact and in each of
them they pioneered numerous advances."[89]

Borrowing extensively from these pioneers, American labor leaders focused
on techniques of "arbitration, conciliation, collective bargaining, centralized
union structure and finance, benefit and welfare programs, profit sharing,
industrial partnerships, various co-operative schemes, a vast range of socioeconomic legislation, legal precedents and statistical information." The "most
prominent feature of British influence," a modern historian concludes, "was
its moderation, its pacific reflexes in the face of opposition or obstacles." Many

of the British labor leaders "thundered against the multiple demons that beset workingmen and raised a terrible din, yet their actual tactics and methods, as distinct from the sound and fury, were pragmatic, and often designed to get back to harmonious relationships with capital."[90]

Evidence of labor's unrest and discontent is plentiful. Workingmen struck again and again for higher wages, reduced hours, improved working conditions, or, sometimes, the right to organize. From 1886 to the end of the century there is only one year in which the number of strikes fell below one thousand, and in several of these years the number was close to two thousand. An annual average of over 380,000 workers took part in them.[91]

All historical events must be placed in their setting. These were years of technological revolution in which there occurred a significant deskilling of ancient crafts, years of intense, bitter, and cutthroat price competition among producers for market share—with wages a favored target for cost reductions[92]— years when the manufacturing labor force, swollen by immigrants, groped in the dim light of an early industrial morning to find its way, to articulate its goals. Despite the bleakness often encountered in the workplace, despite the din, the upheaval, and the pain and suffering often attendant upon strikes and lockouts, the American story also requires us to tell that the tactics and methods of labor leaders were "often designed to get back to harmonious relationships with capital." This period was not the last in which this would be true.

13

Mostly Foreign Affairs

It cannot be said that the foreign trade of the United States provided much of a stimulus to the nation's economic development in the second half of the nineteenth century. Unlike Britain, which looked to outside sources for much of its wheat after the repeal of the Corn Laws in 1846, or France, which had to import the fuel needed to run its factories, the United States, under the technological conditions of the later nineteenth and most of the twentieth century, enjoyed a remarkably high degree of self-sufficiency in foodstuffs, energy sources, and industrial raw materials. The technological caveat is an important one. Resource needs, indeed resources themselves, change over time as technological development redefines them. The precolonial American Indians had no knowledge of coal, limestone, and iron ore—the stuff of steel, symbol of the first Industrial Revolution. Nor, needless to say, did nineteenth-century Americans value the sources of atomic energy. In the absence of conscious need and of knowledge, a nation's physical resources are only potential.

Where resource needs do exist, they may be fulfilled with supplies at hand, traded for, or substituted for; or they may be done without. The possibilities of trade, it is often said, are determined by differences in climate and geography. But this view is incomplete, for it ignores the effects of changes in a nation's factor proportions on its comparative advantage. The latter is redefined again and again as technology affects the mix of land, labor, and capital and opens up new areas of specialization in production and exchange. Nor is this all, for it is really comparative costs which matter. And differences in costs—between Britain and the United States, for example—depend not only on technology but also on entrepreneurship, economies of scale, and other considerations. These issues are not explored here. It is enough to recall the observation that even a Caribbean island which grows nothing for export but bananas may be enabled by modern transportation to export its climate and scenery in winter in the form of a tourist industry. It will then put less of its resources into bananas and more into hotels. In the end it may prove to its comparative advantage to pay its local labor force to work in hotels, and to import bananas from some less fortunate island.[1]

In fact, there is little trade between less-developed islands—or countries. The overwhelming majority of trading transactions, today as well as in the nineteenth century, emanates from the developed economies. Indeed, it is the richest, industrialized countries which are the most dynamic markets for manufactured goods, the demand for which, because of their endless variety, is not subject to the law of diminishing marginal utility. In part because of industrial development in western Europe, the United States, and Japan, but also because of lowered freight rates, improved handling and loading methods for grain, and the use of refrigerated ships for meat, the volume of world trade expanded to unprecedented proportions in the nineteenth century. The American share of that trade increased from roughly 6 percent in 1867–68 to 11 percent in 1913. But while most of the major industrial powers exported substantially increasing proportions of their industrial production, the United States did not. From 1879 to 1914 the American ratio varied between 4.5 percent and 6.6 percent and displayed no overall trend. And this, during a period when the American share of world manufacturing output was advancing from 23.3 percent in 1870 to 35.8 percent in 1913![2]

Despite the small percentage of manufactured output exported, however, so great was the growth in the industrial sector that the real value of those exports rose from an annual average of $664 million in the half-decade ending with 1880 to $2,131 million in the five years before the First World War. In other words, enough manufactured output was exported to justify the statement that the United States had replaced Great Britain as the "workshop of the world" by the eve of the war. This was the more true in view of the doubling of the percentage exported between 1879 and 1914 of major industrial groups such as machinery and iron and steel products. Contemplating American-made sewing machines, reapers, typewriters, cash registers, shoe machinery, pumps, telephone apparatus, electrical machinery, film, and other products, Europeans began talking about an "American invasion." "The invasion," as one Englishman put it, "goes on unceasingly and without noise or show in five hundred industries at once. From shaving soap to electric motors, and from shirt waists to telephones, the American is clearing the field."[3]

But the main field of invasion was not Europe but the markets of the continental United States itself. Americans exported a smaller proportion of their manufactured products than other nations did because the size and diversity of the country's resources opened up far more extensive opportunities for internal specialization and exchange than were available elsewhere. The same considerations governed the distribution of the bulk of the country's agricultural commodities. Altogether, the value of all United States exports averaged only about 6 percent of the gross national product (GNP) from the 1830s till the end of the century, gradually declining after that to 4 percent in the 1960s. It had not always been thus. In the colonial period the export proportion of GNP was much higher—perhaps 20 to 30 percent between 1710 and 1720, and 10 to 15 percent between 1790 and 1800. So far as manufactures were concerned, it took time for population and incomes to grow sufficiently and for transport improvements to enlarge markets geographically, so that manufacturing could be conducted on a scale large enough to permit reductions in cost and price that would enable American-made goods to compete with imports.[4]

The growth of domestic demand for agricultural commodities posed other kinds of problems. That growth depended not only on rising output in the nonagricultural sector of the economy and on the employment and incomes generated by that output. It also depended on a rate of increase in industrial output sufficiently great to offset the extremely rapid rate of growth of agricultural production. In the years between the end of the Civil War and 1896 the rate of industrial growth proved insufficient—mainly because of the vast increase in the size of the agricultural domain during these years, in combination with the capital-deepening process in which industry was engaged— and foreign demand helped take up the slack. About 20 percent of agricultural output went abroad in the form of crude foodstuffs during the period 1870–1900. Wheat, flour, and meat products were increasingly important agricultural exports, although cotton continued, as before the Civil War, to dominate the export stream.[5]

Viewed in the round, the main changes in export categories over the nineteenth century were the relative decline of crude foodstuffs and other raw materials—which made up three-fifths of American exports in the 1870s— and the rise of finished manufactures, changes which reflected the progressive industrialization of the economy (see Table 36).914 the share of raw materials in exports was half its earlier size and the share in imports sharply higher. A pronounced shift also occurred in the nature of manufactured exports. On average, manufactured foods, which accounted for 24 percent of exports during the fiscal years 1876–1880, declined to 14 percent during 1909–1914. In the same intervals finished manufactures and semimanufactured goods rose from 20 percent to 47 percent.[6]

The currents of nineteenth-century American trade flowed mainly to and from Europe, especially Britain and Germany. Nevertheless, trade with Canada, Latin America, and Asia increased steadily before the First World War. Within the Americas, Canada was the largest export market and Cuba the main source of imports, although after 1900 imports from Canada, Brazil and Mexico became increasingly important. By the 1920s total inter-American trade accounted for nearly 40 percent of overall U.S. imports and nearly a third of exports. Meanwhile, trade with Asia, especially Japan, expanded strongly.

The vessels carrying this trade were for the most part chartered ships of foreign registry, a resort to which shippers were driven by the high cost of building and operating American ships. The participation of American flag

Table 36.   Exports and imports of American merchandise, 1860–1920
            (percentages).

Year	Crude materials	Crude foodstuffs	Manufactured food	Semi-manufactured goods	Finished manufactures
			Exports		
1860	68.7	3.8	12.3	4.1	11.4
1870	56.8	11.1	13.5	3.7	14.9
1880	29.5	31.6	23.4	3.5	11.3
1890	36.6	15.6	26.6	5.4	15.7
1900	24.8	16.5	23.3	11.2	24.2
1910	33.6	6.4	15.1	15.7	29.2
1914	34.3	5.9	12.6	16.1	31.1
1920	23.3	11.4	13.8	11.9	39.7
			Imports		
1860	11.3	13.0	16.9	9.9	48.6
1870	13.1	12.4	22.0	12.8	39.9
1880	21.3	15.0	17.7	16.6	29.5
1890	22.8	16.2	16.9	14.8	29.3
1900	33.2	11.5	15.6	15.8	23.9
1910	37.1	9.3	11.7	18.3	23.6
1914	34.3	13.1	12.0	16.8	23.7
1920	33.8	11.0	23.5	15.2	16.6

Source: Bureau of the Census, *Historical Statistics of the United States, Colonial Times to 1970*
(Washington, D.C.: Government Printing Office, 1976), II, 889–890.

vessels in the foreign carrying trades of the country, measured by the value of cargoes carried, fell steadily from 36 percent in 1870, to 17 percent in 1880, 13 percent in 1890, and 9 percent in 1900. The figure stood at 10 percent in 1914. Measured in gross tonnage, the participation declined from 38 percent in 1870 to 26 percent in 1914. In the early nineteenth century the freights earned by American vessels were a significant element in the balance of payments, but their contribution to the costs of imported goods and services obviously declined over time.[7]

Nor was the contribution made by merchandise exports sufficient to close the gap. In all the years from the beginning of American independence to the final quarter of the nineteenth century, merchandise exports did not exceed imports in value a half-dozen times. Americans were able to make up the difference through the earnings of the merchant marine, foreign exchange brought in by immigrants, and borrowing abroad, sources of income which also permitted them to pay interest and dividends on foreign investments and to finance remittances to the relatives of immigrants and the expenditures of Americans traveling in foreign countries. Shipments of gold (every year between 1862 and 1876) also helped finance the trade deficit. In essence, a developing American economy was able by these means to consume more capital goods and consumer goods than it produced.[8]

Between 1874 and the outbreak of the First World War, however, exports of goods exceeded imports in every year but three, indeed, far more so after 1898. Behind this change in trend were productivity advances in manufacturing which, by lowering prices of American goods below those obtaining abroad, made them attractive to foreigners while at the same time discouraging relatively more expensive imports. Export earnings, together with a rising tide of foreign loans, and investments in American railroads, cattle, mines, and bonanza farms provided sufficient foreign exchange to cover heavy immigrant remittances, shipping charges, and interest and dividend payments. In the late 1880s and early 1890s the trade surplus weakened temporarily, and large payments of interest and dividends on foreign loans resulted in heavy shipments of gold, especially in the four years 1892–1895. After 1895, however, the balance on current account moved into a long-term surplus position, and with the outbreak of the First World War the United States became for the first time in its history a creditor on long term. The world's preeminent industrial power was now capital rich, and during most of the time since then the United States has been more often a lender than a borrower overseas.[9]

The statistical record of long-term foreign investment by Americans, though woefully incomplete, indicates a 350 percent increase from $700 million to $2.5 billion in the brief period from 1897 to 1908, and a further leap to $3.5 billion by mid-1914. About three-fourths of this sum represented direct rather than portfolio investment, ownership by Americans not of stocks and bonds but rather of mines, plantations, factories, assembly plants, and other physical properties. They were acquired to improve access to raw materials or to enable American business to operate behind tariff walls erected abroad—partly in response to increasingly protective legislation enacted by a Congress controlled, during most of the years between the Civil War and 1912, by the Republican party. (The Dingley Tariff Act of 1897 imposed the second highest average rate of dutiable goods in American history—52 percent.) Singer sewing machines, McCormick reapers, and Kodak cameras were being manufactured or assembled in Great Britain and elsewhere in the 1880s. The first automobile factories built abroad by U.S. companies or their affiliates were located in Canada. By 1914 Ford Model T assembly plants were also located in England, France, and Argentina. Three years earlier International Harvester had five foreign plants, in Canada, Sweden, France, Germany, and Russia.[10]

Manufacturers were by no means the only representatives of American economic interests in foreign lands. By the beginning of the 1890s Standard Oil, having won a dominant position in foreign markets for its exports, was pushed by competitive pressures to extend its marketing investments as well as its products beyond the national borders. It did so by establishing foreign subsidiaries in Great Britain and Germany and building refineries in Mexico and Cuba. The "Big Three" in American insurance—Equitable, New York Life, and Mutual—were making direct investments in lots and buildings abroad somewhat earlier, in the seventies and eighties. By 1880 New York Life was selling insurance in Canada, England, France, Germany, Scotland, the West Indies, Mexico, British Guiana, Belgium, Venezuela, Russia, Ireland, Switzerland, Italy, and Austria, and in the next decade it added forty more countries to its list—from China to Peru, from South Africa to Australia. Nearly a third of its business was being done outside the United States and Canada. In sum, imaginative entrepreneurs first developed sales organizations covering the national market of the United States and then pushed their products, skills, patents, machinery, and knowledge abroad. In the process their firms became giant multinational concerns.[11]

By the late nineties many American businessmen had become exuberant, brimming with a self-confidence that bordered upon the extravagant. The chairman of the American Steel and Wire Company declared that mergers had taken place in his industry because its organizers "wished to be the wire manufacturers of the world." Sherwin-Williams paints, the slogan ran, "Cover the Earth." "The World," announced the president of the New York Central Railroad, Chauncey Depew, "is ours." But these were sales pitches, expressions of the bravado of market men intent on boosting volume and profits. Are they also evidence of support on the part of the business community for American imperialist ventures at the turn of the century, for the annexation of the Hawaiian Islands and, after a short war with Spain, the taking of Puerto Rico and the Philippines—followed by the acquisition of Guam and part of the Samoan archipelago?[12]

Let us be more specific. Did the Industrial Revolution, as some writers have charged, result in the production of surpluses and generate depressions, violence, and a growing radical literature? And did these developments in turn induce business interests to put pressure on the government to solve the dilemmas by foreign expansion, by going to war with Spain in 1898 for the purpose of obtaining markets in Asia to relieve the glut of goods, and by acquiring Hawaii as a naval base and coaling station essential as support for a dominant American position in the Far East?[13] Editorial trends in the religious as well as business press did run distinctly in the direction of approval of foreign expansion, and these trends were undoubtedly observed by politicians in Washington. However, the trends set in after, rather than before, Admiral George Dewey's victory in Manila Bay. Before that event the business press either opposed the acquisition of new territory or, more often, simply said nothing about the subject. Indeed, both in the business press and elsewhere there is mention of the extent to which businessmen were noncommittal. On August 29, 1898, the *New York Journal of Commerce,* for example, commented regretfully on the "deathlike silence" of most of the business community.[14]

Businessmen had no need, no economic motive, for promoting political control of foreign markets. Trade did not follow the flag. The most important markets by far for American manufactures were developed, industrial countries, not the underdeveloped areas of imperialist interest with their low per capita incomes. Commentary on the "invasion" of their markets by products of American manufacturing came from Europe, especially from Great Britain, original home of the Industrial Revolution.

Nor had businessmen any reason to favor political control of outlying regions in order to augment and safeguard investment outlets. The overwhelming majority of their investments both before and after the dawn of the imperialist era were in developed countries. The dollars that trickled into the newly acquired territories of both the European and American empires largely financed political and military objectives rather than economic ones. Investments in developed countries were made for reasons much akin to those governing domestic investment. Those made in sales operations, for example, had as their objective broadened markets, improved control over distribution, and competitive advantage. Those in finishing, assembling, and manufacturing plants saved on transportation costs and warehousing expenses. In addition, they made it possible to obtain superior customer service, to avoid shipping damage on perishable products—and to take advantage of production costs that were lower abroad than at home. According to one authority, "no basic decision on whether or not to invest involved any action by the United States government."[15]

The forces behind American imperialism were essentially noneconomic in nature—Protestant missionary zeal to convert the heathen, racist nonsense about the "White Man's Burden," Social Darwinist notions about the survival of the fittest, prideful nationalist desire to export American democratic institutions, and still other elements, including economic ones, all poured together and mixed well with Turnerian ruminations on the significance of a closed domestic frontier and Mahanist researches into the influence of sea power on history. To which one need add only an image of Uncle Sam, rather suddenly aware that he was now a young adult, tall, self-confident, strong, and proud—except for the embarrassment of noticing that he was still in short pants. While it is always possible for someone to profit from almost any kind of foreign venture by the government, to ascribe the venture to economic interest is to emphasize a small and probably trivial part of the spectrum of motives.[16]

The results were no less trivial. In the first place, investments made by Americans abroad between 1869 and 1897 were a mere 1 percent of their total investments, domestic and foreign, during those years, a percentage which rose to 6 percent between 1900 and 1929. The latter increase, in United States foreign investment all over the globe, was smaller than the increased investment in California alone. Its impact on the rate of return of U.S. capital was to raise it from a little over 4.8 percent to a little under 4.9 percent. If profit from foreign investment played the role of prop for a sagging capitalism, as Marxists allege, it was a bit part in a theater off-off-Broadway.[17]

Does this mean that the American government was unconcerned about the property interests of Americans in foreign places? Certainly not. At least till the Wilson administration the United States government clearly sought to assist American business abroad. Unlike Woodrow Wilson, who took the position that American dollars invested in turbulent countries must take the chances inseparable from such conditions, President William Howard Taft declared in 1909 that his administration was "lending all proper support to legitimate and beneficial American enterprise in foreign countries." He added that the Department of State was being reorganized to "make it a thoroughly efficient instrument in the furtherance of foreign trade and of American interest abroad." Presidents were not lacking in political support for such actions. The enthusiastic politicians who nudged America into war with Spain, forced from the British the cancellation of the Clayton-Bulwer Treaty, and made plans for the Panama Canal hailed the expansion of American companies abroad. They saw the acquisition of Hawaii as a great spring for business and, along with many businessmen, viewed the conquest of the Philippines as a stepping stone to trade with the Far East. Secretary of State John Hay's Open Door notes of 1899—his insistence on equality of commercial opportunities and his dictum that China was neither to be partitioned nor divided into spheres of influence by Europeans or Japanese—were part of the same vibrant, expansive mood.[18]

Nor were American businessmen innocents abroad. As a community in the large they may have opposed or been indifferent to prospects of enlarging the sphere of American dominion before the war with Spain, but this does not mean that individual economic units such as the Standard Oil Company of New Jersey or the United Fruit Company were indifferent to the potential uses of political, military, and financial methods of promoting their interests. The ownership of foreign assets has always been more heavily concentrated than the ownership of domestic assets, a condition flowing from the fact that the largest U.S. corporations and individual fortunes are disproportionately invested abroad. This concentration enhances the ability of those investors to advance their interests. Hundreds of instances might be cited in which American military or naval forces were employed in defense of American investment bankers or corporate interests in Central America and the Caribbean, for example, in Guatemala, Cuba, Nicaragua, and the Dominican Republic. In the last country alone United States marines landed approximately thirty times from 1902 to 1916. Sometimes governments were overthrown with American aid, as, for example, the José Santos Zelaya government in Nicaragua in 1909. At other times governments were propped up. The flotation of foreign bonds in the New York market during and after the 1890s gave investment bankers a material interest in the continuation of foreign regimes that were the most generous issuers of debt.[19]

Sometimes American firms and governments worked at cross-purposes. Concerned with the threat to American lives, and to investments of approximately $1 billion in Mexico, President Taft in 1911 dispatched American troops to the border and took other actions designed to bolster the crumbling Porfirio Díaz regime. The interests of Standard Oil, however, lay in oil concessions which the company hoped to obtain from Francisco Madero, leader of the revolutionary junta, in the event of his success in overthrowing the Díaz government. Although it cannot be proved that Standard paid money to Madero's people, an examination of recently available documents in the State Department Archives discloses that an "offer of between $500,000 to $1,000,000 by 'representatives' of the Standard Oil Company to the Madero insurrectos was certainly made." Five weeks later Díaz resigned, and in the fall of 1911 Madero was elected president. In the sequel, he served only two years before being himself overthrown and murdered by General Victoriano Huerta (who succeeded him as head of the government) and a nephew of Díaz, a duo whose coup had been encouraged, although to an extent that has not been determined, by the American ambassador to Mexico, Henry Lane Wilson. American foreign policy in Mexico between 1911 and 1913, resting as it did on the conviction that the protection of American lives and property required the restoration of order and stability by a strong military figure, was responsible for these events.[20]

Not all instances of foreign interference by the government are ascribable to concern for the lives and property interests of Americans. President Woodrow Wilson rejected "dollar diplomacy" and substituted for it what his biographer has called missionary diplomacy, a policy of strengthening forces of constitutional government and democracy abroad. His diplomacy succeeded when all that was required of the president was an order to occupy some small republic and to establish a puppet government. It failed miserably in Mexico. At the end of the Wilson administration the United States had hardly a friend in that country. Evidently, foreign meddling is not ennobled by the non-property-interest objectives that set it in motion.[21]

Meddling aside, sovereign governments have generally sought to protect the lives and property of their citizens by rules of law at home, by diplomacy and war abroad. When American lives and property on the high seas were threatened during the Napoleonic wars of the early nineteenth century, President Thomas Jefferson successfully urged upon Congress passage of the Embargo Act (1807), a self-denying ordinance requiring that American shipowners keep their vessels and goods in the safety of their home ports to avoid foreign entanglements that might lead to war. One hundred and ten years later another American president sought to protect American lives and commercial property on the high seas from the devastation of unrestricted submarine warfare by adopting a policy of armed neutrality. The policy proved ineffectual, and in April 1917 President Wilson reluctantly asked Congress for a declaration of war against Germany. What differentiated the two situations, above all, was the economic strength and potential military and naval power at the disposal of the twentieth-century president after five generations of growth in population, wealth, and technological knowledge. In the time of Wilson but not that of Jefferson, the United States was a great power, one that could not submit to what appeared to Wilson and his contemporaries a flagrant assault by Germany on American sovereignty. Submission would have entailed loss of honor and destruction of American influence for constructive work in the world.[22]

Although antiwar sentiment in the country was very wide and deep in 1917, American farmers, shipping interests, industrialists, and investment bankers had been benefiting since near the outbreak of the war in July 1914 from floods of Allied orders for wheat, flour, meat, and munitions and from the need for loans to help finance the imports. During the approximately three years of United States neutrality, American exports to the Allies exceeded imports by a total of no less than $5.3 billion—over $1 billion of this amount representing shipments of munitions in 1916 alone. Besides borrowing about $2.5 billion in United States financial markets, the Allies sold off $1.4 billion in American securities and shipped more than $1 billion in gold to pay for these supplies. Citizens of Allied countries also reduced by $0.5 billion short-term loans to the United States.[23]

By 1917, therefore, the American economy was geared up for an even more effective participation in the war. Steps to expand the army and navy had been taken in 1916 and a Council of National Defense created to advise the president on all aspects of industrial mobilization. The council, composed of six cabinet officials, received technical advice from an advisory commission of seven industrial experts. Its assignment was formidable: to conduct a survey of the resources available to the nation and to recommend plans for their mobilization in time of need.[24]

Formally organized in December 1916, the council did not actively function till the following March, a scant month before the declaration of war. When it did become active, it was the business representatives on the advisory commission rather than the cabinet officials on the council who took the lead in mobilizing the economy. Dividing itself into committees on transportation, raw materials, munitions, manufacturing, and general supplies, the commission then set up over one hundred "cooperative committees," groups of businessmen representing the major firms in various industries, among others, iron and steel, aluminum and brass, copper, lumber, oil, and rubber. These dollar-a-year men helped the commission gather information on the capacity of essential industries, on means for curtailing production for civilian uses, and on rudimentary price, priority, and other controls.[25]

The advisory commission made significant headway in planning for military and civilian supply needs, but as a purely advisory body it could do nothing to affect the distribution or order of precedence in which contracts let by the army, navy, and other claimant agencies were awarded to producers. Lacking was a system for channeling the forces of demand, particularly one capable of controlling the procurement activities of eight uncoordinated bureaus of the army, which led to costly competitive buying, conflict of orders, congestion of purchases, and waste of transport facilities. The economic impact of that department's antiquated supply system was enormous, for between April 1916 and June 1919 the army alone spent nearly half of the $32 billion estimated to have been the cost of the war. After floundering for nearly a year, the Council of National Defense in July 1917 replaced the advisory commission and its structures with the War Industries Board (WIB). The result was that the federal government at last had a centralized organization to control industry. Nevertheless, the WIB was itself to remain an advisory body till May 1918, when President Wilson finally responded to continued chaos in mobilizing the nation's resources by separating the board from the council and placing it directly under himself.[26]

Between August and December 1918 the WIB in turn replaced the cooperative committees with war service committees elected by trade associations or, in industries in which these had not yet been organized, with groups formed with the aid of the United States Chamber of Commerce. The war years thus saw the beginning of the modern trade association movement. Ultimately, over three hundred war service committees were formed, their function being that of advising some fifty-seven so-called commodity committees into which the WIB was subdivided. This commodity committee–war service committee system served as the nerve center and major source of policy for the WIB. Both were representative of the entire spectrum of American industry. Although the chairman of the WIB, as "supreme interpreter of the national good," might veto specific proposals emanating from the committees, it was industry itself that was the source not only of the laws and regulations required by the emergency but also of the sanctions necessary for the enforcement of most of them.[27]

The most important of these regulations was the priority system. Operating on both military and civilian needs for industrial products and transportation, projected as well as current, the WIB managed to set orders of precedence without statutory authority or punitive supports. Although the board sometimes found it necessary to resort to disciplinary measures, its official historian maintained that "almost without exception the announcement of an intention to resort to stern measures was sufficient, not only for the individual case, but for its class." He tells of an instance in which a prominent automobile manufacturer refused to comply with a request from the board that he limit his production—until the chairman of the board threatened to commandeer his coal supplies. A similar threat to commandeer some lumber mills brought their owner into line.[28]

While the WIB served as the general manager of American industry, it was

itself a slender organization dependent on the cooperation of several independent government agencies. The wartime activities of these agencies, together
with those of the WIB, made for a remarkably high degree of governmental
regulation of private business enterprises, far more so than at any previous
time in American history.

> The War Industries Board mobilized production; the War Trade Board li-
> censed imports and exports; the Capital Issues Committee regulated invest-
> ment; the War Finance Corporation lent funds to munitions industries; the
> Railroad Administration unified the nation's railways; the Fuel Administra-
> tion fixed the price of coal and imposed "coal holidays" on eastern industry;
> and the Food Administration controlled the production and consumption of
> food.[29]

The nation's experience in World War I was an important precursor of the
New Deal's involvement in the economy of the 1930s. Despite the breadth
and depth of the government's interposition, however, the business of the
administrative state was not conducted by the kind of bureaucracy which
characterized the New Deal and later years. In World War I bureaucracy was
emergent rather than fully developed. Previous peacetime activities of government had been too few to warrant one, so that there was no choice but to look
to the private sector when war came. Unsurprisingly, the individuals and
private groups recruited for the emergency failed to act like bureaucrats. They
relied on "informal, personal agreements among men of good will, among
whom the gentlemen's code carried more weight than the administrative sanctions of the state." President Wilson's appointee as chairman of the WIB,
Bernard Baruch, exemplifies these practices. A high-minded former businessman with a keen sense of public responsibility, Baruch preferred voluntary
cooperation to political coercion. Refusing to play the part of dictator, he
acted on his settled conviction that businessmen both inside and outside the
board were trustworthy and competent to direct industrial mobilization and
he did not withhold from them full participation in decision making.[30]

The exigencies of war underscored the importance to the nation of the
managerial expertise and productive capacity of major business corporations.
The same exigencies also favored not only the growth of trade associations
but business consolidation as well. Indeed, between 1915 and 1920 there took
place the second great merger movement to occur between 1895 and 1920.
The number of firms disappearing in mergers in 1917 reached a level not
exceeded since 1905. Whereas agencies like WIB provided an institutional
environment favorable to consolidation, rising prices and demand for industrial and military goods provided the necessary economic incentives.[31]

Wartime economic incentives and opportunities affected other sectors of
the American economy as well, especially the workers. Labor was scarce from
the beginning of the war. By the time the United States entered the war in

1917, labor and the other economic resources of the country were virtually fully employed, not least because of the flood of Allied orders for food, munitions, and other supplies during the preceding three years. American participation in the war increased the scarcity of workers, not only because of the drying up of immigration but also because of the induction of nearly 3 million young men into the armed services. Partial compensation for these losses would have been possible by installing improved machines in newly built or expanded manufacturing facilities, and also by adopting work processes capable of raising the productivity of the labor force. The WIB made a contribution to this end by encouraging a more efficient use of available resources and by standardizing products and reducing the number of product designs, not only for the weapons of war but also for a number of civilian products, ranging from baby carriages to coffins.

The contribution of technological innovation, however, was insufficient. There was little alternative, therefore, but to look to increased numbers of workers rather than to growth in output per worker, and to shifts within the labor force from employments of low wartime priority to higher ones. Governmental publicity and policies exempting skilled workers from the draft played a part in the achievement of both objectives, but it is difficult to avoid the conclusion that the market price of labor deserves most of the credit. Annual earnings of full-time employees in agriculture rose every year between 1914 and 1920, from $234 to $528. In manufacturing the record was nearly as consistent—only 1915 shows a dip from the earnings of a previous year—and the earnings were much higher, $696 in 1914 and $1,532 in 1920. Living expenses in the cities where manufacturing employment was concentrated were certainly higher than they were down on the farm—the consumer price index rises rapidly during the war years and doubles between 1914 and 1920—but what counts here is the power of higher wages to attract people from one area of employment to another or from nonwage employment, for example, as a housewife, into the labor force. That power was sufficiently great to induce an important rise in the size of the industrial labor force through the migration of blacks from the South to the North. The employment of women also increased during the war years, but not by much. Rather than going to work in larger numbers, women tended to shift from low- to higher-paying jobs.[32]

In 1919 the total size of the labor force was larger by 1,675,000 persons than it had been in 1914, an interval in which nonfarm employment rose by 3,316,000 and farm employment fell by 447,000. Precisely comparable figures showing the contribution of blacks to nonfarm employment in the North are not available. We do know that the first wave of black migration from the South started in 1916 and that by 1920 the northern black population was 515,000 larger than it had been in 1910. In part, "pushing" factors were behind this movement, for during the war years the ravages of the boll weevil in the cotton crop increased, reaching their height in 1920–21 and bringing heavy reductions in yield per acre. But the main explanation for the great exodus is provided by the increased demand for industrial labor brought about by the war. In consequence, material levels of living rose for blacks not only in the North but also in the South, where the drain to the North led to a decline of the rural population and created a serious labor shortage that led not only to higher wages but also to a general formation of interracial committees to promote more harmonious relations and improved living conditions for southern blacks—including better schools and hospitals and more efficient police protection.[33]

Working opportunities for women in manufacturing also increased during the war. In any one year the maximum increase amounted to 100,000, but except for the year 1988, additions were far fewer than that. Growth in the employment of women in manufacturing did not signify a comparable rise in the total number of women at work. Some of the manufacturing employees merely moved into factories from prior jobs in domestic service, trade, and other industries. The federal census for 1920 shows an increase over 1910 of only 6.3 percent in working females ten years old or over. In contrast, in World War II the rate of increase over the immediate prewar employment level was 50 percent.[34]

One important shift in employment saw white women moving from domestic service, textile mills, and clothing shops into war-related work in iron and steel, metal, chemical, lumber, glass, and leather factories. As they did so, black women filled the vacancies left in domestic, industrial, and clerical jobs. "In a seesaw manner, the number of black female domestics in northern cities went up as the number of white female servants went down." Some black women, however, obtained employment in the tobacco and food-processing industries. Their best jobs, in terms of wages and opportunities for advancement, lay in the garment trades, government arsenals, and the railroad industry. About five thousand black women obtained wartime jobs with the U.S. government as typists, stenographers, bookkeepers, and filing clerks, while another five hundred were trained as billing and addressograph operators or packing and shipping clerks. In general, however, racial prejudice had a deleterious impact on opportunities to develop skills, and because lack of skills closed off to black women many kinds of jobs open to white women, they remained concentrated in the types of jobs traditional to women. Another shift in wartime employment took white women from their jobs as waitresses, clerks, telephone operators, domestic servants, and machine tenders to positions in the transportation industry, where they served as streetcar conductors or as ticket and station agents. Still others moved out of clerical jobs in stores and businesses to similar ones in the railroad industry or in government. In general, movement from one sector of the economy to another could be effected with relative ease because highly routinized skills in factories, offices, and retail stores could be quickly mastered. According to one detailed survey of wartime production made by the government, "women comprised 20 percent or more of all workers manufacturing electrical machinery, airplanes (including seaplanes), optical goods, motion picture and photographic equipment, musical instruments, leather and rubber goods, dental supplies, and food, as well as paper, paper goods, and printed materials."[35]

Women's contribution to the American war effort was a highly important one, but its postwar aftermath left them with little to cheer about. Two patterns emerged. In industries such as tobacco and food processing, where jobs had been slowly but steadily opening for women, the trend continued during the war decade, sometimes with a temporary rise. But when hostilities ended, the numbers of women declined, leaving the gain that might have been predicted in any event. On the other hand, in those industries where women had been losing ground before the war, as in chemical and electrical goods, a pattern of temporary wartime employment developed, only to be followed by the reestablishment of male dominance. "In sum, the emergency expansion of industrial production, and the momentary absence of men, did not alter patterns of employment in manufacturing beyond the war years. With few exceptions, jobs returned to male control when the conflict ended."[36]

It was different though in those sectors of the economy that were expanding in response to the country's growing prominence in international trade and finance, to the needs of corporate sales and advertising programs, and to the spread of telephonic communications. Legions of women found jobs as telephone and telegraph operators and as saleswomen, buyers, designers, decorators, copywriters, clerks, and stenographers. Accelerated gains made by women in these white-collar areas during the war persisted after the war, so that by 1920 a larger percentage of employed women was to be found in the service sector (25.6 percent) than in manufacturing (23.8 percent), domestic service (18.2 percent), or agriculture (12.9 percent). In sum, expanding peacetime opportunities for female employment outside the home owed far more to underlying long-term economic and business changes than they did to the temporary aberration of war.[37]

Nevertheless, women wage earners fared well during the war, as did their male counterparts. All available evidence suggests that increases in the money wages of most workers surpassed a steep rise in the cost of living. This did not happen because men and women were working harder and longer. In fact, productivity per worker went down in both agriculture and manufacturing. Two things enabled people to earn more. One was the tight labor market. The other was governmental support of unions by the National War Labor Board, which President Wilson created in April 1918. In return, labor agreed not to strike, and on the whole it kept its promise. By 1920 the unions, mainly the craft unions of the AFL, had twice as many members as in 1910, and over 12 percent of the labor force belonged to them.[38]

Encouraged to rise, wages encountered few if any obstacles on their upward path. It is true that the WIB's Price-Fixing Committee attempted to control the prices of steel, lumber, copper, and other raw materials, but its method was that of voluntary agreement with producers rather than legal compulsion. The tactic appears to have influenced prices of some items. But since the prices of "controlled" items rose somewhat higher than noncontrolled ones from 1916 to 1918, it is perhaps just as well that volunteerism was not extended across the board to consumer goods. In the absence of restraint, the latter took off. In contrast to the years 1914–1916, when the cost of living rose only a relatively moderate 14.8 percent, the years between 1916 and 1920 saw it soar 83 percent. Food prices advanced 73.8 percent; clothing, 139.6 percent; housing, 31.8 percent; fuel and light, 58.6 percent; furniture and furnishings, 129 percent; and miscellaneous items, 77.8 percent.[39]

Two fundamental factors underlay this wartime inflation: the relative scarcity of productive resources available to the civilian sector and the impact of wartime finance on the money supply. Since the economy was almost fully utilizing its productive resources on the eve of America's entry into the war, and expanded thereafter only on a minor scale and in only a few commodities, part of the resources previously used for civilian production had to be diverted to war production, and consumption sacrificed. The amount diverted depended on the magnitude of the war effort, and this dimension was defined by government expenditures for war purposes. Expenditures rose sharply during the war, from $1.34 billion in 1917 to a high of $18.21 billion in 1919. The production of consumer goods, on the other hand, did not go up at all from 1917 to 1919, and even declined somewhat each year. War expenditures therefore constituted a steadily increasing proportion of the GNP. By fiscal year 1919 that proportion amountd to approximately 25 percent, the money value of which also rose in the same two-year span from $49.9 billion to $65.7 bilion.[40]

These changes in the money value of the national product were due neither to an increase in the volume of physical output nor to improvement in the efficiency with which the factors of production were used. Gains in output were minor ones after 1916, and, as we have seen, productivity in both agriculture and manufacturing declined. The rising money value of the national product was due primarily to increases in the market prices of the goods produced. The latter, in turn, reflected the pressure of demand on scarce goods. All recipients of income helped generate this pressure—employees, entrepreneurs, money lenders, landlords, and corporations. Employees—wage and salary earners—were by far the most important of these groups, for they received over half of the national income from 1915 to 1920. Unfortunately, governmental tax policies did little to abate consumer demand. In 1918, for example, groups with incomes representing 77.7 percent of the taxpayers contributed only 0.6 percent of the individual income tax receipts. Meanwhile, excess-profits taxes on business incomes, imposed by the War Revenue Act of 1917, ranged from 20 to 60 percent. Taxation at these rates, though equitable, discouraged investment in productive facilities which might have retarded inflation by increasing output.[41]

In sum, although the government raised taxes, its receipts fell far short of its expenditures during the period of active warfare. Indeed, from April 1917 to June 1919 federal deficits reached the large sum of $23 billion, or nearly three-quarters of total expenditures of $32 billion. The government financed these deficits by selling Liberty bonds to the public, that is, by borrowing. To encourage the Treasury's bond sales, Congress amended the Federal Reserve Act in 1916 to permit reserve banks not only to rediscount commercial paper, as provided for in the original act of 1914, but also to rediscount loans made on the collateral of government bonds. In essence, the Federal Reserve banks became the bond-selling windows of a Treasury Department intent on encouraging sales by making it easy to borrow for that purpose. It worked this way: a commercial bank that was a member of the Federal Reserve System would lend money to an individual to enable him to buy a bond. The money would take the form either of a credit to the customer's deposit account or of Federal Reserve notes. If then the member bank needed to replenish its reserves in order to expand its loans and discounts, it could either have its Federal Reserve bank rediscount the customer's promissory note or discount its own note secured by the bond. Although the government did not print greenbacks, as it had done during the Civil War, the Federal Reserve notes and deposits arising out of bond sales served the same purpose. By the end of the war they made up most of the nation's money supply, a development also aided by further amendment of the Federal Reserve Act in June 1917 reducing the required reserves of the member banks.[42]

Between April 1917 and June 1919 the stock of money rose 49 percent, and the effect of this large increase was to sharpen the competition for scarce goods and services and drive up their prices. For during the same interval wholesale prices advanced 55 percent. The method chosen by the government to finance the wartime deficit, however, merely altered the instrumentality of an inflation that had begun during the period of American neutrality. Between June 1914 and March 1917 the stock of money had risen by 46 percent, and wholesale prices by 65 percent. What brought on these developments were large inflows of gold to pay for purchases of war materiel by the Allies. The Federal Reserve Board had no way to sterilize this inflow by removing it from the banking system, and, added to the reserves of the Federal Reserve banks, it served as "high power money." The war thus changed the vehicle of inflation but not its course.[43]

A final word. The early years of the European war, like the years of neutrality before American involvement in the wars of the French Revolution, brought prosperity to producers and carriers of goods needed by the belligerents. Did prosperity continue after the U.S. declaration of war in April 1917, and are the rising wages of workers a sign of it? The proposition is a doubtful one. In the first place, governmental financial policies effected a massive shift of productive resources from the civilian to the war sector of the economy. With few if any reserves of idle capital and labor that could be harnessed in 1917 and 1918 to the production of war materiel, increases in the goods of war could come only at the expense of the goods of peace. Between the opening quarter of 1917 and the closing one of 1918—the Armistice came in November 1918—the output of war industries rose at an annual rate of $11 billion whereas that of civilian goods declined by $13 billion. Sharper analyses than any now available must be made of changes in expenditure patterns compelled by shortages of specific civilian goods. Workers' wages more than kept pace with rising living costs, but what goods were available to spend the money on? Food, clothing, housing, and other necessaries, of course, but what of the "extra" above the cost of living? And what of the possibility of wartime deterioration in the quality of the "necessaries"? Finally, one must also consider the possibility that since wage earners undoubtedly invested a considerable part of their gains in Liberty bonds, only a very moderate increase in actual consumption took place between 1917 and 1920. In all probability a decrease occurred.[44]

14

The Undertow of Prosperity

I n the economic sense, the First World War ended for the United States not with the armistice of November 1918 but rather with the onset of the brief, steep depression of 1920–21. Until mid-1920 the peacetime economy proved surprisingly resilient to the impact of demobilization. The latter can only be described as precipitate. The war effort was wound up without thought of the consequences. War contracts were canceled abruptly; major controls, including price controls, were abandoned almost overnight; and demobilization was rushed forward, with the only idea in mind that of getting the boys back home. At the time of the armistice the War Department had $6 billion in manufacturing contracts outstanding, one-third of which were for goods on which production had already been completed. Of the remaining $4 billion, $2.5 billion were canceled within four weeks, with work on the rest tapering to the vanishing point by the spring of 1919. By the first anniversary of the armistice in November of that year, probably between 2 and 3 million workers were no longer needed as producers of guns, planes, ammunition, and other products for which there was no peacetime demand. Joining them during that interval were some 4 million men discharged from the armed services. While these 6 or 7 million persons were being dumped on the peacetime labor market, between 2 and 3 million others withdrew from it. Yet unemployment at the close of 1919 was little greater than it had been at the war's end. It therefore follows that some 3 million peacetime jobs which did not exist at the end of the war were created during the ensuing year.[1]

One of the reasons this development could occur was that the economy had to face only minimal problems of reconversion. For the production of distinctive implements of war such as guns, planes, and ammunition, new plants had been built. But much of the war output was by firms producing goods similar to their peacetime products—uniforms and blankets by textile firms, army shoes by shoe companies, steel sheet and plate and pipe by firms equipped to produce those products. So far as the United States was concerned, it had been a partial rather than total war, with about one-fourth of the national product devoted to war in 1918—in contrast to the Second World War, in which half of the nation's output was so allocated in 1943—and total conversion of a plant and its facilities from peace to war production seems to have been rare.[2] But ease of reconversion does not explain why rapid expansion of peacetime employment took place in 1919 and early 1920. Businessmen expand output when they experience or anticipate a high level of demand. That they in fact did so is attributable to the activity of three forces in particular. Primary among them were the expenditures of the federal government. Many wartime projects—shipbuilding, for example—could not be terminated quickly, and Treasury expenditures reached their peak not during the period of hostilities but after the armistice. Although declining irregularly during 1919, these expenditures were huge by prewar standards. More important, they represented a very large net contribution to the nation's purchasing power. In 1919 they exceeded revenues from taxes and other sources by more than $13 billion. Not only the deficit itself but its unprecedented size worked to sustain income and employment during the period of demobilization.[3]

Two other factors also contributed to this result. Both before and during the war the United States had enjoyed a favorable balance of payments—meaning, of course, that claims by Americans on foreign currencies arising out of sources of earnings such as exports of commodities and services exceeded foreign claims on the dollar. To the extent that exports were not financed by credit extended by the federal government, they acted as a force distinct from the deficit in stimulating employment and economic activity in the United States. During the war private financing was negligible, but after the armistice nongovernmental credit financed exports of cotton and food to a cold and hungry Europe to a significant extent. According to one estimate, private credit in 1919 amounted to $1.7 billion, nearly half the total of $3.58 billion earned by exports of American farm products.[4] These exports were an important source of agricultural prosperity in the United States, and the respending of income earned by farmers provided a substantial demand for the products of industry. Total merchandise exports exceeded imports by no less than $4,896 million. The magnitude of this sum is more clearly seen in relation to a calculation that new investment, including changes in inventories, amounted to only $10,517 million.[5]

The third and final factor in the rapid peacetime expansion of production was the economic activity stimulated by the deficit. In part, this took the form of investment in manufacturing plant and equipment, investment which had risen by mighty leaps from $600 million in 1915 to over four times that amount in 1918. After declining moderately in 1919 the manufacturing industry responded to the enlarged demand for consumer goods by increasing the volume of investment to $3 billion in 1920—a total not equaled until the period of industrial mobilization preceding World War II, not even in 1929.[6]

Nevertheless, manufacturing plant and equipment have never been large components of net capital formation, and the impact of this investment must not be exaggerated. More important in sustaining incomes appears to have been a wave of speculative activity which took the form of inventory accumulation. Of a total gross investment by business concerns of $10 billion in 1919, no less than $3 billion, or 30 percent, was accounted for by an increase in inventories. In contrast, the average percentage for the years 1922–1929 was less than half that—12 percent. Two-thirds of the increase was "real" and took the form of physical volume of stocks held; the other one-third represented price increases. The largest increase was in wholesale and retail inventories, department store stocks, for example, rising 50 percent between May 1919 and April 1920.[7]

Another speculative activity of large proportions consisted of "inventory accumulation" in the form of farmland. In order to meet wartime demands for food and raw materials, American farmers had expanded the number of acres of land in farms by more than 38 million between 1914 and 1919. And while farm mortgage debt, provided by life insurance companies, commercial and savings banks, and private individuals, had increased by nearly $2.5 billion in that interim, net income realized by farm operators from farming had doubled, rising from $649 million in 1914 to $1,395 billion in 1919.[8] Encouraged by the belief that European producers would need a very long time to restore their prewar agricultural capacity, a belief reinforced by statements made by private and public officials, optimistic farmers had high expectations about future farm incomes. In consequence, a farm real estate boom occurred in almost every state of the Union. In 1920 alone, 10 million acres were added to the agricultural domain. That year the national average of farmland values was 22 percent higher than it had been the year before—and 68 percent higher than it had been in 1914.[9] Land values in the central and southern regions of the country were almost double the prewar averages, with over half the gain taking place in most cases between 1918 and 1920. Farm mortgage debt accompanied these rising values, increasing from $6.5 billion in 1918 to $8.4 billion in 1920.[10]

The farmers guessed wrong. Agricultural recovery in Europe and elsewhere proved far more rapid than expected, and between late 1920 and the end of 1921 a sharp collapse in commodity prices and farmland values occurred. Net income was down nearly $200 million in 1920, and many farmers found themselves saddled with a heavy load of fixed debt and diminishing prospects of meeting the interest payments on it. The next year the bottom dropped out, with net income just half of what it had been in 1920. Between their zenith in 1919 and their nadir in 1921, farm incomes had fallen 60 percent.[11]

Farmers were not alone in their troubles. The bubble burst almost everywhere else, too. Prices, income, and output fell sharply, and the country sank into a serious depression in 1920–21. Although decline in construction activity and in the favorable foreign balance[12] contributed to these results, the major part of the explanation lies in the areas of fiscal and monetary policy. In place of the deficit of more than $13 billion in 1919, the Treasury ran a surplus of some $290 million in 1920 and over $500 million the next year. The stimulus caused by peak deficit expenditures gave way to the deflationary influence of surplus.[13] In this situation, the appropriate posture of the Federal Reserve Board would have been that of credit leniency, one of encouraging the member banks to expand their loans and discounts by lowering the discount rate or purchasing government securities on the open market. Instead, the Federal Reserve Board, alarmed by the speculative overtones of the upswing of 1919, put on the brakes—it permitted the Reserve banks to raise their discount rates—thus adopting a policy of monetary restriction rather than one of ease. The action might have been the correct one had it been taken in early or mid-1919 instead of near the end of that year and subsequently, when, as its leading protagonist, Governor Benjamin Strong of the New York Reserve Bank, realized, it was too late for rate increases to have the desired effect. Indeed, "to do it now," he is said to have observed in November 1919, "would be to bring on a crisis."[14]

The remark was a prescient one. By mid-1921 prices had fallen to 56 percent of their level in May 1920, perhaps the sharpest price decline in American history.[15] Unemployment at its peak exceeded 10 percent of the civilian labor force.[16] Had Governor Strong not been on leave for reasons of health after mid-December 1919, the steep increase in the rate of 1.25 percentage points taken in January 1920, the "sharpest single rise in the entire history of the System, before or since," might not have occurred. As it was, the Federal Reserve's first attempt at deliberate monetary policy proved a failure—a harbinger of even more serious failure at the end of the decade.[17]

In between, however, were years of prosperity for many Americans, perhaps for most of them. Behind that prosperity lay significant increases in business investment and in the purchasing power of the public. Table 37 shows the total disposition of the gross national product during the twenties, both the flows to consumers of services and perishable, semidurable, and durable goods, and the components of gross capital formation—producer durables, construction, change in inventories, and foreign investment. Capital formation paved the way for a huge expansion in the output of prepared foods, other perishables, and semidurable goods, as well as durables such as furniture, radios, refrigerators, vacuum cleaners, and automobiles.

Total nonmanufacturing investment, especially in construction, was also impressive, for the twenties witnessed an unprecedented housing boom, which, together with the spreading use of automobiles and investment in highway building—spending by the states on highway construction rose from $70 million in 1918 to $750 million in 1930—resulted in a large increase in suburban single-family houses as well as in city apartments. However, nonresidential structures such as commercial and industrial facilities outnumbered newly built residences all through the twenties.[18] States and cities floated bond

Table 37. Gross national product and its chief components, 1919–1929 (billions of dollars, in 1929 prices).

GNP components	1919	1920	1921	1922	1923	1924	1925	1926	1927	1928	1929
Gross national product	67.8	68.5	65.5	70.4	80.0	81.6	84.3	89.8	90.6	91.9	98.0
Flow to consumers	49.7	51.3	54.1	56.5	61.2	65.3	64.0	68.9	70.7	72.5	76.9
Perishable	19.9	21.0	21.8	22.6	23.5	25.3	25.1	26.3	26.8	26.7	28.0
Semidurable	7.5	6.5	7.8	8.9	9.8	9.0	10.0	10.0	11.2	11.2	11.8
Durable	5.0	4.9	4.0	5.1	6.6	6.9	7.8	8.6	8.2	8.4	8.8
Services	17.3	18.9	20.4	19.9	21.3	24.1	21.2	24.0	24.5	26.2	28.4
Gross capital formation	18.1	17.2	11.4	13.9	18.7	16.2	20.3	20.9	19.9	19.4	21.1
Producer durables	5.5	5.3	3.6	4.2	5.8	5.4	6.0	6.5	6.1	6.5	7.5
Construction	6.3	5.4	6.3	8.8	9.7	10.8	12.1	12.8	12.7	12.3	11.2
Change in inventories	2.8	4.2	0.0	0.3	2.8	-0.9	1.6	1.2	0.4	-0.4	1.7
Claims against foreign countries	3.5	2.3	1.5	0.7	0.5	1.0	0.7	0.4	0.7	1.0	0.8

Source: Simon Kuznets, *Capital in the American Economy: Its Formation and Financing* (New York: National Bureau of Economic Research, 1961), appendix A, pp. 487, 488, 492. (I have used Kuznets' Variant I.) Used with permission.

issues to finance the building of schools, while continued growth in central electric power production and distribution facilities added to the capital available to the American people. Estimated expenditures on materials used in construction rose, in current prices, from $12,158,000 in 1919 to $17,385,000,000 in 1928.[19] That part of the national income arising directly from construction doubled between 1919 and the peak of the construction cycle in 1926, increasing from $2.1 billion to $4.2 billion. These sums were larger than those of any single group of manufacturing industries except metals and, for the first three years of the period, textiles and leather.[20] Taxation financed the public works, but private investments emerged largely out of personal savings.

Had it not been for the rising purchasing power of the public, these increases in investment, in capital formation, would probably not have been made. To begin with, real incomes rose, both per worker and per capita. The former went up from an average of $629 a year between 1909 and 1918 to $738 between 1919 and 1928; the latter, from $517 to $612. But people did not confine their buying to articles for which they were able to pay cash. A remarkable extension of sales "on time" (installment sales) occurred in the 1920s. Finance companies specialized in providing consumer credit in this form in a volume which rose from $1,375 million in 1925 to $3,000 million in 1929. Wide use of the technique was made for the distribution of consumer durables such as automobiles, furniture, radios, and other electrical equipment for the home. An unknown proportion of the consumer's dollar also went to firms providing services, such as transportation companies, beauty shops and purveyors of entertainment and recreation.[21]

However paid for, the twenties witnessed what can only be called a consumer-durable revolution. According to a popular but astute writer on economic subjects during those years, Stuart Chase, the estimated 27 million American homes had durable articles in the following numbers in 1928:

    15,300,000 electric flat irons
     6,828,000 vacuum cleaners
     5,000,000 washing machines
     4,900,000 electric fans
     4,540,000 electric toasters
     2,600,000 electric heaters
       755,000 electric refrigerators
       348,000 ironing machines

In 1920, Chase added, there were sixty-one telephones per thousand city people. In 1928 there were ninety-five per thousand. In the same interval the number of radios increased from just about zero to 10 million. Although Chase doubted that the home of the average American was as comfortable as it had been in 1890, he acknowledged that it nevertheless had running water, a bathtub, electric lights, and probably a radio and telephone—"which makes it a cleaner, better lighted, more strenuous and far noisier home."[22]

A consumer durable parked outside the home was noisy too, especially when the UHOOGAH of its concerted horns flared to protest the traffic jams. But it provided a means for transforming personal and social relations, to say nothing of its impact on patterns of settlement and mobility. The automobile promised romance, adventure, and escape from monotony: "North America lies in the hollow of our hands!" Chase exulted. "Mountain, canyon, pass and glacier; mighty rivers, roaring cataracts, the glint of the sea—jump in, step on it, all are yours." The automobile "fired the blood like wine."[23]

It fired the economy, too. To Chase, the automobile, the production of which rose 255 percent in the twenties—passenger car registration increasing from 9.3 million to 23.1 million between 1921 and 1929—provided the fundamental explanation of the prosperity of that decade. The booming car industry interlocked at one end with large increases in the production of gasoline and oil, rubber products, plate glass, metals, and other inputs, and at the other end with highways, residential and commercial construction, and the cement and lumber industries, among others. Although no single industry, even with these linkages in mind, can contribute more than a small fraction to the total output of an economy, the automobile quickened the long-term rise in national income—the pace of economic growth—by introducing greater efficiency in methods of production. Automobiles were the leading growth industry of the 1920s, and behind the mass production techniques which cheapened their cost and made them affordable by millions of people stands one man in particular, Henry Ford.[24]

Barely literate, bigoted, and ruthless in his labor relations (said to be easily the worst in the auto industry), a man ignorant of the complexities of worlds beyond his chosen domain, Ford was nevertheless an extremely important innovator. He may have been the greatest manufacturer of all time. Ford did not invent the moving assembly line, but he did encourage his assistants, especially Charles Sorenson, Walter Flanders, and Ed Martin, in experiments which culminated in mass production at unprecedented speed and on a scale never seen before. Instead of workmen bringing parts to the point of assembly and putting them together, an assembly belt moved the chassis frame, axles, motor, and other major components past stations at speeds perfectly timed to enable workmen to perform their assigned operations. The work moved to the worker. Ford himself described the process in *My Life and Work*:

> In the chassis assembly are forty-five separate operations or stations. The first men fasten four mudguard brackets to the chassis frame; the motor arrives on the tenth operation. . . Some men do only one or two small operations, others do more. The man who places a part does not fasten it—the part may not be fully in place until after several operations later. The man who puts in

the bolt does not put on the nut; the man who puts on the nut does not tighten it. On operation number thirty-four the budding motor gets its gasoline; it has previously received lubrication; on operation number forty-four the radiator is filled with water, and on operation forty-five the car drives out.

As a rule, one car came out of the Ford factory about every forty-five seconds. By 1926, when Ford discontinued production of his famous Model T, he had sold 15 million cars, half of the nation's entire output of new cars, more than double that of his nearest competitor, General Motors. In 1923 alone Ford had made and sold nearly 1.7 million. The introduction and perfection of the moving assembly line had enabled him to increase his annual output more than 150 times and to lower production costs and the sales prices of his cars.

Famous as Ford became—he may have been more widely known than any other American in the early 1920s—his automobiles did not sell themselves, certainly not at first. Ralph Waldo Emerson said that the world would beat a path to the door of the man who invented a better mousetrap, but he was wrong: the inventor would have to advertise. And Ford did so. Announcing his intended product in 1909, he told the public:

> I will build a motor car for the great multitude. It will be large enough for the family but small enough for the individual to run and care for. It will be constructed of the best materials, by the best men to be hired, after the simplest designs that modern engineering can devise. But it will be so low in price that no man making a good salary will be unable to own one—and enjoy with his family the blessing of hours of pleasure in God's great open spaces.[25]

Not only automobiles had to be advertised but all the other salable products of the economy as well, as manufacturers sought to differentiate their products from those of competitors. Indeed, the 1920s saw the birth of modern advertising, of advertising as an important part of America's secular culture. Not that only secular subjects were grist for its mills. In *The Man That Nobody Knows*, a best-seller in the mid-1920s, Bruce Barton portrayed Jesus as a super-salesman, the parables as "the most powerful advertisements of all time." Jesus was a topnotch businessman: "He picked up twelve men from the bottom ranks of business and forged them into an organization that conquered the world." Anyone doubting that business was His main concern had only to read the Bible. Had not Jesus Himself said, "Wist ye not that I must be about my father's business?" If even Jesus had to be advertised, who or what was immune?[26] What a difference a few decades had made! In the late nineteenth century the warning "No Beggars, Peddlers, or Advertising Men" had appeared on signs affixed to many a shop and office door. Advertising was widely regarded as on the fringe of legitimate business activity. Media advertising revenue in 1865 was on the order of $7.5 million, but by 1921 the revenue amounted to ninety times that sum. By 1929 expenditures on advertising reached a total of $3.4 billion, more than 3 percent of the gross national product.[27]

One consequence of expanded advertising was a severe drop in sales of commodities in bulk as people turned to packaged goods bearing brand names. By the end of the twenties the majority of Americans are believed to have been buying packaged cheese, macaroni, crackers, butter, lard, coffee, and soap flakes. Packaged bacon had been almost unknown in 1920, but by 1930 about 44 percent of American families were buying it. Another aim of advertisers was to stimulate sales by encouraging frequent style changes. Obsolescence rather than durability became their goal, with all the arts of salesmanship being enlisted in campaigns to convince consumers that they ought to want "the latest." The technique had long been employed to sell wearing apparel, but in the twenties it was also applied to automobiles, furniture, and other consumer durables.[28]

In sum, the prosperity of the twenties rode a rising wave of incomes which crested in installment credit and then flowed into channels marked off by salesmen and advertisers. These higher incomes were themselves products of gains realized in the efficiency of production. In the case of Henry Ford's workers, increased wages probably belong among the source springs of productivity advance as well. In 1914 he astonished the business world by doubling the minimum wage of "deserving" workers to five dollars a day—a rate he did not indefinitely maintain, however. The action was followed by a tremendous surge in output at the Ford plants, ascribed by Ford people to skyrocketing morale and by Ford detractors to sheer terror on the part of workers at the possibility of losing jobs which had suddenly become more desirable than any comparable ones anywhere.[29]

Notable gains in productivity were achieved not only in the Ford plants but in those of other manufacturers too. Striking increases occurred also in mining and in transportation. Before the war, during the years of early modern industrialization, the capital-deepening process was characterized by a rapid buildup of capital as mechanized techniques were substituted for hand processes and as plant was constructed in anticipation of increasing demand and rates of utilization. During this phase of modernization, output per unit of capital input declined. Then, after production processes had been made as capital-using as current technology and relative factor prices warranted, resources were devoted primarily to refining equipment and processes of production. Capital-saving innovations became more numerous, and output per unit of capital input began to rise. In short, a dollar invested in manufacturing in the 1920s produced a larger amount of output, which indicates that the new investment of that decade was more productive.[30]

In contrast to the decades 1889–1899, 1899–1909, and 1909–1919, when average rates of change in output per unit of capital input were negative (-1.8 percent, -1.6 percent, and -1.9 percent, respectively), the years between 1919 and 1929 registered a strikingly high positive increase of 4.3 percent in manufacturing. Not only capital but labor as well was used more efficiently, for output per unit of labor input exhibits a similar history of change, although the rates were always positive. In the first three decades, those rates averaged 1.7 percent, 1.1 percent, and 0.8 percent, respectively, but in the twenties they jumped to 5.6 percent. Thus, while average output per unit of labor input enjoyed a higher absolute level of growth during the 1920s than did capital productivity, the latter's rate of increase represented a reversal of the declining trend of earlier years. Its quickening, therefore, was greater than the comparable acceleration in the growth of labor productivity. Furthermore, the quickening was unique. The productivity advance achieved by manufacturing capital in the twenties was larger than during any other period between 1889 and 1953.[31]

Technological innovation lay behind the increased productivity. Technological progress occurs when methods of production are so improved that one is able to achieve more output with the same volume of resources, or the same output with a smaller volume of resources. To effect improvement, new and better tools and equipment (technological "hardware") may be utilized, or economic inputs may be better organized and managed. (These broader forms of innovation constitute improvements in technological "software.")[32] A few examples of innovative hardware in the petroleum refining, paper, and chemical industries will clarify the ways in which the productivity of capital was raised in the 1920s. While a major wave of capital-improving innovations broke over industry in that decade, it took the form of numerous small improvements rather than large breakthroughs.

The introduction of continuous thermal cracking in petroleum refining is estimated to have been the source of 40 percent of the capital-output growth that took place in that industry. The innovation increased the amount of output per unit of capital because it led to higher gasoline yields, more continuous processing, and automation. At the same time, greater refining capacities could be fitted into smaller spaces with less equipment. Nearly 50 percent of capital-output growth in paper making is traceable to the electrification of that industry, which increased output by raising machine speeds and making possible continuous processing methods. Along with electrification, mills were modernized by the installation of space-conserving equipment—thus saving capital—and by the improvement of plant layout so that the pulp could flow more continuously. In the chemical industry, linkage of individual chemical processes, improved material handling, better plant layout, and automatic process control also made for a pronounced trend toward continuous processing. In sum, in contrast to earlier years of capital deepening, years which might well be viewed as the preparatory phase of the Industrial Revolution, when plant, machinery, and equipment essential for mass production were installed, the twenties witnessed a widespread extension of the techniques of mass manufacture—automatic machinery, straight-line production, and automatic control. Technological innovations in the glass, rubber, tobacco, iron and steel, garment, brick, and bread-baking industries seem to confirm this conclusion.[33]

In all these industries factors which are not technological in nature also deserve credit for improvement in the performance of industrial capital. Among them are the shutting down of marginal plants, increased economies of scale, and more efficient utilization of capacity. Some factors were external to the manufacturing sector, for example, advances in communication and transportation, shifts from steam power to central (public utility) electric power, and improvements in techniques of constructing buildings and machinery. Still others were the impact of education, experience, and shorter work days—and why not Henry Ford's five-dollar-a-day wage?—on improved labor quality. Last but far from least were developments in "soft" technology, namely, better organization and management. Even so, it should be kept in mind that it was advances of the "hard" variety—perhaps more the frequency of technical change than the kind of technology employed—that were principally responsible for inducing the latter kinds of change in large industrial enterprises during and after the twenties.[34]

Following the leadership of Pierre S. DuPont of the DuPont Chemical Company—and later president of General Motors—many chemical companies decided in the 1920s to diversify their product lines by setting up large research departments for the purpose of bringing forth new products and improving existing ones, together with the processes by which they were made. They were not alone, for United States Rubber, B. F. Goodrich, and other rubber companies, as well as firms in the electrical, electronics, and, to a somewhat lesser extent, the power machinery and automobile industries, did the same.[35] Alfred D. Chandler, Jr., describes some of the early consequences of this institutionalized research in the following account:

> The great electrical companies, General Electric and Westinghouse, began as makers of a full line of producers' goods for the generation and use of electric power and light. In the 1920's, they moved into the mass consumer market by producing and selling washing machines, refrigerators, vacuum cleaners, stoves, and other household appliances. At the same time, the energies of their research laboratories brought these companies into the making of plastics, alloys, and a variety of products based on the vacuum tube and the science of electronics. The automobile companies, in turn, began to produce tractors, diesels, airplane engines, electrical equipment, and even household appliances—all using the new sources of power, particularly the internal combustion engine. The agricultural implement and other power machinery firms followed much the same road, with the first of them developing construction

equipment and diesels and the second moving into agricultural implements as well as heavy electrical equipment.[36]

Product diversification, however, created a host of problems which could not be addressed successfully by corporate administrations made up of functionally specialized departments for purchasing, accounting, sales, and other activities under the control of a central headquarters. This older type of administration worked well when the firm manufactured a single product or sold in a single market. Product diversification—and territorial expansion into new markets and sources of supply—made for complex difficulties in obtaining materials and supplies and in manufacturing and marketing a number of product lines for different types of customers or in different parts of the world. The older departmental headquarters could not address such problems rationally and systematically, nor, even more important, could it coordinate the flow of products through the several departments or make intelligent appraisals of operating performance of functions such as engineering and research, production, distribution, transportation, and finance when several very different industries or lines of business were involved. Finally, it could not successfully make long-term strategic plans for the use of facilities, personnel, and funds.[37]

These dilemmas required for their solution a higher degree of administrative specialization, one that focused on the individual product, product line, or market, and the new organizational form became known as the multidivisional structure. In this type of structure autonomous operating divisions were set up for each product, product line, or territorial area and made responsible for production, purchasing, sales, research and development, and traffic. Above these line functions, each assigned a different department, were established two large staff divisions, a financial staff and an advisory staff, each under a vice-president. Under the former, the treasurer and his subordinate offices and employees handled matters pertaining to securities, taxes, audits, benefits, and statistics, while the controller's offices took care of accounting, billing and receiving, and cost analysis. The advisory staff was charged with a number of functions: legal, personnel, purchasing, advising, public relations, engineering, development, traffic, real estate, and "services." At the top of the administrative pyramid were the president and other general executives making up the executive committee and the board of directors. In sum, autonomous multifunctional divisions, headed by middle managers, integrated production and distribution "by coordinating flows from suppliers to consumers in different, clearly defined markets." The divisions, in turn, were supervised by a general office of top managers who were assisted by large financial and administrative staffs.[38]

The multidivisional structure, developed in the 1920s by Pierre S. DuPont for the DuPont Company and by DuPont and Alfred P. Sloan, Jr., for General Motors (GM), was slowly adopted by other large industrial enterprises during that decade and in the succeeding one. The burgeoning markets and swiftly advancing technology of the post–World War II years induced company after company to follow suit, and by 1960 it had become the standard managerial form for the most complex and diverse of America's industrial enterprises.[39]

An organizational chart for an innovative administrative device cannot alone suggest the ways in which it contributed to productivity growth. Essentially, the multidivisional structure was a capital-saving innovation, one which, by improving the coordination of activities between and within departments, and between headquarters and field, speeded up the information flows on which decisions rested, thus economizing on expenditures for time and materials— to say nothing of the augmentation in the value of those variables by decisions crowned with success by the market. Sloan of GM, for example, on becoming aware of the development of friction between line and staff executives—line managers thought staff men too theoretical, whereas the latter thought line men too preoccupied by current production schedules—formed "interdivisional relations committees" for major functional activities such as product development, sales, and institutional advertising. Since executives from major divisions were included on these committees, which were usually chaired by a member of the executive committee, top management was able to separate itself from the biases and responsibilities of operations while at the same time keeping itself informed about the widespread operations of the corporation. Policy and planning could be done by general executives with the time, information, and necessary commitment to the enterprise as a whole rather than to one of its parts. Constantly polished and adjusted, the multidivisional structure made a significant contribution to productivity advance, however difficult it may be to measure that contribution.[40]

And so too did the men who managed the structure. Beginning in the twenties, and once more following the leadership of DuPont, the management of large industrial and marketing enterprises by members of the family increasingly gave way to management by outsiders, by men trained not only in the schools of business experience but more and more in academic schools of business. The railroads had shown the way in the 1880s and 1890s. In and after the twenties, the leaven of professionalization spread throughout the empire of business, encouraging the rapid dissemination of new administrative techniques and helping managers to become aware of their own identity as a distinct economic and social group.[41]

There were several ways to the top—expertise in finance, accounting, and even, as the career of Charles ("Boss") Kettering of GM illustrates, invention—but one of the surest was mastery of the market. Indeed, the longevity of the firm itself depended on it. The leading industrial corporations of the twenties went to great pains to estimate the demand for their products and to allocate their financial and other resources accordingly. By 1924 DuPont and Sloan of GM, for example, had their financial staff prepare annual forecasts for each of their divisions. These projections of demand also included all the inputs required for the anticipated output, as well as purchase and delivery schedules for materials and capital equipment, and for labor. Unit costs, prices, and rates of return were estimated for each product, with the staff taking into account national income, the effect of the business cycle, seasonal variations in demand, and, for each of its lines, the division's anticipated share of the market. Forecasts were then adjusted constantly in the light of sales, data on the latter being submitted every ten days by the firm's dealers.

> Besides permitting immediate adjustments of flows to even small changes in demand, this information had other uses. The comparison of actual to estimated results of sales, market share, and rate of return was used to sharpen forecasting techniques. Of more importance, such comparison provided another source of information for the monitoring of divisional performance and the planning and allocating of resources for the future.[42]

Similar techniques for controlling inventory, coordinating flows, and evaluating managerial performance, including interdivisional billing at market prices, were adopted by General Electric, Westinghouse, and Sears Roebuck. Eventually all large modern business enterprises in the United States utilized such methods.[43]

Information. Knowledge. Whether the technology was hard or soft, information was close to the bottom of it, and if the information was sound, it was based on knowledge. Not only knowledge acquired in the way of the nineteenth and earlier centuries, by the crude empiricism of trial-and-error methods, but also systematic knowledge born of controlled experimentation, of science. And since an increasing proportion of the technological changes of the twentieth century have depended on advances in systematic knowledge, it will be evident how important education has become in this century. Science has increased the demand for skilled labor, and education, however defined, is the ultimate source of skills.

American society responded by raising the level of its investment in education. Expenditures for that purpose had claimed only 1.17 percent of the gross national product in 1920, but by 1928 the percentage had nearly doubled to 2.22 percent (by 1964 the percentage, 6.2 percent, was nearly triple that of 1928). A good deal of the increase went into secondary education, for in the same interval the percentage of seventeen year olds who were high school graduates rose from 16.3 percent to 26.2 percent. Meanwhile, new institutions of higher learning were founded—173 of them being four-year colleges—with the graduates of all such institutions, both male and female, increasing in number. The gains of the latter were particularly impressive, for while male recipients of bachelor's or first professional degrees rose from 48,622 in 1920 to 111,161 in 1928, their female counterparts increased from 16,642 to 48,869—nearly tripling. The number of doctorates also came close to tripling, with degrees in chemistry (179) more than twice those in the agricultural sciences (88). Other fields—medicine (67), physics (64), biology (55), psychology (49), engineering (44), and geology (10)—attracted fewer candidates. In 1928, 24 percent of the total population, of all ages, was enrolled in school, a higher percentage than that of any country in Europe.[44] The result was that the proportion of skilled men and women in the population increased in the 1920s, enriching the human capital of the labor force. At the same time, the proportion of the unskilled declined as a result of restrictions on immigration. The latter had fallen off deeply during the war, but in 1924 Congress, responding to the "Red Scare," adopted a quota system in the National Origins Act, which reduced the annual flow of immigrants to less than one-fourth of what it had been before the war. Between 1900 and 1914 immigrants had been responsible for 73 percent of the growth of the labor force, but between 1914 and 1930 the proportion fell to 40 percent. The resulting decline in the numbers of unskilled foreign workers tended to raise the wages of the native unskilled and narrow the gap between those wages and the earnings of the skilled.[45]

Working men and women were better off in other ways as well. Unemployment was low, averaging 5.1 percent of the labor force between 1923 and 1929, and employees worked fewer hours, those in manufacturing, for example, enjoying close to a forty-hour week by 1929. Finally, prices were essentially stable from the end of the 1920–21 depression to the end of the decade.[46]

Undoubtedly this combination of favorable conditions goes far to explain why union membership fell off in the 1920s. Unions had prospered during the war, and by 1920 approximately 5 million workers were members, roughly one-eighth of the labor force. After 1923, however, and despite substantial growth in the labor force, union membership never exceeded 3.7 million, with nearly half the decrease taking place in metals, machinery, shipbuilding, mining, quarrying, and oil. Nevertheless, the traditional opposition of employers to independent unions characterized the 1920s as well and found expression in the organization of company unions and in widespread use of injunctions and yellow dog contracts. These the courts upheld, continuing to confirm the historical failure of the legal system to embrace the interests of a major American constituency—working men and women.[47]

Despite the fact that the Clayton Act (1914) had stipulated that "no restraining order or injunction shall be granted by any court of the United States . . . in any case between an employer and employees . . . unless necessary to prevent irreparable injury to property . . . for which injury there is no adequate remedy at law," unions, their officers, or individual members found themselves defendants, by one count, in seventy-two recorded cases brought under the Sherman Act. In addition, at least twenty-three criminal prosecutions, six damage suits, and forty suits for injunctions were instituted during the twenties. More than half the criminal cases resulted in convictions, and the great majority of the injunction petitions were granted. It would be hard to imagine a more devastating defeat for labor. Instead of holding unions exempt from the operation of the antitrust laws, the courts fashioned the statutes into powerful weapons against labor.[48]

They did so not by contesting the constitutionality of the exemption but by ruling that certain activities undertaken in the interests of labor were illegal. Although workers had the acknowledged right to engage in peaceful persuasion, picketing, even if peaceful, "inevitably leads to intimidation and obstruction." Such was the view of Chief Justice William Howard Taft of the United States Supreme Court. Similarly, strikes undertaken for the purpose of unionizing the unorganized were held to be illegal on the ground that union officials ordering them were engaged in a conspiracy to interfere with the production and shipment of goods in interstate commerce, a manifest violation of the Sherman Act justifying the issuing of an injunction. Even a collective bargaining agreement could be held illegal if it called for the employment of union men who had been granted the right to refuse work on nonunion materials. In contrast, the same court—the Supreme Court of the United States—held lawful an attempt by employers to protect an antiunion arrangement. And in both *Adair v. United States* (1908) and *Coppage v. Kansas* (1915) the Court had held that federal and state laws prohibiting yellow-dog contracts were unconstitutional restraints on personal liberty and private property. Leading students of labor law at the end of the twenties were in agreement that the marriage of the labor injunction with the yellow-dog contract—that is, a yellow-dog contract enforced by an injunction—placed in jeopardy the very existence of trade unionism in the United States.[49]

Not only the law of labor relations but social legislation as well offered inadequate protection to the interests of labor. Minimum wages are a case in point. Originating in the late nineteenth century and led by middle-class reform organizations and individuals influenced in part by the shockingly low wages paid women, and also in part by the example of minimum wage laws enacted in Great Britain and Australia, the movement enjoyed some early success, and by 1920 sixteen states and the District of Columbia had passed the necessary legislation. In no case, however, did the laws apply to men. The sponsors hoped that if the regulatory laws were limited to females, they would be upheld as a legitimate exercise of the police power, not only on the ground that women had little bargaining power but also because concern for the health of future mothers justified interposition on their behalf by the state.

Even this minimal degree of protection against exploitation was felled in 1923 by a Supreme Court wielding the stout club of liberty of contract. In *Adkins v. Children's Hospital,* Justice George Sutherland, speaking for the Court, struck down as unconstitutional the District of Columbia's minimum wage law, which had been enacted by Congress in the interests of children as well as of women. The Children's Hospital was perfectly at liberty to engage a female "at a wage rate which, in the judgment of Congress, was deleterious to her health and morals and she was equally free to seek employment at that rate." Sutherland argued that it was "no longer open to question" that the right to contract was part "of the liberty of the individual protected by" the Fifth Amendment. Despite the fact that the Clayton Act had solemnly declared that "the labor of a human being is not a commodity or article of commerce," he saw "no difference between the case of selling labor and the case of selling goods." Called by constitutional historians a "classic expression of the iden- tification of laissez-faire economics with constitutional right," the decision was repeatedly cited thereafter as "ample precedent for a broad interpretation of the scope of free contract." It was also a precedent under which several state minimum wage laws became inoperative. Although laws did remain on the statute books of a few states, they became dead letters.

Efforts to ameliorate other social evils fared little if any better. The census of 1920 counted more than a million children between the ages of ten and fifteen as gainfully employed, especially in agriculture, textile and glass man- ufacturing, the street trades, and industrial homework. Over the opposition of the National Association of Manufacturers and the owners of southern textile mills, Congress had enacted the first child labor law by overwhelming majorities in 1916. But nine months later, the Supreme Court in *Hammer v. Dagenhart* held the law to be an inappropriate exercise of constitutional power under the commerce clause. Congress tried again, in 1918, but once again the Court invalidated the effort, this time because the law was an unconstitutional exercise of the taxing power (*Bailey v. Drexel Furniture Company*, in 1922). The onus of blame does not fall on the Supreme Court alone, however. The American Farm Bureau Federation bitterly opposed efforts to ratify a consti- tutional amendment giving Congress the power to "limit, regulate, and pro- hibit the labor of persons under 18 years of age." Opponents rallied behind the wrinkled banner of states rights to oppose making the child a ward of the federal government, enlisting prominent persons such as President Abbott Lawrence Lowell of Harvard University and President Nicholas Murray But- ler of Columbia University in the cause. Perhaps not surprisingly, then, in the year of Franklin Delano Roosevelt's triumph over Hoover, the legal system afforded little protection to working children.[50]

Despite the widespread passage of workmen's compensation laws after the mid-1890s—by 1920 forty-three states had enacted them—workers injured on the job and the families of those killed enjoyed little more. The main object of the laws was to transfer the economic burden of work injury and death from the victim to industry and, ultimately, to society. But by the early 1930s only a small fraction of that burden had been shifted. As of the mid-1920s, one-fourth of the compensation states limited benefits to 50 percent of wages; the maximum in any state was 65 percent. Workers who were disabled totally and permanently might receive from $3,000 to $6,000 in aggregate benefits over a period of weeks ranging from 260 to 1,000. Although medical benefits improved, most states imposed time and dollar limits (two weeks to a year, and $100 to $800). Only ten states provided compensation for industrial disease.[51]

In this case it was not courts of law that were responsible for these modest accomplishments. Rather, it was the uncompromising hostility of commercial insurance companies to the establishment of state compensation funds—together with stress on the importance of preventing accidents in the first place, an emphasis which appealed strongly to the employers represented in the National Association of Manufacturers. From the beginning the idea of prevention had taken precedence over the economic needs of injured workers. It was an idea difficult to resist because it testified to the belief in the beneficial effects of economic incentive and competition. As late as the 1950s, twenty-six of the fifty-four compensation jurisdictions remained elective, and estimated compensation payments totaled no more than one-third of income loss. Benefits payable to widows averaged 50 percent of wages; including allowances for dependents, the most common figure was 66.6 percent.[52]

Legislatively, a vigorous campaign to provide pensions for the aged (sixty-five and over) fared poorest of all in the 1920s. Before 1929 eleven states had enacted pension laws. But in two of the states (Pennsylvania and Arizona) they had been declared unconstitutional, and in another three (California, Washington, and Wyoming) they had been vetoed. In the remaining six, the laws were merely optional and locally financed; in a word, either inoperative or defective. In 1929 a grand total of 1,200–odd aged persons in Montana, in a handful of Wisconsin counties, and in Alaska were receiving pensions totaling around $222,000.[53]

Private pension schemes instituted by industrialists and other employers make a somewhat more impressive showing. Alfred Dolge, a New York felt manufacturer, established the first pension plan in a manufacturing establishment in 1882. Other important early programs were those launched for the Carnegie Steel employees in 1901, by Standard Oil of New Jersey in 1903, and by street railway and other public utility companies. By 1905 twelve railroads had pension systems covering 35.4 percent of their employees. The most rapid growth of industrial pensions occurred after 1910, and by 1929 a total of 418 programs were in existence. Railroads, public utilities, banking, metal trades, oil, insurance, and electrical apparatus and supply industries accounted for more than 80 percent of the employees covered. Only one-eighth of all manufacturing employees were potential pensioners, however, and pension programs barely touched mine and construction workers and employees of chain and department stores, hotels, and restaurants. By 1932, 434 pension systems were reported to be in existence, covering about 140,000 industrial workers, but these represented less than 15 percent of all wage and salaried employees in industry.[54]

First and foremost, the industrial pension was a technique of labor control, indifferently funded without actuarial calculations, and vesting employees with no legal rights. Whether justified as benevolence—a reward for long and faithful service—or as a deferred wage, it was an instrument used by capital in its struggle with labor to control the employment market. An employer's underlying purpose in setting up pension systems was to attach his workforce permanently to himself in order to gain independence from both the uncertainties of the labor market and the dominance of unions. Industrial pension plans, in fine, were a staple of the "welfare capitalism" that characterized the 1920s, an expression of an even broader American ideal in that decade, namely, that volunteerism was the most appropriate form of collective action.[55] Unquestionably, there is truth in the allegation that employer hostility to independent trade unions was behind much of the welfare capitalism of the "New Era," behind not only pension plans but also group life insurance programs (it was estimated in October 1928 that 5.8 million workers were covered by $7.5 billion of this insurance), employee stock ownership programs (by 1927 some 800,000 employees of 315 corporations owned more than $1 billion in securities), medical care, recreational facilities, and numerous other benefits made available to many employees. But there was something more behind it, too, for in this New Era of hope, of expectation that the nation had reached a high plateau of permanent prosperity, some businessmen, at least, believed that the camps of capital and labor were not hopelessly separated by valleys of difference, that, in the words of John D. Rockefeller, Jr., "the fundamental idea of Welfare Capitalism [is] that the only solidarity natural in industry is the solidarity which unites all those in the same business establishment."[56] The fundamental objective was survival in the competitive struggle, and loyalty to the firm was viewed as contributory to that end, for a lessening of labor turnover preserved the human capital embedded in experience—the investments of the firm in training, particularly of managerial employees and skilled workers, but not of them alone. The labor management techniques of the 1920s contrast starkly with those of the nineteenth century. Especially in the later decades of that century, when the capital-intensive plant and structural overhead of a modern industrial economy was being put in place, working conditions were often egregiously harsh under the "drive system" maintained by factory foremen. It was a system of close supervision, fear, profanity, and abuse calculated to keep effort levels up and labor costs down. As a rule it was the foreman rather than the employer who did the hiring, made job assignments, determined piece wage rates, maintained discipline, and made decisions about promotions and firings. Indeed, each foreman ran his shop or department as an "autonomous fiefdom." It was he who decided how the job was to be done, what tools and often what materials were to be used, as well as the timing of operations, the flow of work, and the worker's methods and sequences of moves. In sum, after accepting a bribe to give a man a job— perhaps the most common method of obtaining one—the foreman supervised the daily administration of employment and the life and work of the shop floor.

In industries in which skill inputs were strategically important, craft unions were able to place some limits on the power of the foreman through rules governing methods of shop organization and, especially, by fixing output quotas to protect themselves from overexertion. But the unskilled lacked "voice." Their alternative was to "exit," to quit, and the resulting labor turn-over became a matter of increasing concern to growing numbers of reformers and middle-class professionals, as well as to employers. For something more than labor turnover and its replacement cost was seen to be involved. Concern over the decline of the work ethic, over lethargy, absenteeism, and insobriety, over the connection between seasonal unemployment and high turnover rates, and between both of the latter and the growth of unions, on the one hand, and of strikes, violence, and a drift to the political left, on the other, was also present.[57]

In consequence, the reformers—engineers interested in systematic management, welfare workers, vocational guidance counselors, men and women persuaded that rational administration was a social good and that professionals could both mediate and mitigate social conflict—mounted a campaign of study and propaganda to replace foremen by professional employment managers. These were years in which the functions of marketing, production, and sales were evolving toward greater conscious control by the firm, a process in which the "visible hand" of management increasingly replaced the invisible hand of the market.[58] And this was not the only organizational change under way. A similar process was at work after 1910 in the area of employment. An intrafirm, or internal, labor market was developing in which standardized procedures and rules could replace the capriciousness and arbitrariness of the older regime, a market in which workers could be efficiently allocated by bureaucratic mechanisms, by employment departments or personnel managers. The craft unions welcomed the change for the obvious reason that their system of rules, procedures, and protections were a model, in certain respects, of the internal labor market.[59] In the formation of that market the preference of workers for more secure, lawful, and impersonal employment relationships was very important. At the same time, employers viewed the new movement as one which would increase the loyalty of workers to their firms.[60]

The rise of employment management techniques thus dovetailed in their objectives with those of welfare capitalism, the primary goal of which was the enhanced labor productivity which would come from loyalty. But welfarism by no means dates from the 1920s. Indeed, it is as old as American industry itself. As early as 1790 Samuel Slater sought to recruit boys for his mill at Pawtucket, Rhode Island, by offering to open a Sunday school where they could learn on their day off. During the mid-nineteenth century welfare practices were concentrated mainly on housing for workers, but developments of the later nineteenth century brought proliferating activities in their wake. In particular, the growing size of firms resulted in loss of contact between employer and employee. Coupled with the special problems posed by a heavy influx of immigrant labor and growing labor unrest—between 1880 and 1900 nearly 23,000 strikes occurred, an average of three a day for twenty years, with 117,000 establishments being affected by them—many employers not only provided housing for their workers but also opened and operated every form of school short of a college or university, company libraries, restaurants, stores, parks and recreational facilities, gardens and greenhouses, moving-picture houses, bathhouses—even, in the case of United States Steel, a company morgue![61]

In 1916, even before the entry of the United States into the First World War, the federal government itself decided to encourage the spread of welfarism in order to stimulate production and minimize labor unrest and turnover. Three subcommittees of the Council of National Defense Committee on Welfare Work concerned themselves, respectively, with sanitary facilities in factories and company towns, the improvement of housing, and the encouragement of recreational activities. American intervention brought still other governmental agencies onto the side of welfarism. One, the Housing Corporation, spent $194 million to house about six thousand families, in effect constructing a series of "company" towns. Not surprisingly, similar exigencies induced private employers to redouble their efforts to bind their workers to themselves not only by welfare measures but also by establishing personnel management departments in their firms. In a situation marked by recurring industrial relations crises, declining labor productivity widely attributed to worker discontent, and a tight labor market, the economic costs of turnover mounted—and personnel management thrived.[62]

As in the case of welfarism, the federal government, in an effort to maintain uninterrupted production in industries producing and distributing war materiel, assisted the growth of the movement by popularizing employment management and its new techniques and encouraging the formation of employment departments. A committee of the War Industries Board went so far as to establish a crash program of instruction to expand the supply of employment managers, training more than six hundred managers in the short span of fourteen months. In sum, while government regulation of the labor market during the war helped hasten the adoption of employment departments and employment management techniques throughout industry, only a minority of firms had done so by 1921.[63]

The movement reached its peak in 1920, was sharply curtailed in the severe depression of 1920–21, and then proceeded forward, but at a slower pace than before, as turnover rates declined with the development of considerable slack in the manufacturing sector's demand for labor. Not so welfarism. The 1920s were the heyday of welfare capitalism. Contemporaries called it the "new" welfare work. Such quasi-pecuniary programs as profit sharing, stock ownership plans, group insurance, pensions, and paid vacations began to supplant older, more paternalistic practices. Some firms had introduced parts of the new welfare work in a piecemeal fashion before the war. Now they were "implemented *en bloc*" and with such success that, in the judgment of a leading labor historian, welfare capitalism might have continued to dominate industrial relations had it not been for the coming of the Great Depression.[64] The opinion is a controversial one. Certainly the evidence for a lesser degree of labor militancy in the 1920s is clear. By the middle of the decade the number of strikes had declined to a third of what it had been in the years just before the war. The material conditions of work were a good deal better than they had been. The factory, especially the large one, became a safer, cleaner, and more spacious place in which to work, one that was better lighted, heated, and ventilated. With machines and equipment engineered for safe use and plants laid out to avoid hazards, the most dramatic improvements, perhaps, were in the area of safety. These and the numerous other gains under welfare capitalism disposed the factory worker to reject independent unions and to embrace company unions, and, accordingly, membership in the former fell off while rising in the latter. In sum, there are many reasons for believing that the regime of paternalism was widely accepted. But there is also survey and other evidence of worker dissatisfaction with an arrangement under which employees were unable to bargain with their employers for increases in pay and reductions in hours of work. Moreover, the company union, euphemistically known as an employee representation plan, lacked authorization to strike, had no funds to finance a stoppage, and was incapable of coordinating its acts with organizations at other firms in the industry. Whether or not welfare capitalism would have continued if the prosperity of the twenties had lasted, it could not survive the depression. It had always thrived in good times and waned in those of decline.[65]

The roots of that depression are many and they are entangled, some reaching down to consequences of the First World War, others emerging with varying degrees of independence from that conflict in the 1920s. To begin with, not all regions, economic sectors, firms, and individuals—to utter a truism— shared equally in the prosperity of the decade. The lumber industry, for example, first overexpanded in response to a boom in the construction industry, then followed the decline of the latter in the late 1920s. The value of forest products fell sharply from $311 million in 1928 to $173.2 million in 1929.[66] Lumbering, like coal mining, also suffered from depleted resources in various parts of the country, most notably in the northern portions of the Great Lakes states. The railroad industry was hurt by severe competition with newer forms of transit in the 1920s. Trucks deprived them of some of their freight, and buses and private automobiles of some of their passengers. Railroad passenger-miles declined from 47 million in 1920 to 34 million in 1927, and the return on railroad investment exceeded 5 percent in only one year, 1926, when it reached 5.2 percent.[67] Above all, agriculture was afflicted in many ways. Largely because of the difficulties experienced in agriculture and in lumbering and mining, per capita income growth in the West North Central states and those of the mountain West and the South lagged behind gains achieved in other regions (for comparative indexes of regional growth rates, see Table 38).

Scholarly tradition has it that the farmer was the "sick man" of the American economy all through the twenties, that for agriculture the Great Depression began in 1920 rather than in 1929.[68] Recent writers, however, have challenged this pessimistic view. Calling attention to the fact that farm income per capita rose perhaps twice as fast as nonfarm income per capita from their postwar lows in 1921 to their trend apogees in 1929, one historian goes so far as to suggest that the farmer was "one of the few beneficiaries of the prosperity of the twenties."[69] That puts it a bit too boldly, although we must also concede to revisionism that net farm income from 1923 to 1929 was higher every year than it had been in the prewar period 1910–1914. Nevertheless, during those same years of the 1920s farmers' incomes averaged 30 percent lower than in 1919–20.[70] Quite evidently, it is the standard of comparison that matters. It mattered most to the farmers.

Implicit in the pointing out of these comparisons is the historian's insistence that the past be viewed not only in the light of statistical and other facts

Table 38.   Indexes of per capita personal income, by region, 1920 and 1930.

Region	1920	1930
United States	100	100
Northeast	132	138
New England	124	129
Middle Atlantic	134	140
North Central	100	101
Great Lakes	108	111
West North Central	87	82
South	62	55
South Atlantic	59	56
East South Central	52	48
West South Central	72	61
West	122	115
Mountain	100	83
Pacific	135	130

Source: Richard A. Easterlin, "Regional Income Trends, 1840–1950," in *American Economic History,* ed. Seymour Harris (New York: McGraw-Hill, 1961), p. 528. Used with permission.

available to later scholars but also in the light of what contemporaries believed about their situation and about themselves. Otherwise, we cannot fully account for historical change, because it is the historical actors themselves who bring it about. Scholars after the event are right to suggest that demographic, economic, or other forces hidden in the past or only partially understood propelled people into the actions they took. But we also need to know the ways in which these underlying forces entered into the calculations of men and women or affected their behavior. Even misunderstanding and error are important to know. For some purposes, whether the earth is round or flat matters less than what people believe it to be. What these observations amount to in the present case is this: Yes, there was an agricultural depression in the 1920s. But it was one which struck the nation's farmers unevenly. For some, notably those in particular geographic areas, the drop in income was absolute. For others, the decline was a relative one, but its consequences were also severe, for disappointed expectations can also lead to falling demand and values. From the statistics on prices of agricultural commodities and farm incomes, one would never guess that the value of farmland fell through the "prosperous" twenties, or that farm mortgage foreclosures increased and carried many rural banks into insolvency.

The explanation for this anomaly may well be that the value of farmland was less influenced by current income than by the shattering of expectations about the course of income and land values that had been built up before the 1920s, in the immediate postwar period.[71] Of course, other factors also influenced the value of farmland, some tending to enhance it, others to lower it. Yet it is misleading to speak of "the" farmer or of the price of "land." America's many regions and subregions held farmers specializing in numerous forms of enterprise, and the value of the land and its produce varied with the condition of the land, with its suitability for the crops grown on it, and with topography, weather, proximity to markets, farm product prices, and still other factors. Some influences were widespread in their effects. Urban expansion, for example, drove up the price of farmland in many localities; increased demand for dairy and livestock products raised the need for additional acres for feed and pasture. Others had mixed or partially offsetting effects. The advent of the tractor increased the demand for land, especially in the wheat-growing areas of the western plains, by making it possible to cultivate a more extensive acreage with fewer hands. Yet widespread adoption of tractors and tractor-driven implements after the war—the South being the main regional exception—reduced the number of acres needed for crops to feed horses and mules. Much of this acreage, as we shall see, was then devoted to the production of meats and grains, so that the income effect of the change in product mix depended not only on the impact on production costs of the substitution of tractors for work animals, but also on the price and income elasticity of demand for meats and grains.

Between 1918 and 1929 the number of tractors on farms rose from 85,000 to 827,000, and the use of motor trucks, automobiles, grain combines, and corn pickers also rose impressively.[72] Resultant increases in per worker productivity lessened the demand for farmers, and in most years during the twenties the net movement from farms exceeded the natural increase of the farm population. Income from farming represented a declining share of national income. Industrial and commercial expansion far outran expansion in farm output, and between 1919 and 1928 the farm income percentage of national income fell by one-half, from 18.5 percent to 9.5 percent. With fewer people in farming, demand for farmland declined, and with it its price. Yet an additional factor also made for price decline, namely, the lowering of once-high hopes for capital gains on investment in land—an important part of lifetime income for most farmers in the nineteenth century, and probably before as well. As incomes failed to reach high wartime levels, the value of land as an investment declined.[73]

What made the problem worse was the fact that most farmers had not yet fully paid for their land. Most made a small down payment, then took out both a first and a second ("junior") mortgage for the balance. As long as land values were rising, the farmers were able to induce their mortgagee banks and insurance companies for the first mortgage, and either a local bank or an individual lender (often the seller of the land) for the second, to renew their promissory notes. But when values fell, they faced a rapid loss of equity. As a rule, then, it was the declining value of land rather than the inability of the farmer to meet fixed interest payments that led to mortgage foreclosure during the twenties. But there was one set of circumstances in which the cause was insufficient current income.[74] Much of the debt distress that developed in the 1930s as well as the 1920s is traceable to excessive lending on farms which proved to be lacking in long-term earning power because of limitations imposed by soils, climate, topography, or location. Inferior or marginal land was most likely to be overpriced in periods of prosperity and inflation, as in the land boom of 1918–1920. As long as the prices of agricultural products were high, the land might earn a handsome rate of return. But when they declined, mortgages were likely to end in foreclosure. Some of the worst mortgage trouble spots were in areas of recent settlement by people unacquainted with the physical limitations of the regions in which they located. Inexperienced settlers from farther east, where rainfall was more plentiful and dependable, located on farms in the Great Plains that were too small to constitute economic units in a semiarid region. Introducing crop farming into areas that in the long run were unsuited to it, they found themselves in trouble. Similar mistakes were made by settlers in the cutover areas of the Great Lake states, where soils were relatively unproductive and capable of supporting little more than subsistence agriculture in normal times. Farm mortgage distress in this region, especially in northern and central Minnesota, upper Michigan, and a large part of Wisconsin, was of major proportions. Foreclosure rates were also very high in the Corn Belt in the 1920s, but the highest rates occurred in such poor-soil areas as southern and northwestern Iowa, northern Missouri, and southern Indiana.[75]

Farmland is not a homogeneous commodity but a highly variable one, even within a given region, and it is not surprising that the farmland market should have experienced difficulties in setting values which accorded with earnings prospects. In addition, farmers in many areas had to confront difficulties and expenses which only compounded the eventual costs of mistaken appraisals. Where drought was a problem, as in the Great Plains, Rocky Mountain states, and parts of the Northwest, farmers not only had to meet the interest payments due on their mortgages but also to pay taxes for the operation, maintenance, and debt service of irrigation districts. Hot winds, hail, and frost added to other debt difficulties by reducing crop yields. And while insect pests, noxious weeds, and plant and animal diseases lowered production in some cases, in others their costs took the form of cash outlays for control measures.[76] In Louisiana, the mosaic disease almost wiped out the sugar industry before it was conquered in the late 1920s and early 1930s by the introduction of new varieties of cane. Making its appearance in the cotton states of the Southeast in the late teens, the boll weevil blanketed the cotton South by 1923.[77] In Georgia the pest reduced yields by an estimated 45 percent in 1921, 44 percent in 1922, and 37 percent in 1923. In South Carolina the greatest reduction, 40 percent, occurred in 1922.[78]

In both the 1920s and the 1930s the South was a chronic trouble area. In the cotton states of the Mississippi Delta—Arkansas, Mississippi, and Louisiana—there were not only drainage taxes to pay but also regular county and state taxes, as well as additional imposts for levee districts, road districts, and sometimes fence districts. In the eastern Cotton Belt farmers were in serious financial difficulties, even though cotton prices recovered from their lows in 1921–22, because of poor cotton yields and relatively high costs and debt service charges. Had it not been for these low yields, the price of cotton might not have been able to recover as much as it did in the 1920s. This is because technological innovation in the chemical industry, especially the development of rayon and nylon as substitutes for natural fibers, was somewhat diminishing the demand for cotton and exerting downward pressure on its price. The individual farmer could not hope to counter declining demand by lowering his output still more. His product was such a small part of the total that it could exert no effect on price. Given the problems he faced in the twentieth century, the essence of the cotton farmer's predicament was his almost total dependence on cotton as the principal source of farm income. That dependence was one of the important causes of debt distress, not only in the Delta but also in the eastern Cotton Belt, where farm mortgage foreclosures were among the highest in the United States.[79]

Behind this monocultural predicament lay a host of social, demographic, and economic problems; in a word, behind it lay southern history. The relative failure of industry to develop left the South still 67.9 percent rural even in 1930, with 42.8 percent of its workforce still working on farms and earning a per capita income of $189, in contrast with $484 for nonfarm occupations. The rural scene was the old and familiar one of "a patient Negro, driving a mule, and marching endlessly behind a plow for crops which never quite brought freedom from economic slavery." For blacks poverty, ignorance, illiteracy, and superstition remained bitter by-products of racial oppression and parsimonious expenditures on public education. But these characteristics experienced little difficulty in crossing the color line. Application of an effective insecticide, calcium arsenate, to the weevil scourge was frequently resisted by farmers who insisted that the weevil represented a judgment of God. Similarly, obstinate folkways hampered the war on the cattle tick, bearer of Texas fever. In 1930 tenants still operated 55.5 percent of all southern farms.[80] The most difficult aspect of the farm problem, not only in the South but in Appalachia and in the cutover region of the Great Lake states as well—indeed, wherever self-sufficiency and marginal returns were conspicuous features of the agricultural landscape—was a "set of social rigidities" which culminated in inability to induce sufficient numbers of people to migrate from areas of stunted opportunities to others where life chances were better. Fundamentally, the social problem in agriculture reduces to the overpopulation of certain regions in relation to their supply of natural resources.[81]

More generally, farmers faced an economic problem formulated by leaders of farm opinion as one of "overproduction," of "surpluses." Essentially, their formulation was correct. It was a classic case of supply outdistancing demand—demand at prices which would remunerate the farmer's investment of his labor, land, and capital. Supply had received a big boost during the war when 40 million additional acres were placed under cultivation to meet the needs not only of a growing urban America but also those of the Allies. Then, during the 1920s the replacement of horses and mules by tractors released for the production of salable crops some 24 million acres which before had been devoted to the production of oats and hay needed by draft animals.[82.] Demand could not keep up. Domestic demand for meats, grains, and most other major farm products was inelastic with respect to both income and price. (Increases in urban incomes or price reductions did not bring about a proportionate increase in the demand for the commodities.) And foreign markets declined as, first, the return to peacetime conditions restored agricultural production in Europe and, second, as foreign governments sought to protect their markets by tariffs.

The individual farmer responded to declining demand and prices by increasing production in an effort to maintain his income. It would have done him no good to cut back as long as other people did not do so. Unfortunately tens of thousands of his fellows were scattered throughout the country, and it was virtually impossible by voluntary means to induce them to form associations for the purpose of limiting their output. In contrast, industrialists were responding to the encouragement of Secretary of Commerce Herbert Hoover by forming dozens of trade associations. To be sure, these associations were being organized "merely" to exchange information on prices and output. But many of them used this information to restrict competition. And the federal courts did not object unless explicit price fixing activity could be proved.

To make matters worse, industrialists were able to sell their products in an American market protected by tariffs. There were tariffs on farm products too—on wheat, corn, meat, wool, and many other staples— imposed by the Emergency Tariff Act of 1921 and by the Fordney-McCumber Act of 1922.[83] But they were simply irrelevant in view of the flooding of American markets by American farmers themselves. Resulting low prices could hardly entice imports having to bear not only tariffs but shipping costs. Despite the tariff, the world price of wheat determined the domestic price because American surpluses forced the home market down to world levels.[84]

A few thought that the way out of the dilemma was for government to mount "domestic allotment" programs designed to curtail output. But such suggestions were too activist for the twenties. Farm spokesmen had an alternative plan. They would raise the domestic price level by combining high tariffs on farm products with a corporate device for removing surpluses from the American market and dumping them abroad. The overall objective was "fair-exchange" value, or parity, which was defined as the ratio obtaining before the war (1910–1914) between prices received by farmers and prices paid by them. If parity could be achieved, an unfair situation would be corrected, one in which farmers sold their crops in competitive markets while buying their equipment and many of their supplies in a protected one.[85] To restore it, a corporation chartered by the federal government would buy enough of each commodity to raise its price to the computed parity level. The corporation would then sell the commodities abroad at the world price, presumably a lower one. Naturally the corporation would sustain losses, but the farmers would be obliged to make these good by paying a tax (called an equalization fee) on every unit or bushel of a commodity sold. The tax, however, would be less than the amount by which the domestic price would rise.[86]

Following the leadership of George N. Peek and Hugh Johnson of the Moline Plow Company ("You can't sell a plow to a busted customer"), the farm lobby put pressure on Congress, with the result that Senator Charles L. McNary of Oregon and Representative Gilbert N. Haugen of Iowa introduced bills in 1924 and again in 1928 to restore parity. Both passed the Congress only to meet vetoes by President Calvin Coolidge, who had the strong support of Secretary of Commerce Herbert Hoover and Secretary of the Treasury Andrew Mellon, among others. Hoover did not wish, as he expressed it, to "put the government in the business of buying and selling farm products, or deliver the farmers over to government price-fixing." Mellon feared the impact of rising food costs on industrial wages and the effect that the latter would have on the country's ability to compete in industrial markets. Those who favored "McNary-Haugenism" frequently defined their objectives in terms of Jeffersonian agrarianism or other philosophical principles, but the chances are that this was at bottom one more struggle to see whether the economic interests of farmers or those of manufacturers would prevail. There was more than a little truth in Peek's comment in 1928 that "the whole effect of the policies of the last two administrations has been to hasten the industrialization of America at the expense of agriculture." Nevertheless, McNary-Haugenism proved to be an important precedent for the soon-to-be-enacted Agricultural Adjustment Act of the Franklin D. Roosevelt administration, and from that day to this the farm bloc has enjoyed a political power that is extraordinary in a highly postindustrialized society.[87]

The misfortunes experienced by substantial numbers of farmers permit the unsurprising presumption that the distribution of income in the 1920s was something less than equal. It was. The difference between the incomes received by a small minority and by the rest of the population was large at the beginning of the decade and bigger still at its end. In 1920 the real disposable income of the top 1 percent of the population was 15.5 times larger than that of the lower 93 percent. In 1929 it was 30 times larger. The top 1 percent's share of total income rose from 13 percent in 1923 to 19 percent in 1929 (the comparable figure at the end of the Second World War was only 1 percent).[88]

Widely separated farmers could organize only with great difficulty if at all in an effort to influence prices and incomes. Manufacturing firms had an easier time of it, and they not only formed large numbers of trade associations in the twenties but also entered into mergers. Between 1924 and 1929 they engaged in a merger movement second in importance only to the giant turn-of-the-century wave, the number rising during those years from 368 to 1,245.[89] Market control, however, was not the only objective sought. A merger often permitted a firm to diversify, to move into new product lines and markets, and since mergers often brought one or more smaller companies under the wing of a financially powerful, better organized and administered large firm, the movement undoubtedly contributed to productivity growth. Mergers were typically consummated by exchanging the stock of the smaller firm for that of the larger, so that the capital gains afforded by a rising stock market added to the inducement to sell out. The merger movement of the 1920s was not only the largest since the great wave at the turn of the century. It was also marked by the closest correlation between mergers and stock prices in merger history.[90]

The New York Stock Exchange was indeed a buoyant market in the 1920s. From transactions involving 236 million shares in 1923, sales soared in 1929 to 1,125 million shares on January 1 of that year.[91] Adding to the volume of

securities available for purchase or sale were not only the offerings of companies seeking in a favorable market to raise money for general corporate
purposes, but also those brought into existence by the merger movement, for
each new merger required new capital and a new issue of securities to pay for
it.[92] In addition, numerous investment trusts—corporations which sold their
own stock to investors and used the proceeds to purchase shares in other
corporations, thus diversifying the investment risk—were formed, an estimated 186 in 1928 and 265 in 1929. In the latter year they sold an estimated
$3 billion worth of securities. Finally, there were the stocks of the holding
companies, especially in public utilities, firms incorporated for the purpose of
buying control of operating companies, but which sometimes controlled other
holding companies—which in turn controlled still other holding companies—in a maze perhaps best understood by the Samuel Insulls of the period.
New issues of stock in 1929 went disproportionately to mergers and other
financial schemes; new isssues of bonds went disproportionately to real
investment.[93]

Investment in stocks, almost wholly confined to wealthy people before the
war, probably spread in the later 1920s to embrace a significant segment of
the middle class. Legend has it that clerks and bootblacks as well as businessmen, lawyers, doctors, and others of more substantial means engaged in speculating.[94] All recent estimates, however, clearly show that only a small minority
(8 percent) of the population owned stock—although this percentage may
have doubled in the boom years—and that large holdings were heavily concentrated in the hands of the wealthy few, with perhaps 500,000 to 600,000
people owning between 75 and 85 percent of the outstanding shares.[95] Yet if
it is untrue that "virtually the whole population was engaged in a gambling
spree"—one historian thinks it safe to say that the number of active speculators
in 1929 was probably much less than 1 million persons—numbers alone do
not convey the avid public interest in the market: "the striking thing about
the stock market speculation in 1929 was not the massiveness of the participation. Rather it was the way it became central to the culture."[96] Like batting
averages, market news "touched the statistical heart of the country."[97]

The main object of popular attention, of course, was the behavior of stock
prices. Prices began to rise in the last six months of 1924 and continued to do
so through the next year. The market suffered something of a setback in 1926,
resumed its upward course in 1927, and then, after the winter of 1928, took
off in great vaulting leaps. Radio, the "speculative symbol of the time," gained
18 points on March 12, 1928, and on the following day opened 22 points
above the previous close. During the year as a whole it went from 85 to 420.
Numerous other issues also did well that year. DuPont rose from 310 to 525,
Montgomery Ward from 117 to 440, and Wright Aeronautic from 69 to 289.
At the top of the boom, in September 1929, Radio, adjusted for stock splits,
reached 505.[98]

Fueling these upward spiraling prices was not only the cash of the circumspect investor but also a vast volume of credit available to speculators in the form of brokers' loans. These loans enabled purchasers to obtain stock on margin, at some percentage of the purchase price, the loans being subject to call rather than extended for a given period of time. Attracted by interest rates that rose from around 5 percent at the beginning of 1928 to 12 percent the last week of that year, cash flowed into the call money market not only from domestic sources but from abroad as well. The commercial banks, especially those of New York, notably the National City Bank under the chairmanship of Charles E. Mitchell, were one of the sources of speculative funds, but their participation was relatively small. Commercial banks owned less than 1 percent of the outstanding corporate stock in 1929, a total of $1.2 billion. Their "loans on securities" to brokers and dealers or individual speculators were much higher, reaching $8.3 billion in 1929.[99]

Almost all of the increase in brokers' loans in 1928–29 came from nonbank sources, from corporations, foreigners, and wealthy individuals. Standard Oil of New Jersey invested a daily average of $69 million in the call money market in 1929, while Electric Bond and Share averaged over $100 million. A few corporations went so far as to sell their own securities and lend the proceeds in the stock market. As much as $3 billion of corporate funds, including the excess cash balances of many corporations not issuing new stock, may have gone into brokers' loans in the late 1920s. In the early years of that decade the volume of brokers' loans ranged between $1 billion and $1.5 billion a year. During the summer of 1929 they increased by approximately $400 million a month, and by the end of that summer the grand total exceeded $7 billion.[100]

In this developing situation, especially during 1929, monetary policy was largely paralyzed by severe disagreement between the Federal Reserve Board and the Federal Reserve Bank of New York. Both agreed that speculation was cause for concern, but the board refused to allow the New York bank to raise its discount rate—at least it did so till August 1929, by which late date the bank believed the time might have passed for such action. Instead, the Federal Reserve Board favored the use of moral suasion to deter overborrowing by member banks making loans to speculators.[101] It hoped by this tactic to combat speculation without at the same time restricting the flow of credit to legitimate borrowers needing money for productive purposes. In February 1929, for example, the board told the Federal Reserve banks that a member bank—that is, a commercial bank like Mitchell's National City—was "not within its reasonable claims for rediscount facilities at its reserve bank when it borrow[ed] either for the purpose of making speculative loans or for the purpose of maintaining speculative loans." But at the same time the board made it clear that it had "no disposition to assume authority to interfere with the loan practices of member banks, so long as they do not involve the Federal reserve banks."[102] Thus even the use of moral suasion was to be confined to those member banks which lacked excess reserves and in consequence had to use the rediscounting facilities of their reserve banks if they wanted to make loans to speculators.

The Federal Reserve Board's policy was not a bold one. Indeed, the board may justly be said to have set the stage for speculation in 1927, when in an effort to help Britain remain on the gold standard, to which it had returned two years before, the board lowered the discount rate from 4 to 3.5 percent and also purchased government securities in considerable volume.[103] Yet when all is said and done, the river of money on which speculation floated was far too wide for the board to control. What was required was international central bank cooperation, and this was entirely lacking. In view too of the comparatively small amount of bank credit fueling speculation, an earlier, more restrictive policy might not have arrested the mania. Too much of that money was beyond its control. In fact, when the board finally allowed the New York bank to raise its rediscount rate, it may have given a boost to interest rates and in consequence attracted an even larger amount of corporate and individual money to Wall Street.[104]

Had the Reserve Board then possessed the power to set margin rates which Congress was to give it in 1934, it might have used it to sobering effect. But it did not, and the reckoning came. In September and October 1929 the mad structure began to fall apart. In September the industrial averages had stood at 452. Two months later they were half that. By July 1932 they had sunk to 58. According to the New York Stock Exchange, the market value of all listed securities was $89,668 billion in September 1929. Three years later, again in July 1932, their value was $15,663 billion.[105] In those three years GM fell from 73 to 8, U.S. Steel from 262 to 22, Montgomery Ward from 138 to 4.[106] And that was not all. Between 1929 and 1933 the net national product in current prices fell by more than half, in constant prices by over a third. Monthly wholesale prices, too, were down by more than a third.[107] As of 1932–33, industrial production was down by more than half, gross private domestic investment by nearly 90 percent (in constant prices), and farm prices by more than 60 percent. In March 1933 unemployment stood at about 25 percent of the labor force, and the nation was plunged into catastrophic depression, the most severe in its history.[108]

Did the collapse of the stock market trigger the depression? The question is short, the answer long. There are two fundamental reasons for this. One is that the collapse was only one of several interacting causes of the coming of the depression. The other is that the depression itself must be divided into at least two, and probably three, distinct phases. One runs from the collapse itself to the first wave of bank failures in October 1930, another from then till 1933, and the probable third for most of the remainder of the 1930s. In each of these phases different factors, always in combination and never singly, appear to have played either dominant or recessive roles. Yet none of them ever ran out the string and ceased to be a requisite part of a moving causal mosaic. How comforting it would be—perhaps—if it were possible, by either econometric or verbal means, to specify the weight to be assigned each of the factors in each of the phases. Alas! this can never be. History is not a science, and nothing can make it so. But it is precisely because this is true that the men and women who try to reconstruct the past must shoulder a heavy burden of responsibility for the tentative judgments they are required to reach.

Since the appearance in 1963 of Milton Friedman and Anna J. Schwartz' monumental *Monetary History of the United States, 1867-1960,* the debate over the causes of "the great contraction" has concerned the respective roles of monetary and nonmonetary forces. While there are differences among monetarists (and among nonmonetarists too, of course), some of them, at any rate, stress slow monetary growth in 1928 and early 1929, when "M_2" (currency in the hands of the public and checking accounts) grew at an annual rate of only 0.6 percent in contrast to a rate of 5.2 percent in the preceding five quarters, as the underlying cause of the first year's contraction.[109] The position is an extreme one, and it can be effectively countered by pointing to an even larger drop in the money stock between 1924 and 1926 which failed to culminate in depression. Evidently it is the total context in which the stock of money changes that matters, and if this is so, it follows that variables other than the money supply must also be taken into account.[110] Nonmonetarists readily concede a role in the collapse of the market to the easy-money policy of the Federal Reserve Board in 1927, which encouraged speculation, and to its constrictionist reversal in 1929, which sought to discourage speculation but at the same time hampered economic growth by making credit tighten. But they also point to other changes of a negative character in the later 1920s. As one analyst puts it, it is clear that "business was in trouble long before the crash."[111]

Declining investment in both residential and commercial construction appears to have been of particular importance.[112] Private construction activity peaked as early as 1926 and fell by $2 billion between then and 1929.[113] The percentage of full-employment output going to residential fixed investment declined 40 percent during this interval and then fell another 40 percent from 1929 to 1930.[114] The decline was especially sharp in 1928,[115] and in March of the following year the rapid fall in building contracts prompted a Federal Reserve official to note with alarm that this was "always a precursor of a general decline." The development cannot be attributed to falling income, for incomes were rising between 1926 and 1929, at least till August 1929, when they began a slight decline that totaled 5 percent between that month and the crash.[116] It owes something to restrictive immigration laws in 1921 and 1924, which by reducing the number of incoming new families lessened the demand for new homes. However, immigration was small in relation to the increase in the domestic population, so that the effect of the legislation was probably not very large.[117] Yet, although overall population was increasing, it was doing so at a declining rate between 1923 and 1931.[118] The most likely explanation is that the construction industry was unaware of the population trend and simply overbuilt. For six years (1923–1928) the industry achieved a level of residential construction that was more than twice the average annual level of the entire decade before the war. All in all, it is not surprising that supply exceeded demand at prices which would clear the market.[119]

Other industries also showed signs of overcapacity, with a resulting decline in the demand for capital goods.[120] In some of them, accelerating technical change had led to increases in investment which seemed amply justified by a rising marginal propensity to consume—encouraged by the availability of new products, installment credit, advertising, and high-pressure salesmanship. The high levels of spending on consumption and investment masked the excessive capacity that was being built up.[121] The textile industries had been suffering from overcapacity for some time, and by mid-1929 it was clear that the automobile market was also oversold.[122] Automobile production reached its peak in March 1929 at 622,000 and fell to 416,000 in September.[123] The industry was of special importance because of the number of other industries whose production depended significantly on the demand for cars. Output of tires, for example, began to fall sharply the latter part of 1928. Thus investment opportunities were increasingly restricted simply because they had been so thoroughly exploited in the 1920s. The development of buyers' markets in a number of important lines associated with peak production from overbuilt plants probably weakened business expectations and discouraged further investment. Production went down a full 20 percent between August 1929 and the crash, and wholesale prices fell 7.5 percent.[124]

For these reasons the economy was in a sense "set up," highly vulnerable to the psychological effects of the stock market collapse. The crash severely aggravated the situation by precipitating a drastic decline of $3 billion in consumption spending between 1929 and 1930. Behind this decline lay a widespread financial squeeze felt by American consumers as a result of increased liabilities and falling financial-asset values between 1929 and 1932. In the heady atmosphere of the boom year 1929—before the October crash— consumers had purchased durable goods on installment credit and taken out mortgages to buy homes; household liabilities thus incurred increased by 20 percent, in comparison with a rise of only 12 percent the previous year. As a result of the stock market crash, however, the value of financial assets such as bonds, stocks, and life insurance policies fell—by 4 percent in 1929–30, 6 percent in 1930–31, and 8 percent in 1931–32.[125] Price deflation had increased the real burden of indebtedness. The consequence was a sharp decline in aggregate spending by consumers, and this, interacting with and reinforced by the continuing decline in residential housing, turned what might have been a relatively mild recession into the beginnings of a major depression.[126] *The fundamental cause of the Great Depression, then, was the fall in aggregate demand.* Experience in the twentieth century had led businessmen to expect that signs of a resumption in activity would not linger long in the wake of decline, but as the autumn of 1930 wore on and these failed to appear, the effects of the decline spread throughout the economy and businessmen lost the confidence that underlies private investment.[127]

It is possible that the depression lasted as long as it did because the right kinds of investment were not forthcoming in sufficient quantities. Contemporaries were apparently unaware of a fundamental shift that was taking place in the structure of the economy and therefore failed to take the kinds of action required by that change. The higher levels of full-employment income reached in the 1920s were altering the structure of potential consumer demand in the direction of industries producing services and nondurable consumer goods such as food products, beverages, tobacco products, chemicals, petroleum products, and pharmaceuticals. These industries experienced fairly continuous technological change and product innovation in the twenties and thirties and in the latter decade suffered relatively limited decreases in the demand for their products. Unlike steel and other older manufacturing sectors in which concentration ratios were high, these new dynamic sectors were competitive, both as to price and otherwise. Unfortunately, they were also capital intensive and unable to absorb much of the unemployed manpower of the depression decade. Finally, even though the long-run potential for economic growth was represented by the activity of these sectors, their presence in the aggregate economy was still relatively insignificant. Very much the dynamic tail, they could nevertheless not wag the dog.[128]

What of the possibility that consumption demand might have cushioned the shock of the crash had workers' incomes borne a closer relationship to productivity advances? One economist, at least, gives it scant weight. "It can scarcely be argued," he suggests, "that a moderately higher level of consumption could have prevented for very long, if at all, a decline in investment in residential and commercial building, in the automobile and related industries, and in other areas that had been expanding most rapidly. There was overinvestment in the late 1920s in the sense that capacity in numerous lines had been expanding at a rate that could not be maintained indefinitely." Perhaps he is right, perhaps a "moderately higher" level would not have helped for "very long."[129] He may also be wrong. For was not the overinvestment directly related to the possibility that too large a share of the national income was going to savers and too small a portion to the consuming classes—workers and farmers?

It is true that farming accounted for only a quarter of total employment in 1929, and farm exports only 28 percent of farm income. Yet even in 1929 farm exports declined, pulling agricultural revenue down with them. And between that year and 1932 farm exports dropped 66 percent, a consequence of foreign retaliation provoked by the Hawley-Smoot Tariff Act of 1930, which raised the effective rate of duties on imports by nearly 50 percent. The decline not only reduced farm incomes and aggregate demand. Farm prices also fell substantially, helping to pull down rural banks and encouraging hoarding, with a consequent fall in the money supply.[130]

In sum, although we may justly conclude that the collapse of the stock market initiated the Great Depression, the severity and duration of the latter is wound in a causal complex whose filaments are so entwined in gossamer incertitude that they are incapable of bearing weight as single strands. They include lagging wages, falling farm incomes, decline in residential construction, overcapacity in a number of industries, structural shifts, and, as we shall see, the impact of international financial and commercial considerations on spending by consumers and investors. Yet the parts played by these "real" factors by no means rule out a role for monetary ones, for as Friedman and Schwartz well say, "it is hardly conceivable that money income could have declined by over one-half and prices by over one-third in the course of four years if there had been no decline in the stock of money."[131] Behind that decline lay the collapse of the banking system and the failure of the Federal Reserve System both to prevent that collapse and to moderate its effects.

The first of four banking crises came upon the nation in October 1930. From the agricultural areas which had experienced the heaviest impact of bank failures in the 1920s, especially from Missouri, Indiana, Illinois, Iowa, Arkansas, and North Carolina, rose a "contagion of fear" which soon spread to other parts of the country. Within a month 256 banks, with deposits of $180 million, had failed, and by the end of December another 352, with deposits of over $370 million, followed suit. Fortunately this initial "liquidity crisis"— defined by scrambling efforts to convert corporate bonds and other assets into currency to meet the withdrawal demands of depositors and to prepare the institution for future contingencies—was of brief duration. It was over by March 1931, and had the Federal Reserve Board heeded the indicators of economic revival—for example, rising industrial production—by vigorously expanding the money supply, a sustained recovery might have ensued. Instead, it reduced the amount of Federal Reserve credit outstanding, and in March 1931 the total stock of money was lower than it had been in December 1930.[132]

The onset of the second banking crisis came in March 1931 as the public renewed at an increasing rate the conversion of its deposits into currency, a process which led, of course, to a decline in the deposit/currency ratio, the "most sensitive indicator of the public's attitude toward banks." In the five months from March to August the stock of money fell at the phenomenal annual rate of 13 percent as banks sought both to meet the demands of depositors and to add to their reserves relative to their liabilities. Bank failures stepped up sharply in June, but despite "an unprecedented liquidation of the commercial banking system," the Federal Reserve Board undertook only timid, minor open-market purchases between June and August to ease the situation. From February to mid-August no net change occurred in Federal Reserve credit outstanding.[133]

In September 1931 Britain abandoned the gold standard. (It was not really a gold standard but rather a "gold exchange" standard, that is, one in which reserves consisted not only of gold but also of claims on foreign currencies, or foreign exchange.) Anticipating the possibility that the United States might follow Britain, that the gold value of the dollar might not be maintained, foreign holders of dollar assets, especially central banks such as the Bank of France, which had suffered large losses on their sterling holdings and feared a similar experience with their dollars, converted those assets into gold.[134] In consequence, the gold stock—source of reserves of "high power money"— declined by $725 million in the six-week span between September 16 and the end of October. An internal drain on the banking system accompanied this external drain as banks with deposits of $414 million closed their doors in August and September.[135]

In an effort to halt the flight of gold abroad, the Federal Reserve Bank of New York twice raised its rediscount rate within a single week in October, "the sharpest rise within so brief a period in the whole history of the System, before or since." Within two weeks the external drain ceased, at least till the end of December. But the tightening of the money supply was also accompanied by a spectacular increase in bank failures and in runs on banks. All told, in the six months between August 1931 and February 1932, 1,860 banks with deposits of $1,449 million suspended operations. Those institutions which managed to stay afloat saw their deposits fall by nearly five times that amount. In the six months ending in February 1932 the money stock fell at an annual rate of 31 percent, a rate of decline larger by far than for any comparable period in the entire 93–year span for which a continuous statistical series on the money stock is available.[136]

Once again, the reaction of the Federal Reserve Board left something to be desired. Although the reserves of member banks were being heavily drained from two directions—by exports of gold and by internal demands for currency—the board managed to purchase only an additional $500 million in bills, an amount insufficient to offset the outflow of gold, let alone the domestic drain. It made no purchases of government securities at all. Had it done so, had it adopted a policy of monetary ease instead of one of constraint, its open market operations would have permitted a multiple expansion of deposits instead of the multiple contraction that actually occurred.[137]

In the meantime, the broader economic indicators showed a continuation of the steep decline, with personal income down by 31 percent, wholesale prices by 14 percent, and production by 32 percent from the beginning of the second banking crisis in March 1931 through mid-1932. Under heavy congressional pressure to expand the money supply, the Federal Reserve Board in April 1932 finally embarked on a program of large-scale open market purchases. By August its security holdings had increased by roughly $1 billion. Had it not taken this action, it is possible that a renewed flurry of bank failures in mid-1932 would have degenerated into a major crisis. As it was, the arresting of the decline in the money stock and the beginning of the purchase program were shortly followed by encouraging changes in general economic indicators such as wholesale prices, production, factory employment, and railroad ton-miles. Although it cannot be demonstrated that the economic improvement reflected the influence of the monetary improvement, neither can it be denied that such a causal sequence is highly plausible.[138]

The recovery proved to be only a temporary one, and once again bank failures, which began in the last quarter of 1932, mostly in the Midwest and Far West, were a notable feature of the relapse. This time the situation was more serious than it had been before and the panic more widespread. Heavy withdrawals from savings banks, demands for currency from interior banks, speculative accumulation of foreign currencies, and increased earmarkings of gold on the part of banks and individuals who feared a renewal of foreign demand for the metal led to heavy drains of gold, both internal and external. Once again the Federal Reserve System responded with half-measures. It raised discount rates in February 1933 in an effort to stem the outflow of gold, but it failed to make a determined effort to counter either the internal or the external drain by engaging in extensive open market operations. During the four years from 1930 through 1933, more than nine thousand banks suspended operations, imposing losses of approximately $2.5 billion on stockholders, depositors, and other creditors.[139]

Why was the Federal Reserve System so belated in showing concern for bank failures and so inactive in responding to them? Freidman and Schwartz believe the answer lies in the limited understanding of most of the governors of the banks, members of the board, and other administrators, who tended to regard bank failures as "regrettable consequences of bad management and bad banking practices, or as inevitable reactions to prior speculative excesses, or as a consequence but hardly a cause of the financial and economic collapse in process." These deficiencies were not shared by officials of the Federal Reserve Bank of New York. In contrast to the local and regional matters which concerned their counterparts elsewhere, New York technical personnel, officers, and directors had enjoyed years of primary responsibility for the conduct of monetary policy in the central money market of the country and had cooperated with similarly placed men in the leading money markets of the world. In consequence, there were "extraordinary differences between New York and most of the other Banks in the level of sophistication and understanding about monetary matters"—and between New York and the Federal Reserve Board itself, which had no tradition of leadership and had failed throughout the twenties to play a key role in determining the policy of the system. Before

1928 the New York bank was the major source of policy, both domestic and foreign, and the dominant figure in the entire Federal Reserve System was the man who had been its governor from the beginning, Benjamin Strong. After Strong's retirement in August 1928 and death in October, power shifted from New York to the other Federal Reserve banks. Much more parochial in situation and outlook than New York and lacking in a background of leadership and of national responsibility, these regional bankers were more likely to believe that the system must adjust to other forces rather than lead them.[140]

The ultimate explanation for the financial collapse, however, was the existence of a financial system that was susceptible to crises which could only be resolved by leadership such as that provided by Strong. In his absence, the policy of the system after 1929 can only be described as inept. Its hallmarks were drift and indecision, inertia, and passivity. Even the deep devotion of almost everyone, including the officials of the New York bank, to the maintenance of the gold standard does not excuse the actions taken by the system after Britain left the gold standard in September 1931. The sharp rises in the discount rate decided on in an effort to stem the outflow of gold ought to have been accompanied by open market operations. These would have increased the reserves of the member banks and permitted a multiple expansion of deposits instead of the multiple contraction that actually occurred. In short, the situation was one that called for a policy of monetary ease rather than constraint. Claims by monetarists that changes in the money supply lead in the short run to changes in the "real" economy must remain controversial, yet had the Federal Reserve System prevented or moderated the large decline in the money stock between 1929 and 1933, it is reasonable to believe that both the severity and the duration of the Great Depression would have been reduced.[141]

Finally, international capital flows also played a role in both the coming and the worsening of the depression. The First World War marks a major turning point in the direction of those flows. From the beginning of colonial settlement, Americans had been largely dependent on European lenders and investors for the capital required for the development of their resources. While savings by Americans became increasingly important as a source of investment capital, and eventually the dominant source, never before 1914 had Americans invested as much abroad as foreigners had invested in the United States. This situation began to change with the outbreak of the war. First, the European belligerents reduced their investments in American stocks, bonds, and real estate in order to gain command of the dollars necessary for the purchase of war materiel and foodstuffs. Next, they began to borrow, initially from American bankers and private individuals, and then, after the entry of the United States in the war in April 1917, from the federal government. The net result of these transactions was the conversion of the United States from a debtor to a creditor nation. On July 1, 1914, Americans had owed foreigners approximately $3,686,000,000 more than the latter owed Americans, but on December 31, 1919, foreign debts to the United States exceeded by $12,562,000,000 the amount owed by Americans abroad. More than 80 percent of the latter represented sums owed the United States government, principally by Great Britain and France. These war debts would contribute to the unsettled state of international finance in the 1920s.[142]

So too would the reparations owed by Germany to the Allied governments. Although the United States did not demand reparations, set in April 1921 at $33 billion by a Reparations Commission made up of representatives of the Allies, the large annual interest payments on them became connected with the war debts owed the United States when Great Britain in 1922 decided to collect in reparations only such amounts as would equal her war debt payments to the United States. And since France used its share of reparations to repay the large sums it had borrowed from Britain during the war—thus swelling the total reparations receipts of Great Britain—the effect of the British decision was to make the United States the ultimate recipient of reparations.

Nevertheless, Germany's economy, devastated by the effects of military defeat, inflation, and the occupation of the Ruhr by French troops in 1923, yielded an insufficient surplus to permit the required payments. In consequence the Allies decided to scale them down, and did so by accepting the Dawes Plan in 1924. After this, both the German reparations payments and the war debt installments due the United States—also effectually reduced by lowering initial interest rates—were regularly made.[143] What permitted them to be made, however, was the revival of confidence in the international capital markets which the Dawes Plan brought about. The plan contemplated a loan of 800 million marks to Germany that would be floated in the various financial capitals. American interest in the loan was extraordinary. One hundred and ten million dollars of it, underwritten by J. P. Morgan & Company, were sold in New York, with the amount oversubscribed ten times.[144] And this was only the beginning. Very soon thereafter additional New York money poured into bonds issued by German corporations such as those headed by Krupp, Stahlverein, and Thyssen and into the bonds of German municipalities. In effect, the extension of large American loans to Germany enabled that country to make its reparations payments to Great Britain and France, and the latter two nations to pay their war debts to the United States. Thus the money that came to the United States from the Allies only rounded a circle to its point of origin.[145]

American loans to Germany were quickly followed by loans to the rest of Europe and to Latin America, the total reaching some $6,400 million between 1924 and 1929.[146] In earlier nineteenth-century decades, American promoters had scoured Europe for lenders, but between 1925 and 1929 the search was for foreign borrowers. They were found not only in world capitals but also in smaller cities and towns, even in public and parochial school districts and church organizations. Americans pressed their money on borrowers. When American agents discovered that a Bavarian hamlet was in need of about $125,000, they persuaded it to accept a loan of $3 million instead. According to Thomas W. Lamont of J. P. Morgan & Company, the competition between American bankers and firms took place "on almost a violent scale."[147] At one time no fewer than twenty-nine representatives of American financial houses were trying to negotiate loans in Colombia; at another, some thirty-six houses, mostly American, were competing for a city of Budapest loan. Historical versions of the three-martini lunch and instances of douceurs to influential persons were probably common. One American bank, the Chase, managed to find a well-paid position in its Cuban branch for the son-in-law of the president of Cuba during most of the time it was successfully competing with other American banks for the privilege of financing the Cuban government. Another, the National City Bank, joined with the J. & W. Seligman Company in a payment of $450,000 to the president of Peru for his aid in arranging a $50 million loan, which these houses proceeded to market for Peru.[148]

Nevertheless, the loans made possible not only extravagant expenditures and waste on the part of some of the borrowers but also a host of solid works of construction. In the late eighteenth century Robert Morris, financier of the American Revolution, had welcomed Dutch capital "to clear the forests of America."[149] The 1920s saw a reversal of roles: American capital built highways, railroads, public utilities, sanitation works, residential apartment houses, and other public works abroad, including waterworks systems in Athens, stockyards and tramways in Warsaw, irrigation works in Chile, port works in Colombia, a seacoast boulevard in Montevideo, and roads in Argentina, Chile, Colombia, Cuba, and Guatemala. The loans also exerted an accelerator effect on American industry, widening the demand for equipment and materials, for steam shovels and grading machinery, metal pipes and plumbing supplies, steel rails, engines and cars for railroads, and cement and asphalt. They also encouraged the export of human capital, especially in the form of engineers supervising construction works abroad.[150]

These beneficial effects may have disposed lenders to discount occasional warnings against what Thomas W. Lamont in May 1927 called "indiscriminate lending and indiscriminate borrowing." But it was neither the precarious situation of some of the borrowers, nor the onset of depression in some parts of the world, nor even laws such as that of Colombia, which in June 1928 required provincial and municipal governments to obtain the approval of the central government before negotiating further loans, which led to a decisive downturn in American long-term lending after June 1928. Rather, it was the superior prospect of gains in the stock market, either from purchases of stocks or, in the case of financial intermediaries (which were not permitted to buy stocks), from the call loan market. One economist estimates that the decline in U.S. long-term lending during the stock market boom from June 1928 through the first three-quarters of 1929, when compared with the preceding period of similar length, ranged between an estimated $1.3 billion and $5.0 billion.[151] Even if one accepts an alternative "educated guess" that the net change in lending amounted to about $2 billion, the sum remains enormous.[152]

Unfortunately, the decline in foreign lending was soon followed by a reduction of imports into the United States, and the dual impact of this loss of purchasing power exerted deflationary pressure not only on Germany and other European states, but, probably even more severely, on the less developed countries of the world as well. Between September and December 1929 coffee, cotton, rubber, and wheat fell more than 50 percent, "with disastrous consequences for the exports, income and central-bank reserves of Brazil, Colombia, the Netherlands East Indies, Argentina, and Australia." Price declines in these and other primary products—cocoa, copper, corn, hides, lead, silk, tin, and zinc—continued with almost no abatement throughout the following year and into 1931. The deflationary spiral was by no means confined to the developing countries. As price and income declines reduced the latter's imports, aggregate demand in the industrialized countries fell to that extent, and this in turn led to even further reductions in the value of the exports of the developing countries. Thus the spiral widened as it turned down to catch business profits, prices of stocks and bonds, and the security of bank loans throughout Europe, where the weight of foreign short-term indebtedness, in the form of commercial credit extended to the exporters of primary products, was also heavy. The failure of the Austrian Credit-Anstalt in mid-1931 set off runs on banks in Germany, Hungary, Czechoslovakia, Rumania, and Poland, with consequent losses of gold.[153] Britain's abandonment of gold was thus an action taken in response to an international financial crisis which had engulfed central Europe and affected many other countries as well.[154]

Its effect on the United States, as we have seen, was a flight of gold, as European central banks, with confidence in the stability of the dollar imperiled, exchanged their dollar claims for gold. Nor was that all. Defaults on American loans spread rapidly throughout Latin America in 1931—to Peru, Chile, and Brazil—and in 1932 to Uruguay, Colombia, and the Central American republics. Nineteen thirty-two was the year of big defaults in Europe, beginning with Hungary and then moving to Greece, Bulgaria, Austria, Yugoslavia, and Denmark.[155] World depression tightened its grip on dwindling assets and incomes, with significant impact on both the exports and the gross national product of the United States.

Declining export sales lowered the GNP between 1929 and 1930 by $2.3 billion, and between 1930 and 1931 by $2.5 billion. These year-to-year changes represent 24 percent and 44 percent, respectively, of the *total* year-to-year decline in GNP. Surely in the first two years of the depression, then, the export sector of the American economy reinforced and helped prolong the downturn.[156] In contrast, in the earlier 1920s, the value of American exports had risen every year.[157] There was the rub. Had American policy not been wedded to the notion that a favorable balance of trade was a Good Thing, and had that same policy not been bent on returning the major trading nations to the gold standard, Europeans would not have been compelled to resort to the American loan market to the extent that they did. Especially because liquid reserves of gold were insufficient to repay their American debts, and because the dominant size of the American merchant marine limited their prospects of earning dollars as cargo carriers, their main hope of discharging indebtedness was to export more goods to the United States than they imported.

Unfortunately the United States, inexperienced in the role of creditor, did not act as a creditor should. Instead of encouraging imports and pumping dollars into the channels of international trade, it encouraged exports. It did so by passing the Webb-Pomerene Act in 1918, which suspended the application of the antitrust laws to manufacturers who organized export associations that would enable them to compete more effectively in international trade. It did so by passing the Edge Act in 1919 in an effort to promote the organization of corporations which would sell their own bonds in the United States and lend the proceeds to foreign importers, thus helping to finance American exports.[158] And, finally, it did so by passing the Emergency Tariff Act in 1921 and the Fordney-McCumber Tariff in 1922. The rates on manufactured goods imposed by the latter were so high as to be almost prohibitive. In consequence of these various measures, but also partly because of the greater efficiency of the American manufacturing sector, which lowered unit costs and prices of American products in relation to those of competing countries, the value of American merchandise exports exceeded imports throughout the twenties, the favorable balance rising from $400 million in 1923 to $1.09 billion in 1928.[159] In sum, foreigners had little choice but to borrow if they were to repay their debts, and in consequence the severe reduction of American net long-term lending after mid-1928, coupled with the existence of obstacles in the way of an offsetting response by short-term capital markets, helped throw the system of international trade and payments into worldwide disorder. In one economist's judgment, more than any other single factor the decline in long-term lending turned an American depression into a world depression as foreign monetary authorities responded to the reduction with tight money policies in order to maintain their balances of payments.[160]

And since the reduction was caused by the lure of the stock market, we have returned full circle, but one widened to include much of the world in its embrace, to the beginning point of the Great Depression.[161] We must now inquire into the reactions of two American presidents, Herbert Hoover and Franklin Delano Roosevelt, to the events which constitute it.

15

Coping with the Great Depression

Before the Great Depression twentieth century presidents had by no means been wholly passive in the face of problems arising out of economic crisis. For example, during the financial panic of 1907—the "bankers' panic"—President Theodore Roosevelt first assured the country of the essential soundness of the economy and then took steps to ensure that the currency supply of the national banks would be shored up—measures which succeeded in calming the fears of depositors and easing the stringency of money. Similarly, when the outbreak of war in 1914 put heavy pressure on the stock market and on American bankers and merchants, President Woodrow Wilson issued a statement of reassurance and had the Treasury take actions which stabilized the market and stopped runs on banks. Finally, President Warren Harding and his secretary of the Treasury, Andrew Mellon, reacted to the severe recession of 1920–21 by inducing Congress to lower the excess-profits tax and the surtax on individual incomes, to enact an emergency tariff with an antidumping provision and high protective rates on a number of farm commodities, and to expand governmental loans to farmers' cooperatives and livestock growers. Harding's moves were obviously more substantial than those of his predecessors, but just as obviously the crisis he confronted was more serious and prolonged. Even so, his measures were minimal and little affected the country's eventual recovery from the recession.[1]

The depression which filled three of President Herbert Hoover's four years in office was of unprecedented magnitude but he had an arsenal of convictions to fire at it. When Hoover entered the White House in 1929, he brought with him not only a well-earned reputation as one of the world's great humanitarians and perhaps its leading engineer but also a strong set of beliefs about the respective duties of the public and private sectors and the proper relationship between them. Deeply distrusting "big government" as a menace to liberty ("Free speech does not live many hours after free industry and free commerce die"[2]), he also denounced "ruthless individualism" or "individualism run riot" ("You know, the only trouble with capitalism is capitalists; they're too damn greedy")[3] and called for a system of "cooperative individualism" or "ordered liberty" to replace it. To him, the "American system" was one in which the individual discharged his responsibility to the community, the local government its responsibility to the state, and the state to the national government. Above all, it was a cooperative system in which public and private organizations worked together to achieve national objectives. This, suggests a historian with the New Freedom and New Nationalism of the earlier twentieth century in mind, was the "New Individualism," an individualism which "idealized voluntary association to achieve collective ends."[4]

Hoover believed, as he wrote in the earlier twenties, that the country was "in the midst of a great revolution . . . in the whole super-organization of its economic life," that the American people were "passing from a period of extremely individualistic action into a period of associational activities."[5] During his long tenure as secretary of commerce in the cabinets of Harding and Coolidge, he urged that the values of an older industrialism be blended with those of the new, that the energy and creativity generated by individual effort in a system of private enterprise become merged with scientific rationality and social engineering to form a larger synthesis. By social engineering he meant the development and proper use of cooperative institutions, especially trade associations and professional societies, and similar organizations among farmers and workers. These institutions would form a type of private government that would work toward economic and social betterment without inviting the evils associated with governmental bureaucracies. In sum, cooperative association based on mutuality of interests would humanize industrial relationships and raise living standards without the intervention of a coercive state.[6]

During the 1920s Hoover sponsored innumerable promotional and educational conferences, mounted inquiries by fact-finding committees of experts, and set up a host of other ad hoc structures, all of them tied to private groups and associations. His purpose was that of finding private solutions to national problems. One example of his use of private expertise was his reorganization of the Bureau of Foreign and Domestic Commerce along commodity lines and his staffing of it with men from the export industries. The agency thus became an associational system for gathering and disseminating commercial intelligence and for dealing with foreign governments and cartels. A cooperating industrial committee worked in conjunction with each commodity division in efforts to develop and expand markets, the only function of the state being to serve as a clearing house, inspirational force, and protector of international rights. It did not trade, invest, or impose detailed regulations.[7]

Similar growth and transformation also occurred in the Bureau of Standards, which proceeded to sponsor associational reform in the areas of research, housing, and industrial efficiency. The bureau's Building and Housing Division became the nucleus of a network of cooperating committees and study groups, each of them tied to the major trade and professional associations in the housing field, each of them undertaking educational campaigns in an effort to overcome the bottlenecks blocking "modernization" and "rationalization." The Census Bureau, the Bureau of Customs Statistics, the Inter-American High Commission (designed to promote trade in Latin America), the United States Coal Commission, the Federal Oil Conservation Board, the Northeastern Super Power Committee, and still other government agencies, including the Treasury and Labor departments, felt the guiding, transforming hand of the secretary of commerce. Essentially, Hoover made that department an "economic 'general staff,' business 'correspondence school,' and national coordinator, all rolled into one." By implementing its plans through nearly four hundred cooperating committees and numerous private groups, and by appealing to science, community, and morality to bridge the gap between public and private interests, the agency managed to avoid bureaucratic dictation and legal coercion and to preserve the essential of American individualism.[8]

As president, Hoover's methods remained essentially what they had been throughout his years in the Commerce Department. He confronted adversity with his faith in associationalism intact.[9] One of his first acts as president, taken a month after the collapse of the stock market in October 1929, was to summon Henry Ford, Pierre DuPont, Julius Rosenwald, and nineteen other leading industrialists to the White House. What he said to them there typifies the man and his approach to the crisis. Warning the assembled industrialists that the depression must last for some time and that no one could then measure the destructive forces to be met, the president proceeded to point out the urgency of the need to consider the human problem of unemployment and distress. He explained that the immediate response of businessmen in previous depressions had been the laying off of workers. His every instinct opposed that policy, for labor was not a commodity. It represented human homes. The first shock, he said, must fall on profits, not on wages. Reduction in wages would only deepen the depression by suddenly reducing purchasing power and bringing about industrial strife. His fundamental view was that wages should not be cut, that planned construction work should be maintained by industry, that government agencies should increase construction to provide as much employment as possible, that the available work should be spread among all employees by shortening the work week, and that each industry should relieve distress among its own employees. Hoover's own "note for the occasion" discloses that his guests expressed major agreement with his views and that his program was accepted, subject to its approval by labor leaders and their agreement that they would initiate neither strikes nor demands for increased pay during the current situation. After an afternoon conference the same day with the labor leaders William Green, William L. Hutcheson, Matthew Woll, John L. Lewis, and nine others, Hoover obtained the required adherence of labor.[10]

The very next day Hoover called a conference of leaders in the building and construction industries in an effort to maintain investment and output, and the day after that he telegraphed a request to governors and mayors through-out the country to cooperate with him in expanding public works in every practical direction. And so it went. Conference after conference, address after address ("I am convinced with unity of effort we shall recover," he told the Chamber of Commerce in May 1930)—the president seemed to be every-where, talking to bankers, public utility magnates, workers, and federal offi-cials, admonishing, cajoling, trying to stimulate positive responses to the disaster, creating new agencies in a continuing effort, all through 1930, 1931, and into 1932, to obtain constructive cooperative action without resorting to governmental coercion. His objective, once more, was to win agreements to maintain wage rates and industrial peace and to enlarge private investment and governmental expenditures for public works. He tried hard. Walter Lippmann judged him fairly when he wrote in May 1932 that "Mr. Hoover's concern with the problem [of unemployment] has been quite as sincere and his efforts to deal with it quite as persistent as those of any man living."[11]

And he did more than talk. In his budget message of December 1929 Hoover called for a reduction in income tax rates on the ground that experience (in 1924, 1926, and 1928) had shown that such reductions, by encouraging increases in consumer expenditures and business investment, generated in-creased revenues even at the lower rates. Congress responded by reducing rates one percentage point on 1929 incomes. Expenditures for public works also rose, from $2,468 million in 1929 to $2,858 million in 1930. Most of the increase, however, was accounted for by state and local governments, federal spending rising only about a third, from $155 million to $209 million. Unhappily, the public works increase was swamped by a decline in private construction. Despite the president's pleas, private nonresidential construc-tion fell from $5 billion to $4 billion and residential construction from $4 billion to $2.3 billion. Nevertheless, according to an economist who has meas-ured the stimulus imparted by fiscal policy to the total demand for goods and services in the 1930s, that effect was larger in 1931 than in any other year of the 1930s except 1934, 1935, and 1936—of which only 1936 was much larger than 1931. However, this was a case of stimulation by inadvertence. Two developments produced a substantial swing of the budget from surplus to deficit, and Hoover had nothing to do with either of them. In the first place, revenues automatically declined because incomes did. In the second, expenditures rose largely because of the enactment of a law providing for advance payment to veterans of a billion dollars. As Roosevelt was also to do in 1936, Hoover vetoed the bonus bill, both vetoes being overridden by Congress.[12]

Deliberate budget policy before 1932 did little to revitalize the economy, in part because inadequate statistical information and analysis misled the administration into thinking that the economy was improving. "Like most economists," Louis Bean confessed after a long career in the Department of

Agriculture, "we misjudged the information at the end of 1930 and expected that the low point would come in the summer of 1931, and it didn't come until the summer of 1932."[13] Not misinformation but a host of complicating factors explain the administration's recommendation in December 1931 to raise taxes, a proposal which, at first glance, would appear to have been the height of folly in a period of depression. One of these factors was not only Hoover's but also almost everyone else's belief in the need to balance the budget. Balancing the budget, however, is an elastic concept that should not require a balance every year: surplus in some years could make room for deficits in other years. The administration knew this, but it was also aware that reports of tax collections during the spring and summer of 1931 were showing that the deficit was running much higher than had been forecast and that if Congress accepted its proposal, also made in December 1931, to create a Reconstruction Finance Corporation with authority to make loans for a variety of purposes, the deficit would be enlarged still more. Not only would the Treasury buy the capital stock of the corporation, which amounted to $500 million, but the corporation itself would be authorized to borrow up to $3.3 billion in addition, either from the Treasury or elsewhere.

Even the prospect of higher deficits, however, did not bring about a crisis of confidence in the business community, and in the absence of still other developments it is problematical whether increased taxes would have been requested. But when Britain went off the gold standard in September 1931, the financial conditions facing the Treasury changed drastically. Gold began to flow out of the country in large quantities as foreign claimants anticipated the possibility that the United States would also abandon gold. As a result, bank reserves declined, interest rates rose sharply, frightened depositors began withdrawing currency in large quantities, and bank failures soared. Unfortunately, the independent Federal Reserve System, as we have seen, while meeting the foreign drain on bank reserves in the classic way by increasing discount rates, did not at the same time take active measures to ease the internal drain through open market purchases.[14]

In these circumstances, with confidence in the credit of the government and in the dollar at a low ebb, Hoover had little room for choice. Without cooperative monetary policy, even the prospect of continued government borrowing to finance deficits promised to lower security prices still more and raise interest rates still higher, effects which, in turn, promised to add to the difficulties of private business borrowing while reducing the value of bank assets and further diminishing confidence in the banks. In sum, given the widely shared desideratum of a balanced budget, given the monetary facts faced by the president, namely, the threat to the gold standard and to the dollar; and given the depressed state of confidence, the stimulative effects of a budget deficit might have been small, zero, or, depending on the speculative reactions to it, even adverse. These conditions made for a factual ambience hospitable to an increase in taxes. Looking out to the post-Hooverian years, a contemporary economist sums it up: "The government's fiscal policy did not begin to change markedly until after these facts had changed."[15] Had they not changed, neither a Rooseveltian liberation of fiscal policy nor Keynesian doctrine on the beneficial uses of deficits is likely to have arrested the continuing downturn.

Although Hoover's policy alternatives were restricted by what Thomas Carlyle called "facts, immense, indubitable facts," they were not—progressive historiography to the contrary notwithstanding—imprisoned by an ideology of laissez faire. For one thing, when thousands of overseas speculators began converting paper dollars into gold in reaction to the European financial crisis which had driven Britain off the gold standard, Hoover warned the Congress that it must "legislate or go off gold." The congressional response to his urgings took the form of the Glass-Steagall bill, which Hoover signed into law in February 1932. The rules governing the operations of the Federal Reserve System were amended in such a way as to release a large quantity of gold previously required to be held in reserve as backing for Federal Reserve notes. Thus freed, the gold could be used to meet international demands without threatening the gold standard.[16]

This was one instance among many. If Hoover had ever been a devotee of the doctrine of laissez faire, he abandoned it even before becoming secretary of commerce. As he noted in his presidential address of November 1920 before the Federation of American Engineering Societies, the regulation of public utilities was "itself, also proof of the abandonment of the unrestricted capitalism of Adam Smith." Soon after the inauguration of Roosevelt, Hoover commented somewhat bitterly to a friend that "the Brain Trust and their superiors are now announcing to the world that the social thesis of laissez-faire died on March 4. I wish they would add a professor of history to the Brain Trust." Presumably the professor would let Roosevelt's associates know that history had overwhelmed the thesis "half a century ago," and that the "visible proof" of this was the enactment of the Sherman Act, transportation and public utility regulation, the Federal Reserve System, the Eighteenth Amendment, the Federal Farm Board, Home Loan banks, and the Reconstruction Finance Corporation.[17]

He had sponsored the creation of the last three agencies himself, and others besides. In 1931 he signed into law the Bacon-Davis Act, which provided a basic eight-hour day on public construction projects and the payment of "prevailing wages," which meant, essentially, union wages. The Federal Farm Board, originally recommended by President Calvin Coolidge and promised in the Republican platform of 1928, was created by the Hoover-sponsored Agricultural Marketing Act of June 1929. "A nation which is spending ninety billions a year," Hoover had said in accepting the presidential nomination in 1928, "can well afford an expenditure of a few hundred million for a workable program that will give to one-third of its population their fair share of the nation's prosperity."[18] The major purpose of the board was to promote orderly, cooperative marketing of farm products, to "build up," as Hoover himself expressed it, "farmer-owned, farmer-controlled marketing organizations," to enable farmers to obtain better prices for their products. Allotted a revolving fund of $500 million, the board extended loans to cooperatives organized for the marketing of cotton, wheat, and other products in an effort to stabilize prices by purchasing surpluses. Hoover considered the board "the most important agency ever set up in government to assist an industry," and it was with evident satisfaction that he reported in his annual message to Congress in December 1931 that the Federal Farm Board had enabled "farm cooperatives to cushion the fall in prices of farm products in 1930 and 1931," thereby securing "higher prices than would have been obtained otherwise" and averting "the failure of a large number of farmers and country banks." Unhappily, when it became evident that the board was losing money on such purchases without achieving price stabilization, the board decided, with Hoover's approval, to abandon the effort. Ultimately it lost approximately $345 million, mainly because of the depression which began less than six months after the passage of the act creating the board.[19] Meanwhile, in January 1932 Hoover signed an act which provided an additional $125 million in capital for the Federal Land banks in an effort to relieve pressure on farm mortgages.[20]

The purpose of the Home Loan Bank Bill, finally passed by Congress in July 1932 after repeated earlier pleas on the part of Hoover, was to encourage home ownership by making it possible for home owners to obtain long-term loans payable in installments, thus saving existing homes from foreclosure and encouraging both the building of new ones and employment. He considered it "one of the tragedies of this depression" that there had occurred "literally thousands of heart-breaking instances of inability of working people to attain renewal of existing mortgages on favorable terms, and the consequent loss of their homes."[21] Under the act twelve Home Loan banks were established in various parts of the country, each with a minimum capital of $5 million. Building and loan associations, savings banks, and insurance companies were among institutions eligible both to become members in the system and to borrow from the banks upon notes secured by the collateral of home mortgages. It was Hoover's hope that the banks could be expanded into a general mortgage discount system to be owned cooperatively by banks and mortgage companies, thus paralleling in the field of long-term credit the service of the Federal Reserve System for short-term credit. He urged Congress to institute an inquiry into this possibility just two weeks before leaving office.[22]

The most imaginative and probably the most useful of the government agencies created by Congress at the insistence of President Hoover was the Reconstruction Finance Corporation (RFC). Established in January 1932, with a capital stock of $500 million which the Treasury was to purchase, the corporation eventually was authorized to borrow up to an additional $3.5 billion, either from the Treasury or elsewhere. In fact, it borrowed $1,585 million, all from the Treasury, during fiscal years 1932 and 1933. Wholly financed by the federal government, the corporation had as its essential purpose the making of loans to banks, insurance companies, building and loan associations, railroads, and other businesses to enable them to meet their obligations and remain afloat during the depression. In addition, RFC loans established Agricultural Credit banks, helped finance public works, and aided states with inadequate resources "to extend full relief to distress and to prevent any hunger and cold in the United States." In 1931–32 the Department of Agriculture made available to more than 500,000 farmers RFC loans totaling $64 million.[23]

In his campaign for the presidency in the fall of 1932 Roosevelt taunted Hoover by saying that the RFC had been designed to help banks and corporations rather than the common man. Hoover's rejoinder reveals once again the basic premise of his political philosophy. Roosevelt "knows full well," he charged, "that the only purpose of helping an insurance company is to protect the policyholder." "He knows full well," Hoover continued, that

> the only purpose in helping a bank is to protect the depositor and the borrower. He knows full well that the only purpose of helping a farm-mortgage company is to enable the farmer to hold his farm. He knows full well that the only purpose of helping the building and loan association is to protect savings and homes. He knows full well that in sustaining the business man it maintains the worker in his job. He knows full well that in loans to the States it protects the families in distress.[24]

Hoover was not disingenuous in maintaining that the "only purpose" of these federal aids was to help individuals. Of course it is true that RFC loans also helped corporations and their officers and shareholders, as well as officials of state governments and the political parties to which they belonged. But that is precisely the way Hoover believed individuals should be helped, for indirect aid sustained not only the individual but also the independent associations whose viability was essential to the preservation of economic and political liberty.

Hoover opposed direct federal relief to the unemployed because he was afraid it would break down the "sense of responsibility of individual generosity" and "mutual self-help in the country in times of national difficulty," impair "something infinitely valuable in the life of the American people," and strike "at the roots of self-government." He did not feel he should be charged with lack of sympathy for those who suffered. He reminded his critics that he had spent much of his life fighting hardship abroad and, during the great Mississippi flood of 1927, in the southern states. He acknowledged that he had sought the help of Congress in the past for foreign relief, but this was for nations "so disorganized by war and anarchy that self-help was impossible." There was no such paralysis in the United States. The Quaker president was confident that the American people had "the resources, the initiative, the courage, the stamina and kindliness of spirit to meet this situation in the way they have met their problems for generations."

Nevertheless he added, *"I am willing to pledge myself* that if the time should ever come that the voluntary agencies of the country together with the local and state governments are unable to find resources with which to prevent hunger and suffering in my country, *I will ask the aid of every resource of the Federal Government because I would no more see starvation amongst our countrymen than would any senator or congressman."* In February 1931 he said he had "faith in the American people" that such a day would not come, and as late in his administration as October 1932 he obviously believed it had not come, and that RFC loans, together with $2 billion for public works and $300 million for loans to the states "to be used in relieving the hardships resulting from unemployment," funds made available under the Emergency and Relief Construction Act of July 1932, were indeed helping individual people. Undoubtedly some were helped. But some were not enough.[25]

Hoover believed that "nothing has ever been devised in our history which has done more [than the RFC] for those whom Mr. Coolidge has aptly called the common run of men and women."[26] His successor undoubtedly would have managed a less enthusiastic appraisal, but it is noteworthy that Roosevelt retained the RFC, greatly expanded both its resources and the uses to which it was put, and converted it into the government's largest general-purpose institution. It is not without irony that Roosevelt's aide Rexford Guy Tugwell went so far as to remark publicly in an interview in 1974, "We didn't admit it at the time but practically the whole New Deal was extrapolated from programs that Hoover started."[27] The statement is a gross exaggeration, but it does serve to moderate somewhat an older view of a hapless, inactive president.

Hoover's activities in the field of human welfare—in defense of civil liberties, of native Americans, blacks, workers (women as well as men), and children ("If we could have but one generation of properly born, trained, educated, and healthy children, a thousand other problems of government would vanish");[28] in the interests of conservation, public power systems, and public education; as well as in those of still other areas of American life—were so broad as to challenge credulity. Most of these activities, however, serve as evidence of one man's highly refined conscience rather than of public programs calling for legal change. Yet it should be recorded that the RFC was authorized to make loans for slum clearance and that it was Hoover who in 1932 signed into law the Norris-LaGuardia Anti-Injunction Act, a landmark in labor legislation. Among other things, the act outlawed yellow-dog contracts.[29]

It was the tragic fate of Herbert Hoover not only to occupy the White

House during the initial stages of an unprecedented depression but to have had to do so before the emergence of a politically viable mandate for counter-cyclical intervention by the federal government. The traditional way of coping with a depression was to let things run their course. Once inflated values were liquidated the economy would readjust itself. Hoover's secretary of the Treasury, Andrew Mellon, expressed it with succinct brutality: "Liquidate labor, liquidate stocks, liquidate the farmers, liquidate real estate."[30] Even if a clear and insistent call for federal intervention had issued from the public, government officials would have been handicapped by the lack of basic economic information essential for effective action. There was as yet no system of national income accounts, no statistical series on total output or employment. Economists themselves disagreed on what it was that determined the level of national income and employment and what effected change in those levels. The "Keynesian revolution," after all, did not begin till after 1936. And when it did, it little affected what Hoover's successor thought or did.[31]

Given these considerations, the extent of Hoover's activism is remarkable. It far exceeded that of any presidential predecessor in time of peace. Yet this was not the thrust of his leadership. As we have seen, Hoover was deeply committed to a belief in the power of persuasion to move state and local governments and private individuals and organizations, especially businessmen, to undertake measures of relief and economic recovery. The proper function of the presidency was to stimulate and encourage, to indicate what should be done, but not to engage the federal government in the doing of it. Unhappily, persuasion did not work. The private sector failed to respond to the degree that the president had hoped it would. Hoover then wheeled into play some of the resources of the public sector. But he did so reluctantly and insufficiently.

Earlier historians variously called his course "fatalistic and defeatist," lacking in boldness and imagination, inhibited by "a doctrinaire adherence to inherited principles."[32] More recent scholars ones have sought to diminish the differences between his approach and that of his successor. As one writer puts it, "the shift was not from laissez faire to a managed economy, but rather from one attempt at management, that through informal business-government cooperation, to another more formal and coercive attempt."[33] But if it can be said that Hoover, as well as Roosevelt, entered upon the path of activist government, it was not long before the former became a figure dimly perceived in the distance. The differences between the two remain substantive.

In time, Roosevelt's policies alienated many businessmen, who came to despise "that man in the White House." In further time, however, many of the social programs associated with the New Deal came to be regarded by the successors to the businessmen of the 1930s as built-in stabilizers in periods of falling demand. As we shall see, the New Deal marks the beginning not only of the Welfare State but also of the cushioned economy. Hoover preferred other solutions to the nation's economic and social problems. Men and women can attend only to what they understand to be the exigencies of their time. For all we know, Hoover's advocacy of close voluntary cooperation between government, labor, and business enterprise, while ineffective in the early 1930s, may yet prove a useful model for the renewal of American economic leadership and for the preservation of American living standards in the closing years of the twentieth century and beyond. If so, Hoover's place among our presidents will continue to be reassessed, for the shifting judgment of history views a person not only in the context of his or her own present but also in relation to currents of change which bring the future into being.

When Franklin Delano Roosevelt assumed the presidency in March 1933, the nation's economy had all but collapsed. Thirteen million workers, more than a quarter of the labor force, were unemployed, and millions more had only part-time jobs. Joblessness varied from one industry to the next and thus among the communities in which they were concentrated. The automobile industry was extremely hard hit. In March 1929 Willys-Overland had employed 28,000 persons in Toledo, Ohio; by November the number had fallen to 4,000. The Ford Motor Company, dominating Detroit, had 128,142 people on its payroll in March 1929; by August 1931 the number had plummeted to 37,000. Conditions in Pontiac and Flint, Michigan, were no better. Unemployment in the textile industry and its heavily dependent towns were distressing: by the end of 1930, 120,000 of New England's 280,000 mill hands were out of work completely. Many others had part-time jobs, frequently paying less than ten dollars a week. Employment also fell off sharply in Philadelphia, Buffalo, Cincinnati, and other cities boasting diversified industry.[34]

The pall of poverty spread like an evil mist over much of the country. Most families were receiving either inadequate relief or none at all.

Many lived in the primitive conditions of a preindustrial society stricken by famine. In the coal fields of West Virginia and Kentucky, evicted families shivered in tents in midwinter; children went barefoot. In Los Angeles, people whose gas and electricity had been turned off were reduced to cooking over wood fires in back lots. Visiting nurses in New York found children famished; one episode, reported Lillian Wald, "might have come out of the tales of old Russia." A Philadelphia storekeeper told a reporter of one family he was keeping going on credit: "Eleven children in that house. They've got no shoes, no pants. In the house, no chairs. My God, you go in there, you cry, that's all."[35]

These appalling human conditions reflected the snaillike motions of the economy which generated them. In March 1933 the gross national product, in real terms, was down 30 percent from its level in 1929. Debt default or delinquency was widespread, embracing the obligations of state and local governments, business firms, home owners, and farmers. The financial system was virtually prostrate. There was hardly a bank in the country that was not either closed or severely restricted in its operations under bank holidays proclaimed by the governors of the states. Checks could not be cleared, the securities markets were shut down, and transactions in foreign exchange could not be conducted. The international gold standard was gone, international capital movements were at a standstill, and international trade had fallen to a low level, in part because of a drastic decline in world incomes, but also because of tariffs, quantitative limitations, exchange controls, and other restrictions. Elected by a landslide—besides losing the three traditionally Republican states of Maine, New Hampshire, and Vermont, Roosevelt lost only Connecticut, Pennsylvania, and Delaware while polling 472 electoral votes to Hoover's 59—Roosevelt was in a commanding position to respond to a rising public clamor for action against the grinding forces of deflation. The long duration of widespread hardship and economic disruption had cast doubt on the proposition, long entertained by conservatives, that an unaided private sector would eventually restore order out of chaos. The way was now open to a variety and extent of government action which would have been generally disapproved just a few years before.[36]

The variety and extent were to be remarkable, especially during two "hundred-day" periods in 1933 and 1935, when Congress enacted more legislation of far-reaching significance than ever before in American history—with the possible exception of the early years of the Republic. Historians have neatly categorized these laws as designed to bring about relief, reform, or recovery, the latter two objectives being associated with specific institutions or occupational groups. In contrast, relief applied only to individuals. The distinctions are artificial. Many programs served overlapping purposes. Not only individuals but banks and other businesses needed relief, and some of them structural reform, before they could become instruments of recovery. The fundamental fact is this: the president and the Congresses he dominated were engaged in a massive rescue operation affecting not only the poor and unemployed but also the major institutions of economic society. At stake was the viability of American capitalism.[37]

Unemployed men and women were early beneficiaries of the change in presidential attitude toward direct relief represented by Roosevelt. The Federal Emergency Relief Administration (FERA), established by the president in May 1933, funneled a half-billion dollars to states and cities. The latter, in turn, made direct grants of cash to people on the relief rolls. In the eyes of the FERA's administrator, the former social worker Harry Hopkins ("Hunger is not debatable"), the sum was insufficient, and he persuaded the president to create a second agency to take over unemployment relief during the anticipated harsh winter of 1933–34. Unlike FERA, the Civil Works Administration (CWA) was a federal operation throughout. Providing work relief for the unemployed at minimum wages, it made possible the building or improving of some 500,000 miles of roads, 40,000 schools, more than 3,500 play-grounds and athletic fields, and 1,000 airports before succumbing to intense conservative criticism in the spring of 1934.[38]

Hopkins then prevailed upon the president to establish a permanent work relief program. The Emergency Relief Appropriations Act of 1935 granted Roosevelt discretionary authority to spend $5 billion for relief. Although the Works Progress Administration (WPA) received only $1.4 billion of this sum, the rest being siphoned off by the president for use by other agencies, includ-ing the Department of Agriculture, Hopkins' WPA built or improved some 2,500 hospitals, 5,900 school buildings, 1,000 airport landing fields, and nearly 13,000 playgrounds, besides funding the Federal Theatre Project, the Federal Writers Project, the Federal Art Project, and the National Youth Administration. One of the early casualties of the Second World War, WPA eventually spent $10 billion for the relief of 3.5 million desperate blue-collar and professional people.[39]

Convinced that economic recovery was contingent upon the restoration of public confidence in the integrity of the country's financial institutions and practices, Roosevelt applied his salvaging efforts to banks and the nation's securities markets as well as to individuals. His first step, administrative rather than legislative, was to give national recognition to what was in effect already a nationwide bank holiday declared piecemeal by thirty-four individual states. On March 6, acting under authority of the 1917 Trading-with-the-Enemy Act, he issued an executive order temporarily suspending banking activities throughout the country and forbidding dealings in gold. No bank could re-open for business till its condition had been examined by the secretary of the Treasury (in the case of member banks of the Federal Reserve System) or by state banking authorities (in the case of state-chartered nonmember banks) and a license issued permitting it to do so. Adopting a scheme suggested by Hoover's secretary of the Treasury, Ogden Mills, banks were classified into three groups—wholly sound, questionable, and hopeless. Banks that were both safe and liquid could open right away, but those in doubtful condition might look to rehabilitation and subsequent opening. Unsound institutions would be closed and liquidated. The wheat was soon separated from the chaff. At the beginning of 1933 nearly 17,800 commercial banks had been in op-eration. When the banking holiday was terminated on March 9, 17,300 re-mained, but of these fewer than 12,000 were licensed to open and do business. Some 3,000 were reopened later, but more than 2,000 were closed for good—either liquidated or consolidated with other banks.[40]

In the restoration of the banking system, the Reconstruction Finance Cor-poration played a major role. Under the administration of Jesse Jones it not only lent more than $2 billion to some 8,500 endangered banks. It also in-vested more than $1 billion in the capital stock of over 6,000 banks—a sum representing one-third of the total capital of the banks in 1933. For government, this was a new departure. Yet Roosevelt fully supported it. "The government needs the willing and confident cooperation of its banks," he told Jones, "and is willing to go into partnership with them on a limited dividend basis, permitting the banks to end the partnership at will, but in the meantime making it easy for them to furnish the credit necessary for the recovery program."[41]

To Jones, no other emergency action compared in its potential for economic recovery with the government's extension of relief to the banks. "The completion of bank reconstruction," he remarked in June 1934, "will mean more perhaps, in sustaining recovery, than any of the emergency measures. Without a sound banking system and a strong banking structure, we cannot sustain recovery." Reminiscing on the experience in a speech in 1940, he said that it was his "firm conviction that without the RFC's repair work in banks through putting capital into them, our entire banking system would have failed." We shall see how other repair work during the New Deal years by an expanded RFC made that institution the world's largest, most powerful bank.[42]

Prompt government action had saved the commercial banking system, yet something more was needed if future panics were to be avoided, the circulating medium protected, and the interests of depositors and investors safeguarded. The system suffered from fundamental structural defects. For one thing, it was dominated by small, independent unit banks. It always had been. Indeed, the role of small business in the history of American banking may well be greater than that of any other nation. As late as 1920 most of the thirty thousand independent commercial banks in the country conducted their business in small towns, and with only a handful of employees. And most were not members of the Federal Reserve System, which meant that they lacked the ability to supplement their cash positions when faced with problems of liquidity.

The overwhelming majority of banks which suspended during the 1920s were small banks. Eighty-eight percent of them had assets under $1 million; 40 percent started with less than $24,000; and 85 percent were not members of the Federal Reserve. Nearly nine of ten were located in small rural communities, mainly in the West North Central and South Atlantic states, where agriculture was depressed. Indeed, four-fifths of the failures occurred in states which prohibited branch banking. Unlike a branch bank, the small independent could not diversify credit risks, raise additional resources, or draw on more than the local supply of management talent.[43]

It is difficult to determine the significance of the branching prohibition in the larger history of American banking. The laws of many states, and also the National Banking Act of 1864, forbade the establishment of branch banks. Yet in the dozen states which did allow branching at the beginning of the twentieth century, forty-seven banks had a mere total of eighty-five branches. Why was the number not larger than that? The answer may well be that small banks were then more efficient than branches. They had superior sources of information about local conditions and about the creditworthiness of the farmers, tradesmen, and other small businessmen who applied to them for loans, and they could act quickly in a fluid and rapidly developing economy. More generally, despite the deeply lodged belief in their vulnerability, further study of small businesses may reveal that they enjoyed a respectable longevity so long as economies of place, time, and personal service gave them shelter from competition. In sum, given the "personal nature of many banking services, the costs of gathering information in an economy of continental dimensions with millions of small producers who were bank clients, and the well documented reluctance of capital to migrate from surplus to deficit saving sectors during the great expansion of the American economy in the last century," branch banking did not possess a self-evident advantage over independent unit banking. Rather, it was the other way around.[44]

In the 1920s the automobile and other forces began to dismantle the advantages of small unit banks, and they began to fail in large numbers every year, indeed, in numbers that far exceeded those of any year, save one (1893), since 1864. But while the number of branch banks nearly tripled during the same decade, it is evident that small-unit-bank failures cannot be attributed to competition from that source, for, as we have seen, four-fifths of the failures took place in states which prohibited branch banking. Whatever the source—agricultural depression seems to be the best candidate—the weakness of small institutions only underscored the need for improved security for the banking system as a whole.[45]

The answer to this need came in the form of deposit insurance. Although initially opposed by Roosevelt, under the terms of the Glass-Steagall Banking Act of June 1933 a Federal Deposit Insurance Corporation was established. All members of the Federal Reserve System were required to have their deposits insured; nonmembers might also be insured if approved by the corporation. Insurance was limited to a maximum of $2,500, but the limitation was soon raised to $5,000 (in 1934) and subsequently to $10,000 (in 1950) and $100,000 (in 1980). Insurance first became effective on January 1, 1934; within six months some 97 percent of all commercial bank deposits were covered. Since then, federal deposit insurance has been accompanied by a dramatic decline in both commercial bank failures and in losses borne by depositors in banks that did fail. The insurance program represents the most important structural change in the banking system since the taxing out of existence of state banknotes immediately after the Civil War.[46] (Unhappily, massive failures in the nation's savings and loan institutions in the late 1980s revealed deficiencioes in federal deposit insurance, requiring further structural change in the program.)

The Glass-Steagall Banking Act of 1933 also contained provisions designed to increase the security of commercial banks and to blunt the capacity for abuse by investment banks. Many of the nation's largest commercial banks had responded to growing opportunities to profit from transactions in securities by organizing investment affiliates. Subject to common corporate policies and governance—for example, Charles E. Mitchell was chairman of the board of both the National City Bank and the National City Corporation, the world's second largest bank and the largest investment banking house in the country, respectively,—it was possible to use funds deposited in the commercial half of the alliance for speculative ventures in the investment half and thus to jeopardize their safety, as well as provide fuel for the gyrations of the market. Worse, the credit facilities of the former, and their access to the Federal Reserve System, compounded the potential damage. As early as December 3, 1929, President Hoover in his annual message to Congress had recommended that it "consider the advisability of separating commercial and investment banking as part of a larger study of the entire financial system." While Congress was slow to act on the proposal, the increasing number of bank failures, together with Hoover's repeated urgings, finally induced the Senate in 1931 to organize a special subcommittee of the Banking and Currency Committee to investigate the nation's banking system. After his appointment in January 1933, its able counsel, Ferdinand Pecora, soon elicited shocking confessions and documentary evidence of high-handed if not illegal practices on the part of many of the leading bankers in the country.[47]

Unimpeachable testimony disclosed investment affiliates speculating on the stock exchange and participating in pooling agreements which earned large profits for the participants; trading heavily in the stock of their allied commercial banks, advising depositors in commercial banks to purchase the stock of those banks and other securities as well, including dubious foreign bonds and the stocks of firms in which they themselves held extensive stock interests and on whose boards some of their executives sat as officers; and transferring losses on loans from the books of the bank to those of the investment affiliate without informing the latter's stockholders. Like the partners in many private investment banking firms, the executives of an investment affiliate profited handsomely from participating as individuals in the affiliate's flotations. Top executives not only drew substantial salaries but also voted themselves huge annual bonuses which were not reported in annual statements. The abuses, including the transfer of title of securities to a relative to evade income taxes, were flagrant and bitterly resented by a public which had come to look upon them as pillars of rectitude and strength. Although probes into the affairs of private banking houses such as those of J. P. Morgan and Kuhn, Loeb disclosed none of the gross violations of fiduciary trust which disfigured the record of a number of incorporated firms, including Mitchell's National City Company and Albert W. Wiggins' Chase Securities Corporation—the private banking houses, with few exceptions, were run conservatively; they eschewed speculative ventures, dealt mostly with established corporations, and showed a considerable sense of responsibility toward their clients—the revelation that not a single Morgan partner owed any income taxes for the years 1931 and 1932 aroused widespread public indignation.

Not surprisingly, the Banking Act of 1933 required banks belonging to the Federal Reserve System to divorce themselves from their security affiliates, compelled private banks to choose between deposit and investment banking, prohibited partners or executives of security firms from serving as directors or officers of commercial banks that were members of the Federal Reserve, increased the authority of the twelve Federal Reserve district banks to supervise and control the amount of credit extended to their members, and empowered the Federal Reserve Board to regulate bank loans secured by the collateral of stocks or bonds. In addition, the law prohibited their payment of interest on demand deposits in order to discourage outlying banks from sending large sums to metropolitan centers, especially New York, where they might feed speculation by being re-lent on the call loan market. Finally, the Securities Act of 1933, often called the "Truth-in-Securities Act," and the Securities Exchange Act of 1934 were enacted as legislative by-products of the Pecora investigation. The latter regulates trading on the national security exchanges, prohibits various kinds of manipulations and trading abuses, and requires companies whose securities are traded on the exchanges to provide full and accurate financial data.[48]

Abuses cried out for correction, and the federal government had no choice but to respond to the call for reform. Yet the question must be raised whether the laws were unnecessarily stringent, restrictive, and severe, whether the reforms promoted or obstructed financial rehabilitation and economic recovery. Many critics, including at least a few Federal Reserve officials, believed that both the Securities Act and the Securities Exchange Act inhibited recovery by increasing the costs and risks of new flotations and by making officers of issuing companies and underwriters reluctant to assume risks for fear of incurring civil and criminal penalties. Critics also argued that the Banking Act of 1933 got in the way of recovery in at least three ways. Recovery required broadening, not narrowing, the types of loans made by banks, but the act, by indicating official opposition to loans on the collateral of securities, threatened to restrict them. Second, prohibiting the payment of interest on demand deposits led to withdrawals of some correspondent bank deposits from financial centers, thus depriving the latter of funds which they would probably have been able to utilize more effectively than the banks withdrawing them. Finally, the requirement that commercial banks refrain from investment banking activity lessened the number of underwriting facilities at the time when the economy needed all the investment that could be induced.[49]

Another early attack by Roosevelt on the forces making for depression sought economic stabilization and recovery through improved wages and wider employment.[50] In May 1933 he sent a bill to Congress calling for "a great cooperative movement throughout all industry . . . to obtain wide reemployment, to shorten the working week, to pay a decent wage for the shorter week and to prevent unfair competition and disastrous overproduction." Enacted into law the next month, the National Industrial Recovery Act (NIRA) aimed to alleviate business distress by putting a floor under prices and by permitting industry to eliminate "unfair" competitive practices by agreement. The latter required a relaxation of the antitrust laws, but the legislation also sought to protect the interests of working people from the possible consequences of this legalized cartelization of industry by provisions which abolished child labor and established minimum wage standards, maximum hours, and collective bargaining procedures.[51] To carry out the purposes of the act, Roosevelt named Hugh Johnson, a World War I general, to head the National Recovery Administration (NRA).

Industry leaders greeted the legislation with unrestrained enthusiasm. "In Franklin D. Roosevelt," declared the president of the Chamber of Commerce, Henry I. Harriman, in June 1933, "business greets a leader of courage, resourcefulness, and trustworthiness. It glows in the audacious pioneering spirit in which he is tackling our common problems." To the Chamber of Commerce the bill seemed a "Magna Charta of industry and labor," for in the eyes of many of its members excessive competition had destroyed profitable operations, undermined confidence, and reduced the rate of investment. They welcomed the opportunity to negotiate with the government "codes of fair competition" which would establish minimum prices, enlarge employment, and control production through agreements to limit machine or plant hours or the construction of new capacity. But while more than thirty industries succeeded in winning approval for restrictions on productive capacity—by the end of 1934 only a fraction of the eligible industries were uncodified— manufacturers by no means spoke with a single voice. Rather, it was the older, more developed, and larger firms that were most eager to secure government regulation. Located in relatively less profitable industries, usually those making producers' goods, they had been seeking this objective since the late 1920s. In the earlier years of that decade they had pursued the security and profitability promised by cartelization indirectly, through informal understandings with the Justice Department, the Federal Trade Commission, and the federal courts. Now they enjoyed the explicit sanction of the law.[52]

In the textile industries, the larger firms in the North embraced the code worked out by that industry's trade association, whereas the newer, smaller mills of the South did not. In steel, firms with high overhead and excess capacity welcomed the codes, whereas smaller fabricating companies accepted them reluctantly. In the rubber industry, giants such as Firestone Tire and Rubber pushed for NRA price stabilization, as did almost all lumber firms. In sum, it was precisely in the industries where economic conditions were worst that the NRA codes were warmly embraced. But the codes may have impeded recovery by discouraging the newer and more progressive firms. Despite normal incentives to develop labor-saving technology during a depression, the codes, by seeking to bolster employment and raise operating rates, tended to reduce the pace of innovation.[53]

The NIRA appears to have got in the way of recovery in other ways as well. While the codes raised real hourly wage rates, especially those of the unskilled, those higher rates also encouraged employers to lay off workers—thus reducing the redistribution of income toward labor which liberal proponents of the measure had hoped to achieve as a means of increasing purchasing power and getting the wheels of industry turning again. The codes also raised prices and thus reduced the real money supply. In sum, the effect of the codes was contractionary: output, employment, and real wealth, rather than increasing, were diminished. By 1934 an operation initially hailed as a stepping stone to prosperity was being bitterly attacked as a major obstacle to that objective. A program of bewildering complexity, one which generated over seven hundred industrial codes seeking to reconcile the conflicting interests of large and small businessmen, and of labor and consumers, the NRA broke down even before the Supreme Court in May 1935 declared unconstitutional the law which sanctioned its existence.[54]

Fortunately however, a number of the labor provisions of the NIRA (section 7a) were rescued from oblivion three years later with the enactment of the Fair Labor Standards Act. The legislation established a standard work week of forty-four hours—reduced to forty after two years—with time-and-a-half pay for overtime. It also set minimum rates of hourly pay and generally prohibited child labor below the age of sixteen, as well as sweatshop industrial labor at home. The minimum rates were minimal indeed, merely forty cents an hour. Furthermore, the law allowed numerous exemptions from its requirements. Imperfect though it was, the law nevertheless laid foundations on which future Congresses could build. It must be remembered that in 1937, 12 million workers in industries affected by interstate commerce were making less than forty cents an hour.[55]

Section 7a had also placed the power of the federal government and of federal law on the side of labor unions by stipulating that "employees shall have the right to organize and bargain collectively through representatives of their own choosing, and shall be free from the interference, restraint or coercion of employers . . . in the designation of such representatives . . . [and] that no employee and no one seeking employment shall be required as a condition of employment to join any company union or to refrain from joining . . . a labor organization of his own choosing." Soon, however, a loophole was discovered in the law: although the law prevented employers from *forcing* employees to join a company union, it did not prevent them from *encouraging* employees to join one. The encouragement appears to have been considerable, for between 1932 and 1935 the number of workers covered by employee representation plans doubled, rising from 1,263,000 to 2,500,000.[56]

The respite proved a brief one. Two months after the Supreme Court declared the NIRA unconstitutional in May 1935, Congress passed the National Labor Relations Act, commonly called the Wagner Act. The new law reenacted the labor provisions of the NIRA with greater care and eliminated the loophole through which employee representation plans had moved with such ease. For business firms to support or encourage the formation of a company union was declared to be an unfair labor practice, and a National Labor Relations Board (NLRB) was established to enforce compliance. Businessmen nevertheless doubted the constitutionality of the new law, and two months after its passage there were still 672 employee representation plans in operation. With the Supreme Court's ruling in April 1937 in favor of the Wagner Act, employee representation schemes were doomed.

The Wagner Act and the NLRB gave new stimulus to the formation of independent trade unions. A burst of organizing had occurred even before, following the passage of the NIRA, for the AFL had chartered 584 federal unions and its member unions (2,953 locals) between June and October 1933. Industrial unionism increased steadily too, rising from 17 percent of the industrial workforce in 1929 to 27 percent in 1933 and to 33 percent in 1934. By the end of 1934, trade unions boasted a membership of 3,608,600, a gain that nearly equaled the AFL's losses between 1923 and 1933. By mid-1935 an additional 800,000 workers were unionized, and by 1941 total trade union membership stood at approximately 11 million. Despite the withdrawal of industrial unions from the AFL and the formation of the Congress of Industrial Organizations (CIO) in 1938, the former organization boasted a clear majority of union members on the eve of Pearl Harbor.[57]

The growth of unions in the 1930s was the principal force behind a phenomenal expansion of the personnel management movement in that decade. The proportion of firms employing more than 250 workers that had personnel departments, only 25 percent in 1920 and 34 percent in 1929, nearly doubled between 1929 and 1935, rising to 64 percent. The proportion of the entire industrial labor force covered by a personnel department, merely 13 percent in 1920 and 19 percent in 1929, shot up sensationally to 72 percent by 1935. Even firms with company unions required a central agency to deal with them, and this led to the vesting of the labor relations function in the personnel department. Although most personnel managers and independent trade unionists "had no great love for each other, their mutual interest in restraining foremen and developing rules and procedures to guide employment decisions led to a partial coalescence of the goals of the two movements."[58]

Legal recognition of the right of labor to organize and bargain collectively free of employer interference was an enduring achievement of the New Deal. So too were its protective federal laws on labor standards and social insurance. The Social Security Act of 1935 provided a compulsory old-age insurance program, a system of state unemployment compensation plans encouraged by offsetting federal taxes, and a joint federal-state program of financial assistance to needy old people, the blind, and fatherless children. Health insurance, bitterly opposed as "socialized medicine" by the American Medical Association, was not included.

In a famous speech to the Teamsters Union in 1940, President Roosevelt summed up the labor achievements of the New Deal. The foundation of industrial relations for all time, he said, was the right to organize and bargain collectively.

> With that foundation, the last seven years have seen a series of laws enacted to give labor a fairer share of the good life to which free men and women in a free nation are entitled as a matter of right. Fair minimum wages are being established for workers in industry; decent maximum hours and days of labor have been set, to bring about the objective of an American standard of living and recreation; child labor has been outlawed in practically all factories; a system of employment exchanges has been created; machinery has been set up and strengthened and successfully used in almost every case for the mediation of labor disputes. Over them all has been created a shelter of social security, a foundation upon which we are trying to build protection from the hazards of old age and unemployment.[59]

In sum, the New Deal virtually revolutionized national labor-management relations policy and, in addition, laid essential foundations of the Welfare State. In was high time: Germany, Britain, Australia, New Zealand, Sweden, and still other nations had done so long before. Surely the richest country in the world could afford to be no less compassionate.

Roosevelt also sought a fairer share of the good life for the nation's farmers. The worldwide depression fell with cruel force on agriculture, continuing the downturn in the fortunes of the farmer so evident in the 1920s. Exports of farm products declined in volume and even more heavily in price. In 1919 the estimated farm value of exports had constituted 15.8 percent of gross income from farm production. By 1932 that percentage was down to 6.5 percent. Stagnant industrial production brought down domestic demand for fibers and raw materials, while falling incomes reduced consumption of food products. Prices behaved accordingly. Between 1929 and 1932 leading commodities were down 50 percent or more. Wheat, for example, fell from $1.04 a bushel to $.38, corn from $.80 to $.32, oats from $.42 to $.16, and barley from $.54 to $.22. Livestock fell too: beef steers from $13.43 per cwt. to $6.70, hogs from $10.16 to $3.83. Cotton was down from about $.17 a pound to $.065. Taxes, interest charges, rent, wages, and operating expenses, on the other hand, underwent only moderate decline, so that net income from farming shrank even more severely.[60] In 1932 the average net income of farm operators from farming was less than a third of what it had been in 1929.[61]

These drastic declines resulted in a wave of foreclosures and other distress transfers of farms. For example, the fall in cotton, the principal cash crop of the South, led during 1931–1933 to more than twice the annual number of transfers of the preceding six years. In general, however, farm mortgage distress was especially acute in areas that had escaped the ravages of the 1920s, such as the eastern Great Plains and Rocky Mountain region. Other troubles fell on parts of the West, too. Prolonged droughts in some areas—for example, in the Red River valley—produced severe damage in the form of wheat rust, while many parts of the Dust Bowl area of western Kansas and eastern Colorado became uninhabitable, leading to a mass exodus of population. Natural calamities like these intensified the distress of the farm families experiencing them.[62]

Prices of farm products were generally at their lowest and farm distress at its worst during the summer, fall, and winter before Roosevelt was sworn in as president on March 4, 1933. Farmers began taking matters into their own hands. During the winter grim mobs gathered to stop foreclosures while pickets manned the highways to prevent the movement of products to town. Edward A. O'Neal, the head of the Farm Bureau Federation, warned a Senate committee in January 1933: "Unless something is done for the American farmer we will have revolution in the countryside within less than twelve months."[63]

What Roosevelt did was to instruct his supporters in Congress to give priority to agricultural legislation. The upshot was the passage of the Agricultural Adjustment Act of May 1933. Underlying this law was the belief, expressed in the act itself, that the "acute economic emergency" was partly due to "a severe and increasing disparity between the prices of agricultural and other commodities, which disparity has largely destroyed the purchasing power of farmers for industrial products."[64] Since "disparity" implied "parity," Congress defined the latter by declaring it to be the policy of the government:

> to establish and maintain such balance between the production and consumption of agricultural commodities, and such marketing conditions therefore, as will re-establish prices to farmers at a level that will give agricultural commodities a purchasing power with respect to articles that farmers buy, equivalent to the purchasing power of agricultural commodities in the base period. The base period in the case of all agricultural commodities except tobacco shall be the pre-war period, August 1909–July 1914. In the case of tobacco, the base period shall be the post-war period, August 1919–July 1929.[65]

The fundamental assumption on which the act rested was that the prices of "basic" agricultural commodities could be induced to rise by restricting the acreage devoted to their production to a level about one-third lower than in the previous three years. The act designated as "basic" wheat, cotton, field corn, hogs, rice, tobacco, and milk and its products. Farmers were to be encouraged to comply voluntarily with this "domestic allotment" program by being offered contracts calling for a rental-benefit payment for limiting their acreage (or, in the case of hogs, for limiting their marketings)—the payment being financed by taxes levied on the sale of the products to processors. Before the first year was over, however, the Agricultural Adjustment Program departed from its voluntary character with respect to cotton and tobacco and also added price-supporting loans. Loans on cotton and corn made by the secretary of agriculture in the fall of 1933 were made at levels in excess of current market prices—marking the beginning of present-day government price-support loan operations. In the event the market price failed to rise to the level of the loan rate, it was agreed that the producer might deliver his crop to the government in full repayment of this "nonrecourse" loan.[66]

After the Supreme Court in 1936 declared unconstitutional the collection of processing taxes to finance government production-adjustment contracts with individual producers, new legislation (1938) was framed on the basis of the interstate commerce clause. The act directed the secretary of agriculture to make nonrecourse loans available to producers of the major storable crops within a range of 52 percent to 75 percent parity. The law also authorized the secretary "to invoke marketing quotas upon the approval of two-thirds of the producers if supplies reached certain levels in relation to normal marketings." The Court upheld the constitutionality of the new law in 1942, and in the interim since then it has not been successfully challenged.[67]

The impact of the adjustment program on agricultural prices and farm incomes is almost impossible to determine. Consider, for example, the first year of the program. Although prices of basic commodities were substantially higher than they had been—between 1932 and 1933 wheat rose from $.38 to $.74, corn from $.32 to $.52, oats from $.16 to $.34, barley from $.22 to $.43, and cotton from $.065 to over $.10—Mother Nature brought forth adverse weather that year and therefore had a hand in the production of short crops. In addition, a substantial measure of increased business activity and consumer purchasing power must also be credited to some extent, as must purchases of food for purposes of relief. Finally, the depreciation of the dollar in terms of gold and the foreign exchanges directly helped raise prices of crops such as cotton, wheat, and tobacco, of which there were significant exports or imports. Even at the end of the thirties, it is safe to say, the goal of "price parity" was far from being achieved, for in no year during that decade did the farmer's average net income from his farm operation reach the level it had attained in 1929. Although the legislation probably did help raise farm incomes from their low point in 1932, it seems to have done so not by generating increases in national income but by redistributing existing income from consumers, who were obliged to pay higher prices for food products, to farmers. The total impact of the program on purchasing power may therefore have been negative, for farmers were a declining sector of the American economy, both in numbers and in their contribution to aggregate output.[68]

Nevertheless, the policies of the agricultural adjustment acts of the 1930s profoundly altered the structure of the labor markets of the plantation South, and in so doing helped prepare that long-beleaguered area for the modernization that came after the Second World War. Ever since Reconstruction days cotton plantations had been divided into smaller farms operated by sharecroppers and tenants. These institutional arrangements guaranteed a supply of labor throughout the annual cotton cycle, from preharvest ground breaking, planting, and cultivation, especially weed control, to the harvesting of the crop, the time of peak labor demand. The reason why the plantation South was an exception to the rule of widespread adoption of the tractor for preharvest operations in the 1920s was not only that the tenant plots were too small to justify this partial mechanization, but also, and more important, because it would have been uneconomical to displace workers for that part of the cycle when they would be needed to pick the cotton. Because southern economic development lagged and did not generate an adequate supply of casual workers who might have been paid wages to pick the cotton, the agricultural labor supply had to be retained, placed on hold, so to speak, so that it would be available for the harvest, as well as for preharvest operations. Opportunities for nonagricultural employment in the plantation areas during the off-season were insufficient, and this generated a fear that unless a worker had an annual interest in the crop, he would not be available when needed most.

The agricultural adjustment acts from 1933 to 1939 altered this situation by providing incentives to displace tenants. The payment of government subsidies to take cotton land out of production, plus the expectation of a cotton price stabilized by government, lump sum cash payments for use in the purchase of tractors and trucks, and a supply of agricultural labor sufficiently abundant—not least because of the stagnation created by the depression—to meet spurts in demand, reduced the cost of changing the old arrangements, and small plots were consolidated into large enough farms to make the use of tractors economically feasible. The demand for labor during the Second World War, it is true, led to a massive migration of erstwhile farmers and agricultural workers to the industrial centers of the North and South. But the resulting labor shortage, together with the new-found disposition to mechanize represented by adoption of the tractor, increased the cotton planter's receptivity to the mechanical cotton picker—an invention whose basic engineering principle had been patented in 1850 but which was not produced in commercial quantities till the late 1940s and early 1950s.[69]

But we get ahead of our story. On and on dragged the heavy wheels of the Great Depression. Why? What had the president failed to do, and what had he done wrong? He had sought to address the major problems of every sector of the American economy—its banking institutions and financial markets, its industry, workforce, and agriculture. The helping hand of the RFC had extended aid on a massive scale to foundering enterprises of many kinds. For example, after attempting in vain to unfreeze loans on the real estate mortgage market, an attempt, unsupported by private interests, which took the form of an offer to match $25 million of privately raised capital with $75 million in government funds to establish mortgage companies, the government chose to face the task alone. In 1935 the Reconstruction Finance Corporation Mortgage Company was created, and in 1938 that company was supplemented by the Federal National Mortgage Association, owned and operated by the RFC. More generally, when the nation's commercial banks and trust companies declined to make loans to industry, preferring instead the safe and highly liquid securities of the federal government, Congress in June 1934 approved an administration bill authorizing federal loans to small and medium-sized enterprises on a long-term five-year basis (later extended to ten years). The Federal Reserve Board as well as the RFC was permitted to make such loans. By the time the United States entered World War II, the RFC alone had made twelve thousand loans totaling $848,400,000.[70]

And that is not all. The RFC acted as the great engine of relief during the 1930s. It lent over $1 billion to 89 railroads, $90 million to 133 insurance companies, and $1.5 billion to farmers. In creating new agencies such as the Export and Import banks, the Rural Electrification Administration, and the Disaster Loan Corporation it extended its aid to cities, cooperatives, and individuals. The activities of the RFC, Jesse Jones observed, "have reached . . . every citizen of the United States." Not quite. But the reach was wide.

> RFC relief spread out like a rippling wave in a quiet pond. In saving the railroads from bankruptcy and receivership, for example, the RFC also saved those institutions, notably insurance companies, which held the $11 billion in railroad bonds outstanding. In addition it aided localities throughout the country whose income included railroad taxes. Through this interlocking process, RFC relief sustained the nation's property owners and its owners of capital.[71]

The only ones not included in these benefits were people who held no equity in anything, not even a job. It was these people who were ministered to by the relief agencies run by Harry Hopkins.

Despite these massive efforts on the part of the administration, nearly 8 million workers, 14.3 percent of the civilian labor force, were still unemployed even at the peak of the business cycle in 1937. It is true that the most commonly accepted index of economic health, net national product in constant prices, had risen spectacularly during the four preceding years, averaging 12 percent a year—a rate of growth unmatched by any other four-year period from 1869, when recorded figures start, to 1960. Monetary policy deserves most of the credit for this appearance of substantial recovery, but, as we shall see, the nature of the economic activity underlying it prevented it from bringing an end to the depression.

The restoration of a healthy commercial banking system marks the beginning of the rise. Governmental scrutiny of the condition of the commercial banks and the enactment of deposit insurance restored confidence, and the deposits which flowed back into the banks enabled those institutions to expand their loans. Yet that auspicious beginning might have been choked off had it not been for further reform, this time of the Federal Reserve System itself.

The Banking Act of 1935 not only centralized control of the system in the hands of the board of governors but moved the board's locus of power from New York to Washington, where it would be more responsive to the policy goals of the administration. Among the latter was that of raising the domestic price level by devaluing the nation's monetary unit to encourage imports of gold. Increases in bank reserves, multiple-deposit creation, and monetary expansion would result therefrom so long as the Federal Reserve Board did not take action, as it had done between 1929 and 1933, to offset or "neutralize" the imports. Enhancement of the board's political sensitivity was designed to encourage a more cooperative attitude on the part of the Federal Reserve.[72]

Lessening the number of grains of pure gold in the dollar could raise the dollar value of an ounce of gold. This was precisely the purpose of the Gold Reserve Act of January 1934, and President Roosevelt immediately followed its enactment by a proclamation which, by reducing the gold content of the dollar by about 40 percent, raised the price of an ounce of gold from its old official level of $20.67 to $35.00, an increase of nearly 70 percent. The new price level not only encouraged a rise in the world's physical output of gold but also unleashed a golden avalanche upon the United States. From the end of 1933 to the end of 1937 the nation's monetary gold stock rose from $4,036 million to $12,760 million, with more than 63 percent of the increase coming from imports. By the end of 1941 net gold imports accounted for 90 percent of an increase which by then amounted to $18,701 million.[73]

Despite the attractiveness of the new price, net imports of gold would not have flowed into the United States had not the country enjoyed a favorable balance of payments during these years. Had foreign claims on the dollar exceeded American claims on foreign currencies, had Americans owed more to others than the latter owed to them, then the gold which flowed into the country in response to its new price would have flowed out again to extinguish American indebtedness abroad. Exports for such purposes were perfectly legal, for although the Gold Exchange Act had called in all domestically held gold and forbidden its domestic circulation, the federal government was authorized to sell gold for purposes of foreign payments. Fortunately, the latter were unnecessary, for Americans were net creditors during these years. Net claims on account of trade in goods and services form part of the explanation of the creditor position, but only a small part. Far more important were huge net inflows of capital funds, both long term and short term, with the principal component of the latter being foreign funds seeking asylum in the United States from the troubles of Europe. The role of the United States in international capital flows was thus reversed. In the 1920s the nation had been a large net exporter of capital; now it was a large net importer.[74]

The heavy imports of gold had a decisive effect on the stock of money, which rose at an average annual rate of nearly 11 percent, one of the largest rises on record, between April 1933 and March 1937. Roughly comparable increases in the price level and in national income also occurred during these years. Since March 1933, wholesale prices had risen nearly 50 percent. Clearly, the increased money supply, together with the prospect of higher prices, induced people to spend, stimulating demand for goods and services and inducing idled manufacturers to resume production and hire workers, who in turn gave the wheel of demand another turn by spending their wages. Devaluation of the dollar and reform of the Federal Reserve System thus placed the economy on an upward path of recovery.[75]

Yet even at the cyclical peak in 1937 not only did unemployment continue to loom large, but per capita output was lower than it had been in 1929. The rapid increase in net national product that took place between 1933 and 1937 is mainly attributable to the performance of the nondurables component of the index of industrial production. At the cyclical peak in 1937 that component was more than 21 percent above its value at the 1929 peak. In contrast, the durables component was some 6 percent below, a difference largely reflecting an unusually low level of private capital formation. Net private investment remained negative until 1936, and when it did become positive in 1936 and early 1937, an unusually large part consisted of additions to inventories. At its height in early 1937, private construction was only one-third of the peak level of the mid-1920s. In consequence, the most notable feature of the revival after 1933 was not its rapidity but its incompleteness.[76]

The investment that occurred during these years tended to be tied to the current demand for output. These expenditures were required to replace depleted capital stock but were not large enough to enable net additions to be made to productive capacity and output. Yet for consumption expenditures to rise secularly there must be either net private investment or repeated injections of government spending. The latter was wanting too. Federal expenditures—for example, by the Public Works Administration—did rise every year after 1932, except in 1937, and these made some contribution to aggregate demand. The increases, however, filled only a small part of the large gap between actual and potential output. Moreover, their expansionary effects were partially offset by effective tax rates that were higher during these years than they had been before 1933. Rates were pushed up virtually across the board, but notably on the lower- and middle-income groups. Indeed, the Federal Revenue Act of 1932, which came into full effect the next year, approximately doubled full-employment tax yields and essentially set the tax structure for the entire period up to the Second World War. Even within that structure taxes continued to be raised. Corporate tax rates went up gradually to 19 percent, and new payroll taxes were imposed to finance the social security program enacted in 1935.[77]

As this tax and expenditure pattern suggests, the administration had no clearly worked out fiscal policy. Roosevelt did believe that the budget should be balanced: he had denounced Hoover for not balancing it and had promised to perform the feat himself if elected. His failure to do so probably implies that this objective was less important to him than goals which required the running of deficits. The closest he came to it was in requesting and obtaining a special tax levy in 1933 to service debt created in order to finance expenditures that were not paid for immediately out of revenues. This was not close at all; in fact, it represented a kind of dual budget, the taxing part of which was designed to create an aura of sound finance necessary for business confidence and continued public support. In 1937—fearing inflation!—he once again placed a high priority on reducing expenditures, increasing revenues, and balancing the budget, with unfortunate results, as we shall see. In a word, government fiscal policy cannot be said to have failed to end the depression. It was simply not tried.[78]

The impact of governmental tax and spending programs on aggregate demand was positive every year from 1930, but by small and varying amounts, ranging from 0.5 percent (in 1933) to 2.5 percent (in 1936). The latter was largely attributable to a soldiers' bonus of $1.7 billion, which Roosevelt vetoed, as Hoover had before him. The bonus imparted an unusual boost to both consumer incomes and expenditures. Tax revenues also rose substantially, however, not only because of existing taxes but also because of the new social security taxes. The result was a severe decline in the net government contribution to income in early 1937. There ensued in 1937–38 one of the sharpest business contractions on record, a recession reminiscent of that of 1920–21.[79]

Many scholars attribute the recession to these governmental fiscal measures. Some, however, place emphasis on the Treasury's sterilization of gold and the doubling of reserve requirements by the Federal Reserve Board. Banks sought to restore their excess reserve position by curtailing loans, and since the latter took the form of bank-created deposits on which borrowers could draw by check, the ratio of deposits to reserves fell sharply. High-powered money—reserves which generate deposits by a multiple varying with the amount of the reserve requirement—rose, but the rate of growth of the stock of money declined with the curtailment of lending. Indeed, the money stock fell with only minor interruptions from March 1937 to the end of the year. Of the two, the fiscal explanation would appear the more persuasive, especially because, with the mounting of massive defense expenditures and the outbreak of war, the depression finally came to an end. In the year of Pearl Harbor the unemployed portion of the civilian labor force dropped from 14.6 percent to 9.9 percent. A year later, in 1942, it was down to 4.7 percent.[80]

We are left with the question we just raised: what went wrong? Why was private investment so weak during the 1930s? Certainly the answer cannot be found in shortages of available funds for investment. Had supplies been scarce relative to demand, interest rates would have risen to levels above those obtaining when they were more plentiful. But the opposite occurred: rates on short-term commercial paper and yields on corporate bonds—the latter an index of the cost of long-term investment funds—were sharply lower in the 1930s than they had been in the 1920s. The real question concerns not the supply of capital but the demand for it. Why was the demand for capital, especially for long-term investment funds, so low in the 1930s?

One scholar suggests the importance of a gradual shift in the long-run potential for growth to the nondurable goods sectors of the economy, sectors whose capital and labor requirements were as yet too small in relation to the economy as a whole to affect very much the demand for those factors of production.[81] Other analysts, however, emphasize the impact of New Deal policies on business confidence. Those policies tended to promote increases in wages and to reduce profit levels. The former were encouraged by the NIRA, by the National Labor Relations Act, and by the enactment of minimum wage laws. Laws imposing new taxes, particularly social security taxes, also raised labor costs, as did federal provision for unemployment compensation and old age security payments. At the same time, profits were reduced net of taxes by a tax on undistributed corporate profits enacted for the first time in American history in 1936.[82]

But there is more to it than this: attention must be paid not only to costs and profits, not only to partisan rhetoric by ardent New Dealers such as Secretary of the Interior Harold L. Ickes, Secretary of Agriculture Henry A. Wallace, administrator of the Works Progress Administration Harry Hopkins, and the president himself, but to the whole bent of public policy as viewed by the business community. Rhetorical characterizations of them as "economic royalists" unnerved business leaders, and so too did the president's penchant for military analogy to characterize both the economic crisis and the ways in which the government intended to deal with it. This, after all, was a decade of dark dictatorship in Germany, Italy, and Japan. But businessmen were alarmed still more by the establishment in May 1933 of the Tennessee Valley Administration (TVA), a public corporation which produced and sold hydroelectric power and fertilizer in competition with the private sector, and by Roosevelt's attempt to pack the Supreme Court in order to gain legal approval of the reformist legislation he sponsored.

The last was the crux of the matter: the legislation itself. It represented a revolutionary turnabout in American history, an unmistakable placement of federal power in the corner of the underdog. Distrust, fear, and even hate increased the risks and uncertainties of business decisions. Lacking faith in the administration's intentions with respect to business and the private enterprise economy, businessmen chose to confine their risks to short-term investments rather than to incur possible losses in an uncertain future. At bottom, then, reform impeded recovery.[83]

Yet this cannot be the whole story. Businessmen had no reason to be wary of Hoover's administration. Yet they were reluctant to invest then too. "Potential credit is a favorable factor to business recovery," said Hoover's secretary of the Treasury, Ogden Mills, "but until the credit actually goes to work it can affect neither business nor prices. It will go to work only when the lender feels secure enough to lend, and the borrower confident enough of the use he can make of the money to borrow." "What is holding us back," he added, "is uncertainty and lack of confidence." Mills expressed these thoughts in a speech before the Young Republican Club of Missouri on February 11, 1933, before Roosevelt was inaugurated. "How," asks an analyst of the Hoover and Roosevelt presidencies, could Hoover and Mills "overcome that paralyzing compound of fear, timidity, and caution—that lack of confidence—on the part of the business community which had frustrated all of Hoover's previous efforts?"[84]

How indeed? Roosevelt and Jesse Jones of the RFC faced a similar problem in the early days of the New Deal. "There is no ally that President Roosevelt needs quite so much to achieve and maintain recovery," Jones told the New York State Bankers Association in February 1934, "as the banker." Yet the "common cry almost everywhere," he added, "is that the banks are not lending." In part, the explanation is the same then as during the latter days of Hoover. The trauma of the depression made bankers fearful and timid. But businessmen were also fearful, and in consequence the demand for loans was thin.

Banker and business assessments of market risk must therefore be added to the explanation of inadequate investment in the 1930s. But the other factor, uncertainty born of reformist legislation, is there too. As Jones remarked in 1938, "bankers seldom like the way government is run." They especially disliked the way Roosevelt's government was run. "One characteristic of bankers," he declared, "is that probably 95% of them don't like the New Deal, and while they would not intentionally 'cut off their nose to spite their face' . . . they naturally pull back." He might have added that businessmen in general also held back, in all probability partly for the same reason.[85]

Yet, costly as reforms may have been for the short-run prospects of economic recovery, who can doubt that they were necessary? Reform touched not only the nation's securities and financial markets, its labor relations practices, and its treatment of the aged, infirm, sick, and unemployed, but also the egregiously irresponsible, indeed corrupt practices of multilayered utility holding companies. The Public Utilities Holding Company Act of 1935 made such firms illegal if they were more than twice removed from their operating companies. TVA represented reform, too, reform of a dismal situation in which only one Mississippi farm in a hundred enjoyed the uses of electric power in 1932. Indeed, before President Roosevelt's creation of the Rural Electrification Administration in May 1935 nine of ten American farms had no electricity. By 1950 only one of ten lacked it.[86]

Many business leaders were alienated in the 1930s, but the irony is that much of the reform brought about by the New Deal is now an institutionalized part of American life. So too is the relationship of government to the economy: despite regulations of economic conduct which future administrations would both introduce, modify, and even abandon; despite change in the degree to which government would intervene in the economy; despite change, too, in the industrial cast of characters subject to intervention, the basic fact remains that the reaction of both government and business to the trauma of the Great Depression has in all probability ended forever the relatively minimal contact between the two sectors that characterized all of American history before the 1930s.

The New Deal, once again, did not end the Great Depression. But the president's policies did save the American economic system. Moreover, they did much to prepare the major institutions of America's political economy for needs soon to be redefined by rapid technological innovation and social change.

Roosevelt was a bold experimenter and a compassionate man, yet one who lacked a coherent program for economic recovery. He would undoubtedly have been the first to acknowledge the absence of system in his policies. He believed in trying one thing and then turning to another if it failed to work. A man of immense warmth and magnetism, a superb public speaker and consummate politician, he raised hope and instilled confidence in a groping and badly shaken people. Though aristocratic himself, if ever that un-American word may be applied to a figure in public life, he had genuine feeling for the common man, for the worker, and especially for the farmer. Unfortunately, he was less sensitive to the humanity of the businessman, to his need for confidence that public utterances and policies would not undermine the indispensable role which he too must play in the American economic system. Events soon to unfold would reveal once again the importance of that role in war as well as in peace.

16

The Second Great War and Its Aftermath

I n the 1930s the American people only slowly came to accept the fact of their inescapable presence in the larger world.[1] From the Japanese movement into Manchuria in 1931 to the German invasion of Poland in 1939, isolationism was their dominant mood. Hoping to avoid incidents which might lead to American involvement, Congress in 1935 made it unlawful to export arms, ammunition, or implements of war for the use of belligerents, and in 1937 broadened the Neutrality Act to include materials and articles other than munitions when shipped in American vessels. According to a poll taken by the American Institute of Public Opinion in September 1939, just after the German occupation of the Polish Corridor, 88 percent of the American people replied in the negative when asked "whether we should declare war on Germany at once."[2]

Nevertheless, American sympathies were clearly on the side of the Allies, and in November of that year the Neutrality Act was further revised to permit the shipment of arms and munitions to belligerents once the title to them had been transferred to the consignee. With the adoption of this "cash-and-carry" principle, the British and French took steps to enlarge and coordinate their purchasing operations in the United States. Their contracts resulted in the construction of facilities for the production of armaments and thus strengthened American defense capabilities as well. The latter would be strengthened still more after the sweep of German armies across western Europe in the spring and early summer of 1940 cleared the way for additional appropriations for national defense and enabled the president to give precedence to the production of military supplies.[3]

Those events also enabled the president to move warily—partly because of his desire to avoid alarming those millions of Americans who were willing to support the enemies of the Axis but unwilling to enter the "shooting war"— toward administrative arrangements for industrial mobilization, and in the months before Pearl Harbor he revived the First World War's National Defense Advisory Commission (May 1940) and established the Office of Production Management (December 1940; OPM), the Office of Price Administration and Civilian Supply (April 1941), and the Supply Priorities and Allocations Board (August 1941; SPAB). None of these agencies possessed either the authority or the unity to move the country to the degree of industrial mobilization deemed vital by the military and by leading government officials.[4] The OPM, for example, had as its codirectors the labor leader Sidney Hillman and the former General Motors executive William Knudsen, each of whom was solicitous of his former constituents.

Nevertheless, they represent important steps in the development of machinery for coordinating the activities of the government—SPAB, for example, was designed to bring together the responsible officials concerned with the military sphere, with civilian supply, and with export and economic warfare policies—and also signify the rejection of a powerful system of economic controls envisioned by mobilization plans prepared in 1930, 1933, 1936, and 1939 by the War Department (in close collaboration with the navy). These plans proposed the establishment of a superagency, the War Resources Administration, with supervisory power over all other agencies principally charged with functions directly related to economic mobilization. Roosevelt believed that if he approved any such system, he would be turning over the war effort to "complete outsiders who don't know anything about running government." He thought it would be unconstitutional to do so: "The final responsibility is mine and I can't delegate it." "I would simply be abdicating the presidency to some other person," he added.[5]

Despite the halting, makeshift administrative arrangements of the defense period, the nation had gained valuable experience in the letting of contracts, in production, controls, and administrative machinery. When war was declared on December 8, 1941 about 15 percent of the country's industrial output involved military equipment and supplies. The civilian economy was geared for war, and—at last—the Great Depression had begun to sink into history.[6]

The process was painfully slow, the more so because of the New Deal's long restorative efforts, but gradually governmental expenditures during the defense period, and especially in wartime, enabled the economy to regain the levels of output and employment reached in 1929. As late as 1939, some 9.5 million workers remained unemployed, an average rate of unemployment of over 17 percent, and even in 1940 the rate was still 14.6 percent. True, real GNP that year was 9 percent above that of 1929, but this advance was a "historically miserable performance," especially if one took into account the stimulus imparted to the level of the GNP in 1940 by business firms anticipating a preparedness boom.[7] Other indexes of economic activity were also above 1929 levels, but not by much. In real terms, receipts from farm marketings were 15 percent and industrial production 16 percent higher. But real gross private domestic investment was still 18 percent below the corresponding figure for 1929. In fact, the value of the gross stock of business plant and equipment in 1940 was still less than it had been in 1926! Expenditures for national defense, at $1.24 billion in 1939, were merely 1.4 percent of the nation's GNP. Although they rose the next year in response to the launching of Hitler's blitzkrieg of spring and summer, they totaled only $2.2 billion in a GNP of $100 billion.

Even 1941 was a year of transition in which the demands of the civilian economy continued to compete strongly with those of the preparedness program. Domestic investment, still overwhelmingly civilian, was 26 percent higher in 1941 than it had been the preceding year. Real personal consumption also rose from 5.1 percent to 6.2 percent (in 1942 it fell absolutely). Not till the third quarter of the year did outlays on durable consumer goods register a decline; not till the fourth quarter did private domestic investment begin to drop off. And average unemployment throughout the year was still high at 10 percent of the civilian labor force. But in the fourth quarter of 1941 the transition to a war economy gathered speed, for then the level of military expenditures rose to 16 percent of GNP. The Great Depression was over at last. What finally ended it was a huge increase in deficit spending. In 1941 the ratio of the federal deficit to the GNP was twice as high as it had been in 1939.

The onset of war also made it possible for the president to abandon the slow administrative motions of the preparedness period. In January 1942 he issued an executive order which created the War Production Board, delegating to it all the president's powers over industry, production, raw materials, factories, machine tools, priorities, allocations, and rationing. As it turned out, these powers fell into the hands of one man, Donald M. Nelson, a former Sears, Roebuck executive. The board, composed of the top production representatives of the War, Navy, and Commerce departments, the Board of Economic Warfare, and the price administrator, as well as a representative of the White House, was purely advisory, serving as a mechanism for weekly meetings around the council table.[8]

But Nelson had no intention of taking over the contracting and procurement activities of the army and navy. Indeed, he said that he "didn't even consider . . . for 5 minutes" setting up a buying organization independent of theirs.[9] The purchasing officers of the services were experienced and already at work and would undoubtedly be better able than the new agency to withstand charges of favoritism or collusion in letting contracts and defining profits. "Their independence," however, "left him without the authority to define and enforce over-all production priorities which affected not the military only but also lend-lease, other war-related and essential civilian production, and the health of businesses, large and small."[10]

The War and Navy departments naturally turned to Big Business for their needs. Given the urgencies of war, it is difficult to see how they could have done otherwise, most especially if Brehon Somervell, chief of the Army Service

Forces and commanding general of the Services of Supply, spoke truly when he said that "all the small plants of the country could not turn out one day's requirements of ammunition."[11] Big Business, on the other hand, had much of the plant and experience to handle enormous orders for military materials, and also the executives and engineers able to manage new, technologically difficult programs. And if there was truth in the contemporary quip that a small firm could be defined as "any business that is unable to maintain a staff in Washington to represent its interests," Big Business held an obvious advantage in that respect too.[12]

The consequences are hardly surprising. Despite the establishment by Congress of the Smaller War Plants Corporation (SWPC) in June 1942 to make loans to small businesses and otherwise help them obtain procurement orders, of a total $175 billion in prime contracts awarded between June 1940 and September 1944 more than one-half went to the top thirty-three corporations (with size measured by the value of the prime contracts received). The smallest 94 percent of prime supply contracts (those of $9 million or less) got 10 percent of the value of all such contracts during that period. Small enterprises fared no better as recipients of subcontracts from large firms. According to a 1943 survey by the SWPC, although a group of 252 of the largest contracting corporations did subcontract about one-third of the value of their prime contracts, three-fourths of that value went to other large (over five hundred employees) concerns.[13]

Wartime change in the numbers of small manufacturing firms, and in their share of total manufacturing employment, tell much the same story. Companies with fewer than twenty employees accounted for approximately 70 percent of all enterprises in 1939. By 1944, the percentage had risen only seven points, a modest increase indeed during a period which saw manufacturing firms with fewer than one hundred employees account for about 26 percent of total manufacturing employment. Five years later, and in the context of a 55 percent increase in total manufacturing employment, this share had declined to only 19 percent. In sum, it was the biggest companies that gained: those with ten thousand or more workers employed 13 percent of all manufacturing workers in December 1939. By December 1944 that percentage had risen to more than 30 percent. In short, small manufacturing firms emerged from the war in a weakened market position.[14]

Other segments of the small-enterprise sector fared even worse, for between 1940 and 1945, 324,000 firms went out of business—a significant 10 percent of the 1940 total. Exits were especially heavy in construction, retail trade, and service activities, all havens of small business. Both corporations and nonincorporated firms went under, indeed in roughly equal proportions. But the survivors did well, especially in view of wartime constraints (the Revenue Act of 1942, for example, raised the excess profits tax from 60 percent to 90 percent). The profits of both groups, in real, price-deflated terms, rose 60 percent during the five years of war, a proportion almost exactly equal to the rise in real national income during the period. Strangely enough, larger manufacturing corporations do not appear to have done as well. Despite a remark by Henry L. Stimson, secretary of war, that "if you are going to try to go to war, or to prepare for war, in a capitalist country, you have got to let business make money out of the process or business won't work," most industry groups had lower net profits after taxes in the years 1942–1945 than in 1941. The sole exceptions were firms producing beverages and transportation equipment, and, in the case of the largest corporations (assets of $10 million or more), lumber.[15]

At the beginning of the emergency, indeed even after Pearl Harbor, many business leaders had refused to "work." The situation contrasted starkly with that of the First World War, in which private capital had financed 90 percent of the cost of the expansion of industrial facilities. The government had induced the capital flow by permitting owners of facilities built or acquired for war production to write off their cost to the extent to which they possessed no postwar value, a device which would enable them to lower their taxes. Owners of about one-eighth of the nearly $5 billion in private capital invested in new plant and equipment were ultimately provided relief through tax amortization. Seeking a similar response, Congress enacted a tax amortization provision in October 1940 that provided for accelerated depreciation of the full value of all qualified defense facilities at an annual rate of 20 percent—in contrast to standard allowable rates of 5 percent for buildings and 10 percent for equipment. The plan provided less of an incentive than had been hoped, partly for the reason that the legitimacy of fully one-third of the relief through tax amortization had been subsequently challenged by a Senate committee after World War I. In addition, businessmen had other fears.[16]

Even after the nation had entered the "shooting war," many business leaders continued their reluctance to invest, their memories of the recent prolonged depression too keen not to anticipate with apprehension the possibility that increases in plant and equipment would lead to excess capacity, new firm entry, cutthroat competition, and flooded markets after the war. The following exchange between Senator E. H. Moore of Oklahoma and Interior Secretary and Petroleum Administrator for War Harold L. Ickes dramatically illustrates what Harold Vatter with fairness calls a "basic conflict between some industry leaders and the government." The colloquy took place in February 1943 when Ickes testified before the Truman Committee "in behalf of the imperative need for a petroleum pipeline to be constructed from Texas to the East Coast."

> *Secretary Ickes:* I would like to say one thing, however. I think there are certain gentlemen in the oil industry who are thinking of the competitive position after the war.
> *The Chairman:* That is what we are afraid of, Mr. Secretary.

Secretary Ickes: That's all right. I am not doing that kind of thinking.

The Chairman: I know you are not.

Secretary Ickes: I am thinking of how best to win this war with a least possible amount of casualties and in the quickest time.

Senator Moore: Regardless, Mr. Secretary, of what the effect would be after the war? Are you not concerned with that?

Secretary Ickes: Absolutely.

Senator Moore: Are you not concerned with the economic situation with regard to existing conditions after the war?

Secretary Ickes: Terribly. But there won't be any economic situation to worry about if we don't win the war.

Senator Moore: We are going to win the war.

Secretary Ickes: We haven't won it yet.

Senator Moore: Can't we also, while we are winning the war, look beyond the war to see what the situation will be with reference to—

Secretary Ickes (interposing): That is what the automobile industry tried to do, Senator. It wouldn't convert because it was more interested in what would happen after the war. That is what the steel industry did, Senator, when it said we didn't need any more steel capacity, and we are paying the price now. If decisions are left with me, it is only fair to say that I will not take into account any post-war factor—but it can be taken out of my hands if those considerations are paid attention to.

Senator Moore: I think you will find that those of us who do look beyond the war and to the economic situation beyond the war are as much interested now in winning the war as anybody else is, but we must look to the situation developing now that may result in the unnecessary destruction—

Secretary Ickes (interposing): On that point, Senator, the Government will own this pipe line. The Government can scrap it; it can take it up, it can sell it; it can lease it; it can operate it after the war.

Senator Moore: That is what we are afraid of. We are afraid that they will not scrap it; they will not take it up but it will be sold to the people whose power it will be to destroy existing facilities, and that is what we object to.

Secretary Ickes: I am not afraid of my Government yet.

Senator Hatch: I don't think the Secretary has been quite fair to himself, because I have had many conferences with Secretary Ickes about the oil industry and about the preservation of the independent oil producer in this country, and I can say for him, which he will not say for himself, that there isn't a man in this country that is more concerned with the preservation of the independent oil men of this country than is Secretary Ickes.

Senator Moore: I am glad to hear you say that, Senator.

Senator Hatch: I so testify for you, Mr. Secretary.

Senator Moore: I say that when the bald statement is made that, "I am not concerned with anything beyond winning the war"—

Secretary Ickes: That's right; I want to win the war first.[17]

As Secretary Ickes pointed out, the automobile industry was reluctant in 1940–41 to convert to production of military aircraft, and steel industry spokesmen denied the need for additional capacity. Railroad management and the electric power industry are further examples of hesitation in expanding capacity. Shortages of crude materials also set in early, aggravated by wartime curtailment of imports, which fell well below the 1940 level every year from 1942 through 1945. The drops in imports of tin and crude rubber after 1941 was especially critical. The Japanese occupation of the Malay Peninsula and the Netherlands East Indies early in 1942 found the United States with a total stockpile of natural rubber of less than 540,000 tons. The technology for producing synthetic rubber was known, but whether that product could be competitive in either price or quality with natural rubber after the war was far from certain. In these circumstances private capital could not be expected to finance production, and in consequence the government did. Almost all of the new capacity required for synthetic rubber, as well as for magnesium— another item in critically short supply—was financed by the Defense Plant Corporation established in August 1940. Built by the government and leased to private operators for $1.00 a year, these plants increased the output of synthetic rubber from 8,383 long tons in 1941 to 753,111 in 1944.[18]

The device of tax amortization did succeed in inducing the private sector to invest nearly $6.5 billion during the war. Despite early misgivings, makers of automobiles became the largest single group of suppliers to the aircraft industry, in addition to their output of tanks, jeeps, and trucks; the railroads increased their ton-mile volume of intercity traffic 93 percent between 1940 and 1944, and oil pipeline manufacturers their product by 125 percent during the same interval. Steel, too, expanded its ingot capacity between 1940 and 1945 from 81.6 to 95.5 million tons, but in this case it was governmental financing that made the expansion possible. Furthermore, since the production of raw steel rose only 8 percent from 1941 to the wartime peak in 1944, it is clear that a fundamental aspect of the manner in which war-production increases were achieved was through a considerable diversion from civilian use. However, despite the limitations on civilian consumption implied by diversion—production of passenger cars, for example, all but ceased after 1942—the total was higher in 1943 than it had been in 1940, with personal-consumption expenditures per person of the resident civilian population drifting upward throughout the war. The civilian "sacrifice" was surely not very severe, especially in comparison with that of the British.[19]

The private sector supplied roughly one-quarter of the total investment of $25 billion in new and expanded facilities and equipment made during the defense and war periods. The rest was provided by agencies of the federal government. The War Department constructed about $5.4 billion worth of plant and equipment, the Navy Department $2.9 billion, and the Maritime Commission $600 million. Nearly a third of the $25 billion was supplied either directly by the Reconstruction Finance Corporation or, to a far greater extent, by its defense-related subsidiaries. Of the latter, the Defense Plant Corporation (DPC), which made 2,300 investments in plant and equipment totaling nearly $7 billion, was much the most important. The bulk of the investment was in the aircraft and closely related industries—aluminum, magnesium, and aviation gasoline—with large investments also made in the steel and chemical industries and in pipeline transportation. Synthetic rubber, as we have seen, was a new industry, brought by the DPC from infancy to maturity, an amalgam of government capital and private initiative. All told, the DPC increased the nation's wartime productive capacity by more than 10 percent.[20]

The end of the war in 1945 found the government as titleholder in publicly financed industrial facilities valued at approximately $16 billion. Of this sum, the $7 billion investment by the DPC represented the major portion of commercial-type facilities most attractive for peacetime use. DPC was the main instrumentality through which the government owned 90 percent or more of the synthetic rubber, aircraft, and magnesium industries, 55 percent of the nation's aluminum capacity, and the bulk of the nation's machine tools—besides significant percentages in a variety of other industries. Obviously the policy guidelines along which surplus plant and equipment were disposed of would exert important impacts on a number of industries. For one thing, although we do not yet know precisely what equipment was installed in which plants, a calculated increase of 27 percent in labor productivity over the years 1940–1944 lends support to the judgment that plants built during the war were generally more efficient. By the end of the war, it is true, the value of most plants to their operations had fallen considerably; that is to say, the cost of building them had been inflated by the need for haste and the use of less desirable materials. In addition, they had seen hard usage during the war. In consequence, sales of the plants to their operators or to others required price concessions reflecting the cost of readying them for peacetime use.[21]

Machine tools—lathes, planers, milling and grinding machines, cutting tools, and gauges, for example—also had seen hard wear, but in the case of cutting tools, their original manufacturers agreed for a fee to restore them to first-class condition prior to sale. The stock of machine tools had approximately doubled during the war, and about two-thirds of them were owned by the government. They were modern and worked at higher speeds and tolerances than older tools. Firms acquiring these technologically superior tools, either separately or along with the plants in which they were installed, would have a competitive edge over rivals. In addition, if facilities were sold to large firms already accounting for significant shares of output in their industries, the degree of concentration would be increased. On the other hand, increased competition would be the by-product of sales to smaller firms. Not all of the facilities would be declared surplus, however, for the army and navy had an interest in retaining some of them as reserves against future emergencies.[22]

Debate within the administration and Congress on demobilization strategies went on for about two years, with the objective of obtaining a fair return on sales vying with other goals such as discouraging monopoly and aiding small business, fostering postwar employment, avoiding dislocations in the economy, and supporting independent new enterprises. The actual disposal of surplus plants and equipment was "neither neat nor swift," with a large part of the machinery being sold separately. And according to Representative Estes Kefauver, chairman of the Monopoly Subcommittee of the House Committee on Small Business, the disposal process in 1946 was not being used to strengthen the competitive position of small business. It did, however, enable Henry J. Kaiser and his partner, Joseph Frazer, to break into the automobile industry. Although the new firm lasted only a few years, the impact of the disposal program on the aluminum industry was more permanent. Helped by the Supreme Court's conclusion in March 1945 that the Aluminum Corporation of American (Alcoa) was a monopoly, the government was able to break Alcoa's hold on the industry by compelling the corporation to deliver its patents on a royalty-free basis to operators of government-owned alumina plants in Arkansas and Louisiana. This outcome encouraged the Reynolds Metal Company and Kaiser—this time with more lasting success—to purchase several government plants, and by 1956 Alcoa's share of primary capacity in the industry was down to 43 percent, with Kaiser enjoying 27 percent, Reynolds 26 percent, and Anaconda, a newcomer, 4 percent. In addition, the government nurtured the synthetic rubber industry through its years of infancy until the development of "cold rubber" for tire making enabled it to stand on its own feet. Finally, DPC's "Big Inch" and "Little Big Inch" pipelines "helped the natural gas industry to widen its markets, to the mutual benefit of Texas producers and East Coast consumers."[23]

War left its impress on the labor force as well as on the industrial sector. At the beginning, conversion to a war economy was facilitated by the existence of both excess industrial capacity and unemployed labor power. Indeed, before 1943 huge increases in wartime production were won in the main not by enlarging the size of the capital stock but by employing additional labor, energy, and raw materials. Between 1940 and 1943 the civilian labor force rose by about 5 million, or nearly 12 percent, but in addition, the number of labor hours also increased. Average weekly hours worked in manufacturing, for example, rose from 38.1 in 1940 to about 45 in both 1943 and 1944. But not only industry required more labor. The federal government also did, and between 1941 and 1945 it added more than 12 million persons to its payroll—almost 2 million to the Department of Defense and other agencies and over 10 million to the armed forces.[24]

Many hundreds of thousands of the new members of the civilian labor force must have come from agriculture, for in 1940 that sector was harboring excess capacity, marginal entrepreneurs, and disguised unemployment (in addition to the officially unemployed). While only about 600,000 persons transferred out of farm employment between 1940 and 1944, the total farm population fell by 5.7 million! Perhaps a million and a quarter of these men and women who were surplus to the needs of agriculture entered the civilian labor force, with many of the remainder becoming members of the armed forces. Many teenagers and elderly persons also manned the wartime factories, but an increasing proportion of the labor force was composed of women.[25]

That proportion had been rising steadily since 1900, and by 1940 females over fourteen constituted 25.3 percent of all workers. At the peak of wartime production the 11 million working women of 1940 had become the 19.5 million of 1945. Perhaps as many as 1.5 million of these women, however, would have joined the labor force even if there had been no war. Even if no change had taken place in the female participation rate, the increase in the female population by 1945 would have brought an additional 750,000 workers into the labor force. When one also takes into account the number of women unemployed and looking for work in 1940—some 3 million strong—together with an estimated additional 1 million who had abandoned the search out of discouragement, perhaps only about 3.5 million workers who otherwise might not have entered the labor force did so in the war years. Although these considerations are essential if we are to weigh the relative strength of the historical forces underlying the employment of women, it must also be remembered that the war not only added labor demands beyond those of historical trend lines but also ended the depression. Had the latter continued, the number of unemployed would surely have been larger by several millions.[26]

War also enlarged opportunities for older women and black women. Women over forty-five appeared in the labor force in numbers about 20 percent above what normally would have been expected. Three of five new female recruits to the labor force during the war were over thirty-five. Despite the need to take advantage of all available sources of labor during the war, racial prejudice proved costly to the nation as well as to its victims. To his credit, President Roosevelt created the Fair Employment Practices Commission by executive order in July 1941, and, sustained by rulings of the War Manpower Commission as well, black women improved their position before the end of the war. They did so by transferring from low-paid, low-status employment as domestics to jobs in factories. But they never got some of the best-paying jobs—as welders, ship fitters, or riveters, and in steel mills.[27]

Black men also benefited from the opening of urban occupational opportunities, especially in the North, but in the South and West as well. According to the *Negro Year Book* of 1947, during the war almost a million blacks migrated from southern farms and rural communities to northern, southern, and western industrial centers, with black employment in manufacturing increasing by 600,000. Most moved to nonsouthern states—Alabama, Arkansas, Georgia, and Mississippi experiencing absolute declines in their average black male populations over the census decade 1940–1950. In contrast, five large nonsouthern states and the District of Columbia enjoyed a net in-migration of almost half a million blacks. The bulk of the movement out of southern agriculture involved farm laborers rather than operators, the wartime prosperity of agriculture both arresting a decline in operators which had set in after the census of 1920 and making possible "a noteworthy, income-equalizing shift of black operators from tenants and part owners to full owners of farms." It was high time. In 1939 two of every three farm families in the United States whose annual incomes were less than $1,000 were located in the South, and a high proportion of these were black.[28]

Not only blacks but farmers generally benefited from the circumstances of war. Total net income of farm operators from farming rose from $4,482,000 in 1940 to $12,312,000 in 1945, with incomes per farm operator increasing more rapidly than did nonfarm business and professional incomes. The farmer's share of a typical market basket of farm food products jumped from 40 percent to 53 percent, the number of mortgaged farms declined by 29 percent, and total farm indebtedness outstanding fell from $6.6 billion to $4.9 billion. These favorable results would have been difficult to envisage from the vantage point of the depression period, for the outbreak of war in Europe found the country in possession of approximately a two-year supply of major commodities such as wheat, corn, and cotton. With foreign demand reduced by the war, normally large surpluses mounted with each harvest. By the fall of 1942, however, Pacific sources of sugar, oil, fruit, and other foodstuffs had been cut off, and meat, fats, oils, dairy products, and canned foods were in short supply. Thereafter, the needs of the Allies and of American armed forces abroad for manufactured foods would add their impact on agricultural production and food processing industries to that of domestic shortages.[29]

Agriculture responded not so much by increasing the amount of land under crops—crop acreage harvested in 1945 was only 4 percent more than in 1940—as by raising output per acre. It did so not by increasing total inputs of labor hours (which declined slightly during the period) but by enhancing the role of capital, especially of fertilizer and liming materials, mechanical power (including electricity), and machinery. Between 1940 and 1945 the number of tractors on farms rose steadily from 1,567,000 to 2,354,000, the number of motor trucks increased by 42 percent, grain combines by 97 percent, and corn pickers by 53 percent; the amount of commercial fertilizer increased by 62 percent, and lime by 60 percent. An index of productivity in the farm segment of the economy, standing at 115.7 in 1940 (1929 = 100), rose during the war to 127.2 in 1945. The value of farm assets, in constant prices, also rose. Whereas farm real estate registered only a modest 2 percent increase, implements and machinery increased by 65 percent. Horses and mules, not surprisingly, decreased in value by 18 percent, the acquisition of machinery resulting in the disposition of work animals at rates that were without precedent.[30]

Most of the gain in farm income came between 1939 and 1943, when income more than doubled as a result of both rapidly expanding production and higher prices. Only slight further gains were made in 1944 and 1945, with bigger government subsidies rather than price increases their main source. Farmers had suffered from low prices and incomes for so long—at the outbreak of war farm prices averaged only 79 percent of parity (1910–1914 = 100)—that the Farm Bureau and other large organizations representing their interests bitterly opposed the administration's efforts to achieve price stabilization by paying subsidies to farmers and food processors to compensate for the imposition of price controls. They were apprehensive that subsidies would accustom consumers to low prices and deepen the expected postwar depression. As enacted in January 1942, price control legislation gave the secretary of agriculture veto power over ceiling prices on nonprocessed farm commodities and set minimum ceilings at 110 percent of parity—110 percent rather than 100 percent to enable prices, which fluctuated daily, to average 100 percent. In October 1942, at the president's request, Congress lowered the ceilings to 100 percent but also, in enacting the so-called Steagall Amendment, passed legislation which may well have been the most important single farm price action taken during the war period. To avoid the effects of a sudden fall in farm prices after the war, such as had occurred after World War I, the amendment provided that price supports would continue in effect two years after the cessation of hostilities. The wartime supports, as it turned out, proved to be of little importance. The demand for all farm products was so great that prices dropped to support levels in only a few exceptional cases and for very short periods.[31]

Before 1943 prices of farm products rose much higher than those of other commodities. As Table 39 shows, effective price control did not begin until 1942. Thereafter, except for farm prices, which did not cease rising for another

Table 39.   Price behavior during World War II (1947–1949 average = 100).

Year	Wholesale price index		Consumer price index
	All commodities other than farm products and foods	Farm products	
1940	59.4	37.8	59.9
1941	63.7	46.0	62.9
1942	68.3	59.2	69.7
1943	69.3	68.5	74.0
1944	70.4	68.9	75.2
1945	71.3	71.6	76.9

Source: Harold G. Vatter, *The U.S. Economy in World War II* (New York: Columbia University Press, 1985), p. 91. Copyright © 1985 Columbia University Press. Used by permission.

year, the wholesale price index shows a remarkable stability. It is true that indirect but unmeasured price increases such as quality deterioration, elimination of sales, black market transactions, tie-in sales, rationing, and shortages were not fully reflected in the published consumer price index, but a recent analysis of those increases finds the distortions to have been relatively small.[32]

Price control and rationing machinery was not set up till after the issuance of a general maximum-price regulation by the Office of Price Administration (OPA) in April 1942. Price ceilings under "General Max" were set at March 1942 levels. The "Little Steel" formula for settling requests for wage increases was developed even later, in July 1942, with the announcement by the National War Labor Board that requests for wage increases which came to it for settlement would not be granted if wage rates had already been increased 15 percent over 1940 levels. Considering the lateness with which control machinery was installed and the enormous inflationary pressures generated by the scarcities of wartime—in addition, in the two years before the adoption of General Max the money stock had surged upward from $52.8 billion to $67.4 billion, a 28 percent rise—success in holding down prices must be considered a notable achievement. Even Milton Friedman and Anna J. Schwartz, who suggest that the jump in the price index after the elimination of price control in 1946 "reflected largely the unveiling of price increases that had occurred earlier," acknowledge that "prices rose more slowly during the war than before or after." They did indeed. Over the nine-year period between August 1939 and August 1948 they rose 6.4 percent per year, leaping up to 12.5 percent per year between June 1946, when controls were lifted, and August 1948. But during the period of effective control, between May 1943 and June 1946, prices increased only 2.1 percent per year.[33]

Price control, wage control, and rationing of scarce goods were part and parcel of a far more extensive intervention by government in the economy than had ever before occurred in American history. Shortages of raw materials, machine tools, components, ships, freight cars, and other items also necessitated the imposition of controls. In consequence, the freedom of manufacturers to operate their facilities and to use raw materials and fabricated items was severely restricted by the orders of the War Production Board. The same board sharply limited the freedom to buy by issuing priority regulations. The right to choose an occupation or change jobs was curtailed by both the Selective Service System and the War Manpower Commission. Freedom of civilians to travel had to yield to the priority needs of military personnel. Shipping shortages appeared early—within a month after Pearl Harbor demand exceeded supply by better than two to one—and this made it necessary for the War Shipping Administration (WSA) to allocate the available tonnage by a system of priority ratings for cargoes. The WSA had to determine the cargoes to be moved in both the import and the export trades, to coordinate the two, to decide on the ports to be used, and to route the traffic.[34]

Labor too had to be allocated, but only after shortages in unskilled and industrial workers developed in the fall of 1943, especially on the Pacific Coast and in the northeastern states. Congress, however, rejected a proposal made by President Roosevelt in January 1944 to enact national service legislation, the purpose of which was to make "available for war production or for any other essential services every able-bodied adult in the Nation." Rather, labor shortages were met mainly by devices such as occupational deferments from military service, approval of higher wage rates by the War Labor Board to stimulate recruitment, furloughs of trained workers by the army, and shifting of war contracts from points of acute labor shortage to other areas. In addition, new housing and child care facilities were provided in cities in which war production was concentrated, and steps taken to prevent the pirating and hoarding of labor, high absenteeism and turnover, wasteful migration, and discrimination against women and minorities. One minority, however, 120,000 Japanese citizens and resident aliens who lived on the West Coast, fell victim to war hysteria and racial prejudice. Ten weeks after the Japanese attack on Pearl Harbor, President Roosevelt signed an executive order which led to their uprooting and internment in barbed-wire enclosed "relocation camps" in the interior. With masterful logic, the army general responsible for the defense of the West Coast, John L. DeWitt, reasoned that "the very fact that no sabotage has taken place to date is a disturbing and confirming indication that such action will be taken."[35]

Within days of the Japanese surrender in August 1945 President Truman issued an executive order instructing federal agencies "to move as rapidly as possible without endangering the stability of the economy toward the removal of price, wage, production, and other controls and toward the restoration of collective bargaining and the free market."[36] In most agencies plans to do so had been held in readiness since the fall of 1944, and the victory over Japan was celebrated with a very substantial restoration of economic freedom. The very day after the surrender, the War Manpower Commission dropped all controls over manpower, and the OPA removed ration restrictions on gasoline, fuel oil, processed foods, and heating stoves. Other ration orders were lifted during the next few months, and by the end of 1945 only sugar remained. By the end of August the War Production Board had abolished most priority controls, eased industrial construction restrictions, and abandoned all control over metals except tin, lead, and antimony. By then, too, the Office of Defense Transportation had lifted several thousand controls on commercial motor-vehicle traffic and, a few days later, had given up a large portion of the controls over exports. Coastal and intercoastal shipping was resumed, and within approximately three months of VJ-Day the OPA had removed several hundred items from price control.[37]

In what was potentially the most significant peacetime change, government purchases of goods and services declined from $83 billion in 1945 to $30 billion the next year. But while industrial production also fell rapidly, the contraction was brief and relatively mild and the heavy unemployment that was widely feared did not develop. The trough, reached in October 1945, was followed by a vigorous expansion as rapid conversion from wartime to peacetime production offset the decline in government expenditures. Consumer demand for durables fueled the expansion. The unavailability during most of the war period of automobiles, trucks, refrigerators, washing machines, and other electrical appliances, together with an acute shortage of housing, had induced individuals and households to save. So too had the desire to aid the war effort by purchasing bonds, as well as a widespread fear that depression would come in the aftermath of the war. Unlike the case of the First World War, however, it did not. Indeed, unemployment in 1945 never reached 2.5 million, and it remained below that level until after the end of the expansion in November 1945.[38]

The surprising thing about the postwar expansion is that it occurred in the face of a restrictive fiscal policy. Government expenditures continued to decline, and by the end of 1948 they were only a third of what they had been in 1945. Revenues, on the other hand, fell by less than 10 percent, so that the 1946 deficit of $20.7 billion was converted by 1948 into a surplus of $8.4 billion. Throughout these years Republicans in Congress attacked the Democrats as the party of high spending and high taxes and repeatedly sought to reduce both. To President Harry Truman, however, the real enemy was inflation, and the proper goal of fiscal policy a balanced budget ("There is nothing sacred about the pay-as-you-go idea so far as I am concerned except that it represents the soundest principle of financing that I know," he says in his memoirs).[39] Truman therefore opposed and repeatedly vetoed bills calling for tax reduction, only to have a third veto overridden in April 1948. In view of the fact that prices rose at an annual rate of 16.4 percent between June 1946 and their peak in August 1948, fiscal policy was insufficiently restrictive, if anything.

Monetary conditions, on the other hand, were expansive and joined hands with pent-up consumer demand to raise employment and economic activity to high levels during these years. The money stock itself increased at a rather modest rate of approximately 4 percent per year from January 1946 to August 1948, so that the rise in prices and income primarily reflected growth in velocity. Nevertheless, the importance of the increased stock of money itself must not be discounted, nor that of a rise in the gold stock, which, by increasing bank reserves ("high-power money"), helped make it possible. Expenditures of former belligerents (in excess of those financed by American loans and by the Marshall Plan), as well as the demands of neutral countries desiring goods not available during the war, led to the inflow of gold. In addition, the willingness of the public to hold more of its money as deposits and less as currency also helped expand the money stock. Finally, the Federal Reserve System continued its wartime practice of supporting the price of government securities, thereby relinquishing effective control over the quantity of high-power money (its purchases automatically increased member bank reserves).[40]

Thus a set of more or less accidental monetary conditions, rather than monetary policy, characterized the early postwar years. But it was not accidental that clear-cut fiscal and monetary policies were lacking. The Keynesian emphasis on countercyclical strategies had not yet won over the American people or their political leaders. This is reflected in the limitations which characterize the Employment Act of 1946. As the Second World War was drawing to an end, Congress had been flooded with legislative proposals on how to deal with problems of the postwar period. Most of these concerned short-range issues such as contract termination and disposal of war surplus property. Others, however, reflected the bitter experience of the Great Depression and an awareness that government expenditures during the war had finally brought it to an end. Accordingly, some individuals, especially economists whose aid had been sought in drafting and promoting the employment bill, regarded it as a mandate for compensatory deficit spending. Opponents of the measure accused its sponsors of preparing the demise of private enterprise—probably on the ground that government promotion of "full employment" would imply inflation if not accompanied by wage and price controls. The overwhelming majority of congressmen, however, were in agreement that keeping unemployment low was an important national objective and that the federal government had responsibilities to discharge if that goal was to be achieved.[41]

The upshot was compromise on a statement of policy which for the time being proved more symbolic than substantive. The undefinable objective of "full" employment was dropped in favor of "maximum employment, production, and purchasing power," and the government was called upon to use "all its plans, functions, and resources" to achieve them. The act also created a Council of Economic Advisers in the executive office of the president. Its function, in the language of one of its chairmen, was to "put at the President's disposal the best facts, appraisals, and forecasts that economic science, statistics, and surveys can produce." This information would presumably enable the president to discharge his responsibility under the act to specify the levels of activity prevailing in the U.S. economy, the levels expected, and the levels needed to carry out the purposes of the law.[42]

President Truman paid little heed to the council, at least up to the time of the Korean War. He was not at home with either abstract ideas or intellectuals (he is reputed, probably apocryphally, to have remarked that whenever he asked the council chairman for advice, what he customarily received were replies that began "On the one hand, this, but on the other hand that." To which Truman is said to have responded plaintively, "Can anybody get me a one-handed economist?"). But neither the first chairman of the council, Edwin Nourse, nor his vice-chairman and successor, Leon Keyserling, was greatly interested in fiscal policy. Indeed, Keyserling warned congressional committees against preoccupation with overall conditions, like general inflation, or with overall measures of either fiscal or monetary policy. In what may prove to have been prescient advice, however, he acted as a leading advocate of a bill in 1949 which would have empowered the government to promote investment in specific industries where it was clear that private investment was insufficient to generate balanced growth. American governments may yet decide to encourage the development of specific industries that are essential to continued economic growth but which also have to compete in international markets with industries fostered and subsidized by foreign governments.[43]

Under Truman fiscal policy was passive. Such was the president's preoccupation with the danger of inflation that it was not till the seventh month of a recession which began in 1949 that he finally abandoned his effort to induce Congress to raise taxes in order to reduce the deficit. An active policy would have sought increased expenditures and lowered taxes to put more purchasing power in the hands of the public and encourage private investment. Fortunately, the passive policy of relying on the "built-in" response of tax revenues, which decline during recession, and expenditures such as unemployment compensation, which go up, worked out well. A budget surplus which had been running at an annual rate of $3.8 billion in the fourth quarter of 1948 turned into a deficit of $3.9 billion in the second quarter of 1949. Automatic declines in revenues and increases in expenditures account for almost all of this transformation. In a word, the fiscal response to the recession was "almost entirely automatic and unsought."[44]

The election of Dwight D. Eisenhower as president in 1952 brought to Washington the first Republican administration in twenty years and raised the question whether it would accept the responsibility under the Employment Act to use the powers of government, including fiscal policy, to stabilize the economy and maintain high employment. The question was all the more important because, just the year before, the Treasury and the Federal Reserve System had reached an accord which, by releasing the latter from its obligation to support the prices of government bonds, freed it to play the role of partner in fiscal policy. So far as the president's words were concerned, there was no doubt he agreed that the role of partner was the proper one for government to assume. And to a limited degree government did assume that role. But the larger fact is that the new administration, like the one it had replaced, centered its policy on the public's fear of inflation and sought to balance the budget and avoid deficits.

These objectives called for opposition to tax cuts, even those strongly supported by congressional spokesmen for the interests of the Chamber of Commerce and the National Association of Manufacturers. Almost at the beginning of his administration Eisenhower had to confront pressures to allow an excess profits tax of 77 percent, imposed at the outbreak of the Korean War in 1950, to expire on its scheduled date of June 29, 1953. The president wanted the expiration date delayed for the sake of the federal revenues, and he had his way. Nevertheless, when the economy entered recession in the fall of 1953 with the decline of military expenditures, he made it clear that if conditions became worse he would not be deterred by fear of deficits. In October 1953 he showed the flexibility of his attitude on balancing the budget:

> When it becomes clear that the Government has to step in, as far as I am concerned, the full power of Government, of Government credit, and of everything the Government has, will move in to see that there is no wide-spread unemployment and we never again have a repetition of conditions that so many of you here remember when we had unemployment.[45]

The decline never reached the point where the administration thought that strong action was needed, so that it is not possible to say how far it would have gone to use the resources of government to combat it. According to the figures then available, unemployment was only 3 percent in December 1953; the Federal Reserve Board, moreover, was pursuing an expansive monetary policy. At the end of March 1954, however, Congress reduced excise taxes by about $1 billion a year, a move later characterized by Eisenhower's council chairman, Arthur R. Burns, as a cut made "for countercyclical reasons."[46]

Recession came again in 1957–58, and still again in 1960–61, and in the first of these the country came closer than ever before to cutting taxes in order to encourage a general economic expansion. But it did not do so. Inflation continued to be viewed by the administration as the most important long-term problem, with recession representing merely a brief interlude. Moreover, the launching of the Soviet Sputnik in the fall of 1957 had called attention to American weakness in space exploration, missile capability, education, and economic growth, and raised the prospect of strongly rising expenditures— and even of tax increases to support them. If taxes were reduced instead, more than the increasing revenues required by these growing expenditures would be threatened. So too would be the budget surplus needed to combat inflation after the economy returned to its "normal" condition. As it turned out, a slowing of the rate of economic decline in the spring of 1958 weakened the case for a tax cut to combat recession, and, once again, none was made.[47]

Nor was one made in Eisenhower's last two years. This does not mean that the first Republican administration since Hoover was unsympathetic to business and its needs. Eisenhower realized full well that a prosperous, growing economy required a high rate of private investment, and in 1954 he had put the weight of his administration behind a tax reform program which permitted businesses to charge off their investment expenditures more rapidly, giving them more opportunity to balance losses of particular years against the gains of earlier or later years, and reduced the double taxation of dividends. These reforms sought to encourage private investment by raising its prospects of profitability. Four years later the rate of taxation of corporate income remained an elevated 52 percent, but profits had been high in 1955, 1956, and 1957, and many businessmen themselves believed that they were passing on the corporate tax in higher prices. While many continued to grumble over the failure to take further steps to reduce the double taxation of dividends or to liberalize depreciation allowances, businessmen were not a constituency opposed to Eisenhower's fiscal policy.[48]

In the final two years of the administration, 1959 and 1960, the centerpiece of that policy continued to be the fight against inflation, with a large budget surplus its principal weapon. Eisenhower believed that a large surplus would not only help erode the inflationary psychology of the time but also promote economic growth. It needed promoting. In the late fifties the country awoke with a start from its dream that the American rate of increase of total output was not only satisfactory, but the marvel of the world. The fact is that its average annual growth rate between 1948 and 1960 was only 2.9 percent— in comparison with Japan's 8.7 percent, Germany's 7.2 percent, Italy's 5.8 percent, France's 4.2 percent, Sweden's 3.7 percent, Canada's 3.6 percent, and Great Britain's 2.7 percent. As growth rather than mere stability rose in the scale of national objectives, Eisenhower believed his case for running a large budget surplus stronger than ever. Such a surplus would help contain inflation and would also permit retirement of part of the national debt—almost $300 billion in January 1960—and thus reduce the interest burden on the debt. Eisenhower repeatedly referred to the debt in terms of a burden which would be passed on to taxpayers' children and grandchildren, thus overlooking the fact that Americans owned the debt as well as owed it.[49]

A large surplus and the containment of inflation, finally, would strengthen international confidence in the dollar, and with it, America's prestige in the world. Ever since the end of the Second World War, the United States had been running almost continuously a deficit in its balance of payments, discharging its obligation either by exporting gold or by placing dollar assets in the hands of foreigners in the form of U.S. government securities or deposits in U.S. banks. In the late 1950s both American and foreign concern was mounting over the possibility that the loss of gold and increase in liabilities were weakening the U.S. reserve position. "There was talk about loss of confidence in the dollar. In the opinion of many bankers and other financial experts it was necessary that the U.S. should stop its inflation and its budget deficits."[50] A balanced budget or surplus would help restrain inflation, increase the competitiveness of American exports, and improve the balance of payments. Clearly, a stabilization policy of combatting recession and unemployment—nearly 8 percent in 1957–58 and again in 1960–61—by incurring deficits would have compromised these other objectives. Fiscal policy therefore remained essentially passive.

With the election of John F. Kennedy in 1960, the scenario dramatically changed. Called the "first modern economist in the American Presidency,"[51]

Kennedy late in 1960 urged a "return to the spirit as well as the letter of the Employment Act" in order "to deal not only with the state of the economy but with our goals for economic progress."[52] In the main, the economists who influenced his thinking were younger men weaned on the deficit spending and other compensatory doctrines of John Maynard Keynes, men who had come to believe that in a recession the government should spend more and tax less, and that in a boom the reverse of this compensatory policy was the appropriate one. In their eyes, the essential economic problem was full employment and economic growth rather than the curtailment of inflation. As for budget balancing—that was an irrelevancy. In general, they believed the free market worked well and should not be tampered with, yet they acknowledged that government intervention to influence the decisions of businesses and labor unions might be justified if high employment could not be achieved without inflation. As Walter Heller, Kennedy's chairman of the Council of Economic Advisers, later said: "It is hard to study the modern economics of relative prices, resource allocation, and distribution without developing a healthy respect for the market mechanisms . . . But I do not carry respect to the point of reverence."[53] Enormously self-confident, the Kennedy economists believed that steady advances in fact gathering, together with their use of a wider statistical net, improved surveys of consumer and investment intentions, and more refined, computer-assisted methods, would enable them to make reliable forecasts of economic fluctuations and to adopt the fiscal and monetary policy mix appropriate to goals of either stabilization or growth.[54]

It was the latter, rather than the objective of averaging out cyclical periods of prosperity and recession, on which the council fixed its focus. The rate of unemployment when Kennedy came into office was 6.7 percent, but the country, in the eyes of his advisers, was suffering from something even more fundamental. The basic problem was years of slack. The economy was running substantially below its full-employment potential—indeed, since early 1957 what came to be called the "performance gap" between actual and potential GNP had increased from about $10 billion to about $50 billion. The "old orthodoxy" had emphasized the importance of balancing the government's annual budget, but according to the "new economics" this had unbalanced the economy.[55] An expansionist fiscal policy could take the form of increased expenditures or lowered taxes. The latter was more palatable politically, and Kennedy chose that option. In August 1962 he said he would ask the Congress the following January to approve reductions of approximately 20 percent in both individual and corporate taxes. Tax reduction thus became the centerpiece of administration policy, but both Kennedy and his advisers saw the need for a period of gradual reeducation before Congress and the country, "accustomed to nearly sixteen years of White House homilies on the wickedness of government deficits, would approve of an administration deliberately and severely unbalancing the budget." The need was real: by early 1963, with the deficit rising, expenditures rising, and the economy rising, accusations of fiscal irresponsibility reached their peak.[56]

Kennedy did not live to see his major fiscal innovation become law. However, his successor, Lyndon Johnson, fully accepted the commitment to tax reduction and signed the measure into law in early 1964. Later, advocates of the policy hailed an impact on the economy that was "almost exactly in accord with the economic analysis and projections on which it was founded."[57] Evidence supporting the claim appeared impressive. By the first quarter of 1966 over 7 million new jobs had been created, and the unemployment rate had fallen from nearly 7 percent to under 4 percent. Real per capita income, after taxes, was one-fifth higher than it had been in the first quarter of 1961, and the realized growth rate of the economy had doubled, rising from 2.25 percent for the period 1953–1960 to 4.5 percent between 1960 and 1966. Corporate profits after taxes had also doubled, while the total real compensation of all employees was about 30 percent higher. In contrast to the preceding five-year period, when the weekly take-home pay of the average manufacturing worker had fallen 1 percent, pay rose 18 percent. Yet the rise in consumer prices from 1960 to 1965 amounted to only 1.3 percent a year (wholesale prices rose 2 percent)—a record of wage-price moderation assisted by the establishment of guideposts—an essentially educational process of "informing labor, management, and the public of the explicit ways in which wage and price decisions should be geared to productivity advances if they are to be non-inflationary." Surely the record was a remarkable one, and the prestige of the economic advisers to the president rode high.[58]

The bold activism of the Kennedy-Johnson tax cut—once again, made not to counter recession but to lift up a listless economy to a higher growth path—is the first indubitably clear instance in American history of the use of Keynesian fiscal medicine to cure an ailing patient. It worked. But it worked in a context of supportive monetary policy, and perhaps of psychological and unknown other elements conducive to success. Needless to say, if it were certain that in all circumstances some specific fiscal-monetary policy mix would alone generate some specific quantum of growth or degree of stabilization, the problem of economic management would be simple. Unhappily, the world is not so simple. The claim that the economy expanded because of the tax cut is plausible, but it is not unquestionable.[59]

Nevertheless, the expansion was real enough and, in the words of the Economic Report of the President in January 1969, it created a "prosperity without parallel in our history."[60] Even though an upsurge in defense spending for the war in Vietnam after mid-1965 generated strong inflationary pressures, the upward drift in prices from 1959 to 1969 was a moderate 2.32 percent per year in the consumer price index (CPI). From 1962 to 1969 total civilian employment rose 2.24 percent, and labor hours of all persons in the nonfarm business sector 2.27 percent a year. Expenditures on research and development as a proportion of GNP were historically high.[61]

Leading the growth in aggregate demand were two expenditure streams of approximately equal size (other than federal transfers), namely, those made by state and local governments and those made by businesses on nonresidential fixed investment. Between 1962 and 1969 the latter increased by nearly 95 percent, the former by 105 percent. Behind the increased spending by state and local governments were federal grants to those governments, which rose by about 155 percent in the interim. And behind the rise in business expenditures were several "supply-side" inducements, namely, an investment tax credit in 1962, a liberalization of tax depreciation guidelines, low long-term interest rates, a tax cut for corporations, and a reduction of the top tax rates from 91 percent to 70 percent. The role of government was thus a very important one. Indeed, some economists maintain that its role was fundamental in the prosperity of the 1960s, with the rise in business fixed investment being primarily induced by governmental outlays at the federal as well as state and local levels.[62]

Belief in fiscal activism reached its zenith in early 1968. "We now take for granted," proclaimed a buoyant chairman of President Johnson's Council of Economic Advisers, "that the government must step in to provide the essential stability at high levels of employment and growth that the market mechanism, left alone, cannot deliver."[63] Soon, however, inflation began to accelerate far beyond the expectations of the activists. It did so between 1967 and 1969 and did not slow down even in the recession of 1969–70. Here was a new phenomenon—stagflation—for a drop in inflation had been recorded in all earlier postwar recessions. Economists had confidently believed it possible to trade off a given amount of inflation for a given amount of unemployment, that the relationship between the two (as shown by the "Phillips curve") was stable, and that policymakers could select any combination of the two that seemed desirable. Now it appeared that there existed a "natural rate" of unemployment, and that if policy managed to push the rate below this point, inflation would continue to accelerate. In a word, the stage was set for the triumph of monetarism over fiscal activism.[64]

It appeared to be well set, for the relationship between the money supply and national income had been quite close ever since 1959 (changes in the one being paralleled by changes in the other of roughly the same magnitude). Then with the acceleration of monetary growth in 1971, output expanded at a frenetic pace for more than a year. Throughout 1972 the country enjoyed the largest real growth (5.7 percent) since 1966 and the lowest rise in consumer prices (3.3 percent) since 1967. By the end of the year unemployment was down to 5.1 percent. The most remarkable aspect of the boom was the investment by consumers in durable goods and residential construction, expenditures which may have been partly due to optimism engendered by the wage and price control program set in place by Richard Nixon's administration in 1971–72. The importance of expenditures by state and local governments began to decline in comparison to consumer and business investment. After two decades of roughly 6 percent growth in real terms, spending by those levels of government increased at only 4 percent during 1967–1973 and at 2.3 percent between early 1973 and 1978. After early 1973, however, the economy faltered, a victim of "supply shocks," especially those set in motion by the Organization of Petroleum Exporting Countries (OPEC), and with these events the influence of monetarism began to fade. The impact of higher energy and food prices on inflation and output growth seemed more relevant than alterations in the aggregate money supply. And besides, whereas advocates of monetarism had insisted on the need for a constant rate of monetary growth, it now appeared that the demand for money was a stable and predictable function of income and interest rates.[65] But monetarism was far from dead. As we shall see, it was to be revived in the early eighties by the Federal Reserve Board under the chairmanship of Paul Volcker.

The remaining years of the seventies were marked by rising inflation and unemployment and by booming growth followed by recession. At the beginning of 1973 the economy was humming near full capacity, but after the dropping of controls, farm prices exploded, followed by a general commodities boom, soaring inflation, tightened credit conditions, a jump in interest rates to record levels, and, at the end of the year, a fourfold increase in oil prices by OPEC; from an annual rate (CPI) of 3.3 percent in 1972, inflation surged to 11 percent in 1974. The confidence of businessmen and consumers turned to fright, and 1974 became the worst year for the American economy since the end of the Second World War, with real GNP falling by 2 percent.[66]

By 1975 the country seemed well into a depression, but before the year was half over a new boom began that was to continue through Jimmy Carter's election to the presidency in 1976 and to last until 1980. But like the Nixon boom, Carter's soon began to accumulate the "familiar symptoms of America's economic disorder: record inflation, huge trade deficits, a deteriorating dollar, abrupt and rigorous monetary restraint, bounding oil prices and finally a severe recession."[67] The recession was destined to be the longest of the postwar period. Only in early 1983, halfway into the first administration of Ronald Reagan, did the economy show signs of revival. We shall inquire into the nature of the Reagan administration's connection with this recession and, more generally, into the impact of its policies on inflation and other aspects of the economy. But first let us identify some of the fundamental technological and demographic factors which will continue to exert powerful influences on the American economy long after the Reagan administration has passed into history.

17

From Recent Times to the Present and Future

Demography and technology—people and the knowledge, techniques, and mechanisms they bring to bear on their efforts to achieve their goals—are closely related. The nature of the relationship, however, is not easily predictable. Sometimes technology is associated with a rise in population, sometimes with a decline. Let us look first at the former. Technological innovation is a prime source of economic growth, and the higher living standards which growth brings about can lead to an increasing population as young people with confidence in the future marry and have families. Something like that seems to have occurred in the wake of the Second World War, when a "baby boom" took place between 1946 and 1960 (roughly), catching demographers by surprise. They were surprised because the long-term trend, both in the United States and in other developed countries, had been one of declining fertility.[1] Not only had the average American birthrate been declining since the 1870s, but the rate had been an accelerating one, falling from 22.3 per thousand between 1935 and 1955 to 19.5 per thousand in the twenty-three years from 1955 to 1978.[2] The rate has continued to go down. In fact, the years between 1965 and 1976 have been dubbed a period of "baby bust," and in 1976 the fertility rate fell to 1.7 per woman, the lowest in American history at that time. Ten years later the rate fell still more.[3]

The declining trend is easily explicable. Given rising standards of living in the developed countries, millions of couples have opted for smaller families, simultaneously reducing the financial and other burdens on themselves and adding to the resources available to their children. Technology as well as economics has enabled them to do so. Increased medical knowledge and improved health care have made it possible for most newborns to survive, so that parents who want two children, say, need not have a larger number in order to achieve the desired family size. Authorization of the oral birth control pill in 1960, introduction of the intrauterine device (IUD), and widespread liberalization of abortion laws in the late sixties have all played a part. So too has the drastic change in the way young women look upon themselves: many have veered away from traditional paths of marriage and family in favor of career-oriented goals.[4]

In the poorer countries of Asia, Africa, and Latin America the story has been a different one. The poor have always tended to have large families, and it is on these continents that most of the population increases of modern times have taken place. Before then the world had little medical knowledge or expertise in production techniques, and abundant family births did not make for a large population. According to the best estimates, world population had reached only about 800 million by the mid-eighteenth century. That was on the eve of the Industrial Revolution, before the increasing mastery of nature associated with that term had developed. A gradual reduction in mortality then brought far more rapid population growth. By the mid-twentieth century world population had tripled, and in merely another thirty years it had grown by another 80 percent, rising from 2.5 billion to 4.5 billion. It had taken humankind more than a million years to reach a population of 1 billion. The second billion required only 120 years; the third, 32 years; and the fourth, 15 years. Exports from the developed world of medical and public health technology and improved techniques of food production lowered mortality rates and permitted the survival of far higher proportions of the large families characteristically concentrated in those areas.[5] While Ethiopia and other sub-Saharan African nations have experienced large population losses in recent years, principally because of drought, the longer-run difference between the developing and the developed countries lies in fertility rates rather than in mortality rates. This is not the only demographic distinction: the age composition of their populations also differs. The age structure of the developing countries rests more heavily on the young, whereas the opposite is true of their "modernized" counterparts. American society is beginning to age. In 1983 the median age of the population reached 30.9, the oldest ever, and the expectation is that it will reach 36 by the year 2000. The oldest of the baby boomers, one of every three Americans and the largest generation in our history, are now in their forties. The aging process is partly a reflection of the declining birthrate. Women are waiting longer to have children and are having fewer of them. Employment opportunities help account for these choices. In 1960 only 19 percent of women with children under six were in the work-force; by 1985, half of them were. Many working women of childbearing age are deciding against having any children at all.

The most surprising statistic points to significant social problems in the future: for the first time Americans over age sixty-five outnumber teenagers. The percentage of the population over sixty-five is expected to climb moderately from 11.3 percent to 13.1 percent between 1980 and 2000, but to exceed 21 percent by the year 2030. If so, there will be heavy pressure to spend more money on both hospital and long-term care for a generation caught in the coils of degenerative illness. Acute illness is one thing, chronic illness another. Society is organized and financed to treat medical emergencies, but the sad truth is that chronic illness accounts for 80 percent of all deaths and 90 percent of all disabilities among the elderly. A person suffering a heart attack can be sped to the nearest hospital. One with Alzheimer's disease is more likely to go broke. The aging of the population, however, has increased the political clout of "grey power," and there were growing signs in the later eighties of congressional concern for the plight of the elderly, not the least of these signs being the enactment of the Medicare Catastrophic Coverage Act in 1988. But concern was also mounting for the long-term solvency of the social security system.[6]

In general, the population today is both healthier and longer-lived than it was in 1950. Death rates in 1980 were lower at all ages, for all races, and for both sexes, with the decline greater for females than for males and greater for nonwhites than for whites. The decrease in nonwhite death rates is the major factor in the rise in the proportion of nonwhites in the population. Up to the mid-1950s, decline in mortality was due mainly to the diffusion of new antibiotic "wonder drugs." After leveling off, mortality rates once again began to fall in the late 1960s, particularly for older men and women, reversing a historical tendency for improvement to be most marked in younger age groups. Control of cardiovascular and cerebrovascular diseases, especially, and to some extent also infectious diseases, lay behind the drop in mortality at older ages, the decline in the former probably being due in part to new medical care developments permitting the identification as well as treatment of high-risk cases. Tragically, violent death—accidents, homicide, suicide—is the chief killer of young adults, especially males, and for this group mortality has failed to decline. The 1980s saw the emergence of a dread new killer of the young, acquired immune deficiency syndrome (AIDS). While concentrated in the male homosexual population and in intravenous drug users, falling heaviest on blacks and Puerto Ricans, the killer disease also began to spread in the late eighties to the heterosexual population. Public awareness of the potentially decimating consequences of this modern plague increased rapidly in those years.[7]

While total American population had surged to 234 million by 1983, were it not for immigration demographers were predicting that the population would crest at about 243 million in the year 2000 and then start declining.[8] Immigrants have made significant contributions to population growth ever since the end of the Second World War. Their total numbers, however, may never be known because much of the immigration has been illegal. The inflow reached its highest levels in the 1960s. In the 1970s legal and illegal immigration together accounted for perhaps one-third of the nation's estimated increase of 15 million people. The newcomers shifted the occupational composition of the population to higher levels of skill. Only 1 percent of the immigrants of 1901–1910 had been professionals. In the 1960s that percentage was close to 25 percent. Substantially, the new departure was encouraged by the Immigration Act of 1965, which substituted considerations of humanity and labor skills for the national-origins quotas of past legislation.[9]

The immigrant stream of recent years has also differed in other ways from those of the past. Perhaps its closest resemblance is to what the late nineteenth and early twentieth centuries knew as the New Immigration, an influx from southern and eastern Europe rather than from traditional northern European sources, especially Britain. The postwar flow, scholars suggest, might therefore be dubbed the "new" New Immigration, for it too broke with historical precedent, emerging from Asia and Latin America, especially Mexico, and also from the Philippines, Korea, Cuba, India, Taiwan, and the Dominican Republic.[10]

Internally, the population has redistributed itself in significant ways over the American landscape. The story has historically been one of urban growth and rural depopulation as a consequence of technological change in industry and agriculture. Since the mid-twentieth century, however, the United States has been on the brink of still another memorable epoch in geographic settlement, namely, the repopulation of previously rural areas. The first clue to this development appeared in the form of suburbanization in the earlier years of the century. Recently, however, population has been flowing to rural areas which do not border on major cities, and it has also been shifting to the Sun Belt. The latter is evident in net migration rates from the fifties through the seventies. Throughout, the South and West have led in population growth, with the lead widening noticeably over time. Again throughout, in both the Northeast and North Central regions, in-migration has been low or negative.[11]

More recently, however, the population of New England has been rising, partly in response to rapid job growth in "high-technology" manufacturing and in related research and development services, and partly in response to a national defense buildup. By the 1970s, the South and West were virtually tied as leaders in rates of population growth and net in-migration. In the West, growth was particularly marked in the Rocky Mountain states. In mining, advantages in oil and gas extraction, especially in Wyoming and Colorado, and coal mining, particularly in Wyoming, reflected the nation's dependence on the region for part of its energy supply. In durables manufacturing, the advantages in technologically advanced machinery, transportation equipment, fabricated metals, and instruments reflected the area's rapid industrialization, especially in Utah and Colorado. The region was also increasingly self-sufficient in services and in transportation and finance. Finally, in the Rocky Mountain states and in every other region except the South, population growth in areas which do not border on major cities has been higher than in those which do.[12]

What explains the shifts to the Sun Belt and to nonmetropolitan areas? In part, the answer lies in the presence of special factors such as natural resource endowments or governmental decisions regarding the location of military, space, and educational activities. In the case of the South, for example, it appears that large military allocations and technological developments accompanying the Second World War provided the necessary external stimulus for the industrial and population growth long sought by the region's leaders. In the postwar decades an increasing number of businessmen turned southward in response to lower operating costs, especially lower wages, but also lower energy and land costs and lower state and local taxes, together with a growing regional market nurtured by increased federal expenditures. When the space industry boomed in the early 1960s, for example, Florida's population grew by nearly three thousand persons a week. In the region as a whole, industrial development after the war first slowed population losses and then, between 1970 and 1976, spurred a net gain from in-migration of 2.9 million people.[13]

But special circumstances do not explain longer-term developments. "Throughout the history of mankind residence decisions have been dominated by place of work."[14] In long eras of the American past these decisions were governed by farming opportunities opened up by the vast extent of available land. Then with the advent of mechanized production in the nineteenth century, settlement patterns shifted in favor of urban locations. The new technology made possible important economies of scale; unlike colonial shops, factories needed access to substantial markets for their products. Furthermore, the coal and iron ore required by industry were "much less ubiquitous than the agricultural and forest resources on which preindustrial technology was based." For this reason, producers located at or near the sources of these new industrial inputs or at transport points that made them accessible at low cost.

In consequence, new business and job opportunities were opened up in urban centers, places which soon became key junctions in the railroad network. So-called agglomeration economies accentuated the advantages of these centers as workers and consumers flocked to them. Rising per capita incomes then raised consumer demand for high-income-elasticity manufactured products, with the result that still more people were drawn to urban centers in search of job opportunities. The consequence was rural depopulation: in each of the two decades between 1940 and 1960, more than 3,100 American counties experienced absolute declines in their numbers of people.

Modern technology then proceeded to break the ties that bound the consumer's residence to his or her place of work. First the horse-drawn trolley and electric streetcar and then the automobile allowed many urban Americans to exercise their preference for rural or semirural living places, a preference made possible also by the shortened workday brought about by modern economic growth. In addition, the transmission of electricity supplied the power essential for the operation of households in nonurban residential communities. Nor can the open-air recreational facilities of rural areas—camping, picnicking and water sports—be ignored.

Business firms as well as consumers have been affected by the relative advantages of rural locations. They are no longer, as in the nineteenth century, tied to narrow resource requirements. Technological progress has diversified industrial materials, permitting a shift, for example, from ferrous to nonferrous metals and plastics, from coal to petroleum, natural gas, and other sources. Trucks have altered the rigid rail transport network. Above all, information essential to all business decisions is now transmitted by the telephone and the computer. Furthermore, former economies of agglomeration have turned into diseconomies of urban pollution, and congestion has increased. All in all, in this century the location of business firms is far less bound than it was in the past to a limited urban network. It is more responsive than ever before to consumer preferences, not least those of workers for more attractive locations in which to work.[15]

Rural repopulation, in sum, represents a personal or business response to ways of living and working made possible by technological advance. It does not bespeak an increased demand for agricultural labor. Indeed, the opposite is true. Between 1945 and 1981 the farm population fell from 17.5 percent of the total to merely 2.6 percent, with farm employment down from 10 million to about one-third of that. In 1947 more than one family in six lived on a farm, but by 1977 only one in twenty-six continued to do so. As late as 1929, payments for capital, labor, and natural resources by the agricultural, forestry, and fisheries sectors of the economy generated 10 percent of the national income, but by 1978 this percentage had fallen to 2.9 percent. Behind both of these developments in relation to agriculture lay major increases in productivity. The farm sector has shrunk by becoming more efficient. Crop output per hour quintupled between 1950 and 1979; output of livestock and livestock products rose sixfold. Meanwhile, hours of labor required on farms fell by more than two-thirds.[16]

Capital has displaced much of this labor. An index of farm inputs shows labor falling from 217 in 1950 to 65 in 1980. In part, mechanical power and machinery took its place, the index rising from 84 to 128. More important, the index for agricultural chemicals, including fertilizers, lime, and pesticides, jumped from 29 to 174 during the period. Unfortunately, there is no index for another important input, namely, intangible capital in the form of better management and knowledge of improved production techniques. Large public and private investments in education, in schools, colleges, and research organizations, including those of the Department of Agriculture, have generated and spread this knowledge, stimulating new patterns of input use. Growing managerial efficiency and knowledge, then, as well as technology, help explain one of the truly amazing facts of American history: in 1790, at the beginning of America's existence as an independent nation, the labor of perhaps 85 of every 100 persons was required to satisfy the agricultural needs of a population of 4 million, including those met from the proceeds of modest exports. In 1981, in contrast, fewer than 3 persons of every 100 were needed to feed and clothe a population swollen to over 230 million and to generate, besides, huge surpluses. Surely this is a miracle of agricultural science.[17]

Agriculture has become industrialized. Most farms are now firms, some factories. Around the time of the Second World War an agricultural revolution comparable in many ways to the earlier Industrial Revolution began to take place in the United States. One similarity between the two was the tendency for production to become concentrated in fewer, larger units. In 1980 the number of "farms" in the United States was only a third of the total in 1920, but their average size had grown from 147 to 453 acres. Small farms of less than 100 acres still continued to represent 43.5 percent of all farms in 1978, but they harvested only 5 percent of the country's total cropland. They were essentially noncommercial farms. Their annual sales amounted to less than $2,500. In contrast, farms ranging in size from 500 to more than 2,000 acres harvested 60 percent of the cropland. These larger units dominated American agriculture. Scarcely more than one farm in ten boasted annual sales of $100,000 or more, but these giants were responsible for 63 percent of the total sales.[18]

One difference between the agricultural and industrial revolutions is the comparatively small role played by the corporation up to now. As late as 1978, 88 percent of all farms were classified as individual or family proprietorships. Partnerships accounted for 10 percent, corporations for only 2 percent. Industrialists generally incorporate to raise the capital that will enable them to add to their plant and equipment, to expand output, and to achieve economies of scale. More common reasons in agriculture are the existence of tax advantages—corporate rates on taxable income above $25,000 being lower than individual rates, for example—and greater ease in passing securities than in transferring physical assets to heirs. Still, in 1974 corporate farms were responsible for a third of all sales of cattle and calves, nearly a third of the products of horticultural specialty farms—fruits, nuts, and berries—and 60 percent of nursery and greenhouse products. Indeed, they accounted for 18 percent of all sales of farm products that year. And between then and the end of the decade their number came close to doubling. Corporate farms are particularly important in California and Florida, in relation to both the total number of farms and the amount of farmland acreage in those states.[19]

Incorporated or not, in the mid-1970s cash-grain farms, comprising primarily those growing wheat, corn, and soybeans, were the largest single type of commercial farm (34 percent). Next in order came those producing livestock (29 percent); tobacco (5.6 percent); other field crops, principally Irish potatoes and peanuts (4.8 percent), fruit and nuts (3 percent); and poultry (2.5 percent). Vegetable farms round off the list of commercial producers. Average acreages per farm were particularly large in livestock (896) and cotton (580); in general farms, that is to say, large growers of products sold from seed crops, hay, and silage (494); in cash grain (485); and in other field crops (478). In contrast, dairy farms averaged 276 acres; those devoted to vegetables (240), fruit and nuts (149), and tobacco (129) were also smaller. Even these smaller farms, though, exhibited the tendency toward specialization that became marked after the Second World War. As for the large ones, in many counties farm sales of leading commodities had become so concentrated on a few big farms by 1978 that the United States Department of Agriculture was prevented by disclosure laws from publishing the relevant figures in the agricultural census.[20]

What brought about this result was not size alone, but size together with heavy investments of capital in machinery and equipment, fertilizer, chemicals, labor, and other inputs—in a word, mechanization. The two tend to be strongly correlated, of course, and it is this fact that gives the term *agricultural industrialization* its meaning. Heavily capitalized agriculture is to be found today in all major agricultural regions of the United States except the Great Plains. Particularly prominent areas are the Far West, especially the Pacific Southwest and trans-Cascade Pacific Northwest, with their important eastern extensions in the irrigated valleys of southeastern California, southwestern Arizona, and west-central Washington, the Midwest including the western Corn Belt, together with northern Illinois and southeastern Wisconsin; much of the lower Great Lakes littoral; and especially (because of the influence of large urban markets) southern New England and the Middle Atlantic, together with the Florida peninsula. Aside from Florida, the largest area of agricultural capitalization in the South is a belt extending through northern Alabama and Georgia across the entire length of North Carolina. While the investment reflects the needs of large-scale poultry, tobacco, and mixed-farming operations, as well as of cotton, the story of what happened to that traditional southern crop illustrates the broad impact of many of the overall developments that have changed the face of American agriculture since the last great war.[21]

In 1940 the eleven southern states had boasted 2.4 million farms, but by 1974 their number was down to 723,000. In the same interim, though, average farm size grew from 86 to 235 acres. It was on these larger farms—in Arkansas, the Mississippi Delta, and Texas—that cotton was now grown, their owners utilizing machinery, heavier fertilizer, and better seeds to increase production. Tractors had been gradually phasing out mules since the 1930s, especially in areas such as the Mississippi Delta. The hand picking of cotton held on longer, only 3 percent of the crop being harvested by machine in 1948. Twenty years later the percentage had soared to 94 percent, and the old Cotton Belt of the Carolinas and the Black Belt was gone, purged of its tenants. Technological change had at last completed what government—the New Deal's Agricultural Adjustment Administration—had begun, namely, the reduction of the farm population of the South. The Census Bureau confirmed the extinction of the sharecropper by dropping the category in 1959. By that year cotton amounted to more than 50 percent of the crops harvested in only eleven counties of four southern states. Planters throughout the richer flatlands had turned to dairying, beef cattle production, and alternative crops such as hay, grain sorghum, soybeans, and, in the Mississippi Delta, rice.[22]

Cotton moved west. By the 1950s Texas was the number one producer, with California vying with Mississippi for the second spot. Cotton had ridden a westward-moving belt ever since the early decades of the nineteenth century, but that belt would have stopped short had it not been for an important piece of legislation passed by Congress in 1902. The Newlands Act stipulated that 95 percent of the proceeds from the sale of public lands were to flow into a reclamation fund to finance the construction of giant dams and reservoirs to store water for the irrigation of dry lands. This law, and other acts providing for the use of the waters of western states for irrigation, yielded a total of $14 billion by the early 1980s. The low-cost water and power thus made available to the western states made possible not only the displacement of the old Cotton Kingdom by Texas, California, and Arizona but also the movement of the vegetable crop, fruit, canning, and nursery business from New York to California.[23]

Agriculture is big business in California. In 1978 that state alone—called by one scholar "the most powerful agricultural region on the planet"—accounted for nearly 10 percent of the value of the entire nation's agricultural output.[24] And cotton has dominated that output in recent years, exceeding $1.3 billion in value in 1979. Controlled application of irrigation water, its use in measured amounts at the proper time, lowered the incidence of water stress and increased yields. The experience of the cotton South contrasts sharply with that of California, the South's losses in yield from insufficient or excessive moisture being larger than those attributed to the boll weevil in all but ten years between 1909 and 1950. Controlled conditions in the West also reduced greatly the growth of weeds. Weeds, especially Johnson grass (which could stand shoulder high), sapped productivity in much of the South. Tractor-drawn cultivators controlled weeds in the California cotton fields relatively easily. In the South wet weather was far more likely to keep tractors out of the field. These regional differences in weed conditions considerably affected both preharvest and harvest mechanization.[25]

In consequence, cotton farmers in California adopted tractors for preharvest operations—breaking the land, harrowing, planting, and cultivation—earlier and in greater numbers than did southern farmers. By 1950 California farms were four times as likely as those in Mississippi to have a tractor. The need for workers to keep weeds under control by hoeing and chopping also complicated the decision to mechanize picking operations in the South, for that preharvest task of spring and early summer often required nearly as many workers as were needed for the picking season. The situation in California was the reverse of this: the higher yields of irrigated lands, together with the far lesser problem of weed control, led the cotton farmers of that state to employ five times as many workers during the height of the harvest as during the peak of the chopping period. This, in combination with the larger scale of cotton farming in California and greater labor scarcity than in the South, gave the farmers of the state a strong incentive to adopt the mechanical cotton picker.[26]

Fortunately, both International Harvester and the Rust brothers (John and Mack) were able to respond to the interest in mechanical pickers aroused by labor shortages during the Second World War. By the early 1940s both had taken important steps toward perfecting their equipment, but shortages of materials limited manufacturing output to a few experimental machines. By 1948 the first assembly line models were reaching the market, and within three years half of all the spindle picking machines manufactured in the United States were being utilized in California. The percentage has steadily declined since then—it was 11 percent in 1971—but the fact remains that in the nascence of the industry California and the other states of the arid Southwest served both as a proving ground and as a source of income to manufacturers during a crucial period.[27]

Once again, the technological improvements that began about the time of the Second World War and have since continued—widening mechanization, seeds with higher yields, improved breeds of livestock, and the use of herbicides, pesticides, and other products of agricultural chemistry, for example—constitute an agricultural revolution.[28] But the American farmer, his banker, his suppliers, and those who service his equipment, processing, and transport needs—the complex of "agribusiness"—have by no means enjoyed a record of unparalleled financial success. Indeed, significant numbers of farmers and rural bankers faced bankruptcy in the mid-1980s. "I've never seen a year like this," said Dean Jack, president of York State Bank in southeastern Nebraska in February 1985. "Half of our farmers are in good shape, about 25 percent are in trouble and about 25 percent are already broke." He added, "We have good water for irrigation, we have land that is as good as anybody's and we raised as good crops as ever, and half our farmers still can't pay their debts."[29] More broadly, in early 1985 one-third of the nation's farms were encumbered by an average debt of $325,000. The ratio of the debts to the assets of these farms was at least 41 percent and may have been as high as 71 percent and more. Another 29 percent of the farms were only relatively better off. Their average debt of $187,000 represented debt/asset ratios ranging from 11 percent to 40 percent.[30]

The fundamental explanation of the financial predicament in which so many American farmers found themselves in the mid-1980s is simple: they responded incautiously to the price signals of the marketplace. The explanation itself, however, has to be explained, and that is anything but simple. The chronic farm problem in the United States has long been that of excess capacity, of an ability to produce more than domestic and foreign markets can absorb at remunerative prices, even with the aid of goods taken off the market by government support programs. In other words, in the aggregate, demand has been inelastic. Ever since the days of the New Deal, government has tried to cope with this problem by mounting a host of programs—acreage allotments and marketing quotas, purchase agreements, soil banks, and others—

designed to curtail supply by limiting production. And it has tried through commodity loans to farmers or to their cooperative marketing associations to provide floors under market prices. In addition, numerous programs have authorized payments to producers in the form of commodity price supports or in return for adopting soil conservation measures. Analysts generally agree that average farm prices in the 1950s and 1960s would have been considerably lower if these programs had not been in existence, perhaps from 10 to 25 percent lower.

In the late 1960s prices, which with government support had held at reasonably constant levels from 1953 to 1967, began to move upward. And in 1973 they shot skyward to levels never before experienced except during wartime or its aftermath. What had happened? The explanation is that foreign demand rose massively in response to (a) the Nixon administration's approval of the sale of $750 million worth of wheat and feed grains to the Soviet Union in the summer of 1972—a sale which sparked orders from elsewhere in Europe and from Japan—and (b) the Nixon administration's devaluation of the dollar in 1973, which cheapened American exports.

America's farmers responded with enthusiasm to the prospect of upwardly spiraling demand, prices, and profits. Encouraged by their bankers to borrow, and by top officials in the Department of Agriculture to plant "from fence to fence," they increased the area under crops by 54 million acres between 1969 and 1981—and adopted improved production techniques besides to lower costs and raise output. Corn production, for example, went up from 5.6 million bushels in 1972 to 8.4 million in 1982. In the meantime, however, agricultural production abroad also expanded, and American surpluses soared.[31]

Enter the value of the dollar. In the early 1980s, as in the late 1960s, the dollar became grossly overvalued in relation to the currencies of Europe and Japan. Exports of manufactured goods as well as farm commodities were affected. Since they were priced in expensive dollars, they fell. In contrast, imports rose. Indeed, in 1986 the excess of imports over exports soared to a historically high deficit of 169.8 billion.[32] The strong dollar reduced foreign demand for American goods, and the effect of this, of course, was to increase the quantities available for domestic sale. But while this lowered prices to consumers, it also lowered incomes for farmers. Falling incomes, in turn, made it difficult for farmers to repay loans taken out for investments in equipment and supplies, with obvious economic consequences for manufacturers, bankers, and tradesmen. Thus, as always since the rise of industry, the fortunes of the agricultural and manufacturing sectors of the economy were closely entwined.

In some ways, manufacturers had an even harder row to hoe. In contrast with the remarkable record of productivity growth encountered in the postwar history of American agriculture, manufacturing, once the pace-setting embodiment of the "American system," as it was known and envied abroad, could boast no similar accomplishment in recent years. Just the opposite: the rate of increase in productivity had been slowing down. From an annual average of 3.4 percent between 1948 and 1966, the rate fell to 2.3 percent from 1966 to 1973, to 1 percent from 1973 to 1977, and to 0.4 percent in 1977 and 1978. In 1979 and 1980 growth stopped altogether and productivity actually declined.[33]

Economists have been pondering the causes of this strange unhistoric performance since the late sixties. Among the numerous factors cited were an increase in the proportion of youths and women in the labor force ("output per man-hour tends to be relatively low among women and among new entrants into the labor force"); relatively low rates of investment after 1973, which lowered the capital/labor ratio; the costs of compliance with environmental, health, and safety regulations; a decrease in the proportion of the gross national product devoted to research and development in the late 1960s and early 1970s; and the shift of national output away from goods and toward services, where possibilities of productivity growth are more limited.

These by no means exhaust the possibilities. Some economists blame chronic inflation, suggesting that the search for hedges against rising prices may distort the composition of investment. Uncertainty about the value of money shrinks the time horizon and induces managers to avoid long-lived projects embodying large elements of technical change. Some suggest that the solution to the puzzle "might begin by dismantling United States policies that have raised costs, discouraged saving, and protected lame-duck industries and companies."[34] Others emphasize the importance of providing people with skills and knowledge and of inspiring high morale and motivation in the workforce. Productivity in the "era of human capital," writes a scholar in recent times, "will depend largely on collaboration, group learning, and teamwork." According to a study released in the fall of 1983 the work ethic is alive but neglected by employers who fail to see to it that pay is tied directly to performance. "Why should people work hard and live up to their work-ethic ideals," asked the coauthor of the report, "if others who are holding back receive just as much reward and recognition?"[35]

There is another possibility to be considered. How productivity enhancing have been many of the decisions made by business managers, especially those of the largest manufacturing corporations? According to one critic, professional managers, intent on a favorable reading of the "bottom line," have gradually become "paper entrepreneurs" since the mid-1960s. Avoiding the costs and risks of investments in fundamentally new products or processes, their innovations have been neither technological nor institutional. "Rather, they have been based on accounting, tax avoidance, financial management, mergers, acquisitions and litigation. They have been innovations on paper."[36] Instead of creating new wealth, they have merely rearranged industrial assets.

The conglomerate merger movement of the 1960s and 1970s is a case in point. Before then, American business enterprises as a rule confined their expansion to lines of business related to their original products, entering markets appropriate to their managerial, technical, and marketing capabilities in search of competitive advantage. The conglomerate enterprises born after the mid-1960s—Gulf & Western, LTV, Textron, Litton, United Technologies, Northwest Industries, ITT, and Teledyne—were entirely different. Multibusiness giants, they have grown by acquiring existing enterprises, often in wholly unrelated fields. ITT, for example, owns Wonder Bread, Sheraton Hotels, Hartford Insurance, Bobbs-Merrill Publishing, and Burpee Lawn and Garden Products. Conglomerates rarely, if ever, bring managerial, technical, or marketing skills to the companies they acquire, because they lack direct knowledge of these unrelated businesses. Their expertise is in law and finance and their relationship to their subsidiaries that of an investor who diversifies to spread risks.

Conglomeration has been taking place rapidly in recent years, with American companies increasing the amounts spent in acquiring other companies from $22 billion in 1977 to twice that sum two years later. The year 1981 saw record-shattering expenditures of $82 billion for the purpose. Managerial emphasis, in short, has often shifted in recent years from cost-reducing and product-enhancing innovation through research and development to short-run profits from market manipulations of company assets. The consequence has surely been the placing of higher managerial premiums on expertise in law and finance than on engineering and other productivity-enhancing bodies of knowledge.

The productivity slowdown was a major cause of the declining competitiveness of American products in world markets. Exports of American manufactured goods have fallen as a percentage of world manufactured exports ever since 1963. Ironically, the industries affected are those on which the industrial preeminence of the United States has long rested, a superiority due to its ability to produce with growing efficiency standardized goods in high volume. They are its basic steel, textile, automobile, electronics, rubber, and petrochemical industries, together with other high-volume industries dependent on them. The United States proportion of world automobile sales fell by nearly one-third between 1963 and 1981. Sales of industrial machinery also declined by one-third, agricultural machinery by 40 percent, telecommunications machinery by 50 percent, and metalworking machinery by 55 percent.

To some extent these declines reflected the recovery of countries devastated by the war. In contrast to the United States, which escaped with its factories, mines, and transport net intact, industrial capacity in almost every continental European country and in Japan had been destroyed, and that of Great Britain crippled. These circumstances enabled the United States to reverse its historic role as a net importer of consumer goods, the net surplus of exports of those goods in 1947, for example, amounting to $1 billion. In 1950 the United States was producing about 60 percent of the world's manufacturing output.[37]

The distortion in the composition of trade was not destined to last. Public grants of about $15 billion under the Marshall Plan paved the way to a return to traditional trading patterns by contributing significantly to European industrial and economic growth. The European economies recovered and rebuilt capacity in the 1950s. In the next decade Japan entered competitive world markets in a major way. And in the 1970s several developing countries, aided by a gradual reduction of tariff levels after adoption of the General Agreement on Tariffs and Trade in 1947; by relatively easy access to international capital through European, American, and Japanese banks; and also by a new postwar institution, the World Bank, began making important contributions to manufacturing output and trade. By 1979 the share of the United States in world industrial production had fallen from 60 percent to 35 percent, and its share in world exports of manufactured goods from 29 percent (in 1953) to 13 percent (in 1976). By 1980 the share of the developing nations in the latter had soared to one of exact equivalence with that of the United States, while Japan's rose in the 1970s from 6 percent to 10.5 percent. From a transitory position of early postwar dominance of the export trade, the United States thus moved to one of rough equivalence with other industrial countries, in the meantime resuming its historical posture as a net importer of consumer goods.[38]

The growth of industrial capacity in other parts of the world, however, even together with wage differentials favoring production in those areas, does not wholly explain the declining share of American manufactures in world exports which set in after the early 1960s. As we have already seen, the relative values of national currencies must also be taken into account. During the years of decline which began in the late 1960s, the American dollar was strong, overvalued in relation to other currencies, and in consequence foreign sales of American goods were impeded, imports stimulated, and American firms encouraged to invest abroad. But because of the peculiar role which the dollar came to play under the international currency system agreed upon by a United Nations conference at Bretton Woods, New Hampshire, in 1944, devaluation of the dollar was for a long time effectively ruled out. The result was that the United States trade balance, after reaching a peak surplus in the early 1960s, began to deteriorate, turning down dramatically in 1968. By July 1971 the balance-of-payments deficit was rising at the very high rate of $23 billion a year, and this generated increasing pressure to abandon the system.

But this step could not be taken lightly. Bretton Woods represented an experiment in international idealism. American and British postwar planners hoped that a break could be made with the legacy of economic nationalism inherited from the past. The 1930s had been a decade fragmented by bilateral trading agreements, blocked exchanges, efforts to achieve autarchy, and other arrangements inhospitable to efficient international exchanges of goods and services. Persuaded of the close connection between a peaceful and prosperous world and the reconstruction of a trading system in which obstacles to the movement of goods and services would be as few as possible, Secretary of State Cordell Hull had already successfully sponsored the Reciprocal Trade Agreements Act of 1934. Under this legislation, which authorized the president to enter into reciprocal pacts and to modify American tariffs in order to promote the expansion of American foreign trade, some twenty-nine agreements were negotiated by 1947. As an instrument for liberalizing world trade, the act bore the defect of the president's inability to carry out unilateral across-the-board reductions in American tariff rates, but it did take the nation part way along the road to a more open commercial world.[39]

The Second World War quickened the determination of Hull, Harry Dexter White in the Treasury Department, and others to erect a framework in which international trade and exchange could be conducted with minimal friction. Their efforts, especially those of White on the American side and of John Maynard Keynes on the British side, culminated in the adoption of articles of agreement at Bretton Woods which were to last for nearly thirty years. The United Nations conference created two new institutions, the International Monetary Fund and the International Bank for Reconstruction and Development (World Bank), American participation in both being authorized by Congress in July 1945. The bank, with an authorized capital of $10 billion and the ability to enhance that sum by issuing securities, was permitted both to make loans from its own resources and to guarantee private loans to countries to facilitate postwar reconstruction—an initial purpose which was to change to one of promoting the economic development of Third World and other modernizing countries. The objective of the International Monetary Fund, the resources of which amounted to $8.8 billion—the American contribution being $3.175 billion—was to enhance liquidity by making limited amounts of currency available to member countries running a deficit in their balance of payments in order to shorten the duration and lessen the degree of international disequilibrium.[40]

Bretton Woods adopted a regime of fixed exchange rates. The dollar was the system's *numéraire:* all other currencies were valued in terms of the dollar, with the dollar itself being valued in terms of gold. Gold at the fixed price of thirty-five dollars an ounce was supposed to be available from the Federal Reserve when a foreign central bank wished to exchange its dollars. This convertibility of dollars into gold was the system's theoretical anchor. It justified other countries' holding dollars instead of gold in their monetary reserves. The dollar thus served as the principal reserve currency of an arrangement which technically was called the gold exchange standard. To hold exchange rates within bands of specified width around parity values, central banks generally intervened by buying or selling reserves in the foreign-exchange markets.[41]

But central banks were not the only dealers in dollars. Unfortunately, the system was vulnerable to speculation. Private holders of dollars were supposed to be able to buy gold at the official price in the open market. By bidding up the dollar price of gold on that market, traders could speculate against the dollar itself, betting, as it were, that the United States would be unable to provide enough gold to sustain the official price.[42] Three simple numbers show how difficult that would prove to be. In August 1971 the United States held more than $10 billion worth of gold, but foreign official holdings of dollars exceeded $40 billion, and private dollar holdings totaled more than $30 billion.[43]

Domestic inflation and persistent deficits in the balance of payments imperiled the dollar after the mid-1960s. By attracting foreign products and discouraging exports, relatively high domestic prices created deficits in the merchandise trade account. Even larger dollar claims resulted from overseas military expenditures, foreign aid, and direct investments in Europe and in Canada. Those in manufacturing alone rose eightfold, from $3.8 billion to $32.3 billion between 1950 and 1970. Capital expenditures in Europe were partly motivated by the desire of American business to avoid import duties imposed by member countries forming the European Common Market in 1958.[44] In addition, both long- and short-term interest rates were generally well below European levels, and this induced foreigners to borrow in the United States. Fresh deficits in the balance of payments appeared each year and showed no signs of diminishing. Ironically, it was the outflow of dollars made necessary by the deficits which enabled the dollar to function as the principal reserve currency and medium of payment for international transactions.

Following a massive speculative run against the dollar, the Nixon administration in August 1971 suspended indefinitely the dollar's official convertibility into either gold or foreign currencies, a suspension made permanent in 1973. The dollar was devalued against gold, and nearly all the major industrial currencies were revalued against the dollar—the Japanese yen, for example, by approximately 17 percent. The purpose of the devaluation was to produce a major improvement in the United States balance of payments, including the trade balance, and to put an end to the disadvantage under which American export industries were operating, in the belief that this, together with a hoped-for reversal of capital flows, would improve the balance of payments. The Bretton Woods system of fixed parities was abandoned. Floating exchange rates replaced fixed exchange rates, with the price of dollars in terms of gold and other currencies thenceforth being determined by the supply of and demand for dollars.[45]

Ten years later, in 1983, a number of countries, France in particular, were complaining about the strength of the dollar under floating exchange rates and urging a return to the fixed rate system established at Bretton Woods. What made the dollar strong was the effect of large budgetary deficits on real interest rates. In 1986 the deficit reached a record $221 billion, raising the national debt about $2 trillion, double its level when President Reagan took office. Because the government must compete with private borrowers for available savings, the very large government borrowing required to finance the deficit kept interest rates high. This, in turn, together with the perceived stability of the American economy, attracted foreign capital to the United States. Capital-losing countries naturally complained because of the reduced sums available for their own development needs. The reply of the Reagan administration was that a reduced rate of inflation was responsible for the dollar's strength, and it urged other industrialized countries around the world to follow the example of the United States![46]

If falling manufacturing productivity and relative currency values go far to explain the decline in American manufactured exports as a proportion of world sales, they also throw light on the ability of foreign imports to win larger shares of the domestic market.

> By 1981 America was importing 26 percent of its cars, 25 percent of its steel, 60 percent of its televisions, radios, tape recorders and phonographs, 43 percent of its calculators, 27 percent of its metal-forming machine tools, 35 percent of its textile machinery, and 53 percent of its numerically controlled machine tools. Twenty years before, imports had accounted for less than 10 percent of the U.S. market for each of these products.[47]

Productivity and currency, however, are not the only relevant considerations. Since the 1960s a major structural change has been taking place in the world economy. Access to capital, technological knowledge, and innovations, and global channels of sales and marketing, have permitted less-developed countries to participate in that economy far more actively than before. Their participation, in turn, and that of Third World countries as well, has permitted an international rationalization of the location of production to take place. The globe is thus becoming a single marketplace, with goods being made wherever they can be produced the cheapest. Real wages are lower in the Third World, and many of the countries also have a favored access to cheap materials. In addition, the availability of data processing machines, microprocessors, and satellite communications facilities has made it possible for manufacturers to divide the process of production into separate operations that can be performed at different sites and then integrated into a single product. Developing countries such as Korea, Hong Kong, Taiwan, Singapore, Brazil, and Spain have been ideally suited for manufacturing standardized parts that are assembled into end-products elsewhere. Sometimes the process is reversed. Since 1970, for example, the United States has been increasing its exports of auto parts and its imports of complete cars, its exports of industrial textiles and its imports of consumer textiles. South Korea's textile exports rose by 436 percent between 1970 and 1975, while those of Taiwan and Hong Kong increased by 347 percent and 191 percent, respectively. Imports to the United States from developing nations rose nearly tenfold from 1970 to 1980, from $3.6 billion to $30 billion (in constant dollars).[48]

One consequence of this structural change in the world economy has been an intensification of competition in the American marketplace, where, by 1980, foreign-made goods were competing with more than 70 percent of those produced in the United States.[49] Another has been a progressive shift in competitive advantage in high-volume standardized production to the newly developed and developing countries. The upshot of these rapid changes is that a number of old-line American industries, including textiles, steel, automobiles, petrochemicals, electrical machinery, and metal-forming machinery, found themselves in trouble in the early 1980s.[50]

Many of them had become stable oligopolies of three or four major firms (although it is also true that only a slight increase in concentration in the manufacturing industry has taken place since World War II).[51] Unaccustomed to price competition, adhering to a system of administered prices and guaranteed wage increases, management often refused to allow prices to respond to market conditions. Technologically backward and reluctant to innovate, steelmakers clung to open hearth and ingot-casting techniques while their Japanese counterparts were investing heavily in superior basic oxygen furnaces and continuous casting. American automakers also held back, toying with changes in style while their Japanese counterparts were adopting new stamping technologies and experimenting with more efficient engines and pollution control devices.[52] The competitive threat came not only from the Japanese but also from West German machine tool companies, French radial tire manufacturers, Swedish makers of precision instruments, and textile manufacturers in developing countries. The list of American companies experiencing sharply reduced profits in the early 1980s included ghostly giants of the past: United States Steel, General Motors, International Harvester, and RCA.[53]

American producers in the steel, automobile, consumer electronics, and other industries sought protection from imports by forming political coalitions with organized labor, petitioning the executive branch, lobbying Congress, and seeking support through the federal courts. Various sorts of trade restrictions followed, one example being the marketing agreement negotiated with Japan by the United States government limiting imports of Japanese color televisions to approximately 1.6 million sets a year, and similar agreements subsequently negotiated with Taiwan and South Korea. Besides quotas, protection has also been obtained through increased duties and a wide assortment of government subsidies, special tax credits and depreciation allowances, and subsidized loans and loan guarantees. According to one computation, the total cost to the federal government of special tax provisions for the benefit of specific industries rose from $7.9 billion in 1950 to $62.4 billion in 1980. During the same interval, the cost of subsidized loans and loan guarantees, as measured by interest charges and loan defaults, increased from only $300 million to $3.6 billion. Altogether, government subsidies and tax expenditures increased from $77.1 billion in 1950 to $303.7 billion in 1980. In addition, government subsidies have taken the form of *ad hoc* bailouts of particular failing firms, for example, Lockheed and Chrysler.[54]

One recent critic views such responses as efforts to preserve an old and outmoded industrial base. He urges, instead, adoption of an industrial policy promoting skill-intensive production. And since he sees little hope of eliciting from the private sector the quality of information that industrial policymakers would need, he looks to government leadership for the promotion of economic development. "Ultimately," he writes, "America's capacity to respond to economic change will depend on the vitality of its political institutions," with investments in skills, knowledge, and team learning emerging as the key determinants of national well-being. The United States must accept that economic advantage in high-volume production of standardized products has moved to the developing countries. The challenge of the "new American frontier" is to promote the growth of "flexible-system" production by technically advanced, skill-intensive industries, a highly integrated system that can respond quickly to new opportunities.[55]

The answer to economic decline, then, is to fashion "a new productive organization requiring a different, less rigidly delineated relationship between management and labor and a new relationship with government."[56] The marketplace is far from being an apolitical arena.

> Every major industry in America is deeply involved with and dependent on government. The competitive position of every American firm is affected by government policy. No sharp distinction can validly be drawn between private and public sectors within this or any other industrialized country; the economic effects of public policies and corporate decisions are completely intertwined.[57]

The thesis is an engaging one. Throughout American history government and law have deeply influenced the behavior of economic actors and the contours of development. Through concessions, grants of special privilege, or capital contributions, these agents of the community encouraged the creation of colonial docks, salt mines, gristmills and sawmills, and nineteenth-century turnpikes, canals, and railroads. And in the twentieth century, tariffs, quotas, marketing orders, price supports, bailouts, federal loans and loan guarantees, subsidized insurance, and special tax breaks have continued an American tradition of public aid to private enterprise. It is calculated that government programs that promote particular industries or businesses amounted to 13.9 percent of the gross national product in 1982.[58]

The idea of an industrial policy had numerous supporters in the early 1980s, but it also had many critics, perhaps especially among economists. One was

Charles Schultze, former chairman of the Council of Economic Advisers under President Carter. Writing in 1983, Schultze pointed out that the essential purpose of such a policy was the production of an industrial structure different from what the market would have produced. Its techniques were twofold: protecting the losers and picking the winners. Both represented a "dangerous solution for an imaginary problem."[59] Protecting losers meant supporting major declining industries by such means as trade barriers, subsidies, favorable regulatory treatment, tax breaks, and subsidized loans. Protectionism, inefficiencies, and higher prices for consumers would soon manifest themselves.

As for picking winners, or providing government aid to specific companies and industries that are fast growers, big employers or exporters, or technological leaders, Schultze wanted to know how government bureaucrats could be expected to be better judges of the likelihood of success than private investors. He feared such a policy would turn into a vast boondoggle for every industry with political clout. More fundamentally, he challenged the basic contention of industrial policy advocates that the American economy was deindustrializing. Although American manufacturing output moved up slightly less than gross national product in the 1970s, the phenomenon was a worldwide one. Two major industries, steel and autos, he conceded, were in serious structural trouble, but their difficulties should not be generalized into a national malady.

Schultze's views were broadly shared by his counterpart under President Nixon, Herbert Stein, who wrote in 1984 that the idea of an industrial policy "has possible ramifications that could seriously impair the efficiency and adaptability of the American economy." It provided a rationale for ad hoc interventions to assist American industry in the necessary adjustments required by a changing world economy. Experience, however, showed that assistance overwhelmingly involved protecting existing industries rather than encouraging adaptation to new ones. Such was the nature of politics, of bureaucracy. Stein's prescription for the continued success of the American economy was straightforward:

> The main requirement is an environment in which private enterprise will invest in change, providing attractive opportunities to draw workers out of the fading industries. To reduce the economic uncertainties that accompany inflation, to avoid absorbing an enormous share of the national saving in financing a deficit and to relieve the tax burdens that have borne most heavily on investment—these things will most surely contribute to the adaptation of the American economy.

He reminded his readers of past successes: "With a stable and nonhostile environment, American private enterprise has been quite energetic in moving into new technologies and new markets. In retrospect one can point to cases in which these adjustments seem to have been too slow. But that is not the same as saying that government intervention in the process would have made these adjustments better or quicker."[60] America was not Japan. The policy question was a significant political issue of the 1980s, and only time would tell the outcome of the debate.

In the meantime, the stability of the economy appeared to some viewers to be in jeopardy because of the rising mountain of debt, both public and private. As we have seen, public borrowing had created a national debt of $2 trillion by 1986, but private borrowing by businesses, much of it to finance highly leveraged mergers and acquisitions, and by farmers, real estate investors, and consumers pushed total indebtedness to nearly $9 trillion, more than twice its level at the beginning of the decade. A growing part of the debt was owed abroad. As recently as 1982 the United States was the world's largest creditor, but just four years later the tables were turned and the country had emerged as the largest debtor, with a foreign debt at the end of 1986 of $263.6 billion. The line from creditor to debtor had been crossed in 1985, for the first time in over seventy years, but the debt at the end of that year was only $111.9 billion. In just one year it rose by 135 percent, compounding interest charges and raising concern that living standards in the United States would be reduced as more of the country's wealth was transferred to foreign hands.[61]

Once again, the main reason why the debt was so large was the attraction of relatively high real interest rates to foreign investors, an elevation chiefly due to the enormous deficits in the government's budget. Rising from 2.5 percent of the gross national product in 1980 to more than 6 percent in 1983, the deficit absorbed virtually all of the net saving generated by the nation's households, businesses, and state and local governments. The sharp rise in government borrowing pushed up the real rate of interest on long-term government bonds and attracted funds from around the world to invest in dollar securities. In consequence, the exchange value of the dollar—that is, the value of the dollar in relation to the yen and other foreign currencies—went up. As we have seen, the strong dollar,in turn, dampened American exports and encouraged imports, but the latter, by increasing the supply of available products, did tend to reduce inflationary pressures. The offset to this desirable result, however, was a merchandise trade deficit which reached a record high of $152.7 billion in 1986. The deficit was financed by an inflow of foreign capital, but should that inflow be reversed, Americans would no longer be able to consume more than they produced.

Although no one could say for sure what the prospects were for a continuation of this round of interconnected phenomena, one view of the future was by no means a bleak one. Martin Feldstein, former chairman of the Council of Economic Advisers, was optimistic because of the sharp drop in the exchange value of the dollar which began to take place in the spring of 1985. The reason for the drop was this: increasing numbers of foreign investors had come to the conclusion that the high value of the dollar could not be sustained indefinitely because of mounting political pressures to do something about the budget deficit. Enactment in the fall of that year of the Gramm-Rudman-Hollings law, which provided for an orderly reduction in the annual deficit and the achievement of a balanced budget by 1991, confirmed their conclusion. As a result, the real interest rate and the interest differential in favor of United States bonds narrowed significantly, and this encouraged a continuation of the dollar's decline. Between February 1985 and December 1986 the dollar fell by more than 40 percent against the currencies of the major industrial powers.

Even with this decline, however, the level of the dollar remained so high as to place in sharp doubt the notion that foreigners would find it to their interest to continue to finance the persistent trade deficit by their investments in American securities. Now that the United States had become a debtor nation, now that foreign loans to American borrowers plus foreign equity investments in the United States exceeded the sum of United States loans and investments abroad, the combination of interest and dividends on this debt would, according to estimates made by the International Monetary Fund, quadruple by 1990 from $200 billion to $800 billion. The annual cost of interest and dividends on these obligation would be some $60 billion. Debt of this magnitude, in Feldstein's judgment, would be unsustainable. He believed that increasing risks of fluctuation in the value of the dollar and in dollar interest rates would make additional investments in dollar securities less attractive to foreigners. In all likelihood they would shift their investments from dollar bonds to securities denominated in other currencies. In consequence, the value of the dollar would be driven down even further, and this would bring the United States trade balance closer to a sustainable level. Not intervention in foreign-exchange markets by finance ministers or central bankers, or "jawboning" by government officials, it should be emphasized, but rather the perceived interest of private investors, was expected to bring about this result. Within a few years the United States would begin to meet the cost of servicing its overseas debt by exporting more than it imported, so that by the early 1990s, Feldstein predicted, the United States would again be running a merchandise trade surplus.[62]

In sum, if indeed the main reason for the decline in American manufacturing exports and the mounting deficits in merchandise trade has been the declining value of the dollar rather than the loss of a historical advantage in productivity, the American economy could confidently be expected to survive the turmoil of the 1980s. Supporting this view, and reinforcing faith in free markets as opposed to a governmental industrial policy, was the fact that the United States exported $150 billion of manufactured products to the rest of the world in 1986. Furthermore, over 70 percent of the American demand for manufactured goods was satisfied by products made in the United States.

When we turn from American foreign debt to the external obligations of other countries, the question arises whether free markets alone can be depended on to preserve international economic stability. Leonard Silk, the economic columnist of the *New York Times,* has argued strongly that they cannot. Emphasizing the world's economic interdependence and the troublesome problem of Third World debt, which by the end of 1986 amounted to $1 trillion, Silk found the international financial system to be in peril. The need was for an international lender of last resort, a role played by Great Britain through most of the nineteenth and early twentieth centuries. Unless the United States regained its ability to sustain nations in danger of default or built a collective defense with Japan and others to do so, there could be a financial disaster comparable to that of 1929, or an even greater one.

It was the developing nations of Latin America, sub-Saharan Africa, and East Asia that were essentially in need of loans and investments from the industrialized countries. Only development could raise their standards of living and their health and literacy levels, and this required savings in sums beyond the capacity of their economies to generate. It required capital from external sources, and the commercial banks of the United States were quick to respond, even aggressively eager to do so. Charles P. Kindleberger has sketched a scenario in which "multinational banks swollen with dollars tumbled over one another in trying to uncover new foreign borrowers and practically forced money on the less-developed countries.[63] Especially after the early 1970s they plied the public and private sectors of Mexico, Argentina, Brazil, and other Latin American nations, providing in the following decade more than two-thirds of the capital inflow into the region.

Their loans were made at commercial interest rates, that is, at short-term rates which varied with changes in the market. The ensuing "debt problem" of the developing countries was largely a Latin American one. Dependent on exports to earn the foreign exchange with which to service their debts, these countries were vulnerable to recessions abridging demand in foreign markets for their products and to upward movements in interest rates. All were therefore hard hit in 1981–82 by the conjuncture of rising interest rates and an unexpectedly deep and enduring international recession. In August 1982 Mexico announced that it would be unable to repay the principal of its debt; Brazil soon followed, and in the ensuing debt crisis of 1982–83 international commercial-bank lending ground to a halt, forcing renegotiation of part of the external commercial-bank debt of Brazil, Chile, Venezuela, Ecuador, Peru, and Uruguay.

Unhappily, potential crises remained. Mexico was soon to be rocked once again, this time by a severe earthquake, falling oil prices, and government mismanagement. Under the leadership of the United States Treasury, a money package supported by the International Monetary Fund, the World Bank, and commercial-banks was quickly put together to help. The commercial banks, however, remained reluctant to increase their exposure in the debtor countries. Indeed, the largest American commercial-bank lender, Citibank, decided in

May 1987 to increase drastically its provision for losses on loans to developing countries. Essentially, it wrote off a large part of the loans. Chemical Bank of New York followed by establishing "loan-loss reserves" of $1.1 billion.

These episodes illustrate the interconnectedness of trade, finance, and economic policy, some of the intersections between the public and private domains. "The line between domestic and international economic policy," Silk writes, "has been rubbed out." A nation's monetary, fiscal, and trade policies have an impact not only on its own citizens but also on those of other countries. Restrictive monetary policies to combat inflation in one nation and protect the exchange value of its currency lower the level of its prices and inhibit imports from other countries. Dependent developing countries face narrowed markets and difficulties of meeting interest payments on external debt. Foreign lending institutions find their profit-and-loss accounts affected as a result. Protectionist measures produce similar consequences. Silk reminded his readers of the connection between policies like these and an earlier cataclysm: "At the end of the 1920s it was the resort by individual nations to unduly restrictive monetary and fiscal policies and to 'beggar-thy-neighbor' protectionism, in the presumed self-interest of each, that caused the Great Depression." It followed that the "greatest change needed to preserve stability and growth is for the world economy, rather than the national economy, to become the unit for policy thinking." Needed most was "political will."[64]

Given the generous response of Americans in the 1980s to televised scenes of starvation and disease among the children of Ethiopia and elsewhere, was it too much to believe that they would be willing to accept some reduction in their own elevated standards of living for the sake of the rest of humanity? The history is yet to be written. When it is, history may record that when the reduction came, willingness had nothing to do with it.

Of their historic willingness to devote public funds to ameliorate the lot of disadvantaged Americans, however, there was little doubt. Even so dedicated a proponent of free market solutions as Herbert Stein acknowledged the need for government to provide a safety net consisting of income assistance programs such as unemployment compensation, food stamps, and Aid to Families with Dependent Children for low-income people. Such an idea would have found few supporters before the debut of the Welfare State during the anguished years of the Great Depression. Most looked to a healthy economy to provide jobs and income and to private charity to help the victims of misfortune.

The New Deal marks the triumph of a more compassionate philosophy, namely, that it is a legitimate responsibility of the federal government to aid in the provision of the minimal needs of the disadvantaged. The new viewpoint was evidenced by enlarged government expenditures for social security programs such as those providing for old age, survivors', invalidity, and public health insurance; for workmen's compensation, unemployment insurance, family allowances, public assistance, and public employee programs. The Welfare State of the Age of Roosevelt was extended but not reshaped under Truman (who supported legislation making social security available to 10 million additional people; authorizing new public housing for the slum dweller; and expending public funds on public power, rural electrification, soil conservation, and flood control projects), and found its richest expression in the twentieth century thus far in the Great Society programs of Lyndon Johnson.

Some of the legislation of the Johnson years, such as medical care for the aged, had been bottled up in Congress since the Truman administration. Other programs bore Johnson's personal stamp, and of these probably the most important was the War on Poverty. In 1962 Michael Harrington had written movingly about the 40 million or so people (one-fifth of the American population) who had "dropped out of sight," who dwelt in a "culture of poverty." They made up a more or less permanent underclass including the elderly, the nonwhites, the poorly educated and unproductive small farmers, the inhabitants of urban ghettos and of Appalachia.[65] Although poverty is not only an absolute but also a relative concept, and one whose definition necessarily changes over time, roughly half of all these groups were at or below the poverty line as defined by the Social Security Administration in 1964 (that is, having annual incomes of $3,000 or less to support a family of four).

Acting on the belief that poverty of this kind was impacted, that it was the result of social problems little affected by broad economic forces and hence could not be eliminated by indirect methods which stimulated overall economic growth, Johnson put the weight of his presidential authority behind direct approaches to the problem. The Economic Opportunity Act of 1964, which established ten programs, among which were Head Start, the Job Corps, and Vista, amounted to the first concerted attack on poverty since New Deal days. Other major programs followed: Medicare and Medicaid, federal aid for elementary and secondary education, federal scholarships for college students, a multimillion-dollar program for medical research, legislation providing rent subsidies, demonstration cities, a teachers' corps, regional medical centers, "vest pocket" parks, a rescue operation for the economically depressed region of Appalachia, and an assortment of consumer protection laws, including those designed to increase auto and highway safety.[66]

Standing as a halfway marker between the Roosevelt and Johnson administrations, the creation of a cabinet-level Department of Health, Education and Welfare in 1953 symbolized the continuing enlargement of the federal presence in the area of human melioration. From 1950 to 1964, federal expenditures for these purposes nearly tripled, rising, in constant dollars, from $35.1 billion to $108 billion. Unhappily, the War on Poverty fell victim to the war in Vietnam, the escalating funding requirements of which induced Johnson, as early as the beginning of 1966, to reduce or eliminate his budgetary requests for the maintenance of civilian programs he came to regard as ones of lower priority. Nevertheless, the evidence of the past half-century of governmental interest in the preservation and improvement of human capital is unmistakable.[67]

In this the United States is not alone. While elements of welfare or social security programs vary from one country to another, reflecting differences in governmental structure, tradition, and historical development, the major industrial powers have devoted increasing portions of their gross national product to welfare objectives in recent decades. Despite differences in the nature of their political societies, all have responded to underlying social pressures engendered by an advanced state of industrialization. As Table 40 shows, however, government expenditures by the United States from 1957 to 1977 represented a smaller share of GNP than those of any other country except Japan. Even this portion was subjected to deep budgetary cuts by the Reagan administration. The slicing of expenditures on education aid and loans, job training and retraining, and nutrition benefits for expectant mothers placed in serious jeopardy the nation's future stock of human capital.[68]

In the early 1980s the question of poverty also became ensnarled in statistical and definitional controversy. The Census Bureau reported that 34.4 million Americans whose cash incomes in 1982 were less than $9,862 for a family of four fell below the official poverty level. The poverty rate that year was 15 percent of the American people, up from 14 percent in 1981, and the highest rate reported since the start of President Johnson's antipoverty campaign in 1965. The director of the Office of Management and Budget, David Stockman, disputed these figures, however. In testimony before the House Ways and Means Committee in November 1983 he rejected the definition of poverty used by the Census Bureau and other federal agencies since 1964. "The official poverty count based on money income," he said, "substantially overstates the rate of poverty because it ignores $107 billion in in-kind medical, housing, food and other aid that tangibly raises the living standard of many

Table 40. Government expenditures for social security programs as a percentage of GNP: selected countries, 1957–1977.

Country	1957	1960	1963	1966	1971	1974	1977
Canada	6.5	8.7	9.4	9.0	14.8	13.7	14.6
France	14.3	13.7	15.4	16.6	n.a.	22.4	26.5
West Germany	16.6	16.2	16.9	18.4	18.8	22.5	26.5
Japan	4.3	4.7	5.1	5.6	5.6	6.4	8.7
Sweden	10.5	10.9	12.2	14.5	20.6	24.4	30.7
United Kingdom	10.0	11.0	11.1	12.3	13.5	14.1	17.1
United States	5.0	6.29	6.8	7.7	11.1	12.1	13.7

Source: David P. Calleo, *The Imperious Economy* (Cambridge, Mass.: Harvard University Press, 1982), p. 96. Used with permission.

low-income families." When noncash benefits are counted as income, he added, the poverty rate for 1982 is reduced from 15 percent to 9.6 percent, the number of poor people from 34.4 million to 22 million. The point was not a new one. Scholars had emphasized the relevance of in-kind aid nearly a decade before, if not earlier. The influence on policy was delayed, but in 1983 the Census Bureau at least planned to issue future reports simultaneously displaying the official poverty rate, using the usual definition, and calculating what the rate would be if noncash benefits were counted as income.[69]

According to Stockman, poor people in 1982 fell into four categories. The elderly (sixty-five and older) formed 10.9 percent of the total; female-headed households, 32.8 percent; young singles between sixteen and twenty-four years of age, 3.9 percent; and other adults between twenty-five and sixty-four years of age, 52.3 percent. The rising tide of economic growth would lift many boats, but not all. It would alleviate poverty for people in their prime working years but would be largely irrelevant to the elderly poor, many of whom had retired. Cash welfare programs, on the other hand, were of less value to young singles than to poor people in female-headed households, for whom government checks were of "critical and overwhelming significance." The conjunction of family instability, race and ethnicity, and poverty were painfully apparent. Only 56.1 percent of black families were husband-wife families in 1978, in contrast to 85.9 percent in the case of whites. In 1981 the poverty rate for female-headed families with children under eighteen was about 68 percent for blacks, 67 percent for Hispanics, and 43 percent for whites.[70] A task force appointed by President Reagan to investigate the question of hunger in the United States reported early in 1984 that "quantitative information about the extent of the problem is not available." In a final report characterized by the *New York Times* as one of "chilly, bloodless neutrality," the task force acknowledged "the sad truth" that "there is hunger in America" but concluded that "general claims of widespread hunger can neither be positively refuted nor definitively proved." Early in 1984 the nation awaited the course of action by a president who in November 1983 had said: "If there is one person in this country hungry, that is one too many, and we're going to see what we can do to alleviate the situation.[71]

As is evident from a comparison of the amount of cash income demarcating the official poverty line for a family of four in 1964 ($3,000) and 1982 ($9,862), something more than inflation has affected the definition of poverty. Undoubtedly the most important additional ingredient has been the rising standard of living. "Need" today is defined at a higher level than in the past because of the very success of the American economic system in providing for the material wants of the average family.

> In 1900 15 percent of U.S. families had flush toilets; today [1976] 86 percent of our poor families do. In 1900 3 percent had electricity; today 99 percent

of our poor do; in 1900 1 percent had central heating; today 62 percent of the poor do. In 1900 18 percent of our families had refrigeration, ice refrigeration; today 99 percent of our poor have refrigerators, virtually all mechanical.[72]

It is this "upward trend in the reference standard" that makes the end of poverty "an ever-retreating goal, and an unachievable one."[73] In sum, government has done much and must do more to alleviate the absolute poverty of hunger; in the relative sense, the biblical admonition that "the poor ye have always with you" will continue to be true as long as American capitalism generates not only more and more goods and services but also the desire to have them. For in creating wealth, it at the same time creates want.

Like other countries, whether noncapitalist or capitalist, America has its rich as well as its poor. But that is a trivial observation: the important question is whether the gaps between them have narrowed or widened with the passage of time. More than a century ago Karl Marx asserted that the overriding tendency of capitalism is toward an ever-increasing inequality in the distribution of income and wealth.[74] Recent studies, however, indicate strongly that he was wrong. According to one study, the outstanding fact about income inequality is its display of considerable variance ever since the seventeenth century. After showing no clear trend toward concentration before 1820, nonhuman wealth (excluding ownership of slaves as a form of wealth) became much more concentrated across the nineteenth century as skilled labor, professional groups, and urban wealthholders prospered much faster than farm hands, and the urban unskilled. Earnings and total incomes became even more markedly unequal between the 1890s and the First World War, leveled dramatically but briefly during the war, and resumed the trend toward inequality in the 1920s. Incomes moved toward greater equality between 1929 and the Korean War—the leveling before taxes and transfers being at least as large as the entire equalizing effect of governmental redistribution. After Korea, income inequality showed little trend till the advent of the Reagan administration, as we shall see.[75]

Other studies confirm variance over time. One estimate covers almost the entire sweep of independent America. Between 1774 and 1966, it suggests, average wealth per capita rose nearly tenfold, from $1,133 to $11,032.[76] A number of analyses address change in the twentieth century. One reveals that the top 1 percent of wealthholders owned about 32 percent of the wealth in 1922, 36 percent in 1929, and 21 percent in 1949, with the main shift toward a more egalitarian distribution occurring—once more—between the Great Depression and the Korean War.[77] As with wealth, so with income: in 1900 median real family income totaled $705; in 1971, the median reached $10,285. Racial discrimination and its employment and productivity effects, however, limited the gains of nonwhite families, which rose from 52 percent of white family incomes to only 63 percent in the seventy-one years.[78] One study, though confined to a single year (1970), uses Internal Revenue Service tax returns to provide a comprehensive view of the distribution of wealth among consumer units earning incomes ranging from less than $1,000 to more than $1,000,000. The disparities between lower and upper percentiles are gargantuan. But there is every reason, founded either in a division of estates among heirs or in their dissipation by profligate heirs, for believing that over the long run the rich are not getting richer. Rather, "the children of the rich in America tend to regress toward mean incomes—and thereby prevent the increasing concentration of wealth."[79] As for the lower ends of the distribution, it is worth remembering that in the mid-seventies probably two-thirds of the population of the rest of the world had incomes below the levels which define poverty in the United States.[80]

Many influences bear upon inequalities in income and wealthholding, some of them natural, others manmade. In addition to racial and ethnic prejudice and the effects of inheritance laws and practices, individual differences in native intelligence, health, ambition, strength of will, educational attainment, and family connections must be taken into account. Age, sex, and marital status matter, as well as geographic location and occupation.[81] Higher fertility and population growth appear to reduce the quality of the labor force by lessening the amount of resources devoted by families and public schools to each child.[82] Finally, not all Irishmen have the luck of the Irish.

Although comparison of the income and wealth experience of other industrialized countries, in particular, is essential if the American record is to be fully explained, it may well be, as has been suggested by the economist Simon Kuznets, that inequality first rises and then falls with modern economic growth.[83] Part of the reason for this must surely lie in the declining contribution of physical capital formation to growth. Measured in constant prices, the proportion of net capital formation in net national product has fallen from somewhat less than 15 percent in the early decades following the 1820s to 7 percent in the 1930s–1950s period.[84] In the early stages of modern industrial growth a proportionately larger share of current product must be saved rather than consumed if the manufacturing plant and equipment, residential and commercial structures, transport media, gas, lighting, water supply, sewage disposal, and other utilities essential to the urban needs of labor force mobilization are to be laid down, and if the agricultural hinterland and its food, raw materials, and excess labor supplies are to be linked with urban demand.

Capital in all these forms represents the real savings of the nation, but the money savings that are invested to form the capital originate in highly unequal proportions in the different segments of the population. It is this fact which supplies the linkage between capital needs and income inequality. Personal savings, of individuals and unincorporated enterprises, both farm and nonfarm, account for over 70 percent of total savings—the rest originating in the undistributed profits of corporations (about 20 percent) and in the excess of current revenues over expenditures by government (7 percent).[85] And since merely the top 5 percent of all income recipients are the source of 50 percent of these personal savings—the other 50 percent being saved by the remaining 95 percent of the population—it will be evident that an unequal income distribution has made a highly disproportionate contribution to capital formation.[86]

Recognition of this fact played an important part in the elaboration of the "supply-side" economics with which the Reagan administration proposed to tackle the nation's economic problems. The way to increase the supply of real capital and of goods and services, the argument ran, was to reduce taxes, especially on higher incomes. The consequence would be increased saving, investment, employment, and economic growth. The approach was the opposite to that of Keynesianism, which held that it was demand that paved the way to growth. Supply-siders thus believed they had brought "a new perspective to fiscal policy." In the words of an "insider," Paul Craig Roberts:

> Instead of stressing the effects on spending, supply-siders showed that tax rates directly affect the supply of goods and services. Lower tax rates mean better incentives to work, to save, to take risks, and to invest. As people respond to the higher after-tax rewards, or greater profitability, incomes rise and the tax base grows, thus feeding back some of the lost revenue to the Treasury. The saving rate also grows, providing more financing for governmental and private borrowing.

"Keynesian analysis," Roberts continued, "left out such effects."[87]

Persuaded by these arguments, President Reagan at the beginning of his administration induced the Congress to adopt a tax policy which would foster saving, investment, and productivity growth. The Economic Recovery Tax Act of 1981 reduced individual income tax rates by 25 percent over a period of three years and cut the top rate on unearned income from 70 percent to 50 percent. Other provisions of the law were designed to encourage new investment more directly, for example, an expanded investment tax credit and a system of allowances making it possible to recover capital costs more rapidly.[88]

The bait failed to take. Instead of increasing, the household saving rate declined. And although investment recovered sharply from the recession of 1981–82, the tax cuts appear to have had nothing to do with it. The reduced rates, that is to say, affected structures rather than equipment, but the recovery in investment in 1983–84 "came mainly in equipment and thus apparently could not be attributed to the tax cut."[89] Longer-range effects were even more dispiriting. Real per capita income growth between 1980 and 1986 averaged only 1.5 percent, lower than in the 1970s (1.8 percent) or 1960s (2.5 percent). Output per hour fell from an annual increase of 1.3 percent in the 1970s to an even lower 1.1 percent between 1980 and 1985.[90]

The legislation did bring about a redistribution of income—from the poor and the middle class to the better-off segments of society. Many observers, including David Stockman, the exceptionally able head of the Office of Management and Budget, have identified the redistribution as one of the hidden agendas of the Reagan administration, the supply-side rationale as a "Trojan Horse" to justify tax cuts for those in the highest bracket. "I've never believed," Stockman confided to an editor of the *Washington Post* in 1981, "that just cutting taxes alone will cause output and employment to expand."[91]

The cuts, together with effective rates of state and local taxes, continued a twenty-year trend (1966–1985) of steadily lower taxes on unearned income (in the form of dividends and rents) and steadily higher taxes on income from labor.[92] The dramatic tax reform bill of 1986, however, which lowered individual tax rates, removed many loopholes, and raised the corporation income tax, benefited not only the wealthy but also those with low incomes. Together with the taming of inflation, tax reform was a major accomplishment of the administration.[93]

Reagan made the conquest of inflation an objective of high priority. At least in the early years of his administration he warmly supported the efforts of the Federal Reserve Board, under its remarkable chairman Paul Volcker, to attack the problem by monetarist means. That is to say, Volcker and the president believed that the root cause of inflation was a rapid rise in the money supply. They wished to abandon the stop-and-go policies of the 1970s in favor of a constant supply of money. A monetarist experiment seemed justified by the situation. Inflation had risen rapidly in the late 1970s, and when it reached 13.4 percent in 1979, Volcker and the board decided to curb monetary growth, bringing down the money supply by 2.7 percent in 1980 and by 3.3 percent in 1981. The rate of inflation appeared to respond accordingly, falling from a level of 12.4 percent in 1980 to 3.8 percent in 1982. Lower oil and food prices, however, provided an assist. Between 1982 and 1986 the inflation rate averaged 3.3 percent, but in early 1989 it threatened to rise above that level somewhat.[94]

Unfortunately, there also occurred an unanticipated drop in the velocity of money in the early 1980s, and partly for this reason the nation was plunged into the longest and deepest recession since the Great Depression. Unemployment rose from 5.8 percent in 1979 to 9.7 percent in 1982. Between 1980 and 1986 it averaged 7.8 percent, a figure representing about 9 million workers. Not till 1987 did the rate drop back to 6 percent. Loss of output during the recession amounted to an estimated $886 billion. The price was therefore high, and the president was increasingly reluctant to pay it, but the victory was a real one.[95]

Probably the major goal of the administration was reduction in the size of government. In speech after speech Reagan urged the need to "get the government off the backs of the people." Realization of the objective would require two things: substantial reductions in expenditures, and initiatives to roll back government regulation of private business. The former would prove difficult because of the simultaneous need to continue increases in defense spending begun under President Carter, partly in response to an extensive arms buildup by the Soviet Union. To compensate for those increases, which rose from 25.8 percent of the total budget in 1980 to 30.2 percent in 1987, the president induced the Congress to reduce expenditures on domestic programs, which fell during the same interval from 34.8 percent to 32.4 percent of the budget. Most of the reductions occurred during the first two years of the administration, the so-called honeymoon period. After the 1982 elections, when Democrats registered gains in the House and five Republican Senators won by less than 2 percent of the vote, little further erosion took place.[96]

The Reagan administration tried several times to cut back on various aspects of the social security program but achieved only marginal success because of the opposition of both Congress and public opinion. Health and income security payments actually rose between 1980 and 1987, from 16.8 percent of the budget to 18.8 percent, although the rate of increase slowed in comparison with the 1970s. So too did general government and law-enforcement spending levels, the increase between 1980 and 1987, however, being a modest rise from 1.3 percent to 1.5 percent. Other domestic programs such as transportation, agriculture, education, natural resources, and community development fell from 16.8 percent of the federal budget to 12.1 percent between 1980 and 1987.[97]

The Reagan administration continued initiatives taken earlier by Presidents Ford and Carter to deregulate industry. Convinced by numerous economists and others that burdensome and costly regulation was helping to sustain inflation, the Ford administration gained passage of laws deregulating the brokerage industry and repealing federal fair trade laws, besides initiating legislation to reform financial institutions. Not least, it established a Commission on Federal Paperwork. The Carter administration saw the successful passage of laws deregulating trucking, railroads, and the airlines and, in addition, a revision of natural gas legislation that set specific dates for the decontrol of prices. Both presidents believed it important to study the economic impact of regulation to ascertain whether its benefits exceeded its costs.

So too did President Reagan, whose administration deregulated interstate bus lines and succeeded in achieving the passage of legislation accelerating the deregulation of financial institutions and eliminating controls on interest rates paid to savers and checking account customers. The administration also undertook a retrospective analysis of over one hundred regulations of business and industry, with the result that its revisions or eliminations brought savings in regulatory costs estimated at $14 billion a year.[98]

While both the Carter and Reagan administrations saw deregulation as a way to lower costs to consumers by encouraging competition among producers and ease of entry into business, they differed significantly in their attitudes toward Big Business and antitrust. The former focused its antitrust machinery on large firms in major industries, in the process demonstrating its conviction that a high degree of concentration was a proper measure of monopoly behavior, indeed, that the existence of "shared monopoly" should prompt enforcement of the antitrust statutes. During the Reagan years, in contrast, the Justice Department "moved sharply away from the tendency to prosecute primarily on the basis of size of firm, as in the case of mergers, or on levels of concentration, where an industry might be dominated by a few domestic producers." The department made headlines when it abandoned a thirteen-year-old effort—300 lawyers and 66 million pages of record later!—to prosecute International Business Machines (IBM). The decision reflected "the emergence of new meaningful competition across IBM's major product lines." That competition was clearly seen to have been intensely international as well as domestic.[99] Whether the dimensions of international competition will operate in the future to induce the American legal system to encourage firms of large size is a question not only of economic but also of political and social significance for the American democracy.

In the area of what the political scientist Paul Peretz calls consumer regulation, that is to say, regulation protecting the environment and ensuring the safety of products, utilities, and food and drugs—an area in which the purpose of regulation is "to constrain actors in the market system from causing harm to the public"—it is clear that the Reagan administration's actions bespeak the conviction that the costs of the protection far outweigh the benefits. By appointing to the regulatory agencies strong proponents of deregulation such as Mark Fowler (chairman of the Federal Communications Commission) and Ann Gorsuch-Burford (director of the Environmental Protection Agency); by reducing the budgets of the regulatory agencies (by 14 percent between 1980 and 1985, leading to a decline in staffing of around one-sixth); and by relying on "dubious executive orders aimed at reducing the costs to industry of compliance with regulations," the president achieved some successes despite the opposition of the public, public interest groups, and a Democratic House of Representatives. Many of the executive orders, however, were later reversed by the courts.[100]

Although the quality of historical judgments will benefit from the additional evidence and reflection permitted by the passage of time, an interim assessment of the Reagan years—in the nature of what accountants call a trial balance—may even now be made. The president entered the White House with the most far-reaching economic program in half a century. The program called for a lessening of the rate of growth of government expenditures, a progressive reduction in the size of the federal deficit, a scaling back and reform of government regulation, and the containment of inflation.[101] The first three of these objectives represent specific modes of addressing what the president regarded as the central domestic problem of the late twentieth century—Big Government.

His efforts do not appear to have succeeded. Surprisingly, in view of the president's emphasis on free market solutions to economic problems, his administration achieved less in the way of deregulation than Carter's.[102] And despite the substantial cuts made in domestic programs, the expenditures involved affected only about one-third of the budget. Spending rose on social security and Medicare, on national security, and on interest payments on the national debt, and these increases exceeded the reductions in domestic spending. Far from diminishing, the role of government in the economy increased during the Reagan years. It increased at an even faster rate than had occurred in recent earlier administrations. Under the Republican administrations of Nixon and Ford, government expenditures as a percentage of GNP rose from 31.3 percent in 1970 to 33 percent in 1976, and under the Democratic administration of Carter between 1976 and 1980 they actually fell, from 33 percent to 32.6 percent. Under Reagan, a dedicated foe of growth in government, the percentage rose from 32.6 percent in 1980 to 35.3 percent in 1985.[103]

The natural consequence of increased expenditures and lowered taxes was growth in the federal deficit. The Reagan administration managed to double in just eight years a national debt which had taken a century and a half to cumulate to the sum reached by 1981. It is true that the national debt which the Jackson administration actually extinguished in the 1830s was comparatively very small, and that the gross national product, as well as the debt, has grown greatly since then. But it is also true that the national debt hangs like a sword of Damocles over the American economy and society in the closing decade of the twentieth century.

The assignment of relatively low priority to some of the domestic programs may also come back to haunt the American people. Take, for example, the environment. Despite the Reagan administration's relative lack of sympathy for expenditures on behalf of the environment, the fact is that modern industrialization has heightened consciousness in many lands to the environmental consequences of economic growth, namely, to pollution of air by automobiles, factories, electric-power plants, and garbage incinerators; and to pollution of water by chemicals washed into rivers by factories, using it as a coolant, by oil spills which kill marine life and damage property, and by insecticides washed off numerous farms into the national water supply. Concern about the environment is by no means confined to those countries that are relatively rich. In their efforts to raise the living standards of their peoples, developing countries have destroyed millions of acres of forests and invited soil erosion on a vast scale. The fact that planet Earth lost about a quarter of its closed canopy in the twenty years between 1962 and 1982 helps explain why 102 developing countries, including China and Indonesia, had established environmental ministries or similar top-level agencies by the early 1980s.[104] In the United

States the federal government first gave official recognition to the problem of air pollution in 1955, when the Congress enacted legislation authorizing research under federal auspices and technical assistance to the states. The Clean Air Act of 1963 then broadened the federal role by establishing a program of grants to the states to assist them in setting up or maintaining agencies for the control of pollution. Not till 1965, however, did amendments to this act mention the automobile, the largest single source of air pollution, by authorizing the promulgation of federal standards for the control of emissions from cars beginning with model year 1968. Legislation enacted in 1967 strengthened substantially the powers of local, state, and federal authorities and authorized the secretary of the Health, Education, and Welfare Department to enforce air quality standards in designated federally financed regions throughout the country.[105]

Environmental alarums were sounding throughout the country in the 1960s in response to the warnings of the biologist Barry Commoner, the French oceanographer Jacques Cousteau, and others that the damage being done by industrial society might prove irreversible. Popular interest in ecology snapped into focus on April 22, 1970, with the celebration of Earth Day, a day marked by teach-ins, various clean-up projects, and adjournment by Congress to permit its members to address rallies across the nation. The next four years produced the broadest and most expensive environmental legislation in the nation's history. Congress at last established firm deadlines for the reduction of pollutants from automobiles, enacted a comprehensive water pollution control measure aimed at cleaning up the nation's waters by 1985, made petroleum companies liable for the costs of cleaning up oil spills, and acted on a host of other environmental issues, including the banning of hunting from aircrafts, conservation of wildlife, reforestation of national forests, and the creation or expansion of national wilderness, historical, or recreational areas. It even shifted the priorities of President Nixon by appropriating more money for pollution control than he had asked for, and less for defense than he had proposed![106]

It was the high point. At the same time that Congress was churning out environmental legislation in unprecedented volume, a new problem was emerging: shortage of energy. The issue became real for millions of Americans in the winter of 1972–73, when the United states suddenly seemed unable to muster enough fuel to heat its homes and power its factories. "Popeye is running out of cheap spinach," quipped former commerce secretary Peter G. Peterson. Then, between October 1973 and January 1974, the cost of imported "spinach" went up nearly 400 percent as a result of the embargo on oil shipments imposed by the Organization of Petroleum Exporting Countries (OPEC). More and more, it seemed that the solution to the nation's dwindling supply of power might be in conflict with the concerns of environmentalists.[107]

As the first environmental decade came to a close, the race to clean up the country, begun in such earnest on Earth Day 1970, began to slow down. Economic concerns, as well as the problems of energy, were tempering the nation's commitment to a clean environment. Shrinking oil supplies, soaring inflation, slowing economic growth, and rising unemployment were forcing serious consideration of the questions: how clean? how fast? at what cost? In the early 1980s the Reagan administration, as we have seen, gave decisive evidence of its preference for renewed growth over environmental renewal, the Steel Compliance Act of 1981, for example, amending the Clean Air Act to allow steel companies to defer compliance for three years. Whether the rollbacks on environmental and worker-safety regulations, as well as on commitments to improved educational opportunity and to health, housing, and nutrition programs, were justifiable on grounds of the excessive costs of "social luxuries" or, rather, represented foolhardy reductions in the nation's investment in human capital, is one of the great political questions for Americans to confront in the 1990s and beyond.[108]

The answers given that question will go far toward determining the strength and resiliency of American capitalism in the twenty-first century. Healthy and well-educated working men and women are likely to become ever more important sources of the nation's economic well-being. That is because of the increasingly crucial role of scientific, technical, and managerial knowledge in economic growth. Even in the first half of the twentieth century, advances in knowledge contributed an estimated 40 percent of the total rise in income per person employed.[109] In all likelihood, the contribution has risen since then and will continue to do so. For in the second half of the century the American economy began to experience a second Industrial Revolution, a revolution in the organization and processing of information and knowledge.[110]

At the center of this revolution is the electronic digital computer. Unlike the calculator, the computer has a memory, a set of preprogrammed instructions or mathematical rules which it applies automatically to new data introduced at a later time. Like radar, jet aircraft, and other complicated high-technology developments incorporating state-of-the-art scientific knowledge, the electronic computer was a product of governmental need during World War II. The first large electronic digital computer (the ENIAC) was built to enable the army's Ballistic Research Laboratory to calculate trajectories for field artillery and bombing tables, a tedious task previously requiring large numbers of mathematicians using desk calculators. It was an enormous contraption, 100 feet long, 3 feet wide, and 10 feet high, and it contained about 18,000 vacuum tubes. Even though technical improvement was soon forthcoming, computers remained very costly after the war; they were difficult to program, and they were vulnerable to failure because of the dependence of their complex circuitry on vacuum tube technology. Many companies had both the knowledge and the resources to build them, but great uncertainty over the size of the potential market made them reluctant to invest the substantial scientific, technical, and financial resources required if they were to become commercial suppliers of computer systems.

Even the company that was subsequently to dominate the computer market,

International Business Machines (IBM), held back at first. Under the leadership of Thomas J. Watson, Sr., IBM had grown from a small, struggling manufacturer of punch-card products and time-recording equipment in 1914, when cash items amounting to $35,000 were supplemented by less than $200,000 in treasury bonds used as collateral for short-term loans, to a firm whose U.S. revenues in 1949 were approximately $180 million. Watson was certainly interested in electronics; between 1937 and 1944 IBM had sponsored research in the techniques of electromechanical computation and by 1947 had developed and built a partially electronic and partially electromechanical stored-program digital computer. But faced with internal opposition on the part of engineers and executives, with continuing uncertainty over the likelihood of demand for a computer, with technical problems, and with the high profitability of the traditional product line, he hesitated. Perhaps his age—he was seventy-one in 1945—also had something to do with it. At any rate, it was his son, Thomas, Jr., only thirty-six years old in 1950, who eventually authorized the development of a high-performing general-purpose computer (the 701). Shipments began in 1953 at the rate of one a month, a production record unmatched at the time by any other company. Manufactured on an assembly-line basis, the 701 was from ten to one hundred times faster than the ENIAC.

It was also much smaller and cheaper; indeed, it was the first general-purpose computer that did not have to be built in the customer's own computer room. Subsequent machines—both those produced by IBM and those produced by early competitors such as Remington Rand and Burroughs, as well as by later ones such as General Electric, RCA, and Control Data—became still smaller, cheaper, and increasingly versatile as types of uses and users multiplied. Eventually, in the late 1970s Apple, Commodore, and Tandy emerged as leaders among firms manufacturing microcomputers. The technology of the industry had changed dramatically. First transistors, then silicon chips, replaced vacuum tubes. Chips no larger than the head of a thumbtack could hold the equivalent of 100,000 transistors, and work on a far larger integration of circuitry was proceeding apace.

It will be many years before the full impact of computers—on business decision making, the structure of the firm, labor unions and employment, the legal system, the home, the school, learning, leisure, and privacy—can be assessed. Yet it is already clear that its influence in some areas has become very great. The ability to link a personal computer with huge quantities of data stored in a central data base (by means of a modem, or modulation/demodulation device, enabling it to communicate over telephone lines) helped transform information processing into information communication. Both the curricula of hundreds of high schools and colleges and the operations of small businessmen and professionals have been affected. The business office is in the process of being changed radically, not only by the use of "teleconferencing" to save the time and expense of bringing together people from distant places for face-to-face discussions and by use of electronic mail, word processing, and even electronic filing, but also by calling on the computer for routine business functions such as the assembly of financial data and the preparation of quarterly financial and actuarial reports, statistical analyses, and payrolls. The public at large has familiar encounters with the effects of computers at the check-out counters of supermarkets or when making flight reservations, renting an automobile, or buying an insurance policy. In manufacturing, it seems likely that the computer will assist more and more in product design and in the control of welding robots and assembly line equipment.

It is sometimes said that the United States has been entering a postindustrial era since the end of World War II, that it is now best described as an "information economy." If so, this would represent the most recent in a series of fundamental changes in the structure of the American economy. Change was slow at first, certainly relatively so, for agriculture dominated American economic life during its first three centuries. But certainly from 1889 on, the value of manufactured goods regularly exceeded that of agricultural products. From the point of view of national income generated by payments for labor, land, and natural resources, manufacturing continues to be the largest and most conspicuous sector of the economy. But its proportional size has declined somewhat in the years after the Second World War. In contrast, the service industries—trade, transportation, utilities, finance, insurance, real estate, education, health, and government—have increased their share of national income. The provision of information alone, according to a recent calculation, accounted for 46 percent of the net income of the economy in 1967 and for an even large proportion, 53 percent, of all employee income.[111]

Ever since the end of the last great war industries producing goods—namely, agriculture, forestry, fishing, manufacturing, mining, and construction—have employed fewer people than those producing services.[112] In the two decades between 1947 and 1968 employment in services grew ten times as fast and brought about a massive shift from blue-collar work, including farming, to white-collar work, especially in professional, technical, and clerical jobs. Increasingly high levels of educational attainment accompanied these developments. In contrast to the prewar period, high school graduation became common among the young, with rising proportions of both men and women going on to college. The number of bachelor degrees granted doubled between 1966 and 1974, with master's degrees and doctorates increasing at nearly the same rate. As always, some fields of study enjoyed preferred status, law and business schools undergoing extraordinary growth. Engineering fared less well—until the boom in the popularity of computer science in recent years.

Other changes in the industrial distribution and composition of the workforce are no less arresting. The share of state and local governments in employment has doubled in the postwar period. By 1977 those governments were employing one of every seven workers, in contrast to one of fourteen three decades before. The most notable alteration in labor force composition has been the postwar influx of women into the job market, particularly married women with children. In 1978, 41 percent of the workforce consisted of women, nearly half of them less than thirty-five years of age, about one-fourth between sixteen and twenty-four, one in six a college graduate, and over 70 percent high school graduates.

Some of these developments were not unrelated to the decline in industrial unionism in postwar America, for unions have historically been blue-collar phenomena. But it is also true that unions have rarely thrived in the absence of the support of the legal system. Between passage of the Wagner Act in 1935 and the end of World War II union membership made a fourfold gain, but from 1947 to 1970 membership as a proportion of the total nonagricultural workforce remained exactly the same. The Taft-Hartley amendment to the National Labor Relations Act in 1947 reflected a growing belief that the law should protect not only the right of a worker to join a union but also his right to refrain from joining one if he so chose. It was followed by a number of National Labor Relations Board (NLRB) and Supreme Court decisions favoring management's right to "free speech" in opposition to unionism. Encouraged by these rulings to contest NLRB elections, managements made extensive efforts to convince workers to vote against union organization of the workplace. They were often successful, however, because of the growing similarity in personnel practices between organized and nonorganized companies. Many large nonunion firms, for example, paid union level wages and maintained work conditions comparable to those in organized plants.

Unionism in the public sector has fared differently, growing rapidly in states with laws favorable to collective bargaining, and also at the federal level following the issuance of Executive Order 10988 by President Kennedy. The State, County, and Municipal Workers Union is the largest in the AFL-CIO. Public school teachers form one of the most highly organized occupational groups in the nation, and in most cities policemen and firemen negotiate over wages and working conditions. About half of the workers in the federal government are organized. These developments have changed the face of the American labor movement. They have also brought the United States closer to other developed nations, where unionization of government employees has long been practiced. There as well as here, unions in the public sector rely on political rather than economic power to achieve their objectives.

Should business firms do the same? Should they rely on government rather than on the market in their effort to compete with foreign producers? Perhaps the question whether or not such a partnership or alliance should be entered into is the most important issue confronting the American political economy

today. However—if a historian may be permitted to run the risks of prog-
nostication—an alliance might well replace economic competition with political competition, might well politicize all economic decision making, and,
in the words of a former chairman of Citicorp, Walter Wriston, create "an
environment in which a corporation's well-being depends less and less on its
ability to produce a saleable product or service and more and more on its
ability to secure a favorable interpretation of some obscure paragraph in the
Federal Register."[113] Even worse, it might lead to an erosion of the soil of
private ownership and control in which the power of political dissent sinks its
roots.

There is one last consideration, by no means the least. Although the public
sector has played an important part in aiding the historical development of
the American economy, the truth must remain that the overwhelming majority of decisions on what to produce and on how, where, and when to produce
it have been made by private persons and businesses, that is to say, by the
market. The powerful persistence of the nation's democracy is in part cause
and in part effect of that truth. The high standards of living that most of its
people have been able to achieve owe much to it too, which is another way of
saying that the wealth of the nation has been created by its people because
they have been free to work, save, invest, and innovate. But they have been
free to do these things only because they have believed it important that they
be free to do them. In the end, then, the nation's wealth has been the product
of the nation's values, and of the people and institutions in which they are
embodied.

We have come a long way in our survey of the institutions, values, and laws
which have gone into the making of the American economy. Long before
America was a glint in the eye of Columbus, Europeans had worked out
techniques necessary to the conduct of capitalist enterprise, essential to
stretching the width of choice beyond the limitations of subsistence. They
were of course not practiced everywhere at once. Fanning out north and west
from their points of origin in early-fourteenth-century Italy, they slowly transformed ways of thought and behavior, first in Europe, then in America, and
increasingly throughout the world. The process was by no means an automatic
one. Everywhere it required a willingness to take risks, but nowhere was there
a total absence of people willing to take them.

The farm family moving to an unfamiliar environment or trying a new
technique in the one it knew; the businessman or worker with a new idea or
an improvement on an old one; the jurist venturing down a different legal
path to sharpen incentives to invest; the lawmakers of all kinds risking tenure
of office by giving priority to measures designed to entice capital and labor to
their jurisdictions—all partook of the entrepreneurial spirit. And so too did
families who dared the unknown ocean to the west and the perils of the farther

west as the American people loosened their hold on the eastern seaboard and sought a more fruitful life in the interior. It was such as these, enterprisers all, who provided the leaven which gradually lifted the living standards of the average person to heights unknown anywhere in the past.

Can America keep those heights? There are many doubters, and their names are neither Thomas nor Cassandra. Rather, they are patriot voices sounding of pride in who we are, where we have come from, and what we have made. But for all that they are also voices of deep concern: over the fact that it is others who sustain us and not we ourselves; over the fact that we are living beyond our means and laying the bills over for the next generation to pay.

They are concerned over the huge budget deficit and our dependence on foreign borrowing to pay the interest. They are concerned over the decline in personal saving—the rate of which fell in 1986 to only 3.9 percent, the lowest since 1949—and over the reliance on household debt to sustain expenditure levels. Much has been made of the long economic expansion after 1982, too little of the fact that it was fueled by consumption spending financed by debt. In the second quarter of 1986 the ratio of debt to disposable personal income reached a postwar high of 86.2 percent. Finally, they are concerned over the fact that the decline in the national saving rate has made the United States increasingly dependent on net capital inflows to finance *investment*. In 1986 those inflows and the associated buildup of foreign claims on the United States accounted for one-half of net capital formation in this country.[114]

Has America lost its competitive edge? Some economists deny it. They maintain that the deterioration of international cost competitiveness in American manufacturing during the first half of the 1980s was "the result of the real appreciation of the dollar, not sagging productivity growth or excessive wage increases." From the third quarter of 1980 through the first quarter of 1985, they point out, "the real value of the trade weighted dollar appreciated by some 47 percent and the relative price of imports declined by 22 percent."[115] The argument cannot be dismissed. A sharp rise of the dollar did occur, caused mainly by the growing borrowing needs of the federal government.

The strong dollar aggravated America's competitive decline, but one must look elsewhere for the long-term, more fundamental causes of the erosion. Former governor Richard D. Lamm of Colorado maintains that one must look to American society, that it is society itself that is uncompetitive. "The U.S. must make all of its *institutions* more competitive," he writes, "or else lose its place in the new international marketplace."[116] He cites education, for example. The United States has more functional illiterates than any other industrial country. A twelve-nation study of seven subjects, including math, science, reading comprehension, and literature, found the national average comprehensive scores of Americans ranking in the lower third. American students were poorer in math than those of any other nation tested. They tied with Irish students for the lowest average score in civic education among industrialized nations. "Homework in Japan is almost two hours a day, compared to approximately half an hour in the U.S. Japanese students go to school 240 days a year while U.S. students go 180 days a year. By the time a Japanese student graduates from high school, he or she has as much classroom time as an American college student." In its report, *A Nation at Risk,* the National Commission on Excellence said that the United States is committing an "act of unilateral education disarmament" by letting its educational system deteriorate.

The costs of America's extraordinary litigiousness ("two thirds of all the lawyers in the world practice in the United States"); of a health care system which spends more per capita than any other country (yet the United States still ranks fifteenth in life expectancy at birth for males and eighth for females, "The leading causes of premature death in the United States are not the lack of health care, but smoking too much, drinking too much alcohol, not wearing seat belts, and not eating the right foods. We will bring far better health to Americans by seriously addressing these social problems than merely by pouring endless resources into doctors and hospitals"); of a tax system which encourages consumption; and of very high crime rates ("the United States is the most violent and crime-ridden society in the industrialized world") add significantly to the competitive problems of American producers and point to institutional deficiencies of a serious nature. "The wealth of nations is not found in its Dow Jones average; it is in the productivity of its workers, cost of its capital, excellence of its education, cost of its health care, efficiency of its institutions, patterns of its investment, and the viability of its political system." By these standards, Lamm concludes, America is becoming increasingly uncompetitive. What is required is "a major sustained reform of all its institutions." The indictment is a powerful one.

There can be no doubt that the American economy is in a state of relative decline. However, the important word in this sentence, as Paul Kennedy reiterates time and again in his major book *The Rise and Fall of the Great Powers,* is "relative."[117] Because growth rates vary from one country to another, just as they vary from one geographic region, economic sector, or industry to another within any one country, some countries (regions, sectors, industries) are bound to be growing more rapidly than others. The "gross world product," after all, like any nation's gross national product, is only an average of the differential rates of the individual components. And just as the growth rates of individual regions (and economic sectors and industries) have varied over time, so too have the growth rates of nations.

At the end of the Second World War the United States alone accounted for roughly half of the world's manufacturing output. Given the weakened condition of other nations, some of them with plants devastated by the war, that is hardly surprising. It should not be surprising either that the share of countries other than the United States in world manufacturing production should have increased with the postwar recovery. And since this is the case, as we have seen, the *relative* share of the United States naturally declined, to an estimated 31.5 percent by 1980. It is not that Americans produced significantly less in the interval since the war, "except in industries generally declining in the western world," but rather that "others were producing much more." The strength of the United States vis-à-vis the rest of the world in 1945 was "both unprecedented and artificial." And that is "the most important fact in understanding the American relative decline."[118]

But that is not the only fact. The average annual rate of growth in output per capita in the United States in recent years has been significantly lower than those of a number of other countries, most notably West Germany and Japan. There are several reasons for this, and we have already looked at some of them, from tax policies encouraging consumption but not personal saving, to industrial sector complacency with the existing state of things, and a corresponding deemphasis on the importance of research and development to improve conditions. There is an additional reason, and it is an important one: America's defense expenditures were, and remain, larger than those of any other Western country, especially those of Japan.[119] The latter just has more funds free to devote to civilian investment. If this pattern continues, Kennedy suggests, and

> if the Pentagon's spending drains off the majority of the country's scientists and engineers from the design and production of goods for the world market while similar personnel in other countries are primarily engaged in bringing out better products to the civilian consumer, then it seems inevitable that the American share of world manufacturing will steadily decline, and also likely that its economic growth rates will be slower than in those countries dedicated to the marketplace and less eager to channel resources into defense.[120]

The relative economic decline of the United States in recent years is thus a reflection not only of all the factors we have discussed which have reduced its competitiveness in world markets. It is a reflection also of our national priorities. The United States has accumulated over the years a vast array of strategic commitments across the globe. Like other Great Powers in history, from ancient Rome to sixteenth-century Spain and nineteenth-century Great Britain, the nation runs the risk of "imperial overstretch," of an inability, given the relative decline of its economic strength, to defend all its widespread interests and obligations.[121]

The question would therefore appear to be this: which of these strategic commitments are more important to the national security of the United States and its allies than others? Difficult choices will undoubtedly have to be made by the American political system. Among those choices, only dimly perceivable in the distance, may be those made possible by continuing international rapprochement, especially between the United States and the Soviet Union, which would permit a scaling back of the massive expenditures on weapons systems and a devotion of the resources saved to the human needs of peace— to homes for the homeless, food for the hungry, better education and training for the nation's farmers and workers, and a reaching out in compassion to the needy everywhere.

Relative economic decline in the lives of Great Powers is all but inevitable, and with that decline a lessened degree of military, diplomatic, and political influence in the world. Whether the latter should take priority over opportunities to exchange guns for butter and investment is a question which should occupy public attention during the rest of this century and into the next. The historic enterprise of a free people is capable of giving a different meaning to the term *Great Power*.

Abbreviations
Notes
Index

Abbreviations

AER	*American Economic Review*
AH	*Agricultural History*
AHR	*American Historical Review*
AJS	*American Journal of Sociology*
AQ	*American Quarterly*
BHR	*Business History Review*
CLR	*Columbia Law Review*
EDCC	*Economic Development and Cultural Change*
EEH	*Explorations in Economic History*
EHR	*Economic History Review*
EJ	*Economic Journal*
ESQ	*Economic Studies Quarterly*
FA	*Foreign Affairs*
JAH	*Journal of American History*
JEBH	*Journal of Economics and Business History*
JEH	*Journal of Economic History*
JFE	*Journal of Farm Economics*
JIH	*Journal of Interdisciplinary History*
JPE	*Journal of Political Economy*
JSH	*Journal of Social History*
JSoH	*Journal of Southern History*
LH	*Labor History*
MVHR	*Mississippi Valley Historical Review*
NAR	*North American Review*
NEQ	*New England Quarterly*
PAH	*Perspectives in American History*
PMHB	*Pennsylvania Magazine of History and Biography*
PP	*Past and Present*
PSQ	*Political Science Quarterly*
QJE	*Quarterly Journal of Economics*
RES	*Review of Economics and Statistics*

SCB	*Survey of Current Business*
SCSH	*Smith College Studies in History*
SEJ	*Southern Economic Journal*
WMQ	*William and Mary Quarterly*

Notes

1. The Road to Jamestown

1. Edmund S. Morgan, "The Labor Problem at Jamestown, 1607–18," *AHR*, 76 (1971), 595.

2. Ibid., p. 597. On the importance of incentives, see Sigmund Diamond, "From Organization to Society: Virginia in the Seventeenth Century," *AJS*, 63 (1958), 457–475; and idem, "Values as an Obstacle to Economic Growth: The American Colonies," *JEH*, 27 (1967), 561–575.

3. Richard S. Dunn, *Sugar and Slaves: The Rise of the Planter Class in the English West Indies, 1624–1713* (Chapel Hill: University of North Carolina Press, 1972), pp. 9–10, 16–19, 50. According to Lawrence Stone, the "rich and well-born were idle almost by definition" *(Crisis of the Aristocracy* [Oxford: Clarendon Press, 1965], p. 331).

4. Bernard Bailyn, "Politics and Social Structure in Virginia," in *Seventeenth Century America*, ed. James M. Smith (Chapel Hill: University of North Carolina Press, 1959), pp. 98–100.

5. Wesley Frank Craven, *The Colonies in Transition, 1660–1713* (New York: Harper & Row, 1968), p. 175.

6. Stewart Mitchell, ed., *Winthrop Papers*, 5 vols. (Boston: Massachusetts Historical Society, 1947), II, 126 (spelling and punctuation modernized); Darrett B. Rutman, *Winthrop's Boston: Portrait of a Puritan Town, 1630–1649* (Chapel Hill: University of North Carolina Press, 1965), pp. 87–90.

7. David W. Galenson, *White Servitude in Colonial America: An Economic Analysis* (Cambridge: Cambridge University Press, 1981), pp. 34–50.

8. Mildred L. Campbell, *The English Yeoman* (New Haven: Yale University Press, 1942), pp. 104, 220, 73; Lawrence Stone, "Social Mobility in England, 1500–1700," *PP*, 33 (1966), 16–55.

9. Mildred L. Campbell, "Social Origins of Some Early Americans," in Smith, *Seventeenth Century America*, p. 84; Bailyn, "Politics and Social Structure," pp. 98–100.

10. Bureau of the Census, *Historical Statistics of the United States, Colonial Times to 1957* (Washington, D.C.: Government Printing Office, 1966), p. 756; Dunn, *Sugar and Slaves*, pp. 16, 19.

11. J. H. Elliott, *The Old World and the New, 1492–1650* (Cambridge: Cambridge University Press, 1970), pp. 76–77.

12. Bernard Bailyn, *Voyagers to the West: A Passage in the Peopling of America on the Eve of the Revolution* (New York: Alfred A. Knopf, 1986), pp. 199–200.

13. Marc Bloch, *French Rural History: An Essay in Its Basic Characteristics,* trans. Janet Sondheimer from *Les Caractères originaux de l'histoire rurale française* (Berkeley: University of California Press, 1966), pp. 4–5.

14. Karl F. Helleiner, "The Population of Europe from the Black Death to the Eve of the Vital Revolution," in *The Economy of Expanding Europe in the 16th and 17th Centuries,* ed. E. E. Rich and C. H. Wilson, vol. 4 of *The Cambridge Economic History of Europe* (Cambridge: Cambridge University Press, 1967), pp. 5–20; Richard Koebner, "The Settlement and Colonisation of Europe," in *The Agrarian Life of the Middle Ages,* ed. J. H. Clapham and Eileen Power, vol. 1 of *The Cambridge Economic History of Europe* (Cambridge: Cambridge University Press, 1941), pp. 53–56; E. A. Wrigley, *Population and History* (New York: McGraw-Hill, 1969), p. 78; F. L. Ganshof, *Feudalism* (London: Longmans, Green, 1952), p. xv; Douglass C. North and Robert Paul Thomas, *The Rise of the Western World: A New Economic History* (Cambridge: Cambridge University Press, 1973), p. 103.

15. Joseph R. Strayer, "Feudalism in Western Europe," in *Feudalism in History,* ed. R. Coulborn (Princeton: Princeton University Press, 1956), pp. 15–25; Lynn White, Jr., *Medieval Technology and Social Change* (Oxford: Clarendon Press, 1962), pp. 135–136.

16. Ganshof, *Feudalism,* pp. 54–57, 151; for a succinct analysis of the origins and nature of feudalism, see Peter Gay and R. K. Webb, *Modern Europe to 1815* (New York: Harper & Row, 1973), pp. 30–31.

17. Ganshof, *Feudalism,* p. xvii; Gay and Webb, *Modern Europe,* p. 31; J. W. Thompson, *The Middle Ages, 300–1500* (New York: Alfred A. Knopf, 1931), I, 302–303.

18. North and Thomas, *Rise of the Western World,* pp. 11, 26.

19. White, *Medieval Technology,* p. 71.

20. Ibid., pp. 69–71. Fifty acres reclaimed represented one-eighth of the 400 acres already under cultivation.

21. Ibid., p. 41; G. Duby, "La Révolution agricole médievale," *Revue de géographie de Lyon,* 29 (1954), 363.

22. White, *Medieval Technology,* pp. 43–44, 53–54, 57–59, 61–73.

23. North and Thomas, *Rise of the Western World,* p. 26; Michael M. Postan, "The Trade of Medieval Europe: The North," in *Trade and Industry in the Middle Ages,* ed. M. Postan and E. E. Rich, vol. 2 of *The Cambridge Economic History of Europe* (Cambridge: Cambridge University Press, 1952), pp. 157–168.

24. Postan, "Trade of Medieval Europe: North," pp. 171–172.

25. Robert Lopez, "The Trade of Medieval Europe: The South," in Postan and Rich, *Trade and Industry,* p. 295.

26. White, *Medieval Technology,* pp. 77–78.

27. North and Thomas, *Rise of the Western World,* p. 25.

28. Raymond de Roover, "The Development of Accounting Prior to Luca Pacioli According to the Account-Books of Medieval Merchants," in *Studies in the History of*

Accounting, ed. A. C. Littleton and Basil S. Yamey (Homewood, Ill.: Richard D. Irwin, 1956), pp. 159, 165.

29. Lopez, "Trade of Medieval Europe: South," p. 299.

30. Robert-Henri Bautier, *The Economic Development of Medieval Europe* (New York: Harcourt, Brace, Jovanovich, 1971), p. 106.

31. Lopez, "Trade of Medieval Europe: South," pp. 289, 302–303.

32. Ibid., p. 291.

33. Raymond de Roover, "The Commercial Revolution of the Thirteenth Century," in *Enterprise and Secular Change,* ed. Frederick C. Lane and Jelle Riemersma (Homewood, Ill.: Richard D. Irwin, 1953), p. 82.

34. Lopez, "Trade of Medieval Europe: South," p. 291.

35. De Roover, "Commercial Revolution," p. 82.

36. For a standard textbook description of these forms of business organization, see Herbert Heaton, *An Economic History of Europe,* rev. ed. (New York: Harper & Bros., 1948), pp. 165, 170–171. For more on the fairs and on traveling merchants, see Lopez, "Trade of Medieval Europe: South," p. 316, and de Roover, "Commercial Revolution," p. 80.

37. J. A. Houtte, "The Rise and Decline of the Market at Bruges," *EHR,* 37 (April 1966), pp. 29–48; de Roover, "Commercial Revolution," p. 80.

38. Michael M. Postan, "The Rise of a Money Economy," in *Essays in Economic History,* ed. E. M. Carus-Wilson (London: Edward Arnold, 1954), p. 6. For the agricultural innovations, see White, *Medieval Technology,* ch. 3, esp. pp. 128–129.

39. De Roover, "Development of Accounting," p. 116.

40. De Roover makes it clear that the sedentary merchant "relied on partners, agents or correspondents to secure representation abroad" (ibid., p. 123). Lopez says that employees were sometimes sent abroad ("Trade of Medieval Europe: South," p. 335; see also p. 316); North and Thomas, *Rise of the Western World,* p. 55.

41. Lopez, "Trade of Medieval Europe: South," pp. 323, 330.

42. Frederic C. Lane, "Family Partnerships and Joint Ventures in the Venetian Republic," in Lane and Riemersma, *Enterprise and Secular Change,* pp. 93, 97; Stuart Bruchey, *Robert Oliver, Merchant of Baltimore, 1783–1819* (Baltimore: Johns Hopkins Press, 1956), ch. 3.

43. De Roover, "Development of Accounting," p. 120.

44. Raymond de Roover, *L'Evolution de la lettre du change* (Paris: A. Colin, 1953), passim.

45. De Roover, "Development of Accounting," p. 116. De Roover adds that the shift from movement to residency gave rise to a need to record credit transactions and to the use of agency. But could not credit entries continue to be made on scraps of paper, as had long been done for sales at the Champagne fairs? De Roover also suggests that agency may explain the appearance of merchandise accounts (ibid., pp. 116–117).

46. Ibid., pp. 115, 139.

47. De Roover, "Commercial Revolution," p. 81.

48. According to G. E. M. de Ste. Croix, "the Greeks and Romans, far from reaching the advanced stage of accounting at which double-entry becomes possible, thought, and kept their books, mainly in terms of receipts and expenditures rather than debit and credit; and furthermore . . . never even got as far as the habitual

separation of what we should call debit and credit entries by inserting them in two separate columns, let alone on opposite pages of an account." ("Greek and Roman Accounting," in Littleton and Yamey, *History of Accounting*, p. 14).

49. De Roover, "Development of Accounting," passim.

50. Werner Sombart, "Medieval and Modern Commercial Enterprise," in Lane and Riesmersma, *Enterprise and Secular Change*, p. 38.

51. Max Weber, *General Economic History*, trans. Frank H. Knight (New York: Crowell, 1961), pp. 207, 260.

52. Postan, "Trade of Medieval Europe: North," pp. 191–233.

53. Lopez, "Trade of Medieval Europe: South," p. 339; North and Thomas, *Rise of the Western World*, p. 73.

54. Postan, "Trade of Medieval Europe: North," p. 214.

55. C. G. A. Clay, *Economic Expansion and Social Change: England, 1500–1700*, 2 vols., vol. 1, *People, Land and Towns* (Cambridge: Cambridge University Press, 1984), pp. 15–16; Helleiner, "Population of Europe," p. 20; Frank C. Spooner, "The Economy of Europe, 1559–1609," in *The Counter-Reformation and Price Revolution, 1559–1610*, ed. R. B. Wernham, vol. 3 of *The New Cambridge Modern History* (Cambridge: Cambridge University Press, 1968), p. 34; Ralph Davis, *The Rise of the Atlantic Economies* (Ithaca: Cornell University Press, 1973), p. 91.

56. Helleiner, "Population of Europe," p. 31.

57. Quoted in ibid., p. 31.

58. Ibid.

59. Clay, *Economic Expansion and Social Change*, p. 17.

60. E. M. Jope, "Agricultural Implements," in *A History of Technology*, ed. Charles Singer, E. J. Holmyard, A. R. Hall, and Trevor I. Williams, vol. 2, *The Mediterranean Civilizations and the Middle Ages, c. 700 B.S. to c. A.D. 1500* (Oxford: Clarendon Press, 1956), pp. 81–101; Spooner, "The Economy of Europe, 1559–1609," p. 34; D. C. Coleman, "Labour in the English Economy of the Seventeenth Century," in Carus-Wilson, *Essays in Economic History*, II, 291–308; in his introduction to vol. 3 of *The New Cambridge Modern History*, R. B. Wernham observes that "the Men of the late sixteenth-century lacked the technical invention and the scientific advancement to answer the challenges of growing population, rising demand, and rising prices" (p. 11).

61. John U. Nef, "The Progress of Technology and the Growth of Large Scale Industry in Great Britain, 1540–1640," *EHR*, 5 (1934), 4–16.

62. Peter Bowden, "Agricultural Prices, Farm Profits, and Rent," in *The Agrarian History of England and Wales*, ed. Joan Thirsk (Cambridge: Cambridge University Press, 1967), IV, 607–609.

63. Ibid., pp. 598–608; Coleman, "Labour in the English Economy," pp. 299–300.

64. Joan Thirsk, "The Farming Regions of England," in Thirsk, *Agrarian History*, pp. 2–5.

65. Bowden, "Agricultural Prices," pp. 690–695.

66. Joan Thirsk, "Enclosing and Engrossing," in Thirsk, *Agrarian History*, p. 219.

67. Ibid., pp. 232–255.

68. Ibid., pp. 200–201.

69. Eric Kerridge, *The Agricultural Revolution* (London: Allen & Unwin, 1967), pp. 15, 40, 347–348; E. L. Jones, *Agriculture and the Industrial Revolution* (New York: John Wiley, 1974), p. 93; Bowden, "Agricultural Prices," pp. 606–607.

70. Bowden, statistical appendix in Thirsk, *Agrarian History,* tables 1 and 2, pp. 815–828; Joan Thirsk, "Farming Techniques," in ibid., pp. 195–197; and Alan Everitt, "The Marketing of Agricultural Produce," in ibid., pp. 510–511.

71. Bowden, "Agricultural Prices," pp. 599–600.

72. Ibid., pp. 596–597.

73. J. Hurstfield, "Social Structure, Office-Holding and Politics, Chiefly in Western Europe," in *The New Cambridge Modern History,* III, 126–128; Spooner, "The Economy of Europe," in ibid., pp. 14–43; Peter Ramsay, *Tudor Economic Problems* (London: Victor Gollancz, 1965), pp. 14, 113–120, 145; Robert Gray, *A Good Speed to Virginia* (London, 1609), p. 4.

74. F. J. Fisher, "Commercial Trends and Policy in Sixteenth-Century England," *EHR,* 10 (1940), 96–97, 108–109.

75. Ibid., pp. 97–98, 103–104.

76. Ramsay, *Tudor Economic Problems*, pp. 47–69; Robert Brenner, "The Social Basis of English Commercial Expansion, 1550–1650," *JEH,* 32 (1972), 363.

77. Brenner, "Social Basis," pp. 363–364.

78. J. H. Parry, "Colonial Development and International Rivalries Outside Europe," in *The New Cambridge Modern History,* III, 520–524.

79. Ibid., pp. 517, 525–526; J. H. Parry and P. M. Sherlock, *A Short History of the West Indies* (New York: St. Martin's Press, 1956), pp. 27–28, 45.

80. Parry, "Colonial Development and International Rivalries," p. 528.

81. *A Discourse of the Commonweal of This Realm of England, Attributed to Sir Thomas Smith,* ed. Mary Dewar (Charlottesville: University Press of Virginia, 1969), pp. 63, 122–123, 125. For emphasis on the importance of safeguarding and increasing treasure, see also pp. 63–65, 69, 91, 95, 111.

82. Immanuel Wallerstein, *The Modern World System* (New York: Academic Press, 1974), pp. 96, 281, 45.

83. Wesley Frank Craven, *Dissolution of the Virginia Company* (New York: Oxford University Press, 1932), p. 29.

84. Parry, "Colonial Development and International Rivalries," p. 528.

85. Richard Hakluyt, *A Discourse of Western Planting,* ed. Charles Deane (Cambridge: Press of John Wilson & Son, 1877), pp. 19, 36–37 (spelling modernized).

86. Theodore K. Rabb, *Enterprise and Empire: Merchant and Gentry Investment in the Expansion of England, 1575–1630* (Cambridge, Mass.: Harvard University Press, 1967), pp. 41, 60, 66, 90.

87. Brenner, "Social Basis," pp. 376, 375, 380.

2. The Promised Land

1. Curtis P. Nettels, *The Roots of American Civilization* (New York: Appleton-Century-Crofts, 1963), p. 224.

2. W. Stitt Robinson, Jr., *Mother Earth, Land Grants in Virginia, 1607–1699* (Williamsburg: Virginia 350th Anniversary Celebration Corporation, 1957), p. 2.

3. Marshall Harris, *Origin of the Land Tenure System in the United States* (Ames: Iowa State College Press, 1953), pp. 163–164, 166–168.

4. *The Colonial Laws of New York: From the Year 1664 to the Revolution* (Albany, N.Y., 1896), I, 149.

5. Robinson, *Mother Earth*, pp. 32–33.

6. Ibid., pp. 37–42.

7. Harris, *Land Tenure System*, pp. 219, 232–236.

8. Clarence P. Gould, *The Land System in Maryland, 1720–1765*, Johns Hopkins University Studies in Historical and Political Science, series 31, no. 1 (Baltimore: Johns Hopkins Press, 1913), pp. 58, 91.

9. Harris, *Land Tenure System*, pp. 209, 212–214.

10. Robinson, *Mother Earth*, p. 43; Philip A. Bruce, *Economic History of Virginia in the Seventeenth Century* (New York: Macmillan, 1935), pp. 528–532.

11. Robinson, *Mother Earth*, pp. 45–47, 74.

12. Ibid., p. 59.

13. Stuart Bruchey, ed., *The Colonial Merchant: Sources and Readings* (New York: Harcourt, Brace & World, 1966), p. 97.

14. Harris, *Land Tenure System*, pp. 99–100, 106.

15. Sumner Chilton Powell, *Puritan Village: The Formation of a New England Town* (Middletown, Conn.: Wesleyan University Press, 1963), p. 83.

16. Mildred Campbell, *The English Yeoman under Elizabeth and the Early Stuarts* (New Haven: Yale University Press, 1942), pp. 21–26.

17. Bruchey, *Colonial Merchant*, p. 95.

18. Kenneth A. Lockridge, *A New England Town, the First Hundred Years: Dedham, Massachusetts, 1636–1736* (New York: W. W. Norton, 1970), p. 72.

19. Philip J. Greven, Jr., "Family Structure in Seventeenth-Century Andover, Massachusetts," *WMQ*, 23 (1966), 235; idem, *Four Generations: Population, Land and Family in Colonial Andover, Massachusetts* (Ithaca: Cornell University Press, 1970), p. 45.

20. Powell, *Puritan Village*, p. 136.

21. Richard L. Bushman, *From Puritan to Yankee* (Cambridge, Mass.: Harvard University Press, 1967), p. 42.

22. Lockridge, *A New England Town*, p. 71; Greven, "Family Structure," p. 235.

23. Powell, *Puritan Village*, p. 74.

24. Greven, *Four Generations*, pp. 42–44.

25. Lockridge, *A New England Town*, pp. 12, 71.

26. Greven, *Four Generations*, p. 58; Powell, *Puritan Village*, p. 94.

27. Lockridge, *A New England Town*, p. 71; Greven, "Family Structure," p. 235; idem, *Four Generations*, p. 57.

28. Powell, *Puritan Village*, p. 95; Lockridge, *A New England Town*, p. 82; Greven, *Four Generations*, pp. 52–55.

29. Bushman, *From Puritan to Yankee*, p. 41.

30. Richard B. Morris, *Studies in the History of American Law: With Special Reference to the Seventeenth and Eighteenth Centuries*, 2d ed. (New York: Octagon Books, 1964), pp. 77–78.

31. Harry Carman, ed. *American Husbandry* (Port Washington, N.Y.: Kennikat Press, 1964), p. 35; Nettels, *Roots,* pp. 147–150.

32. J. Russell Smith, *North America: Its People and the Resources, Development, and Prospects of the Continent as an Agricultural, Individual, and Commercial Area* (New York: Harcourt, Brace, 1925), pp. 62–64.

33. Carman, *American Husbandry,* pp. 98, 71, 111–119.

34. Ibid., pp. 363–364, 155, 237, 270–271, 273, 335.

35. Quoted in Stevenson W. Fletcher, *Pennsylvania Agriculture and Country Life, 1640–1840* (Harrisburg: Pennsylvania Historical and Museum Commission, 1950), p. 2.

36. Darrett B. Rutman, *Husbandmen of Plymouth: Farms and Villages in the Old Colony, 1620–1692* (Boston: Beacon Press, 1967), p. 42; Charles F. Carroll, *The Timber Economy of Puritan New England* (Providence: Brown University Press, 1973), p. 59.

37. Rutman, *Husbandmen of Plymouth,* p. 42.

38. Everett E. Edwards, "American Agriculture—The First 300 Years," in *USDA Yearbook of Agriculture, 1940: Farmers in a Changing World* (Washington, D.C.: Government Printing Office, 1940), p. 174.

39. Lewis C. Gray, *History of Agriculture in the Southern United States to 1860* (Washington, D.C.: Carnegie Institute, 1933), I, 27.

40. Edwards, "American Agriculture," p. 174.

41. Rutman, *Husbandmen of Plymouth,* pp. 11, 43–46; Gray, *Agriculture in the Southern United States,* p. 27; Percy Wells Bidwell and John I. Falconer, *History of Agriculture in the Northern United States, 1620–1860* (Washington, D.C.: Carnegie Institute, 1925), pp. 34–35.

42. Gray, *Agriculture in the Southern United States,* pp. 215–216.

43. Avery O. Craven, *Soil Exhaustion in Virginia and Maryland, 1606–1860* (Urbana: University of Illinois Press, 1925), pp. 34–35.

44. Aubrey C. Land, "The Tobacco Staple and the Planter's Problems: Technology, Labor and Crops," *AH,* 43 (1969), 80; Gloria L. Main, *Tobacco Colony: Life in Early Maryland, 1650–1720* (Princeton: Princeton University Press, 1982), pp. 76–77.

45. Robert R. Walcott, "Husbandry in Colonial New England," *NEQ,* 9 (1936), 218–252; Craven, *Soil Exhaustion,* p. 34.

46. Rutman, *Husbandmen of Plymouth,* p. 34.

47. Fletcher, *Pennsylvania Agriculture,* pp. 89–91.

48. Aubrey C. Land, "Economic Base and Social Structure: The Northern Chesapeake in the Eighteenth Century," *JEH,* 25 (1965), 642; idem, "Tobacco Staple," p. 74; Main, *Tobacco Colony,* pp. 76–77.

49. Carman, *American Husbandry,* p. 249.

50. James T. Lemon, *The Best Poor Man's Country* (Baltimore: Johns Hopkins University Press, 1972), p. 208.

51. Nettels, *Roots,* p. 236.

52. Craven, *Soil Exhaustion,* p. 22.

53. Richard B. Morris, *Government and Labor in Early America* (New York: Columbia University Press, 1946), p. 45.

54. Carman, *American Husbandry*, p. 54.

55. Abbott Emerson Smith, *Colonists in Bondage: White Servitude and Convict Labor in America, 1607–1776* (Chapel Hill: University of North Carolina Press, 1947), p. 337; Winthrop D. Jordan, *White over Black* (Chapel Hill: University of North Carolina Press, 1968), p. 66.

56. Rutman, *Husbandmen of Plymouth*, pp. 49–52; Nettels, *Roots*, p. 236.

57. Walcott, "Husbandry in Colonial New England," pp. 250–251.

58. Quoted in Bidwell and Falconer, *Agriculture in the Northern United States*, p. 116.

59. Lemon, *Best Poor Man's Country*, pp. 29, 233, 125, 154.

60. Edmund S. Morgan, *American Slavery, American Freedom: The Ordeal of Colonial Virginia* (New York: W. W. Norton, 1975), pp. 106–107.

61. Smith, *Colonists in Bondage*, pp. 16, 336.

62. Russell R. Menard, *Economy and Society in Early Colonial Maryland* (New York and London: Garland, 1985), pp. 244–261; Edwin J. Perkins, *The Economy of Colonial America* (New York: Columbia University Press, 1980), p. 72; David W. Galenson, *White Servitude in Colonial America* (Cambridge: Cambridge University Press, 1981), p. 153; Gavin Wright, *The Political Economy of the Cotton South* (New York: W. W. Norton, 1978), p. 11.

63. James B. Hedges, *The Browns of Providence Plantations: Colonial Years* (Cambridge, Mass.: Harvard University Press, 1952), ch. 4, esp. pp. 75–80.

64. Jordan, *White over Black*, pp. 80, 101, 104–106, 322–323.

65. Morris, *Government and Labor*, p. 482.

66. Morgan, *American Slavery, American Freedom*, ch. 8.

67. Land, "The Tobacco Staple," pp. 73, 79.

68. Peter Coclanis, "Economy and Society in Colonial Charleston: The Early Years, 1670 to 1719" (Ph.D. diss., Columbia University, 1983), pp. 32, 36, 39, 40.

69. Jared Eliot, *Essays upon Field Husbandry in New England, and Other Papers, 1748–1762*, ed. Harry J. Carman and Rexford G. Tugwell (New York: Columbia University Press, 1934), p. 137.

70. Carman, *American Husbandry*, p. 123.

71. Bidwell and Falconer, *Agriculture in the Northern United States*, pp. 84, 115–121.

72. Ibid., pp. 458–459.

73. Carman, *American Husbandry*, pp. 112–113.

74. Eliot, *Field Husbandry*, p. 9; Bidwell and Falconer, *Agriculture in the Northern United States*, pp. 70, 458.

75. Carman, *American Husbandry*, pp. 93, 315.

76. Craven, *Soil Exhaustion*, p. 21.

77. Bidwell and Falconer, *Agriculture in the Northern United States*, p. 84.

78. Lemon, *Best Poor Man's Country*, p. 223.

79. Gray, *Agriculture in the Southern United States*, p. 466.

80. Craven, *Soil Exhaustion*, p. 56.

81. Walcott, "Husbandry in Colonial New England," p. 224; Carroll, *Timber Economy*, p. 125.

82. Fletcher, *Pennsylvania Agriculture*, p. 3.

83. Carroll, *Timber Economy*, pp. 126–127.

84. Gray, *Agriculture in the Southern United States*, p. 446.

85. Rutman, *Husbandmen of Plymouth*, p. 17.

86. Fletcher, *Pennsylvania Agriculture*, pp. 127–130.

87. Carman, *American Husbandry*, p. 113.

88. Lemon, *Best Poor Man's Country*, p. 154.

89. Bidwell and Falconer, *Agriculture in the Northern United States*, p. 101; Rutman, *Husbandmen of Plymouth*, pp. 52–53.

90. Bidwell and Falconer, *Agriculture in the Northern United States*, p. 119.

91. Craven, *Soil Exhaustion*, pp. 158–159; see also pp. 20, 36.

92. Carole Shammas, "How Self-Sufficient Was Early America?" *JIH*, 13 (1982), 247–272; Winifred B. Rothenberg, "The Market and Massachusetts Farmers, 1750–1855," *JEH*, 41 (1981), 3100–12.

93. Lemon, *Best Poor Man's Country*, pp. 150–151, 220; Lockridge, *A New England Town*, pp. 69–70.

94. James A. Henretta, "Families and Farms: Mentalite in Pre-Industrial America," *WMQ*, 3d ser., 35 (1978), 3–32.

95. Main, *Tobacco Colony*, pp. 54, 62, 167–168.

96. Land, "Economic Base and Social Structure," pp. 642–643.

97. Lemon, *Best Poor Man's Country*, p. 219.

98. Greven, *Four Generations*, p. 225.

99. Lockridge, *A New England Town*, pp. 69–70.

100. Bernard Bailyn, *The New England Merchants in the Seventeenth Century* (Cambridge, Mass.: Harvard University Press, 1955), pp. 81–82, 95–96.

101. Carroll, *Timber Economy*, p. 75.

102. *Winthrop's Journal, "History of New England," 1630–1649*, ed. James K. Hosmer, 2 vols. (New York: Charles Scribner's Sons, 1908), II, 6.

103. Carroll, *Timber Economy*, p. 75.

104. Ibid., p. 76; Bailyn, *New England Merchants*, pp. 65–69, 71.

105. Bailyn, *New England Merchants*, pp. 26–27, 55–59, 71.

106. Carroll, *Timber Economy*, pp. 70, 110, 84–85.

107. Curtis P. Nettels, *The Money Supply of the American Colonies before 1720* (Madison: University of Wisconsin Press, 1934), pp. 101–103; Bernard Bailyn and Lotte Bailyn, *Massachusetts Shipping, 1697–1714: A Statistical Study* (Cambridge, Mass.: Harvard University Press, 1959), p. 21; Carl Bridenbaugh, *Cities in the Wilderness: The First Century of Urban Life in America* (New York: Alfred A. Knopf, 1955), pp. 6, 143.

108. Nettels, *Money Supply*, pp. 102–103; Bailyn and Bailyn, *Massachusetts Shipping*, pp. 78–79; Bruchey, *Colonial Merchant*, p. 11.

109. Carroll, *Timber Economy*, pp. 77–78, 87–91.

110. Ibid., pp. 80–81.

111. Ibid., pp. 81–82; Richard S. Dunn, *Sugar and Slaves: The Rise of the Planter Class in the English West Indies, 1624–1713* (Chapel Hill: University of North Carolina Press, 1972), pp. 59–67, 51–52.

112. Jordan, *White over Black*, p. 67.

113. Carroll, *Timber Economy*, pp. 83–84.

114. Ibid., pp. 84–85, 87, 90; Bailyn and Bailyn, *Massachusetts Shipping,* p. 130.

115. Carroll, *Timber Economy,* pp. 87, 85–86, 89.

116. Ibid., pp. 87–89.

117. Ibid., p. 89.

118. Ibid., pp. 87, 142.

119. Bruchey, *Colonial Merchant,* p. 12; Dunn, *Sugar and Slaves,* pp. 111–116; Carroll, *Timber Economy,* p. 90.

120. Carroll, *Timber Economy,* p. 90.

121. Nettles, *Money Supply,* pp. 171, 175, 276–277.

122. James A. Henretta, "Economic Development and Social Structure in Colonial Boston," *WMQ,* 22 (1965), 78–79.

123. Bruchey, *Colonial Merchant,* p. 129.

124. Main, *Tobacco Colony,* pp. 87–91, ch. 6, and p. 125; Land, "Economic Base and Social Structure," p. 646; idem, "The Tobacco Staple," p. 71.

3. A Growing People

1. Alice Hanson Jones, *Wealth of a Nation to Be: The American Colonies on the Eve of the Revolution* (New York: Columbia University Press, 1980), pp. 34–37.

2. I use the rate of £1 equals ca. $54, which Jones, *Wealth,* uses by implication on p. 55.

3. Jones, *Wealth,* pp. 97–100, 129.

4. James Potter, "The Growth of Population in America, 1700–1860," in *Population in History,* ed. D. V. Glass and D. E. C. Eversley (London: Edward Arnold, 1965), pp. 631–632.

5. Ibid., pp. 639–640. The estimates were prepared by the chief clerk of the Census Bureau, W. S. Rossiter, and appear in W. S. Rossiter, *A Century of Population Growth* (Washington, D.C.: Bureau of the Census, 1909), pp. 9–11. The percentages are those worked out by Potter, "Growth of Population," pp. 638–639. For the form in which the table is presented, I am indebted to W. Elliott Brownlee, *Dynamics of Ascent: A History of the American Economy* (New York: Alfred A. Knopf, 1974), p. 46.

6. Potter, "Growth of Population," p. 642; Philip D. Curtin, *The Atlantic Slave Trade: A Census* (Madison: University of Wisconsin Press, 1969), pp. 72–75.

7. Potter, "Growth of Population," p. 644; Daniel Scott Smith, "The Demographic History of Colonial New England," *JEH,* 32 (1972), 165.

8. James T. Shepherd and Gary M. Walton, *Shipping, Maritime Trade, and the Economic Development of Colonial North America* (Cambridge: Cambridge University Press, 1972), p. 35; Max Savelle and Robert Middlekauff, *A History of Colonial America,* rev. ed. (New York: Holt, Rinehart & Winston, 1964), p. 453.

9. Potter, "Growth of Population," pp. 645–646.

10. James M. Cassedy, *Demography in Early America* (Cambridge, Mass.: Harvard University Press, 1969), p. 153.

11. Kenneth A. Lockridge, "The Population of Dedham, Massachusetts, 1636–1736," *EHR,* 10 (1965), 319; Maris A. Vinovskis, "Mortality Rates and Trends in Massachusetts before 1860," *JEH,* 32 (1972), 185–190.

12. Cassedy, *Demography in Early America,* p. 124; Smith, "Demographic History," p. 176.

13. Vinovskis, "Mortality Rates," p. 196.

14. Potter, "Growth of Population," p. 646; Brownlee, *Dynamics of Ascent,* pp. 45–46.

15. Arthur W. Calhoun, *A Social History of the American Family* (New York: Barnes & Noble, 1945), p. 87.

16. Brownlee, *Dynamics of Ascent,* pp. 44–46; Robert Higgs and H. Louis Stettler III, "Colonial New England Demography: A Sampling Approach," *WMQ,* 27 (1970), 285–291.

17. Potter, "Growth of Population," p. 660, 646; Brownlee, *Dynamics of Ascent,* p. 46; Cassedy, *Demography in Early America,* pp. 121–122, 140, 142, 104.

18. Philip J. Greven, Jr., *Four Generations: Population, Land, and Family in Colonial Andover, Massachusetts* (Ithaca: Cornell University Press, 1970), pp. 269–272.

19. Lockridge, "Population of Dedham," p. 328.

20. Potter, "Growth of Population," p. 663.

21. Brownlee, *Dynamics of Ascent,* pp. 46–47.

22. Higgs and Stettler, "Colonial New England Demography," p. 288.

23. Potter, "Growth of Population," pp. 660, 649.

24. Higgs and Stettler, "Colonial New England Demography," p. 286.

25. Brownlee, *Dynamics of Ascent,* pp. 45–46.

26. Smith, "Demographic History," p. 171; Potter, "Growth of Population," p. 648; Cassedy, *Demography in Early America,* pp. 40, 156.

27. Potter, "Growth of Population," pp. 640, 652, 661.

28. David Galenson, *White Servitude in Colonial America* (Cambridge: Cambridge University Press, 1968), p. 63.

29. Potter, "Growth of Population," p. 641.

30. According to Philip Curtin, by the end of the eighteenth century North American slave populations were reproducing at nearly the same rate as that of the settler populations in Europe; the implication is that the rate of natural increase was even lower before this (*Atlantic Slave Trade,* p. 73).

31. Potter, "Growth of Population," pp. 638–641; Jones, *Wealth* p. 104.

32. Harry R. Merrens, *Colonial North Carolina in the 18th Century* (Chapel Hill: University of North Carolina Press, 1964), pp. 122–123.

33. Ibid., p. 125.

34. Leilla Sellers, *Charleston Business on the Eve of the American Revolution* (Chapel Hill: University of North Carolina Press, 1934), p. 53.

35. Merrens, *Colonial North Carolina,* pp. 89–90, 125–126.

36. Jacob M. Price, "Economic Function and the Growth of American Port Towns in the 18th Century," *PAH,* 8 (1974), 163; Bureau of the Census, *Historical Statistics of the United States, Colonial Times to 1957* (Washington, D.C.: Government Printing Office, 1966), p. 761.

37. Lewis C. Gray, *History of Agriculture in the Southern United States to 1860* (New York: Peter Smith, 1941), I, 275.

38. Russell R. Menard, "Secular Trends in the Chesapeake Tobacco Industry," *Working Papers from the Regional Economic History Research Center,* 1 (1978), 1–35.

39. Charles M. Andrews, *The Colonial Period of American History* (New Haven: Yale University Press, 1938), IV, 85–89; Jacob M. Price, *France and the Chesapeake*

(Ann Arbor: University of Michigan Press, 1973), I, 591, xviii; *Historical Statistics to 1957*, p. 766.

40. Price, *France and the Chesapeake*, pp. 509, 664; Jacob M. Price, "The Economic Growth of the Chesapeake and the European Market, 1697–1775," *JEH*, 24 (1964), 498–508.

41. An alternative system was of great antiquity but "of least importance for the tobacco trade," namely, sales by planters to independent merchant residents of the Chesapeake. Men of meager capital, they preferred using their limited resources in the West Indian and southern European trades; Price, *France and the Chesapeake*, p. 661.

42. Price, "Economic Growth of the Chesapeake," pp. 507–509.

43. Price explains the mechanism as follows: "The availability of . . . credit diminished the need for savings for disaster, permitted the expenditure of scarce cash for the purchase of slaves as well as the diversion of labor from subsistence to market activities" (*France and the Chesapeake*, pp. 662–663); ibid., pp. 665–666; idem, "Economic growth of the Chesapeake," pp. 508–509. See also idem, "The Rise of Glascow in the Chesapeake Tobacco Trade, 1707–75," *WMQ*, 1 (1954), 198.

44. James H. Soltow, "Scottish Traders in Virginia, 1750–75," *EHR*, 12 (1959), 85–86; Price, "Economic Growth of the Chesapeake," p. 509.

45. Price, *France and the Chesapeake*, pp. 662–663; Gary M. Walton, "Sources of Productivity Change in American Colonial Shipping, 1675–1775," *EHR*, 20 (1967), 74–76.

46. Converse D. Clowse, *Economic Beginnings in Colonial South Carolina, 1670–1730* (Columbia: University of South Carolina Press, 1971), pp. 63, 121, 125, 130–132; Gray, *Agriculture in the Southern United States*, pp. 277–279.

47. Merrens, *Colonial North Carolina*, pp. 125–129.

48. Gray, *Agriculture in the Southern United States*, p. 289; *Historical Statistics*, pp. 762, 769; William Range, "The Agricultural Revolution in Royal Georgia, 1752–1775," *AH*, 21 (1947), 250–253.

49. Gray, *Agriculture in the Southern United States*, p. 283.

50. Clowse, *Economic Beginnings*, pp. 123, 139, 243–244; *Historical Statistics to 1957*, pp. 761, 768.

51. Clowse, *Economic Beginnings*, pp. 132–134, 174–175; Merrens, *Colonial North Carolina*, p. 86; exports from Charleston of tar, pitch, and turpentine from 1725 to 1774 are given in *Historical Statistics to 1957*, p. 770. Brief discussion of naval stores, despite the relatively small value of exports, is presented because of the relation of slave labor to production.

52. Shepherd and Walton, *Shipping, Maritime Trade*, pp. 39, 100; in 1772 total exports from the southern colonies were as follows: North Carolina, 1,304 lb; Virginia and Maryland, 2,423 lb; South Carolina and Georgia, 770,000 lb (Merrens, *Colonial North Carolina*, p. 127, table 13).

53. Shepherd and Walton, *Shipping, Maritime Trade*, p. 96. A typographical error appears in the sentence "Exports to Great Britian were valued at more than those *from* all other regions combined." The context makes it clear that the word should be *to* instead of *from*.

54. Price, "American Port Towns," pp. 163–164, 173.

55. Price, "American Port Towns," pp. 164–165. See also Stuart Bruchey, ed., *The Colonial Merchant: Sources and Readings* (New York: Harcourt, Brace & World, 1966), pt. 3, "The Southern Staple Trade."

56. Price, "American Port Towns," p. 167.

57. Ibid., p. 172.

58. Ibid.

59. David Klingaman, "The Significance of Grain in the Development of the Tobacco Colonies," *JEH*, 29 (1969), 269.

60. Price, "American Port Towns," pp. 165, 176.

61. Ibid., pp. 162–163, 176.

62. Sellers, *Charleston Business*, pp. 58, 62, 83.

63. Shepherd and Walton, *Shipping, Maritime Trade*, pp. 96–97.

64. Max. G. Schumacher, *The Northern Farmer and His Markets during the Late Colonial Period* (New York: Arno Press, 1975), p. 122.

65. Shepherd and Walton, *Shipping, Maritime Trade*, pp. 96–97.

66. Quoted in Lowell Joseph Ragatz, *The Fall of the Planter Class in the British Caribbean, 1763–1833* (New York: Octagon Books, 1963), p. 88.

67. B. R. Mitchell and Phyllis Deane, *Abstract of British Historical Statistics* (Cambridge: Cambridge University Press, 1962), pp. 285–286.

68. Shepherd and Walton, *Shipping, Maritime Trade*, pp. 41, 94, 96, 98–99, 170–171, 211–227; Schumacher, *Northern Farmer*, pp. 158, 161, 128–129; wood products from all three regions were also of some importance, as were spermaceti candles from New England.

69. Schumacher, *Northern Farmer*, pp. 123–128; Shepherd and Walton, *Shipping, Maritime Trade*, pp. 25, 98; Arthur L. Jensen, *The Maritime Commerce of Colonial Philadelphia* (Madison: University of Wisconsin Press, 1963), p. 91. See also William S. Sacks, "Agricultural Conditions in the Northern Colonies before the Revolution," *JEH*, 12 (1953), 284–285.

70. Schumacher, *Northern Farmer*, p. 143.

71. James T. Lemon, *The Best Poor Man's Country* (Baltimore: Johns Hopkins University Press, 1972), p. 205; Charles Kuhlmann, *The Development of the Flour Milling Industry in the United States* (Boston: Houghton Mifflin, 1929), pp. 33–34.

72. These counties were Philadelphia, Bucks, Berks, Northhampton, and the eastern and northern parts of Chester and Lancaster. Mary Alice Hanna, "Trade of the Delaware District before the Revolution," *SCSH*, 2, no. 4 (1917), 242–248.

73. Jensen, *Maritime Commerce*, pp. 7–8.

74. Hanna, "Trade of the Delaware District," p. 244; Kuhlmann, *Flour Milling Industry*, pp. 15–17.

75. Schumacher, *Northern Farmer*, p. 127, introduction.

76. Lemon, *Best Poor Man's Country*, pp. 154, 182, 223.

77. Duane Ball and Gary M. Walton, "Eighteenth Century Agricultural Productivity Change in the Middle Atlantic Region" (Mimeograph, August 1975), p. 18.

78. Schumacher, *Northern Farmer*, p. 139.

79. Ibid., pp. 131, 144.

80. Shepherd and Walton, *Shipping, Maritime Trade*, pp. 101, 94–95, 211–227, 116.

81. Jacob Price, "A Note on the Value of Colonial Exports of Shipping," *JEH,* 36 (1976), 721.

82. Shepherd and Walton, *Shipping, Maritime Trade,* pp. 117–136, 156–157.

83. Ibid., p. 152. Although the British standing army in the colonies was considerably smaller in the first half of the eighteenth century, there is no indication that naval protection was less. Therefore sterling earned from British expenditures for civil and defense purposes may well have constituted "about the same percentage of total trade over most of the 18th century. Furthermore, the official values (for trade) suggest relatively small deficits with England for earlier years" (ibid., pp. 154–155). In fact, during thirty-one of the forty-six years between 1700 and 1745, the value of colonial exports to Great Britain exceeded the value of imports (*Historical Statistics to 1957,* p. 757).

84. Richard A. Lester, *Monetary Experiments: Early American and Recent Scandinavian* (New York: Augustus M. Kelley, 1939), pp. 17, 25, 29–30. Franklin defended the colonies' use of paper money by telling the British Parliament that "if the inhabitants of those countries are glad to have the use of paper among themselves, that they may thereby be enabled to spare, for remittances hither, the gold and silver they obtain by their commerce with foreigners, one would expect that no objection against their parting with it could arise here, in the country that receives it." According to Lester, in the early nineteenth century Ricardo also agreed with Franklin on the advantages of paper money: "The introduction of the precious metals for the purpose of money may with truth be considered one of the most important steps toward the improvement of commerce and the arts of civilized life; but it is not less true that, with the advancement of knowledge and science, we discovered that it would be another improvement to banish them again from the employment to which, during a less enlightened period, they had been so advantageously applied." Modern economists also agree.

85. Leslie V. Brock, *The Currency of the American Colonies, 1700–64* (New York: Arno Press, 1975), p. 4; Lester, *Monetary Experiments,* p. 18.

86. Oliver P. Chitwood, *A History of Colonial America* (New York: Harper & Bros., 1961), p. 403; Brock, *Currency of American Colonies,* p. 5–7; Curtis P. Nettels, *The Money Supply of the Colonies before 1720* (Madison: University of Wisconsin Press, 1934), p. 180.

87. Lester, *Monetary Experiment,* p. 18.

88. Brock, *Currency of American Colonies,* p. 8; Lester, *Monetary Experiments,* p. 20; Ross M. Robertson, *History of the American Economy,* 3d ed. (New York: Harcourt Brace Jovanovich, 1973), pp. 76–77.

89. Nettels, *Money Supply,* pp. 162–181, 229–249.

90. Brock, *Currency of American Colonies,* pp. 10–14.

91. Ibid., p. 17.

92. Lester, *Monetary Experiments,* p. 46; E. James Ferguson, *The Power of the Purse* (Chapel Hill: University of North Carolina Press, 1961), p. 24.

93. Ferguson, *Power of the Purse,* pp. 5–7.

94. Brock, *Currency of American Colonies,* pp. 18–20.

95. Richard A. Lester, "Currency Issues to Overcome Depression in Delaware, New Jersey, New York, and Maryland, 1715–1737," *JPE,* 47 (1939), 215. See also

idem, "Currency Issues to Overcome Depression in Pennsylvania, 1723–29," *JPE*, 46 (1938), 324–375.

96. Joseph Albert Ernst, *Money and Politics in America, 1755–1775: A Study in the Currency Act of 1764 and the Political Economy of Revolution* (Chapel Hill: University of North Carolina Press, 1973), ch. 1, esp. pp. 8–10.

97. Ferguson, *Power of the Purse*, pp. 5–6.

98. Lester, "Currency Issues to Overcome Depression in Pennsylvania," p. 325.

99. Ferguson, *Power of the Purse*, p. 7.

100. Brock, *Currency of American Colonies*, p. 8.

101. Ferguson, *Power of the Purse*, p. 8.

102. Ibid., p. 9; Lester, *Monetary Experiments*, pp. 27–28, 31; Nettels, *Money Supply*, p. 277.

103. Brock, *Currency of American Colonies*, pp. 95, 557.

104. Whatever the relative volume of Boston's transactions, the specie imported by Massachusetts merchants was sufficiently large to enable the province to do what no other colony did, namely, to adopt a specie-backed paper (in 1751) and to place its reliance therefore on voluntary loans. Ferguson attributes Massachusetts' ability to do so in part to a "pecuniary zeal," "always more exacting" fiscal administrations than in other colonies.

105. Lester, *Monetary Experiment*, p. 27.

106. Ferguson, *Power of the Purse*, pp. 13–14; Brock, *Currency of American Colonies*, pp. 99–100.

107. Brock, *Currency of American Colonies*, pp. 466–476.

108. See also Roger Weiss, "The Issue of Paper Money in the American Colonies, 1720–74," *JEH*, 30 (1970), 770–783.

109. Isaac Weld, Jr., *Travels through the States of North America during the Years 1795–97* (London: John Stockdale, 1799), I, 53.

110. Price, "American Port Towns," appendix C. "In his recent study of the New England merchant, Bernard Bailyn has pointed out that they shared the aversion of Philadelphia merchants to selling goods on commission for English merchants and aspired to conduct this trade on their own account. New York merchants presumably had the same attitude. This method of conducting the English trade in the northern colonies is in sharp contrast to the pattern in Virginia and Maryland where the imports of dry goods were handled mostly through resident Scots factors" (Jensen, *Maritime Commerce*, pp. 97–98).

111. Sellers, *Charleston Business*, pp. 102–104.

112. Glenn Weaver, *Jonathan Trumbull, Connecticut Merchant Magistrate, 1710–1785* (Hartford: Connecticut Historical Society, 1956), pp. 11–20; Chitwood, *History of Colonial America*, p. 404.

113. "Journal of Col. John May, of Boston, Relative to a Journey to the Ohio Country, 1789," *PMHB*, 45 (1921), 144.

114. Jensen, *Maritime Commerce*, p. 89, takes for granted that the trade of Pennsylvania was that of Philadelphia. James F. Shepherd and Samuel H. Williamson, "The Coastal Trade of the British North American Colonies, 1768–72," *JEH*, 32 (1972), 797–801.

115. *Historical Statistics*, p. 757.

116. Virginia D. Harrington, *The New York Merchant on the Eve of the Revolution* (Gloucester, Mass.: Peter Smith, 1964), pp. 200, 189–190.

117. Jensen, *Maritime Commerce,* p. 43

118. James A. Henretta, *The Evolution of American Society, 1700–1815: An Interdisciplinary Analysis* (Lexington, Mass.: D. C. Heath, 1973), pp. 78–79.

119. Jones, *Wealth,* pp. 50, 129.

120. Ibid., pp. 129, 51–53, 109.

121. Ibid., pp. 22–25.

122. Ibid., pp. 90, 96–97.

123. Thomas Jefferson to Arthur Young, quoted in Avery O. Craven, *Soil Exhaustion as a Factor in the Agricultural History of Virginia and Maryland, 1606–1860* (Urbana: University of Illinois Press, 1925), p. 34.

124. Terry L. Anderson, *The Economic Growth of 17th Century New England: A Measurement of Regional Income* (New York: Arno Press, 1975). See also idem, "Economic Growth in the Colonies of New England: Statistical Renaissance," *JEH,* 39 (1979), 243–257. See also Terry L. Anderson and Robert P. Thomas, "White Population, Labor Force, and Extensive Growth of the New England Economy in the 17th Century," *JEH,* 33 (1973), 634–661.

125. Gloria L. Main and Jackson T. Main, "Economic Growth and the Standard of Living in Southern New England, 1640–1774," *JEH,* 48 (1988), 27–46.

126. Menard, "Secular Trends," pp. 1–34.

127. Alan Kulikoff, "The Economic Growth of the 18th Century Chesapeake Colonies," *JEH,* 39 (1979), 275–288.

128. Lois Green Carr and Lorena S. Walsh, "Changing Life Styles in Colonial St. Mary's County," *Working Papers from the Regional Economic History Research Center,* 1 (1978), 73–118.

129. Gloria L. Main, "Personal Wealth in Colonial America: Explorations of Probate Records of Maryland and Massachusetts, 1650–1720" (Ph.D. diss., Columbia University, 1972).

130. Marc Egnal, "The Development of the 13 Continental Colonies, 1720–1775," *WMQ,* 32 (1975), 191–222.

131. Jones, *Wealth,* p. 78.

132. Robert Gallman, "The Pace and Pattern of American Economic Growth," in *American Economic Growth,* ed. Lance Davis, Richard Easterlin, and William Parker (New York: Harper & Row, 1972), pp. 15–60.

133. Thomas J. Wertenbaker, *The Planters of Colonial Virginia* (Princeton: Princeton University Press, 1922), pp. 158–159.

134. Jones, *Wealth,* p. 162.

135. Main and Main, "Economic Growth and the Standard of Living," pp. 27–46, esp. pp. 29, 39, 41–42. See also p. 29n6 for "some of the more important" work on the "consumer revolution."

136. Jackson Turner Main, *The Social Structure of Revolutionary America* (Princeton: Princeton University Press, 1965), pp. 7–8, 18, 17, 20.

137. Ibid., pp. 25, 31–32, 34.

138. Ibid., pp. 34–38.

139. Gary B. Nash, *The Urban Crucible: Social Change, Political Conciousness, and*

the Origins of the American Revolution (Cambridge, Mass.: Harvard University Press, 1979), p. 257. See also Gary B. Nash, ed., *Class and Society in Early America* (Englewood Cliffs, N.J.: Prentice-Hall, 1970), passim.

140. Main, *Social Structure,* pp. 41–42.

141. Nash, *Urban Crucible,* p. ix.

142. James T. Lemon and Gary B. Nash, "The Distribution of Wealth in 18th Century America: A Century of Change in Chester County, Pa., 1693–1802," *JSH,* 2 (1968), 10–13.

143. Bruce C. Daniels, "Long Range Trends of Wealth Distribution in 18th Century New England," *EEH,* 11 (1973–74), 132–133.

144. Thomas J. Archdeacon, "The Age of Leisler: New York City, 1689–1710: A Social and Demographic Interpretation" (Ph.D. diss., Columbia University, 1971), p. 50.

145. Edwin J. Perkins, *The Economy of Colonial America* (New York: Columbia University Press, 1980), p. 155, table 8.4 (compiled from data in Jones, *Wealth*).

4. Independence

1. Probably the Currency Act of 1751 is the main exception. See Joseph A. Ernst, *Money and Politics in America, 1755–1775: A Study in the Currency Act of 1764 and the Political Economy of Revolution* (Chapel Hill: University of North Carolina Press, 1973), p. 41. See also Jack P. Greene, "An Uneasy Connection: An Analysis of the Preconditions of the American Revolution," in *Essays on the American Revolution,* ed. Stephen G. Kurtz and James H. Hutson (Chapel Hill: University of North Carolina Press, 1973), esp. pp. 35–45.

2. For further discussion, see Stuart Bruchey, *Roots of American Economic Growth, 1607–1861* (London: Hutchinson, 1965), pp. 70–71; Oliver M. Dickerson, *The Navigation Acts and the American Revolution* (New York: Octagon, 1978), ch. 1.

3. E. James Ferguson, ed., *The Papers of Robert Morris, 1781–1784* (Pittsburgh: University of Pittsburgh Press, 1973), I, 130.

4. Ibid., pp. 133–134.

5. Dickerson, *Navigation Acts,* pp. 29–299.

6. In a letter containing a discussion of reasons why the inhabitants of various colonies had gone to war, Francis Kinloch of South Carolina made the interesting observation that "the gentlemen of Carolina were grown too opulent to be confined to the care of their estates, and stood in need of some skope to that ambition which of itself takes place in the breasts of those who are rich, idle, and well educated" ("Letters of Francis Kinloch to Thomas Boone, 1782–1786," ed. Felix Gilbert, *JSoH,* 8 [1942], 102). Interestingly enough, Alexander Hamilton believed much the same thing. In "The Farmer Refuted" (February 1775) he wrote: "But what merits still more serious attention is this. There seems to be, already, a jealousy of our dawning splendour. It is looked upon as portentous of approaching independence. This we have reason to believe is one of the principal incitements to the recent rigorous and unconstitutional proceedings against us. And though it may have chiefly originated in the calumnies of designing men, yet it does not entirely depend upon adventitious or partial causes; but is also founded in the circumstances of our country and situation.

The boundless extent of territory we possess, the wholesome temperament of our climate, the luxuriance and fertility of our soil, the variety of our products, the rapidity of our population, the industry of our countrymen and the commodiousness of our ports, naturally lead to a suspicion of independence, and would always have an influence pernicious to us" (*The Papers of Alexander Hamilton*, ed. Harold C. Syrett, 26 vols. [New York: Columbia University Press, 1961–1973], I, 93–94; hereafter *Hamilton Papers*). For other contemporary expressions of this idea, see Edwin Burrows and Michael Wallace, "The American Revolution: The Ideology and Psychology of National Liberation," *PAH*, 6 (1972), 208–215.

7. Phyllis Deane and W. A. Cole, *British Economic Growth, 1688–1959: Trends and Structure* (Cambridge: Cambridge University Press, 1962), pp. 34, 86.

8. Greene, "An Uneasy Connection," pp. 32–80.

9. In the opinion of Alexander Hamilton, Britain's "true motive" in failing to relinquish control of the western forts after the Revolutionary War was "the prodigious advantage which the monopoly of the fur trade affords to the commerce of the English Nation" ("New York Assembly Remarks on an Act Acknowledging the Independence of Vermont, March 28, 1787," *Hamilton Papers*, IV, 136).

10. J. Franklin Jameson, *The American Revolution Considered as a Social Movement* (Princeton: Princeton University Press, 1967), pp. 32–33; Bernard Bailyn, *The Ideological Origins of the American Revolution* (Cambridge, Mass.: Harvard University Press, 1967), p. 119; Edmund S. Morgan, *The Birth of the Republic, 1763–1789, rev. ed.* (Chicago: University of Chicago Press, 1977), p. 59; E. James Ferguson, *The American Revolution: A General History, 1763–1790* (Homewood, Ill.: Dorsey Press, 1979), ch. 3.

11. Stuart Bruchey, ed., *The Colonial Merchant: Sources and Readings* (New York: Harcourt, Brace & World, 1966), pp. 42, 67–78.

12. Quoted in Morgan, *Birth of the Republic*, p. 17.

13. Gilman M. Ostrander, "The Colonial Molasses Trade," *AH,* 30 (1956), 77–84.

14. Arthur L. Jensen, *The Maritime Commerce of Colonial Philadelphia* (Madison: University of Wisconsin Press, 1963), p. 217.

15. Bailyn, *Ideological Origins,* pp. 97, viii. In the case of Virginia, Thad W. Tate emphasizes not only the threat to the colonists' "ancient, legal, and constitutional rights" but also the challenge to some provinces' governing elites ("The Coming of the Revolution in Virginia: Britain's Challenge to Virginia's Ruling Class, 1763–1776," *WMQ,* 3d ser., 19 [1962], 323–343).

16. Bailyn, *Ideological Origins,* p. 95. As early as 1930, Richard B. Morris wrote that 'the resort to the rights of Englishmen' was more influential even in the Revolutionary Era than the appeal to the 'rights of man' " (*Studies in the History of American Law* [New York: Columbia University Press, 1930], p. 68).

17. Ferguson, *The Papers of Robert Morris,* I, 131.

18. Carl L. Becker, *The History of Political Parties in the Province of New York* (Madison: University of Wisconsin Press, 1909), p. 5; Jack P. Greene, "The Social Origins of the American Revolution: An Evaluation and Interpretation," *PSQ,* 88 (1973), 2–4.

19. Gordon S. Wood, "Rhetoric and Reality in the American Revolution," *WMQ*, 3d ser., 23 (1966), 21, 26–27.

20. Kenneth L. Lockridge, "Land, Population and the Evolution of New England Society, 1630–1790," *PP*, 39 (1968), 66, 68–69.

21. Charles S. Grant, *Democracy in the Connecticut Frontier Town of Kent* (New York: Columbia University Press, 1961), p. 99.

22. Lockridge, "Land, Population," pp. 71–74; Grant, *Democracy in Kent*, p. 98. See also Lockridge's interesting speculations in "Social Change and the Meaning of the American Revolution," *JSH*, 6 (1973), 403–439.

23. Lockridge, "Land, Population," p. 80.

24. William S. Sacks, "Agricultural Conditions in the Northern Colonies before the Revolution," *JEH*, 13 (1953), 274–290.

25. Philip J. Greven, Jr., *Four Generations: Population, Land, and Family in Colonial Andover, Massachusetts* (Ithaca: Cornell University Press, 1970), pp. 125–126, 281–282.

26. In his study of Concord, Massachusetts, Robert A. Gross confirms Grevens' account of migration as a safety valve for population pressure (*The Minutemen and Their World* [New York: Hill & Wang, 1976], esp. pp. 79–88).

27. Greene, "Social Origins," p. 16, makes a similar point. Recently Lockridge concluded a series of thoughtful speculations by saying, "I must admit that I have not drawn in precisely the links between my suggested social changes and the more intense social and geographic conflicts which I claim followed from these changes" ("Social Change and the Meaning of the American Revolution," pp. 418–419).

28. The causal insufficiency of these internal changes is discussed by Greene, "Social Origins," pp. 1–22. Marc Egnal and Joseph A. Ernst make a case, rather narrowly I think, for "An Economic Interpretation of the American Revolution," *WMQ*, 3d ser., 29 (1972), 3–32. The argument, in part, is that dry-goods merchants resented British exports direct to shopkeepers, which bypassed established importers, and they resented also an increasing resort to vendue (auction) sales. The authors maintain that American repugnance for these practices "merged with grievances to form an inseparable part of the protest against the new parliamentary enactments." What established merchants, and tobacco planters too, wanted was "economic sovereignty" and control over the economy (p. 18). This somewhat overstates the case.

29. Jameson, "American Revolution," pp. 13–17; Frederick B. Tolles, "The American Revolution Considered as a Social Movement: A Re-evaluation," *AHR*, 60 (1954), 4.

30. Tate, "Coming of the Revolution in Virginia," pp. 4–5.

31. Jameson, "American Revolution," pp. 34–35; Tolles, "American Revolution as a Social Movement," pp. 7–9.

32. Tolles, "American Revolution as a Social Movement," pp. 6–9; this view is supported by a prominent American legal historian: "Just as primogeniture proved inapplicable to American conditions, so the attempt to restrict alienation by entailing estates was very early found adverse to colonial interests" (Morris, *Studies in History of American Law,* p. 86).

33. Morris, *Studies in History of American Law,* pp. 78–79, 81. Rhode Island was an exception to the rule in New England.

34. Rowland Berthoff and John M. Murrin, "Feudalism, Communalism, and the Yeoman Freeholder: The American Revolution Considered as a Social Accident," in Kurtz and Hutson, *Essays on the American Revolution,* pp. 256–288.

35. *Hamilton Papers,* XII, 362 (September 1792).

36. The quotations from John Jay through Samuel Curwen are from Robert A. East, *Business Enterprise in the American Revolutionary Era* (New York: Columbia University Press, 1933), pp. 213–214.

37. David Hackett Fischer, *The Revolution of American Conservatism: The Federalist Party in the Era of Jeffersonian Democracy* (New York: Harper & Row, 1965), p. 203.

38. Francis Kinloch to Thomas Boone, July 8, 1786, in Gilbert, "Letters of Francis Kinloch," p. 109.

39. W. Elliot Brownlee, *Dynamics of Ascent: A History of the American Economy* (New York: Alfred A. Knopf, 1974), p. 74.

40. John Holroyd (Lord Sheffield), *Observations on the Commerce of the American States* (London, 1783), pp. 70–71, 74–75.

41. For examples of retaliatory state legislation, see the following: *Acts and Laws of Connecticut,* Act of May 1784, pp. 271ff.; *Massachusetts Acts and Resolves* (session laws), ch. 8, pp. 439ff.; New Hampshire, *Laws,* June 23, 1785 (Metcalf 1916), ch. 8, pp. 78–81.

42. *The Federalist No. 11,* November 24, 1787, *Hamilton Papers,* IV, 340.

43. Lord Sheffield, *Observations,* pp. 68–69.

44. Brownlee, *Dynamics of Ascent,* pp. 74–75, 79n7; Bureau of the Census, *Historical Statistics of the United States, Colonial Times to 1957* (Washington, D.C.: Government Printing Office, 1966), p. 772. The index of wholesale prices declined each year from 139.6 in 1782 to 94 in 1789 (except for a slight rise between 1785 and 1786). The interpretation that exclusion of American vessels from the West Indies added to deflationary pressures is my own.

45. "This is one of the states where taxation has been carried furthest" (Hamilton to Robert Morris, April 30, 1781, *Hamilton Papers,* II, 612); Massachusetts "threw her Citizens into Rebellion by heavier taxes than were paid in any other state" (Hamilton to Washington, August 18, 1792, ibid., XII, 238).

46. Curtis P. Nettels, *The Emergence of a National Economy, 1775–1815* (New York: Holt, Rinehart & Winston, 1962), pp. 81–88.

47. William E. Nelson, *Americanization of the Common Law: The Impact of Legal Change on Massachusetts Society, 1760–1830* (Cambridge, Mass.: Harvard University Press, 1975), pp. 117–120.

48. *Letters and Other Writings of James Madison,* 4 vols. (Philadelphia: J. B. Lippincott, 1867), I, 226–227.

49. Edward Mead Earle, ed., *The Federalist; A Commentary on the Constitution of the United States* (New York: Modern Library, Random House, 1941), p. 62.

50. While Morris' statement probably exaggerates, Gerry, Mason, Yates, Pinckney, and Ellsworth were among the influential delegates to the convention who joined Madison in opposition to state paper (Max Ferrand, ed., *The Records of the Federal Convention* [New Haven: Yale University Press, 1911], I, 142, 154, 317, 165, 327; II, 309).

51. *Ogden v. Saunders,* 7 U.S. (12 Wheaton) 132, 215 (1827).

52. *Hamilton Papers,* IV, 715.

53. John Locke, *Two Treatises of Government,* ed. Thomas I. Cook (New York: Hafner, 1947), pp. 184, 191–192; Charles Francis Adams, ed., *The Works of John Adams, Second President of the United States . . . ,* 10 vols. (Boston: Charles C. Little & James Brown, 1851), VI, 280; "The Defense of the Funding System," July 1795, *Hamilton Papers,* XIX, 47.

54. Edward S. Corwin, "The Progress of Constitutional Theory between the Declaration of Independence and the Meeting of the Philadelphia Convention," in *American Constitutional History: Essays by Edward S. Corwin,* ed. Alpheus T. Mason and Gerald Garvey (New York: Harper & Row, 1964), p. 24.

55. The following discussion of the public debt leans heavily on E. James Ferguson, *The Power of the Purse* (Chapel Hill: University of North Carolina Press, 1961), pp. 114, 114n13, 145; ch. 9, esp. pp. 179–188. This superb study of the origins and growth of the public debt surpasses anything else in print. Anyone who reads the more than eleven thousand pages of the *Hamilton Papers* covering Hamilton's career till his resignation from Treasury (vols. 1–19) will be fully persuaded of the correctness of Ferguson's observation that "the funding of the public debt consummated the Nationalist effort [of the 1780s] to achieve political centralization by fiscal reform" (p. 292).

56. Nettels, *Emergence of a National Economy,* pp. 76–77, 94–98, 115; Paul Studenski and Herman E. Krooss, *Financial History of the United States,* 2d ed. (New York: McGraw-Hill, 1963), pp. 37–38.

57. "Defense of the Funding System," July 1795, *Hamilton Papers,* XIX, 5.

58. Introductory note (by the editor) to "Report on Public Credit," ibid., VI, 57–58. Wolcott's letter, dated November 29, 1789, is in ibid., V, 564–568.

59. Ferguson, *Power of the Purse,* p. 241 (the "cheap" method), p. 180 (as early as 1780), p. 311 (levying taxes payable in securities), pp. 329–330 (increase in size of debt), p. 330 (debt in 1791); *American State Papers,* I, 482–483 (size of debt as of January 1, 1790; the foreign debt amounted to $12,198,189.85 and the entire national debt to $75,414,238.12 on that date). I think it highly unlikely the debt could have been retired "cheaply." Acceptability for tax purposes would have increased the demand for those securities and raised their price, probably to par.

60. "Defense of the Funding System," July 1795. *Hamilton Papers,* XIX, 19–26.

61. Hamilton to Nathaniel Chipman, September–December 1788, ibid., V, 218.

62. The remark appears equally applicable to the excise on distilled spirits (whiskey tax) which had been recommended for imposition, as Hamilton told Washington, so that "the authority of the National Government should be visible in some branch of internal Revenue; lest a total non-exercise of it should beget an impression that it was never to be exercised & next to that it ought not to be exercised" (Hamilton to Washington, August 18, 1792, ibid., XII, 236–237). While the government wished to tap additional sources of revenue—and later turned to carriages, domestically manufactured snuff and refined sugar, auction sales, dividends on bank stock, and a few other items in Hamilton's time—Hamilton probably also had in mind the desirability of providing an internal domestic exhibition of the presence and power of the federal government. I suspect this is why he avidly sought from Tench Coxe on-the-scene reports of disaffection in western Pennsylvania and personally accompanied militia

sent to quell the Whiskey Rebellion in 1794. (Hamilton lists sources of current revenues in his "Report on Public Credit" in January 1795.) See ibid., XVIII, 77.

63. Hamilton to Washington, August 18, 1792, ibid., XII, 235; "Defense of the Funding System," July 1795, ibid., XIX, 31–32.

64. "Report on Public Credit," January 9, 1790, ibid., VI, 80; "Defense of the Funding System," July 1795, ibid., XIX, 40–41; ibid., XIX, 5.

65. "Defense of the Funding System," ibid., XIX, 65–69, esp. 68. To Hamilton "capital" was money or any kind of property, indeed, "everything that has value is Capital" (ibid., XII, 246). Economists today would disagree, of course. Consumption goods certainly have "value" but are not capital, precisely because they are consumed rather than used for production in the future.

66. "Defense of the Funding System," July 1795, ibid., XIX, 66. See also Hamilton to Washington, August 18, 1792, ibid., XII 243–244. Growing insecurity in wartime Europe and European interest rates, as well as the stability of the American government and debt and the interest rate thereon, would also influence the volume of foreign investment in the American debt.

67. "Report on Public Credit," ibid., VI, 73–78.

68. At least this was the view of the brilliant Philadelphia businessman William Bingham, whose views appear clearly to have influenced Hamilton. See Bingham to Hamilton, November 25, 1799, ibid., V, 538–557, esp. pp. 540, 545. See also Dorfman, *Economic Mind*, I, 289 (Hamilton "had long been convinced of the soundness of Bingham's logic").

69. Ferguson, *Power of the Purse*, p. 326. In his "Report on Public Credit," Hamilton had remarked that "from three to four per cent is deemed good interest in several parts of Europe. Even less is deemed so, in some places. And it is on the decline; the increasing plenty of money tending to lower it" (*Hamilton Papers*, VI, 89). Curtis P. Nettels, *The Emergence of a National Economy, 1775–1815* (New York: Holt, Rinehart & Winston, 1962), p. 115.

70. Washington to David Humphreys, July 20, 1791, *Writings of George Washington*, ed. John C. Fitzpatrick, 39 vols. (Washington, D.C.: Government Printing Office, 1931–1944), XXXI, 318.

71. John Fry to Hamilton, November 2, 1791, *Hamilton Papers*, IX, 451.

72. James O. Wettereau, "New Light on the First Bank of the United States," *PMHB*, 61 (1937), 269.

73. "Report on Additional Sums Necessary for the Support of the Government," August 5, 1790, *Hamilton Papers*, VI, 524.

74. 1 *Stat.*, 186 (August 12, 1790); "Meeting of the Commissioners of the Sinking Fund," August 27, 1790, *Hamilton Papers*, VI, 571; Hamilton to Samuel Meredith, ibid., p. 576; Hamilton to Benjamin Lincoln, February 1, 1791, ibid., VIII, 1–2; "Meeting of the Commissioners of the Sinking Fund," August 15, 1791, ibid., IX, 67–68.

75. The characterization of Duer is that of Joseph Dorfman; see *Economic Mind*, p. 292. For the authorization to use the sinking fund for this purpose, see "Meeting of the Commissioners of the Sinking Fund," March 26, 1792, *Hamilton Papers*, XI, 193–194.

76. Hamilton to William Seton, March 25, 1792, *Hamilton Papers*, XI, 190–192.

77. "Defense of the Funding System," July 1795, ibid., XIX, 66; Hamilton to Seton, April 4, 1792, ibid., XI, 225–226.

78. Hamilton to Seton, January 18, 1792, ibid., X, 525.

79. Hamilton to Seton, March 25, 1792, ibid., XI, 192.

80. "Report on a National Bank," December 13, 1790, ibid., VII, 325, 331.

81. Hamilton to Rufus King, April 2, 1793, ibid., XIV, 274–276. King was a member of the board of directors.

82. "Further Provision for Public Credit," December 13, 1790, ibid., VII, 235.

83. "Report on the State of the Treasury . . . during the Years 1791 and 1792 . . . ," February 19, 1793, ibid., XIV, 113.

84. *Americus No. II,* February 7, 1794, ibid., XVI, 13.

85. Hamilton to Otho H. Williams, March 28, 1792, ibid., XI, 204.

86. "Report on Foreign Loans," February 1793, ibid., XIV, 46.

87. "Treasury Department Circular to the Presidents and Directors of the Offices of Discount and Deposit of the Bank of the United States," February 23–March 5, 1793, ibid., XIV, 137–138.

88. *Debates and Proceedings in the Congress of the United States, 1789–1824* (Washington, D.C., 1824–1856), 1789–1791, p. 2209.

89. Hamilton to Speaker of House, "Report on Defects in the Laws of Revenue," April 22, 1790, *Hamilton Papers,* VI, 373–397, esp. 386–388.

90. Hamilton to Seton, January 24, 1792, ibid., X, 562–563; for the price of bank script, see Wettereau, "New Light," p. 275.

91. Hamilton to Seton, March 19, 1792, *Hamilton Papers,* XI, 154–155; Seton to Hamilton, March 21, 1792, ibid., pp. 163–164.

92. Papers of James O. Wettereau, Special Collections, Columbia University, folder 225, p. 40.

93. Hamilton to Seton, June 11, 1792, *Hamilton Papers,* XI, 505–506.

94. Henry W. Domett, *A History of the Bank of New York, 1784–1884* (New York, 1884), p. 48.

95. S. Bruchey, "Alexander Hamilton and the State Banks," *WMQ,* 27 (1970), 374–375.

96. Hamilton to Washington, April 8, 1783, *Hamilton Papers,* III, 318.

97. Hamilton to Washington, September 9, 1792, ibid., XII, 349.

98. Hamilton to Jeremiah Olney, April 2, 1793, ibid., XIV, 277.

99. "Further Provision for Public Credit," December 13, 1790, ibid., VII, 232.

100. Hamilton to Thomas Willing, September 13, 1789, ibid., V, 371.

101. "Defense of the Funding System," July 1795, ibid., XIX, 47.

102. For example, *Fletcher v. Peck,* 10 U.S. (6 Cranch) 87 (1810), and *Dartmouth College v. Woodward* (4 Wheaton) 518 (1819).

103. *Hamilton Papers,* X, 230–240.

104. John R. Nelson, Jr., "Alexander Hamilton and American Manufacturing: A Reexamination," *JAH,* 65 (1979), 977, 981–982, 986, 994.

105. John Thom Holdsworth and Davis R. Dewey, *The First and Second Banks of the United States* (Washington, D.C.: Government Printing Office, 1910), p. 45.

106. James O. Wettereau, *The Statistical Records of the First Bank of the United States* (New York: Garland, 1985), pp. 229–305. Unfortunately, it cannot be determined

whether figures for deposits represent lodged deposits or those created by the bank in making loans.

107. James O. Wettereau, "The Branches of the First Bank of the United States," *JEH,* 2 (1942), 70.

108. Richard Hildreth, *The History of the United States of America* (New York: Harper Bros., 1856), I, 276.

109. Victor S. Clark, *History of Manufacturing in the United States, 1607–1860,* 3 vols. (Washington, D.C.: Carnegie Institute, 1929), I, 47–53.

110. Joseph S. Davis, *Essays in the Earlier History of American Corporations,* 2 vols. (Cambridge, Mass.: Harvard University Press, 1917), II, 20; Lawrence M. Friedman, *A History of American Law* (New York: Simon & Schuster, 1973), p. 33.

111. Morris, *Studies in History of American Law,* pp. 62–63.

112. Friedman, *History of American Law,* p. 14.

113. Clark, *History of Manufacturing,* I, 26; Davis, *Essays,* pp. 25–27.

114. Davis, *Essays,* pp. 25–29.

115. Nelson, *Americanization of the Common Law,* pp. 133–135.

116. Ibid., pp. 90–92.

117. Clark, *History of Manufacturing,* I, 27–28. "Being distant from foreign intercourse, the people of Virginia [living west of the mountains] depend principally upon home manufactures" (Edward Carrington to Hamilton, October 4, 1791, *Hamilton Papers,* IX, 276).

118. Clark, *History of Manufacturing,* I, 7–8, 87–88, 175–179.

119. *Hamilton Papers,* I, 127.

120. Jacob Cooke, "Tench Coxe, Alexander Hamilton, and the Encouragement of American Manufacturing," *WMQ,* 32 (1975), 380.

121. I am indebted for this summary to David John Jeremy, ed., *Henry Wansey and His American Journal* (Philadelphia: American Philosophical Society, 1970), p. 30.

122. Ibid., pp. 82–83.

5. The Early American Industrial Revolution

1. Among numerous excellent studies of the Industrial Revolution, the most useful for present purposes were David S. Landes, "Technological Change and Development in Western Europe, 1750–1914," in *The Cambridge Economic History of Europe,* vol. 6, pt. 1, ed. M. M. Postan and H. J. Habbakkuk (Cambridge: Cambridge University Press, 1965), pub. separately with an additional chapter as *The Unbound Prometheus* (Cambridge: Cambridge University Press, 1969); Paul Mantoux, *The Industrial Revolution in the Eighteenth Century,* ed. and intro. T. S. Ashton (New York: Harper & Row, 1961); T. S. Ashton, *The Industrial Revolution, 1760–1830* (London: Oxford University Press, 1948); Phyllis Deane, *The First Industrial Revolution* (Cambridge: Cambridge University Press, 1965); Herbert Heaton, "Industrial Revolution," *Encyclopedia of the Social Sciences,* vol. 8 (New York, 1937).

2. Arnold Toynbee, *The Industrial Revolution* (Boston: Beacon Press, 1956), pp. 7–45.

3. Peter Mathias, *The First Industrial Nation* (New York: Charles Scribner's Sons, 1969). Also valuable is the author's discussion titled "Industrial Revolution—Identity and Beginning," in ibid., pp. 1–18.

4. Ashton, *Industrial Revolution,* pp. 1–22.

5. Mathias, *First Industrial Nation,* p. 3.

6. Mantoux, *Industrial Revolution in the Eighteenth Century;* Ashton, *Industrial Revolution;* W. W. Rostow, *The Stages of Economic Growth* (Cambridge: Cambridge University Press, 1960). The quoted passages from these works are in Deane, *First Industrial Revolution,* pp. 2–3. In their study of British economic growth Phyllis Deane and W. A. Cole point out that "it was not until economic expansion was well under way, in the 1760s and 1770s, when the pressures of a growing population were beginning to stimulate investment in measures designed to economise other resources, such as land (enclosures) and coal (canals), that the great labor-saving inventions of the eighteenth century laid the basis for the revolution in the textile industries and the introduction of the factory system" (*British Economic Growth, 1688–1959: Trends and Structure* [Cambridge: Cambridge University Press, 1964], p. 97).

7. Deane, *First Industrial Revolution,* p. 4.

8. Ashton, *Industrial Revolution,* p. 66.

9. Landes, *Unbound Prometheus,* pp. 3, 41.

10. Nathan Rosenberg, "Innovative Responses to Materials Shortages," in *Perspectives on Technology,* ed. Rosenberg (Cambridge: Cambridge University Press, 1976), p. 251. See also p. 183.

11. Nathan Rosenberg, "Selection and Adaptation in the Transfer of Technology: Steam and Iron in America, 1800–1870," in ibid., p. 183.

12. Rosenberg, "Innovative Responses," p. 251.

13. See the superb prize-winning dissertation by Carolyn C. Cooper, "Thomas Blanchard's Patent Management," summarized in *JEH,* 47 (1987), 487–488.

14. Nathan Rosenberg, *The American System of Manufactures* (Edinburgh: Edinburgh University Press, 1969), pp. 8–14.

15. Ibid., p. 28.

16. The phrase is Rosenberg's. See his article "America's Rise to Woodworking Leadership," in Rosenberg, *Perspectives,* p. 43.

17. Rosenberg, *American System,* pp. 28, 14.

18. Ibid., pp. 28–29.

19. All the studies of the Industrial Revolution listed in note 1 discuss the textile innovations in detail (for example, see Deane, *First Industrial Revolution,* ch. 6); for statistics on cotton imports, see Stuart Bruchey, ed., *Cotton and the Growth of the American Economy* (New York: Harcourt, Brace & World, 1967).

20. Dolores Greenberg, "Reassessing the Power Patterns of the Industrial Revolution: An Anglo-American Comparison," *AHR,* 87 (1982), esp. 1237, 1258.

21. David John Jeremy, ed., *Henry Wansey and His American Journal* (Philadelphia: American Philosophical Society, 1970), pp. 82–83, 141.

22. Ibid., p. 83n99 (see last para.); Joseph S. Davis, *Essays in the Earlier History of American Corporations,* 2 vols. (Cambridge, Mass.: Harvard University Press, 1917), I, 497–501; Adam Seybert, *Statistical Annals: Embracing Views of the Population, Commerce, Navigation . . . of the United States of America* (Philadelphia, 1818), pp. 59–60.

23. Timothy Pitkin, *A Statistical View of the Commerce of the United States of America* (New York, 1817), pp. 32–33.

24. Douglass C. North, *The Economic Growth of the United States, 1790 to 1860* (Englewood Cliffs, N.J.: Prentice-Hall, 1961), p. 46.

25. Ibid., p. 38.

26. The basic source for the impact of the European wars on American commerce remains Anna C. Clauder, "American Commerce as Affected by the Wars of the French Revolution and Napoleon" (Ph.D. diss., University of Pennsylvania, 1932), but the analysis of a modern economist, Douglass C. North, is also valuable (see chs. 4 and 5 of his *Economic Growth*). Older, but still useful, are H. See, "Commerce between France and the United States, 1783–1784," *AHR*, 31 (1926), 732–752; F. L. Benns, *The American Struggle for the British West India Carrying Trade, 1815–1830* (Bloomington: Indiana University Press, 1923); R. M. Martin, *History of the West Indies*, 2 vols. (London, 1836–37); and A. L. Burt, *The United States, Great Britain and British North America from the Revolution to the Establishment of Peace after the War of 1812* (New Haven: Yale University Press, 1940).

27. Pitkin, *Commerce of the United States*, ch. 11.

28. Byron Fairchild, *Messrs. William Pepperell: Merchants of Piscataqua* (Ithaca: Cornell University Press, 1954); James B. Hedges, *The Browns of Providence Plantations, Colonial Years* (Cambridge, Mass.: Harvard University Press, 1952); Samuel Eliot Morison, *Maritime History of Massachusetts, 1783–1860* (Boston: Houghton Mifflin, 1921) (for Thomas Boylston); Tyler Dennett, *Americans in Eastern Asia* (New York: Macmillan, 1922) (for Elias Hasket Derby); Stuart Bruchey, *Robert Oliver, Merchant of Baltimore, 1783–1819* (Baltimore: Johns Hopkins Press, 1956).

29. Morison, *Maritime History*, p. 125. The account of flourishing times after 1793 owes much to North, *Economic Growth*, pp. 47–51.

30. North, *Economic Growth*, ch. 12, esp. pp. 156, 170.

31. George Rogers Taylor, *The Transportation Revolution, 1815–1860* (New York: Holt, Rinehart, & Winston, 1951), pp. 207–214; Rolla M. Tryon, *Household Manufactures in the United States, 1640–1860* (Chicago: University of Chicago Press, 1917); N. S. B. Gras, "Stages in Economic History," *JEBH*, 2 (1930), 395–418.

32. Caroline F. Ware, *The Early New England Cotton Manufacture* (New York: Russell & Russell, 1966), pp. 37–38; U.S. Congress, *American State Papers*, II, 427; ibid., III, 53; ibid., IV, 22–28; Pitkin, *Statistical View*, pp. 482, 526; Robert Zevin, "The Growth of Cotton Production after 1815," in *The Reinterpretation of American Economic History*, ed. Robert W. Fogel and Stanley L. Engerman (New York: Harper & Row, 1972); Robert W. Fogel, *Railroads and American Economic Growth: Essays in Econometric History* (Baltimore: Johns Hopkins University Press, 1964), pp. 122–128.

33. Arthur H. Cole, *The American Wool Manufacture*, 2 vols. (Cambridge, Mass.: Harvard University Press, 1926), I, 249; U.S. Census Office, *Eighth Census of the United States, Manufactures* (Washington, D.C., 1865), pp. liv–lv; Arthur H. Cole and Harold F. Williamson, *The American Carpet Manufacture* (Cambridge, Mass.: Harvard University Press, 1941), pp. 12–14; U.S. Census Office, *Tenth Census of the United States, Report on the Agencies of Transportation* (Washington, D.C., 1883), IV, 662; Victor S. Clark, *History of Manufactures in the United States*, 3 vols. (Washington, D.C.: Carnegie Institute, 1929), I, 507 (rpr. New York: Peter Smith, 1949).

34. Diane Lindstrom, *Economic Development in the Philadelphia Region* (New York: Columbia University Press, 1978), pp. 8–9; Lawrence A. Herbst, "Interregional Com-

modity Trade from the North to the South and American Economic Development in the Antebellum Period," *JEH,* 35 (1975), 266–267; Paul Uselding, "A Note on the Inter-Regional Trade in Manufactures in 1840," *JEH,* 36 (1976), 428–435. (Herbst's earlier estimate was 16.4 percent. Uselding revised this upward.) Herbst, *Interregional Commodity Trade from the North to the South and American Economic Development in the Antebellum Period* (New York: Arno Press, 1978); Richard Easterlin, "Interregional Differences in Per Capita Income, Population, and Total Income, 1840–1950," in *Trends in the American Economy in the Nineteenth Century,* ed. William Parker, National Bureau of Economic Research, vol. 24, *Studies in Income and Wealth* (Princeton: Princeton University Press, 1960), pp. 73–140.

35. Taylor, *Transportation Revolution,* pp. 215–217.

36. Blanche Evans Hazard, *The Organization of the Boot and Shoe Industry in Massachusetts before 1875* (Cambridge, Mass.: Harvard University Press, 1921); Clark, *History of Manufactures,* I, 444–445.

37. Clark, *History of Manufactures,* I, 438–463; Taylor, *Transportation Revolution,* pp. 232–233.

38. Barry Poulson, "Estimates of the Value of Manufacturing Output in the Early Nineteenth Century," *JEH,* 29 (1969), 522.

39. Albert Fishlow has emphasized the important "spread effects" of the processing of agricultural products in the West. That is to say, it disseminated a modern technology within the interior and predominantly agricultural parts of the country and thus introduced the beginnings of industrialization in a natural and automatic way. Subsequent transition to a more sophisticated industrial structure thus became easier (*American Railroads and the Transportation of the Antebellum American Economy* [Cambridge, Mass.: Harvard University Press, 1965], pp. 226–229).

40. Fishlow, *American Railroads,* p. 228; Greenberg, "Reassessing the Power Patterns," p. 1258.

41. George S. Gibb, *The Saco-Lowell Shops* (Cambridge, Mass.: Harvard University Press, 1950); Nathan Rosenberg, "Anglo-American Wage Differences in the 1820's," *JEH,* 27 (1967), 221–228; idem, *The American System;* Lance E. Davis and H. Louis Stettler III, "The New England Textile Industry, 1825–60: Trends and Fluctuations," in *Output, Employment, and Productivity in the United States after 1800,* ed. Dorothy Brady, National Bureau of Economic Research, vol. 30, *Studies in Income and Wealth* (New York: Columbia University Press, 1966), p. 228. The quotation which concludes the paragraph will be found in H. J. Habbakkuk, *American and British Technology in the Nineteenth Century* (Cambridge: Cambridge University Press, 1962), p. 106.

42. Thomas Dublin, *Women at Work* (New York: Columbia University Press, 1979), p. 59; Habbakkuk, *American and British Technology,* pp. 102–103; Taylor, *Transportation Revolution,* p. 228; "Report of the Commissioner of Patents Showing the Operations of the Patent Office during the Year 1843," *Patent Office Report,* February 13, 1844, 28th Cong., 1st sess., Senate, p. 6 (copy in Public Search Room of the Patent and Trademark Office, Arlington, Va.).

43. Ware, *New England Cotton Manufacture,* p. 211; Nathan Rosenberg, *Technology and American Economic Growth* (New York: Harper & Row, 1972), pp. 117–127.

44. Alexander Hamilton, "Report on Manufactures," *Hamilton Papers*, X, 256; Habbakkuk, *American and British Technology*, p. 115.

45. North, *Economic Growth*, p. 133; Carl F. Kaestle and Maris A. Vinovskis, *Education and Social Change in Nineteenth-Century Massachusetts* (Cambridge: Cambridge University Press, 1980), pp. 10, 46–50.

46. Maris A. Vinovskis, "Quantification and the History of Education: Observations on Ante-Bellum Educational Expansion, School Attendance, and Educational Reform" (Paper prepared for the US-USSR Colloquium on Quantitative Research in History, May–June 1981); for a more extended discussion of the growth of educational institutions, see Stuart Bruchey, *Roots of American Economic Growth* (New York: Harper & Row, 1965), pp. 83–93; Paul Monroe, *The Founding of the American Public School System: A History of Education in the United States*, vol. 1 (New York: Macmillan, 1940); H. G. Good, *A History of American Education* (New York: Macmillan, 1956); Lawrence A. Cremin, *American Education: The National Experience, 1783–1876* (New York: Harper & Row, 1980).

47. Albert Fishlow, "The American Common School Revival: Fact or Fancy," in *Industrialization in Two Systems*, ed. Henry Rosovsky (New York: John Wiley, 1966), pp. 40–67; Vinovskis, "Quantification and the History of Education," p. 6.

48. Eric E. Lampard, "The Evolving System of Cities in the United States: Urbanization and Economic Development," in *Issues in Urban Economics*, ed. Harvey S. Perloff and Lowdon Wingo, Jr. (Baltimore: Johns Hopkins University Press, 1968), pp. 108, 117; Jeffrey G. Williamson, "Urbanization in the American Northeast, 1820–1870," in Fogel and Engerman, *Reinterpretation of American Economic History*, p. 468.

49. Lindstrom, *Economic Development in the Philadelphia Region*, pp. 13, 23; Clark, *History of Manufactures*, I, 449.

50. George Rogers Taylor, ed., *The Early Development of the American Cotton Textile Industry* (New York: Harper & Row, 1969), p. xxiii.

51. Lindstrom, *Economic Development in the Philadelphia Region*, pp. 27, 123; Dublin, *Women at Work*, pp. 5–6.

52. Thomas Dublin, *Farm to Factory: Women's Letters, 1830–1860* (New York: Columbia University Press, 1981), p. 14; Richard M. Bernard and Maris Vinovskis, "The Female Schoolteacher in Ante-Bellum Massachusetts," *JSH*, 10 (1977), 332–345; Dublin, *Women at Work*, pp. 65–66 (1836 is the year given by Dublin in support of the statement that the daily earnings of men were more than twice those of women); Howard M. Gitelman, "The Waltham System and the Coming of the Irish," *LH*, 8 (1967), 231–232.

53. Dublin, *Women at Work*, pp. 86–122, 163.

54. Ibid., pp. 86–87, 112–113.

55. Walter Hugins, *Jacksonian Democracy and the Working Class* (Stanford: Stanford University Press, 1960).

56. Stuart Bruchey, "Corporations," in *Encylopaedia Britannica*, 1963 ed.; W. Paul Strassman, *Risk and Technological Innovation: American Manufacturing Methods during the Nineteenth Century* (Ithaca: Cornell University Press, 1959); Norman Ware, *The Industrial Worker, 1840–60* (New York: Houghton Mifflin, 1924).

57. Susan E. Hirsch, "From Artisan to Manufacturer: Industrialization and the

Small Producer in Newark, 1830–60," in *Small Business in American Life*, ed. Stuart Bruchey (New York: Columbia University Press, 1980), pp. 80–99.

58. John Higham, *From Boundlessness to Consolidation: The Transformation of American Culture, 1848–1860* (Ann Arbor, Mich.: William L. Clements Library, 1969).

59. It was Douglass C. North who characterized early censuses—before 1840—as "so poor" as to be "almost worthless" (*Economic Growth*, p. 165); the emphasis on the "deficiency of the available evidence" is that of Robert E. Gallman, "The Statistical Approach: Fundamental Concepts as Applied to History," in *Approaches to American Economic History*, ed. George Rogers Taylor and Lucius F. Ellsworth (Charlottesville: University Press of Virginia, 1971); Gallman's studies provide the basic quantitative data on antebellum economic growth (see his "Commodity Output, 1839–1899," in Parker, *Trends in the American Economy*, pp. 13–72; Gallman, "The Statistical Approach"; idem, "Gross National Product in the United States, 1834–1909," in Brady, *Output, Employment, and Productivity*, pp. 3–76; idem, "The Pace and Pattern of American Economic Growth," in *American Economic Growth*, ed. Lance E. Davis et al. (New York: Harper & Row, 1972), pp. 15–60. My discussion of antebellum economic growth owes a great deal to a critical synthesis of recent work prepared by Stanley L. Engerman and Robert E. Gallman. See their "Economic Growth, 1783–1860," in *Research in Economic History*, ed. Paul Uselding (Greenwich, Conn.: JAI Press, 1983), VIII, 1–46. Their references to the literature are far fuller than can be provided here.

60. James F. Shepherd and Gary M. Walton, "Economic Change after the American Revolution: Pre- and Post-War Comparisons of Maritime Shipping and Trade," *EEH*, 13 (1976), 397–422; Alice Hanson Jones, *The Wealth of a Nation to Be* (New York: Columbia University Press, 1980), pp. 79–83; North, *Economic Growth;* idem, "Early National Income Estimates of the United States before 1840: New Evidence and Controlled Conjecture," *JEH*, 27 (1967), 151–197; Robert E. Lipsey, "Foreign Trade," in Davis et al., *American Economic Growth*, pp. 548–581; Irving B. Kravis, "The Role of Exports in Nineteenth-Century United States Growth," *EDCC*, 20 (1972), 387–404.

61. Paul A. David, "The Growth of Real Product in the United States before 1840: New Evidence, Controlled Conjectures," *JEH*, 27 (1967), 151–198.

62. Notably, Gallman; see esp. his "Statistical Approach."

63. W. W. Rostow, "The Take-off into Self-Sustained Growth," *EJ*, 66 (1956), 25–49.

64. Engerman and Gallman, "Economic Growth, 1783–1860."

65. Gallman, "Pace and Pattern," in Davis et al., *American Economic Growth*, p. 53; Stanley Lebergott, *Manpower in American Economic Growth: The American Record since 1800* (New York: McGraw-Hill, 1964), pp. 510–512; Lance E. Davis and Robert E. Gallman, "Capital Formation in the United States during the Nineteenth Century," in *The Cambridge Economic History of Europe*, vol. 7, pt. 2, ed. H. J. Habbakkuk and Peter Mathias (Cambridge: Cambridge University Press), p. 5.

66. Kenneth L. Sokoloff, "Investment in Fixed and Working Capital during Early Industrialization: Evidence from U.S. Manufacturing Firms," *JEH*, 44 (1984), 545–556.

67. Davis and Gallman, "Capital Formation."

68. G. Heberton Evans, Jr., *Business Incorporations in the United States, 1800–1943* (New York: National Bureau of Economic Research, 1948).

6. Money and Banking before the Civil War

1. Joseph A. Schumpeter, *The Theory of Economic Development: An Inquiry into Profits, Capital, Credit, Interest, and the Business Cycle,* trans. Redvers Opie (Cambridge, Mass.: Harvard University Press, 1949), ch. 2; Lance E. Davis, "Banks and Their Economic Effects," in *American Economic Growth: An Economist's History of the United States,* ed. Lance E. Davis et al. (New York: Harper & Row, 1972), esp. pp. 348, 365.

2. Paul B. Trescott, *Financing American Enterprise: The Story of Commercial Banking* (New York: Harper & Row, 1963), pp. 10, 25; Richard Sylla, "American Banking and Growth in the Nineteenth Century: A Partial View of the Terrain," *EEH,* 9 (1971), 211.

3. George Rogers Taylor, *The Transportation Revolution* (New York: Holt, Rinehart & Winston, 1951), p. 328. As Taylor says, Matthew Carey pointed out in 1816 that "deposits rather than bank notes or specie furnished the chief medium of payment in the great commercial cities."

4. Peletiah Webster, *Political Essays: An Essay on Credit* (Philadelphia, 1791), pp. 434, 440–441.

5. Alexander Hamilton, "Report on a National Bank," in *Hamilton Papers,* VII, 305–342.

6. Eric Bollman, *Paragraphs on Banks* (Philadelphia, 1810), p. 21; quoted in Harry E. Miller, *Banking Theories in the United States before 1860* (Cambridge, Mass.: Harvard University Press, 1927), pp. 114, 117.

7. For Oliver's use of checks, see, for example, "Oliver Record Book" (the day-book of Oliver and Thompson for the years 1794–1799) part of the Robert Oliver collection in the Maryland Historical Society), II, 1–2, entries of December 8, 1794. On p. 2 alone are five instances of payment by check. In addition, checks are mentioned in article 19 of the Constitution of the Bank of New York, drawn up by Hamilton in 1784. (See Henry W. Domett, *A History of the Bank of New York, 1784–1884* [New York: Greenwood Press, 1969], p. 14; orig. pub. 1884.)

8. Ralph C. H. Catterall, *The Second Bank of the United States* (Chicago: University of Chicago Press, 1903), p. 96.

9. George D. Green, *Finance and Economic Development in the Old South, Louisiana Banking, 1804–1861* (Stanford: Stanford University Press, 1972), pp. 26, 118–119.

10. American State Papers, *Finance* (Washington, D.C.: Gales & Seaton, 1932), I, 93.

11. J. Laurence Laughlin, *The History of Bimetallism in the United States,* 3d ed. (New York, 1896), pp. 13–24, 264; Lance E. Davis and J.R.T. Hughes, "A Dollar-Sterling Exchange, 1803–1895," *EHR,* 13 (1960), 52–78.

12. Green, *Finance and Economic Development,* pp. 74–75; Bray Hammond, *Banks and Politics in America from the Revolution to the Civil War* (Princeton: Princeton University Press, 1957), pp. 72–78, 279–285, 315–318.

13. J. G. Gurley and E. W. Shaw, "Money," in *American Economic History,* ed. Seymour Harris (New York: McGraw-Hill, 1961), p. 108.

14. Hammond, *Banks and Politics,* pp. 47–49.

15. T. Willing to Alexander Hamilton, October 1, 1789, *Hamilton Papers,* V, 418.

16. Edwin Burrows, "Albert Gallatin and the Political Economy of Republicanism" (Ph.D. diss., Columbia University, 1974), pp. 193, 199.

17. John Thom Holdsworth and Davis R. Dewey, *The First and Second Banks of the United States* (Washington, D.C.: Government Printing Office, 1910), p. 45.

18. James O. Wettereau, "New Light on the First Bank of the United States," *PMHB,* 61 (1937), 263–285; *Hamilton Papers,* VII, 235, 270–272, 279.

19. Jonathan Burrall to President and Directors of the Bank of the United States, Office of Discount and Deposit at New York, January 17, 1800, in Papers of James O. Wettereau, Special Collections, Columbia University, Box 18, folder 347.

20. Papers of Wettereau, box and folder nos. unavailable. To Hamilton, the Bank was "an indispensable engine in the administration of the finances"; quoted in Wettereau, "New Light," p. 263.

21. Minutes of the Board of Directors, October 27, 1795, Papers of Wettereau, Box 18, folder 345. These minutes are verbatim copies made by Wettereau; the originals are in the Cadwalader Mss. in the Historical Society of Pennsylvania.

22. Ibid., February 12, 1805, Box 18, folder 347; this document, which I annotated some years ago, is now (May 1984) missing from the folder.

23. Ibid.

24. Ibid., April 22, 1800.

25. The statistics on numbers of banks and their capital stock given in this chapter are from J. Van Fenstermaker, *The Development of American Commercial Banking: 1782–1837* (Kent, Ohio: Bureau of Economic and Business Research, 1965), p. 13, and appendixes A and B.

26. "The creation of new banks," wrote Albert Gallatin, "was a natural consequence of the dissolution of the Bank of the United States"; quoted in Hammond, *Banks and Politics,* p. 227; see also pp. 228–229; Leon M. Schur, "The Second Bank of the United States and the Inflation after the War of 1812," *JPE,* 68 (1960), 119–120.

27. Schur, "Second Bank," pp. 118–121, 132; Van Fenstermaker, *American Commercial Banking,* p. 13; Catterall, *Second Bank,* pp. 54–56.

28. Schur, "Second Bank," pp. 130–132; Catterall, *Second Bank,* pp. 62–64.

29. Catterall, *Second Bank,* pp. 61–63.

30. Arthur H. Cole, "Cyclical Variations in the Sale of Public Lands," *RES,* 9 (1927), 45, 45n8.

31. Bureau of the Census, *Historical Statistics of the United States, Colonial Times to 1970,* 2 vols. (Washington, D.C.: Government Printing Office, 1976), I, 518.

32. Lance E. Davis, "The New England Textile Mills and the Capital Markets: A Study of Industrial Borrowing, 1840–60," *JEH,* 20 (1960), 1–30. The conclusions given in the text were derived from materials supplied by Davis to Paul Trescott and cited by the latter in *Financing of American Enterprise,* p. 36.

33. Albert Gallatin, *Considerations on the Currency and Banking System of the United States* (New York: Greenwood Press, 1968), pp. 67–68 (orig. pub. 1831); quoted in Sylla, "American Banking and Growth," p. 214.

34. Sylla, "American Banking and Growth," pp. 214–215.

35. Van Fenstermaker, *American Commercial Banking,* p. 94; Green, *Finance and Economic Development,* p. 21.

36. Catterall, *Second Bank,* p. 101.

37. Quoted in ibid., p. 95.

38. Ibid., p. 98.

39. Ibid., pp. 100, 109, 134; Thomas P. Govan, "Fundamental Issues of the Bank War," *PMHB,* 82 (1958), 305–315.

40. Catterall, *Second Bank,* p. 142; Schur, "Second Bank," p. 133; Jean Wilburn, *Biddle's Bank, The Crucial Years* (New York: Columbia University Press, 1967), ch. 8.

41. Thomas P. Govan, *Nicholas Biddle, Nationalist and Public Banker, 1786–1844* (Chicago: University of Chicago Press, 1959), pp. 26, 70–71, 102, 214, 215n2, 285, 353; Catterall, *Second Bank,* p. 134; Govan, *Nicholas Biddle,* p. 285; Walter B. Smith, *Economic Aspects of the Second Bank of the United States* (Cambridge, Mass.: Harvard University Press, 1953), p. 179.

42. Nicholas Biddle to John C. White, March 3, 1828, in *John Campbell White Papers,* Maryland Historical Society.

43. Smith, *Economic Aspects of the Second Bank,* p. 140; Peter Temin, *The Jacksonian Economy* (New York: W. W. Norton, 1969), pp. 54–57.

44. Taylor, *Transportation Revolution,* pp. 308–309; Smith, *Economic Aspects of the Second Bank,* pp. 143–144.

45. Temin, *Jacksonian Economy,* pp. 56–57. After citing Temin, I also agree with him that "this" judgment should not be interpreted to mean that there was no room for improvement!

46. For the mechanism, see Hammond, *Banks and Politics,* p. 198.

47. Quoted in Govan, *Nicholas Biddle,* pp. 85–86.

48. The bank's charter is given in full in Catterall, *Second Bank,* appendix 2. For the functions described in the text, see secs. 16, 15, 10.

49. Quoted in Govan, *Nicholas Biddle,* p. 50.

50. Gurley and Shaw, "Money," p. 105.

51. The international specie standard functioned in the following way: As prices rose in the United States, imports were encouraged and exports dampened; the resulting deficit on current account was followed in certain circumstances (a rise of exchange rates above the gold export point) by specie exports and a rising price level in recipient countries (especially in England, the main trading partner), followed in turn by a reversal of the flows of goods and specie.

52. Frederick Jackson Turner, *Rise of the New West, 1819–1829* (New York: Harper & Bros., 1906), pp. 35–40; Arthur M. Schlesinger, Jr., *The Age of Jackson* (Boston: Little, Brown, 1946), ch. 7, esp. p. 79; Richard Hofstadter, *The American Political Tradition and the Men Who Made It* (New York: Alfred A. Knopf, 1959), pp. 54–61.

53. Hammond, *Banks and Politics,* ch. 12; Marvin Meyers, *The Jacksonian Persuasion, Politics and Belief* (Stanford: Stanford University Press, 1957), pp. 6–9.

54. Schlesinger, *Age of Jackson,* p. 109.

55. The following account of the "Bank War" closely follows that of Thomas P. Govan *(Nicholas Biddle),* although I disagree with his exculpation of Biddle; see esp. chs. 13–14.

56. Quoted in Govan, *Nicholas Biddle,* p. 112.

57. Ibid., p. 115.

58. Ibid.

59. The account of Jackson's experience as a storekeeper is from Fritz Redlich, *The Molding of American Banking: Men and Ideas*, 2 vols. (New York: Johnson Reprint, 1968), I, 164; Schlesinger, *Age of Jackson*, p. 90.

60. Except for the final quotation, all of Jackson's statements are in Govan, *Nicholas Biddle*, pp. 232, 125; the last is in Schlesinger, *Age of Jackson*, p. 89.

61. September 1829 to Asbury Dickens, quoted in Govan, *Nicholas Biddle*, p. 112.

62. Quoted in ibid., p. 118.

63. Quoted in Hammond, *Banks and Politics*, p. 290.

64. Quoted in Carl B. Swisher, *Roger B. Taney* (Hamden, Conn.: Archon Books, 1961), p. 168.

65. Catterall, *Second Bank*, p. 275; Redlich, *Molding*, p. 161; Smith, *Economic Aspects*, pp. 13–17; Hammond, *Banks and Politics*, pp. 297–298; Govan, *Nicholas Biddle*, pp. viii–lx. Only Govan fails to find in Biddle any fault of character serious enough to cause his political defeat. But he reaches this judgment, I think, by turning his back on his own evidence.

66. Hammond, *Banks and Politics*, p. 374.

67. Govan, *Nicholas Biddle*, pp. 124–125.

68. Ibid., ch. 18. Govan argues that Biddle did not favor the introduction of the recharter bill in Congress in 1832 because he thought Jackson's expected veto would cause him to lose the election. He was certain, as was every informed political observer in the United States, that Jackson would win in the fall of 1832. His hope was that raising the bank issue before the election would force candidates for Congress to express themselves during their campaigns in regard to the recharter. Since he judged public opinion to be in favor of the bank, he hoped the voting public would return enough Congressmen committed to vote for recharter that a two-thirds majority would override Jackson's veto. This interpretation may be wrong, however. Some of Biddle's remarks to Clay, quoted in the text, sound as if he thought Jackson would be defeated.

69. Samuel R. Gammon, *The Presidential Campaign of 1832* (Baltimore: Johns Hopkins Press, 1922), pp. 149, 152–153.

70. Catterall, *Second Bank*, p. 235.

71. Wilburn, *Biddle's Bank*, pp. 8–11, 131; Peter Passell and Gavin Wright, "The Effects of Pre-Civil War Territorial Expansion on the Price of Slaves," *JPE*, 80 (1972), 1188–1202; Susan P. Lee, *The Westward Movement of the Cotton Economy: 1840–1860: Perceived Interests and Economic Realities* (New York: Arno Press, 1975), pp. 119–130; Gavin Wright, "An Econometric Study of Cotton Production and Trade, 1830–1860," *RES*, 53 (1971), 119.

72. Hammond specifies six factors responsible for the demise of the Bank, the "most important" being "the impatience of the state banks and of business enterprise with the federal Bank's restraint upon bank credit" (see *Banks and Politics*, p. 443); the Brown firm was second in importance to the bank itself in the foreign-exchange business (Smith, *Economic Aspects*, p. 46). Smith believes the "most significant failure of the Bank" was "a failure of political strategy" (p. 250).

73. Govan, *Nicholas Biddle*, pp. 124–125; Schlesinger, *Age of Jackson*, p. 81n13.

74. These figures are given in the *Speech of Mr. John Quincy Adams on the Removal of the Public Deposits . . .* (Washington, D.C.: Gales & Seaton, 1834), p. 35.

75. Richard P. McCormick, *The Second American Party System: Party Formation in the Jacksonian Era* (Chapel Hill: University of North Carolina Press, 1966).

76. Wilburn, *Biddle's Bank,* esp. ch. 8.

77. Temin, *Jacksonian Economy,* p. 15.

78. Ibid., pp. 17–23, 174.

7. Values, Law, and the Developing Economy

1. Theodore W. Schultz, "Capital Formation by Education," *JPE,* 68 (1960), 571–583.

2. David C. McClelland, *The Achieving Society* (Princeton, N.J.: Van Nostrand, 1961), pp. 39–46. See also David C. McClelland et al., *The Achievement Motive* (New York: Appleton-Century-Crofts, 1953), esp. pp. 102, 139, 145–146, 162–164, 181, and appendixes 1 and 3.

3. George Rogers Taylor, *The Transportation Revolution* (New York: Holt, Rinehart & Winston, 1951), p. 4.

4. Quoted in Carl N. Degler, *Out of Our Past: The Forces That Shaped Modern America* (New York: Harper & Row, 1959), p. 47.

5. Irwin G. Wyllie, *The Self-Made Man in America: The Myth of Rags to Riches* (New Brunswick, N.J.: Rutgers University Press, 1954), pp. 12–13.

6. William N. Parker, "From Northwest to Mid-West: Social Bases of a Regional History," in *Essays in Nineteenth Century Economic History: The Old Northwest,* ed. David C. Klingaman and Richard K. Vedder (Athens: Ohio University Press, 1975), p. 13.

7. Quoted in John William Ward, *Andrew Jackson, Symbol for an Age* (New York: Oxford University Press, 1955), pp. 169–171.

8. Wyllie, *Self-Made Man,* pp. 9–10.

9. "Success in Life," *Harper's New Monthly Magazine,* 7 (1853), 238; quoted in Wyllie, *Self-Made Man,* p. 9.

10. Quotations in Wyllie, *Self-Made Man,* pp. 55–66.

11. Ibid., p. 9.

12. The quotation from McGuffey is in ibid., p. 42; Frances Trollope, *Domestic Manners of the Americans,* ed. Donald Smalley (New York: Vintage Books, 1949), p. 121. Mrs. Trollope added that this was "the only feature in American society that I recognize as indicative of the equality they proffess *[sic].*"

13. Wyllie, *Self-Made Man,* p. 44; Robert Oliver to Lemuel Taylor, October 9, 1832, "Oliver Record Book," VIII, 525–526; October 22, 1788, I, 266. The former is a letter book, the latter a daybook. Both volumes are part of the Robert Oliver collection in the Maryland Historical Society, which spans the years 1783–1819.

14. Charles L. Sanford, "The Intellectual Origins and New-Worldliness of American Industry," *JEH,* 18 (1958), 1–16.

15. Ibid.; Robert Oliver to Robert S. Wilson, January 4, 1814, "Oliver Record Book," VII.

16. The phrase "a people in motion" is Glyndon Van Deusen's. See his *The Jacksonian Era, 1828–1848* (New York: Harper & Bros., 1959), p. 1; Alexis de Tocqueville,

Democracy in America, trans. Henry Reeve, 2 vols. (New York: Colonial Press, 1899), I, 51, 298–299; II, 166.

17. The following discussion of the role of government in promoting "internal improvements" is based substantially on Carter Goodrich, *Government Promotion of American Canals and Railroads* (New York: Columbia University Press, 1960); see esp. pp. 19–48. See also Carter Goodrich, ed., *Canals and American Economic Development* (New York: Columbia University Press, 1961).

18. Harry Ammon, *James Monroe: The Quest for National Identity* (New York: McGraw-Hill, 1971), pp. 387–392. This is an instance in which action speaks louder than words.

19. Charles S. Sydnor, *The Development of Southern Sectionalism, 1819–1848* (Baton Rouge: Louisiana State University Press, 1948), p. 150.

20. Goodrich, *Government Promotion,* pp. 169–171. See also Benjamin H. Hibbard, *History of Public Land Policies* (New York: Macmillan, 1924); Payson J. Treat, *The National Land System, 1785–1820* (New York: E. B. Treat, 1910); Louis Hartz, *Economic Policy and Democratic Thought: Pennsylvania, 1776–1860* (Cambridge, Mass.: Harvard University Press, 1948); Milton S. Heath, *Constructive Liberalism; The Role of the State in Economic Development in Georgia, to 1860* (Cambridge, Mass.: Harvard University Press, 1954); James Neal Primm, *Economic Policy in the Development of a Western State: Missouri, 1820–1860* (Cambridge, Mass.: Harvard University Press, 1954); Oscar Handlin and Mary Flug Handlin, *Commonwealth: A Study of the Role of Government in the American Economy: Massachusetts, 1774–1861* (New York: New York University Press, 1947); Robert A. Lively, "The American System: A Review Article," *BHR,* 29 (1955), 81–96; Harry N. Scheiber, *Ohio Canal Era: A Case Study of Government and the Economy, 1820–1861* (Athens: Ohio University Press, 1969); Hugh G. J. Aitken, ed., *The State and Economic Growth* (New York: Social Science Research Council, 1959).

21. Quoted in Sydnor, *Southern Sectionalism,* p. 139.

22. *NAR,* 12 (1821), 17–20; quoted in Goodrich, *Government Promotion,* p. 45.

23. The following account of Virginia's activities is based on Carter Goodrich, "The Virginia System of Mixed Enterprise: A Study of State Planning of Internal Improvements," *PSQ,* 64 (1949), 355–387.

24. Taylor, *Transportation Revolution,* p. 383.

25. Guy Stevens Callender, "The Early Transportation and Banking Enterprises of the States in Relation to the Growth of Corporations," *QJE,* 17 (1902), 142–143. The financial data are summarized by Lively, "American System," p. 86.

26. Joseph S. Davis, *Essays in the Earlier History of American Corporations,* 2 vols. (Cambridge, Mass.: Harvard University Press, 1917), II, passim; see also Stuart Bruchey, "Corporations—Historical Development," in *Encyclopaedia Britannica,* 1963 ed.

27. Bruchey, "Corporations"; G. Heberton Evans, *Business Incorporations in the United States, 1800–1943* (New York: National Bureau of Economic Research, 1948), p. 17, table 9; Hartz, *Economic Policy,* p. 38.

28. Bruchey, "Corporations"; Hartz, *Economic Policy;* Callender, "Early Transportation and Banking," pp. 161–162.

29. Hartz, *Economic Policy,* p. 291.

30. Carter Goodrich, "The Revulsion against Internal Improvements," *JEH,* 10 (1950), 145–169.

31. Harry H. Pierce, *Railroads of New York: A Study of Government Aid, 1826–1875* (Cambridge, Mass.: Harvard University Press, 1953); Lively, "American System," pp. 86–88, and sources cited therein.

32. Lively, "American System," pp. 91, 93; Hartz, *Economic Policy,* pp. 39–42; Evans, *Business Incorporations,* p. 31.

33. Lee Benson speaks of the "egalitarian impulse" of the age of Jackson. See his *The Concept of Jacksonian Democracy: New York as a Test Case* (Princeton: Princeton University Press, 1961), ch. 1.

34. Quoted in Bray Hammond, *Banks and Politics in America from the Revolution to the Civil War* (Princeton: Princeton University Press, 1957), p. 338.

35. Bureau of the Census, *Historical Statistics of the United States, Colonial Times to 1970,* 2 vols. (Washington, D.C.: Government Printing Office, 1976), II, 1020.

36. Quoted in Carl B. Swisher, *Roger B. Taney* (Hamden, Conn.: Archon Books, 1935), pp. 366–367.

37. Ibid., p. 373; *The Proprietors of the Charles River Bridge v. The Proprietors of the Warren Bridge,* 36 U.S. (11 Peters) 420 (1837).

38. *Bank of Augusta v. Earle,* 38 U.S. (13 Peters) 519 (1839); *Louisville, Cincinnati and Charleston Railroad Co. v. Letson,* 43 U.S. (2 Howard) 497 (1844); *Briscoe v. Bank of Kentucky,* 36 U.S. (11 Peters) 257 (1837); *Woodruff v. Trapnall,* 51 U.S. (10 Howard) 190 (1851); *Curran v. Arkansas,* 56 U.S. (15 Howard) 304 (1853); Stuart Bruchey, "Economy and Society in an Earlier America," *JEH,* 17 (1987), esp. 311–314.

39. Tony Allan Freyer, *Forums of Order: The Federal Courts and Business in American History* (Greenwich, Conn.: JAI Press, 1979), chs. 1–5, esp. pp. xx, 37, 93; Thomas C. Cochran, *Frontiers of Change: Early Industrialism in America* (New York: Oxford University Press, 1981), passim.

40. *Fletcher v. Peck* 10 U.S. (6 Cranch) 87 (1810); *Dartmouth College v. Woodward,* 17 U.S. (4 Wheaton) 518 (1819); *Ogden v. Saunders,* 25 U.S. (12 Wheaton) 213 (1827).

41. See the excellent discussion of the Charles River Bridge case in Morton Horwitz, *The Transformation of American Law* (Cambridge, Mass.: Harvard University Press, 1977), pp. 130–139. See also Stanley I. Kutler, *Privilege and Creative Destruction: The Charles River Bridge Case* (Philadelphia: Lippincott, 1971), esp. pp. 85–101.

42. The discussion which follows summarizes the main thesis of Horwitz, *Transformation;* see esp. ch. 3, "Subsidization of Economic Growth through the Legal System."

43. Charles F. Holt, *The Role of State Government in the Nineteenth Century American Economy, 1820–1902: A Quantitative Study* (New York: Arno Press, 1977), p. 50 (adapted from table 17).

44. Goodrich, *Government Promotion,* esp. chs. 1, 8. See also his *Canals and American Economic Development,* esp. the introduction and conclusion.

45. Goodrich, *Government Promotion.*

46. Roger Ransom, "Canals and Development: A Discussion of the Issues," *AER,* 54 (1964), 375; Fishlow, *American Railroads,* esp. chs. 4, 8.

8. The Agricultural Republic

1. Paul W. Gates, *History of Public Land Law Development* (Washington, D.C.: Government Printing Office, 1968), pp. 49–57, 86.

2. Ibid., pp. 124–126; Edward H. Rastatter, "Nineteenth Century Public Land Policy: The Case for the Speculator," in *Essays in Nineteenth Century Economic History: The Old Northwest,* ed. David C. Klingaman and Richard K. Vedder (Athens: Ohio University Press, 1975), pp. 119, 135.

3. *Statistical Atlas of the United States, 1900* (Washington, D.C.: U.S. Census Office, 1903), pp. 26–27.

4. Ibid., p. 28.

5. Gates, *Public Land Law,* pp. 130–131.

6. Frederick Jackson Turner, *The Frontier in American History* (New York: Henry Holt, 1920), p. 134. When Connecticut ceded its western lands to the federal government, it reserved a strip of land lying between the forty-first parallel and Lake Erie. The area extended 120 miles westward from the Pennsylvania line and was known as the Western Reserve.

7. Ibid., p. 136; *Statistical Atlas, 1900,* p. 27.

8. Quoted in Guy S. Callender, "The Early Transportation and Banking Enterprises of the States in Relation to the Growth of Corporations," *QJE,* 17 (1902), 123.

9. Ibid., pp. 111–162.

10. George Rogers Taylor, *The Transportation Revolution, 1815–1860* (New York: Holt, Rinehart & Winston, 1951), pp. 158–160, 135–136.

11. See Louis C. Hunter, *Steamboats on the Western Rivers* (Cambridge, Mass.: Harvard University Press, 1949), passim; Taylor, *Transportation Revolution,* pp. 63–64, 136; Gates, *Public Land Law,* p. 165.

12. Taylor, *Transportation Revolution,* p. 58.

13. Ibid., pp. 22, 27, 58.

14. Ibid., pp. 133–135.

15. Bureau of the Census, *Historical Statistics of the United States, Colonial Times to 1970,* 2 vols. (Washington, D.C.: Government Printing Office, 1976), I, 209; Douglass C. North, "International Capital Flows and the Development of the American West," *JEH,* 16 (1956), 500n; Gates, *Public Land Law,* pp. 136–137; Stuart Bruchey, ed., *Cotton and the Growth of the American Economy* (New York: Harcourt, Brace & World, 1967), pp. 89–98.

16. Bruchey, *Cotton,* p. 7.

17. Ibid., p. 45.

18. Lewis C. Gray, *History of Agriculture in the Southern United States to 1860,* 2 vols. (Gloucester, Mass.: Peter Smith, 1958), II, 679, 1032.

19. Ibid., pp. 678–680; Matthew B. Hammond, *The Cotton Industry; An Essay in American Economic History,* n.s. vol. 1, *Publications* (New York: American Economic Association, 1897), pp. 24–27.

20. Gray, *Agriculture in Southern United States,* pp. 610–611, 816–817; Ulrich B. Phillips, *American Negro Slavery* (Gloucester, Mass.: Peter Smith, 1959), p. 150.

21. Gray, *Agriculture in Southern United States,* pp. 683, 686–688.

22. Callender, "Early Transportation and Banking," pp. 124–125.

23. *Statistical Atlas of the United States, 1890* (Washington, D.C.: U.S. Census

Office, 1800), pp. 29–30. For the number of western settlers in 1820, I used Timothy Pitkin, *A Statistical View of the Commerce of the United States of America* (New York, 1835), pp. 589–590, including in "West" his population figures for Kentucky, Tennessee, Ohio, Indiana, Mississippi, Illinois, Louisiana, Missouri, Alabama, Michigan, and Arkansas.

24. *Statistical Atlas, 1890,* pp. 29–31; Gates, *Public Land Law,* p. 145; *Historical Statistics to 1970,* I, 8.

25. *Historical Statistics to 1970,* I, 8; *Statistical Atlas, 1890,* p. 31; Klingaman and Vedder, *Nineteenth Century Economic History,* pp. ix–x.

26. Paul W. Gates, *The Farmer's Age: Agriculture, 1815–1860* (New York: Holt, Rinehart & Winston, 1960), pp. 164–167, 269–270; Gray, *Agriculture in Southern United States,* II, p. 910; Lee Benson, *Merchants, Farmers, and Railroads: Railroad Regulation and New York Politics, 1850–1887* (Cambridge, Mass.: Harvard University Press, 1955), ch. 4.

27. *Statistical Atlas, 1900,* p. 32; Gates, *Public Land Law,* pp. 180–183; Ray Allen Billington, *Westward Expansion: A History of the American Frontier* (New York: Macmillan, 1967), pp. 405–410, 473–480, 688–696, 708–712; Paul W. Gates, *Landlords and Tenants on the Prairie Frontier: Studies in American Land Policy* (Ithaca: Cornell University Press, 1973), passim; John G. Clark, *The Grain Trade in the Old Northwest* (Urbana: University of Illinois Press, 1966), chs. 11–13.

28. Notably, Robert W. Fogel; see his *Railroads and American Economic Growth: Essays in Econometric History* (Baltimore: Johns Hopkins University Press, 1964), p. vii.

29. Albert Fishlow, *American Railroads and the Transformation of the Ante-Bellum Economy* (Cambridge, Mass.: Harvard University Press, 1965), ch. 4.

30. Ibid., ch. 5; Clarence H. Danhof, "Farm-making Costs and the 'Safety-Valve': 1850–1860," *JPE,* 49 (1941), 317–359; William N. Parker and Judith L. V. Klein, "Productivity Growth in Grain Production in the United States, 1840–60 and 1900–10," in *Output, Employment, and Productivity in the United States after 1800,* ed. Dorothy Brady, National Bureau of Economic Research, vol. 30, *Studies in Income and Wealth* (New York: Columbia University Press, 1966), pp. 523–579. Robert E. Gallman believes that the higher yields in the West were the almost exclusive source of an increase of about 13 percent in the value of grain yields (oats, corn, and wheat) between 1800 and 1850; see his "The Agricultural Sector and the Pace of Economic Growth: U.S. Experience in the Nineteenth Century," in Klingaman and Vedder, *Nineteenth Century Economic History,* p. 45.

31. Gallman, "Agricultural Sector," pp. 44, 47–49.

32. Marvin W. Towne and Wayne D. Rasmussen, "Farm Gross Product and Gross Investment in the Nineteenth Century," in *Trends in the American Economy in the Nineteenth Century,* ed. William N. Parker, National Bureau of Economic Research, vol. 24, *Studies in Income and Wealth* (Princeton: Princeton University Press, 1960), pp. 255–312; Leo Rogin, *The Introduction of Farm Machinery and Its Relation to the Productivity of Labor in the Agriculture of the United States during the Nineteenth Century* (Berkeley: University of California Press, 1931), pp. 125–126.

33. Gates, *Farmer's Age,* pp. 287–288.

34. According to Gavin Wright, about 86 percent of the cotton was grown on

farms of more than 100 acres, and these farms contained 90 percent of the slaves; see his *The Political Economy of the Cotton South: Households, Markets, and Wealth in the Nineteenth Century* (New York: W. W. Norton, 1978), pp. 27–28.

35. Ibid.; Gray, *Agriculture in Southern United States,* pp. 689–690, 700–708, 729–730, 750.

36. Eugene Genovese, *Roll, Jordan, Roll: The World the Slaves Made* (New York: Pantheon, 1974), pp. 11, 13; Phillips, *American Negro Slavery,* chs. 12–14; Bruchey, *Cotton,* pp. 165–188. Among scholars doubtful of the thesis of scale economies are William N. Parker and Gavin Wright; see Parker's "The Slave Plantation in American Agriculture," in *Contributions to the First International Conference of Economic History* (Paris: Mouton, 1960), pp. 321–331, and Wright, *Political Economy of Cotton South,* pp. 44–55, 74–87. Among those arguing in support of the thesis are Robert W. Fogel and Stanley L. Engerman; see their *Time on the Cross: The Economics of American Negro Slavery* (New York: Little, Brown, 1974), pp. 137–143, 204, 208–209, 234–237. See also Douglass C. North, *The Economic Growth of the United States, 1790–1860* (Englewood Cliffs, N.J.: Prentice-Hall, 1961), p. 125. Fogel and Engerman refine their position in "Explaining the Relative Efficiency of Slave Agriculture in the Antebellum South," *AER,* 67 (1977), 275–296.

37. Gallman, in Klingaman and Vedder, *Nineteenth Century Economic History,* pp. 45–48; Robert E. Gallman and Ralph V. Anderson, "Slaves as Fixed Capital: Slave Labor and Southern Economic Development," *JAH,* 64 (1977), 24–46, esp. 39–46.

38. John Steele to David Anderson, October 1808, Papers of James O. Wettereau, Special Collections, Columbia University, box and folder nos. unavailable.

39. Kenneth Stampp, *The Peculiar Institution* (New York: Alfred A. Knopf, 1956), pp. 404–405; Gavin Wright, "New and Old Views on the Economics of Slavery," *JEH,* 33 (1973), 452–466; Ulrich B. Phillips, "The Economic Cost of Slaveholding in the Cotton Belt," *PSQ,* 20 (1905), 257–275.

40. Stampp, *Peculiar Institution,* pp. 383–418.

41. Alfred H. Conrad and John Meyer, "The Economics of Slavery in the Antebellum South," *JPE,* 66 (1958), 95–122.

42. Wright, "New and Old Views," p. 460; Edward Saraydar, "A Note on the Profitability of Antebellum Slavery," *SEJ,* 30 (1964), 325–332; Noel Butlin, *Antebellum Slavery* (Canberra: Australian National University Press, 1971). The critic of the estimated costs of animals was Eugene Genovese. The exchange with Conrad occurred orally at the annual meeting of the Economic History Association in 1967.

43. Raymond Battalio and John Kagel, "The Structure of Antebellum Southern Agriculture: South Carolina, A Case Study," *AH,* 44 (1970), 25–37; Robert Evans, Jr., "The Economics of American Negro Slavery," in National Bureau of Economic Research, *Aspects of Labor Economics* (Princeton: Princeton University Press, 1962), pp. 185–243; Hugh G. J. Aitken, *Did Slavery Pay? Readings in the Economics of Black Slavery in the United States* (Boston: Houghton Mifflin, 1971), pp. 225–226. Richard Sutch was the scholar who pointd out the large capital gains from holding slaves; see his "The Profitability of Ante-Bellum Slavery—Revisited," *SEJ,* 31 (1965); Wright, *Political Economy of Cotton South,* p. 2.

44. Yasukichi Yasuba, "The Profitability and Viability of Plantation Slavery in the United States," *ESQ,* 12 (1961), 60–67 (rpr. Robert W. Fogel and Stanley L. Enger-

man, *The Reinterpretation of American Economic History* [New York: Harper & Row, 1971], pp. 362–368).

45. Morton Rothstein, "The Cotton Frontier of the Antebellum South: A Methodological Battleground," in *The Structure of the Cotton Economy of the Antebellum South,* ed. William N. Parker (Baltimore: Waverly Press, 1970), p. 161.

46. Diane Lindstrom, "Southern Dependence upon Interregional Grain Supplies: A Review of the Trade Flows, 1840–1860," in Parker, *Structure of Cotton Economy,* pp. 101–115; Albert Fishlow, "Antebellum Interregional Trade Reconsidered," in *New Views in American Economic Development,* ed. Ralph Andreano (Boston: Schenkman, 1965) (orig. pub. in *AER,* 54, 1964); Robert Gallman, "Self-Sufficiency in the Cotton Economy of the Antebellum South," *AH,* 44 (1970), 5–23, esp. 19 (rpr. in Parker, *Structure of Cotton Economy,* pp. 5–25).

47. Gavin Wright and Howard Kunreuther, "Cotton, Corn and Risk in the Nineteenth Century," *JEH,* 35 (1975), 526–551.

48. Wright, *Political Economy of Cotton South,* pp. 55–74.

49. Ibid., pp. 74–87; William N. Parker, "Slavery and Southern Economic Development: An Hypothesis and Some Evidence," *AH,* 44 (1970), 115–125; Gavin Wright, "Slavery and the Cotton Boom," *EEH,* 12 (1975), 439–451.

50. Ulrich B. Phillips, *Life and Labor in the Old South* (New York: Grosset & Dunlop, 1929), pp. 288–289.

51. Fogel and Engerman, *Time on the Cross,* pp. 25–29; Richard Sutch, "The Care and Feeding of Slaves," in Paul A. David et al., *Reckoning with Slavery: A Critical Study in the Quantitative History of American Negro Slavery* (New York: Oxford University Press, 1976), pp. 234–235.

52. Paul A. David and Peter Temin, "Slavery: The Progressive Institution?" in David et al., *Reckoning with Slavery,* pp. 223–224; Sutch, "Care and Feeding," in ibid., pp. 265–268.

53. Sutch, "Care and Feeding," p. 300.

54. Richard Sutch, "The Breeding of Slaves for Sale and the Westward Expansion of Slavery, 1850–1860," in *Race and Slavery in the Western Hemisphere: Quantitative Studies,* ed. Stanley L. Engerman and Eugene D. Genovese (Princeton: Princeton University Press, 1975), pp. 173–210; Herbert Gutman and Richard Sutch, "The Slave Family: Protected Agent of Capitalist Masters or Victim of the Slave Trade?" in David et al., *Reckoning with Slavery,* pp. 94–133; Willie Lee Rose, ed., *A Documentary History of Slavery in North America* (New York: Oxford University Press, 1976), p. 151.

55. Gavin Wright and Peter Passell, "The Effects of Territorial Expansion on the Price of Slaves," *JPE,* 80 (1972), 1188–1202; Susan Previant Lee, *The Westward Movement of the Cotton Economy, 1840–1860: Perceived Interests and Economic Realities* (New York: Arno Press, 1977), passim.

56. Robert W. Fogel and Stanley L. Engerman, "The Economics of Slavery," in idem, *Reinterpretation,* p. 335.

57. Gavin Wright, "Prosperity, Progress, and American Slavery," in David et al., *Reckoning with Slavery,* pp. 325–326.

58. Ibid., pp. 324–325.

59. Ibid., p. 309.

60. Phillips, *American Negro Slavery*, p. 375.

61. Eugene Genovese, *The Political Economy of Slavery: Studies in the Economy and Society of the Slave South* (New York: Pantheon, 1965), passim.

62. Thomas F. Huertas, "Damnifying Growth in the Antebellum South," *JEH*, 39 (1979), 91–92.

63. Wright, *Political Economy of Cotton South*, pp. 107–127; Claudia Goldin, *Urban Slavery in the American South, 1820–1860* (Chicago: University of Chicago Press, 1976), ch. 5.

64. Rothstein, "Cotton Frontier," p. 154; Edwin J. Perkins, *Financing Anglo-American Trade: The House of Brown, 1800–1880* (Cambridge, Mass.: Harvard University Press, 1975), ch. 7; Marilyn Lavin, "William Bostwick: Connecticut Yankee in Antebellum Georgia" (Ph.D. diss., Columbia University, 1977).

65. Wright, *Political Economy of Cotton South*, p. 35. Wright points out, however, that the distribution of cotton output was just as concentrated as were slaveholdings (pp. 27–28).

66. Robert E. Gallman, "The Pace and Pattern of American Economic Growth," in *American Economic Growth, An Economist's History of the United States*, ed. Lance Davis et al. (New York: Harper & Row, 1972), p. 30; idem, "Trends in the Size Distribution of Wealth in the Nineteenth Century: Some Speculations," in *Six Papers on the Size Distribution of Wealth and Income*, ed. Lee Soltow, National Bureau of Economic Research, vol. 33, *Studies in Income and Wealth* (New York: Columbia University Press, 1969), pp. 1–30, esp. pp. 3–4, 8–9, 15, 24–25, 28–30; Wright, *Political Economy of Cotton South*, pp. 24–42; Fogel and Engerman, *Reinterpretation*, p. 335.

67. Stephan Thernstrom, *Poverty and Progress: Social Mobility in a Nineteenth Century City* (Cambridge, Mass.: Harvard University Press, 1964), chs. 5–6.

68. Gallman, "Trends in Size Distribution of Wealth," pp. 1–30.

69. Genovese, *Roll, Jordan, Roll*, p. 59.

9. In the Wake of the Civil War

1. Charles and Mary Beard, *The Rise of American Civilization* (New York: Macmillan, 1927), p. 99.

2. Louis Hacker, *The Triumph of American Capitalism* (New York: Simon & Schuster, 1940), p. 373.

3. Peter Temin, "Manufacturing," in *American Economic Growth: An Economist's History of the United States*, ed. Lance Davis et al. (New York: Harper & Row, 1972), p. 447. Temin notes, however, that the magnitude of the effects are controversial.

4. Robert E. Gallman, "Commodity Output, 1839–1899," in *Trends in the American Economy in the Nineteenth Century*, ed. William N. Parker, National Bureau of Economic Research, vol. 24, *Studies in Income and Wealth* (Princeton: Princeton University Press, 1960), pp. 13–72; idem, "Fundamental Concepts of Statistical Studies as Applied to Economic History," in *Approaches to Economic History*, ed. George Rogers Taylor and Lucius F. Ellsworth (Charlottesville: University Press of Virginia, 1971), pp. 63–86; idem, "Gross National Product in the United States, 1834–1909," in *Output, Employment, and Productivity in the United States after 1800*, ed. Dorothy

Brady, National Bureau of Economic Research, vol. 30, *Studies in Income and Wealth* (New York: Columbia University Press, 1966), pp. 3–76; Robert E. Gallman, "The Pace and Pattern of American Economic Growth," in Davis et al., *American Economic Growth,* pp. 15–60.

5. Thomas C. Cochran, "Did the Civil War Retard Industrialization?" in *The Economic Impact of the Civil War,* ed. Ralph Andreano (Cambridge, Mass.: Schenkman, 1962), pp. 148–161.

6. Stanley L. Engerman, "The Economic Impact of the Civil War," *EEH,* 3 (1966), 176–199.

7. Jeffrey G. Williamson, *Late Nineteenth-Century American Development: A General Equilibrium Analysis* (London: Cambridge University Press, 1974), p. 3.

8. Paul A. David has come closer than any predecessor to demonstrating the favorable impact of protective tariffs on the growth of the cotton textile industry. After the tariff of 1824, tariffs provided subsidies leading to income redistribution favoring the manufacturers; see David's "Learning by Doing and Tariff Protection: A Reconsideration of the Case of the Antebellum United States Cotton Textile Industry," *JEH,* 30 (1970), 521–601.

9. See Cochran, "Did the Civil War Retard Industrialization?"

10. Stephen J. DeCanio and Joel Mokyr, "Inflation and the Wage Lag during the American Civil War," *EEH,* 14 (1977), 311–336; Paul B. Trescott, "Federal Government Receipts and Expenditures, 1871–1875," *JEH,* 26 (1966), 206–222; Paul Studenski and Herman E. Kroos, *Financial History of the United States,* 2d ed. (New York: McGraw-Hill, 1963), pp. 147–157. Earlier scholars, especially Wesley C. Mitchell, emphasized heavily the role of the greenbacks in producing Civil War inflation; see Mitchell's *A History of the Greenbacks, with Special Reference to the Economic Consequences of their Issue, 1862–1865* (Chicago: University of Chicago Press, 1903). More recent analysts, such as DeCanio and Mokyr, and Studenski and Kroos, point to the role of the banking system in monetizing the debt and to the probability that liquid assets were closer substitutes for money than for tangible capital in assetholders' portfolios.

11. DeCanio and Mokyr, "Inflation and the Wage Lag," pp. 324–325.

12. W. Elliot Brownlee, *Dynamics of Ascent* (New York: Alfred A. Knopf, 1974), p. 183.

13. Bureau of the Census, *Historical Statistics of the United States, Colonial Times to 1970,* 2 vols. (Washington, D.C.: Government Printing Office, 1975), I, 8.

14. Ansley J. Coale and Melvin Zelink, *New Estimates of Fertility and Population in the United States: A Study of Annual White Births from 1855 to 1960 and of Completeness of Enumeration in the Censuses from 1880 to 1960* (Princeton: Princeton University Press, 1963), p. 35.

15. *Historical Statistics to 1970,* I, 76, 54; Richard A. Easterlin, *Population, Labor Force, and Long Swings in Economic Growth: The American Experience* (New York: Columbia University Press, 1968), p. 228; idem, "The American Population," in *American Economic Growth: An Economist's History of the United States,* ed. Lance E. Davis et al. (New York: Harper & Row, 1972), pp. 146–147, 166–167, and sources cited on p. 167.

16. Easterlin, "American Population," pp. 135, 142–143.

17. Figures given for arrivals in the study by Kuznets and Rubin cited below differ

from those in *Historical Statistics to 1970*. Since the latter source presents no figures for departures, the percentages given in Table 20 were calculated on the basis of the Kuznets and Rubin arrival–departure figures and then applied to the arrival figures in *Historical Statistics*. Official figures for departures are available only since 1908, so that the Kuznets and Rubin projections back to 1870 are estimates. See Simon Kuznets and Ernest Rubin, *Immigration and the Foreign Born*, Occasional Paper 46 (New York: National Bureau of Economic Research, 1954), p. 19.

18. *Historical Statistics to 1970*, I, 106–107; Kuznets and Rubin, *Immigration and the Foreign Born*, p. 3.

19. Williamson, *Late Nineteenth Century American Development*, p. 246.

20. Hope T. Eldridge and Dorothy Swain Thomas, *Population Redistribution and Economic Growth*, 3 vols. (Philadelphia: American Philosophical Society, 1964), III, 64–89.

21. Stanley Lebergott, *Manpower in Economic Growth: The American Record since 1800* (New York: McGraw-Hill, 1964), p. 13.

22. The discussion of the railroad sector is based on two intensive analyses by Albert Fishlow. See his "Internal Transportation," in Davis et al., *American Economic Growth*, pp. 468–547, and "Productivity and Technological Change in the Railroad Sector, 1840–1910," in Brady, *Output, Employment, and Productivity*, pp. 583–646. See also Alfred D. Chandler, Jr., ed., *The Railroads: The Nation's First Big Business* (New York: Harcourt, Brace & World, 1965).

23. Fishlow, "Internal Transportation," p. 501.

24. Robert W. Fogel, *Railroads and American Economic Growth: Essays in Econometric History* (Baltimore: Johns Hopkins University Press, 1964).

25. C. Vann Woodward, *The Burden of Southern History* (Baton Rouge: Louisiana State University Press, 1960), p. 17; Richard A. Easterlin, "Interregional Differences in Per Capita Income, Population, and Total Income, 1840–1950," in Parker, *Trends in the American Economy*, pp. 85–89; Easterlin, "Regional Income Trends, 1850–1950," in *American Economic History*, ed. Seymour Harris (New York: McGraw-Hill, 1961), 528.

26. James L. Sellers, "The Economic Incidence of the Civil War in the South," in *The Economic Impact of the American Civil War*, 2d ed., ed. Ralph Andreano (Boston: Schenkman, 1967), p. 106; Robert Higgs, *The Transformation of the American Economy, 1865–1914* (New York: John Wiley, 1971), p. 114.

27. Eugene M. Lerner, "Southern Output and Agricultural Income," in Andreano, *Economic Impact*, pp. 109–122; Paul W. Gates, *Agriculture and the Civil War* (New York: Alfred A. Knopf, 1965), pp. 108, 371–373; E. Merton Coulter, *The South during Reconstruction, 1865–1877* (Baton Rouge: Louisiana State University Press, 1947), ch. 1.

28. Gavin Wright, "The Strange Career of the New Southern Economic History," in *The Promise of American History: Progress and Prospects*, ed. Stanley I. Kutler and Stanley N. Katz (Baltimore: Johns Hopkins University Press, 1982), p. 169; Roger L. Ransom and Richard Sutch, *One Kind of Freedom: The Economic Consequences of Emancipation* (Cambridge: Cambridge University Press, 1977), ch. 3; Stanley L. Engerman, "The Economic Impact of the Civil War," in Andreano, *Economic Impact*, pp. 188–209; Claudia G. Goldin and Frank D. Lewis, "The Economic Cost of the Civil

War: Estimates and Consequences," *JEH*, 35 (1975), 303; Peter Temin, "The Post-Bellum Recovery of the South and the Cost of the Civil War," *JEH*, 36 (1976), 898–907, esp. 898–904.

29. Ransom and Sutch, *One Kind of Freedom*, pp. 48–50.

30. Ibid., pp. 53–54.

31. Ibid., pp. 192–199; Easterlin, "Interregional Differences," pp. 85–88; Gavin Wright, *The Political Economy of the Cotton South: Households, Markets, and Wealth in the Nineteenth Century* (New York: W. W. Norton, 1978), pp. 183–184.

32. C. Vann Woodward, *Origins of the New South, 1877–1913* (Baton Rouge: Louisiana State University Press, 1951), p. 292.

33. Eric Foner, *Politics and Ideology in the Age of the Civil War* (New York: Oxford University Press, 1980), p. 125.

34. Harold D. Woodman, "Sequel to Slavery: The New History Views the Postbellum South," *JSH*, 43 (1977), 523–554; Foner, *Politics and Ideology*, pp. 99, 106.

35. Harold D. Woodman, "Post–Civil War Agriculture and the Law," *AH*, 53 (1979), 321–322; Ransom and Sutch, *One Kind of Freedom*, pp. 60–61.

36. Ransom and Sutch, *One Kind of Freedom*, pp. 57, 66–67; Woodman, "Post–Civil War Agriculture," p. 323.

37. Woodman, "Post–Civil War Agriculture," pp. 323–327, 327n3.

38. Ibid., pp. 326–328; see the cases cited on p. 327n3.

39. Ibid., pp. 329–332.

40. Ibid., pp. 332–336.

41. Wright, "Strange Career," p. 168.

42. Gavin Wright and Howard Kunreuther, "Cotton, Corn, and Risk in the Nineteenth Century," *JEH*, 35 (1975), 526–551; Wright, *Political Economy of Cotton South*, pp. 183–184.

43. Ransom and Sutch, *One Kind of Freedom*, ch. 8, esp. pp. 162–165; Woodman, "Post–Civil War Agriculture," p. 326.

44. Ransom and Sutch, *One Kind of Freedom*, ch. 7, esp. pp. 126–137, 161.

45. Robert Higgs, *Competition and Coercion: Blacks in the American Economy, 1865–1914* (Cambridge: Cambridge University Press, 1977), p. 59.

46. Ibid., pp. 57, 61.

47. Ibid., p. 55; Wright, "Strange Career," p. 173.

10. Three Frontiers

1. Gilbert C. Fite, *The Farmer's Frontier, 1865–1900* (New York: Holt, Rinehart & Winston, 1966), p. 2.

2. The account of western settlement given here follows closely that of Hope T. Eldridge and often reflects the same language. Eldridge acknowledges that her own account is "based largely" on that given in *Statistical Atlas of the United States* (Washington, D.C.: Bureau of the Census, 1914), pp. 12–23. See Hope T. Eldridge and Dorothy Swaine Thomas, *Demographic Analyses*, vol. 3 of *Population Redistribution and Economic Growth, United States, 1850–1950*, ed. Everett S. Lee et al., 3 vols. (Philadelphia: American Philosophical Society, 1957), pp. 3–5. The physical and other characteristics of the Great Plains are described superbly in the classic by Walter P. Webb, *The Great Plains* (Boston: Ginn, 1931), pp. 5–6.

3. Rodman Paul, *Mining Frontiers of the Far West: 1848–1880* (New York: Holt, Rinehart & Winston, 1963), pp. 2, 96; Richard A. Easterlin, "Interregional Differences in Per Capita Income, Population, and Total Income, 1840–1950," in *Trends in the American Economy in the Nineteenth Century*, ed. William N. Parker, National Bureau of Economic Research, vol. 24, *Studies in Income and Wealth* (Princeton: Princeton University Press, 1960), p. 183.

4. Paul, *Mining Frontiers*, pp. 19, 28–33, 63–64, 79–83; Israel Borenstein, *Capital and Output Trends in Mining Industries, 1870–1948: Studies in Capital Formation and Financing*, Occasional Paper 45 (New York: National Bureau of Economic Research, 1954), pp. 36–37.

5. Gary D. Libecap, *The Evolution of Private Mineral Rights: Nevada's Comstock Lode* (New York: Arno Press, 1978), pp. 8, 27–28; Robert W. Swenson, "Legal Aspects of Mineral Resources Exploitation," in *History of Public Land Law Development*, ed. Paul W. Gates (Washington, D.C.: Government Printing Office, 1968), ch. 23, esp. pp. 702, 706, 711.

6. Libecap, *Private Mineral Rights*, p. 29; Swenson, "Legal Aspects," p. 709.

7. Libecap, *Private Mineral Rights*, pp. 37–38, 127.

8. The territorial legislature's declaration is quoted in ibid., p. 61; see also pp. 96, 135.

9. Ibid., pp. 53–55, 96, 158.

10. The indentured quotation is from ibid., p. 245; see also pp. 155, 172. Libecap says the mineral rights structure was well established by 1867 (p. 128).

11. Paul, *Mining Frontiers*, pp. 50–51, 110, 138, 150, 159.

12. Webb, *Great Plains*, pp. 26, 50.

13. Ibid., pp. 224–227; Louis Pelzer, *The Cattlemen's Frontier: A Record of the Trans-Mississippi Cattle Industry from Open Trains to Pooling Companies, 1850–1890* (New York: Russell & Russell, 1969), pp. 37–42 (orig. pub. 1936).

14. George W. Rollins, *The Struggle of the Cattleman, Sheepman and Settler for Control of Lands in Wyoming, 1867–1910* (New York: Arno Press, 1979), pp. 45–46.

15. Ibid., pp. 56–57.

16. Ibid., pp. 54–55, 59–61.

17. Ibid., pp. 67–73.

18. Ibid., pp. 169, 171. Although a number of Land Office reports pointed out the inadequacies of the land laws, "very few" changes were made, "especially those dealing with grazing, until after the turn of the century" (pp. 175–176). By then, the ranges were badly overstocked and depleted.

19. Webb, *Great Plains*, ch. 8, esp. pp. 313, 317, 322–324, 328, 348.

20. Fred Shannon, *The Farmer's Last Frontier: Agriculture, 1860–1897* (New York: Farrar & Rinehart, 1945), p. 27; Fite, *Farmer's Frontier*, pp. 12, 91–112.

21. Fite, *Farmer's Frontier*, pp. 1–23, 135–136.

22. Ibid., pp. 81–83; Shannon, *Farmer's Last Frontier*, p. 155.

23. Fite, *Farmer's Frontier*, pp. 81–86; Shannon, *Farmer's Last Frontier*, pp. 158–159.

24. Fite, *Farmer's Frontier*, pp. 89–90; H. J. Habbakkuk, *American and British Technology in the Nineteenth Century: The Search for Labour-Saving Inventions* (Cambridge: Cambridge University Press, 1962), pp. 13, 38–39.

25. Fite, *Farmer's Frontier*, p. 93; Shannon, *Farmers' Last Frontier*, pp. 139–140; William N. Parker and Judith L. V. Klein, "Productivity Growth in Grain Production in the United States, 1840–60 and 1900–10," in *Output, Employment, and Productivity in the United States after 1800*, ed. Dorothy Brady, National Bureau of Economic Research, vol. 30, *Studies in Income and Wealth* (New York: Columbia University Press, 1966), p. 543. Parker finds power generation to have been "strikingly absent from agriculture in the nineteenth century. Despite much talk and experimentation on the steamplow, the steam engine made no significant impact in the field" ("Sources of Agricultural Productivity in the Nineteenth Century," *JFE*, 49 [1967], 1463); Peter Temin and Franklin Knight believe the westward movement was more important as a source of productivity growth than do Parker and Klein, but they acknowledge their inability to assign that movement a numerical value.

26. Ray A. Billington, in foreword to Fite, *Farmer's Frontier*, p. vi; Martin L. Primack, *Farm Formed Capital in American Agriculture, 1850 to 1910* (New York: Arno Press, 1977), pp. 6, 11. Percentages calculated from figures on p. 11. Although the five prairie states "all contained significant amounts of forest," they were "completely prairie and not affected by large amounts of forest land" (p. 7).

27. Shannon, *Farmer's Last Frontier*, pp. 163–165; Robert Klepper estimates both partial and total gross agricultural product for thirty states and makes the justifiable assumption that the higher the ratio between the two estimates, the greater the degree of specialization. New England and the mountain states are excluded from the analysis. Klepper finds his measure of specialization "highly correlated with regions as it is greatest in states where cotton and wheat were important cash crops" (*The Economic Bases for Agrarian Protest Movements in the United States, 1870–1900* [New York: Arno Press, 1978], pp. 37–38, 57).

28. Shannon, *Farmer's Last Frontier*, pp. 259–261, esp. table on p. 260.

29. Paul Glenn Munyon, *A Reassessment of New England Agriculture in the Last Thirty Years of the Nineteenth Century* (New York: Arno Press, 1978), pp. 5, 194–206, 214–217. For the traditional view of the area's decline, see Harold F. Wilson, *The Hill Country of Northern New England* (New York: Columbia University Press, 1936), p. 95.

30. *Slaughter-House Cases*, 16 Wall 36 (1873); *Minnesota v. Barber*, 136 U.S. 313 (1890).

31. Shannon, *Farmer's Last Frontier*, p. 148; Guy A. Lee, "The Historical Significance of the Chicago Grain Elevator System," *AH*, 11 (1937), 16–32; Morton Rothstein,"America in the International Rivalry for the British Wheat Market, 1860–1914," *MVHR*, 47 (1960), 411.

32. Rothstein, "British Wheat Market," pp. 401–402, 411.

33. Ibid., p. 403; Lee, "Chicago Grain Elevator System," p. 27.

34. Ann Mayhew, "A Reappraisal of the Causes of Farm Protest in the United States, 1870–1900," *JEH*, 32 (1972), 465; Harold D. Woodman, "Chicago Businessmen and the 'Granger' Laws," *AH*, 36 (1962), 4n, 26, 5; Shannon, *Farmer's Last Frontier*, ch. 14; John D. Hicks, *The Populist Revolt* (Minneapolis: University of Minnesota Press, 1931), p. 23.

35. Shannon, *Farmer's Last Frontier*, p. 140 (see table "Prices of Typical Machines, 1860–1900").

36. Allan G. Bogue, *Money at Interest: Farm Mortgages on the Middle Border* (New York: Russell & Russell, 1955), pp. 1–6, 262–276; Douglass C. North, *Growth and Welfare in the American Past* (Englewood Cliffs, N.J.: Prentice-Hall, 1966), p. 286; Robert W. Fogel and Jack Rutner, "The Efficiency Effects of Federal Land Policy, 1850–1900: A Report of Some Provisional Findings," University of Chicago, Report 7027 (Mimeograph, June 1970), p. 19. The quotation is from Klepper, *Agrarian Protest Movements*, p. 4. Freight rates are from Shannon, *Farmer's Last Frontier*, p. 298, and North, *Growth and Welfare*, pp. 139–141.

37. Klepper, *Agrarian Protest Movements*, pp. 7–55, esp. pp. 7, 19, 22, 32–33, 55. In the quoted passage, Klepper is discussing estimates of "partial" gross product, which "account for well over 50 percent of total gross product for most of the 30 states in 1879, 1889, 1899, and 1909—years for which estimates of total gross product were made." He explains how he goes from partial to total estimates in these words: "Annual estimates of partial gross product [the ratios are given in tabular form on p. 33] in census years provide annual estimates of total gross product, and a similar computation gives estimates of year to year changes in total gross product" (p. 33). The crucial assumption of this useful study is that "gross revenue fluctuated more than costs" (p. 32). The study, therefore, while addressing the question of fluctuating farm output (income), does not directly confront the specific agrarian complaints about extortionate railroad rates, and so on; Shannon, *Farmer's Last Frontier*, pp. 298–299.

38. George H. Miller, *Railroads and the Granger Laws* (Madison: University of Wisconsin Press, 1971), pp. 55–56.

39. Shannon, *Farmer's Last Frontier*, pp. 300–301. The points made in the final two sentences were stressed by Hanry Varnum Poor, long-time late-nineteenth-century editor of *Railway Age*, in introductions to his frequent statistical compilations. I am indebted to Alfred D. Chandler, Jr., the biographer of Poor, for this information.

40. John F. Stover, *American Railroads* (Chicago: University of Chicago Press, 1961), p. 114.

41. U.S. Industrial Commission, *Report of the Industrial Commission on the Relations and Conditions of Capital and Labor in Manufacturing and General Business . . . ,* 2 vols. (Washington, D.C.: Government Printing Office, 1901), II, 142.

42. Edward C. Kirkland, *Industry Comes of Age: Business, Labor, and Public Policy, 1860–1897* (New York: Holt, Rinehart & Winston, 1961), p. 80.

43. Lee, "Chicago Grain Elevator System, p. 28.

44. Ibid., pp. 28–29.

45. Solon J. Buck, *Agrarian Crusade: A Chronicle of the Farmer in Politics* (New Haven: Yale University Press, 1920), pp. 52–55.

46. *Munn v. Illinois*, 94 U.S. 113 (1876), pp. 85–86, 90.

47. *Chicago, Milwaukee and St. Paul Railway Company v. Minnesota*, 134 U.S. 418 (1890).

48. *Wabash, St. Louis & Pacific Railway Company v. Illinois*, 118 U.S. 557 (1886). See also I. L. Sharfman, *The Interstate Commerce Commission; A Study in Administrative Law and Procedure*, 4 vols. (New York: Commonwealth Fund, 1935–36), I, 14–19.

49. Edward A. Purcell, Jr., "Ideas and Interests: Businessmen and the Interstate Commerce Act," *JAH*, 54 (1961), 561.

50. Thomas C. Cochran, *Railroad Leaders, 1845–1890: The Business Mind in Action* (Cambridge, Mass.: Harvard University Press, 1953), p. 185.

51. In *Interstate Commerce Commission v. Cincinnati, New Orleans and Texas Pacific Railway Company* (the "Maximum Rate" case), for example, the Court held that Congress had not conferred upon the ICC the power either to prescribe maximum or minimum rates or to determine whether or not some past rate was just and reasonable. See 167 U.S. 479 (1897).

52. In *Railroads and Regulation, 1877–1916* (New York: W. W. Norton, 1965), p. 3, Gabriel Kolko argues that the railroads were the "most important single advocates of federal regulation," but Edward Purcell, in his "Ideas and Interests," while appearing on one page (561) to accept Kolko's thesis, points out on another page (577) that there existed a "widespread and vocal opposition to the . . . Act on the part of many railroad executives." This opposition is confirmed by Cochran's examination of the correspondence of many railroad presidents (see his *Railroad Leaders,* pp. 197–201).

53. *I.C.C. v. Illinois Central R.R.,* 215 U.S. 452, 470, 30 S.Ct. 155, 160, 54 L.Ed. e80 (1910); William K. Jones, *Cases and Materials on Regulated Industries* (Brooklyn: Foundation Press, 1967), pp. 57–64.

54. In 1905 Henry Carter Adams, the ICC's economist and statistician, reported that "with very few exceptions witnesses before the Commission declared that 'rebates' have either wholly ceased or are much less frequent than formerly"; quoted in Albro Martin, *Enterprise Denied: Origins of the Decline of American Railroads, 1897–1917* (New York: Columbia University Press, 1970), p. 39.

55. Quoted in ibid., p. 51. The argument in the text follows the persuasive case made by Martin; see esp. pp. vii–xiv, chs. 7–12, and appendix.

11. The Maturing of American Industry

1. The value-added and sector-share calculations are in constant prices; see Robert E. Gallman and Edward S. Howle, "Trends in the Structure of the American Economy since 1840," in *The Reinterpretation of American Economic History,* ed. Robert W. Fogel and Stanley L. Engerman (New York: Harper & Row, 1971), p. 26; Gallman, "Commodity Output, 1839–1899," in *Trends in the American Economy in the Nineteenth Century,* ed. William N. Parkes, National Bureau of Economic Research, vol. 24, *Studies in Income and Wealth* (Princeton: Princeton University Press, 1960), p. 26; Stanley Lebergott, "Labor Force and Employment, 1800–1960," in *Output, Employment, and Productivity in the United States after 1800,* ed. Dorothy Brady, National Bureau of Economic Research, vol. 30, *Studies in Income and Wealth* (New York: Columbia University Press, 1966), p. 119.

2. Many of these data are summarized by Robert W. Fogel in *Railroads and American Economic Growth: Essays in Econometric History* (Baltimore: Johns Hopkins University Press, 1964), pp. 121–127. Fogel also deserves credit for the idea that a swift industrial change amounts to a "coup d'état. "One should not," he writes, ". . . require [an industrial] revolution to have the swiftness of a coup d'état" (ibid., p. 229). The recent research referred to is that of Jonathan Prude; see his *The Coming of Industrial Order: Town and Factory Life in Rural Massachusetts, 1810–1860* (Cambridge: Cambridge University Press, 1983).

3. Gallman, "Commodity Output, 1839–1899," p. 24; idem, "The Statistical Approach: Fundamental Concepts as Applied to History," in *Approaches to American Economic History,* ed. George Rogers Taylor and Lucius F. Ellsworth (Charlottesville: University Press of Virginia, 1971), pp. 63–86, esp. pp. 65–67, 86; G. Heberton Evans, *Business Incorporations in the United States, 1800–1943* Publications of the National Bureau of Economic Research, no. 49 (New York, 1948), p. 10, ch. 3; Alfred D. Chandler, Jr., *The Railroads, America's First Big Business* (New York: Harcourt, Brace & World, 1965), p. 13; W. Paul Strassmann, *Risk and Technological Innovation: American Manufacturing Methods during the Nineteenth Century* (Ithaca: Cornell University Press, 1959), passim. The imagery of "take-off" refers to W. W. Rostow's well-known hypothesis that all economies pass through a number of distinct stages in the course of their development, the most critical of which is the "take-off" into self-sustained growth; see his *The Stages of Economic Growth* (Cambridge: Cambridge University Press, 1960).

4. Charles M. McCurdy, "American Law and the Marketing Structure of the Large Corporation, 1875–1890," *JEH,* 38 (1978), 631–649.

5. Moses Abramovitz and Paul A. David, "Reinterpreting Economic Growth: Parables and Realities," *AER,* 63 (1973), 428–439, esp. 429.

6. Robert E. Gallman, "The Pace and Pattern of American Economic Growth," in *American Economic Growth; An Economist's History of the United States,* ed. Lance E. Davis et al. (New York: Harper & Row, 1972), p. 34.

7. Lewis C. Solmon, *Capital Formation by Expenditures on Formal Education, 1880 and 1890* (New York: Arno Press, 1977); Donald R. Winkler, *The Production of Human Capital: A Study of Minority Achievement* (New York: Arno Press, 1977).

8. Lance E. Davis, "Capital Formation in the United States during the Nineteenth Century," in *The Cambridge Economic History of Europe,* vol. 7, *The Industrial Economies, Capital, Labour, and Enterprise,* pt. 2, *The United States, Japan, and Russia,* ed. Peter Mathias and M. M. Postan (Cambridge: Cambridge University Press, 1978), p. 1.

9. Jeffrey G. Williamson, *Late Nineteenth-Century American Development: A General Equilibrium History* (Cambridge: Cambridge University Press, 1974), p. 2; Lance E. Davis, "Savings Sources and Utilization," in Davis et al., *American Economic Growth,* ch. 9, esp. pp. 311–314.

10. Davis, "Savings Sources"; Raymond W. Goldsmith, *A Study of Savings in the United States,* 3 vols. (Princeton: Princeton University Press, 1955), I, 3–22. The sum for net capital imports, 1870–1895, was calculated from figures given by Matthew Simon, "The United States Balance of Payments, 1861–1900," in Parker, *Trends in the American Economy,* pp. 689–705, table 27 (see line 30, "Net international capital movements"; plus signs indicate imports, minus signs exports).

11. John A. James, *Money and Capital Markets in Postbellum America* (Princeton: Princeton University Press, 1978). Here and in the pages which follow, my discussion of the market for short-term capital follows closely the splendid analyses of this book, often with little alteration of language.

12. H. G. Moulton, "Commercial Banking and Capital Formation," *JPE,* 1–4 (1918), 484–508, 638–663, 705–731, 849–881.

13. In 1874 an act abolished the required reserve against note circulation and

replaced it with a redemption fund on deposit with the Treasury (James, *Money and Capital Markets*, p. 98).

14. James, *Money and Capital Markets*, p. 175.

15. While the spread of the commercial paper market "may have been" instrumental in the erosion of local monopoly and thus in the decline of local interest rates (ibid., p. 175), the net flow of capital from west to east makes it essential to place special emphasis on the growth of state banks in the local market as the effective counter to monopoly, (ibid., pp. 197, 199–200, and esp. p. 242).

16. Ibid., p. 124. See also Richard Sylla, "The United States, 1863–1913," in *Banking and Economic Development*, ed. Rondo Cameron (New York: Oxford University Press, 1972), p. 247.

17. Lance E. Davis, "The Investment Market, 1870–1914: The Evolution of a National Market," *JEH*, 25 (1965), 355–399, esp. 387. For the Boston market's thinness even in the 1880s, see idem, "The Capital Markets and Industrial Concentration: The U.S. and the U.K., a Comparative Study," *EHR*, 2d ser., 19 (1966), 262.

18. The apt characterization of New York as a "financial intermediary" is that of Richard Sylla, "The United States, 1863–1913," p. 247.

19. Alfred H. Conrad, "Income Growth and Structural Change," in *American Economic History*, ed. Seymour Harris (New York: McGraw-Hill, 1961), pp. 39–42; Douglass C. North, "Capital Accumulation in Life Insurance between the Civil War and the Investigation of 1905," in *Men in Business*, ed. William Miller (Cambridge, Mass.: Harvard University Press, 1952), pp. 238–253; Davis, "The Investment Market," pp. 380–385; Gerald T. White, *A History of the Massachusetts Hospital Life Insurance Company* (Cambridge, Mass.: Harvard University Press, 1955), chs. 3–4.

20. Allan G. Bogue, *Money at Interest: The Farm Mortgage on the Middle Border* (Lincoln: University of Nebraska Press, 1955), pp. 77–204; Davis, "The Investment Market," pp. 385–386.

21. Davis, "Savings Sources and Utilization" and "Banks and Their Economic Effects," in Davis et al., *American Economic Growth*, pp. 311–365.

22. Edward Meeker, "The Social Rate of Return on Investment in Public Health, 1880–1910," *JEH*, 34 (1974), 392–421, esp. 392–393 and notes.

23. Albert Fishlow, "Levels of Nineteenth-Century American Investment in Education," *JEH*, 26 (1966), 419–420.

24. Quoted in ibid., p. 426.

25. Ibid., p. 427.

26. Sol Cohen, "The Industrial Education Movement, 1906–17," *AQ*, 20 (1968), 97.

27. Ibid., p. 95.

28. Lawrence A. Cremin, *The Transformation of the School: Progressivism in American Education, 1876–1957* (New York: Alfred A. Knopf, 1961), p. 22.

29. Ibid., pp. 26–28.

30. Cohen, "Industrial Education Movement," pp. 98–100.

31. Ibid., pp. 101–102.

32. Ibid., pp. 105–106, 109; Cremin, *Transformation of the School*, pp. 50–51; John Higham, *History* (Englewood Cliffs, N.J.: Prentice-Hall, 1965), p. 113.

33. Higham, *History*, pp. 8–9; Louis Galambos, "The American Economy and

the Reorganization of the Sources of Knowledge," in *The Organization of Knowledge in Modern America, 1860–1920,* ed. Alexandra Oleson and John Voss (Baltimore: Johns Hopkins University Press, 1979), p. 269; Cohen, "Industrial Education Movement," p. 101.

34. Galambos, "Reorganization of Sources of Knowledge," pp. 269–270. The phrase "the age of consolidation" is Higham's apt characterization; see his *From Boundlessness to Consolidation: The Transformation of American Culture, 1848–1860* (Ann Arbor, Mich.: William L. Clements Library, 1969).

35. Nathan Rosenberg, *Technology and American Economic Growth* (New York: Harper & Row, 1972), pp. 118, 53–54.

36. Ibid., pp. 120–122.

37. Strassmann, *Risk and Technological Innovation,* pp. 1–2; Peter Temin, *Iron and Steel in Nineteenth Century America* (Cambridge, Mass.: M.I.T. Press, 1964), appendix C, table c4.

38. This account of Carnegie is based almost entirely on the definitive biography by Joseph Frazier Wall; see his *Andrew Carnegie* (New York: Oxford University Press, 1970), esp. chs. 5–6, 8–11. For the statement that Carnegie Steel alone was producing nearly one-fourth of the country's entire steel output by 1901, I am indebted to the fine sketch of Carnegie in Jonathan Hughes, *The Vital Few: American Economic Progress and Its Protagonists* (Boston: Houghton Mifflin, 1965), pp. 230–232.

39. Temin, *Iron and Steel,* appendix C, table c4; idem, "Manufacturing," in Davis et al., *American Economic Growth,* pp. 441–446; Rosenberg, *Technology,* p. 32.

40. Temin, "Manufacturing," pp. 433, 447; Strassmann, *Risk and Technological Change,* p. 1.

41. Temin, "Manufacturing," p. 438; David Montgomery, *Beyond Equality* (New York: Alfred A. Knopf, 1967), p. 205.

42. Rosenberg, *Technology,* pp. 97–98.

43. Ibid., pp. 98–99.

44. Ibid., pp. 100, 100n, 101.

45. Rosenberg, "Technological Change in the Machine Tool Industry, 1840–1910," *JEH,* 23 (1963), 423.

46. Rosenberg, *Technology,* p., 100.

47. Allen H. Fenichel, "Growth and Diffusion of Power in Manufacturing, 1838–1919," in Brady, *Output, Employment, and Productivity,* pp. 443–451 and appendixes.

48. Nathan Rosenberg, "Selection and Adaptation in the Transfer of Technology: Steam and Iron in America, 1800–1870," in *Perspectives on Technology,* ed. Nathan Rosenberg (Cambridge: Cambridge University Press, 1976), p. 184.

49. Alfred D. Chandler, Jr., *The Visible Hand: The Managerial Revolution in American Business* (Cambridge, Mass.: Harvard University Press, 1977), p. 245; quotation, p. 246.

50. Rosenberg, "Selection and Adaptation," p. 185.

51. Chandler, *Visible Hand,* p. 246.

52. Rosenberg, *Technology,* pp. 90–96; quoted definition, p. 90.

53. David A. Hounshell, *From the American System to Mass Production: The Development of Manufacturing in the United States, 1800–1932* (Baltimore: Johns Hopkins University Press, 1984), introduction, pp. 1–13, esp. p. 10.

54. Rosenberg, *Technology,* pp. 108–109.

55. Chandler, *Visible Hand,* p. 243.

56. Rosenberg, *Technology,* pp. 111–112.

57. Chandler, *Visible Hand,* pp. 241, 244, 280.

58. Ibid., pp. 272–280.

59. Daniel Nelson, *Managers and Workers, Origins of the New Factory System in the United States, 1880–1920* (Madison: University of Wisconsin Press, 1975), pp. 56–61; Galambos, "Reorganization of Sources of Knowledge," p. 274.

60. Nelson, *Managers and Workers,* p. 70.

61. Galambos, "Reorganization of Sources of Knowledge," p. 274; John W. Kendrick, *Productivity Trends in the United States,* National Bureau of Economic Research, General Series, no. 71 (Princeton: Princeton University Press, 1961), pp. 136–137.

62. Alfred D. Chandler, Jr., "The Beginnings of Big Business in American Industry," *BHR,* 33 (1959), 1–32.

63. Ibid., p. 7.

64. Ibid.

65. *Minnesota v. Barber* 136 U.S. 313 (1890); the quotation is from McCurdy, "American Law and the Marketing Structure of the Large Corporation," p. 646.

66. Quoted in ibid., pp. 646–647.

67. Rendigs Fels, *American Business Cycles, 1865–1897* (Chapel Hill: University of North Carolina Press, 1959), pp. 107, 112.

68. *Bankers' Magazine,* February 1883, p. 568.

69. Quoted in Fels, *American Business Cycles,* pp. 128–129.

70. Ibid., pp. 137, 165, 185, 194.

71. Quoted in ibid., p. 129.

72. Chandler, *Visible Hand,* p. 279.

73. Quoted in Victor S. Clark, *History of Manufactures in the United States,* 3 vols. (New York: Peter Smith, 1949), II, 175 (orig. pub. 1929). See also the excellent discussion of the forces behind the combination movement in Alfred S. Eichner, *The Emergence of Oligopoly: Sugar Refining as a Case Study* (Baltimore: Johns Hopkins University Press, 1969), pp. 1–2, 93–119; Donald Dewey's invaluable *Monopoly in Economics and Law* (Chicago: Rand McNally, 1959), passim.

74. Clark, *History of Manufactures,* p. 175.

75. Gentlemen's agreements, pools, and other forms of combination are discussed in Hans B. Thorelli, *The Federal Antitrust Policy: Origination of an American Tradition* (Baltimore: Johns Hopkins Press, 1955), pp. 72–85, 254–272.

76. Ralph L. Nelson, *Merger Movements in American Industry, 1895–1956,* National Bureau of Economic Research, General Series, no. 66 (Princeton: Princeton University Press, 1959), pp. 33–105.

77. Henry R. Seager and Charles A. Gulick, Jr., *Trust and Corporation Problems* (New York: Harper & Bros., 1929), pp. 60–61; Nelson, *Merger Movements,* pp. 161–162.

78. William Z. Ripley, *Railroads, Finance and Organization* (New York: Longmans, Green, 1915), pp. 377–378.

79. Quoted in Albro Martin, *Enterprise Denied: Origins of the Decline of American Railroads, 1897–1917* (New York: Columbia University Press, 1971), pp. 20–21.

80. Ripley, *Railroads, Finance, and Organization*, p. 426; Martin, *Enterprise Denied*, pp. 18–21.

81. The discusson of Morgan's railroad activities is from Vincent P. Carosso's magisterial study *The Morgans: Private International Bankers, 1854–1913* (Cambridge, Mass.: Harvard University Press, 1987), chs. 7, 10.

82. William Letwin, *Law and Economic Policy in America* (New York: Random House, 1965), p. 59.

83. Richard Hofstadter, "What Ever Happened to Antitrust?" in *The Business Establishment*, ed. Earl Cheit (New York: John Wiley, 1964), pp. 113–151.

84. John Sherman, *Recollections of Forty Years in the House, Senate and Cabinet*, 2 vols. (Chicago: Werner, 1895), II, 1072.

85. Thorelli, *Federal Antitrust Policy*, p. 221. For the quotations, see Thomas C. Cochran and William Miller, *The Age of Enterprise: A Social History of Industrial America* (New York: Macmillan, 1951), pp. 171–172.

86. According to Letwin, "public concern at the end of the 1880's was serious enough to make immediate federal action against the trusts a clear desideratum, if not an absolute necessity"; *Law and Economic Policy*, p. 143.

87. Ibid., pp. 103–106; Thorelli, *Federal Antitrust Policy*, p. 229.

88. Thorelli, *Federal Antitrust Policy*, pp. 590–591; *United States v. E. C. Knight Co.*, 156 U.S. 1 (1895).

89. Quoted in Thorelli, *Federal Antitrust Policy*, p. 388.

90. Charles W. McCurdy, "The Meaning of United States v. E. C. Knight Co., Formalism, Inertia, and the 'Modernization' of American Corporation Law, 1869–1903," *BHR*, 53 (1979), 304–342.

91. *Addyston Pipe & Steel Co. v. United States*, 175 U.S. 211 (1899); *Northern Securities Co. v. United States*, 193 U.S. 197 (1904). In the latter case the Court held that "it cannot be said that any State may give a corporation, created under its laws, authority to restrain interstate or international commerce against the will of the nation as lawfully expressed by Congress" (p. 346).

92. Letwin, *Law and Economic Policy*, pp. 244–247; Merle Fainsod, Lincoln Gordon, and Joseph C. Palamountain, Jr., *Government and the American Economy*, 3d ed. (New York: W. W. Norton, 1959), pp. 454–455.

93. Dewey, *Monopoly in Economics and Law*, p. 143.

94. *United States v. Standard Oil Co. of New Jersey*, 221 U.S. 1 (1911); *United States v. American Tobacco Co.*, 221 U.S. 106 (1911); Letwin, *Law and Economic Policy*, pp. 253–265; Fainsod, Gordon, and Palamountain, *Government and American Economy*, pp. 455–459.

12. Workers in Industry

1. J. H. Clapham, *An Economic History of Modern Britain*, 2 vols. (Cambridge: Cambridge University Press, 1964), I, x (orig. pub. 1926). The quoted passages are from the second preface to the reprint of 1939.

2. Melvyn Dubovsky, *Industrialism and the American Worker, 1865–1920* (New York: Thos. Crowell, 1975), p. 23.

3. Jacob Riis, *How the Other Half Lives* (New York: Scribner's, 1890), pp. 123–

124; quoted in Robert Higgs, *The Transformation of the American Economy, 1865–1914: An Essay in Interpretation* (New York: John Wiley, 1971), p. 115.

4. John A. Garraty, *The New Commonwealth, 1877–1890* (New York: Harper & Row, 1968), pp. 136–137.

5. Higgs, *Transformation of American Economy,* p. 115.

6. Dubovsky, *Industrialism and American Worker,* pp. 25–26.

7. Bureau of the Census, *Historical Statistics of the United States, Colonial Times to 1970,* 2 vols. (Washington, D.C.: Government Printing Office, 1976,) I, 129.

8. Maurine Weiner Greenwald, *Women, War, and Work: The Impact of World War I on Women Workers in the United States* (Westport, Conn.: Greenwood Press, 1980), p. 5; Stanley Lebergott, *Manpower in Economic Growth: the American Record since 1800* (New York: McGraw–Hill, 1964), pp. 72–73.

9. Greenwald, *Women, War, and Work,* p. 6.

10. Lebergott, *Manpower,* p. 70.

11. W. Elliot Brownlee and Mary M. Brownlee, eds., *Women in the American Economy: A Documentary History, 1675–1929* (New Haven: Yale University Press, 1976), pp. 32–33; Department of Health, Education, and Welfare, *Biennial Survey of Education in the United States, 1950–1952,* (Washington, D.C.: Government Printing Office, 1955), ch. 5, p. 6.

12. W. Elliot Brownlee, *Dynamics of Ascent: A History of the American Economy* (New York: Alfred A. Knopf, 1974), p. 217.

13. Greenwald, *Women, War, and Work,* pp. 7–8.

14. Brownlee, *Dynamics,* p. 217.

15. Brownlee and Brownlee, *Women,* pp. 27–28; Lebergott, *Manpower,* p. 70; Greenwald, *Women, War, and Work,* pp. 9, 11.

16. Brownlee and Brownlee, *Women,* pp. 33–34; Brownlee, *Dynamics,* p. 217.

17. Alba M. Edwards, "Comparative Occupation Statistics for the United States, 1870–1940," in *Sixteenth Census of the United States, Population* (Washington, D.C.: Government Printing Office, 1940), p. 97.

18. Caroline F. Ware, *The Early New England Cotton Manufacture* (New York: Russell & Russell, 1966), p. 211.

19. Lebergott, *Manpower,* p. 126.

20. "Report on Women and Child Wage Earners, 1910," *Senate Documents,* vol. 6, no. 645 (s.n. 5690), 61st Cong., 2d sess., pp. 45–46; Bureau of the Census, *Abstract of the Census of the United States* (Washington, D.C.: Government Printing Office, 1900), pp. 300–301.

21. *Eleventh Census of the United States, Population* (Washington, D.C.: U.S. Census Office, 1908), pt. 2, p. cxxii.

22. Lebergott, *Manpower,* pp. 28–29; *Ninth Census of the United States, Population* (Washington, D.C.: U.S. Census Office, 1870), pt. 1, table 29; *Eleventh Census,* pt. 2, p. cxlviii.

23. Peter Jensen Hill, *The Economic Impact of Immigration into the United States* (New York: Arno Press, 1975), pp. 64–76.

24. Jeffrey G. Williamson, *Late Nineteenth-Century American Development: A General Equilibrium History* (Cambridge: Cambridge University Press, 1974), p. 249.

25. Higgs, *Transformation,* pp. 116–118.

26. Ibid., pp. 114–119.

27. Peter J. Hill, "Relative Skill and Income Levels of Native and Foreign Born Workers in the United States," *EEH*, 12 (1975), 47–60; Peter R. Shergold, "Relative Skill and Income Levels of Native and Foreign Born Workers: A Reexamination," *EEH*, 13 (1976), 451–461.

28. Shergold, "Relative Skill and Income Levels," pp. 451–461.

29. Robert E. Gallman, "Trends in the Size Distribution of Wealth in the Nineteenth Century: Some Speculations," in *Six Papers on the Size Distribution of Wealth and Income,* ed. Lee Soltow, National Bureau of Economic Research, vol. 33, *Studies in Income and Wealth,* (New York: Columbia University Press, 1969), pp. 11, 15; Peter H. Lindert and Jeffrey G. Williamson, "Three Centuries of American Inequality," in *Research in Economic History,* ed. Paul Uselding (Greenwich, Conn.: JAI Press, 1976), I, 99. The quoted words are Gallman's, "Trends in Size Distribution of Wealth," p. 11.

30. Lebergott, *Manpower,* pp. 161–162.

31. Clarence D. Long, *Wages and Earnings in the United States, 1860–1890* (Princeton: Princeton University Press, 1960), pp. 50–68.

32. Albert Rees, *Real Wages in Manufacturing, 1890–1914* (Princeton: Princeton University Press, 1961), pp. 4–5.

33. Lebergott, *Manpower,* pp. 178–179, 180–183.

34. *Historical Statistics,* I, 168.

35. Rees, *Real Wages in Manufacturing,* p. 12.

36. Dubovsky, *Industrialism and American Worker,* p. 19.

37. Gompers quoted in Garraty, *New Commonwealth,* p. 129.

38. Long, *Wages and Earnings,* p. 118.

39. Dubovsky, *Industrialism and American Worker,* pp. 19–20.

40. Paul Uselding, "In Dispraise of the Muckrakers: U.S. Occupational Mortality, 1890–1910," in Uselding, *Research in Economic History,* pp. 336–339, 350.

41. Ibid., pp. 343, 350.

42. Ibid., pp. 336, 351–358.

43. Dubovsky, *Industrialism and American Worker,* p. 19.

44. Uselding, "In Dispraise of Muckrakers," p. 350.

45. Lawrence M. Friedman and Jack Ladinsky, "Social Change and the Law of Industrial Accidents," *CLR,* 67 (1967), 49–82; rpr. in *American Law and the Constitutional Order,* ed. Lawrence M. Friedman and Harry N. Scheiber (Cambridge, Mass.: Harvard University Press, 1978), pp. 269–272.

46. Ibid., pp. 273–279.

47. Ibid., p. 278.

48. Ibid.

49. Charles O. Gregory, *Labor and the Law* (New York: W. W. Norton, 1946), pp. 99, 100–103.

50. Quoted in Felix Frankfurter and Nathan Greene, *The Labor Injunction* (New York: Macmillan, 1930), pp. 1–24.

51. Ibid., pp. 8–10.

52. The *Duplex* case is in 254 U.S. 349 (1921) and the *Tri-City* case in 257 U.S. 189 (1921).

53. Lawrence M. Friedman, *A History of American Law* (New York: Simon & Schuster, 1973), p. 489.

54. Ibid., pp. 491–492.

55. Edward C. Kirkland, *Industry Comes of Age: Business, Labor, and Public Policy, 1860–1897* (New York: Holt, Rinehart & Winston, 1961), 328–330.

56. *Muller v. Oregon*, 208 U.S. 422 (1908).

57. Friedman, *History of American Law*, pp. 492–493; *Hammer v. Dagenhart*, 247 U.S. 251 (1918); *Bailey v. Drexel Furniture Co.*, 259 U.S. 20 (1922).

58. *Holden v. Hardy*, 169 U.S. 367, 391, 395, 397 (1898).

59. *Lochner v. New York*, 198 U.S. 942, 946–947 (1905).

60. Ibid., pp. 941, 949.

61. *Santa Clara County v. Southern Pacific Railroad Company*, 118 U.S. 394 (1886).

62. Edward S. Corwin, "The Supreme Court and the Fourteenth Amendment," in *American Constitutional History: Essays by Edward S. Corwin*, ed. Alpheus T. Mason and Gerald Garvey (New York: Harper & Row, 1964), p. 96.

63. *Lochner v. New York*, pp. 942, 949. According to Corwin (ibid., p. 95), Holmes's agreement or disagreement concerned the effects on health of long hours of work in bakeries, but I believe this interpretation to be in error.

64. *Slaughter-House Cases*, 16 Wall 36 (1873); *Munn v. Illinois*, 94 U.S. 113 (1876); Corwin, "Supreme Court," pp. 71–74.

65. *Munn v. Illinois*, pp. 136, 140, 142.

66. Arnold M. Paul, *Conservative Crisis and the Rule of Law* (Ithaca: Cornell University Press, 1960), pp. 1–5.

67. Ibid., pp. 12–14.

68. Ibid., pp. 15–16.

69. Ibid., pp. 16–18.

70. Ibid., p. 1.

71. Ibid., pp. 1–5.

72. Garraty, *New Commonwealth*, p. 145. See ch. 4, passim, for the best overall discussion of the working man in this period.

73. "Industrial Commission Report, VII," pp. 756–757, quoted in ibid., p. 145.

74. Garraty, *New Commonwealth*, p. 144.

75. Ibid., p. 146.

76. Ibid., pp. 156–157.

77. Kirkland, *Industry Comes of Age*, p. 357.

78. Garraty, *New Commonwealth*, pp. 161–162.

79. Ibid., pp. 164–167; Henry David, *The History of the Haymarket Affair*, 2d ed. (New York: Russell & Russell, 1958), passim.

80. Garraty, *New Commonwealth*, p. 162.

81. Ibid., pp. 162–163, 171–172.

82. Ibid., p. 170.

83. Kirkland, *Industry Comes of Age*, p. 362.

84. Henry Pelling, *American Labor* (Chicago: University of Chicago Press, 1960), pp. 83–84.

85. *Historical Statistics to 1970*, II, 177.

86. Ibid., pp. 126, 127.

87. Pelling, *American Labor,* pp. 87–88.

88. See, for example, David, *History of the Haymarket Affair,* chs. 13, 20.

89. Clifton K. Yearley, Jr., *Britons in American Labor: A History of the Influence of the United Kingdom Immigrants on American Labor, 1820–1914* (Baltimore: Johns Hopkins Press, 1957), p. 311.

90. Ibid., pp. 312–314.

91. John I. Griffin, *Strikes: A Study in Quantitative Economics* (New York: Columbia University Press, 1939), pp. 38, 43, 73.

92. David Brody, *Steelworkers in America, The Nonunion Era* (Cambridge, Mass.: Harvard University Press, 1960), chs. 1–2.

13. Mostly Foreign Affairs

1. Jonathan Hughes, *American Economic History* (Glenview, Ill.: Scott, Foresman, 1983), p. 400.

2. For a thoughtful review of the literature and an analysis of rival theories of trade and economic growth, see Mary Locke Eysenbach, *American Manufactured Exports, 1879–1914: A Study of Growth and Comparative Advantage* (New York: Arno Press, 1976), pp. 2, 7; Folke Hilgerdt, *Industrialization and Foreign Trade* (Geneva: League of Nations, 1945), tables 7, 8, 9, 13.

3. Eysenbach, *American Manufactured Exports,* pp. 3, 7. The quotations are from Mira Wilkins, *The Emergence of Multinational Enterprise: American Business Abroad from the Colonial Era to 1914* (Cambridge, Mass.: Harvard University Press, 1970), p. 70. By the early 1980s the export proportion of GNP had tripled, rising to more than 12 percent.

4. Robert E. Lipsey, "Foreign Trade," in *American Economic Growth: An Economist's History of the United States,* ed. Lance E. Davis et al. (New York: Harper & Row, 1972), p. 554. Lipsey calls his colonial period estimates rough.

5. Bureau of the Census, *Historical Statistics of the United States, Colonial Times to 1970,* 2 vols. (Washington, D.C.: Government Printing Office, 1976), II, 889–890, 898–899.

6. Ibid., 889–890. For the conversion of dollar figures into percentages, I am indebted to Robert C. Puth, *American Economic History* (Chicago: Dryden Press, 1982), p. 320; Eysenbach, *American Manufactured Exports,* p. 2.

7. *Historical Statistics to 1970,* II, 903; John G. B. Hutchins, *The American Maritime Industries and Public Policy, 1789–1914: An Economic History* (Cambridge, Mass.: Harvard University Press, 1941), pp. 402–403, 537–540.

8. *Historical Statistics to 1970,* II, 885–886.

9. Ibid., pp. 864–865.

10. Wilkins, *Multinational Enterprise,* pp. 67–69, 97, 103; Sidney Ratner, *Taxation and Democracy in America* (New York: John Wiley, 1927). "The average rate of duties under the Dingley Act rose to heights unparalleled even under the Civil War tariffs" (p. 224).

11. Wilkins, *Multinational Enterprise,* pp. 64–65, 83.

12. The quotations are from ibid., p. 71.

13. Walter LaFeber, *The New Empire: American Expansion, 1860–1898* (Ithaca: Cornell University Press, 1963), pp. 60–61, 408–410.

14. Ernest R. May, "American Imperialism: A Reinterpretation," in *Perspectives in American History,* ed. Bernard Bailyn and Donald Fleming (Cambridge, Mass.: Harvard University Press, 1967), I, 125–126, 126n.

15. Wilkins, *Multinational Enterprise,* pp. 66–67.

16. Herbert Feis, *Europe, the World's Banker, 1870–1914* (New York: W. W. Norton, 1965); W. Woodruff, *The Impact of Western Man* (New York: St. Martin's Press, 1967), ch. 2; J. R. T. Hughes, *Industrialization and Economic History* (New York: McGraw-Hill, 1970), ch. 2, esp. p. 189; Stanley Lebergott, "The Returns to U.S. Imperialism, 1890–1929," *JEH,* 40 (1980), 229–252; Robert B. Zevin, "An Interpretation of American Imperialism," *JEH,* 32 (1972), 316–360.

17. Lebergott, "Returns to U.S. Imperialism," p. 231.

18. Wilkins, *Multinational Enterprise,* pp. 73–74.

19. Zevin, "American Imperialism," p. 350.

20. Jules David, *American Political and Economic Penetration of Mexico, 1877–1920* (New York: Arno Press, 1976), pp. 246, 257–286; Arthur S. Link, *Woodrow Wilson and the Progressive Era, 1910–1917* (New York: Harper & Row, 1963), pp. 111–112n9.

21. Link, *Wilson,* pp. 107, 113.

22. Arthur S. Link, *Wilson's Campaigns for Progressivism and Peace, 1916–1917* (Princeton: Princeton University Press, 1965), pp. 411–412, 423.

23. Ibid., p. 429n103; Milton Friedman and Anna J. Schwartz, *A Monetary History of the United States* (Princeton: Princeton University Press, 1963), p. 199.

24. Paul A. C. Koistinin, "The 'Industrial-Military Complex' in Historical Perspective: World War I," *BHR,* 41 (1967), 383–385; Grosvenor B. Clarkson, *Industrial America in the World War: The Strategy behind the Line, 1917–1918* (Boston: Houghton Mifflin, 1923), p. 491.

25. Koistinin, "Industrial-Military Complex," p. 386. The committees and their membership are listed in Clarkson, *Industrial America,* pp. 495–500.

26. Clarkson, *Industrial America,* p. 112; Koistinin, "Industrial-Military Complex," pp. 389–391, 396.

27. Clarkson, *Industrial America,* pp. 98, 303–311; Koistinin, "Industrial-Military Complex," p. 394.

28. Clarkson, *Industrial America,* pp. 140–141, 98–100, 482. A modern scholar agrees. The board, writes Robert D. Cuff, "assumed unprecedented significance in the industrial economy" (*The War Industries Board: Business-Government Relations during World War I* [Baltimore: Johns Hopkins University Press, 1973], p. 6).

29. William E. Leuchtenberg, "The New Deal and the Analogue of War," in *Change and Continuity in Twentieth Century America,* ed. John Braeman et al. (Athens: Ohio State University Press, 1966), p. 85.

30. Cuff, *War Industries Board,* pp. 5, 7, 269, 272; Robert D. Cuff, "Bernard Baruch: Symbol and Myth in Industrial Mobilization," *BHR,* 43 (1969), 130–133.

31. Cuff, *War Industries Board,* pp. 272, 274n14; Ralph Nelson, *Merger Movements in American Industry, 1895–1956* (Princeton: Princeton University Press, 1959), p. 35.

32. Stanley Lebergott, *Manpower in American Economic Growth: The American*

Record since 1800 (New York: McGraw-Hill, 1964), pp. 512, 525; *Historical Statistics to 1970*, II, 164.

33. Lebergott, *Manpower*, p. 513; John Maurice Clark, *The Cost of the World War to the American People* (New Haven: Yale University Press, 1931), pp. 257–259; *Historical Statistics to 1970*, I, 126.

34. Lebergott, *Manpower*, p. 396; Maurine Weiner Greenwald, *Women, War and Work: The Impact of World War I on Women Workers in the United States* (Westport, Conn.: Greenwood Press, 1980), p. 13.

35. Greenwald, *Women, War, and Work*, pp. 21–26.

36. Ibid., pp. 21–22.

37. Alice Kessler-Harris, *Out to Work: A History of Wage-Earning Women in the United States* (New York: Oxford University Press, 1982), pp. 219–224.

38. Paul H. Douglas, *Real Wages in the United States, 1890–1926* (New York: Houghton Mifflin, 1930), p. 178; National Industrial Conference Board, "Wartime Changes in Wages, September 1914–March 1919," in *Research Report*, no. 20 (Boston, 1919), pp. 100–106; Clark, *Cost of World War*, pp. 132–133; Charles Gilbert, *American Financing of World War I* (Westport, Conn.: Greenwood Press, 1970), p. 204.

39. Clark, *Cost of World War*, pp. 161–168; Gilbert, *American Financing*, p. 213; *Statistical Abstract of the United States, 1924* (Washington, D.C.: Government Printing Office, 1925), p. 310.

40. Gilbert, *American Financing*, pp. 205, 211.

41. Ibid., pp. 96–99, 202–205; Simon Kuznets, *National Product in Wartime* (New York: National Bureau of Economic Research, 1945), p. 141.

42. Friedman and Schwartz, *Monetary History*, pp. 192, 205, 216–220.

43. Ibid.

44. Kuznets, *National Product in Wartime*, p. 105; Clark, *Cost of World War*, pp. 132–133.

14. The Undertow of Prosperity

1. Paul A. Samuelson and Everett E. Hagen, *After the War, 1918–1920 Military and Economic Demobilization of the United States, Its Effect upon Employment and Income* (Washington, D.C.: National Resources Planning Board, 1943), pp. 21, 6, 11. Even now, this work remains a superb analysis and explanation of the economy's behavior during the years in question.

2. Ibid., p. 12.

3. Ibid., pp. 21–22.

4. Ibid., p. 28; Bureau of the Census, *Historical Statistics of the United States, Colonial Times to 1957* (Washington, D.C.: Government Printing Office, 1960), p. 482.

5. Simon Kuznets, *National Income and Capital Formation, 1919–35* (New York: National Bureau of Economic Research, 1938), no. 34, table 10 (in current dollars).

6. Samuelson and Hagen, *After the War*, pp. 28–29.

7. Ibid., p. 33; Kuznets, *National Income*, p. 40.

8. *Historical Statistics to 1957*, pp. 457, 483, 491.

9. H. Thomas Johnson, "Postwar Optimism and the Rural Financial Crisis of the 1920's," *EEH*, 11 (1973), 178, 179n.

10. *Historical Statistics to 1957,* p. 491.

11. Johnson, "Postwar Optimism," pp. 178, 175.

12. For a brief discussion of the timing and the effect of deterioration of the foreign trade position, see Thomas Wilson, *Fluctuations in Income and Employment* (New York: Pitman, 1948), p. 99. Part 2 of this book is a valuable analysis of cyclical fluctuations from 1919 to 1937 and is especially useful for its comparisons between the depressions of 1920–21 and 1929–1937.

13. Samuelson and Hagen, *After the War,* p. 35; *Historical Statistics to 1957,* p. 1104.

14. Milton Friedman and Anna J. Schwartz, *A Monetary History of the United States, 1867–1960* (Princeton: Princeton University Press, 1963), pp. 225–228.

15. See ibid., pp. 222–239, for a discussion of the period 1919–20.

16. Elmus L. Wicker, "A Reconsideration of Federal Reserve Policy during the 1920–21 Depression," *JEH,* 26 (1966), 223.

17. Friedman and Schwartz, *Monetary History,* pp. 229–230.

18. Robert A. Gordon, *Economic Instability and Growth: the American Record* (New York: Harper & Row, 1974), pp. 22–27.

19. Simon Kuznets, *Commodity Flow and Capital Formation* (New York: National Bureau of Economic Research, 1937), I, 375.

20. George Soule, *Prosperity Decade, From War to Depression, 1917–29* (New York: Holt, Rinehart & Winston, 1962), p. 170.

21. Ibid., pp. 116, 157.

22. Stuart Chase, *Prosperity, Fact or Myth* (New York: Charles Boni, 1929), pp. 62–63.

23. Ibid., p. 45.

24. John Herman Lorant, *The Role of Capital-Improving Innovations in American Manufacturing during the 1920s* (New York: Arno Press, 1975), p. 25; Soule, *Prosperity Decade,* pp. 147, 286.

25. This account of Henry Ford is drawn from Jonathan Hughes's admirable distillation of numerous biographies, mostly bad, and other sources; see Hughes, *The Vital Few: American Economic Progress and Its Protagonists* (Boston: Houghton Mifflin, 1965), pp. 274–356.

26. Quoted in William E. Leuchtenburg, *The Perils of Prosperity* (Chicago: University of Chicago Press, 1958), p. 189.

27. Daniel Pope, *The Making of Modern Advertising* (New York: Basic Books, 1983), p. 23; Elliot Brownlee, *Dynamics of Ascent: A History of the American Economy* (New York: Alfred A. Knopf, 1979), p. 392.

28. Soule, *Prosperity Decade,* p. 149.

29. Hughes, *Vital Few,* pp. 301–305.

30. John W. Kendrick, *Productivity Trends in the United States* (Princeton: Princeton University Press, 1961), pp. 140–141.

31. Ibid., pp. 166, 152.

32. Nathan Rosenberg, *Technology and American Economic Growth* (New York: Harper & Row, 1972), pp. 1–8.

33. Lorant, *Capital Improving Innovations,* pp. 211, 143–145, 206–208.

34. Rosenberg deserves credit for the suggestion that the variation in organiza-

tional forms might be more closely related to the frequency with which technology changes than to the kind of technology employed (*Technology,* p. 186n).

35. Alfred D. Chandler, Jr., *Strategy and Structure: Chapters in the History of Industrial Enterprise* (Cambridge, Mass.: M.I.T. Press, 1962), pp. 42–43.

36. Ibid., p. 43.

37. Ibid., p. 44.

38. Alfred D. Chandler, Jr., *The Visible Hand: The Managerial Revolution in American Business* (Cambridge, Mass.: Harvard University Press, 1977), pp. 457–458; see esp. the organizational chart on p. 458 showing the multidivisional structure used by large manufacturing firms.

39. Ibid., p. 463; Chandler, *Strategy and Structure,* pp. 44, 49.

40. Chandler, *Visible Hand,* pp. 462–463.

41. Ibid., p. 456.

42. Ibid., pp. 460–461.

43. Ibid., p. 461.

44. Rosenberg, *Technology,* pp. 35, 38n; Bureau of the Census, *Historical Statistics of the United States, Colonial Times to 1970,* 2 vols. (Washington, D.C.: Government Printing Office, 1976), II, 379, 383, 386–387. Switzerland is a possible exception to the generalization expressed in the final sentence. The percentage of its population enrolled is unknown.

45. Brownlee, *Dynamics,* pp. 385–386.

46. Robert M. Coen, "Labor Force and Unemployment in the 1920's and 1930's: A Re-examination Based on Postwar Experience," *RES,* 55 *(1973),* 40–55; *Historical Statistics to 1970,* I, 200, 210–211.

47. *Historical Statistics to 1970,* I, 177–178.

48. Irving Bernstein, *The Lean Years* (Baltimore: Penguin Books, 1960), pp. 206–215.

49. Ibid., pp. 196, 199.

50. Ibid., pp. 225–237.

51. Roy Lubove, *The Struggle for Social Security, 1900–1935* (Cambridge, Mass.: Harvard University Press, 1968), pp. 53–54, 59–60.

52. Ibid., pp. 60–61.

53. Ibid., pp. 135–137.

54. Ibid., pp. 242n60; 127–128.

55. Ibid., pp. 128–132.

56. Quoted in Bernstein, *Lean Years,* p. 170.

57. Sanford D. Jacoby, "The Origins of Internal Labor Markets in American Manufacturing Firms, 1910–1940" (Ph.D. diss., University of California, Berkeley, 1981), pp. 27, 52–62.

58. Chandler, *Visible Hand.*

59. Jacoby, "Internal Labor Markets," p. 25.

60. Ibid., pp. 20, 89.

61. Stuart D. Brandes, *American Welfare Capitalism, 1880–1940* (Chicago: University of Chicago Press, 1976), pp. 1–5, 10–11.

62. Ibid., pp. 25–26.

63. Jacoby, "Internal Labor Markets," pp. 22, 370, 426–427, 431, 442, 488.

64. David Brody, "The Rise and Decline of Welfare Capitalism," in *Change and Continuity in Twentieth-Century America: The 1920s*, ed. John Braeman et al. (Columbus: Ohio State University Press, 1968), pp. 147–148; see also Brody, *Workers in Industrial America* (New York: Oxford University Press, 1980), ch. 2.

65. Brandes, *American Welfare Capitalism*, pp. 136–141; as we shall see, this was not to be the fate of the personnel management movement, which underwent a phenomenal rate of growth in the thirties.

66. Frederick Strauss and Louis H. Bean, *Gross Farm Income and Indices of Farm Production and Prices in the United States, 1869–1937*, U.S. Department of Agriculture, Technical Bulletin no. 703 (Washington, D.C.: Government Printing Office, 1940), p. 14.

67. Soule, *Prosperity Decade*, p. 162.

68. Robert L. Heilbroner, *The Making of Economic Society*, 4th ed. (Englewood Cliffs, N.J.: Prentice-Hall, 1972), ch. 8, esp. p. 143.

69. Charles F. Holt, "Who Benefitted from the Prosperity of the Twenties?" *EEH*, 14 (1977), 283–284.

70. Lawrence A. Jones and David Durand, *Mortgage Lending Experience in Agriculture* (Princeton: Princeton University Press, 1954), p. 10; *Historical Statistics to 1970*, I, 483.

71. Johnson, *Postwar Optimism*, pp. 179–182, concedes that rising incomes after 1922 had a major impact on farmland values *at the margin* and that those values were falling at a decreasing rate.

72. *Historical Statistics to 1970*, I, 469.

73. Joseph S. Davis, *On Agricultural Policy, 1926–38* (Stanford: Stanford University Food Research Institute, 1939), p. 242. The income estimates are those of the National Bureau of Economic Research and the Department of Agriculture; Johnson, *Postwar Optimism*, p. 182.

74. Johnson, *Postwar Optimism*, pp. 186–191.

75. Jones and Durand, *Mortgage Lending*, pp. 192–193, 186–188, 107, 121–122.

76. Ibid., pp. 188–189.

77. George B. Tindall, *The Emergence of the New South, 1913–45* (Baton Rouge: Louisiana State University Press, 1967), p. 121n40.

78. Jones and Durand, *Mortage Lending*, p. 189.

79. Ibid., pp. 196, 103–104, 190.

80. Tindall, *New South*, ch. 4, esp. pp. 111, 122, 124, 125.

81. Brownlee, *Dynamics*, pp. 398–399.

82. *Historical Statistics to 1970*, II, 510.

83. Tindall, *New South*, p. 136.

84. Gilbert C. Fite, *George N. Peek and the Fight for Farm Parity* (Norman: University of Oklahoma Press, 1954), pp. 38–39.

85. Ibid.; Tindall, *New South*, p. 137.

86. Fite, *Peek*, pp. 59–60; Tindall, *New South*, pp. 137–138. See also Darwin N. Kelly, "The McNary-Haugen Bills, 1924–28: An Attempt to Make the Tariff Effective for Farm Product," *AH*, 14 (1940), 170–180.

87. Fite, *Peek*, pp. 165, 130.

88. Holt, "Prosperity of Twenties," pp. 277–279, 283. Holt's article derives most of its data from Kuznets' *Shares of Upper Income Groups in Income and Savings* (New York: National Bureau of Economic Research, 1953).

89. Willard Thorp, *The Structure of Industry*, Temporary National Economic Committee, Investigation of Concentration of Economic Power Monograph Series no. 27 (Washington, D.C.: Government Printing Office, 1941), p. 233.

90. Ralph Nelson, *Merger Movements in American Industry, 1895–1956* (Princeton: Princeton University Press, 1959), pp. 121–122.

91. Leuchtenburg, *Perils,* p. 242.

92. John Kenneth Galbraith, *The Great Crash: 1929* (Boston: Houghton Mifflin, 1954), pp. 48–49.

93. Ibid., pp. 54–55, 50.

94. Leuchtenburg, *Perils,* p. 241; Soule, *Prosperity Decade,* p. 293, calls it a legend that "virtually the whole population was engaged in a gambling spree."

95. George D. Green, "The Economic Impact of the Stock Market Boom and Crash of 1929" (paper presented to the Federal Reserve Bank of Boston, Conference Series no. 5, Monetary Conference June 1971, *Consumer Spending and Monetary Policy: The Linkages),* p. 198.

96. Galbraith, *Great Crash,* p. 83.

97. Leuchtenburg, *Perils,* p. 243.

98. Galbraith, *Great Crash*, pp. 12, 17, 22; Leuchtenburg, *Perils,* p. 243; Green, "Economic Impact," pp. 207–209.

99. Galbraith, *Great Crash*, pp. 36, 72–74.

100. Ibid.; Green, "Economic Impact," p. 208.

101. Friedman and Schwartz, *Monetary History,* pp. 254–255.

102. Ibid., p. 257; Wilson, *Fluctuation in Income and Employment,* p. 147.

103. Friedman and Schwartz, *Monetary History,* pp. 291–292; see also Galbraith, *Great Crash,* pp. 14–16, for a different point of view.

104. Elmus R. Wicker, *Federal Reserve Monetary Policy, 1917–1933* (New York: Random House, 1966), chs. 9, 10.

105. *New York Stock Exchange Yearbook, 1932–33,* pp. 110–113, 117, 157.

106. Leuchtenberg, *Perils,* p. 245.

107. Friedman and Schwartz, *Monetary History,* p. 299.

108. Gordon, *Economic Instability and Growth,* pp. 46-48.

109. Robert J. Gordon and James A. Wilcox, "Monetary Interpretations: An Evaluation and Critique," in *The Great Depression Revisited,* ed. Karl Brunner (Boston: Martinus Nijhoff, 1980), p. 66.

110. More precisely, the growth of M2 slowed from an annual rate of 8.8 percent in seven quarters preceding the fourth quarter of 1925 to a 0.5 rate in the next four quarters (ibid.).

111. Charles P. Kindleberger, *The World in Depression* (London: Penguin Books, 1973), p. 117.

112. Gordon, *Economic Instability and Growth,* p. 71.

113. Peter Temin, *Did Monetary Forces Cause the Great Depression?* (New York: W. W. Norton, 1976), p. 66.

114. Gordon and Wilcox, *Monetary Interpretations,* pp. 77–79, as summarized by

Allan H. Meltzer, "Comments on Monetarist Interpretations of the Great Depression," in Brunner, *Great Depression Revisited*, p. 156.

115. Gordon, *Economic Instability and Growth*, p. 70.

116. Kindleberger, *World in Depression*, p. 117; Friedman and Schwartz, *Monetary History*, p. 306; Temin, *Monetary Forces*, p. 66.

117. Temin, *Monetary Forces*, pp. 66–67. In their critique of Temin, Gordon and Wilcox unaccountably ignore his discussion of this point and accept as valid an earlier study by B. S. Hickman emphasizing the effects of immigration restriction on housing demand.

118. Meltzer, "Comments," p. 156. The rate began to slow in 1919. Michael A. Bernstein, "Long Term Economic Growth and the Problem of Recovery in American Manufacturing: A Study of the Great Depression in the United States, 1929–39" (Ph.D. diss., Yale University, 1982); Gordon and Wilcox, "Monetary Interpretation," p. 78.

119. Gordon and Wilcox, "Monetary Interpretation," p. 78.

120. Instead of the term *general overcapacity*, Erik Lundberg prefers a formulation which stresses "a lower average degree of incentives to increase capacity in relation to earlier years" (p. 76), but this seems to me a distinction without a difference. See Lundberg, *Instability and Economic Growth* (New Haven: Yale University Press, 1968), pp. 75–76.

121. Joseph Paul Waters, *Technological Acceleration and the Great Depression* (New York: Arno Press, 1977), pp. 220–221.

122. Gordon, *Economic Instability and Growth*, pp. 43–44.

123. Kindleberger, *World in Depression*, p. 117.

124. Gordon, *Economic Instability and Growth*, pp. 44, 74; Friedman and Schwartz, *Monetary History*, p. 306.

125. Frederic S. Mishkin, "The Household Balance Sheet and the Great Depression," *JEH*, 38 (1978), 918–937.

126. Gordon and Wilson, *Monetary Interpretations*, p. 80.

127. Temin, *Monetary Forces*, p. 172.

128. Bernstein, "Long-Term Economic Growth," pp. 53–55.

129. Gordon, *Economic Instability and Growth*, p. 71.

130. Kindleberger, *World in Depression*, p. 85; Temin, *Monetary Forces*, p. 172; Gordon and Wilcox, *Monetary Interpretations*, p. 82.

131. Friedman and Schwartz, *Monetary History*, p. 301.

132. Ibid., pp. 308–313.

133. Ibid., pp. 343, 344, 314.

134. Lester V. Chandler, *American Monetary Policies, 1928–41* (New York: Harper & Row, 1971), p. 170.

135. Friedman and Schwartz, *Monetary History*, p. 317.

136. Ibid., pp. 317–320.

137. Ibid., p. 399.

138. Ibid., pp. 322–324.

139. Ibid., pp. 324–326, 351.

140. Ibid., pp. 358, 374, 411, 415–416.

141. Ibid., pp. 411, 414, 418, 380–382, 396–399, 301.

142. Cleona Lewis, *America's Stake in International Investments* (Washington, D.C.: Brookings Institution, 1938), pp. 447, 450; Soule, *Prosperity Decade,* pp. 252–254.

143. Soule, *Prosperity Decade,* pp. 259–264.

144. Kindleberger, *World in Depression,* p. 38n16.

145. Ibid.; Soule, *Prosperity Decade,* p. 264.

146. Kindleberger, *World in Depression,* p. 56.

147. Lewis, *America's Stake,* pp. 376–380.

148. Ibid., ch. 18, esp. pp. 376–397.

149. Office of Finance to Congress, July 29, 1782, in *Journals of the Continental Congress,* ed. Gaillard Hunt, 33 vols. (Washington, D.C.: Government Printing Office, 1914), XXII, 433.

150. Lewis, *America's Stake,* ch. 18, esp. pp. 378-379.

151. Heywood W. Fleisig, *Long-Term Capital Flows and the Great Depression: The Role of the United States, 1927–33* (New York: Arno Press, 1975), p. 8. The figure $1.4 on this page is evidently a typographical error. The figure $1.3 appears elsewhere throughout the book.

152. Kindleberger, *World in Depression,* pp. 72–74.

153. Ibid., pp. 142–144, 146.

154. Chandler, *American Monetary Policies,* pp. 160-161.

155. Lewis, *America's Stake,* pp. 399–403.

156. George D. Green, "The International Economy and the Causation of the United States Depression," paper presented to the American Historical Association, December 29, 1971.

157. *Historical Statistics to 1970,* II, 864.

158. Paul P. Abrahams, "American Bankers and the Economic Tactics of Peace: 1919," *JAH,* 56 (1969), 572–593.

159. *Historical Statistics to 1970,* II, 864.

160. Fleisig, *Long-Term Capital Flows,* pp. 165–166. The latter inhibited long-term foreign lending and borrowing as an offset to the decline in American lending. Fleisig's sophisticated analysis is far more detailed than this reference to his emphasis would indicate. For a fine article on the effect of security inflation on the psychological climate of the business community, Giulio Pontecorvo, "Investment Banking and Security Speculation in the Late 1920's," *BHR,* 32 (1958), 166–191.

161. For a superb humanistic treatment of the intertwined international character of the depression, see John A. Garraty, *The Great Depression: An Inquiry into the Causes, Course, and Consequences of the Worldwide Depression of the Nineteen-Thirties, as Seen by Contemporaries and in the Light of History* (New York: Harcourt Brace Jovanovich, 1986).

15. Coping with the Great Depression

1. Unfortunately, the Budget and Accounting Act of 1921, which established a budget bureau, also cut government expenditures substantially, just the opposite of what it should have done. See Albert U. Romasco, "Herbert Hoover's Policies for Dealing with the Great Depression: The End of the Old Order or the Beginning of the New?" in *The Hoover Presidency: A Reappraisal,* ed. Martin L. Fausold and George

T. Mazuzam (Albany: State University of New York Press, 1974), pp. 69–86, esp. pp. 79–84.

2. Campaign speech, New York, October 31, 1932; in William Starr Myers and Walter H. Newton, *The Hoover Administration: A Documented Narrative* (New York: Charles Scribner's Sons, 1936), p. 520.

3. Joan Hoff Wilson, *Herbert Hoover, Forgotten Progressive* (Boston: Little, Brown, 1975), p. 166.

4. Ibid., pp. 7, 127; Myers and Newton, *Hoover Administration*, pp. 517–518.

5. Ellis W. Hawley, "Herbert Hoover, the Commerce Secretariat, and the Vision of an 'Associative State,' 1921–1928," *JAH*, 61 (1974), 116–140.

6. Ibid.

7. Ibid.

8. Ibid.

9. Ellis W. Hawley, "Herbert Hoover and American Corporatism, 1929–1933," in Fausold and Mazuzam, *Hoover Presidency*, pp. 101–119, esp. p. 104.

10. Myers and Newton, *Hoover Administration*, pp. 26-27. According to Joseph Dorfman, Hoover's decision to maintain wage rates was "unparalleled in the history of the Presidency" (*The Economic Mind in American Civilization*, 5 vols. [New York: Viking Press, 1959], V, 608).

11. Myers and Newton, *Hoover Administration*, pp. 28, 36; Wilson, *Hoover, Forgotten Progressive*, pp. 139–145; Herbert Stein, *The Fiscal Revolution in America* (Chicago: University of Chicago Press, 1969), pp. 16-17; Lippmann quoted on p. 8.

12. E. Cary Brown, "Fiscal Policies in the Thirties: A Reappraisal," *AER*, 46 (1956), 857; Stein, *Fiscal Revolution*, pp. 10, 17–18, 22–26.

13. Quoted in Stein, *Fiscal Revolution*, p. 22.

14. Milton Friedman and Anna J. Schwartz, *A Monetary History of the United States, 1857–1960* (Princeton: Princeton University Press, 1963), pp. 395–406.

15. Stein, *Fiscal Revolution*, p. 37.

16. For a clear discussion of the technical issues involved, see Albert U. Romasco, *The Poverty of Abundance: Hoover, the Nation, the Depression* (New York: Oxford University Press, 1965), pp. 191–194. See also David Burner, *Herbert Hoover, a Public Life* (New York: Alfred A. Knopf, 1979), p. 270.

17. Stein, *Fiscal Revolution*, pp. 7–8, 469n2.

18. *The New Day: Campaign Speeches of Herbert Hoover, 1928* (Stanford: Stanford University Press, 1928), p. 22.

19. Myers and Newton, *Hoover Administration*, pp. 24, 38–39, 148, 388, 392; Burner, *Hoover*, pp. 236–244.

20. Romasco, *Poverty of Abundance*, p. 190.

21. Myers and Newton, *Hoover Administration*, p. 506.

22. Romasco, *Poverty of Abundance*, pp. 190–191; Myers and Newton, *Hoover Administration*, pp. 231, 233-234.

23. Romasco, *Poverty of Abundance*, pp. 189–190; Myers and Newton, *Hoover Administration*, pp. 158, 231-234, 252, 539. Initially loans were made to banks, although Hoover wanted them to be made to public bodies and industries as well. It took eight months for these proposals to be authorized. As Burner points out, James Olson's discussion of the origins of the RFC replaces Gerald D. Nash's older interpre-

tation "that shows Eugene Meyer persuading a grumbling, foot-dragging President to accept it." See Burner, *Hoover*, pp. 268–279, esp. p. 401n43; James Olson, *Herbert Hoover and the Reconstruction Finance Corporation, 1931–1933* (Ames: University of Iowa Press, 1977), pp. 24–32.

24. Myers and Newton, *Hoover Administration*, pp. 265–266.

25. Ibid., pp. 62–64, 496; Wilson, *Forgotten Progressive*, pp. 150–151.

26. Myers and Newton, *Hoover Administration*, p. 266.

27. Quoted in Burner, *Hoover*, p. 244.

28. Myers and Newton, *Hoover Administration*, pp. 455–457.

29. Burner, *Hoover*, ch. 10.

30. Quoted in Romasco, *Poverty of Abundance*, p. 25; see also pp. 4–5.

31. Lester V. Chandler, *American Monetary Policy, 1928–1941* (New York: Harper & Row, 1971), pp. 116–117, 251.

32. Carl N. Degler, *Out of Our Past: The Forces That Shaped Modern America* (New York: Haprer & Row, 1959), pp. 384–391, 412–416; Richard Hofstadter, *The Age of Reform* (New York: Alfred A. Knopf, 1955), p. 304; Lester V. Chandler, *America's Greatest Depression, 1929–1941* (New York: Harper & Row, 1970), p. 126.

33. Ellis W. Hawley, "The New Deal and Business," in *The New Deal, the National Level*, 2 vols., ed. John Braeman et al. (Columbus: Ohio State University Press, 1975), I, 57.

34. Irving Bernstein, *The Lean Years* (Boston: Houghton Mifflin, 1960), pp. 254–256.

35. William E. Leuchtenburg, *Franklin D. Roosevelt and the New Deal, 1932–1940* (New York: Harper & Row, 1963), pp. 1–2.

36. Chandler, *American Monetary Policy*, pp. 243–244, 260, 270; Vincent P. Carosso, *Investment Banking in America: A History* (Cambridge, Mass.: Harvard University Press, 1970), p. 352.

37. Albert U. Romasco, *The Politics of Recovery: Roosevelt's New Deal* (New York: Oxford University Press, 1983), pp. 52–54, 217–218.

38. Ibid., pp. 64–65; Leuchtenburg, *Roosevelt and New Deal*, p. 121.

39. Romasco, *Politics of Recovery*, p. 65; Leuchtenburg, *Roosevelt and New Deal*, pp. 125–130.

40. Chandler, *American Monetary Policy*, p. 221. Hoover had refused to take similar action because he doubted its constitutionality under 1917 law. Even after Roosevelt's proclamation, powerful members of the House and Senate Banking and Currency committees argued that the president lacked constitutional power to close state nonmember banks and that "only the grave emergency justified such action" (Susan Estabrook Kennedy, *The Banking Crisis of 1933* [Lexington: University Press of Kentucky, 1973], pp. 230, 185).

41. Chandler, *American Monetary Policy*, p. 221; Kennedy, *Banking Crisis*, pp. 231, 229; Romasco, *Politics of Recovery*, p. 56; Friedman and Schwartz, *Monetary History*, pp. 422–425.

42. Romasco, *Politics of Recovery*, p. 57; Jesse H. Jones with Edward Angly, *Fifty Million Dollars* (New York: Macmillan, 1951), p. 3; Friedman and Schwartz, *Monetary History*, pp. 427–428.

43. Richard E. Sylla, "Small Business Banking in the United States, 1780–1920,"

in *Small Business in American Life,* ed. Stuart Bruchey (New York: Columbia University Press, 1980), p. 240.

44. Ibid., pp. 241–242, 259.

45. Bureau of the Census, *Historical Statistics of the United States, Colonial Times to 1970,* 2 vols. (Washington, D.C.: Government Printing Office, 1976), II, 1038.

46. Friedman and Schwartz, *Monetary History,* pp. 436-437, 434, and tables on pp. 438–439.

47. Carosso, *Investment Banking,* pp. 331–332, 368-369.

48. Ibid., pp. 322–351, 371; Kennedy, *Banking Crisis,* pp. 103–128; Chandler, *American Monetary Policy,* p. 270.

49. Chandler, *American Monetary Policy,* p. 271.

50. Robert F. Himmelberg, *The Origins of the National Recovery Administration: Business, Government, and the Trade Association Issue, 1921–1933* (New York: Fordham University Press, 1976), p. 2.

51. Kenneth D. Roose, *The Economics of Recession and Revival* (New Haven: Yale University Press, 1954), p. 60.

52. *New York Times,* June 25, 1933, sec. 8, p. 1; Ellis W. Hawley, *The New Deal and the Problem of Monopoly* (Princeton: Princeton University Press, 1966), pp. 26, 57–61; Michael M. Weinstein, *Recovery and Redistribution under the NIRA* (New York: North-Holland, 1980), p. 9; Michael Alan Bernstein, "Long-Term Economic Growth and the Problem of Recovery in American Manufacturing: A Study of the Great Depression in the United States, 1929–1939" (Ph.D. diss., Yale University, 1982), p. 439; Himmelberg, *Origins of National Recovery Administration,* pp. 221–222. Himmelberg uses the word *conspiracy* to characterize the "understandings" of the early 1920s. But probably nothing more than shared values accounts for tolerance of uncompetitive behavior on the part of trade associations.

53. Bernstein, "Long-Term Economic Growth," pp. 439–440, 367.

54. Weinstein, *Recovery and Redistribution,* pp. 63, 112.

55. Milton Derber, "The New Deal and Labor," in Braeman et al., *New Deal,* I, 110–132; Leuchtenburg, *Roosevelt and New Deal,* pp. 262–263.

56. Joseph G. Rayback, *A History of American Labor* (New York: Free Press, 1966), p. 327; Stuart D. Brandes, *American Welfare Capitalism, 1880–1940* (Chicago: University of Chicago Pres, 1976), p. 143; Sanford D. Jacoby, "The Origins of Internal Labor Markets in American Manufacturing Firms, 1910–1940" (Ph.D. diss., University of California, Berkeley, 1981), p. 543.

57. Jacoby, "Internal Labor Markets," pp. 541–542; Derber, "New Deal and Labor," p. 115. Derber's figures show a 2-to-1 advantage in favor of the AFL in 1939.

58. Jacoby, "Internal Labor Markets," pp. 543–544.

59. Quoted in Derber, "New Deal and Labor," p. 121.

60. Arthur M. Schlesinger, Jr., *The Coming of the New Deal* (Boston: Houghton Mifflin, 1959), p. 27.

61. Joseph S. Davis, *On Agricultural Policy, 1926-1938* (Stanford: Stanford University Food Research Institute, 1939), p. 245; *Historical Statistics to 1970,* I, 511, 517, 521, 483.

62. Lawrence A. Jones and James V. Durand, *Mortgage Lending Experience in*

Agriculture, National Bureau of Economic Research, Studies in Agricultural Finance (Princeton: Princeton University Press, 1954), pp. 71, 76–97.

63. Davis, *On Agricultural Policy,* p. 246; quoted in Schlesinger, *Coming of New Deal,* p. 27.

64. Davis, *On Agricultural Policy,* p. 233.

65. Quoted in Walter W. Wilcox, Willard W. Cochran, and Robert W. Herdt, *Economics of American Agriculture,* 3d ed. (Englewood Cliffs, N.J.: Prentice-Hall, 1974), p. 440.

66. Davis, *On Agricultural Policy,* p. 248; Wilcox, Cochran, and Herdt, *Economics of American Agriculture,* pp. 437–438.

67. Wilcox, Cochran, and Herdt, *Economics of American Agriculture,* pp. 439–440; *Wickard v. Filburn,* 317 U.S. 111 (1942), 128–129.

68. Davis, *On Agricultural Policy,* pp. 259–260; *Historical Statistics to 1970,* I, 483. The farmer's average net income in 1929 was $945. The highest income in the 1930s, $905, was achieved in 1937. In no other year did it reach the $800 level. In only two years, 1935 and 1940, did it get as high as the $700s.

69. Warren C. Whatley, "Institutional Change and Mechanization in the Cotton South: The Tractorization of Cotton Farming," Ph.D. diss., Stanford University, 1982, pp. 7–8, 179–180.

70. Romasco, *Politics of Recovery,* pp. 62–63.

71. Ibid., pp. 53, 63–64.

72. Friedman and Schwartz, *Monetary History,* pp. 504-505.

73. Chandler, *American Monetary Policy,* pp. 289–291, 298.

74. Ibid., pp. 298–300.

75. Friedman and Schwartz, *Monetary History,* pp. 497-499.

76. Ibid., pp. 493–495.

77. Chandler, *American Monetary Policy,* p. 253.

78. Stein, *Fiscal Revolution,* pp. 43–47; Brown,
"Fiscal Policies in Thirties," pp. 863–866.

79. Brown, "Fiscal Policies in Thirties," pp. 863–869.

80. Friedman and Schwartz, *Monetary History,* pp. 526-527, 8–9; Stanley Lebergott, *Manpower in Economic Growth: The American Record since 1800* (New York: McGraw-Hill, 1964), p. 512. "It took the massive expenditures forced on the nation by the second world war to realize the full potentialities of fiscal policy. Until then, the record fails to show its effective use as a recovery measure" (Brown, "Fiscal Policies in Thirties," p. 869).

81. Bernstein, "Long-Term Economic Growth," pp. 47-53.

82. Friedman and Schwartz, *Monetary History,* pp. 495-496; Roose, *Economics of Recession and Revival,* pp. 45-47. Other legislation adversely affecting business confidence created the Tennessee Valley Authority in 1933, the Resettlement Administration and Rural Electrification Administration in 1935, the Social Security Board in 1935, the Home Owners Loan Corporation in 1933, and the Federal Farm Mortgage Corporation in 1934—all instances of expanded government activity in competition with private enterprise.

83. Romasco reaches the same conclusion. "Businessmen," he writes, "repeatedly complained that government, by penetrating economic affairs, was creating business

uncertainty and a depressing lack of business confidence. In sum, the federal government's ventures in reform served only to discourage recovery . . . In retrospect, the
conservative business critics were correct. The New Deal years from 1933 through
1938 represented a genuine watershed in the evolution of the political control of the
economy" (*Politics of Recovery*, p. 219).

84. Romasco, *Poverty of Abundance*, pp. 196–198.

85. Romasco, *Politics of Recovery*, pp. 60–61.

86. Leuchtenburg, *Roosevelt and New Deal*, pp. 154–158.

16. The Second Great War and Its Aftermath

1. I wish to acknowledge my deep indebtedness to Harold G. Vatter, without
whose book *The U.S. Economy in World War II* (New York: Columbia University
Press, 1985), available to me in manuscript before publication, much of this chapter
would not have been written.

2. Americans "were more inclined to feel annoyance with the march of events
. . . than to consider seriously the implications to themselves" (Bureau of the Budget,
*The United States at War: Development and Administration of the War Program by the
Federal Government* [Washington, D.C.: Government Printing Office, 1946], p. 5;
hereafter *U.S. at War*). Though written by a committee of historians and political
scientists before many records of the war became available, this account remains a
valuable history on which all subsequent accounts must lean. (For the poll, see p.
17n1.)

3. Ibid., pp. 18, 20–21. A year later Congress authorized priorities for essential
civilian goods as well; see Richard Polenberg, *War and Society: The United States,
1941–1945* (Philadelphia: J. B. Lippincott, 1972), p. 8.

4. John Morton Blum, *V Was for Victory: Politics and American Culture during
World War II* (New York: Harcourt Brace Jovanovich, 1976), p. 117. Blum's discussion of "War Lords and Vassals" is brief but perceptive. The former included Henry
L. Stimson, Harry Hopkins, Harold Ickes, Henry Morgenthau, Jr., and Henry Wallace
(pp. 119–121); *U.S. at War*, p. 378.

5. For the industrial mobilization plans, see R. Elberton Smith, *The Army and
Economic Mobilization* (Washington, D.C.: Government Printing Office, 1959), pp.
74–97. The first of the two quotations from FDR is in Smith, ibid., pp. 102–103,
the second in Polenberg, *War and Society*, p. 6.

6. *U.S. at War*, p. 103.

7. The data in this paragraph and in the one following are from Vatter, *U.S.
Economy*, pp. 7-13.

8. *U.S. at War*, p. 105.

9. Ibid., p. 107.

10. Blum, *V Was for Victory*, p. 121.

11. Robert Wood Johnson, *"But, General Johnson"* (Princeton: Princeton University Press, 1944), p. 17.

12. Ibid., p. 9; Blum, *V Was for Victory*, p. 122.

13. U.S. Congress, Smaller War Plants Corporation, *Economic Concentration and
World War II*, Senate Doc. no. 206, 79th Cong., 2d sess. (Washington, D.C.: Government Printing Office, 1946), p. 29.

14. Harold G. Vatter, "The Position of Small Business in the Structure of American Manufacturing, 1870–1970," in *Small Business in American Life,* ed. Stuart Bruchey (New York: Columbia University Press, 1980), p. 154; Vatter, *U.S. Economy,* pp. 59–61.

15. Bureau of the Census, *Historical Statistics of the United States, Colonial Times to 1970,* 2 vols (Washington, D.C.: Government Printing Office, 1976), II, 911, 914. As Vatter notes, "Estimates of the business population are notoriously crude" ("Position of Small Business," pp. p. 177n16); Polenberg, *War and Society,* p. 28; Vatter, *U.S. Economy,* pp. 55–56. Federal Trade Commission, *Report on Wartime Costs and Profits for Manufacturing Corporations, 1941 to 1945* (Washington, D.C.: Government Printing Office, 1947), p. 29. The report is based on data submitted to OPA by 4,107 companies operating in twenty-two industry groups in 1941. For the smallest corporations (assets of $250,000 to $1 million), net earnings were higher in each war year than in 1941 in the food, beverages, tobacco, and transportation-equipment industry groups. Corporations in the next to smallest group ($1 million to $5 million) were also much more profitable during the war in the beverages and tobacco industries. In the $5-million-to-$10-million group, corporations in only two industries had higher profits after federal taxes during the war than in 1941, namely, the automobile and equipment industries; Secretary Stimson's remark is quoted in Polenberg, ibid., p. 12.

16. Gerald T. White, *Billions for Defense: Government Financing by the Defense Plant Corporation during World War II* (Tuscaloosa: University of Alabama Press, 1980), pp. 2, 7–8.

17. U.S. Congress, Senate, Special Commission to Investigate the National Defense Program [the Truman Committee], 78th Cong., 1st sess., pt. 17, "Pipe Line Transportation," *Hearings,* February 17, 1943, pp. 6918–19; quoted in full by Vatter, *U.S. Economy,* pp. 24–25.

18. Vatter, *U.S. Economy,* pp. 24–29. See the Truman Committee's interim *Report on Steel,* Report no. 10, pt. 3, February 4, 1943, p. 2; Donald M. Nelson, *Arsenal of Democracy* (New York: Harcourt, Brace, 1946), pp. 290-293; *U.S. at War,* p. 296n8.

19. White, *Billions for Defense,* p. 9; John B. Rae, *Climb to Greatness: The American Aircraft Industry, 1920–1960* (Cambridge, Mass.: M.I.T. Press, 1968), p. 157; *Historical Statistics to 1970,* II, 265, 693, 707; Edward L. Allen, *Economics of American Manufacturing* (New York: Henry Holt, 1952), p. 79; Vatter, *U.S. Economy,* pp. 29–31, 20.

20. White, *Billions for Defense,* pp. vii, 6, 10.

21. Ibid., pp. 89–90, 94–95; Vatter, *U.S. Economy,* pp. 18–19. To reach his estimate of a 27 percent increase in labor productivity, Vatter divided the sum of civilian production and military commodities purchased by the federal government by private civilian labor hours. However, he points out that "labor productivity" is deceptive because it ignores the influence of other inputs and of technological improvements, and, in this case, because rising rates of utilization may have brought increasing marginal output rates. (Inventories of installed equipment exist and are being analyzed by George Sweeting, a graduate student in the Department of History, Columbia University.)

22. White, *Billions for Defense,* pp. 110–112.

23. Ibid., pp. 90, 102–103, 106–107, 123. The disposal of surplus plants and tools was largely accomplished by 1949 (p. 112).

24. Vatter, *U.S. Economy*, pp. 14–17.

25. Ibid., pp. 17–19.

26. Alice Kessler-Harris, *Out to Work: A History of Wage-Earning Women in the United States* (New York: Oxford University Press, 1982), pp. 275–277.

27. Ibid., p. 278.

28. Tuskegee Institute, Department of Records and Research, *Negro Year Book, 1947*, p. 134; Vatter, *U.S. Economy*, pp. 127–130; Everett S. Lee et al., *Population Redistribution and Economic Growth, United States, 1870–1950*, 3 vols. (Philadelphia: American Philosophical Society, 1957), I, 107–231, reference table P-1.1 (calculated by Vatter, ibid., p. 129); Walter W. Wilcox, *The Farmer in the Second World War* (Ames: Iowa State University Press, 1947), p. 13.

29. *Historical Statistics to 1970*, I, 466–467, 483; Geoffrey G. Moore, "Secular Changes in the Distribution of Income," *AER*, 42 (1952), 541n9; *U.S. at War*, p. 321; Vatter, *U.S. Economy*, pp. 51–55.

30. *Historical Statistics to 1970*, I, 469, 827, 830; John W. Kendrick, *Productivity Trends in the United States*, National Bureau of Economic Research (Princeton: Princeton University Press, 1961), p. 364 (the index slipped badly in 1943, from 130.4 the previous year to 124.6); Alvin S. Tostlebe, *Capital in Agriculture: Its Formation and Financing since 1870* (Princeton: Princeton University Press, 1957), p. 71. On the other hand, the sources of animal products (livestock other than horses and mules) increased 17 percent. Indeed, the war years witnessed a dramatic shift from cropland to pastureland, the latter rising by 22 percent (Vatter, *U.S. Economy*, pp. 52–54, 176n4).

31. Wilcox, *Farmer in Second World War*, pp. 120-122, 128–129, 246, 249; Barton J. Bernstein, "Clash of Interests: The Postwar Battle between the Office of Price Administration and the Department of Agriculture," *AH*, 41 (1967), 46–47; *U.S. at War*, p. 235. The "agricultural authorities" referred to are Walter W. Wilcox, Willard W. Cochrane, and Robert W. Herdt, *Economics of American Agriculture*, 3d ed. (Englewood Cliffs, N.J.: Prentice-Hall, 1951), p. 441. The postwar price supports, for "basic commodities" and those for which the secretary of agriculture had asked for an expansion of output, were set at 90 percent of parity (Wilcox, ibid., p. 129).

32. Vatter, *U.S. Economy*, p. 91; Hugh Rockoff, "Indirect Price Increases and Real Wages during World War II," *EEH*, 15 (1978), 407–420.

33. Vatter, *U.S. Economy*, pp. 89–101; W. Elliot Brownlee, *Dynamics of Ascent: A History of the American Economy*, 2d ed. (New York: Alfred A. Knopf, 1979), p. 454.

34. *U.S. at War*, pp. 143, 173–189, 431, 439–452.

35. Ibid., pp. 429–455; Vatter, *U.S. Economy*, pp. 17–18; *New York Times*, February 25, 1983, sec. A, p. 12.

36. Executive Order no. 9599, August 18, 1945, *Federal Register*, X, 10155–58.

37. *U.S. at War*, pp. 492–493.

38. Milton Friedman and Anna J. Schwartz, *A Monetary History of the United States* (Princeton: Princeton University Press, 1963), pp. 569, 574.

39. Quoted in Herbert Stein, *The Fiscal Revolution in America* (Chicago: University of Chicago Press, 1969), p. 207.

40. Ibid., p. 195; Friedman and Schwartz, *Monetary History,* pp. 566, 575.

41. Stein, *Fiscal Revolution,* pp. 201–202.

42. Ibid., pp. 199–201; Walter E. Heller, *New Dimensions of Political Economy* (Cambridge, Mass.: Harvard University Press, 1966), pp. 16, 175.

43. Stein, *Fiscal Revolution,* pp. 205–206.

44. Ibid., p. 239.

45. Quoted in ibid., p. 299.

46. Ibid., pp. 298, 304.

47. Ibid., pp. 319–345.

48. Ibid., pp. 300–301, 320.

49. Ibid., p. 368; Brownlee, *Dynamics,* p. 458.

50. Stein, *Fiscal Revolution,* p. 352.

51. Ibid., p. 375.

52. Quoted in Heller, *New Dimensions,* p. 61.

53. Ibid., p. 8.

54. Stein, *Fiscal Revolution,* p. 383.

55. Ibid., pp. 385–386; Robert Warren Stevens, *Vain Hopes, Grim Realities* (New York: New Viewpoints, 1976), p. 43.

56. Ibid., p. 46; The quoted words are those of Theodore Sorensen; see his *Kennedy* (New York: Harper & Row, 1965), p. 413; Heller, *New Dimensions,* p. 64.

57. Heller, *New Dimensions,* p. 64.

58. Ibid., pp. 43, 46, 76–77.

59. Stein, *Fiscal Revolution,* p. 456. Stein adds that the "general acceptance of compensatory finance as a basic principle of fiscal policy did not rest on any conclusive scientific demonstration that a policy of compensatory finance had worked or would work. The scientific issues were still unsettled in the mid-1960s when the history related here ends" (p. 463).

60. *Economic Report of the President* (Washington, D.C.: Government Printing Office, 1969), p. 4.

61. U.S. Joint Committee, Subcommittee on Economic Growth, *Economic Growth and Total Capital Formation,* 94th Cong., 2d sess. (Washington, D.C.: Government Printing Office, 1976), p. 4.

62. Harold G. Vatter and John F. Walker, "Can the Good Performance of the 1960s Be Repeated in the 1980s?" (paper presented at the annual meeting of the American Economic Association, December 1982). The percentages given in the text were calculated by Vatter and Walker.

63. The chairman was Walter Heller; see his *New Dimensions,* p. 9.

64. Ibid., p. 140. Even the imposition of a temporary surcharge on income taxes in July 1968 failed in its purpose of dampening the expenditures of consumers (ibid., p. 136); Robert J. Gordon, "Postwar Macroeconomics: The Evolution of Events and Ideas," in *The American Economy in Transition,* ed. Martin Feldstein (Chicago: University of Chicago Press, 1980), pp. 133–140.

65. Gordon, ibid., pp. 135–156; David P. Calleo, *The Imperious Economy* (Cambridge, Mass.: Harvard University Press, 1982), p. 64.

66. Calleo, *Imperious Economy,* p. 106; Bureau of the Census, *Statistical Abstract*

of the United States, 1982 (Washington, D.C., Government Printing Office, 1982), 459.

67. Calleo, *Imperious Economy,* p. 139.

17. From Recent Times to the Present and Future

1. Richard A. Easterlin, "American Population since 1940," in *The American Economy in Transition,* ed. Martin Feldstein (Chicago: University of Chicago Press, 1980), pp. 275–321; for the dating of the "baby boom" (1946–1960), see p. 311.

2. Simon Kuznets, "Notes on Demographic Change," in Feldstein, *American Economy,* pp. 334–340.

3. *Bangor Daily News,* June 10, 1987, p. 10.

4. Easterlin, "American Population," p. 277.

5. Robert S. McNamara, "Time Bomb or Myth: The Population Problem," *FA,* 62 (1984), 1107–31.

6. Easterlin, "American Population"; according to the Census Bureau, the proportion of never-married single women rose from 36 percent to 56 percent between 1970 and 1983 ("Snapshot of a Changing America," *Time Magazine,* September 2, 1985, pp. 16–18).

7. "Snapshot of a Changing America," pp. 16–18; Easterlin, "American Population," pp. 299–301.

8. "Snapshot of a Changing America," p. 17.

9. Easterlin, "American Population," pp. 302–305.

10. Ibid.

11. Ibid., pp. 305–311.

12. Kenneth P. Johnson and Howard L. Friedenberg,"Regional and State Projections of Income, Employment, and Population to the Year 2000," *SCB,* 65 (1985), 39–48.

13. James C. Cobb, *The Selling of the South: The Southern Crusade for Industrial Development, 1936–1980* (Baton Rouge: Louisiana State University Press, 1982), esp. ch. 7.

14. Easterlin, "American Population," p. 308.

15. Ibid., p. 310.

16. Bureau of the Census, *Statistical Abstract of the United States, 1982–1983* (Washington, D.C.: Government Printing Office, 1983), p. 649; Richard E. Caves, "The Structure of Industry," in Feldstein, *American Economy in Transition,* p. 503; *Statistical Abstract, 1982–1983,* p. 674.

17. *Statistical Abstract, 1982–1983,* p. 673; Forrest McDonald, *We the People* (Chicago: University of Chicago Press, 1958), p. 359; Luther S. Tweeten, *Roots of the Farm Problem: Changing Technology, Changing Capital Use, Changing Labor Needs* (Ames: Iowa State University Press, 1965), pp. 4–8.

18. Bureau of the Census, *Statistical Abstract of the United States, 1984,* (Washington, D.C.: Government Printing Office, 1983), pp. 651, 654. In 1974 the Census Bureau changed the 1969 definition of "farm"; see p. 648.

19. Ibid., p. 653; Gail L. Cramer and Clarence W. Jensen, *Agricultural Economics and Agribusiness,* 2d ed. (New York: John Wiley, 1982), p. 24; Howard F. Gregor,

Industrialization of U.S. Agriculture: An Interpretive Atlas (Boulder, Colo.: Westview Press, 1982), p. 8.

20. Cramer and Jensen, *Agricultural Economics*, pp. 22–33; Morton D. Wineberg, "Agricultural Specialization in the United States Since World War II," *AH*, 56 (1982), 694–695.

21. Gregor, *Industrialization of U.S. Agriculture*, pp. 1–10, 35–36, 161–165. Although the thrust of Gregor's argument is that intensity of capitalization is a more reliable indicator of agricultural industrialization than is size or value of output (industrialization of small farms may be increased by placing them under the same management and integrating their operations vertically, for example), he acknowledges that "changing technologies . . . put a premium on larger units" (p. 229) and that in the"privileged center of American agriculture, the Middle West," farms are "becoming ever larger at the expense of other operators, the same as has occurred in the often-criticized 'factory farm' areas" (p. 234).

22. Donald Holley, "The Sharecropper," in *Farmers, Bureaucrats, and Middlemen: Historical Perspectives on American Agriculture*, ed. Trudy Huskamp (Washington, D.C.: Howard University Press, 1980), pp. 133–134; Pete Daniel, "The Transformation of the Rural South, 1930 to the Present," *AH*, 55 (1981), 244.

23. Moses S. Musoke and Alan L. Olmstead, "The Rise of the Cotton Industry in California: A Comparative Perspective," *JEH*, 42 (1982), 385; Paul W. Gates, "Pressure Groups and Recent Land Policies," *AH*, 55 (1981), 104.

24. Donald Worster, "Hydraulic Society in California: An Ecological Interpretation," *AH*, 56 (1982), 503.

25. Musoke and Olmstead, "Cotton Industry in California," pp. 385, 389.

26. Ibid., pp. 393–397.

27. Ibid., pp. 398–401.

28. Wayne D. Rasmusen, "The Impact of Technological Change on American Agriculture, 1862–1962," *JEH*, 22 (1962), 578–591.

29. *New York Times*, February 3, 1985, sec. 1, p. 30.

30. Ibid., February 10, 1985, sec. 1, p. 30.

31. Willard W. Cochrane and Mary E. Ryan, *American Farm Policy, 1948–1973* (Minneapolis: University of Minnesota Press, 1976), pp. ix, xiv, 1–17, 66–67, 223.

32. *New York Times*, April 1, 1978, sec. 1, p. 1.

33. Robert B. Reich, *The Next American Frontier* (New York: Times Books, 1983), p. 118; Edwin Mansfield, Ruben F. Mettler, and David Packard, "Technology and Productivity in the United States," in Feldstein, *American Economy*, pp. 564-568.

34. Robert J. Gordon, "Postwar Macroeconomics: The Evolution of Events and Ideas," in Feldstein, *American Economy*, p. 158; Reich, *New American Frontier*, p. 356.

35. Daniel Yankelovich, as quoted in *New York Times*, September 5, 1984, p. 8. The report, coauthored by Yankelovich and John Immerwahr, is titled "Putting the Work Ethic to Work: A Public Agenda Report on Restoring America's Competitive Vitality."

36. Reich, *New American Frontier*, pp. 118, 122; William H. Branson, "Trends in United States International Trade and Investment since World War II," in Feldstein, *American Economy*, p. 231.

37. Branson, "Trends," pp. 183–186; Reich, *New American Frontier*, p. 122.

38. *Congress and the Nation, A Review of Government and Politics,* III, 1969–1972 (Washington, D.C.: Congressional Quarterly Service, n.d.), p. 127; Branson, "Trends," p. 203.

39. Richard N. Gardner, *Sterling-Dollar Diplomacy; Anglo-American Collaboration and Reconstruction of Multilateral Trade* (Oxford: Clarendon Press, 1956), p. 13. In "Commercial Conflict and Foreign Policy: A Study in Anglo-American Relations, 1932–1938" (Ph.D. diss., Johns Hopkins School of Advanced International Studies, Washington, D.C., 1975), Benjamin M. Rowland makes the point that Hull was probably the greatest of America's economic determinists during this era and argues persuasively that a major, if not the primary, goal of Hull's reciprocity program from 1934 onward was to breach Britain's Commonwealth preference system. America's pressures for an open economic system unaccompanied by a commitment to assume responsibility for the security of the system were major destabilizing forces in interwar diplomacy.

40. Gardner, *Sterling-Dollar Diplomacy,* pp. 110–144.

41. Branson, "Trends," p. 249.

42. David P. Calleo, *The Imperious Economy* (Cambridge, Mass.: Harvard University Press, 1982), p. 46.

43. Leonard Silk, *Nixonomics, How the Dismal Science of Free Enterprise Became the Black Art of Controls* (New York: Praeger, 1972), p. 107.

44. Calleo, *Imperious Economy,* pp. 31–32; Branson, "Trends," pp. 240–243.

45. Calleo, *Imperious Economy,* pp. 45, 59, 63–64.

46. *Annual Report of the Council of Economic Advisers* (Washington, D.C.: Government Printing Office, 1988), p. 337, table B-76, and pp. 109–115; *New York Times,* April 21, sec. 4, p. 13; Bureau of the Census, *Statistical Abstract of the United States, 1988* (Washington, D.C.: Government Printing Office, 1987), p. 291.

47. Reich, *New American Frontier,* pp. 121–122.

48. Ibid., pp. 117–139, esp. pp. 121–124; Branson, "Trends," pp. 231–232;

49. Reich, *New American Frontier,* p. 121.

50. Ibid., p. 140.

51. Caves, "Structure of Industry," p. 516.

52. Reich, *New American Frontier,* p. 176.

53. Ibid., pp. 176, 126.

54. Ibid., p. 178.

55. Ibid., pp. 184, 194–195, 196, 255, 266, 129–130, 133.

56. Ibid., p. 134.

57. Ibid., p. 233.

58. Ibid., p. 245.

59. *New York Times,* September 16, 1983 (as reported in Leonard Silk's column in sec. D, p. 2).

60. Herbert Stein, *Presidential Economics: The Making of Economic Policy from Roosevelt to Reagan and Beyond* (New York: Simon & Schuster, 1984), pp. 346, 345, 375.

61. Leonard Silk, "The United States and the World Economy," *FA,* 65 (1987), 458-476; *Bangor Daily News,* June 24, 1987, p. 20; Arthur F. Burns, "The American Trade Deficit in Perspective," *FA,* 62 (1984), 1058-69.

62. Martin Feldstein, "Correcting the Trade Deficit," *FA,* 65 (1987), 795–806; *Statistical Abstract, 1988,* p. 768.

63. Charles P. Kindleberger, *Manias, Panics, and Crashes, A History of Financial Crisis* (New York: Basic Books, 1978), pp. 23–24.

64. Silk, "United States and World Economy," pp. 475–476; Pedro-Pablo Kuczynski, "Latin American Debt: Act Two," *FA,* 62 (1983), 17–38; *New York Times,* April 10, 1988, sec. 3, p. 6; ibid., May 22, 1988, sec. 4, pt. 1.

65. Michael Harrington, *The Other America* (New York: Macmillan, 1982), pp. 169, 186; Robert Warren Stevens, *Vain Hopes, Grim Realities* (New York: New Viewpoints, 1976), pp. 46–61.

66. *Congress and the Nation,* I, 1945–1964, II, 1965-1968, esp. pp. 663–666.

67. Ibid., I, 1945–1964, p. 1113.

68. Reich, *New American Frontier,* p. 206.

69. *New York Times,* November 4, 1983, sec. D, p. 1; Edgar K. Browning, *Redistribution and the Welfare System* (Washington, D.C.: American Enterprise Institute for Public Policy Research, 1975), pp. 1–2, 21–25; Irving B. Kravis, *The Structure of Income: Some Quantitative Essays* (Philadelphia: University of Pennsylvania, Wharton School of Finance and Commerce, Industrial Research Unit, 1962), ch. 6.

70. *New York Times,* November 27, 1983, sec. E, p. 4; Bureau of the Census, *The Social and Economic Status of the Black Population in the United States: An Historical View, 1790–1978,* Current Population Reports, Social Studies Series P-23, no. 80 (Washington, D.C.: Government Printing Office, n.d.), p. 175, table 125.

71. *New York Times,* January 11, 1984, sec. A, p. 16; ibid., January 12, 1984, sec. A, p. 30.

72. Stanley Lebergott, *The American Economy: Income, Wealth and Want* (Princeton: Princeton University Press, 1976), p.7.

73. Ibid., p. 9.

74. Robert J. Lampman, *The Share of Top Wealth-Holders in National Wealth, 1922–56,* National Bureau of Economic Research Studies, General Series, no. 74, (Ann Arbor, Mich.: University Microfilms, 1967), p. 1.

75. Jeffrey G. Williamson and Peter H. Lindert, "Three Centuries of American Inequality," in *Research in Economic History,* ed. Paul Uselding (Greenwich, Conn.: JAI Press, 1976), I, 69–123. See also James D. Smith and Stephen D. Franklin, "The Concentration of Personal Wealth, 1922–1969," *AER,* 64 (1974), 162–174.

76. Alice Hanson Jones, "Wealth Estimates for the American Middle Colonies, 1774," in *EDCC,* 18 (1970), pt. 2.

77. Lampman, *Share of Top Wealth-Holders,* pp. 1–32.

78. Lebergott, *American Economy,* p. 301.

79. Ibid., pp. 179–211.

80. Browning, *Redistribution and Welfare System,* pp. 11–12.

81. Herman P. Miller, *Income of the American People* (New York: John Wiley, 1955), p. 1.

82. Peter H. Lindert, *Fertility and Scarcity in America* (Princeton: Princeton University Press, 1978), p. 258.

83. Simon Kuznets, "Economic Growth and Income Inequality," *AER,* 45 (1955), 1–28.

84. Simon Kuznets, *Capital in the American Economy, Its Formation and Financing* (Princeton: Princeton University Press, 1961), p. 9.

85. Raymond Goldsmith, *A Study of Saving in the United States* (Princeton: Princeton University Press, 1955), p. 271, table S-12; Kuznets, *Capital in the American Economy*, pp. 100, 459.

86. Goldsmith, *Study of Saving*, p. 271, table S-12.

87. Paul Craig Roberts, *The Supply-Side Revolution: An Insider's Account of Policymaking in Washington* (Cambridge, Mass.: Harvard University Press, 1984), p. 25. For a strong critique, see Stephen Rousseas, "The Ideology of Supply-Side Economics," in *Reagonomics in the Stagflation Economy*, ed. Sidney Weintraub and Marvin Goodstein (Philadelphia: University of Pennsylvania Press, 1983), pp. 21–33.

88. Joel Slemrod, "Taxation and Business Investment," in *Essays in Contemporary Economic Problems, 1986*, ed. Philip Cagan (Washington, D.C.: American Enterprise Institute for Public Policy Research, 1986), p. 47.

89. Cagan, introduction in Cagan, *Essays*, p. 2.

90. Paul Peretz, "Economic Policy in the 1980s," in *The Politics of American Economic Policy Making*, ed. Peretz (Armonk, N.Y.: M. E. Sharpe, 1986), p. 447.

91. Ibid., p. 449; William Greider, *The Education of David Stockman and Other Americans* (New York: E. P. Dutton, 1986), p. 49.

92. Joseph Pechman, "Who Paid the Taxes, 1966–85?" in Peretz, *Politics*, pp. 278–280.

93. Peretz, "Economic Policy," p. 443.

94. Ibid., p. 446; John L. Palmer and Isabel V. Sawhill, eds., *The Reagan Experiment, An Examination of Economic and Social Policies under the Reagan Administration* (Washington, D.C.: Urban Institute, 1982), p. 5.

95. Peretz, "Economic Policy," pp. 441, 447.

96. Ibid., pp. 444–445.

97. Ibid., pp. 445–449.

98. Bruce Yandle, "The Evolution of Regulatory Activities in the 1970s and 1980s," in Cagan, *Essays*, pp. 118–123.

99. Ibid., pp. 124–129.

100. Peretz, "Economic Policy," pp. 438–439. See also Murray L. Weidenbaum, "Regulating Reform under the Reagan Administration," in *The Reagan Regulatory Strategy*, ed. George C. Eads and Michael Fix (Washington, D.C.: Urban Institute, 1984).

101. Cagan, introduction, in Cagan, *Essays*, p. 1.

102. David J. Lemak, "Social Regulation: A Swing of the Pendulum," in *Regulatory Reform Reconsidered*, ed. Gregory A. Daneke and David J. Lemak (Boulder, Colo.: Westview Press, 1985).

103. Peretz, "Economic Policy," pp. 444–448; *Economic Report of the President, Together with Annual Report of Council of Economic Advisers* (Washington, D.C.: Government Printing Office, 1987), pp. 331–332.

104. A. W. Clausen, *The Development Challenge of the Eighties* (Washington, D.C.: World Book, 1986), pp. 24–27.

105. John C. Esposito et al., *Vanishing Air* (New York: Grossman, 1970), pp. 21–22; *Congress and the Nation*, III, 1969–1972, p. 759.

106. *Congress and the Nation,* III, 1969–1972, p. 745.

107. The embargo applied to the United States and to several European countries whose pro-Israeli policies during the October (1973) Middle East war affronted the Arabs.

108. *Congress and the Nation,* V, 1977–1980, p. 533.

109. The precise years covered by the estimate are 1929–1957; Edward F. Denison, *The Sources of Economic Growth in the United States and the Opportunities before Us* (New York: Committee for Economic Development, 1962).

110. The following discussion of the computer is based on Franklin M. Fisher, Richard B. Mancke, and James W. McKie, *IBM and the U.S. Data Processing Industry: An Economic History* (New York: Praeger, 1983), ch. 1, and Robert Sobel, *I.B.M., Colossus in Transition* (New York: Quadrangle/New York Times Books, 1983), passim, esp. chs. 3, 5, 6, 14.

111. Caves, "Structure of Industry," pp. 502–507; Bureau of the Census, *Historical Statistics of the United States, Colonial Times to 1970,* 2 vols. (Washington, D.C.: Government Printing Office, 1976), I, 482 (gross output and product of agriculture), II, 654 (value added by manufacturing).

112. The following discussion of the service economy, labor force, and unionism is based on Daniel Bell, *The Coming of Post-Industrial Society: A Venture in Social Forecasting* (New York: Basic Books, 1973), pp. 130–140, and Richard B. Freeman, "The Evolution of the American Labor Market, 1948–80," in Feldstein, *American Economy in Transition,* pp. 349–396, esp. pp. 349–374.

113. Walter B. Wriston, "The Structure of Industry," in Feldstein, *American Economy in Transition,* p. 550.

114. *Economic Report of the President,* pp. 43, 112.

115. Ibid., p. 118.

116. The following discussion of Governor Lamm's views on the need for institutional renovation is based on Richard D. Lamm, "Crisis: The Uncompetitive Society," in *Global Competitiveness: Getting the U.S. Back on Track,* ed. Martin K. Starr (New York: W. W. Norton, 1988), pp. 12–42, esp. pp. 17, 19, 24–26, 29, 41–42.

117. Paul Kennedy, *The Rise and Fall of the Great Powers, Economic Change and Military Conflict from 1500 to 2000* (New York: Random House, 1987). For the emphasis on "relative," see p. 432 and esp. p. 536.

118. Ibid., p. 432.

119. "According to the latest report from the Defense Department, the United States spent 6.8 percent of its gross domestic product on military power in 1986. Germany spent 3.1 percent and Japan 1 percent" (*New York Times,* August 7, 1988, sec. A, p. 6.)

120. Kennedy, *Rise and Fall,* p. 532.

121. On p. 515 Kennedy speaks of American inability to defend all its interests "simultaneously," but on pp. 519–521 he acknowledges that it is "hardly likely" it would be called upon to do so (ibid.).

Index

Abbott, Lyman, 195
Accounting methods, 15–18, 329, 334, 335, 338
Achievement motivation, 193–195
Achieving Society, The (McClelland), 193
Act of Union (1707), 76
Act to Regulate Commerce. *See* Interstate Commerce Act
Adams, John, 117, 118
Adams, John Quincy, 200
Adair v. United States (1908), 414
Addyston Pipe & Steel Co. v. U.S., 347
Administration. *See* Management
Advertising, 406–407
AFL. *See* American Federation of Labor
Age: at marriage, 70, 71, 72, 110; of population, 261, 312, 257, 497–498; of workers, 352, 355
Agribusiness, 221, 294–295, 505
Agricultural Adjustment Act (1933), 427, 463–464, 465
Agricultural Adjustment Administration, 503
Agricultural Adjustment Program, 463–465
Agricultural commodities: trade, 63–64, 400, 425, 433–434, 442, 447–448, 462, 463, 506. *See also* Trade under specific commodities, e.g., Corn, trade
Agricultural costs, 21, 24, 55, 243, 424
Agricultural Credit banks, 449
Agricultural innovations, 8–10, 23–24, 68, 99, 235, 237, 290, 292–293, 501, 503, 504–505. *See also* Mechanization, of agriculture
Agricultural labor, 25, 294–295, 356; regional, 49, 73–74, 85, 274–280, 297, 465; scarcity of, 256, 279, 504–505; loss

of, 308, 433, 481–483, 501. *See also* Farmers; Indentured servants; Labor productivity, in agriculture; Slavery
Agricultural machinery industry, 296, 298, 301, 409–410, 426, 505, 508
Agricultural Marketing Act (1929), 447–448
Agricultural prices, 25, 56, 85, 174, 227, 422, 423, 425; decline in, 175, 301, 434, 440, 462; rise of, 232, 462, 495. *See also* Prices under specific commodities, e.g., Cotton, prices
Agricultural price supports, 426–427, 448, 463–464, 484–485, 505–506
Agricultural productivity, 47, 59, 99–100, 162, 296, 308, 382, 463–465, 501. *See also* Crop yields; Subsistence farming
Agricultural revolution, 24, 237, 502
Agriculture, 221, 294–295, 301, 421–425, 455, 456; in the Middle Ages, 14, 19, 21; in colonial period, 44–49, 52–58, 84–85. *See also* specific crops, e.g., Tobacco; and agriculture under places, e.g., South, agriculture in
Alabama, 176, 238, 275, 277
Alexander Brown and Sons of Baltimore, 190
Aluminum Corporation of America (Alcon), 481
American Farm Bureau Federation, 415, 463, 484
American Federation of Labor (AFL), 378, 395, 461
American Husbandry, 42, 43, 46, 47, 52–53, 54
American Institute of Public Opinion, 473